Survival Communications in Pennsylvania: Central Region

John E. Parnell, KK4HWX

13 ISBN 978-1-62512-071-7

Cover design by:
Lynda Colón
FREELANCE GRAPHIC DESIGN &
MARKETING COMMUNICATIONS
www.hirelynda.webs.com

I do wish to acknowledge the hard work of **Angie Shirley** in putting together the database required for this book. Without her efforts, this book could not have been done.

Titles available in this series:

Survival Communications in Alabama
Survival Communications in Alaska
Survival Communications in Arizona
Survival Communications in Arkansas
Survival Communications in California
Survival Communications in Colorado
Survival Communications in Connecticut
Survival Communications in Delaware
Survival Communications in Florida
Survival Communications in Georgia
Survival Communications in Hawaii
Survival Communications in Idaho
Survival Communications in Illinois
Survival Communications in Indiana
Survival Communications in Iowa
Survival Communications in Kansas
Survival Communications in Kentucky
Survival Communications in Louisiana
Survival Communications in Maine
Survival Communications in Maryland
Survival Communications in Massachusetts
Survival Communications in Michigan
Survival Communications in Minnesota
Survival Communications in Mississippi
Survival Communications in Missouri

Survival Communications in Montana
Survival Communications in Nebraska
Survival Communications in Nevada
Survival Communications in New Hampshire
Survival Communications in New Jersey
Survival Communications in New Mexico
Survival Communications in New York
Survival Communications in North Carolina
Survival Communications in North Dakota
Survival Communications in Ohio
Survival Communications in Oklahoma
Survival Communications in Oregon
Survival Communications in Pennsylvania
Survival Communications in Rhode Island
Survival Communications in South Carolina
Survival Communications in South Dakota
Survival Communications in Tennessee
Survival Communications in Texas
Survival Communications in Utah
Survival Communications in Vermont
Survival Communications in Virginia
Survival Communications in Washington
Survival Communications in West Virginia
Survival Communications in Wisconsin
Survival Communications in Wyoming

The above titles are available from your favorite online or brick-and-mortar bookstore or directly from the publisher at Tutor Turtle Press LLC, 1027 S. Pendleton St. – Suite B-10, Easley, SC 29642.

TABLE OF CONTENTS

Appendix A – Pennsylvania Ham Radio Clubs

ARRL Affiliated Amateur and Ham Radio Clubs – By City

Appendix B – Pennsylvania: Central Region
Amateur Radio Licensees by City

Survival Communications in Pennsylvania

Perhaps you have prepared for WTSHTF or TEOTWAWKI with respect to food, water, self-defense and shelter. But what about communication?

Whenever there is a disaster (hurricane, earthquake, economic collapse, nuclear war, EMF, solar eruption, etc.), the normal means of communication that we're all reliant upon (cell phone, land line phone, the Internet, etc.) will probably be, at best, sporadic and at worst, non-existent.

As this author sees it, short of smoke signals and mirrors, there are three options for communication in "trying times": (1) GMRS or FRS radios; (2) CB radios; and (3) ham or amateur radio. Let's consider each of these options to come up with the most acceptable one.

GMRS (General Mobile Radio Service) / FRS (Family Radio Service)

GMRS (General Mobile Radio Service) / FRS (Family Radio Service) radios work optimally over short distances where there is minimal interference. Originally designed to be used as pagers, particularly inside a building or other such confined area, these radios are low-cost and convenient to carry. Unfortunately their small size and light weight comes with a trade-off – short range and short battery life. These radios are supposed to be able to communicate for up to 25-30 miles. Right. That's on level terrain, without buildings or trees getting in the way. While battery life technology is constantly improving, you will need spare batteries to keep communicating or someway of recharging the ones in the radio. In this author's opinion, GMRS/FRS radios are not first choice when concerned with medium or long range communication.

CB (Citizens Band)

CB (Citizens Band) radios operate in a frequency range originally reserved for ham or amateur radio operation. Because of the overwhelming number of people wishing quick, low-cost, regulation-free communication, the FCC (Federal Communication Commission) split off a portion of the frequency spectrum and allowed anyone to purchase a CB radio and start communicating. No test. No license. Just personal/business communication. Today, CB radios are readily available in such outlets as eBay and Craigslist. This author has seen them at yard/garage/tag sales and at flea markets.

CB radios come in a variety of "flavors." Fixed units, sometimes referred to as base units are intended for home use. For the most part, they derive their power from the utility company. In the event of loss of electricity, most base units can also be connected to a 12-volt battery, like that in your car/truck. If you choose to obtain a fixed unit, make sure you know how to connect the unit to the battery – ahead of time. Trying to figure this out when you're under extra stress is not a good situation.

A second type of CB radio is designed to be mobile, that is, installed in your car/truck. It gets its power from the vehicle's battery. You can either attach an antenna permanently to the vehicle or have a removable, magnetic type antenna.

The third type of CB radio is designed for handheld use. They are small and light. Most weigh less than a pound and operate on batteries. Yes, using batteries in a CB poses the same limitations as those by the GMRS/FRS radios, but have the added advantage that most handheld units come with a cigarette lighter adapter. Comes in handy when you are on the move and wish to be able to communicate both from a vehicle and also when you have to abandon it.

While they have a greater range than GMRS/FRS radios, CB radios are, legally, limited to operate on 40 channels, with a power rating of four (4) watts or less. Yes, it is possible to alter CB radios to get around these limitations, but not legally,

Ham/Amateur Radio

Ham/Amateur radio is very appealing. With a ham radio, you are not limited to less than 50 miles, but can communicate with anyone in the world (who also has access to a ham radio, of course).

Standardized Amateur Radio Prepper Communications Plan

In the event of a nationwide catastrophic disaster, the nationwide network of Amateur Radio licensed preppers will need a set of standardized meeting frequencies to share information and coordinate activities between various prepper groups. This Standardized Amateur Radio Communications Plan establishes a set of frequencies on the 80 meter, 40 meter, 20 meter, and 2 meter Amateur Radio bands for use during these types of catastrophic disasters.

Routine nets will not be held on all of these frequencies, but preppers are encouraged to use them when coordinating with other preppers on a routine basis. Routine nets may be conducted by The American Preparedness Radio Net (TAPRN) on these or other frequencies as they see fit. However, TAPRN will promote the use of these standardized frequencies by all Amateur Radio licensed preppers during times of catastrophic disaster. The promotion of this Standardized Amateur Radio Communications Plan is encouraged by all means within the prepper community, including via Amateur Radio, Twitter, Facebook, and various blogs.

Standardized Frequencies and Modes
80 Meters – 3.818 MHz LSB (TAPRN Net: Sundays at 9 PM ET) 40 Meters – 7.242 MHz LSB 40 Meters Morse Code / Digital – 7.073 MHz USB (TAPRN: Sundays at 7:30 PM ET on CONTESTIA 4/250) 20 Meters – 14.242 MHz USB 2 Meters – 146.420 MHz FM

Nets and Network Etiquette

In times of nationwide catastrophic disaster, the ability of any one prepper to initiate and sustain themselves as a net control may be limited by the availability of power and other resource shortages. However, all licensed preppers are encouraged to maintain a listening watch on these frequencies as often as possible during a catastrophic disaster. Preppers may routinely announce themselves in the following manner:

• This is [Your Callsign Phonetically] in [Your State], maintaining a listening watch on [Standard Frequency] for any preppers on frequency seeking information or looking to provide information. Please call [Your Callsign Phonetically]. Preppers exchanging information that may require follow up should agree upon a designated time to return to the frequency and provide further information. If other stations are utilizing the frequency at the designated time you return, maintain watch and proceed with your communications when those stations are finished. If your communications are urgent and the stations on frequency are not passing information of a critical nature, interrupt with the word "Break" and request use of the frequency.

For More Information

Catastrophe Network: http://www.catastrophenetwork.org or @CatastropheNet on Twitter The American Preparedness Radio Network: http://www.taprn.com or @TAPRN on Twitter

© 2011 Catastrophe Network, Please Distribute Freely

In order to use a ham radio, legally, one must be licensed to do so by the FCC (other countries have analogous governmental bodies to regulate ham radio). To obtain a license is quite easy – take a test and pay your license fee. There are currently three classes of license – Technician, General, and Amateur Extra. With each of these licenses come specific abilities.

Technician class is the beginning level. The exam consists of 35 multiple choice questions randomly drawn from a pool of 395 questions. The question pool is readily available online for free downloading (http://www.ncvec.org/downloads/Revised%20Element%202.Pdf) or in such publications at *Ham Radio License Manual Revised 2nd Edition* (ISBN 978-0-87259-097-7). The current Technician pool of questions is to be used from July 1, 2010 to June 30, 2014. Be sure the question pool you are studying from is current. You will need to score at least 26 correct to pass. (Do not worry, Morse Code is no longer on the test, although many ham operators use it anyway.) You do not need to take a formal class in order to qualify to take the exam. You can learn the material on your own. Most people spend 10-15 hours studying and then successfully take the exam. The cost of taking the exam is under $20. The exam is given in MANY locations throughout the US. Usually the exam is given by area ham clubs. You do not have to belong to the club to take the exam. Check Appendix A for a listing of clubs in Pennsylvania.

Topics for the Technician License in Amateur Radio

The Technician license exam covers such topics as basic regulations, operating practices, and electronic theory, with a focus on VHF and UHF applications. Below is the syllabus for the Technician Class.

Subelement T1 – FCC Rules, descriptions and definitions for the amateur radio service, operator and station license responsibilities

[6 Exam Questions – 6 Groups]

T1A – Amateur Radio services; purpose of the amateur service, amateur-satellite service, operator/primary station license grant, where FCC rules are codified, basis and purpose of FCC rules, meanings of basic terms used in FCC rules

T1B – Authorized frequencies; frequency allocations, ITU regions, emission type, restricted sub-bands, spectrum sharing, transmissions near band edges

T1C – Operator classes and station call signs; operator classes, sequential, special event, and vanity call sign systems, international communications, reciprocal operation, station license licensee, places where the amateur service is regulated by the FCC, name and address on ULS, license term, renewal, grace period

T1D – Authorized and prohibited transmissions

T1E – Control operator and control types; control operator required, eligibility, designation of control operator, privileges and duties, control point, local, automatic and remote control, location of control operator

T1F – Station identification and operation standards; special operations for repeaters and auxiliary stations, third party communications, club stations, station security, FCC inspection

---

Subelement T2 – Operating Procedures

[3 Exam Questions – 3 Groups]

T2A – Station operation; choosing an operating frequency, calling another station, test transmissions, use of minimum power, frequency use, band plans

T2B – VHF/UHF operating practices; SSB phone, FM repeater, simplex, frequency offsets, splits and shifts, CTCSS, DTMF, tone squelch, carrier squelch, phonetics

T2C – Public service; emergency and non-emergency operations, message traffic handling

---

Subelement T3 – Radio wave characteristics, radio and electromagnetic properties, propagation modes

[3 Exam Questions – 3 Groups]

T3A – Radio wave characteristics; how a radio signal travels; distinctions of HF, VHF and UHF; fading, multipath; wavelength vs. penetration; antenna orientation

T3B – Radio and electromagnetic wave properties; the electromagnetic spectrum, wavelength vs. frequency, velocity of electromagnetic waves

T3C – Propagation modes; line of sight, sporadic E, meteor, aurora scatter, tropospheric ducting, F layer skip, radio horizon

Subelement T4 - Amateur radio practices and station setup

[2 Exam Questions – 2 Groups]

T4A – Station setup; microphone, speaker, headphones, filters, power source, connecting a computer, RF grounding

T4B – Operating controls; tuning, use of filters, squelch, AGC, repeater offset, memory channels

Subelement T5 – Electrical principles, math for electronics, electronic principles, Ohm's Law

[4 Exam Questions – 4 Groups]

T5A – Electrical principles; current and voltage, conductors and insulators, alternating and direct current

T5B – Math for electronics; decibels, electronic units and the metric system

T5C – Electronic principles; capacitance, inductance, current flow in circuits, alternating current, definition of RF, power calculations

T5D – Ohm's Law

Subelement T6 – Electrical components, semiconductors, circuit diagrams, component functions

[4 Exam Groups – 4 Questions]

T6A – Electrical components; fixed and variable resistors, capacitors, and inductors; fuses, switches, batteries

T6B – Semiconductors; basic principles of diodes and transistors

T6C – Circuit diagrams; schematic symbols

T6D – Component functions

Subelement T7 – Station equipment, common transmitter and receiver problems, antenna measurements and troubleshooting, basic repair and testing

[4 Exam Questions – 4 Groups]

T7A – Station radios; receivers, transmitters, transceivers

T7B – Common transmitter and receiver problems; symptoms of overload and overdrive, distortion, interference, over and under modulation, RF feedback, off frequency signals; fading and noise; problems with digital communications interfaces

T7C – Antenna measurements and troubleshooting; measuring SWR, dummy loads, feedline failure modes

T7D – Basic repair and testing; soldering, use of a voltmeter, ammeter, and ohmmeter

Subelement T8 – Modulation modes, amateur satellite operation, operating activities, non-voice communications

[4 Exam Questions – 4 Groups]

T8A – Modulation modes; bandwidth of various signals

T8B – Amateur satellite operation; Doppler shift, basic orbits, operating protocols

T8C – Operating activities; radio direction finding, radio control, contests, special event stations, basic linking over Internet

T8D – Non-voice communications; image data, digital modes, CW, packet, PSK31

Subelement T9 – Antennas, feedlines

[2 Exam Groups – 2 Questions]

T9A – Antennas; vertical and horizontal, concept of gain, common portable and mobile antennas, relationships between antenna length and frequency

T9B – Feedlines; types, losses vs. frequency, SWR concepts, matching, weather protection, connectors

Subelement T0 – AC power circuits, antenna installation, RF hazards

[3 Exam Questions – 3 Groups]

T0A – AC power circuits; hazardous voltages, fuses and circuit breakers, grounding, lightning protection, battery safety, electrical code compliance

T0B – Antenna installation; tower safety, overhead power lines

T0C – RF hazards; radiation exposure, proximity to antennas, recognized safe power levels, exposure to others

Once your name and call sign are available in the FCC database, you have the privilege of operating on all VHF (2 m) and UHF (70 cm) frequencies above 30 megahertz (MHz) and HF frequencies 80, 40, and 15 meter, and on the 10 meter band using Morse code (CW), voice, and digital mode. For a Technician license in Pennsylvania, your call sign will consist of a two-letter prefix beginning with K or W, the number three (3), and a three-letter suffix. The single digit number in the call sign is determined according to which area of the US you obtain your first license. Even though you may move to another state, you keep this number in your call sign. This is also true should you upgrade to a higher license and get a new call sign. The numeral portion of your call sign stays the same.

Call Sign Numbers

Below is a chart showing the various numbers and the state(s) in which you would obtain the number.

Call Sign Number	State(s)
0	CO, IA, KS, MN, MO, NE, ND, SD
1	CT, ME, MA, NH, RI, VT
2	NJ, NY
3	DE, DC, MD, PA
4	AL, FL, GA, KY, NC, SC, TN, VA
5	AR, LA, MS, NM, OK, TX
6	CA
7	AZ, ID, MT, NV, OR, WA, UT, WY
8	MI, OH, WV
9	IL, IN, WI

Residents of Alaska may have any of the following call sign prefixes assigned to them: AL0-7, KL0-7, NL0-7, or WL0-7. Likewise, residents of Hawaii may have the prefix AH6-7, KH6-7, NH6-7, or WH6-7 assigned.

Once you obtain your Technician license, do not stop there. Go and get your General license.

General is the second of three ham license classes. Like the Technician license, to get a General license, you merely have to take a 35-question multiple choice exam and pay your license fee. Passing is still at least 26 correct answers and the fee is the same (less than $20). Again the question pool is available for free online (http://www.ncvec.org/page.php?id=358). It is also available in such print publications as *The ARRL General Class License Manual 7th Edition* (ISBN 978-0-87259-811-9). The current General pool of questions is to be used from July 1, 2011 to June 30, 2015. Be sure the question pool you are using is current. Being a bit more comprehensive than the Technician license, the General license usually requires 15-20 hours of study to learn the material. Check Appendix A for a listing of clubs in Pennsylvania where you might take your exam. Once your name and NEW call sign is listed in the FCC database, you're good to go. For a General license in Pennsylvania, your call sign will consist of a one-letter prefix beginning with K, N or W, the number three (3), and a three-letter suffix.

Topics for the General License in Amateur Radio

The General license exam covers regulations, operating practices and electronic theory. Below is the syllabus for the General Class.

Subelement G1 – Commission's Rules
(5 Exam Questions – 5 Groups)
G1A – General Class control operator frequency privileges; primary and secondary allocations
G1B – Antenna structure limitations; good engineering and good amateur practice, beacon operation; restricted operation; retransmitting radio signals
G1C – Transmitter power regulations; data emission standards
G1D – Volunteer Examiners and Volunteer Examiner Coordinators; temporary identification
G1E – Control categories; repeater regulations; harmful interference; third party rules; ITU regions

Subelement G2 – Operating procedures
(5 Exam Questions – 5 Groups)
G2A – Phone operating procedures; USB/LSB utilization conventions; procedural signals; breaking into a OSO in progress; VOX operation
G2B – Operating courtesy; band plans, emergencies, including drills and emergency communications

G2C – CW operating procedures and procedural signals; Q signals and common abbreviations; full break in

G2D – Amateur Auxiliary; minimizing interference; HF operations

G2E – Digital operating; procedures, procedural signals and common abbreviations

Subelement G3 – Radio wave propagation

(3 Exam Questions – 3 Groups)

G3A – Sunspots and solar radiation; ionospheric disturbances; propagation forecasting and indices

G3B – Maximum Usable Frequency; Lowest Usable Frequency; propagation

G3C – Ionospheric layers; critical angle and frequency; HF scatter; Near Vertical Incidence Sky waves

Subelement G4 – Amateur radio practices

(5 Exam Questions – 5 Groups)

G4A – Station Operation and setup

G4B – Test and monitoring equipment; two-tone test

G4C – Interference with consumer electronics; grounding; DSP

G4D – Speech processors; S meters; sideband operation near band edges

G4E – HF mobile radio installations; emergency and battery powered operation

Subelement G5 – Electrical principles

(3 Exam Questions – 3 Groups)

G5A – Reactance; inductance; capacitance; impedance; impedance matching

G5B – The Decibel; current and voltage dividers; electrical power calculations; sine wave root-mean-square (RMS) values; PEP calculations

G5C – Resistors; capacitors and inductors in series and parallel; transformers

Subelement G6 – Circuit components

(3 Exam Questions – 3 Groups)

G6A – Resistors; capacitors; inductors

G6B – Rectifiers; solid state diodes and transistors; vacuum tubes; batteries

G6C – Analog and digital integrated circuits (ICs); microprocessors; memory; I/O devices; microwave ICs (MMICs); display devices

Subelement G7 – Practical circuits

(3 Exam Questions – 3 Groups)

G7A – Power supplies; schematic symbols

G7B – Digital circuits; amplifiers and oscillators

G7C – Receivers and transmitters; filters, oscillators

Subelement G8 – Signals and emissions

(2 Exam Questions – 2 Groups)

G8A – Carriers and modulation; AM; FM; single and double sideband; modulation envelope; overmodulation

G8B – Frequency mixing; multiplication; HF data communications; bandwidths of various modes; deviation

Subelement G9 – Antennas and feed lines

(4 Exam Questions – 4 Groups)

G9A – Antenna feed lines; characteristic impedance and attenuation; SWR calculation, measurement and effects; matching networks

G9B – Basic antennas

G9C – Directional antennas

G9D – Specialized antennas

Subelement G0 – Electrical and RF safety

(2 Exam Questions – 2 Groups)

G0A – RF safety principles, rules and guidelines; routine station elevation

G0B – Safety in the ham shack; electrical shock and treatment, safety grounding, fusing, interlocks, wiring, antenna and tower safety

With a General license, you can use all VHF and UHF frequencies and most of the HF frequencies. You would have access to the 160, 30, 17, 12, and 10 meter bands and access to major parts of the 80, 40, 20, and 15 meter bands. Of course, this is in addition to all bands available to Technician license holders.

Amateur Extra is the third of three ham license classes. Like the Technician and General classes, you merely have to pass a test and pay your fee to get your Amateur Extra license. This class of license is more comprehensive than the lower license classes. The exam is longer – 50 questions – and the minimum passing score is higher – 37. However, once you get your Amateur Extra license, all ham frequencies, VHF, UHF and HF are available for your enjoyment. The Extra exam covers regulations, specialized operating practices, advanced electronics theory, and radio equipment design.

Like for the other license classes, the question pool for the Amateur Extra license is available online for downloading (http://www.ncvec.org/downloads/REVISED%202012-2016%20Extra%20Class%20Pool.doc). It is also available in print form in such publications as *The ARRL Extra Class License Manual Revised 9th Edition* (ISBN 978-0-87259-887-4).

Topics for the Extra License in Amateur Radio

Below is the syllabus for the Amateur Extra Class for July 1, 2012 to June 30, 2016.

Subelement E1 – Commission's Rules

[6 Exam Questions – 6 Groups]

E1A – Operating Standards: frequency privileges; emission standards; automatic message forwarding; frequency sharing; stations aboard ships or aircraft

E1B – Station restrictions and special operations: restrictions on station location; general operating restrictions, spurious emissions, control operator reimbursement; antenna structure restrictions; RACES operations

E1C – Station control: definitions and restrictions pertaining to local, automatic and remote control operation; control operator responsibilities for remote and automatically controlled stations

E1D – Amateur Satellite service: definitions and purpose; license requirements for space stations; available frequencies and bands; telecommand and telemetry operations; restrictions, and special provisions; notification requirements

E1E – Volunteer examiner program: definitions, qualifications, preparation and administration of exams; accreditation; question pools; documentation requirements

E1F – Miscellaneous rules: external RF power amplifiers; national quiet zone; business communications; compensated communications; spread spectrum; auxiliary stations; reciprocal operating privileges; IARP and CEPT licenses; third party communications with foreign countries; special temporary authority

Subelement E2 – Operating procedures

[5 Exam Questions – 5 Groups]

E2A – Amateur radio in space: amateur satellites; orbital mechanics; frequencies and modes; satellite hardware; satellite operations

E2B – Television practices: fast scan television standards and techniques; slow scan television standards and techniques

E2C – Operating methods: contest and DX operating; spread-spectrum transmissions; selecting an operating frequency

E2D – Operating methods: VHF and UHF digital modes; APRS

E2E – Operating methods: operating HF digital modes; error correction

Subelement E3 – Radio wave propagation

[3 Exam Questions – 3 Groups]

E3A – Propagation and technique, Earth-Moon-Earth communications; meteor scatter

E3B – Propagation and technique, trans-equatorial; long path; gray-line; multi-path propagation

E3C – Propagation and technique, Aurora propagation; selective fading; radio-path horizon; take-off angle over flat or sloping terrain; effects of ground on propagation; less common propagation modes

Subelement E4 – Amateur practices

[5 Exam Questions – 5 Groups]

E4A – Test equipment: analog and digital instruments; spectrum and network analyzers, antenna analyzers; oscilloscopes; testing transistors; RF measurements

E4B – Measurement technique and limitations: instrument accuracy and performance limitations; probes; techniques to minimize errors; measurement of "Q"; instrument calibration

E4C – Receiver performance characteristics, phase noise, capture effect, noise floor, image rejection, MDS, signal-to-noise-ratio; selectivity

E4D – Receiver performance characteristics, blocking dynamic range, intermodulation and cross-modulation interference; 3rd order intercept; desensitization; preselection

E4E – Noise suppression: system noise; electrical appliance noise; line noise; locating noise sources; DSP noise reduction; noise blankers

Subelement E5 – Electrical principles

[4 Exam Questions – 4 Groups]

E5A – Resonance and Q: characteristics of resonant circuits: series and parallel resonance; Q; half-power bandwidth; phase relationships in reactive circuits

E5B – Time constants and phase relationships: RLC time constants: definition; time constants in RL and RC circuits; phase angle between voltage and current; phase angles of series and parallel circuits

E5C – Impedance plots and coordinate systems: plotting impedances in polar coordinates; rectangular coordinates

E5D – AC and RF energy in real circuits: skin effect; electrostatic and electromagnetic fields; reactive power; power factor; coordinate systems

Subelement E6 – Circuit components

[6 Exam Questions – 6 Groups]

E6A – Semiconductor materials and devices: semiconductor materials germanium, silicon, P-type, N-type; transistor types: NPN, PNP, junction, field-effect transistors: enhancement mode; depletion mode; MOS; CMOS; N-channel; P-channel

E6B – Semiconductor diodes

E6C – Integrated circuits: TTL digital integrated circuits; CMOS digital integrated circuits; gates

E6D – Optical devices and toroids: cathode-ray tube devices; charge-coupled devices (CCDs); liquid crystal displays (LCDs); toroids: permeability, core material, selecting, winding

E6E – Piezoelectric crystals and MMICs: quartz crystals; crystal oscillators and filters; monolithic amplifiers

E6F – Optical components and power systems: photoconductive principles and effects, photovoltaic systems, optical couplers, optical sensors, and optoisolators

Subelement E7 – Practical circuits

[8 Exam Questions – 8 Groups]

E7A – Digital circuits: digital circuit principles and logic circuits: classes of logic elements; positive and negative logic; frequency dividers; truth tables

E7B – Amplifiers: Class of operation; vacuum tube and solid-state circuits; distortion and intermodulation; spurious and parasitic suppression; microwave amplifiers

E7C – Filters and matching networks: filters and impedance matching networks: types of networks; types of filters; filter applications; filter characteristics; impedance matching; DSP filtering

E7D – Power supplies and voltage regulators

E7E – Modulation and demodulation: reactance, phase and balanced modulators; detectors; mixer stages; DSP modulation and demodulation; software defined radio systems

E7F – Frequency markers and counters: frequency divider circuits; frequency marker generators; frequency counters

E7G – Active filters and op-amps: active audio filters; characteristics; basic circuit design; operational amplifiers

E7H – Oscillators and signal sources: types of oscillators; synthesizers and phase-locked loops; direct digital synthesizers

Subelement E8 – Signals and emissions

[4 Exam Questions – 4 Groups]

E8A – AC waveforms: sine, square, sawtooth and irregular waveforms; AC measurements; average and PEP of RF signals; pulse and digital signal waveforms

E8B – Modulation and demodulation: modulation methods; modulation index and deviation ratio; pulse modulation; frequency and time division multiplexing

E8C – Digital signals: digital communications modes; CW; information rate vs. bandwidth; spread-spectrum communications; modulation methods

E8D – Waves, measurements, and RF grounding: peak-to-peak values, polarization; RF grounding

Subelement E9 – Antennas and transmission lines

[8 Exam Questions – 8 Groups]

E9A – Isotropic and gain antennas: definition; used as a standard for comparison; radiation pattern; basic antenna parameters: radiation resistance and reactance, gain, beamwidth, efficiency

E9B – Antenna patterns: E and H plane patterns; gain as a function of pattern; antenna design; Yagi antennas

E9C – Wire and phased vertical antennas: beverage antennas; terminated and resonant rhombic antennas; elevation above real ground; ground effects as related to polarization; take-off angles

E9D – Directional antennas: gain; satellite antennas; antenna beamwidth; losses; SWR bandwidth; antenna efficiency; shortened and mobile antennas; grounding

E9E – Matching: matching antennas to feed lines; power dividers

E9F – Transmission lines: characteristics of open and shorted feed lines: 1/8 wavelength; 1/4 wavelength; 1/2 wavelength; feed lines: coax versus open-wire; velocity factor; electrical length; transformation characteristics of line terminated in impedance not equal to characteristic impedance

E9G – The Smith chart

E9H – Effective radiated power; system gains and losses; radio direction finding antennas

[1 exam question – 1 group]
E0A – Safety: amateur radio safety practices; RF radiation hazards; hazardous materials

Once your new call sign is listed in the FCC database, you are good to go. For an Amateur Extra license in Pennsylvania, your call sign will consist of a prefix of K, N or W, the number three (3), and a two-letter suffix, or a two-letter prefix beginning with A, N, K or W, the number three (3), and a one-letter suffix, or a two-letter prefix beginning with A, the number three (3), and a two-letter suffix.

Ham radio equipment can be expensive or you can do it "on the cheap." The cost will run from a couple hundred dollars to well in the thousands, depending on what you have available. eBay, and Craigslist are good places to start looking. Most ham clubs do some sort of hamfest annually wherein club members or others are willing to part with older equipment. See Appendix A for a list of clubs in Pennsylvania.

Another excellent source of equipment, as well as advice on setting the equipment up and how to use it properly, is current ham operators. In Appendix B, the author has listed all the FCC licensed ham operators in Pennsylvania, listed by city, and then sorted by street and house number on the street. Who knows, maybe someone who lives close to you is a ham operator. Be a good neighbor, stop by and have a chat with him/her.

Like CB radios, ham radios come in three formats – base, mobile, and handheld. They can use the electric company for power, or operate off a car battery. In the opinion of this author, in spite of the slightly higher cost of the equipment and having to take a test to legally use the equipment, ham radio is the way to go when concerned about communication during times of crisis.

Canadian Call Sign Prefixes

Because of our proximity to Canada, many times ham contact is made with our northern neighbors. Below is a chart showing the origin of Canadian call sign prefixes.

Call Sign Prefix	Provence or Territory
CY0	Sable Island
CY9	St. Paul Island
VA1, VE1	New Brunswick, Nova Scotia
VA2, VE2	Quebec
VA3, VE3	Ontario
VA4, VE4	Manitoba
VA5, VE5	Saskatchewan
VA6, VE6	Alberta
VA7, VE7	British Columbia
VE8	North West Territories
VE9	New Brunswick
VO1	Newfoundland

VO2	Labrador
VY0	Nunavut
VY1	Yukon
VY2	Prince Edward Island

Common Radio Bands in the United States

Certain radio bands are more popular with ham radio enthusiasts than others. Below is a chart showing these bands and when they are most popular.

	Band (meter)	Frequency (MHz)	Use
HF	160	1.8 – 2.0	Night
	80	3.5 – 4.0	Night and Local Day
	40	7.0 – 7.3	Night and Local Day
	30	10.1 – 10.15	CW and Digital
	20	14.0 – 14.350	World Wide Day and Night
	17	18.068 – 18.168	World Wide Day and Night
	15	21.0 – 21.450	Primarily Daytime
	12	24.890 – 24.990	Primarily Daytime
	10	28.0 – 29.70	Daytime during Sunspot highs
VHF	6	50 – 54	Local to World Wide
	2	144 – 148	Local to Medium Distance
UHF	70 cm	430 – 440	Local

Common Amateur Radio Bands in Canada

160 Meter Band - Maximum bandwidth 6 kHz
1.800 - 1.820 MHz - CW
1.820 - 1.830 MHz - Digital Modes
1 830 - 1.840 MHz - DX Window
1.840 - 2.000 MHz - SSB and other wide band modes

80 Meter Band - Maximum bandwidth 6 kHz
3.500 - 3.580 MHz - CW
3.580 - 3.620 MHz - Digital Modes
3.620 - 3.635 MHz - Packet/Digital Secondary
3.635 - 3.725 MHz - CW
3.725 - 3.790 MHz - SSB and other side band modes*
3.790 - 3.800 MHz - SSB DX Window
3.800 - 4.000 MHz - SSB and other wide band modes

40 Meter Band - Maximum bandwidth 6 kHz
7.000 - 7.035 MHz - CW
7.035 - 7.050 MHz - Digital Modes
7.040 - 7.050 MHz - International packet

7.050 - 7.100 MHz - SSB
7.100 - 7.120 MHz - Packet within Region 2
7.120 - 7.150 MHz - CW
7.150 - 7.300 MHz - SSB and other wide band modes

30 Meter Band - Maximum bandwidth 1 kHz
10.100 - 10.130 MHz - CW only
10.130 - 10.140 MHz - Digital Modes
10.140 - 10.150 MHz - Packet

20 Meter Band - Maximum bandwidth 6 kHz
14.000 - 14.070 MHz - CW only
14.070 - 14.095 MHz - Digital Mode
14.095 - 14.099 MHz - Packet
14.100 MHz - Beacons
14.101 - 14.112 MHz - CW, SSB, packet shared
14.112 - 14.350 MHz - SSB
14.225 - 14.235 MHz - SSTV

17 Meter Band - Maximum bandwidth 6 kHz
18.068 - 18.100 MHz - CW
18.100 - 18.105 MHz - Digital Modes
18.105 - 18.110 MHz - Packet
18.110 - 18.168 MHz - SSB and other wide band modes

15 Meter Band - maximum bandwidth 6 kHz
21.000 - 21.070 MHz - CW
21.070 - 21.090 MHz - Digital Modes
21.090 - 21.125 MHz - Packet
21.100 - 21.150 MHz - CW and SSB
21.150 - 21.335 MHz - SSB and other wide band modes
21.335 - 21.345 MHz - SSTV
21.345 - 21.450 MHz - SSB and other wide band modes

12 Meter Band - Maximum bandwidth 6 kHz
24.890 - 24.930 MHz - CW
24.920 - 24.925 MHz - Digital Modes
24.925 - 24.930 MHz - Packet
24.930 - 24.990 MHz - SSB and other wide band modes

10 Meter Band - Maximum band width 20 kHz
28.000 - 28.200 MHz - CW
28.070 - 28.120 MHz - Digital Modes
28.120 - 28.190 MHz - Packet

| 28.190 - 28.200 MHz - Beacons |
| 28.200 - 29.300 MHz - SSB and other wide band modes |
| 29.300 - 29.510 MHz - Satellite |
| 29.510 - 29.700 MHz - SSB, FM and repeaters |

160 Meters (1.8-2.0 MHz)

| 1.800 - 2.000 CW |
| 1.800 - 1.810 Digital Modes |
| 1.810 CW QRP |
| 1.843-2.000 SSB, SSTV and other wideband modes |
| 1.910 SSB QRP |
| 1.995 - 2.000 Experimental |
| 1.999 - 2.000 Beacons |

80 Meters (3.5-4.0 MHz)

| 3.590 RTTY/Data DX |
| 3.570-3.600 RTTY/Data |
| 3.790-3.800 DX window |
| 3.845 SSTV |
| 3.885 AM calling frequency |

40 Meters (7.0-7.3 MHz)

| 7.040 RTTY/Data DX |
| 7.080-7.125 RTTY/Data |
| 7.171 SSTV |
| 7.290 AM calling frequency |

30 Meters (10.1-10.15 MHz)

| 10.130-10.140 RTTY |
| 10.140-10.150 Packet |

20 Meters (14.0-14.35 MHz)

| 14.070-14.095 RTTY |
| 14.095-14.0995 Packet |
| 14.100 NCDXF Beacons |
| 14.1005-14.112 Packet |
| 14.230 SSTV |
| 14.286 AM calling frequency |

17 Meters (18.068-18.168 MHz)

| 18.100-18.105 RTTY |
| 18.105-18.110 Packet |

15 Meters (21.0-21.45 MHz)

| 21.070-21.110 RTTY/Data |

21.340 SSTV

12 Meters (24.89-24.99 MHz)

24.920-24.925 RTTY
24.925-24.930 Packet

10 Meters (28-29.7 MHz)

28.000-28.070 CW
28.070-28.150 RTTY
28.150-28.190 CW
28.200-28.300 Beacons
28.300-29.300 Phone
28.680 SSTV
29.000-29.200 AM
29.300-29.510 Satellite Downlinks
29.520-29.590 Repeater Inputs
29.600 FM Simplex
29.610-29.700 Repeater Outputs

6 Meters (50-54 MHz)

50.0-50.1 CW, beacons
50.060-50.080 beacon subband
50.1-50.3 SSB, CW
50.10-50.125 DX window
50.125 SSB calling
50.3-50.6 All modes
50.6-50.8 Nonvoice communications
50.62 Digital (packet) calling
50.8-51.0 Radio remote control (20-kHz channels)
51.0-51.1 Pacific DX window
51.12-51.48 Repeater inputs (19 channels)
51.12-51.18 Digital repeater inputs
51.5-51.6 Simplex (six channels)
51.62-51.98 Repeater outputs (19 channels)
51.62-51.68 Digital repeater outputs
52.0-52.48 Repeater inputs (except as noted; 23 channels)
52.02, 52.04 FM simplex
52.2 TEST PAIR (input)
52.5-52.98 Repeater output (except as noted; 23 channels)
52.525 Primary FM simplex
52.54 Secondary FM simplex
52.7 TEST PAIR (output)
53.0-53.48 Repeater inputs (except as noted; 19 channels)
53.0 Remote base FM simplex
53.02 Simplex
53.1, 53.2, 53.3, 53.4 Radio remote control

53.5-53.98 Repeater outputs (except as noted; 19 channels)
53.5, 53.6, 53.7, 53.8 Radio remote control
53.52, 53.9 Simplex

2 Meters (144-148 MHz)

144.00-144.05 EME (CW)
144.05-144.10 General CW and weak signals
144.10-144.20 EME and weak-signal SSB
144.200 National calling frequency
144.200-144.275 General SSB operation
144.275-144.300 Propagation beacons
144.30-144.50 New OSCAR subband
144.50-144.60 Linear translator inputs
144.60-144.90 FM repeater inputs
144.90-145.10 Weak signal and FM simplex (145.01,03,05,07,09 are widely used for packet)
145.10-145.20 Linear translator outputs
145.20-145.50 FM repeater outputs
145.50-145.80 Miscellaneous and experimental modes
145.80-146.00 OSCAR subband
146.01-146.37 Repeater inputs
146.40-146.58 Simplex
146.52 National Simplex Calling Frequency
146.61-146.97 Repeater outputs
147.00-147.39 Repeater outputs
147.42-147.57 Simplex
147.60-147.99 Repeater inputs

1.25 Meters (222-225 MHz)

222.0-222.150 Weak-signal modes
222.0-222.025 EME
222.05-222.06 Propagation beacons
222.1 SSB & CW calling frequency
222.10-222.15 Weak-signal CW & SSB
222.15-222.25 Local coordinator's option; weak signal, ACSB, repeater inputs, control
222.25-223.38 FM repeater inputs only
223.40-223.52 FM simplex
223.52-223.64 Digital, packet
223.64-223.70 Links, control
223.71-223.85 Local coordinator's option; FM simplex, packet, repeater outputs
223.85-224.98 Repeater outputs only

70 Centimeters (420-450 MHz)

420.00-426.00 ATV repeater or simplex with 421.25 MHz video carrier control links and experimental
426.00-432.00 ATV simplex with 427.250-MHz video carrier frequency

432.00-432.07 EME (Earth-Moon-Earth)
432.07-432.10 Weak-signal CW
432.10 70-cm calling frequency
432.10-432.30 Mixed-mode and weak-signal work
432.30-432.40 Propagation beacons
432.40-433.00 Mixed-mode and weak-signal work
433.00-435.00 Auxiliary/repeater links
435.00-438.00 Satellite only (internationally)
438.00-444.00 ATV repeater input with 439.250-MHz video carrier frequency and repeater links
442.00-445.00 Repeater inputs and outputs (local option)
445.00-447.00 Shared by auxiliary and control links, repeaters and simplex (local option)
446.00 National simplex frequency
447.00-450.00 Repeater inputs and outputs (local option)

33 Centimeters (902-928 MHz)

902.0-903.0 Narrow-bandwidth, weak-signal communications
902.0-902.8 SSTV, FAX, ACSSB, experimental
902.1 Weak-signal calling frequency
902.8-903.0 Reserved for EME, CW expansion
903.1 Alternate calling frequency
903.0-906.0 Digital communications
906-909 FM repeater inputs
909-915 ATV
915-918 Digital communications
918-921 FM repeater outputs
921-927 ATV
927-928 FM simplex and links

23 Centimeters (1240-1300 MHz)

1240-1246 ATV #1
1246-1248 Narrow-bandwidth FM point-to-point links and digital, duplex with 1258-1260.
1248-1258 Digital Communications
1252-1258 ATV #2
1258-1260 Narrow-bandwidth FM point-to-point links digital, duplexed with 1246-1252
1260-1270 Satellite uplinks, reference WARC '79
1260-1270 Wide-bandwidth experimental, simplex ATV
1270-1276 Repeater inputs, FM and linear, paired with 1282-1288, 239 pairs every 25 kHz, e.g. 1270.025, .050, etc.
1271-1283 Non-coordinated test pair
1276-1282 ATV #3
1282-1288 Repeater outputs, paired with 1270-1276
1288-1294 Wide-bandwidth experimental, simplex ATV
1294-1295 Narrow-bandwidth FM simplex services, 25-kHz channels
1294.5 National FM simplex calling frequency

1295-1297 Narrow bandwidth weak-signal communications (no FM)
1295.0-1295.8 SSTV, FAX, ACSSB, experimental
1295.8-1296.0 Reserved for EME, CW expansion
1296.00-1296.05 EME-exclusive
1296.07-1296.08 CW beacons
1296.1 CW, SSB calling frequency
1296.4-1296.6 Crossband linear translator input
1296.6-1296.8 Crossband linear translator output
1296.8-1297.0 Experimental beacons (exclusive)
1297-1300 Digital Communications

2300-2310 and 2390-2450 MHz

2300.0-2303.0 High-rate data
2303.0-2303.5 Packet
2303.5-2303.8 TTY packet
2303.9-2303.9 Packet, TTY, CW, EME
2303.9-2304.1 CW, EME
2304.1 Calling frequency
2304.1-2304.2 CW, EME, SSB
2304.2-2304.3 SSB, SSTV, FAX, Packet AM, Amtor
2304.30-2304.32 Propagation beacon network
2304.32-2304.40 General propagation beacons
2304.4-2304.5 SSB, SSTV, ACSSB, FAX, Packet AM, Amtor experimental
2304.5-2304.7 Crossband linear translator input
2304.7-2304.9 Crossband linear translator output
2304.9-2305.0 Experimental beacons
2305.0-2305.2 FM simplex (25 kHz spacing)
2305.20 FM simplex calling frequency
2305.2-2306.0 FM simplex (25 kHz spacing)
2306.0-2309.0 FM Repeaters (25 kHz) input
2309.0-2310.0 Control and auxiliary links
2390.0-2396.0 Fast-scan TV
2396.0-2399.0 High-rate data
2399.0-2399.5 Packet
2399.5-2400.0 Control and auxiliary links
2400.0-2403.0 Satellite
2403.0-2408.0 Satellite high-rate data
2408.0-2410.0 Satellite
2410.0-2413.0 FM repeaters (25 kHz) output
2413.0-2418.0 High-rate data
2418.0-2430.0 Fast-scan TV
2430.0-2433.0 Satellite
2433.0-2438.0 Satellite high-rate data
2438.0-2450.0 WB FM, FSTV, FMTV, SS experimental

3300-3500 MHz
3456.3-3456.4 Propagation beacons

5650-5925 MHz
5760.3-5760.4 Propagation beacons

10.00-10.50 GHz
10.368 Narrow band calling frequency 10.3683-10.3684 Propagation beacons
10.3640 Calling frequency

Now that you have your license (you do, don't you?), and your equipment, you are ready to go live. Below is a suggested start.

1) Assuming you have the HT set up to the appropriate frequency, and offset, press the mic button on the HT and say, "KK4HWX listening." Replace the KK4HWX with your own call sign, the one assigned to you by the FCC (it's the law). If no one responds to your call, you may wish to try again. Hopefully someone will respond to your call.

2) Once you get a response, it will be in the form of something like, "KK4HWX this is ??1??? in Eastport returning. My name is Florence. Back to you. ??1???" then a tone. Let us examine the response more closely. She first acknowledged your call sign (KK4HWX), then identified hers (??1???). From the 1 in her call sign, you know that she first got her license in Region 1, meaning she got it while a resident of CT, ME, MA, NH, RI, or VT. She then told you where she's transmitting from (Eastport). The term "returning" means that she is returning your call. Her name is Florence. The phrase, "Back to you" indicates that she is turning over the conversation to you. She then repeats her call sign. The tone indicates to you that it is okay to proceed with your response. BTW if she had used the term "Over" instead of "Back to you," it would mean the same thing, just fewer words.

3) At this point, press the mic button and continue with the conversation. You should restate your call sign often during the conversation (perhaps every 10 minutes or less and whenever you begin transmitting). Don't forget to say, "Over" or "Back to you" whenever you are giving Florence control of the conversation again.

4) When you are ready to stop the conversation, you should say goodbye or use the phrase "73", meaning "best wishes." Your conversation would end something like, "??1??? 73, this is KK4HWX clear and monitoring." The "clear and monitoring" indicates that you are going to continue to monitor the frequency. If you are not going to continue monitoring, you may wish to end the conversation with Florence with, "clear and QRT" instead. The QRT means that you are stopping transmissions.

Call Sign Phonics

Because of different accents of various people, sometimes it is difficult to understand call sign letters when spoken. For this reason, most ham operators verbalize their call sign using phonics. Below is a table listing the accepted phonics for letters and numbers.

A = ALFA	S = SIERRA
B = BRAVO	T = TANGO
C = CHARLIE	U = UNIFORM
D = DELTA	V = VICTOR
E = ECHO	W = WHISKEY
F = FOXTROT	X = X-RAY
G = GOLF	Y = YANKEE
H = HOTEL	Z = ZULU (ZED)
I = INDIA	1 = ONE
J = JULIETT	2 = TWO
K = KILO	3 = THREE (TREE)
L = LIMA	4 = FOUR
M = MIKE	5 = FIVE (FIFE)
N = NOVEMBER	6 = SIX
O = OSCAR	7 = SEVEN
P = PAPA (PA-PA')	8 = EIGHT
Q = QUEBEC (KAY-BEK')	9 = NINE (NINER)
R = ROMEO	0 = ZERO

The words in parentheses are the pronunciation or the alternate pronunciations for the words or numbers, but you will hear both used. With the letter Z, (ZED) is by far the most commonly used. With the number 9, NINER is the most common and easiest to understand ON THE AIR.

If you wish to use Morse code (CW) instead of voice communication, the "conversation" would follow the same steps, with a few modifications. To type out each word would require a lot of typing and translating. If you are like this author, more means more, i.e., more typing means more typos are likely. To help with this situation, CW enthusiasts have developed a language all their own – they use abbreviations for common phrases. Below is a chart showing some of these abbreviations.

Abbreviation	Use
AR	Over
de	From or "this is"
ES	And
GM	Good Morning
K	Go
KN	Go only
NM	Name
QTH	Location
RPT	Report
R	Roger
SK	Clear

tnx	Thanks
UR	Your, you are
73	Best Wishes

Morse Code and Amateur Radio

If you wish to use CW, but are concerned about accuracy, you might consider purchasing a Morse code translator. This is an electronic device that you place in front of your speakers. It takes the CW sounds and translates them into English and displays the transmission on an LCD display. For the reverse, you can pick up a CW keyboard. With the keyboard, you type in your message and it converts the text to Morse code. The translator does not need to be attached to your ham equipment, whereas the keyboard would.

For your convenience, below is a table showing the Morse code signals and their meaning.

Character	Code
A	· —
B	— · · ·
C	— · — ·
D	— · ·
E	·
F	· · — ·
G	— — ·
H	· · · ·
I	· ·
J	· — — —
K	— · —
L	· — · ·
M	— —
N	— ·
O	— — —
P	· — — ·
Q	— — · —
R	· — ·
S	· · ·
T	—
U	· · —
V	· · · —
W	· — —
X	— · · —
Y	— · — —
Z	— — · ·
0	— — — — —
1	· — — — —

2	· · — — —
3	· · · — —
4	· · · · —
5	· · · · ·
6	— · · · ·
7	— — · · ·
8	— — — · ·
9	— — — — ·
Ampersand [&], Wait	· — · · ·
Apostrophe [']	· — — — — ·
At sign [@]	· — — · — ·
Colon [:]	— — — · · ·
Comma [,]	— — · · — —
Dollar sign [$]	· · · — · · —
Double dash [=]	— · · · —
Exclamation mark [!]	— · — · — —
Hyphen, Minus [-]	— · · · · —
Parenthesis closed [)]	— · — — · —
Parenthesis open [(]	— · — — ·
Period [.]	· — · — · —
Plus [+]	· — · — ·
Question mark [?]	· · — — · ·
Quotation mark ["]	· — · · — ·
Semicolon [;]	— · — · — ·
Slash [/], Fraction bar	— · · — ·
Underscore [_]	· · — — · —

An advantage of using Morse Code is that when broadcasting CW, you are using reduced power, thereby saving your battery. Your battery is used only while actually transmitting or receiving.

International Call Sign Prefixes

As was stated earlier, all ham radio call signs begin with letters (or numbers) taken from blocks assigned to each country of the world by the *ITU - International Telecommunications Union,* a body controlled by the United Nations. The following chart indicates which call sign series are allocated to which countries.

Call Sign Series	Allocated to
AAA-ALZ	**United States of America**
AMA-AOZ	Spain
APA-ASZ	Pakistan (Islamic Republic of)
ATA-AWZ	India (Republic of)
AXA-AXZ	Australia
AYA-AZZ	Argentine Republic

A2A-A2Z	Botswana (Republic of)
A3A-A3Z	Tonga (Kingdom of)
A4A-A4Z	Oman (Sultanate of)
A5A-A5Z	Bhutan (Kingdom of)
A6A-A6Z	United Arab Emirates
A7A-A7Z	Qatar (State of)
A8A-A8Z	Liberia (Republic of)
A9A-A9Z	Bahrain (State of)
BAA-BZZ	China (People's Republic of)
CAA-CEZ	Chile
CFA-CKZ	Canada
CLA-CMZ	Cuba
CNA-CNZ	Morocco (Kingdom of)
COA-COZ	Cuba
CPA-CPZ	Bolivia (Republic of)
CQA-CUZ	Portugal
CVA-CXZ	Uruguay (Eastern Republic of)
CYA-CZZ	Canada
C2A-C2Z	Nauru (Republic of)
C3A-C3Z	Andorra (Principality of)
C4A-C4Z	Cyprus (Republic of)
C5A-C5Z	Gambia (Republic of the)
C6A-C6Z	Bahamas (Commonwealth of the)
C7A-C7Z	World Meteorological Organization
C8A-C9Z	Mozambique (Republic of)
DAA-DRZ	Germany (Federal Republic of)
DSA-DTZ	Korea (Republic of)
DUA-DZZ	Philippines (Republic of the)
D2A-D3Z	Angola (Republic of)
D4A-D4Z	Cape Verde (Republic of)
D5A-D5Z	Liberia (Republic of)
D6A-D6Z	Comoros (Islamic Federal Republic of the)
D7A-D9Z	Korea (Republic of)
EAA-EHZ	Spain
EIA-EJZ	Ireland
EKA-EKZ	Armenia (Republic of)
ELA-ELZ	Liberia (Republic of)
EMA-EOZ	Ukraine
EPA-EQZ	Iran (Islamic Republic of)
ERA-ERZ	Moldova (Republic of)
ESA-ESZ	Estonia (Republic of)
ETA-ETZ	Ethiopia (Federal Democratic Republic of)
EUA-EWZ	Belarus (Republic of)
EXA-EXZ	Kyrgyz Republic
EYA-EYZ	Tajikistan (Republic of)

EZA-EZZ	Turkmenistan
E2A-E2Z	Thailand
E3A-E3Z	Eritrea
E4A-E4Z	Palestinian Authority
E5A-E5Z	New Zealand - Cook Islands (WRC-07)
E7A-E7Z	Bosnia and Herzegovina (Republic of) (WRC-07)
FAA-FZZ	France
GAA-GZZ	United Kingdom of Great Britain and Northern Ireland
HAA-HAZ	Hungary (Republic of)
HBA-HBZ	Switzerland (Confederation of)
HCA-HDZ	Ecuador
HEA-HEZ	Switzerland (Confederation of)
HFA-HFZ	Poland (Republic of)
HGA-HGZ	Hungary (Republic of)
HHA-HHZ	Haiti (Republic of)
HIA-HIZ	Dominican Republic
HJA-HKZ	Colombia (Republic of)
HLA-HLZ	Korea (Republic of)
HMA-HMZ	Democratic People's Republic of Korea
HNA-HNZ	Iraq (Republic of)
HOA-HPZ	Panama (Republic of)
HQA-HRZ	Honduras (Republic of)
HSA-HSZ	Thailand
HTA-HTZ	Nicaragua
HUA-HUZ	El Salvador (Republic of)
HVA-HVZ	Vatican City State
HWA-HYZ	France
HZA-HZZ	Saudi Arabia (Kingdom of)
H2A-H2Z	Cyprus (Republic of)
H3A-H3Z	Panama (Republic of)
H4A-H4Z	Solomon Islands
H6A-H7Z	Nicaragua
H8A-H9Z	Panama (Republic of)
IAA-IZZ	Italy
JAA-JSZ	Japan
JTA-JVZ	Mongolia
JWA-JXZ	Norway
JYA-JYZ	Jordan (Hashemite Kingdom of)
JZA-JZZ	Indonesia (Republic of)
J2A-J2Z	Djibouti (Republic of)
J3A-J3Z	Grenada
J4A-J4Z	Greece
J5A-J5Z	Guinea-Bissau (Republic of)
J6A-J6Z	Saint Lucia
J7A-J7Z	Dominica (Commonwealth of)

J8A-J8Z	Saint Vincent and the Grenadines
KAA-KZZ	**United States of America**
LAA-LNZ	Norway
LOA-LWZ	Argentine Republic
LXA-LXZ	Luxembourg
LYA-LYZ	Lithuania (Republic of)
LZA-LZZ	Bulgaria (Republic of)
L2A-L9Z	Argentine Republic
MAA-MZZ	United Kingdom of Great Britain and Northern Ireland
NAA-NZZ	**United States of America**
OAA-OCZ	Peru
ODA-ODZ	Lebanon
OEA-OEZ	Austria
OFA-OJZ	Finland
OKA-OLZ	Czech Republic
OMA-OMZ	Slovak Republic
ONA-OTZ	Belgium
OUA-OZZ	Denmark
PAA-PIZ	Netherlands (Kingdom of the)
PJA-PJZ	Netherlands (Kingdom of the) - Netherlands Antilles
PKA-POZ	Indonesia (Republic of)
PPA-PYZ	Brazil (Federative Republic of)
PZA-PZZ	Suriname (Republic of)
P2A-P2Z	Papua New Guinea
P3A-P3Z	Cyprus (Republic of)
P4A-P4Z	Netherlands (Kingdom of the) - Aruba
P5A-P9Z	Democratic People's Republic of Korea
RAA-RZZ	Russian Federation
SAA-SMZ	Sweden
SNA-SRZ	Poland (Republic of)
SSA-SSM	Egypt (Arab Republic of)
SSN-STZ	Sudan (Republic of the)
SUA-SUZ	Egypt (Arab Republic of)
SVA-SZZ	Greece
S2A-S3Z	Bangladesh (People's Republic of)
S5A-S5Z	Slovenia (Republic of)
S6A-S6Z	Singapore (Republic of)
S7A-S7Z	Seychelles (Republic of)
S8A-S8Z	South Africa (Republic of)
S9A-S9Z	Sao Tome and Principe (Democratic Republic of)
TAA-TCZ	Turkey
TDA-TDZ	Guatemala (Republic of)
TEA-TEZ	Costa Rica
TFA-TFZ	Iceland
TGA-TGZ	Guatemala (Republic of)

THA-THZ	France
TIA-TIZ	Costa Rica
TJA-TJZ	Cameroon (Republic of)
TKA-TKZ	France
TLA-TLZ	Central African Republic
TMA-TMZ	France
TNA-TNZ	Congo (Republic of the)
TOA-TQZ	France
TRA-TRZ	Gabonese Republic
TSA-TSZ	Tunisia
TTA-TTZ	Chad (Republic of)
TUA-TUZ	Côte d'Ivoire (Republic of)
TVA-TXZ	France
TYA-TYZ	Benin (Republic of)
TZA-TZZ	Mali (Republic of)
T2A-T2Z	Tuvalu
T3A-T3Z	Kiribati (Republic of)
T4A-T4Z	Cuba
T5A-T5Z	Somali Democratic Republic
T6A-T6Z	Afghanistan (Islamic State of)
T7A-T7Z	San Marino (Republic of)
T8A-T8Z	Palau (Republic of)
UAA-UIZ	Russian Federation
UJA-UMZ	Uzbekistan (Republic of)
UNA-UQZ	Kazakhstan (Republic of)
URA-UZZ	Ukraine
VAA-VGZ	Canada
VHA-VNZ	Australia
VOA-VOZ	Canada
VPA-VQZ	United Kingdom of Great Britain and Northern Ireland
VRA-VRZ	China (People's Republic of) - Hong Kong
VSA-VSZ	United Kingdom of Great Britain and Northern Ireland
VTA-VWZ	India (Republic of)
VXA-VYZ	Canada
VZA-VZZ	Australia
V2A-V2Z	Antigua and Barbuda
V3A-V3Z	Belize
V4A-V4Z	Saint Kitts and Nevis
V5A-V5Z	Namibia (Republic of)
V6A-V6Z	Micronesia (Federated States of)
V7A-V7Z	Marshall Islands (Republic of the)
V8A-V8Z	Brunei Darussalam
WAA-WZZ	**United States of America**
XAA-XIZ	Mexico
XJA-XOZ	Canada

XPA-XPZ	Denmark
XQA-XRZ	Chile
XSA-XSZ	China (People's Republic of)
XTA-XTZ	Burkina Faso
XUA-XUZ	Cambodia (Kingdom of)
XVA-XVZ	Viet Nam (Socialist Republic of)
XWA-XWZ	Lao People's Democratic Republic
XXA-XXZ	China (People's Republic of) - Macao (WRC-07)
XYA-XZZ	Myanmar (Union of)
YAA-YAZ	Afghanistan (Islamic State of)
YBA-YHZ	Indonesia (Republic of)
YIA-YIZ	Iraq (Republic of)
YJA-YJZ	Vanuatu (Republic of)
YKA-YKZ	Syrian Arab Republic
YLA-YLZ	Latvia (Republic of)
YMA-YMZ	Turkey
YNA-YNZ	Nicaragua
YOA-YRZ	Romania
YSA-YSZ	El Salvador (Republic of)
YTA-YUZ	Serbia (Republic of) (WRC-07)
YVA-YYZ	Venezuela (Republic of)
Y2A-Y9Z	Germany (Federal Republic of)
ZAA-ZAZ	Albania (Republic of)
ZBA-ZJZ	United Kingdom of Great Britain and Northern Ireland
ZKA-ZMZ	New Zealand
ZNA-ZOZ	United Kingdom of Great Britain and Northern Ireland
ZPA-ZPZ	Paraguay (Republic of)
ZQA-ZQZ	United Kingdom of Great Britain and Northern Ireland
ZRA-ZUZ	South Africa (Republic of)
ZVA-ZZZ	Brazil (Federative Republic of)
Z2A-Z2Z	Zimbabwe (Republic of)
Z3A-Z3Z	The Former Yugoslav Republic of Macedonia
2AA-2ZZ	United Kingdom of Great Britain and Northern Ireland
3AA-3AZ	Monaco (Principality of)
3BA-3BZ	Mauritius (Republic of)
3CA-3CZ	Equatorial Guinea (Republic of)
3DA-3DM	Swaziland (Kingdom of)
3DN-3DZ	Fiji (Republic of)
3EA-3FZ	Panama (Republic of)
3GA-3GZ	Chile
3HA-3UZ	China (People's Republic of)
3VA-3VZ	Tunisia
3WA-3WZ	Viet Nam (Socialist Republic of)
3XA-3XZ	Guinea (Republic of)
3YA-3YZ	Norway

3ZA-3ZZ	Poland (Republic of)
4AA-4CZ	Mexico
4DA-4IZ	Philippines (Republic of the)
4JA-4KZ	Azerbaijani Republic
4LA-4LZ	Georgia (Republic of)
4MA-4MZ	Venezuela (Republic of)
4OA-4OZ	Montenegro (Republic of) (WRC-07)
4PA-4SZ	Sri Lanka (Democratic Socialist Republic of)
4TA-4TZ	Peru
4UA-4UZ	United Nations
4VA-4VZ	Haiti (Republic of)
4WA-4WZ	Democratic Republic of Timor-Leste (WRC-03)
4XA-4XZ	Israel (State of)
4YA-4YZ	International Civil Aviation Organization
4ZA-4ZZ	Israel (State of)
5AA-5AZ	Libya (Socialist People's Libyan Arab Jamahiriya)
5BA-5BZ	Cyprus (Republic of)
5CA-5GZ	Morocco (Kingdom of)
5HA-5IZ	Tanzania (United Republic of)
5JA-5KZ	Colombia (Republic of)
5LA-5MZ	Liberia (Republic of)
5NA-5OZ	Nigeria (Federal Republic of)
5PA-5QZ	Denmark
5RA-5SZ	Madagascar (Republic of)
5TA-5TZ	Mauritania (Islamic Republic of)
5UA-5UZ	Niger (Republic of the)
5VA-5VZ	Togolese Republic
5WA-5WZ	Samoa (Independent State of)
5XA-5XZ	Uganda (Republic of)
5YA-5ZZ	Kenya (Republic of)
6AA-6BZ	Egypt (Arab Republic of)
6CA-6CZ	Syrian Arab Republic
6DA-6JZ	Mexico
6KA-6NZ	Korea (Republic of)
6OA-6OZ	Somali Democratic Republic
6PA-6SZ	Pakistan (Islamic Republic of)
6TA-6UZ	Sudan (Republic of the)
6VA-6WZ	Senegal (Republic of)
6XA-6XZ	Madagascar (Republic of)
6YA-6YZ	Jamaica
6ZA-6ZZ	Liberia (Republic of)
7AA-7IZ	Indonesia (Republic of)
7JA-7NZ	Japan
7OA-7OZ	Yemen (Republic of)
7PA-7PZ	Lesotho (Kingdom of)

7QA-7QZ	Malawi
7RA-7RZ	Algeria (People's Democratic Republic of)
7SA-7SZ	Sweden
7TA-7YZ	Algeria (People's Democratic Republic of)
7ZA-7ZZ	Saudi Arabia (Kingdom of)
8AA-8IZ	Indonesia (Republic of)
8JA-8NZ	Japan
8OA-8OZ	Botswana (Republic of)
8PA-8PZ	Barbados
8QA-8QZ	Maldives (Republic of)
8RA-8RZ	Guyana
8SA-8SZ	Sweden
8TA-8YZ	India (Republic of)
8ZA-8ZZ	Saudi Arabia (Kingdom of)
9AA-9AZ	Croatia (Republic of)
9BA-9DZ	Iran (Islamic Republic of)
9EA-9FZ	Ethiopia (Federal Democratic Republic of)
9GA-9GZ	Ghana
9HA-9HZ	Malta
9IA-9JZ	Zambia (Republic of)
9KA-9KZ	Kuwait (State of)
9LA-9LZ	Sierra Leone
9MA-9MZ	Malaysia
9NA-9NZ	Nepal
9OA-9TZ	Democratic Republic of the Congo
9UA-9UZ	Burundi (Republic of)
9VA-9VZ	Singapore (Republic of)
9WA-9WZ	Malaysia
9XA-9XZ	Rwandese Republic
9YA-9ZZ	Trinidad and Tobago

Third-Party Communications and Amateur Radio

If all of this information about ham radios is somewhat intimidating, do not despair. "You" can still use ham radios for communications without being a licensed operator. Yes, you do have to have a ham license in order to legally transmit by ham equipment (or be under the direct supervision of someone else who is licensed), but there is an alternative – third-party communication.

Third-party communications occur when a licensed operator sends either written or verbal messages on behalf of unlicensed persons or organizations. There are two "controls" on third-party communication.

First, the communication must be noncommercial and of a personal nature. Asking a ham operator to contact another ham operator located in an area just hit by tornados and, because of being without power, phones do not work in Grandma Sally's city so you can check up on her, is okay. Asking a ham to send a message out that you have an old Chevy for sale would not be okay.

Second, the message must be going to a permitted area. Transmitting from a US location to another US location is okay, but transmitting from the US to another country may not. Because third-party communications bypass a country's normal telephone and postal systems, many foreign governments forbid such communications. In order to transmit from one country to another, the other country must have signed a third-party agreement with the US. What follows is a list of those countries that do have third-party a communications agreement with the US.

V2	Antigua / Barbuda
LU	Argentina
VK	Australia
V3	Belize
CP	Bolivia
T9	Bosnia-Herzegovina
PY	Brazil
VE	Canada
CE	Chile
HK	Colombia
D6	Comoros (Federal Islamic Republic of)
TI	Costa Rica
CO	Cuba
HI	Dominican Republic
J7	Dominica
HC	Ecuador
YS	El Salvador
C5	Gambia, The
9G	Ghana
J3	Grenada
TG	Guatemala
8R	Guyana
HH	Haiti
HR	Honduras
4X	Israel
6Y	Jamaica
JY	Jordan
EL	Liberia
V7	Marshall Islands
XE	Mexico
V6	Micronesia, Federated States of
YN	Nicaragua
HP	Panama

ZP	Paraguay
OA	Peru
DU	Philippines
VR6	Pitcairn Island
V4	St. Christopher / Nevis
J6	St. Lucia
J8	St. Vincent and the Grenadines
9L	Sierra Leone
ZS	South Africa
3DA	Swaziland
9Y	Trinidad / Tobago
TA	Turkey
GB	United Kingdom
CX	Uruguay
YV	Venezuela
4U1ITUITU	Geneva
4U1VICVIC	Vienna

Remember, before TSHTF, keep your pantry well stocked, your powder dry, and your batteries fully charged. 73

APPENDIX A

American Radio Relay League

Affiliated Amateur Radio Clubs in

Pennsylvania

ARRL Affiliated Club	Keystone Amateur Radio Club
City:	Abington, PA
Call Sign:	W3PSH
Section:	EPA

ARRL Affiliated Club	PHIL-MONT Mobile Radio Club, Inc.
City:	Abington, PA
Call Sign:	W3QV
Section:	EPA
Links:	www.phil-mont.org

ARRL Affiliated Club	Mt Airy VHF Radio Club Inc.
City:	Abington, PA
Call Sign:	W3CCX
Section:	EPA
Links:	www.packratvhf.com

ARRL Affiliated Club	Frankford Radio Club
City:	Alburtis, PA
Call Sign:	W3FRC
Section:	EPA
Links:	www.gofrc.org

ARRL Affiliated Club	Horseshoe Amateur Radio Club
City:	Altoona, PA
Call Sign:	W3QZF
Section:	WPA
Links:	www.harc1.org

ARRL Affiliated Club	Young Ladies Radio League
City:	Altoona, PA
Section:	WPA
Links:	www.ylrl.org

ARRL Affiliated Club	Adams County Amateur Radio Society
City:	Arendtsville, PA
Section:	EPA

ARRL Affiliated Club	Mobile Sixers Radio Club Inc
City:	Aston, PA
Call Sign:	W3AWA
Section:	EPA

ARRL Affiliated Club	Eastern Pennsylvania Amateur Radio Association (EPARA)
City:	Bartonsville, PA
Call Sign:	N3IS
Section:	EPA
Links:	www.qsl.net/n3is

ARRL Affiliated Club	Bedford County Radio Society
City:	Bedford, PA
Call Sign:	K3NQT
Section:	WPA
Links:	www.bcars.org

ARRL Affiliated Club	Columbia-Montour Amateur Radio Club
City:	Berwick, PA
Call Sign:	KB3BJO
Section:	EPA
Links:	www.qsl.net/cm-arc/

ARRL Affiliated Club	The Christmas City Amateur Radio Club
City:	Bethlehem, PA
Call Sign:	KB3KKZ
Section:	EPA
Links:	thechristmascityarc.org

ARRL Affiliated Club	Punxsutawney Area Amateur Radio Club
City:	Big Run, PA
Call Sign:	K3HWJ
Section:	WPA

ARRL Affiliated Club	Indiana County Amateur Radio Club
City:	Blairsville, PA
Call Sign:	W3BMD
Section:	WPA
Links:	www.qsl.net/w3bmd/index.htm

ARRL Affiliated Club	McKean County Amateur Radio Club
City:	Bradford, PA
Call Sign:	W3VV
Section:	WPA
Links:	www.mcarc.net

ARRL Affiliated Club	Butler County Amateur Radio Association
City:	Butler, PA
Call Sign:	W3UDX
Section:	WPA
Links:	www.w3udx.org

ARRL Affiliated Club	Steel City Amateur Radio Club Inc
City:	Carnegie, PA
Call Sign:	W3KWH
Section:	WPA
Links:	www.w3kwh.com

ARRL Affiliated Club	T.D.F. Radio Club
City:	Catasauqua, PA
Section:	EPA
Links:	www.ka3kdl/tdfradioclub

ARRL Affiliated Club	Lehigh Valley Amateur Radio Club Inc
City:	Catasauqua, PA
Call Sign:	W3OI
Section:	EPA
Links:	www.w3oi.org

ARRL Affiliated Club	Cumberland Valley Amateur Radio Club
City:	Chambersburg, PA
Call Sign:	W3ACH
Section:	WPA
Links:	www.w3ach.org

ARRL Affiliated Club	Anthracite Repeater Assn. Inc
City:	Conyngham, PA
Call Sign:	W3OHX
Section:	EPA
Links:	www.qsl.net/ara

ARRL Affiliated Club	Radio Amateurs of Corry
City:	Corry, PA
Call Sign:	W3YXE
Section:	WPA
Links:	www.w3yxe.wordpress.com, www.w3yxe.org

ARRL Affiliated Club	Triple 'A' Amateur Radio Assn., Inc.
City:	Darlington, PA
Call Sign:	N3TN
Section:	WPA
Links:	taararadio.com

ARRL Affiliated Club	Cumberland Amateur Radio Club
City:	Dillsburg, PA
Call Sign:	K3IEC
Section:	EPA
Links:	home.comcast.net/~carc-k3iec/

ARRL Affiliated Club	Keystone VHF Club Inc.
City:	DOVER, PA
Call Sign:	W3HZU
Section:	EPA
Links:	www.w3hzu.com

ARRL Special Service Club	Warminster Amateur Radio Club
City:	Doylestown, PA
Call Sign:	K3DN
Section:	EPA
Links:	www.k3dn.org

ARRL Affiliated Club	David A. Dewire Amateur Radio Assn.
City:	Eagles Mere, PA
Call Sign:	N3CDC
Section:	EPA
Links:	www.qsl.net/n3cdc

ARRL Special Service Club	Mid-Atlantic Amateur Radio Club
City:	Eagleville, PA
Call Sign:	WB3JOE
Section:	EPA
Links:	www.marc-radio.org/

ARRL Affiliated Club	Pocono Amateur Radio Klub
City:	East Stroudsburg, PA
Call Sign:	W3PRK
Section:	EPA
Links:	www.w3prk.org/

ARRL Affiliated Club	Ellwood City Amateur Radio Association
City:	Ellwood City, PA
Call Sign:	N3EC
Section:	WPA
Links:	www.qsl.net/ecara/

ARRL Affiliated Club	Central Pennsylvania Repeater Assoc. Inc.
City:	Enola, PA
Call Sign:	W3ND
Section:	EPA
Links:	www.w3nd.org

ARRL Affiliated Club	Ephrata Area Repeater Soc., Inc
City:	Ephrata, PA
Call Sign:	W3XP
Specialties:	Repeaters
Section:	EPA

ARRL Affiliated Club   Wattsburg Wireless Association
City: Erie, PA
Call Sign: K3WWA
Section: WPA
Links: www.wattsburg-wireless.us

ARRL Affiliated Club   Radio Association of Erie
City: Erie, PA
Call Sign: W3GV
Section: WPA
Links: www.w3gv.org

ARRL Affiliated Club   West County Amateur Radio Association
City: Fairview, PA
Call Sign: KB3PSL
Section: WPA
Links: groups/yahoo.com/group/westcountyamateurradioassociation1

ARRL Special Service Club   Quad County Amateur Radio Club
City: Falls Creek, PA
Call Sign: N3QC
Section: WPA
Links: The Quad-County Amateur Radio Club

ARRL Affiliated Club   Hilltop Transmitting Assn.
City: Felton, PA
Call Sign: W3ZGD
Section: EPA
Links: www.qsl.net/w3zgd/

ARRL Affiliated Club   South Hills Brass Pounders & M
City: Finleyville, PA
Call Sign: W3PIQ
Section: WPA

ARRL Affiliated Club   Welaurel Reading Works Amateur Radio Club
City: Fleetwood, PA
Call Sign: WE3ATV
Section: EPA

ARRL Affiliated Club   Headwaters Amateur Radio Club
City: Genesee, PA
Call Sign: N3PC
Section: WPA
Links: www.n3pc.com

ARRL Affiliated Club   Two Rivers Amateur Radio Club
City: Greenock, PA
Call Sign: W3OC
Section: WPA

ARRL Affiliated Club   Foothills Amateur Radio Club
City: Greensburg, PA
Call Sign: W3LWW
Section: WPA
Links: www.W3LWW.org/

ARRL Affiliated Club   Westmoreland Emergency Amateur Radio Service
City: Greensburg, PA
Call Sign: WC3PS
Section: WPA
Links: www.wc3ps.org

ARRL Affiliated Club   Harrisburg Radio Amateur Club
City: Halifax, PA
Call Sign: W3UU
Section: EPA
Links: www.w3uu.org, hrac.tripod.com/

ARRL Affiliated Club   Hanover Area Hamming Assn.
City: Hanover, PA
Call Sign: KF3M
Section: EPA
Links: www.qsl.net/haha/

ARRL Affiliated Club   Penn-Mar Radio Club
City: Hanover, PA
Call Sign: W3MUM
Section: EPA
Links: www.w3mum.org

ARRL Affiliated Club   Camp Watonka Amateur Radio Club
City: Hawley, PA
Call Sign: KB3BUM
Section: EPA
Links: www.watonka.com

ARRL Affiliated Club   Unisys Amateur Radio Club-Blue Bell
City: Horsham, PA
Call Sign: KB3BKH
Section: EPA

ARRL Affiliated Club	Susquehanna Valley Amateur Radio Club
City:	Hummels Wharf, PA
Call Sign:	W3VPJ
Section:	EPA
Links:	www.svarc.net

ARRL Affiliated Club	Tri-County CW Amateur Radio Club
City:	Irwin, PA
Call Sign:	W3TCW
Section:	WPA
Links:	www.qsl.net/w3tcw

ARRL Affiliated Club	Southern Pennsylvania Amateur Radio Club Inc.
City:	Lancaster, PA
Call Sign:	K3IR
Section:	EPA
Links:	www.k3ir.org

ARRL Affiliated Club	Red Rose Repeater Assn.
City:	Lancaster, PA
Call Sign:	W3RRR
Section:	EPA
Links:	w3rrr.org

ARRL Affiliated Club	Marple Newtown Amateur Radio Club
City:	Lansdowne, PA
Call Sign:	K3MN
Section:	EPA
Links:	www.mnarc.org

ARRL Affiliated Club	Lebanon Valley Soc of Radio Amateurs, Inc.
City:	Lebanon, PA
Call Sign:	K3LV
Section:	EPA
Links:	lvsra.org

ARRL Affiliated Club	Dauberville DX Association
City:	Leesport, PA
Call Sign:	K3TI
Section:	EPA
Links:	www.ddxa.org

ARRL Affiliated Club	Carbon Amateur Radio Club
City:	Lehighton, PA
Call Sign:	W3HA
Section:	EPA
Links:	carc.wb3w.net

ARRL Affiliated Club	Tri-State Amateur Radio Association, Inc
City:	Matamoras, PA
Call Sign:	K3TSA
Section:	EPA
Links:	www.k3tsa.com

ARRL Affiliated Club	Crawford Amateur Radio Society
City:	Meadville, PA
Call Sign:	W3MIE
Section:	WPA
Links:	w3mie.org

ARRL Affiliated Club	Tuscarora Amateur Radio Association
City:	Mifflintown, PA
Call Sign:	K3TAR
Section:	EPA
Links:	tara.yolasite.com

ARRL Affiliated Club	Cambria Radio Club
City:	Mineral Point, PA
Call Sign:	WA3WGN
Section:	WPA
Links:	www.cvarc.info, www.cambriaradio.com

ARRL Affiliated Club	Penn Wireless Assn. Inc.
City:	Morrisville, PA
Call Sign:	W3SK
Section:	EPA
Links:	www.pennwireless.org

ARRL Affiliated Club	South Mountain Radio Amateurs
City:	Mount Holly Springs, PA
Call Sign:	N3TWT
Section:	EPA
Links:	www.n3twt.org

ARRL Affiliated Club	Huntingdon County Amateur Radio Club
City:	Mount Union, PA
Call Sign:	W3VI
Section:	WPA
Links:	www.localnet.com/~aketner/hcar.htm

ARRL Affiliated Club	Delaware-Lehigh Amateur Radio Club
City:	Nazareth, PA
Call Sign:	W3OK
Section:	EPA
Links:	dlarc.org

ARRL Affiliated Club	Amateur Radio League of Lawrence County
City:	New Castle, PA
Call Sign:	NC3LC
Section:	WPA
Links:	www.qsl.net/arllc/, www.arllc.org

ARRL Affiliated Club	Lawrence County ARES
City:	New Castle, PA
Call Sign:	KB3YBB
Section:	WPA

ARRL Affiliated Club	Skyview Radio Society
City:	New Kensington, PA
Call Sign:	K3MJW
Section:	WPA
Links:	www.skyviewradio.net

ARRL Special Service Club	R F Hill Amateur Radio Club Inc.
City:	Perkasie, PA
Call Sign:	W3AI
Section:	EPA
Links:	www.rfhill.ampr.org

ARRL Affiliated Club	University of PA Amateur Radio Club
City:	Philadelphia, PA
Call Sign:	W3ABT
Section:	EPA
Links:	www.seas.upenn.edu/~uparc/

ARRL Affiliated Club	Temple University Amateur Radio Club
City:	Philadelphia, PA
Call Sign:	K3TU
Section:	EPA
Links:	www.temple.edu/k3tu

ARRL Affiliated Club	Holmesburg Amateur Radio Club
City:	Philadelphia, PA
Call Sign:	WM3PEN
Section:	EPA

ARRL Affiliated Club	Philipsburg Amateur Radio Association
City:	Philipsburg, PA
Call Sign:	W3PHB
Section:	WPA
Links:	www.philipsburg-ara.org

ARRL Affiliated Club	North Hills Amateur Radio Club
City:	Pittsburgh, PA
Call Sign:	W3EXW
Section:	WPA
Links:	www.nharc.org

ARRL Affiliated Club	Breeze Shooters Amateur Radio Club
City:	Pittsburgh, PA
Call Sign:	K3BRZ
Section:	WPA
Links:	www.breezeshooters.net

ARRL Affiliated Club	Wireless Association of South Hills
City:	Pittsburgh, PA
Call Sign:	WA3SH
Section:	WPA
Links:	www.n3sh.org

ARRL Affiliated Club	Carnegie Tech Radio Club
City:	Pittsburgh, PA
Call Sign:	W3VC
Section:	WPA
Links:	www.andrew.cmu.edu/user/ar99/

ARRL Affiliated Club	Schuylkill Amateur Repeater Association
City:	Pottsville, PA
Call Sign:	W3SC
Section:	EPA
Links:	www.w3sc.org

ARRL Affiliated Club	Butler County Amateur Radio Public Service Group
City:	Prospect, PA
Call Sign:	K3PSG
Section:	WPA

ARRL Special Service Club	Washington Amateur Comm. Inc
City:	Prosperity, PA
Call Sign:	WA3COM
Section:	WPA
Links:	www.wacomarc.org

ARRL Affiliated Club	Reading Radio Club Inc.
City:	Reading, PA
Call Sign:	W3BN
Section:	EPA
Links:	www.readingradioclub.org

ARRL Affiliated Club   Scranton/Pocono Amateur Radio Klub
City: Scranton, PA
Call Sign: K3CSG
Section: EPA
Links: www.k3csg.org

ARRL Affiliated Club   Atlantic Wireless Society Inc.
City: Sharon, PA
Call Sign: K3AWS
Section: WPA
Links: www.k3aws.org

ARRL Affiliated Club   Mercer County Amateur Radio Club
City: Sharon, PA
Call Sign: W3LIF
Section: WPA
Links: www.mcarc.info, www.mcarc.info OR
                              groups.yahoo.com/group/MercerCountyARC

ARRL Affiliated Club   Spark Lodge Amateur Radio Club
City: Sharon Hill, PA
Call Sign: K3BSA
Section: EPA
Links: www.k3bsa.org

ARRL Affiliated Club   South Mountain Contest Club
City: Shippensburg, PA
Call Sign: K3EAR
Section: EPA

ARRL Affiliated Club   Southern PA Comm. Group
City: Shrewsbury, PA
Call Sign: K3AE
Section: EPA
Links: www.qsl.net/w6orz/

ARRL Affiliated Club   Susquehanna County Amateur Radio Club
City: Simpson, PA
Section: EPA

ARRL Affiliated Club   Somerset County Amateur Radio Club
City: Somerset, PA
Call Sign: K3SMT
Section: WPA
Links: www.k3smt.org

ARRL Affiliated Club	Beaver Valley Amateur Radio Association
City:	South Heights, PA
Call Sign:	W3SGJ
Section:	WPA
Links:	www.w3sgj.org

ARRL Affiliated Club	Pottstown Area Amateur Radio Club
City:	Spring City, PA
Call Sign:	K3ZMC
Section:	EPA
Links:	www.paarc.net/

ARRL Affiliated Club	York Hamfest Foundation
City:	Spring Grove, PA
Section:	EPA
Links:	www.yorkhamfest.org

ARRL Affiliated Club	Nittany Amateur Radio Club
City:	State College, PA
Call Sign:	W3YA
Section:	WPA
Links:	www.nittany-arc.net/

ARRL Affiliated Club	Tamaqua Wireless Association
City:	Tamaqua, PA
Call Sign:	W3CMA
Section:	EPA
Links:	w3cma.org

ARRL Affiliated Club	Irwin Area Amateur Radio Association
City:	Trafford, PA
Call Sign:	W3NDP
Section:	WPA

ARRL Affiliated Club	Union City Wireless Assn
City:	Union City, PA
Call Sign:	WA3UC
Section:	WPA
Links:	www.ucwa.org

ARRL Affiliated Club	Uniontown Amateur Radio Club
City:	Uniontown, PA
Call Sign:	W3PIE
Section:	WPA
Links:	www.w3pie,org

ARRL Affiliated Club	Penn-Del Amateur Radio Club
City:	Upper Chichester, PA
Section:	EPA
Links:	www.PennDelARC.org

ARRL Affiliated Club	Philadelphia Area Repeater Association
City:	Valley Forge, PA
Call Sign:	W3PHL
Section:	EPA
Links:	www.w3phl.org

ARRL Affiliated Club	WRC Amateur Radio Club of Doylestown
City:	Warminster, PA
Call Sign:	WA3EPA
Section:	EPA
Links:	www.qsl.net/wrc/

ARRL Affiliated Club	Cowanesque Valley School Amateur Radio Club
City:	Westfield, PA
Call Sign:	KB3BRT
Section:	EPA
Links:	users.penn.com/~k3ltm/cvsarc.html#CVSARC

ARRL Affiliated Club	Allegheny Valley Radio Association
City:	Wexford, PA
Call Sign:	W3WPA
Section:	WPA
Links:	www.alleghenyvalley.net

ARRL Special Service Club	Murgas Amateur Radio Club
City:	Wilkes Barre, PA
Call Sign:	K3YTL
Section:	EPA
Links:	murgasarc.org

ARRL Affiliated Club	Bald Eagle Repeater Association
City:	Williamsport, PA
Call Sign:	KB3HLL
Section:	EPA
Links:	www.baldeaglerepeater.org

ARRL Affiliated Club	West Branch Amateur Radio Association
City:	Williamsport, PA
Call Sign:	W3AVK
Section:	EPA

APPENDIX B

Amateur Radio License Holders

in

Pennsylvania: Central Region
(by City)

FCC Amateur Radio Licenses in Aaronsburg

Call Sign: KB3PWF
John W Hawkins II
146 N Rachels Way
Aaronsburg PA 16820

Call Sign: K3JWH
John W Hawkins II
146 N Rachels Way
Aaronsburg PA 16820

Call Sign: KB3RAK
Daniel A Schulin
Aaronsburg PA 16820

Call Sign: KB3TKB
Vincent S Montlick
Aaronsburg PA 16820

FCC Amateur Radio Licenses in Abbottstown

Call Sign: N3MMY
Sandra L Viands
203 Berwich Rd
Abbottstown PA 17301

Call Sign: KA3ZKH
Jason A Viands
203 Berwick Rd
Abbottstown PA 17301

Call Sign: KB3AIT
Brad A Viands
203 Berwick Rd
Abbottstown PA 17301

Call Sign: KE3FN
Gary L Viands
203 Berwick Rd
Abbottstown PA 17301

Call Sign: WB3HYO

James C Brady Sr
Box 54
Abbottstown PA 17301

Call Sign: KA3OGL
Donald J Falls
509 Bullet Way
Abbottstown PA 17301

Call Sign: K3AEE
Warren T MacAdams
324 Crystal Creek
Crossing
Abbottstown PA 17301

Call Sign: K3URJ
Penny MacAdams
324 Crystal Creek
Crossing
Abbottstown PA 17301

Call Sign: N3DAS
Scott E MacAdams
324 Crystal Creek
Crossing
Abbottstown PA 17301

Call Sign: W3ALR
Warren T Macadams
324 Crystal Creek
Crossing
Abbottstown PA 17301

Call Sign: KS3M
Warren T Macadams
324 Crystal Creek
Crossing
Abbottstown PA 17301

Call Sign: K3GRL
Allen E Egger Jr
740 Forest Dr
Abbottstown PA 17301

Call Sign: KB3IYE

Christopher E Sorensen
4 Home Rd
Abbottstown PA 17301

Call Sign: KB3IYF
Shannon E Sorensen
4 Home Rd
Abbottstown PA 17301

Call Sign: KB3VLZ
Daniel J Ecker
76 Hughes Dr
Abbottstown PA 17301

Call Sign: KB8LEQ
Mark W Sorensen
115 Jacobs Mill Rd
Abbottstown PA 17301

Call Sign: KB8LQB
Beverly A Sorensen
115 Jacobs Mill Rd
Abbottstown PA 17301

Call Sign: K2LFG
Manuel B Greco
7429 Lincoln Hwy
Abbottstown PA 17301

Call Sign: KA4KOT
Charles E Falkenstein
7433 Lincoln Hwy
Abbottstown PA 17301

Call Sign: KB3DCJ
Joseph R Crawn
281 Mummerts Church Rd
Abbottstown PA 17301

Call Sign: N3OSW
Scott K Stauffer
85 Pine Rd
Abbottstown PA 17301

Call Sign: N3XDK

Todd M Funke
1079 Racet Rack Rd
Abbottstown PA 17301

Call Sign: WA3UQH
Earl S Davis Jr
221 Runaway Rd
Abbottstown PA 17301

Call Sign: KA3UQM
William T Fortney Sr
103 W King St
Abbottstown PA 17301

Call Sign: N3PIU
Daniel J Pitman
54 Chestnut St
Adamstown PA
195010396

**FCC Amateur Radio
Licenses in Addison**

Call Sign: KB3AGA
Von W Mosser
Box 114A
Addison PA 15411

**FCC Amateur Radio
Licenses in Airville**

Call Sign: N3ZOY
Anthony E Marc
248 Bruce Rd
Airville PA 17302

Call Sign: N3XUD
David D All
219 Center Rd
Airville PA 173029253

Call Sign: KB3STA
Angel C All
219 Center Rd
Airville PA 173029253

Call Sign: NV9B
Mark S Bell
66 Flaharty Rd
Airville PA 17302

Call Sign: K3ZX
Mark S Bell
66 Flaharty Rd
Airville PA 17302

Call Sign: K3MSB
Mark S Bell
66 Flaharty Rd
Airville PA 17302

Call Sign: W3ZGD
Hilltop Transmitting Assn
Inc
66 Flaherty Rd
Airville PA 17302

Call Sign: KB3RGM
Dillon L Whitehead
754 Frosty Hill Rd
Airville PA 17302

Call Sign: KO3T
Bradley E Kline
156 Furnace Rd
Airville PA 173020021

Call Sign: KE3HD
Garrett D Robinson
836 Furnace Rd
Airville PA 173029601

Call Sign: N3LMD
Heather E Robinson
836 Furnace Rd
Airville PA 173029601

Call Sign: WB3FQH
Margery E Robinson
836 Furnace Rd

Airville PA 173029601

Call Sign: WB3FQI
Russell A Robinson
836 Furnace Rd
Airville PA 173029601

Call Sign: WB3AFL
Palmer K Glunt
28 Good Rd
Airville PA 173028803

Call Sign: KB3JSV
Daniel C Melato
54 Mitchell Rd
Airville PA 17302

Call Sign: K3YLG
Joseph F Smith Jr
363 Norris Rd
Airville PA 173029550

Call Sign: KB3NQO
Gregory A Glos
709 Norris Rd
Airville PA 17302

Call Sign: KB3QKL
Gregory A Glos
709 Norris Rd
Airville PA 17302

Call Sign: K3LDG
Gregory A Glos
709 Norris Rd
Airville PA 17302

Call Sign: KB3QVM
Samantha L Lewis
709 Norris Rd
Airville PA 17302

Call Sign: K3DHL
Samantha L Lewis
709 Norris Rd

Airville PA 17302

Call Sign: W3WOC
Gary L Kurtz
76 Stewart Rd
Airville PA 17302

Call Sign: KA3GWD
John R Mettee
7951 Woodbine Rd
Airville PA 17302

Call Sign: N3BWO
Margaret M Mettee
7951 Woodbine Rd
Airville PA 17302

Call Sign: K3QXW
Carl J Rohacek
Airville PA 17302

Call Sign: N3JDQ
Bradley E Kline
Airville PA 173020021

FCC Amateur Radio Licenses in Akron

Call Sign: N3WMF
Donald E Troutman
Colonial Dr
Akron PA 175011223

Call Sign: KB3QYW
Kenneth W May
1206 Diamond St
Akron PA 17501

Call Sign: N3WMD
John K Stauffer
70 E Farmersville Rd
Akron PA 17501

Call Sign: N3ZKS
Christopher H Brubaker

45 Fulton St
Akron PA 17501

Call Sign: N3ZKD
Charles J Hilzinger
Green Acres Mhp
Akron PA 17501

Call Sign: KB3TSR
Don W Ziegler
817 High St
Akron PA 17501

Call Sign: WA3QQX
Terry W Reber
940 High St
Akron PA 17501

Call Sign: KB3ATZ
Elizabeth A Stewart
943 High St
Akron PA 17501

Call Sign: K3MEO
Clyde W Wealand
207 Main St
Akron PA 17501

Call Sign: N3RFZ
Lowell E Strickler
1153 Main St
Akron PA 17501

Call Sign: WA3HNA
G Craig Forney
219 Miller Rd Apt E
Akron PA 17501

Call Sign: KB3ETH
Ryan T Foulk
94 N 10th St
Akron PA 17501

Call Sign: WA3SVX
Alan R Frisbie

312 S 10th St
Akron PA 17501

Call Sign: KB3OEH
Mitch B Bender
39 S 11th St
Akron PA 17501

Call Sign: WA3BAR
Ephrata Hs ARC
212 S 11th St
Akron PA 17501

Call Sign: K3WMH
Robert E Montgomery
212 S 11th St
Akron PA 175011512

Call Sign: N3OAW
Robert L Weidman
477 S 9th St
Akron PA 17501

Call Sign: N3RCH
Mary F Weidman
477 S 9th St
Akron PA 17501

Call Sign: N3FDV
James R Morrison
124 Vista Dr
Akron PA 17501

Call Sign: N3KNZ
John D Gbur
511 W View Dr
Akron PA 17501

Call Sign: N3UCW
Mary J Gbur
511 W View Dr
Akron PA 17501

Call Sign: KA3YVH
Carol L Dietrich

Akron PA 17501

Call Sign: N3JPB
Richard J Dietrich
Akron PA 17501

FCC Amateur Radio Licenses in Alexandria

Call Sign: KA3TFU
Richard G Parmely
Box 155
Alexandria PA 16611

Call Sign: WA3UFA
Shelley S Swigart
Main
Alexandria PA 16611

Call Sign: K4PFF
Richard L Phillips Sr
301 Shelton Ave
Alexandria PA 16611

Call Sign: K3BPF
Robert E Eichelberger
Alexandria PA 16611

Call Sign: KA3SFE
Charles W Weko III
Alexandria PA 16611

Call Sign: N3IAA
Ron L Dively
Alexandria PA 16611

FCC Amateur Radio Licenses in Allensville

Call Sign: KB3BOH
Timothy L Yoder
139 E Main St
Allensville PA 17002

FCC Amateur Radio Licenses in Allenwood

Call Sign: KA0YUZ
Jerry L Kingery Jr
1753 Devitt Camp Rd
Allenwood PA 17810

Call Sign: KB3GWR
Jesse J Baker
201 Ladd Rd
Allenwood PA 17810

Call Sign: KB3KUN
Kathryn R Baker
201 Ladd Rd
Allenwood PA 17810

Call Sign: N3PFG
Terry L Alexander
1155 Lehman Rd
Allenwood PA 17810

Call Sign: KB3MHI
Benjamin J Showers
1195 Mill Rd
Allenwood PA 17810

Call Sign: KB3IGS
Kenneth R Bloomer
16512 US Rt 15
Allenwood PA 17810

FCC Amateur Radio Licenses in Altoona

Call Sign: KE3AQ
David E Ehredt Jr
1827 11th Ave Juniata
Altoona PA 16601

Call Sign: N0MSB
Robert S Juroszek
806 11th St
Altoona PA 16602

Call Sign: KA3VLM
Robert P Malovich
1100 11th St Apt 805
Altoona PA 166014644

Call Sign: KA3MFB
Margaret M Kintz
1919 13th Ave
Altoona PA 16601

Call Sign: W3LKB
Raymond F Rauchle
1311 13th St
Altoona PA 16601

Call Sign: NS3D
Fred R Fields
118 14th Ave Juniata
Altoona PA 16601

Call Sign: WB3EUG
Merwin B Updyke
1813 14th St
Altoona PA 16601

Call Sign: KB3IDH
Merwin B Updyke
1813 14th St
Altoona PA 16601

Call Sign: W3MUK
Merwin B Updyke
1813 14th St
Altoona PA 16601

Call Sign: N3JXI
Daryl E White
1204 15th Ave
Altoona PA 16601

Call Sign: N3KNC
John E Bonifati Jr
1210 15th Ave
Altoona PA 16601

Call Sign: KA3VWC
David P Barr
2501 15th St
Altoona PA 16601

Call Sign: KB3HBK
Sara A Myers
1114 20th Ave
Altoona PA 166013057

Call Sign: KB3YHM
Gregory L Heuston
1117 22nd Ave
Altoona PA 16601

Call Sign: K3BMG
Dennis J Auerbeck
2002 16th Ave
Altoona PA 16601

Call Sign: WB3HDV
David A Pencinger
1115 20th Ave
Altoona PA 16601

Call Sign: WB3EYH
Rick D Scott
1710 24th Ave
Altoona PA 16601

Call Sign: KB3CVN
Lawrence V Koelle
1615 17th Ave
Altoona PA 16601

Call Sign: KA3UEJ
Eugene K Otto
1117 20th Ave
Altoona PA 16601

Call Sign: W3EYH
Rick D Scott
1710 24th Ave
Altoona PA 16601

Call Sign: N3ZQY
Brian W Fornwalt
1521 18th St
Altoona PA 16601

Call Sign: W3BSR
John F Cuzzolina Jr
1417 20th Ave
Altoona PA 16601

Call Sign: KB3OPZ
Caleb J Drenning
1020 25th Ave
Altoona PA 16601

Call Sign: WA3QPE
James E Watchey
2412 18th St
Altoona PA 16601

Call Sign: N3TKV
Michael L Hemberger
1618 20th Ave
Altoona PA 16601

Call Sign: KB3EWG
Christopher W Mika
319 26th Ave
Altoona PA 16601

Call Sign: KB3CWW
Patrick I Nottingham
1803 1st Ave
Altoona PA 16602

Call Sign: KC2WLF
Charles G Weidow
1328 20th Ave Fl2
Altoona PA 16601

Call Sign: KB3FBS
Brian D Farabaugh
317 27th Ave
Altoona PA 16601

Call Sign: K3QFB
William H Long
2119 1st Ave
Altoona PA 16602

Call Sign: KB3IWK
Jolene S Gerlach
530 22nd Ave
Altoona PA 16601

Call Sign: NO3A
Michael G Boehly
2102 2nd Ave
Altoona PA 16602

Call Sign: N3RIW
Markland E Dunn
607 20th Ave
Altoona PA 16601

Call Sign: KB3ING
Thomas C Gerlach
530 22nd Ave
Altoona PA 16601

Call Sign: NX3X
Larry E Staley
2114 2nd Ave
Altoona PA 16602

Call Sign: KB3EVO
Robert A Myers
1114 20th Ave
Altoona PA 16601

Call Sign: N3VJS
Michael Drobnoek
1110 22nd Ave
Altoona PA 16601

Call Sign: KB3GHV
Edward R Fleck
1006 35th St
Altoona PA 16601

Call Sign: W3ERF
Edward R Fleck
1006 35th St
Altoona PA 16601

Call Sign: N3IAF
Lloyd W Harris
5418 4th Ave
Altoona PA 16602

Call Sign: N3ZTX
Mark A Merritt
1202 5th Ave Juanita
Altoona PA 16601

Call Sign: KB3TMU
Matthew J Franco
3010 3rd Ave
Altoona PA 16602

Call Sign: WA3ZRU
David L Ickes
1511 4th Ave Juniata
Altoona PA 16601

Call Sign: N3ZZT
Geraldine A Sipe
3322 6th Ace
Altoona PA 16602

Call Sign: KB3NZO
Mark N Hunter
1917 3rd Ave
Altoona PA 16602

Call Sign: KA3THS
Patrick A Kelley
527 56th St
Altoona PA 16602

Call Sign: K3LYK
George F Brantlinger
2703 6th Ave
Altoona PA 16602

Call Sign: KA3KHC
Peter V Brooks
513 4th Ave
Altoona PA 16602

Call Sign: WZ3M
Marilyn L Kelley
527 56th St
Altoona PA 16602

Call Sign: K3OIH
James W Brantlinger
2703 6th Ave
Altoona PA 16602

Call Sign: KB3CQX
Byron M Sell
2301 4th Ave
Altoona PA 16602

Call Sign: N3SDM
James C Wingate
1012 58th St
Altoona PA 16601

Call Sign: WA3IQT
Jay M Sipe
3322 6th Ave
Altoona PA 16602

Call Sign: W3VPF
Byron S Sell
2301 4th Ave
Altoona PA 16602

Call Sign: KB3PIQ
James C Wingate
1012 58th St
Altoona PA 16601

Call Sign: KB3OUL
John W Miles
2407 7th Ave Apt 2
Altoona PA 16602

Call Sign: N3IHN
Robert E Hoover
4902 4th Ave
Altoona PA 16602

Call Sign: K3QFK
Robert C Loibl
2315 5th Ave
Altoona PA 16602

Call Sign: KB3OIH
Wilbur L Walk
425 Ash St
Altoona PA 16602

Call Sign: N3CHU
Lynn D Norman
5311 4th Ave
Altoona PA 166021305

Call Sign: KB3UUE
Michael E Pfister
5300 5th Ave
Altoona PA 16602

Call Sign: W3ULM
Thomas D Cooney Sr
277 Avalon Rd
Altoona PA 166019768

Call Sign: N3ZZE
Ada J Norman
5311 4th Ave
Altoona PA 166021305

Call Sign: K3MEP
Michael E Pfister
5300 5th Ave
Altoona PA 16602

Call Sign: KB3LMI
Jason A Staph
753 Avalon Rd
Altoona PA 16601

Call Sign: N3CVP
Peter A Gallace
3812 Beale Ave
Altoona PA 16601

Call Sign: N3RXN
Jason S Campbell
Box 411
Altoona PA 16601

Call Sign: N3HJF
Mary E Guyer
Box 616
Altoona PA 166019349

Call Sign: KB3IWJ
Frank R Harchak
105 Bell Ave
Altoona PA 16602

Call Sign: N3IBR
John E Lennox
Box 44
Altoona PA 16601

Call Sign: WA3WGY
John W Blatt
Box 795A
Altoona PA 16601

Call Sign: WB3KPC
James E Stein
Box 191
Altoona PA 16602

Call Sign: N3IBS
Arlene A Lennox
Box 44
Altoona PA 16601

Call Sign: K3QHG
Paul J Reimer
Box 808
Altoona PA 16601

Call Sign: N3CZD
Kenneth D Reed
Box 206
Altoona PA 16601

Call Sign: KB2OPC
Patrick A Crocitto
Box 455
Altoona PA 166019788

Call Sign: N3PUD
George G Husick
Box 889
Altoona PA 16601

Call Sign: K3PGF
James T McIntire
Box 224
Altoona PA 16601

Call Sign: WB3GVB
Merrill S Doran
Box 501
Altoona PA 16601

Call Sign: WB3KQB
Joseph M Hughes
2412 Broad Ave
Altoona PA 16601

Call Sign: KB3CRX
James E Glenn
Box 224 D
Altoona PA 16601

Call Sign: KB3KWD
Blue Knob Repeater Assn
Box 509
Altoona PA 16601

Call Sign: KA3SHV
John R McCoy
2706 Broadway
Altoona PA 16601

Call Sign: N3CZI
Shirley J Van Ormer
Box 241
Altoona PA 16601

Call Sign: KB3FML
Jeffrey J Blake
Box 509
Altoona PA 16601

Call Sign: W3RCS
Robert C Staph
204 Caroline Ave
Altoona PA 16602

Call Sign: WB3FIB
Richard A Forgas
Box 394
Altoona PA 16601

Call Sign: N8UBU
Thomas J Hesley
Box 564
Altoona PA 16601

Call Sign: N3NKR
Edgar E Schoening Sr
520 Caroline Ave
Altoona PA 16603

Call Sign: KB3KXB
Kellie D Campbell
Box 411
Altoona PA 16601

Call Sign: KA3WRM
Paul Guyer
Box 616
Altoona PA 16601

Call Sign: AB7AF
James C Marlin
617 Clairmont Dr
Altoona PA 16601

Call Sign: KR3S
Raymond L Beck
797 Clarion Ln
Altoona PA 166027414

Call Sign: N2ZDE
John A Schwittek
303 Coleridge Ave
Altoona PA 16602

Call Sign: W3QC
Edward S McCauley
3572 Colonel Drake Hwy
Altoona PA 16601

Call Sign: KB3WUV
Carl J Destefano
435 Coral Dr
Altoona PA 16601

Call Sign: KB3JVN
Horseshoe ARC Inc
4006 Cortland Ave
Altoona PA 16601

Call Sign: KB3JVO
Horseshoe ARC Inc
4006 Cortland Ave
Altoona PA 16601

Call Sign: W3QW
Horseshoe ARC Inc
4006 Cortland Ave
Altoona PA 16601

Call Sign: K3HRC
Horseshoe ARC Inc
4006 Cortland Ave
Altoona PA 16601

Call Sign: KD3SA
Thomas D Cooney Jr
4006 Cortland Ave
Altoona PA 16601

Call Sign: N3MAZ
Tammy L Cooney
4006 Cortland Ave
Altoona PA 16601

Call Sign: W3QZF
Horseshoe ARC
4006 Cortland Ave
Altoona PA 16601

Call Sign: KB3KRG
Inc Horseshoe ARC
4006 Cortland Ave
Altoona PA 16601

Call Sign: W3VU
Inc Horseshoe ARC
4006 Cortland Ave
Altoona PA 16601

Call Sign: KB3KQV
Inc. Horseshoe ARC
4006 Cortland Ave
Altoona PA 16601

Call Sign: W3VO
Inc. Horseshoe ARC
4006 Cortland Ave
Altoona PA 16601

Call Sign: KB3LGS
Justin T Cooney
4006 Cortland Ave
Altoona PA 16601

Call Sign: W3SF
Thomas D Cooney Jr
4006 Cortland Ave
Altoona PA 16601

Call Sign: KB3IXH
Horseshoe ARC
4006 Cortland Ave
Altoona PA 16601

Call Sign: KB3DEH
James D Mowery
819 Crawford Ave
Altoona PA 16602

Call Sign: W3QKK
Frank C Baluka
1543 Crawford Ave
Altoona PA 16602

Call Sign: N3JFD
John A March
129 E 22nd Ave
Altoona PA 16601

Call Sign: N3PMO
Edward W Ryan III
516 E 26 Ave
Altoona PA 16601

Call Sign: K3AHG
Stephen W Dolak
400 E Bell Ave
Altoona PA 16602

Call Sign: K3BDI
Domenic A Caminiti
117 E Caroline Ave
Altoona PA 16602

Call Sign: AA3JN
Peter A Robinson
430 E Crawford Ave
Altoona PA 16602

Call Sign: N3UIA
Eric Davies
430 E Crawford Ave
Altoona PA 16602

Call Sign: N3UIB
David Waterworth
430 E Crawford Ave
Altoona PA 16602

Call Sign: WB3DER
Ronald E Strasser
616 E Crawford Ave
Altoona PA 16602

Call Sign: N3VRO
Harry R McGunigal Jr
205 E Fairview Ave
Altoona PA 16601

Call Sign: N3LUA
William J Costanza Jr
604 E Hudson Ave
Altoona PA 166025423

Call Sign: KA3MFC
Michael A Mauk
900 E Hudson Ave
Altoona PA 16602

Call Sign: WA3WED
Michael E Mauk
900 E Hudson Ave
Altoona PA 16602

Call Sign: KB3MAG
Michael A Mauk
900 E Hudson Ave
Altoona PA 166026909

Call Sign: N3QBV
Stephen E Fouse
310 E Southey Ave
Altoona PA 16602

Call Sign: K5WWJ
Jane L Fields
1001 E Walton Ave Apt
305
Altoona PA 16602

Call Sign: WA3CJF
Fred R Fields

1001 E Walton Ave Apt
305
Altoona PA 16602

Call Sign: WA3WEE
Jane L Fields
1001 E Walton Ave Apt
305
Altoona PA 16602

Call Sign: KB3RGG
Blair ARS
112 E Wopsononock Ave
Altoona PA 16601

Call Sign: W3PN
Blair ARS
112 E Wopsononock Ave
Altoona PA 16601

Call Sign: W3BTX
Robert G Gutshall
112 E Wopsononock Ave
Altoona PA 16601

Call Sign: KB3FXS
Robert C Staph
711 East St
Altoona PA 16602

Call Sign: N3QBO
Kevin L Campbell
170 Graham Dr
Altoona PA 16601

Call Sign: KB3FSB
Theresa M Campbell
170 Graham Dr
Altoona PA 16601

Call Sign: KB3FMK
Travis A Lunglhofer
178 Graham Dr
Altoona PA 16601

Call Sign: N8PSU
Jeffrey J Blake
574 Grandview Rd
Altoona PA 16601

Call Sign: KA3JHH
Walter R Hurm
500 Hudson Ave
Altoona PA 166024811

Call Sign: KB3OIK
Michael R Geishauser
201 Ivyside Ests Ln
Altoona PA 16601

Call Sign: KB3OIE
Martin B Horten
710 Jackson Ave
Altoona PA 16602

Call Sign: WB3ADR
Kenneth R Wolfinger II
3930 Juniata Gap Rd
Altoona PA 16601

Call Sign: N3TKU
Constant J Evanoski III
2602 Lark Ave
Altoona PA 16602

Call Sign: N3JYI
Thomas E Clifford
616 Lehigh Ln
Altoona PA 16602

Call Sign: W3DMG
William E Herman
401 Leslie St Lakemont
Altoona PA 16602

Call Sign: KB3QQS
Roy L Brazzle
707 Lincoln Manor
Altoona PA 16602

Call Sign: N3NZL
Mark A Hazlett
697 Lower Riggles Gap Rd
Altoona PA 166018835

Call Sign: KE3TJ
Eric G Hilbert
1231 Madison Ave
Altoona PA 16602

Call Sign: KA3ICZ
Michael R Wall
3940 Maple Ave
Altoona PA 16601

Call Sign: W3MRW
Michael R Wall
3940 Maple Ave
Altoona PA 16601

Call Sign: N3LEW
Andrew H Johnson
603 McMullen Rd
Altoona PA 16601

Call Sign: W7ELW
Paul B Settlemyer
5301 Montrose Ave
Altoona PA 16602

Call Sign: W3ELW
Paul B Settlemyer
5301 Montrose Ave
Altoona PA 16602

Call Sign: KA3MHM
John E Stine
603 N 10th Ave
Altoona PA 16601

Call Sign: N3HKT
Jane L Fields
118 N 14th Ave
Altoona PA 166015610

Call Sign: KB3ML
Paul E Summers
1633 Notre Dame Rd
Altoona PA 16602

Call Sign: N3BZP
Carol A Bollinger
4904 Oak Ave
Altoona PA 16601

Call Sign: N3EXC
Ricky A Croyle
Old Rte 220
Altoona PA 16601

Call Sign: KC5EEN
Charles H Osterhout Jr
Overlook Pl
Altoona PA 16602

Call Sign: W3BZN
Thomas S Gutshall
130 Perry Ln
Altoona PA 16601

Call Sign: WB3EFQ
Lois J Gutshall
130 Perry Ln
Altoona PA 16601

Call Sign: WA3BSK
Harry E Miller
2629 Quail Ave
Altoona PA 16602

Call Sign: K3CEV
Donald L Schucker
Rd 4
Altoona PA 16601

Call Sign: K3BMH
Ralph E Force
503 Ridge Ave
Altoona PA 16602

Call Sign: KD3IR
Samuel M Brassington
607 Ruskin Dr
Altoona PA 16602

Call Sign: KB3DRK
Patricia A Johnson
1209 S 27th St Apt 2A
Altoona PA 16602

Call Sign: KA3LOO
John F Dietrich
640 S Dartmouth Ln
Altoona PA 16602

Call Sign: N3BZW
James L Metzler
737 S Temple Ln
Altoona PA 16602

Call Sign: KB3LGT
Douglas A Whitfield
915 South St
Altoona PA 16602

Call Sign: WA3GPE
Glenn R Thomas
142 Sunny Crest Ln
Altoona PA 16601

Call Sign: KD3XS
Thomas C Streb II
409 Tennyson Ave
Altoona PA 16602

Call Sign: N3LZN
Patricia M Streb
409 Tennyson Ave
Altoona PA 16602

Call Sign: N3JIY
Alan G Fay
1613 Timberline Dr
Altoona PA 16601

Call Sign: KA3EJV
Drew R McGhee
1832 Timberline Rd
Altoona PA 16601

Call Sign: WB3JJG
Robert L Rabenstein
2904 W Pine Ave
Altoona PA 16601

Call Sign: KB3RQU
Scott M Zillinger
3022 Walnut Ave
Altoona PA 16601

Call Sign: KB3QGD
John J Antonik
548 Wharton Ave
Altoona PA 16602

Call Sign: N2BAD
John J Antonik
548 Wharton Ave
Altoona PA 16602

Call Sign: KB3QPA
Joshua M Antonik
548 Wharton Ave
Altoona PA 16602

Call Sign: N3PUA
Carl W Eisel
104 Willow Ave
Altoona PA 16601

Call Sign: W3LQD
Leo C Kelley
618 Yale Ln
Altoona PA 16602

Call Sign: KA3ANA
Thomas M Stein
Altoona PA 16603

Call Sign: KF6MRB

Scott A Campanaro
Altoona PA 16603

Call Sign: W3SO
Wopsononock
Mountaintop Operators
Altoona PA 16603

FCC Amateur Radio Licenses in Alum Bank

Call Sign: KB3PCN
Ryan T Young
515 Belles Rd
Alum Bank PA 15521

Call Sign: KB3CNJ
Jamie L Wentz
1295 Dunkard Hollow Rd
Alum Bank PA 15521

Call Sign: KB3MGO
Branden W Carson
223 Locust St
Alum Bank PA 15521

Call Sign: KB3FBO
Matthew B Crist
2283 Lovely Rd
Alum Bank PA 15521

Call Sign: KB3GXW
Chelciee R Fischer
184 Main St
Alum Bank PA 15521

Call Sign: KB3GEE
Paul R Fischer
184 Main St
Alum Bank PA 15521

Call Sign: KB3GEG
Craig R Hammer
133 Old Mill St
Alum Bank PA 15521

FCC Amateur Radio Licenses in Annville

Call Sign: KA3RGC
Kurt R Showers
Box 255C
Annville PA 17003

Call Sign: KB3UNY
Robert M Long
764 Bricker Ln
Annville PA 17003

Call Sign: N3PXA
Suanne M Long
764 Bricker Ln
Annville PA 170032424

Call Sign: N3JOY
Robert C Long
764 Bricker Ln
Annville PA 170032424

Call Sign: KB3TLP
Richard A Sorensen
15 Crooked Rd
Annville PA 17003

Call Sign: N3WWK
Thomas G Gartlan
22 Crooked Rd
Annville PA 17003

Call Sign: KB3MMR
Ryan M Laird
19 Dianna Dr
Annville PA 176039511

Call Sign: WB3AMC
Richard M Harris
514 E Main St
Annville PA 17003

Call Sign: KB3HQF

Brian L Heilman
1074 E Main St
Annville PA 17003

Call Sign: KA3YVB
Fay M Simmons
1405 E Queen St
Annville PA 17003

Call Sign: KA3YVC
Robert L Simmons
1405 E Queen St
Annville PA 17003

Call Sign: KD4QPK
Brian R Mosier
334 E Sheridan Ave Apt1
Annville PA 17003

Call Sign: N3OLI
James R Safford
1325 E Walnut St
Annville PA 17003

Call Sign: N3CAS
Earl W Wagner
1335 E Walnut St
Annville PA 17003

Call Sign: N3JUS
Henry H Emrich Jr
159 Gingrich Ave
Annville PA 17003

Call Sign: KA3UES
James R Monteith
4505 Hill Church Rd
Annville PA 17003

Call Sign: KB3DXB
Harold A Reist
55 Kindred Pl
Annville PA 17003

Call Sign: KA3PYL

William E Stephens Jr
848 Locust Rd
Annville PA 170032319

Call Sign: N2ZJQ
Richard A Muniz
1491 Louser Rd
Annville PA 17003

Call Sign: N3OUH
Richard J Wolfe
224 N Lancaster St
Annville PA 17003

Call Sign: K3ZCP
Arnold C Smith
766 Ono Rd
Annville PA 17003

Call Sign: KA3HAA
Michael L Hepford
32 Palm City Park
Annville PA 17003

Call Sign: KB3QNJ
Michael Tshudy
762 Palmyra Bellegrove
Rd
Annville PA 17003

Call Sign: N3OZV
Dennis L Zellers
910 Palmyra Bellegrove
Rd
Annville PA 170039652

Call Sign: KB3OWC
Elizabeth A Miorin
225 Parliament Dr
Annville PA 17003

Call Sign: KA3YVD
Kris D Gongloff
Rd 2
Annville PA 17003

Call Sign: KA3YVN
Kory T Gongloff
Rd 2
Annville PA 17003

Call Sign: KB3VLQ
Seth J Shaheen
600 S White Oak St
Annville PA 17003

Call Sign: N3JUT
Carol A Yeagley
750 School House Plaza
Annville PA 17003

Call Sign: KB3HKZ
Ted A Nichols II
102 Spruce Ct
Annville PA 170039313

Call Sign: KB3MFU
Dustin L Hostetter
1660 Thompson Ave
Annville PA 17003

Call Sign: W3WGN
Henry P Ficco
34 Valley Dr Rd 3
Annville PA 17003

Call Sign: N3DMU
Jay K Bell II
321 W Main St
Annville PA 17003

Call Sign: N3UHE
Charles J Gianoulos
1143 W Main St
Annville PA 17003

Call Sign: KE6FQS
Adam J Kirkessner
116 W Main St
Annville PA 17003

Call Sign: N3RWP
Dennis C Reppert
Annville PA 17003

FCC Amateur Radio Licenses in Antes Fort

Call Sign: AC3E
Edgar J Willits Sr
New Corner Front & Main St
Antes Fort PA 17720

FCC Amateur Radio Licenses in Arendtsville

Call Sign: KB3OGJ
Barbara L Baller
Arendtsville PA 17303

Call Sign: W3AVQ
Barbara L Baller
Arendtsville PA 17303

Call Sign: KB3IQH
Howard T Williams
Arendtsville PA 17303

FCC Amateur Radio Licenses in Aristes

Call Sign: N2AP
Anthony Paulina
Aristes PA 17920

FCC Amateur Radio Licenses in Arnot

Call Sign: WB3AGJ
Richard H Smith
73 Pine St
Arnot PA 16911

FCC Amateur Radio Licenses in Artemas

Call Sign: KB3CAE
Russell I Clingerman Jr
1693 Clear Ridge Rd
Artemas PA 172119757

Call Sign: N3WNN
Rick C Robinson
1829 Clear Ridge Rd
Artemas PA 17211

FCC Amateur Radio Licenses in Ashville

Call Sign: N4DCL
Wayne E Nelms
146 High Meadow Ln
Ashville PA 16613

Call Sign: KB3NRZ
Judith C Nelms
146 High Meadow Ln
Ashville PA 16613

FCC Amateur Radio Licenses in Aspers

Call Sign: N3XSE
Duane D Duerr
1086 Bendersville
Wenksville Rd
Aspers PA 17304

Call Sign: KC3CS
Thomas L Brumbeloe
1202 Bull Valley Rd
Aspers PA 17304

Call Sign: N3MII
Paul J Osborn
1260 Center Mills Rd
Aspers PA 17304

Call Sign: KB3EUV
Robert F Mcneill III
540 Company Farm Rd
Aspers PA 17304

Call Sign: KB3HLB
John M Kelly
736 Cranberry Rd
Aspers PA 17304

Call Sign: KB3BFO
Mary J Hush
15 Ed Ave
Aspers PA 17304

Call Sign: KB3BJL
Dawn R Showers
340 Middle Rd
Aspers PA 17304

Call Sign: WA3VYP
Roger L Frazier
1006 Old Carlisle Rd
Aspers PA 17304

Call Sign: KB3VIV
Carl A Seils
151 Orchard Ln
Aspers PA 17304

Call Sign: KB3BKM
Christopher D Turner
25 Prostect St
Aspers PA 17304

FCC Amateur Radio Licenses in Atlas

Call Sign: KB3PIO
Deborah L Weaver
478 W Girard St
Atlas PA 17851

Call Sign: KB3IVP
Robert R Murray

492 W Girard St
Atlas PA 17851

**FCC Amateur Radio
Licenses in Austin**

Call Sign: N3SJM
Judith L Leonard
10 Maple Dr
Austin PA 16720

Call Sign: KB3KVT
Glenn G Williams
720 S Ayers Hill Rd
Austin PA 16720

Call Sign: KB3KVU
Linda P Williams
720 S Ayers Hill Rd
Austin PA 16720

Call Sign: N3PVH
Walter W Blythe
Summit St
Austin PA 16720

Call Sign: N2COD
Michael T Perry
118 Thorn St
Austin PA 16720

Call Sign: N3QDO
Brian L Wotowicz
Austin PA 167200219

Call Sign: AA3XP
Brian L Wotowicz
Austin PA 167200219

**FCC Amateur Radio
Licenses in Avis**

Call Sign: N3QWG
Michael D Seiler
113 E Summit St

Avis PA 17721

Call Sign: KA3YJU
Charles L Brungard
104 Prospect Ave
Avis PA 17721

Call Sign: KE4MHE
Scott S Horton
3093 Woodworth Ave
Avis PA 17721

Call Sign: KB3LAT
James W Kreighbaum Jr
Avis PA 17721

**FCC Amateur Radio
Licenses in Bainbridge**

Call Sign: KB3HZT
Matthew F Davidson
1309 Amosite Rd
Bainbridge PA 17502

Call Sign: W3CYN
Cynthia L Davidson
1309 Amosite Rd
Bainbridge PA 17502

Call Sign: N3MFP
Donna L Culbertson
1343 Amosite Rd
Bainbridge PA 17502

Call Sign: KB3UJD
David R Auch
1403 Keener Rd
Bainbridge PA 17502

Call Sign: W3PLC
Timothy F Davidson
100 Market St
Bainbridge PA 17502

Call Sign: KB3BTH

Randal E Zartman
126 Meadowview Ln
Bainbridge PA 17502

Call Sign: KB3IHX
Stephen F Hulse
135 Risser Rd
Bainbridge PA 17502

Call Sign: N3LZT
Ronald D Smith
426 S 2nd St
Bainbridge PA 17502

Call Sign: WA3OOW
Robert S Zorger
3431 Tpke Rd
Bainbridge PA 17502

Call Sign: KB3YDP
Michael W Weaver
Bainbridge PA 17502

**FCC Amateur Radio
Licenses in Barnesboro**

Call Sign: KB3DMK
Robert W Butterworth
299 Morris St
Barnesboro PA 15714

Call Sign: WB3FBG
Russell H Woods Sr
Barnesboro PA 15714

**FCC Amateur Radio
Licenses in Bausman**

Call Sign: KB3QZE
Dee Utz
Rosedale Ave
Bausman PA 17504

FCC Amateur Radio Licenses in Beaver Springs

Call Sign: KB3ICN
Park E Wagner
Box 424
Beaver Springs PA 17812

Call Sign: KB3ICO
Denyelle D Heiser
Box 492
Beaver Springs PA 17812

Call Sign: KB3UNW
Joseph M Kramer Sr
1006 Center Ave
Beaver Springs PA 17812

FCC Amateur Radio Licenses in Beaverdale

Call Sign: N3MBK
Paul M Bonfanti
716 Cedar St
Beaverdale PA 15921

FCC Amateur Radio Licenses in Beavertown

Call Sign: KB3FSX
Charles F Chandler
247 S Thomas St
Beavertown PA 17813

Call Sign: K3CFC
Charles F Chandler
247 S Thomas St
Beavertown PA 17813

Call Sign: K3DP
Robert C Bitting Jr
231 Thomas St
Beavertown PA 17813

Call Sign: KA4DDE
George McIntosh
223 Walnut St
Beavertown PA 17813

FCC Amateur Radio Licenses in Bedford

Call Sign: N3WMQ
Ronald E Hampton
140 Bedford Valley Rd
Bedford PA 15522

Call Sign: K3MIU
Arden E Moser
3197 Bedford Valley Rd
Bedford PA 15522

Call Sign: W1FHC
John K Timm
4734 Bedford Valley Rd
Bedford PA 155225900

Call Sign: KB3LSH
June A Dolly
4774 Bedford Valley Rd
Bedford PA 155225900

Call Sign: KB3VZC
Glen S Mason
7612 Bedford Valley Rd
Bedford PA 15522

Call Sign: KB3TKC
Truster U Shade Jr
156 Betsy Ave
Bedford PA 15522

Call Sign: N3MZQ
Rena B Cunard
Box 104
Bedford PA 15522

Call Sign: KD0LX
Leonard J Ogle
Box 147
Bedford PA 15522

Call Sign: N0FED
Yolanda D Ogle
Box 147
Bedford PA 15522

Call Sign: N3IUD
Josef A Orosz Jr
Box 450
Bedford PA 15522

Call Sign: KE3ZT
Stephen G Wurm
Box 586H
Bedford PA 15522

Call Sign: K3SAK
C Arnold Moorehead
429 Briar Valley Rd
Bedford PA 15522

Call Sign: W3PA
David W Jefferies
193 Cemetery Rd
Bedford PA 155225776

Call Sign: WB3HDZ
Raymond H Baumiller Jr
2685 Chalybeate Rd
Bedford PA 15522

Call Sign: KB3DFZ
John T Hogenmiller
300 Cumberland Rd
Bedford PA 15522

Call Sign: KA3PNK
Carl E Cseko
2068 Cumberland Rd
Bedford PA 155226441

Call Sign: WB3KSD
Reube B Moorehead

214 Donahoe Manor Rd
Apt 136
Bedford PA 15522

Call Sign: KD2D
Robert J Johnson
220 Donahue Manor Rd
Bedford PA 15522

Call Sign: KB3HUA
William R Turner
326 E Penn St
Bedford PA 155221433

Call Sign: K3NQT
Bedford County ARS
326 E Penn St
Bedford PA 155226459

Call Sign: WB3IEL
Wade A Reffner
4428 Evitts Creek Rd
Bedford PA 15522

Call Sign: K3YNL
Albert D Clites Jr
Evitts Creek Rd
Bedford PA 15522

Call Sign: KB3LBH
Kivins R Beecher II
1024 Hillview Dr
Bedford PA 15522

Call Sign: WA3UXP
Jay B Cessna
7898 Main Rd
Bedford PA 155223854

Call Sign: KB3FXR
James H Peight
525 Messiah Church Rd
Bedford PA 15522

Call Sign: WB3JEK

Kenneth L Burtnett
409 N Richard St
Bedford PA 15522

Call Sign: N3GOV
Steven P Spiker
1079 Narrow Ln
Bedford PA 15522

Call Sign: KA3EBS
J Frank Williams
139 Orchard Way
Bedford PA 155221137

Call Sign: AB3NR
David J Vanecek
386 Patio Ranch Rd
Bedford PA 15522

Call Sign: KB3RJB
Karl F Wenger Jr
499 Pigeon Hill Rd
Bedford PA 15522

Call Sign: WN4ZNS
Karl F Wenger Jr
499 Pigeon Hill Rd
Bedford PA 15522

Call Sign: KA3PNL
Jeffrey D Guyer
572 Pine Ridge Rd
Bedford PA 155225206

Call Sign: N4EEX
Guy E Hyre
800 Preston St Apt O
Bedford PA 15522

Call Sign: NK3A
Mahlon U Dimond
338 S Bedford St
Bedford PA 15522

Call Sign: N3KVL

Archimede Ziviello III
610 S Juliana St
Bedford PA 15522

Call Sign: N3ZMZ
Dawn M Ziviello
610 S Juliana St
Bedford PA 15522

Call Sign: KC4JGN
Rudy E Plummer
244 S Richard St
Bedford PA 15522

Call Sign: KB3UEK
Randy A Snair
1206 Sherry Rd
Bedford PA 15522

Call Sign: KB3RJA
Robert A Patterson
2247 Teaberry Rd
Bedford PA 15522

Call Sign: N3AHW
James L Whisner
112 Union St
Bedford PA 15522

Call Sign: KB3TR
Joel C Cunard
9343 US Rt 220
Bedford PA 155226215

Call Sign: W3ZWJ
Bedford County Amat
Radio Scty
9453 US Rt 220
Bedford PA 155226459

Call Sign: K3SCM
R Jay Williams
9453 US Rt 220
Bedford PA 155226459

Call Sign: W3TF
Thomas J Folan
141 Woodside St
Bedford PA 155226608

Call Sign: K3MKX
Claude E Koontz
Bedford PA 15522

Call Sign: KB3TQ
Harold E Manges
Bedford PA 15522

Call Sign: KA3FOJ
John F Feeney
Bedford PA 155220419

Call Sign: N3VCH
Edward J Brown
Bedford PA 155220519

FCC Amateur Radio Licenses in Beech Creek

Call Sign: KB3FUN
Jay E Martin Jr
410 Laurel Run Rd
Beech Creek PA 16822

Call Sign: N3JIT
Thomas S Beatty
2569 Laurel Run Rd
Beech Creek PA 16822

FCC Amateur Radio Licenses in Bellefonte

Call Sign: KB3SMN
Thomas N Eby
232 Armagast Rd
Bellefonte PA 16823

Call Sign: W3TNE
Thomas N Eby
232 Armagast Rd

Bellefonte PA 16823

Call Sign: N3SBJ
Richard J Cabral
1340 Axemann Rd
Bellefonte PA 16823

Call Sign: KR3C
Richard J Cabral
1340 Axemann Rd
Bellefonte PA 16823

Call Sign: K3OOR
Joan H Clark
1604 Axemann Rd
Bellefonte PA 168238111

Call Sign: KB3WPG
Domonique A Allen
1329 Axemann Rd Apt 2
Bellefonte PA 16823

Call Sign: KB3SHV
Leroy E Straley
125 Bel Air Hills Rd
Bellefonte PA 16823

Call Sign: KB3NDK
Alex M Lauri
151 Bel Air Hills Rd
Bellefonte PA 16823

Call Sign: N3EWR
Paul T Hunter
252 Benner Rd
Bellefonte PA 16823

Call Sign: N3HGM
Jeffrey M Catchmark
493 Blanchard St
Bellefonte PA 16823

Call Sign: KD3MY
Frances R Haube
830 Blanchard St

Bellefonte PA 16823

Call Sign: W3LNG
Edmund D Haube
830 Blanchard St
Bellefonte PA 16823

Call Sign: WB3EKL
Robert N Sagett
1152 Blue Spruce Dr
Bellefonte PA 168239457

Call Sign: W3SVI
John T Fisher
2929 Buffalo Run
Bellefonte PA 16823

Call Sign: W3CCC
Thomas W Widmann
2092 Buffalo Run Rd
Bellefonte PA 168238015

Call Sign: KB3LGV
Jerry L Bierly
2144 Buffalo Run Rd
Bellefonte PA 16823

Call Sign: KB3GUP
James H Karl
2924 Buffalo Run Rd
Bellefonte PA 16823

Call Sign: KB3RTQ
Eugene W Dupler
103 Darrell St
Bellefonte PA 16823

Call Sign: N3WXZ
Byron C Forsythe
1251 Daruss Dr
Bellefonte PA 16823

Call Sign: KB3FZK
Christopher Baughman
451 Davidson Rd

Bellefonte PA 16823

Bellefonte PA 16823

Bellefonte PA 16823

Call Sign: N3SOY
Dennis N Pagen
368 Dunkle Rd
Bellefonte PA 16823

Call Sign: K3SBA
Shannon B Allison
106 Fieldstone Ln
Bellefonte PA 16823

Call Sign: K2LBB
Everett I Mundy
106 Lewis St
Bellefonte PA 16823

Call Sign: KE8MH
Michael D Bester
405 E Bishop St
Bellefonte PA 16823

Call Sign: N9FXZ
David W De Vilbiss
103 Flint Ct
Bellefonte PA 16823

Call Sign: WA3JTU
Everett I Mundy
106 Lewis St
Bellefonte PA 16823

Call Sign: KB3CTL
Alyssa L Caldwell-Gill
437 E Bishop St
Bellefonte PA 16823

Call Sign: WA3KVQ
Raymond C Wilson
906 Green Ave
Bellefonte PA 16823

Call Sign: K3BJZ
Brian L Jones
393 Meadow Flower Cir
Bellefonte PA 16823

Call Sign: KB3CTG
John F Fusco
460 E Cherry Ln
Bellefonte PA 15823

Call Sign: WB3HKM
Joseph B Johnson Sr
426 Gregory Ln
Bellefonte PA 16823

Call Sign: N3VKS
Richard D Groff
273 Meadow Ln
Bellefonte PA 16823

Call Sign: WB3GDY
Donald E Crust
521 E Linn St
Bellefonte PA 16823

Call Sign: K3TJW
Frank A Capperella
330 Harmony Forge E
Bellefonte PA 16823

Call Sign: N3MVA
Michael L Edmonds
329 Meadow Ln
Bellefonte PA 16823

Call Sign: KB3VDG
Ryan C Vanauken
210 Edward Dr
Bellefonte PA 16823

Call Sign: KB3CZD
Roy A Long
122 Jenjo Dr
Bellefonte PA 16823

Call Sign: W3GAH
Gregg A Houck
717 N Allegheny St
Bellefonte PA 168232609

Call Sign: KC0QJX
Gordon C Vanauken
210 Edward Dr
Bellefonte PA 16823

Call Sign: KB1BH
Kenneth H Johnson
1322 Joanna Dr
Bellefonte PA 16823

Call Sign: AA3O
Gregg A Houck
717 N Allegheny St
Bellefonte PA 168232609

Call Sign: N3XHY
Matt A Corey
329 Feidler Rd
Bellefonte PA 16823

Call Sign: N3BXP
Donald L Wilson Jr
114 Kathryn Dr
Bellefonte PA 16823

Call Sign: KB3EFD
James G Stewart II
129 N Monroe St Apt C
Bellefonte PA 16823

Call Sign: N3XIA
Bobbin W Corey
329 Feidler Rd

Call Sign: N3PIX
John L Coder
170 Kathryn Dr

Call Sign: WB3JNE
Nicholas Pelick
225 Nittany Valley Dr

Bellefonte PA 16823

Bellefonte PA 16823

Bellefonte PA 16823

Call Sign: KA3MLK
Jon P Barnhart
1794 Nittany Valley Dr
Bellefonte PA 16823

Call Sign: K3UGW
Richard K Witmer
1309 Summit Dr
Bellefonte PA 16823

Call Sign: KB3HQG
Brent A Beauseigneur
1110 W Springfield Dr
Bellefonte PA 16823

Call Sign: N3EHT
Terrance R Lindquist II
410 Oak Ln
Bellefonte PA 16823

Call Sign: K3YGD
Phyllis J Robison
257 Thomas Hill Rd
Bellefonte PA 16823

Call Sign: KA3IUT
William C Culp Sr
950 W Water St
Bellefonte PA 16823

Call Sign: KB3CBU
Randy L Grove
1192 Purdue Mtn Rd
Bellefonte PA 16823

Call Sign: W3GKD
John J Robison
257 Thomas Hill Rd
Bellefonte PA 16823

Call Sign: KA1VXX
James T Lomartire
197 Washington Ave
Bellefonte PA 16823

Call Sign: KB3RXT
Ronald F Eichenlaub
110 Rosewood Cove
Bellefonte PA 16823

Call Sign: N3XNO
Johanna L Sedgwick
710 Valentine St Apt 2
Bellefonte PA 16823

Call Sign: W3TU
Ronald L Holt
297 Weaver Hill Rd
Bellefonte PA 168236908

Call Sign: KB3DSZ
Richard K Peters
967 Runville Rd
Bellefonte PA 16823

Call Sign: KD3AA
Gary S Settles
2053 Valley View Rd
Bellefonte PA 16823

Call Sign: WB2CIR
Neil J Nitzberg
133 White Pine Ln
Bellefonte PA 168236115

Call Sign: KB3EFA
Randall W Kilmer
163 Songbird Ln
Bellefonte PA 16823

Call Sign: KA3DEC
W David Files
519 W Lamb St
Bellefonte PA 16823

Call Sign: N3CCD
Herbert W Blair
155 Willow Dr
Bellefonte PA 16823

Call Sign: KB3QGC
Eric D Prescott
728 Spring Creek Rd
Bellefonte PA 168238454

Call Sign: W3SAY
W David Files
519 W Lamb St
Bellefonte PA 16823

Call Sign: N3OKC
Joseph J Rokita
306 Wiltshire Dr
Bellefonte PA 16823

Call Sign: N3VMV
Kathryn P Miller
501 St Paul Cir
Bellefonte PA 16823

Call Sign: WA3EFJ
William D Kuzio
1013 W Springfield Dr
Bellefonte PA 16823

Call Sign: KA3NHF
Matthew J Burns
1070 Zion Rd
Bellefonte PA 16823

Call Sign: WB3AEI
Charles E Mulfinger
131 Stover Rd

Call Sign: K3UZ
William D Kuzio
1013 W Springfield Dr

**FCC Amateur Radio
Licenses in Belleville**

Call Sign: KB3BIX
Joseph R Habbershon
4501 E Main St C11
Belleville PA 17004

Call Sign: K3PPO
Junior L Heaster
606 Erie Dr
Belleville PA 17004

Call Sign: W3SBX
Leroy E Pearson
34 Orchard Apts 2nd St
Belleville PA 17004

Call Sign: N8CRX
Charles G Rhodes Sr
45 Seneca Rd
Belleville PA 17004

Call Sign: W3YW
Jack L Walker
Valley View Ter
Belleville PA 17004

Call Sign: N3MDO
Michael B Ziviello
90 Walnut St
Belleville PA 17004

**FCC Amateur Radio
Licenses in Bellwood**

Call Sign: W3TEF
Roy B Goshorn
521 Bellview Ave
Bellwood PA 166172026

Call Sign: K3REV
Robert J Dill
606 E 3rd St
Bellwood PA 16617

Call Sign: KB3LGW
Heidi R Schratzmeier

600 E 4th St
Bellwood PA 16617

Call Sign: WB3FID
Kent R Willson
502 Martin St
Bellwood PA 16617

Call Sign: KB3JYE
Christopher E Creek
602 N 10th St
Bellwood PA 16617

Call Sign: KA3HQR
James F Hoffman Jr
610 N 4th St
Bellwood PA 16617

Call Sign: N3PIY
Mark N Hunter
908 N 6th St
Bellwood PA 16617

Call Sign: KB3MPU
Leroy F Dively III
611 N 9th St
Bellwood PA 16617

Call Sign: W3LFD
Leroy F Dively III
611 N 9th St
Bellwood PA 16617

Call Sign: WA2KDF
Gerard J Michaud
611 Orchard St
Bellwood PA 16617

Call Sign: KA3YRT
Richard A Kemp
423 S 1st St
Bellwood PA 16617

Call Sign: KB3GUS
Patricia A Kemp

423 S 1st St
Bellwood PA 16617

Call Sign: KE3UN
George J Oswald
Bellwood PA 16617

**FCC Amateur Radio
Licenses in Bendersville**

Call Sign: N3NFD
Anthony C Helman
103 Kime Ave
Bendersville PA 17306

**FCC Amateur Radio
Licenses in Benton**

Call Sign: KB3FZH
Bryan E Puderbaugh
Box 111
Benton PA 17814

Call Sign: N3AVW
Harold M Steege
Box 233
Benton PA 17814

Call Sign: KA3SKS
Mark R Seward
Box 94 D1
Benton PA 178149586

Call Sign: N3OSY
Walter E Minto Sr
81 E Piper Ln
Benton PA 17814

Call Sign: WB3CTT
William H Cunningham
11 Grassmere Park Rd
Benton PA 17814

Call Sign: K3JLM
Dennis D McHenry Sr

485 Kramer Hill Rd
Benton PA 17814

Call Sign: WA3VSP
Edward J Laubach
4082 Maple Grove Rd
Benton PA 17814

Call Sign: WB3JIA
William H McHenry
400 Mendenhall Ln
Benton PA 17814

Call Sign: K3KEL
David H Wenner
38 Mitchell Rd
Benton PA 178147779

Call Sign: N3QCZ
Matt Seward
20 Mossville Rd
Benton PA 17814

Call Sign: W3UF
Clemence M Misavage
6 Old Green Creek Rd
Benton PA 17814

Call Sign: N3GEL
Alberta A McHenry
480 Park St
Benton PA 17814

Call Sign: N3LVT
Robert C Wolfgang Jr
72 Peterman Rd
Benton PA 17814

Call Sign: N3WFE
Gerard E Mattive
Po Box 106 Jc
Benton PA 17814

Call Sign: K3BEP
Bryan E Puderbaugh

3751 State Rt 239
Benton PA 17814

Call Sign: AA3TT
Andrew P Pavalonis
178 Swamp Rd
Benton PA 17814

Call Sign: KB3RLW
James F Helisek
88 Youngs Hill Rd
Benton PA 17814

Call Sign: N3MWC
Karen M Musitano
Benton PA 17814

Call Sign: KA3MGG
Charles A Musitano
Benton PA 17814

Call Sign: WB3CQM
James F Seibel
Benton PA 17814

Call Sign: N3UMQ
Grace A Cragle
Benton PA 17814

**FCC Amateur Radio
Licenses in Berlin**

Call Sign: KB3VME
James P Froehlich
229 Beachdale Rd
Berlin PA 15530

Call Sign: WB3ITP
Joseph F Simpson
1496 Beachdale Rd
Berlin PA 15530

Call Sign: KB3RHQ
Nicholas A Trulick
1823 Brotherton Rd

Berlin PA 15530

Call Sign: KB3IKO
Michael A Livengood
1602 Brubaker St
Berlin PA 15530

Call Sign: KB3JXZ
Joel D Landis
118 Cumberland St
Berlin PA 155300064

Call Sign: AB3MT
Joel D Landis
118 Cumberland St
Berlin PA 155300064

Call Sign: K3YVS
Roy C Bucher
719 Division St
Berlin PA 15530

Call Sign: WA3BHM
John F Jenista
161 Fochtman Rd
Berlin PA 15530

Call Sign: WB3HRJ
Sandra A Jenista
161 Fochtman Rd
Berlin PA 15530

Call Sign: KB3MFT
Cody C Miller
8945 Glades Pike
Berlin PA 15550

Call Sign: KB3MBJ
Terry L Metzgar
10122 Glades Pike
Berlin PA 15530

Call Sign: W1RON
Ronald I Trench Jr
4436 Huckleberry Hwy

Berlin PA 155307100

Call Sign: KB3NSY
Kenneth D Flick
818 Main St
Berlin PA 15530

Call Sign: K3DPM
Daniel L Wilson
Rr 1
Berlin PA 15530

Call Sign: KE3VO
David L Hochard
354 S Pike View Rd
Berlin PA 15530

Call Sign: K3UMB
Charles E La Bute
506 South
Berlin PA 15530

Call Sign: N3FWT
James L Burcaw
611 Swallow St
Berlin PA 155301513

Call Sign: KA3YOZ
Charles R Mowry
701 Swallow St
Berlin PA 15530

Call Sign: KB3BZB
Ty T Will
1092 Tunnel Rd
Berlin PA 155305221

Call Sign: W3WDZ
William G Mothersbaugh
180 W Main St
Berlin PA 15530

FCC Amateur Radio Licenses in Berrysburg

Call Sign: W3BBT
Leroy A Moppin Jr
205 S 2nd St
Berrysburg PA 170050011

Call Sign: N3GEW
Leroy A Moppin Jr
205 S 2nd St
Berrysburg PA 170050018

FCC Amateur Radio Licenses in Berwick

Call Sign: N3DCV
Frank R Ferrera
1415 2nd Ave
Berwick PA 18603

Call Sign: KC8LHI
John M Lewallen
3 3rd Ln
Berwick PA 186036643

Call Sign: N3GQM
Dennis E Freeman
1141 7th Ave
Berwick PA 18603

Call Sign: N3XUQ
Keith J Oliveri
1227 7th Ave
Berwick PA 18603

Call Sign: N3NOP
Robert Fulton Jr
1342 7th Ave
Berwick PA 18603

Call Sign: N3PEK
Carol A Fulton
1342 7th Ave
Berwick PA 18603

Call Sign: N3PEJ
Richard R Wehry

Box 2588
Berwick PA 18603

Call Sign: KA3NRO
Lawrence L Feissner II
Box 3135
Berwick PA 18603

Call Sign: W3ESC
La Rue S Eddinger
Box 3427
Berwick PA 18603

Call Sign: N3UHW
Kerry K Kishbaygh
Box 4075
Berwick PA 18603

Call Sign: N3JRF
Richard A Bognar Sr
Box 4083
Berwick PA 18603

Call Sign: KY3W
David A Stout
546 Cemetery Rd
Berwick PA 18603

Call Sign: KB3MJI
Patricia A Camillocci
202 E 10th St
Berwick PA 18603

Call Sign: KA3BPN
Anthony J Camillocci
202 E 10th St
Berwick PA 18603

Call Sign: KA3UWZ
Sean M Minahan
809 E 2nd St
Berwick PA 18603

Call Sign: KA3TKC
David E Schuppert

E 2nd St
Berwick PA 18603

907 E 6th St
Berwick PA 18603

2508 Heights Rd
Berwick PA 18603

Call Sign: KA3ULG
David J Zimmerman Jr
711 E 3rd St
Berwick PA 18603

Call Sign: N3FIP
Jerzy M Gizowski
1230 E 6th St
Berwick PA 18603

Call Sign: KB3MEQ
Conway G Hosler Sr
125 Hosler Rd
Berwick PA 18603

Call Sign: WB3HDE
Mark S Hanna
1006 E 4 1/2 St
Berwick PA 18603

Call Sign: N3XXJ
James D Cherrington
332 E 8th St
Berwick PA 18603

Call Sign: N3ZFB
Christopher P Bauslaugh
227 Iron St
Berwick PA 18603

Call Sign: KA3TST
Pierce H Morgan
500 E 4th St
Berwick PA 18603

Call Sign: W3LKN
Wilson G Helt
404 E 9th St
Berwick PA 18603

Call Sign: K3EVQ
Michael J Leffler
229 Iron St
Berwick PA 18603

Call Sign: KB3ECH
Roy D Row
729 E 5th St
Berwick PA 18603

Call Sign: KB3IPX
Wayne W Varner
237 E Front St
Berwick PA 18603

Call Sign: N3OAP
Alexander E Kishbaugh
20 Joy Ln
Berwick PA 18603

Call Sign: KB4EIB
Roy E Row
729 E 5th St
Berwick PA 18603

Call Sign: N3NDP
Helen C Hoover
1137 E Ft St
Berwick PA 18603

Call Sign: N3QLW
Yvonne C Young
764 Knob Mtn Rd
Berwick PA 18603

Call Sign: N3QLY
Joseph J Maynard
925 E 5th St
Berwick PA 18603

Call Sign: N3OMA
Andrew M Shecktor
1308 Fairview Ave
Berwick PA 18603

Call Sign: N3QOH
Neil A Young
764 Knob Mtn Rd
Berwick PA 186035853

Call Sign: KB3FJI
Thomas J Talanca
306 E 6th St
Berwick PA 18603

Call Sign: N3EUQ
John C Petty
1209 Good Ave
Berwick PA 18603

Call Sign: KA3UWP
Kenneth B Ahearn
Lasalle St
Berwick PA 18603

Call Sign: KA3BVF
Steven J Hampton
316 E 6th St
Berwick PA 18603

Call Sign: N3PNG
Michael R Seward
720 Green St
Berwick PA 18603

Call Sign: N3BUD
Michael K Hoover
45 Lights Rd
Berwick PA 186035532

Call Sign: KA3CWK
Donald C Shoemaker Sr

Call Sign: N3JPV
Randall C Kishbaugh

Call Sign: WA3ESX
Frederick W Briggs

1414 Market
Berwick PA 18603

100 Mulberry St Apt 15
Berwick PA 186034742

Pine St
Berwick PA 18603

Call Sign: WA3DQI
David M Clark
333 Martzville Rd
Berwick PA 18603

Call Sign: N3SEQ
Sheldon A Norris
109 Municipal Rd
Berwick PA 186035216

Call Sign: KB3EJV
Frank S Barren Jr
813 Poplar St
Berwick PA 186031527

Call Sign: KB3GXO
Matthew J Harris
545 Martzville Rd
Berwick PA 18603

Call Sign: WA3PGQ
Richard P Cocklin
1945 N Market St
Berwick PA 18603

Call Sign: AK3V
Robert B Price
1120 Salem Blvd
Berwick PA 18603

Call Sign: K3USY
Louis S Trapane Jr
Monroe St
Berwick PA 18603

Call Sign: KA3NSG
Alana M Golomb
2015 N Market St
Berwick PA 18603

Call Sign: KB3JPW
Matthew R Price
1120 Salem Blvd
Berwick PA 18603

Call Sign: AK3U
Louis S Trapane Jr
Monroe St
Berwick PA 18603

Call Sign: K3DYU
James F Makar
1726 N Vine St
Berwick PA 18603

Call Sign: WA3PGU
Donald Z Kishbach
55 Shelhamer Rd
Berwick PA 18603

Call Sign: KA3LMG
Clifford M Kishbaugh III
61 Moores Hill Rd
Berwick PA 18603

Call Sign: KB3KCJ
Wayne S Hamilton
1119 Orange St
Berwick PA 18603

Call Sign: N3VXA
Paula M Benjamin
234 Slowick Rd
Berwick PA 18603

Call Sign: KA3DWA
Clifford M Kishbaugh Jr
374 Moores Hill Rd
Berwick PA 18603

Call Sign: KA3SLT
Michael B Billy
1416 Orange St
Berwick PA 18603

Call Sign: K3QIA
Robert L Foster
1586 State Rt 93
Berwick PA 18603

Call Sign: KA3LMF
Cheryl L Kishbaugh
374 Moores Hill Rd
Berwick PA 18603

Call Sign: N3YGK
Jesse L Fulkersin
6110 Park Rd
Berwick PA 18603

Call Sign: KB3BJO
Columbia Montour ARC
1586 State Rte 93
Berwick PA 18603

Call Sign: W3KUJ
Robert A M Fulton
310 Mulberry St
Berwick PA 18603

Call Sign: WB3HDQ
John Zerance
205 Pearl St
Berwick PA 18603

Call Sign: KB3KGU
Barry E Freeman
41 Stone Church Rd
Berwick PA 18603

Call Sign: N3LQS
Lester G Roth Jr

Call Sign: N3WIF
Michael K Barna

Call Sign: KB3FJH
Matthew J Harris

467 Stone Church Rd
Berwick PA 18603

Call Sign: N3EUI
David A Slusser
327 Summerhill Ave
Berwick PA 18603

Call Sign: N3PEO
John E Gallagher
525 Summerhill Rd
Berwick PA 18603

Call Sign: N3EZS
Garry L John
160 Thomas Rd
Berwick PA 18603

Call Sign: N3TFD
Donald T Lynn
128 Valley Rd
Berwick PA 18603

Call Sign: KA3PGA
Richard G Mabie
422 W 2nd St
Berwick PA 18603

Call Sign: KA3PTZ
Patrick J Mabie
422 W 2nd St
Berwick PA 18603

Call Sign: W3RGQ
Sheldon C Cleaver
427 W 2nd St
Berwick PA 18603

Call Sign: KD3IT
Alice A Talanca
543 W 2nd St
Berwick PA 18603

Call Sign: NQ3G
Peter J Talanca Jr

543 W 2nd St
Berwick PA 18603

Call Sign: WC3A
David R Schack
602 W Front St
Berwick PA 18603

Call Sign: N3PED
Lawrence W Lahr
718 W Front St
Berwick PA 18603

Call Sign: KB3UZF
Lawrence L Feissner II
1133 W Front St
Berwick PA 18603

Call Sign: W3KRZ
Lawrence L Feissner
1133 W Front St
Berwick PA 18603

Call Sign: KB3GUC
Edward L Bertollo Jr
210 Walnut St
Berwick PA 18603

Call Sign: K3AHD
Edward L Bertollo Jr
210 Walnut St
Berwick PA 18603

Call Sign: WB3CQE
Larry E Grasley
Berwick PA 18603

Call Sign: KB3TZD
Heather D Butera-Howell
Berwick PA 18603

Call Sign: KB3SQV
Jason M Bonsall
Berwick PA 186030001

FCC Amateur Radio Licenses in Big Cove Tannery

Call Sign: KA3UFF
Albert K Wuertenberg
387 Basil Ln
Big Cove Tannery PA 17212

FCC Amateur Radio Licenses in Biglerville

Call Sign: KB3THQ
Paul J Hawthorn
10 Boyds Schoolhouse Rd
Biglerville PA 17307

Call Sign: KB3DDJ
Steven E Taylor
151 Conewago St
Biglerville PA 17307

Call Sign: W3YPL
Charles E Kranias
5 Diane Ln
Biglerville PA 173070508

Call Sign: KA3ONO
Barbara J Mahoney
362 Dug Hill Rd
Biglerville PA 17307

Call Sign: N3ERB
Jerry A Mahoney
362 Dug Hill Rd
Biglerville PA 17307

Call Sign: KB3TUJ
Kevin D Biesecker
24 Penn St
Biglerville PA 17307

Call Sign: KB3EMA
Kevin D Biesecker

24 Penn St
Biglerville PA 17307

Call Sign: KA3NRB
Kimberly S Paull Frank
59 Rocky Rd
Biglerville PA 17307

Call Sign: N3HMI
Derek T Frank
59 Rocky Rd
Biglerville PA 17307

Call Sign: W0AMX
William J Toeller
90 S Main St
Biglerville PA 17307

Call Sign: N3PJD
Michael J Clingan
15 Woodview Rd
Biglerville PA 17307

Call Sign: KA3MQB
Robert G Witten
725 Yellow Hill Rd
Biglerville PA 17307

Call Sign: N1JLW
Jack L Weber
1245 Zeigler Mill Rd
Biglerville PA 17307

Call Sign: K1PMW
Patricia M Weber
1245 Zeigler Mill Rd
Biglerville PA 17307

Call Sign: K3PMW
Patricia M Weber
1245 Zeigler Mill Rd
Biglerville PA 17307

Call Sign: KB3TUI
Samuel A Biesecker

Biglerville PA 17307

FCC Amateur Radio Licenses in Bird In Hand

Call Sign: N3XAN
Shawn R Berry
371 Monterey Rd
Bird In Hand PA 17505

FCC Amateur Radio Licenses in Blain

Call Sign: N3NRS
Guy N Shanafelter
Blain PA 170060163

FCC Amateur Radio Licenses in Bloomsburg

Call Sign: KB3GUF
Josh B Sponenberg
3553 1st St
Bloomsburg PA 17815

Call Sign: KF3BH
Stephen E Richendrfer
3771 2nd St
Bloomsburg PA 17815

Call Sign: KB3TNZ
Bradley L Butler
6270 3rd St
Bloomsburg PA 17815

Call Sign: KA3KZJ
Donna C Levan
20 Amron Dr
Bloomsburg PA
178158745

Call Sign: KA2NVF
Robert P Marande
106 Arbutus Park Rd

Bloomsburg PA
178158512

Call Sign: N3VSU
Dennis A Miller
202 Arbutus Park Rd
Bloomsburg PA
178158508

Call Sign: KB3KJC
Scott C Markley
20 Blue Jay Dr
Bloomsburg PA 17815

Call Sign: KB3JQM
Jonathan M Coady
Box 16
Bloomsburg PA 17815

Call Sign: KB3HCO
Matthew K Minnig
Box 464
Bloomsburg PA 17815

Call Sign: KB3CWM
James V Mattive
Box 46A
Bloomsburg PA 17815

Call Sign: KA3SJF
Rebecca Bozarth
Box 549J
Bloomsburg PA 17815

Call Sign: WB3GPA
Bruce A Bozarth
Box 549J
Bloomsburg PA 17815

Call Sign: N3ZEX
Amy M Rubenstein
Box 75 A
Bloomsburg PA 17815

Call Sign: N3ZDE

Eric D Rubenstein
Box 75A
Bloomsburg PA 17815

Call Sign: N3MJG
Charles L Miller
39 Buckhorn Rd
Bloomsburg PA 17815

Call Sign: WB3KUV
Clarence E Long
66 Buckhorn Rd
Bloomsburg PA 17815

Call Sign: N1HB
Howard W Brochyus Jr
95 Buckhorn Rd
Bloomsburg PA 17815

Call Sign: KB3LWF
Michael B Hamilton
1105 Catherine St
Bloomsburg PA 17815

Call Sign: KA3GGV
Edward S Halfmann
1247 Chestnut St
Bloomsburg PA 17815

Call Sign: K3YIW
Nelson R Whitenight
14 Chrysty Hill Rd
Bloomsburg PA 17815

Call Sign: N3IIQ
Cory J Conklin
2 Clifton Dr
Bloomsburg PA 17815

Call Sign: WC3H
Richard W Conklin
2 Clifton Dr
Bloomsburg PA 17815

Call Sign: KA3SJQ

Joseph C Manning
294 County Line Dr
Bloomsburg PA 17815

Call Sign: KB3CBH
Jeremy P Snyder
7 Dietterick Hill Rd
Bloomsburg PA 17815

Call Sign: N3UMN
Thomas A Ross
352 Draketown Rd
Bloomsburg PA 17815

Call Sign: KC3DR
Richard N Clark
530 Dutch Hill Rd
Bloomsburg PA 17815

Call Sign: K3GQT
Joseph P Bomboy
2 E 11th St
Bloomsburg PA 17815

Call Sign: N3XTS
Terry L Lemon Sr
147 E 11th St
Bloomsburg PA 17815

Call Sign: KA3UXN
David W Clarke
230 E 1st St
Bloomsburg PA 17815

Call Sign: KB3BRW
Bloomsburg U ARC
400 E 2nd St Bloomsburg U
Bloomsburg PA 17815

Call Sign: KB3TTD
John M Lewis
564 E 3rd St
Bloomsburg PA 17815

Call Sign: N3QVQ
Joseph Hadida
610 E 3rd St
Bloomsburg PA 17815

Call Sign: K3ARY
Harvey G Smith Sr
42 E 4th St
Bloomsburg PA 17815

Call Sign: KA3QZT
Mark S Blass
346 E 7th St
Bloomsburg PA 17815

Call Sign: KB3MAJ
William P Herald
227 Fair St
Bloomsburg PA
178151413

Call Sign: WB3KIZ
Gaylen M Gerrish
305 Fair St
Bloomsburg PA 17815

Call Sign: KB3ZI
Donald F Shollenberger
120 Forest Rd
Bloomsburg PA 17815

Call Sign: KB3IGU
Kyle E Martin
134 Frosty Valley Rd
Bloomsburg PA 17815

Call Sign: N3VMM
Dennis W Nichols
331 Glenn Ave
Bloomsburg PA 17815

Call Sign: KC3HP
Douglas L Rubenstein
114 Hedge Rd
Bloomsburg PA 17815

Call Sign: KA7LIO
Kimberly A Peters
1190 Highland Dr
Bloomsburg PA 17815

Call Sign: WA3SVY
Paul M Cain Jr
6195 Hughes St
Bloomsburg PA
178158712

Call Sign: KB3HMU
James D Davis
100 Irondale Ave
Bloomsburg PA 17815

Call Sign: KB3HMV
Joshua B Davis
100 Irondale Ave
Bloomsburg PA 17815

Call Sign: KB3FGS
Jose A Lopez
434 Jefferson St
Bloomsburg PA 17815

Call Sign: KA3FTG
Edward A Kelly
2622 Johnson Rd
Bloomsburg PA
176159020

Call Sign: KA3SJG
Patricia A Grubb
2622 Johnson Rd
Bloomsburg PA
178159020

Call Sign: WA3UAT
Jeffrey R Shearer
212 Juniper St
Bloomsburg PA 17815

Call Sign: KA3KVR

Bruce L Snyder
239 Leonard St
Bloomsburg PA 17815

Call Sign: K3JSM
James S Mason
837 Lightstreet Rd
Bloomsburg PA 17815

Call Sign: W3PSY
Marion G Mason
837 Lightstreet Rd
Bloomsburg PA 17815

Call Sign: N3BUG
Edward H Crossley
1100 Market St
Bloomsburg PA
178153712

Call Sign: KB3WQ
Dennis D Young
9 Meadow Ln
Bloomsburg PA 17815

Call Sign: N3CDK
Sally R Young
9 Meadow Ln
Bloomsburg PA 17815

Call Sign: KF4NTY
James F Makar
10 Michael Dr
Bloomsburg PA 17815

Call Sign: N3BFX
Marvin A Houseknecht
1024 Mountain St
Bloomsburg PA 17815

Call Sign: N3POA
Michael L Cook
5761 New Berwick Hwy
Lot 38
Bloomsburg PA 17815

Call Sign: KB3PNI
James W Magill
25 Nottingham Rd
Bloomsburg PA 17815

Call Sign: N3GEH
Linda A Carl
2008 Old Berwick Rd
Bloomsburg PA 17815

Call Sign: N3YGL
Richard A Maynard Jr
4459 Old Berwick Rd
Bloomsburg PA 17815

Call Sign: NQ3Y
Richard A Maynard Jr
4459 Old Berwick Rd
Bloomsburg PA 17815

Call Sign: N3EUP
Kathleen R Pratt
707 Park St
Bloomsburg PA 17815

Call Sign: N3ZDC
Evan R Brophy
400 Railroad St 10
Bloomsburg PA 17815

Call Sign: KB3LHA
Joshua T Turner
253 Reading St
Bloomsburg PA 17815

Call Sign: KA3FFT
William P Hall
340 Reading St
Bloomsburg PA 17815

Call Sign: WA3IIA
Charles F Wasko
3726 Red Maple Ln
Bloomsburg PA 17815

Call Sign: KD3TE
James R Hufford Sr
3402 Ridge Rd
Bloomsburg PA 17815

Call Sign: W3KE
Eugene Breech
Riverhill Dr
Bloomsburg PA 17815

Call Sign: N3BJS
Michael C Hutnick Jr
450 Riverview Ave
Bloomsburg PA 17815

Call Sign: N3KLL
Albert J Gallagher
460 Riverview Ave
Bloomsburg PA 17815

Call Sign: KB3WDO
Jared R Diehl
515 Riverview Ave
Bloomsburg PA 17815

Call Sign: N3PBG
Thomas R Johnson
193 Rupert Dr
Bloomsburg PA 17815

Call Sign: W3HVG
Patrick E Taylor
1200 S Market St
Bloomsburg PA 17815

Call Sign: WA3HVP
Thomas A Baker
630 Scenic Ave
Bloomsburg PA 17815

Call Sign: N3POB
Dorene E Miguelez
1079 Schoolhouse Rd
Bloomsburg PA 17815

Call Sign: N3IRN
Michael O Miguelez
1079 Schoolhouse Rd
Bloomsburg PA
178159782

Call Sign: KB3IBB
Rodney D Hosler
98 Scotch Valley Dr
Bloomsburg PA 17815

Call Sign: KB3JZB
Nathan A Smith
7205 Shaffer Hollow Rd
Bloomsburg PA 17815

Call Sign: W3QBA
Howard H Holbrook
Shafter Rd
Bloomsburg PA 17815

Call Sign: WA3UNU
Gary E Norton
2213 Shasta Dr
Bloomsburg PA 17815

Call Sign: N3EKV
John C Speicher
27 Shawnee Rd
Bloomsburg PA 17815

Call Sign: KB3ASL
Connie B Shuman
88 State Rd
Bloomsburg PA 17815

Call Sign: KB3AUA
Mark A Balla
297 Summit Ave
Bloomsburg PA 17815

Call Sign: K3TFF
William M Shaffer
420 Valley Rd

Bloomsburg PA
178158444

Call Sign: N3XLG
John K Martin
185 W 12th St
Bloomsburg PA 17815

Call Sign: KB3GYQ
Charlyne M Eichner
474 W 3rd St
Bloomsburg PA 17815

Call Sign: KB3GTY
Jeffrey D Eichner Sr
474 W 3rd St
Bloomsburg PA 17815

Call Sign: WB3FLG
Stephen Levan Jr
330 W 3rd St Apt 402
Bloomsburg PA 17815

Call Sign: N3KFM
Eugene D Radice
144 W 4th St
Bloomsburg PA 17815

Call Sign: W3QVT
Jack F Kountz
323 W 4th St
Bloomsburg PA 17815

Call Sign: KA3OKK
Jeremy J De Prisco
136 W Anthony Ave
Bloomsburg PA 17815

Call Sign: N3KYZ
George S Law
10 Whitenight Ln
Bloomsburg PA 17815

Call Sign: N3MIE
Steve W Graves

255 Whites Church Rd
Bloomsburg PA 17815

Call Sign: N3MXP
Ronnie G Ulmer
266 Whites Church Rd
Bloomsburg PA 17815

Call Sign: KB3WGY
Jeffrey C Brunskill
3014 Woods Edge Dr
Bloomsburg PA 17815

Call Sign: KB3DH
Edwin L Adams
Bloomsburg PA 17815

Call Sign: KB3IGR
James F Youngkin
Bloomsburg PA 17815

FCC Amateur Radio Licenses in Blossburg

Call Sign: KA3IBV
Edward J Modrzejewski Jr
562 Gulick St
Blossburg PA 16912

Call Sign: KB1EVN
David P Milligan
141 Main St
Blossburg PA 16912

Call Sign: WB3CKA
Charles M Pierce
137 Maple Hill Rd
Blossburg PA 16912

Call Sign: WB3AJY
Donald F Smith
319 NW Williamson Rd
Blossburg PA 16912

Call Sign: KB3TQY

Richard B King
448 Ruah St
Blossburg PA 16912

Call Sign: KB3DQR
Richard L Williams
107 S Williamson Rd
Blossburg PA 169121008

Call Sign: WB3BIP
Jerome L Ogden
262 S Williamson Rd
Blossburg PA 16912

FCC Amateur Radio Licenses in Blue Ball

Call Sign: KA3KPO
Donald W Maitland
Blue Ball PA 17506

FCC Amateur Radio Licenses in Blue Ridge Summit

Call Sign: KA3ORQ
Melvin L Wolff Jr
11845 Furnace Rd
Blue Ridge Summit PA 17214

Call Sign: KD5OLE
Roy H Kent
13601 Maryland Ave
Blue Ridge Summit PA 17214

Call Sign: KB3PHT
William A Kent
13601 Maryland Ave
Blue Ridge Summit PA 17214

Call Sign: N3TVD
Amanda L Daywalt

15393 Norwood Ve
Blue Ridge Summit PA 17214

Call Sign: KA3DEU
William N Schlosser
14701 Pa Ave Box 208
Blue Ridge Summit PA 17214

Call Sign: WB9FMP
James O Brockhouse
15441 Sabillasville Rd
Blue Ridge Summit PA 17214

Call Sign: KB3UIA
Phyllis L Presley
15448 Summit Farms Dr
Blue Ridge Summit PA 17214

Call Sign: KB3UIB
Randall S Humphrey
15448 Summit Farms Dr
Blue Ridge Summit PA 17214

Call Sign: WA4IBY
Douglas L Lunde Sr
Blue Ridge Summit PA 17214

FCC Amateur Radio Licenses in Boalsburg

Call Sign: KB3PNT
Eric J Struble
1011 Anna St
Boalsburg PA 16827

Call Sign: K3EJS
Eric J Struble
1011 Anna St
Boalsburg PA 16827

Call Sign: KB3IOT
Walter F Paxton
794 Ashworth Ln
Boalsburg PA 16872

Call Sign: WB3ELI
John P De Barber
405 Ella Dr
Boalsburg PA 16827

Call Sign: KA9LRL
Laura A King
1402 Estate Dr
Boalsburg PA 16827

Call Sign: N3AAF
John T Guss
809 Hemlock St
Boalsburg PA 168271116

Call Sign: N3GU
John T Guss
809 Hemlock St
Boalsburg PA 168271116

Call Sign: KC3N
Dante P Bonaquist
171 Indian Hill Rd
Boalsburg PA 16827

Call Sign: N1XUS
Rachel P Thompson
221 Liberty St
Boalsburg PA 16827

Call Sign: W6YWN
Richard Stern
1150 Linden Hall Rd
Boalsburg PA 16827

Call Sign: K3BIG
Thomas C Miller
306 Montclair Ln
Boalsburg PA 168271653

Call Sign: WB3CEO
Roderick S Thomas
108 Pine Tree Ave
Boalsburg PA 16827

Call Sign: K3TMB
Edward J Sickora
138 Pine Tree Ave
Boalsburg PA 16827

Call Sign: KA0NGT
Allan G Sonsteby
1314 Springfield Cir
Boalsburg PA 16827

Call Sign: K3SJS
Josephine Chesworth
913 Tressler St
Boalsburg PA 16827

Call Sign: W3IA
E Thomas Chesworth
913 Tressler St
Boalsburg PA 16827

Call Sign: KB3QJT
Amateur Radio Elmers
Assn Of Central PA
924 Tressler St
Boalsburg PA 16827

Call Sign: KB3SCG
Hungry Hams ARC
924 Tressler St
Boalsburg PA 16827

Call Sign: N3HIC
Sharon L Gaisler
924 Tressler St
Boalsburg PA 16827

Call Sign: W3PD
John J Portelli
949 Tressler St

Boalsburg PA 16827

Call Sign: WB3GDZ
Joan T Portelli
949 Tressler St
Boalsburg PA 16827

Call Sign: KB3TQK
John P Johnston
345 W Crestview Ave
Boalsburg PA 16827

Call Sign: AB4WO
Jeffrey D Caldwell
348 W Crestview Ave
Boalsburg PA 16827

Call Sign: KB0VTW
Daniel W Sellers
317 W Main St
Boalsburg PA 168271328

Call Sign: KB3PDJ
Dale I Neff
512 West Dr
Boalsburg PA 16827

Call Sign: KB3BPL
Ernest J Oelbermann
1444 Willowbrook Dr
Boalsburg PA 16827

Call Sign: W3HPX
Emil E Hrivnak
1457 Willowbrook Dr
Boalsburg PA 16827

Call Sign: N3EH
Emil E Hrivnak
1457 Willowbrook Dr
Boalsburg PA 16827

Call Sign: WA3ZYO
Christopher J Potalivo
1465 Willowbrook Dr

Boalsburg PA 16827

Call Sign: AL7GK
Douglas D Dougherty
Boalsburg PA 16827

FCC Amateur Radio Licenses in Boiling Springs

Call Sign: KB3KNO
Zachary D Zawisa
114 4th St
Boiling Springs PA 17007

Call Sign: KB3MXG
Emily J Whisel
7 Ashley Ct
Boiling Springs PA 17007

Call Sign: KB3OVS
Alexandra E Schiavoni
104 Creamery Rd
Boiling Springs PA 17007

Call Sign: KB3RYN
Daniel C Blichasz
652 Deer Rd
Boiling Springs PA 17007

Call Sign: KB3NET
Frank D Sears
117 E Countryside Dr
Boiling Springs PA 17007

Call Sign: KA3SGY
Paul R Matter Jr
401 Front St
Boiling Springs PA 17007

Call Sign: KB3PAT
Michael W Sheehan
5 Hickory Ct
Boiling Springs PA 17007

Call Sign: K3EYK
Garry L Fasick
107 Hilltop Rd
Boiling Springs PA 17007

Call Sign: WN3H
Charles W Brucks
1323 Horick Dr
Boiling Springs PA 17007

Call Sign: WA2ZTH
Wayne L Pier
1257 Indian Peg Rd
Boiling Springs PA 17007

Call Sign: KB3LQZ
Ryan J Loesch
1344 Kuan Rd
Boiling Springs PA 17007

Call Sign: KB3PAV
Tyler J Storch
1094 Kuhn Rd
Boiling Springs PA 17007

Call Sign: KD3HJ
Jeffrey K Orner
1485 Lutztown Rd
Boiling Springs PA 17007

Call Sign: W3JKO
Jeffrey K Orner
1485 Lutztown Rd
Boiling Springs PA 17007

Call Sign: KB3SUA
Michael P Orsinger
5 Mulberry Ct
Boiling Springs PA 17007

Call Sign: KB3LRX
Adriana M Spizuoco
6 N Pin Oak Dr
Boiling Springs PA 17007

Call Sign: KB3UWH
Jay F Vogel
6 Persimmon Dr
Boiling Springs PA 17007

Call Sign: N3UZQ
Daniel J Rakes
5 Pewter Ln
Boiling Springs PA 17007

Call Sign: KB3PFS
Brendan D Barnes
41 S Pin Oak Dr
Boiling Springs PA 17007

Call Sign: KB3IUQ
Sean D Barnes
41 S Pin Oak Dr
Boiling Springs PA 17007

Call Sign: N3JQ
Sean D Barnes
41 S Pin Oak Dr
Boiling Springs PA 17007

Call Sign: N3EPY
Richard R Johnson
45 S Pin Oak Dr
Boiling Springs PA 17007

Call Sign: N1NWU
James G Geruntho
1276 Sandy Ln
Boiling Springs PA 17007

Call Sign: N2EMQ
Dominic A De Ricco
667 Spring Ln
Boiling Springs PA
170079648

Call Sign: WA3BKK
Bobbe L Rothermel
346 W 1st St

Boiling Springs PA
170079744

Call Sign: N3NBA
Casey L Shearer
219 W Springville Rd
Boiling Springs PA 17007

Call Sign: N1IOB
Allen G Gates
Boiling Springs PA 17007

Call Sign: N3BWS
James H Ulman
Boiling Springs PA 17007

Call Sign: KB3KLU
Stacey M Brandt
Boiling Springs PA 17007

FCC Amateur Radio Licenses in Boswell

Call Sign: KB9WCX
Elisha R Zimmerman
474 Barnett Rd
Boswell PA 15531

Call Sign: N3XCC
Michael S Zimmerman
474 Barnett Rd
Boswell PA 15531

Call Sign: KB3JYB
Dennis M Zimmerman
610 Barnett Rd
Boswell PA 15531

Call Sign: K3DAD
Dennis M Zimmerman
610 Barnett Rd
Boswell PA 15531

Call Sign: KB3JYA
Jane C Zimmerman

610 Barnett Rd
Boswell PA 15531

Call Sign: K3MOM
Jane C Zimmerman
610 Barnett Rd
Boswell PA 15531

Call Sign: KB3ADD
Robert R Lint
564 Barnick Rd
Boswell PA 15531

Call Sign: N3OND
Robert R Lint Jr
564 Barnick Rd
Boswell PA 15531

Call Sign: KE4EJC
Herbert R Maurer
800 Center St
Boswell PA 15531

Call Sign: N5MPM
Thomas D Gelpi
138 Godin Dr
Boswell PA 15531

Call Sign: KB3UUR
John A Collins
2076 Lincoln Hwy
Boswell PA 15531

Call Sign: NS3HS
North Star High School
ARC
400 Ohio St
Boswell PA 15531

Call Sign: KB3TUA
North Star High School
ARC
400 Ohio St
Boswell PA 15544

Call Sign: W3JKC
Daniel V Couture
Boswell PA 15531

FCC Amateur Radio Licenses in Bowmandale

Call Sign: KB3KMT
Susan M Mumma
Bowmansdale PA 17008

FCC Amateur Radio Licenses in Bowmansville

Call Sign: KB3QWP
Robert N Keffer
Maple Grove Rd
Bowmansville PA 17507

Call Sign: K3DLG
Derrick L Groves
Reading Rd
Bowmansville PA 17507

Call Sign: KA3YPI
Earl J Fox
Bowmansville PA 17507

Call Sign: N3PTY
Don D Riccio Jr
Bowmansville PA 17507

Call Sign: KA3TTC
Linda P Korpi
Bowmansville PA 17507

Call Sign: KD3HH
Kenneth S Korpi
Bowmansville PA 17507

FCC Amateur Radio Licenses in Boynton

Call Sign: N3RUT
Dennis K Critchfield

Boynton PA 15532

FCC Amateur Radio Licenses in Bradford

Call Sign: K3SMS
Stacy S Wallace Esq
26 Bedford St
Bradford PA 16701

Call Sign: KB3SFQ
Debra A Morris
477 Bolivar Dr
Bradford PA 16701

Call Sign: KB3POF
Tyler D Morris
477 Bolivar Dr
Bradford PA 16701

Call Sign: N3HSY
Kelly J Copley
28 Burnside Ave
Bradford PA 16701

Call Sign: N3ZMA
Raymond J Casper
34 Clarence St
Bradford PA 16701

Call Sign: KB3CUD
Carleton Campbell
15 Cole Ave
Bradford PA 167010634

Call Sign: KB3LEI
Brandy R Coffman
172.5 Congress St
Bradford PA 16701

Call Sign: WA3UWT
Joseph E Fedorko
265 Congress St
Bradford PA 16701

Call Sign: N3VLH
William A Harder
428 Congress St
Bradford PA 16701

Call Sign: KB3GSX
David B Higgs
15 Creekside Dr
Bradford PA 16701

Call Sign: K3WL
David B Higgs
15 Creekside Dr
Bradford PA 16701

Call Sign: K3FRQ
Martha A Milks
40 Cross Dr
Bradford PA 167013155

Call Sign: N4DNT
Herbert Doynow
181 Davis St
Bradford PA 16701

Call Sign: KA3UER
Jeffrey R Nuhfer
174 E Main St
Bradford PA 16701

Call Sign: N3PYX
Paul J Troskosky
228 E Main St
Bradford PA 16701

Call Sign: KB3ABW
Sheila A Lane
800 E Main St
Bradford PA 16701

Call Sign: KB3ADH
Todd L Hogue
800 E Main St
Bradford PA 16701

Call Sign: KB3ADY
Heidi M Karst
800 E Main St
Bradford PA 16701

Call Sign: N3PEZ
James E Robinson
1221 E Main St
Bradford PA 16701

Call Sign: N3ELI
Donald R Pistner
1250 E Main St
Bradford PA 16701

Call Sign: N3HPL
Sandra L Pistner
1250 E Main St
Bradford PA 16701

Call Sign: N3IPS
Molly S Pistner
1250 E Main St
Bradford PA 16701

Call Sign: KB3SVG
Pamela M Edgar
807 E Main St Apt 4
Bradford PA 16701

Call Sign: N3LJX
Cindy C Graham
35 Fernwood Dr
Bradford PA 16701

Call Sign: KB3IGC
Brandon L Graham
35 Fernwood Dr
Bradford PA 16701

Call Sign: KD3OH
Nathaniel L Graham
35 Fernwood Dr
Bradford PA 167012902

Call Sign: KB3QFV
Brittany B Reese
61 Garlock Hallow
Bradford PA 16701

Call Sign: KB3BJX
Dominick Rossi Jr
43 Gregory Ave
Bradford PA 167012834

Call Sign: KB3LTR
Sheryl A Wallace
17 Hawthorne Rd
Bradford PA 16701

Call Sign: KA3WLT
Thomas F Eddy
121 Hemlock St
Bradford PA 16701

Call Sign: N3YXE
Michael W Fitzsimmons
100 Holley Ave
Bradford PA 16701

Call Sign: KB3INN
Bernard R Henniger
627 Interstate Pkwy
Bradford PA 16701

Call Sign: KB3BVA
McKean County Public
Service Group
22 Jackson Ave
Bradford PA 16701

Call Sign: N3LLR
William C Edgar
22 Jackson Ave
Bradford PA 16701

Call Sign: KA3YJF
Richard P Pecora Jr
190 Jackson Ave
Bradford PA 16701

Call Sign: KB3IGB
John W Bryner III
330 Langmaid Ln
Bradford PA 16701

Call Sign: KB3NFU
Julie A Malanowski
427 Langmaid Ln
Bradford PA 16701

Call Sign: W3CLD
Julie A Malanowski
427 Langmaid Ln
Bradford PA 16701

Call Sign: KA2MJU
James S Malanowski
427 Langmaid Ln
Bradford PA 16701

Call Sign: W3SKI
James S Malanowski
427 Langmaid Ln
Bradford PA 16701

Call Sign: KB3LAF
Thomas E Urban
34 Laurel Dr
Bradford PA 16701

Call Sign: KB3ADE
John A Labashousky
104 Leonard Ave
Bradford PA 16701

Call Sign: WA3MDY
David W Dolaway
21 Lorana Ave
Bradford PA 16701

Call Sign: KA3ZGY
Adam R Laughlin
145 Lorana Ave
Bradford PA 16701

Call Sign: KA3ZZD
James W Witherow
145 Lorana Ave
Bradford PA 16701

Call Sign: KD3LJ
David J Knight
10 McKune Ave
Bradford PA 16701

Call Sign: KA3OLP
Kenneth L Dunkerley
21 McKune Ave
Bradford PA 16701

Call Sign: N3PYM
Nelson G Gault
32 Melvin Ave
Bradford PA 16701

Call Sign: N3ZLZ
Michael J Shannon
33 Melvin Ave
Bradford PA 16701

Call Sign: N2VXH
David A Johnson
9 Morianna Ave
Bradford PA 16701

Call Sign: KA3YID
Jay J Pecora
10 Nelson Ave
Bradford PA 16701

Call Sign: N3HYN
Joseph S Frontino
150 Nelson Ave
Bradford PA 16701

Call Sign: KA3HZE
Arthur E Bishop
11 Niles Hollow
Bradford PA 16701

Call Sign: KB3RHT
Jordan L Webster
32 North St
Bradford PA 16701

Call Sign: KA3RTX
Melvin W Graffius
97 Orchard Valley Rd
Bradford PA 16701

Call Sign: KD0FCY
Maurice R Waldeck
25 Oxford St
Bradford PA 16701

Call Sign: K3TGK
James A Bryner
50 Parkway Ln
Bradford PA 16701

Call Sign: KA3ZJI
Russell C Nagel
11 Potter St
Bradford PA 16701

Call Sign: KB3PJF
Jason M Bange
81 Pratt Hollow
Bradford PA 16701

Call Sign: KB3QFS
Katie M Bange
81 Pratt Hollow
Bradford PA 16701

Call Sign: KB3JKT
Glenn F Flynn
99 Rob Roy Rd
Bradford PA 16701

Call Sign: WA3GYL
Michael J Matto
26 S 2nd St
Bradford PA 16701

Call Sign: N2ISQ
Theodore M Leonard
20 S 3rd St
Bradford PA 16701

Call Sign: N3YLO
Peggy Mc Gee Leonard
20 S 3rd St
Bradford PA 16701

Call Sign: W3VG
Theodore M Leonard
20 S 3rd St
Bradford PA 16701

Call Sign: KB3QFT
Timothy J Bange
1056 S Kendall Ave
Bradford PA 16701

Call Sign: N2NCE
Kevin E Kilpatrick
685 South Ave
Bradford PA 16701

Call Sign: N3XSU
Andrew L Sanderson
8 Spring St
Bradford PA 16701

Call Sign: KB3JKS
William K Adkins
154 Summer St
Bradford PA 16701

Call Sign: K3IKD
Willard M Ames
298 Summit Rd
Bradford PA 16701

Call Sign: KB3LET
Benjamin M Autieri
105 Tuna Crossroads
Bradford PA 16701

Call Sign: N3JVQ
Hal F Kenyon
435.5 W Washington St
Bradford PA 16701

Call Sign: AB4XS
Roy F Heimel II
774 W Washington St
Bradford PA 16701

Call Sign: NJ2V
William V McCloskey
1007 W Washington St
Bradford PA 16701

Call Sign: N3VLI
James I Fetterman
1145 W Washington St
Bradford PA 16701

Call Sign: KB3GGQ
Ryan P Close
617 W Washington St
Bradford PA 16701

Call Sign: KJ4KTU
Christina A Close
617 W Washington St
Bradford PA 16701

Call Sign: KD3IJ
Wesley A Nicholas
21 Woodlawn Ave
Bradford PA 16701

Call Sign: K3TWO
Allegheny Mountains
Amateur Radio Group
26 York St
Bradford PA 167011646

Call Sign: N3KTA
Anthony M Doriguzzi
26 York St

Bradford PA 167011646

Call Sign: KB3LEH
John M Bacha
43 York St
Bradford PA 16701

Call Sign: WB3GXN
David E Zuckerman
1 Zucks Nook
Bradford PA 16701

Call Sign: W3VV
McKean County ARC Inc
Bradford PA 16701

FCC Amateur Radio Licenses in Breezewood

Call Sign: KA3YBU
Irwin L Brambley
Box 124B
Breezewood PA 15533

Call Sign: N3JZH
Barbara R Grover
Box 156A
Breezewood PA 15533

Call Sign: N3EYF
William L Grover Jr
172 Linda Vista Ln
Breezewood PA 15533

FCC Amateur Radio Licenses in Broad Top

Call Sign: K3BDU
David B Hofreiter
Shady Maple Rd
Broad Top PA 166210164

Call Sign: KA3RFD
Gale B Hofreiter
Shady Maple Rd

Broad Top PA 166210164

FCC Amateur Radio Licenses in Brodbecks

Call Sign: KA3EXQ
Tony L Dubs
Box 12
Brodbecks PA 17329

Call Sign: KA3OFN
Thomas A Lisa
Box 1682
Brodbecks PA 17329

FCC Amateur Radio Licenses in Brogue

Call Sign: N3WVJ
Francisco D Adler
Box 281
Brogue PA 17309

Call Sign: KA3TFG
James E Hileman Jr
Box 357
Brogue PA 17309

Call Sign: K3DAC
Dennis E Warner
12060 Collinsville Rd
Brogue PA 173099197

Call Sign: KB3PFV
Rebecca C Witham
13035 Collinsville Rd Unit 8
Brogue PA 17309

Call Sign: K3COA
Max V Pickel
2250 Delta Rd
Brogue PA 173099102

Call Sign: WB3JBE

Robert G Biester
49 Goram Rd
Brogue PA 17309

Call Sign: KA7TBB
Harold M Hartley
2246 Jacobs Rd
Brogue PA 17309

Call Sign: KB3RWX
Jacob J Beck
12211 Lucky Rd
Brogue PA 17309

Call Sign: W3WCL
Charles J Maguire
32 Maguire Ln
Brogue PA 17309

Call Sign: WA3DJM
Barbara A Maguire
32 Maguire Ln
Brogue PA 17309

Call Sign: KB3JXX
Charles I Hepfer Sr
11921 Pomraning Rd
Brogue PA 17309

FCC Amateur Radio Licenses in Brownstown

Call Sign: N3FNU
Kathy A Alexander
111 E Main St
Brownstown PA 17508

Call Sign: N3VCP
Michael A Gross
264 E Main St
Brownstown PA 175081012

Call Sign: K3KYW
Jonathan R Briggs

19 N State St
Brownstown PA 17508

Call Sign: N3OI
Jonathan R Briggs
19 N State St
Brownstown PA 17508

Call Sign: N3WQN
H Duane Eby
32 N State St
Brownstown PA 17508

Call Sign: W8JRB
Jonathan R Briggs
19 N State St
Brownstown PA 17508

Call Sign: KB3SCE
Nancy A Southwick
27 N State St Apt 2
Brownstown PA 17508

Call Sign: KB3JBC
Geary L Southwick
27 N State St Apt 2
Brownstown PA
175080121

Call Sign: KB3PBT
George G Burnley
Brownstown PA 17508

FCC Amateur Radio Licenses in Buena Vista

Call Sign: N3CBL
Gary W Thompson
22 Oak Dr
Buena Vista PA 15018

Call Sign: N3FZZ
Daniel A Handley
206 Shields St
Buena Vista PA 15018

Call Sign: W3LYQ
Conrad J Maley
3131 Wildcat Rd
Buena Vista PA 15018

FCC Amateur Radio Licenses in Burnham

Call Sign: W3PVZ
Joseph M Olnick
300 3rd Ave
Burnham PA 17009

Call Sign: KB3KIZ
Darwin P Shawver Jr
231 8th Ave
Burnham PA 17009

Call Sign: WB3IPG
Donald S Hirakis
300 9th Ave
Burnham PA 17009

Call Sign: KB3OUO
Ralph E Shields
831 E Freedom Ave
Burnham PA 17009

Call Sign: N3SOV
Alan W Van Art
208 N Beech St
Burnham PA 17009

FCC Amateur Radio Licenses in Burnt Cabins

Call Sign: N3GLJ
Robert D Finley
Main St Box 97
Burnt Cabins PA 17215

Call Sign: KA3TSW
Robert D Finley III
Burnt Cabins PA 17215

FCC Amateur Radio Licenses in Cainbrook

Call Sign: KA3ZSD
Arleen E Gaudry
Box 220
Cairnbrook PA 15924

FCC Amateur Radio Licenses in Calvin

Call Sign: WA3UTB
C Richard Karstetter
Dd K Farm
Calvin PA 16622

FCC Amateur Radio Licenses in Cammal

Call Sign: W3WRX
Paul R Laubscher
311 Ross Siding Dr
Cammal PA 17723

FCC Amateur Radio Licenses in Camp Hill

Call Sign: N4CAK
Steven D Linn
201 Allendale Way
Camp Hill PA 17011

Call Sign: KB3RYR
Elizabeth A Kiral
224 Allendale Way
Camp Hill PA 17011

Call Sign: KB3OZZ
Matthew A Kiral
224 Allendale Way
Camp Hill PA 17011

Call Sign: N3WL

Charles T Greiner
403 Allendale Way
Camp Hill PA 17011

Call Sign: KB3KLR
Howard D Allen
414 Allendale Way
Camp Hill PA 17011

Call Sign: KB3SDV
Jared A Haidet
13 Amhurst Dr
Camp Hill PA 17011

Call Sign: W3KB
Keith G Beebe
108 April Dr
Camp Hill PA 17011

Call Sign: KA3HYG
Genevieve R Hancock
3414 Bedford Dr
Camp Hill PA 17011

Call Sign: KB3PAC
Jeongeun Lee
358 Beverly Rd
Camp Hill PA 17011

Call Sign: KB3TIA
Peter J Lindhome
333 Blacklatch Ln
Camp Hill PA 17011

Call Sign: KB3RZX
Michael S Schappe
9 Blackmere Ct
Camp Hill PA 17011

Call Sign: N3SEC
James G Binkley
264 Blacksmith Rd
Camp Hill PA 17011

Call Sign: KA3OAJ

James E Lee
341 Blacksmith Rd
Camp Hill PA 170118422

Call Sign: KB3LRQ
Brian R Osborne
101 Brentwater Rd
Camp Hill PA 17011

Call Sign: KB3LRJ
Jacob A Millward
2 Brentwood Rd
Camp Hill PA 17011

Call Sign: WA3LKZ
Thomas J Salonick
3 Briarwood Ct
Camp Hill PA 17011

Call Sign: KB3OVE
Austin C Alexander
1 Brighton Ln
Camp Hill PA 17011

Call Sign: N3NMC
Jennifer A Hoffman
3834 Carriage House Dr
Camp Hill PA 17011

Call Sign: W3TH
Ted L Hoffman
3834 Carriage House Dr
Camp Hill PA 17011

Call Sign: KD4YIT
Bruce L Barnhart
4 Cedar Cliff Dr
Camp Hill PA 17011

Call Sign: KE4GPY
Karen H Barnhart
4 Cedar Cliff Dr
Camp Hill PA 17011

Call Sign: N3QMQ

Glenn C Barnhart
4 Cedar Cliff Dr
Camp Hill PA 17011

Call Sign: KB3KAT
Alex J Palkovic
5 Charisma Dr
Camp Hill PA 17011

Call Sign: KB3OVM
Ryan M Lombardo
7 Charisma Dr
Camp Hill PA 17011

Call Sign: KB3MVY
Gregory T Desomer
4044 Cherokee Ave
Camp Hill PA 17011

Call Sign: KB3SQX
Vivek Wadhawan
3109 Chestnut St
Camp Hill PA 17011

Call Sign: WB4KFS
Pinky L Evans
4312 Chestnut St
Camp Hill PA 17011

Call Sign: N3LNR
Peter V Hall
2 Citadel Dr
Camp Hill PA 17011

Call Sign: KN4EE
Michael W Dirle
9 Colgate Dr
Camp Hill PA 17011

Call Sign: KB3UBM
Bryan R Haas
513 Colony Rd
Camp Hill PA 170112010

Call Sign: KB3KNH

Kimberly A Stoner
521 Colony Rd
Camp Hill PA 17011

Call Sign: KB3OIV
Patrick T Mccormick
3024 Columbia Ave
Camp Hill PA 17011

Call Sign: KB3IUR
Meagan A Mccormick
143024 Columbia Ave
Camp Hill PA 17011

Call Sign: N3URL
Wesley A MacDonald
3804 Conestoga Rd
Camp Hill PA 17011

Call Sign: KB3KMN
Courtney A Lawson
3825 Conestoga Rd
Camp Hill PA 17011

Call Sign: KB3MWN
Bradley C Lawson
3825 Conestoga Rd
Camp Hill PA 17011

Call Sign: WV8WG
Beryl W Given Dds
1046 Country Club Rd
Camp Hill PA 17011

Call Sign: KB3OIX
Sean M Munchel
1075 Country Club Rd
Camp Hill PA 17011

Call Sign: KB3QYB
Kelsey E Verbos
1080 Country Club Rd
Camp Hill PA 17011

Call Sign: KB3OIR

Meghan T Cavanaugh
1080 Country Club Rd
Camp Hill PA 17011

Call Sign: KA3YYC
Marc A Jacobson
9 Countryside Ct
Camp Hill PA 17011

Call Sign: N3EDG
Scott D Palmer
3532 Countryside Ln
Camp Hill PA 17011

Call Sign: KB3RZJ
Breton M Asken
5 Creekside Ln
Camp Hill PA 17011

Call Sign: KB3NLA
Tristen R Asken
5 Creekside Ln
Camp Hill PA 17011

Call Sign: N3ESC
Todd L Snyder
141 Deerfield Rd
Camp Hill PA 17011

Call Sign: KB3PAM
Alexander Y Piscioneri
257 Deerfield Rd
Camp Hill PA 17011

Call Sign: KB3NBN
Bradley S Boore
2920 Dickenson Ave
Camp Hill PA 17011

Call Sign: KE3YC
William C Rawlings
1936 E Chatham Dr
Camp Hill PA 17011

Call Sign: KB3LWO

Brandon R Piper
425 E Crestwood Dr
Camp Hill PA 17011

Call Sign: KB3QQB
Rodrigo A Trevino
6.5 E Green St
Camp Hill PA 170116552

Call Sign: KB3MWW
David J Norton
125 E Lauer Ln
Camp Hill PA 170111313

Call Sign: KB3OJD
John J Troy
504 Ellen Rd
Camp Hill PA 17011

Call Sign: AB3FM
John J Troy
504 Ellen Rd
Camp Hill PA 17011

Call Sign: KB3KRF
Sean P Earnest
344 Equus Dr
Camp Hill PA 17011

Call Sign: KB3RZO
Nathaniel W Hachten
358 Equus Dr
Camp Hill PA 17011

Call Sign: KB3LPU
Maurice G Awng
222 Erford Rd
Camp Hill PA 17011

Call Sign: KB3RYW
William T Phillipy V
236 Erford Rd
Camp Hill PA 17011

Call Sign: KB3MQL

Timothy P Portzline
850 Erford Rd
Camp Hill PA 17011

Call Sign: N9KFR
H C Kelley
72 Fairway Dr
Camp Hill PA 170112064

Call Sign: KB3QDU
Alex S Weis
83 Fairway Dr
Camp Hill PA 17011

Call Sign: KB3QPR
Quintin B Gabler
8 Farmhouse Ln
Camp Hill PA 17011

Call Sign: KB3RYQ
William A Kerr
140 Forest Dr
Camp Hill PA 17011

Call Sign: N3CAY
Patricia A M Ulman
352 Furlong Ln
Camp Hill PA 17011

Call Sign: KB3LQV
Brandon L Jarman
350 Futurity Dr
Camp Hill PA 17011

Call Sign: KB3PAR
Erika E Rowe
365 Futurity Dr
Camp Hill PA 17011

Call Sign: K3VBB
William P Kirkland
51 Gale Rd
Camp Hill PA 17011

Call Sign: KB3QXB

Meghan B Elliott
602 Gale Rd
Camp Hill PA 17011

Call Sign: KB3JAW
Michael J Machinist
205 Garrett Ln
Camp Hill PA 17011

Call Sign: KB3OIQ
Ashley L Bierzonski
232 Glenn Rd
Camp Hill PA 17011

Call Sign: N3VPI
Jerry A Koehler
Glenwood Dr
Camp Hill PA 17011

Call Sign: N3XRI
Nancy A Koehler
Glenwood Dr
Camp Hill PA 17011

Call Sign: KB3KMW
Stephen W Panko
516 Grandview Ave
Camp Hill PA 17011

Call Sign: KB3PBE
Barry J Rowan
515 Grant Dr
Camp Hill PA 17011

Call Sign: KC0KIZ
Wendy S Foltz
515 Grant Dr
Camp Hill PA 17011

Call Sign: N3FQH
Jonathan E Bupp
201 Green Ln Dr
Camp Hill PA 17011

Call Sign: KB3NBY

Jamal V Smith
215 Green Ln Dr
Camp Hill PA 17011

Call Sign: K9BW
Michael J Morra
14 Hartzdale Dr
Camp Hill PA 170117930

Call Sign: KA3GRD
Katherine A Shank
2012 Harvard Ave
Camp Hill PA 17011

Call Sign: W3LTI
William J Diehl
2706 Harvard Ave
Camp Hill PA 17011

Call Sign: KB3LRK
Rebecca P Moore
3427 Hawthorne Dr
Camp Hill PA 17011

Call Sign: KA3NCF
Lisa J Obradovich
12 Hickory Pl
Camp Hill PA 17011

Call Sign: N3GLD
John Telencio Jr
1678 High St
Camp Hill PA 17011

Call Sign: N3DUN
Gerald V Petrasic
86 Hillside Cir
Camp Hill PA 17011

Call Sign: KB3KNC
Jared E Rossman
520 Joyce Rd
Camp Hill PA 17011

Call Sign: KB3LQT

Diana K Huynh
6 Karen Ct
Camp Hill PA 17011

Call Sign: KB3MMA
David M Murdoch
44 Kensington Dr
Camp Hill PA 17011

Call Sign: W3ND
Anthony A Manning
410 Lamp Post Ln
Camp Hill PA 17011

Call Sign: KB3VVM
Donald R Mccallin
501 Lamp Post Ln
Camp Hill PA 17011

Call Sign: KB3QXN
Marianna S Koerner
826 Landau Ct
Camp Hill PA 17011

Call Sign: KB3MJA
Paul D Walterick Sr
1914 Lenox St
Camp Hill PA 17011

Call Sign: KB3VIC
Jeffrey A Best
1920 Lincoln St
Camp Hill PA 17011

Call Sign: K3WC
Wilton K Chapman
2009 Lincoln St
Camp Hill PA 17011

Call Sign: ND3X
Mark Prentice
2920 Lincoln St
Camp Hill PA 17011

Call Sign: K3HIT

Vernon J Shaffer
905 Lisburn Rd
Camp Hill PA 17011

Call Sign: W3YRB
William W Blessing
824 Lisburn Rd Apt 308
Camp Hill PA 170117103

Call Sign: W3ETN
Edward H Sawyer
824 Lisburn Rd Apt 423
Camp Hill PA 17011

Call Sign: KB3LQF
Maureen P Delaney
57 Little Run Rd
Camp Hill PA 17011

Call Sign: KB3OIU
Daniel J Grimme
67 Little Run Rd
Camp Hill PA 17011

Call Sign: KB3TJI
Chrac
3425 Logan St
Camp Hill PA 17011

Call Sign: KY3X
Chrac
3425 Logan St
Camp Hill PA 17011

Call Sign: NE3H
Joseph B Shuey
3425 Logan St
Camp Hill PA 17011

Call Sign: KB3OVQ
Emily J Overstreet
816 Mandy Ln
Camp Hill PA 17011

Call Sign: NI3K

Richard J Thibeault
823 Mandy Ln
Camp Hill PA 17011

Call Sign: KB3PAA
Devin Q Langan
841 Mandy Ln
Camp Hill PA 17011

Call Sign: KB3LSB
George F Sullenberger III
212 Maple Ave
Camp Hill PA 17011

Call Sign: K3UKO
John G Kurzenknabe
3600 March Dr
Camp Hill PA 170115013

Call Sign: WB3DWP
Brandt T Bell
3504 Margo Rd
Camp Hill PA 17011

Call Sign: KB3NGK
Francis X Kuntz
2902 Market St
Camp Hill PA 17011

Call Sign: N3QCA
Winton A Miller
3437 Market St
Camp Hill PA 17011

Call Sign: KA3YCW
William C Myers
2804 Market St Apt 5
Camp Hill PA 17011

Call Sign: KB3KMH
Michael W Holder
359 Martingale Dr
Camp Hill PA 17011

Call Sign: KC3QL

John R Suggs
4 Meadow Dr
Camp Hill PA 17011

Call Sign: KA3QHX
John A Levin
23 Meadow Dr
Camp Hill PA 17011

Call Sign: KB3PAN
Alexandra L Priar
27 Meadow Dr
Camp Hill PA 17011

Call Sign: N3MZP
Daniel W De Arment
806 Meadow Ln
Camp Hill PA 17011

Call Sign: KB3IOB
Daniel W De Arment
806 Meadow Ln
Camp Hill PA 17011

Call Sign: KB3IZI
David L Davis
829 Meadow Ln
Camp Hill PA 17011

Call Sign: KB3MXW
Anthony J Carroll
2950 Morningside Dr
Camp Hill PA 17011

Call Sign: KC3BZ
Harold E Frantz
136 N 15th St
Camp Hill PA 17011

Call Sign: N3NMB
Kathleen M Frantz
136 N 15th St
Camp Hill PA 17011

Call Sign: KB3QFB

Frank T Conners
223 N 23rd St
Camp Hill PA 17011

Call Sign: WA9NVF
Curt E Bowen
320 N 24th St
Camp Hill PA 170113605

Call Sign: KB3QLB
Neil T Devlin
328 N 24th St
Camp Hill PA 17011

Call Sign: KB3LQH
Chelsea S Diehl
434 N 25th St
Camp Hill PA 17011

Call Sign: KB3OIW
Jeanne M Mcnally
399 N 26th St
Camp Hill PA 17011

Call Sign: KB3OVN
Duyen M Mai
126 N 33rd St
Camp Hill PA 17011

Call Sign: KB3ERO
Matthew S Bryda
409 Norman Rd
Camp Hill PA 17011

Call Sign: KB3LRE
Christopher R Maydick
115 Northgate Dr
Camp Hill PA 17011

Call Sign: W3DP
Richard D Jaeger
130 Northgate Dr
Camp Hill PA 17011

Call Sign: KB3LQQ

Michelle M Gill
140 Northgate Dr
Camp Hill PA 17011

Call Sign: KB3QQF
Anne K Sniscak
225 Northgate Dr
Camp Hill PA 17011

Call Sign: KB3QQE
Anne K Sniscak
225 Northgate Dr
Camp Hill PA 17011

Call Sign: KB3KNG
Matthew T Sniscak
225 Northgate Dr
Camp Hill PA 17011

Call Sign: KB4TP
Dalton A Bell
106 November Dr Apt 1
Camp Hill PA 17011

Call Sign: KO1D
Daniel J Sullivan
101 Oak Dr
Camp Hill PA 17011

Call Sign: KB3UYP
Kirsten S Sullivan
101 Oak Dr
Camp Hill PA 17011

Call Sign: K3ZIA
Kirsten S Sullivan
101 Oak Dr
Camp Hill PA 17011

Call Sign: KB3LWU
Matthew E Kantes
7 Oakwood Ct
Camp Hill PA 17011

Call Sign: KB3NBR

Sarah C Kantes
7 Oakwood Ct
Camp Hill PA 17011

Call Sign: N3DGL
Mitchell R Davis
532 Orrs Bridge Rd
Camp Hill PA 17011

Call Sign: K3EYO
Kenneth H Mullen
3807 Oxbow Dr
Camp Hill PA 17011

Call Sign: N3UVW
Pete P Millvan
17 Paddock Ln
Camp Hill PA 17011

Call Sign: WB3DIL
Joseph S Swartz
38 Palmer Dr
Camp Hill PA 17011

Call Sign: KB3IYV
Drew C Tuma
435 Parkview Ct
Camp Hill PA 17011

Call Sign: KB3QPP
Matthew B Cherewka
125 Pelham Rd
Camp Hill PA 17011

Call Sign: KG4BBA
Roy C Cox II
Richland Ln Apt 101
Camp Hill PA 170110000

Call Sign: K3RCC
Roy C Cox II
Richland Ln Apt 101
Camp Hill PA 170110000

Call Sign: AA3UQ

David W Curtis
Richland Ln Apt 103
Camp Hill PA 17011

Call Sign: KB3RON
Arun Natarajan
Richland Ln Apt 201
Camp Hill PA 17011

Call Sign: KB3ROO
Natarajan Palaniappan
Richland Ln Apt 201
Camp Hill PA 17011

Call Sign: KB3LQK
Kailey L Egbert
145 Rodney Ln
Camp Hill PA 17011

Call Sign: KB3OZO
Matthew M Egbert
145 Rodney Ln
Camp Hill PA 17011

Call Sign: KB3IXB
Siriphan Jestakhom
1921 Rutland St
Camp Hill PA 17011

Call Sign: KC8HZM
Marten T Roberts Beels
6 S 17th St 2
Camp Hill PA 17011

Call Sign: KB3KRE
Christopher J Reyes
136 S 18th St
Camp Hill PA 17011

Call Sign: KB3QXY
Mariana C Reyes
136 S 18th St
Camp Hill PA 17011

Call Sign: KA3GRE

Michael S Shank
307 S 24th St
Camp Hill PA 170115308

Call Sign: W3MH
Ray E De Walt
928 S 28th St
Camp Hill PA 17011

Call Sign: N3URM
Allan E Brown
4602 S Clearview Dr
Camp Hill PA 17011

Call Sign: KB3QWY
John M Crotty III
101 S Stoner Ave
Camp Hill PA 17011

Call Sign: KB3QXO
Mina S Kokos
3 Saratoga Pl
Camp Hill PA 17011

Call Sign: K3NLX
Richard H Altenburg
10 Scarsdale Dr
Camp Hill PA 17011

Call Sign: N3HJV
Robert C Altenburg
10 Scarsdale Dr
Camp Hill PA 17011

Call Sign: KB3UVM
Justin E Hoyer
3545 September Dr
Camp Hill PA 17011

Call Sign: WB3BCU
Joseph M Olnick
1193 Shoreham Rd
Camp Hill PA 17011

Call Sign: KB3JAG

Trinity High School ARC
3601 Simpson Ferry Rd
Camp Hill PA 17011

Call Sign: N3THS
Trinity High School ARC
3601 Simpson Ferry Rd
Camp Hill PA 17011

Call Sign: KB3KME
Brandon W Gibellino
320 Somerset Dr
Camp Hill PA 17011

Call Sign: KB3MXC
Jillian R Shenk
4 Spartan Cir
Camp Hill PA 17011

Call Sign: KB3PAD
Emily L Martinelli
413 Spring House Rd
Camp Hill PA 17011

Call Sign: N3JRR
Richard W Dillahey
400 Springhouse Rd
Camp Hill PA 17011

Call Sign: N3AQB
Charles B Fager Jr
645 St Johns Dr
Camp Hill PA 170111338

Call Sign: K3RNH
Robert P Homer
5 Stailey Cir
Camp Hill PA 17011

Call Sign: W8IJ
David O Barrows
25 Stephen Rd
Camp Hill PA 170111159

Call Sign: KB3JTL

Kieran J OLeary
12 Sunfire Ave
Camp Hill PA 17011

Call Sign: KB3PAL
Dena L Parada
816 Surrey Ct
Camp Hill PA 17011

Call Sign: KB3KMX
Eric D Parada
816 Surrey Ct
Camp Hill PA 17011

Call Sign: AI5I
Frederick B Kimble
18 Tall Tree Dr
Camp Hill PA 17011

Call Sign: KB3MJY
John M Pritchett
502 Thomas Rd
Camp Hill PA 17011

Call Sign: KA1SMU
Marie C Caputo
505 Thomas Rd
Camp Hill PA 170111261

Call Sign: KB3KMY
Fredric S Prestine
11 Victoria Way
Camp Hill PA 17011

Call Sign: KB3STS
Donald F Herzog Jr
35 Victoria Way
Camp Hill PA 17011

Call Sign: KB3KML
Joshua M Lacoco
49 Victoria Way
Camp Hill PA 17011

Call Sign: N3YLG

Mark T Kertulis
3806 Vine St
Camp Hill PA 17011

Call Sign: KB3MWM
Allen J Kline
55 W Lauer Ln
Camp Hill PA 17011

Call Sign: KB3RZM
Erica M Dickey
2 W Red Gold Cir
Camp Hill PA 17011

Call Sign: KB3KMA
Erica M Dolson
7 Walnut St
Camp Hill PA 17011

Call Sign: W3ROQ
William A Robinson
3407 Walnut St
Camp Hill PA 17011

Call Sign: KB3HGB
Adrian C Maniu
2580 Waterford
Camp Hill PA 170111274

Call Sign: N1EKG
Adrian C Maniu
2580 Waterford
Camp Hill PA 170111274

Call Sign: KB3PAJ
Brian J Murren
206 Willow Ave
Camp Hill PA 17011

Call Sign: KB3QXP
Frank M Kostyal
244 Winding Way
Camp Hill PA 17011

Call Sign: KB3DLE

Edward L Nichols III
4 Windsor Way
Camp Hill PA 17011

Call Sign: K3HIH
William A Dean
213 Wood St
Camp Hill PA 170112640

Call Sign: WA3RAX
William E B Snyder
225 Wood St
Camp Hill PA 17011

Call Sign: KB3QPO
Kaitlyn J Chajkowski
1602 Wyndham Rd
Camp Hill PA 17011

Call Sign: W3SMF
Edward D Crossley
2017 Yale Ave
Camp Hill PA 17011

Call Sign: KA3ZIE
John R Diehl
2616 Yale Ave
Camp Hill PA 17011

Call Sign: KB3SUI
Sarah E Spishock
148 Yellow Breeches Dr
Camp Hill PA 17011

Call Sign: KA8EKN
Andrew A Martin
Yverdon Dr
Camp Hill PA 17011

**FCC Amateur Radio
Licenses in
Campbelltown**

Call Sign: N3KDX
Robert A Brown

148 W Main St
Campbelltown PA 17010

Call Sign: WA3ZFM
John A Valentic
Campbelltown PA 17010

Call Sign: KB3FND
Charles W Tapley
Campbelltown PA 17010

Call Sign: N3JRQ
Matthew J Ondo
Campbelltown PA
170100415

**FCC Amateur Radio
Licenses in Carlisle**

Call Sign: KB3TDQ
Michael E Baker
121 A St
Carlisle PA 17013

Call Sign: KB3YGN
Zachary K Rosborough
306 Acre Dr
Carlisle PA 17013

Call Sign: KB3SUE
Forrest X Schwartz
1007 Acre Dr
Carlisle PA 17013

Call Sign: KB3KMK
Brendan M Kane
629 Adams Rd
Carlisle PA 17013

Call Sign: KB3STU
Sean A Kane
629 Adams Rd
Carlisle PA 17015

Call Sign: N3RYZ

Daniel E Thomas
25 Alexander Ave
Carlisle PA 17013

Call Sign: KA3GLQ
John L Himes
200 Amherst Ln
Carlisle PA 17015

Call Sign: KB3PQS
Stephen L Miller
167 Amy Dr
Carlisle PA 17013

Call Sign: N3LCY
Adolphus R Bartges
9 Annedale Dr
Carlisle PA 17013

Call Sign: W3ATJ
George E Bartges
9 Annendale Dr
Carlisle PA 17013

Call Sign: KB3QEC
Dana S Kellis
9 Appaloosa Way
Carlisle PA 17015

Call Sign: KB3QDR
David J Smith IV
18 Appaloosa Way
Carlisle PA 17015

Call Sign: KB3VID
Contance E Bires
257 Arch St
Carlisle PA 17013

Call Sign: KB3UWF
Joseph J Gaskin
426 Arch St
Carlisle PA 17013

Call Sign: KB3SYZ

Robert L Wardecker
429 Arch St
Carlisle PA 17013

Call Sign: N2NPM
Joseph Ragno
12 Arlington Dr
Carlisle PA 17013

Call Sign: N2NPN
Alba J Ragno
12 Arlington Dr
Carlisle PA 17013

Call Sign: WB3FPC
Paul B Adams
57 Bears School Ln
Carlisle PA 17013

Call Sign: N1GQK
Gilbert F Bake III
220 Birch Ln
Carlisle PA 17015

Call Sign: WD9GFH
Edward F Armistead
111 Birch Rd
Carlisle PA 17013

Call Sign: WD3M
Michael A Helwig
345 Bonnybrook Rd
Carlisle PA 17015

Call Sign: KB3BOV
Matthew G Yanos
160 Boyer Rd
Carlisle PA 17013

Call Sign: N3NOF
John B Campbell
185 Boyer Rd
Carlisle PA 17013

Call Sign: KB3HUC

David R Yoder
1422 Bradley Dr C 313
Carlisle PA 17013

Call Sign: WA3GEL
Ray R Thomas
10 Buckthorn Dr
Carlisle PA 170134303

Call Sign: WA3KRG
Ray R Thomas
10 Buckthorn Dr
Carlisle PA 170134303

Call Sign: KB3SNK
Deborah A Morrison
504 Burgners Rd
Carlisle PA 17015

Call Sign: K3BZQ
Delbert L Hawbaker
807 Burnthouse Rd
Carlisle PA 170159107

Call Sign: KB3SFP
Mt Holly Dx Assn
826 Burnthouse Rd
Carlisle PA 17015

Call Sign: NY3DX
Mt Holly Dx Assn
826 Burnthouse Rd
Carlisle PA 17015

Call Sign: K3SV
William L Gillenwater
826 Burnthouse Rd
Carlisle PA 17015

Call Sign: KB3SZB
Theodore J Pluta III
130 C St
Carlisle PA 17013

Call Sign: WB3FQS

Richard J Jacoby
150 C St
Carlisle PA 170131918

Call Sign: W3JEU
Frank Stets
530 C St
Carlisle PA 170131835

Call Sign: KA3AGY
Gerald J Reber
7043 Carlisle Pike Lot 308
Carlisle PA 170158829

Call Sign: K3NLY
Kay I Brenneman
30 Cave Hill Dr
Carlisle PA 17013

Call Sign: KA3JDI
James J Webster Sr
184 Cedar Ln
Carlisle PA 17013

Call Sign: N3NHY
Richard E Sickmon
102 Charles St
Carlisle PA 17013

Call Sign: N3NAL
Barry M Gosthnian
6 Cobblestone Dr
Carlisle PA 17013

Call Sign: KB3QXQ
Katharina C Mangan
27 Cobblestone Dr
Carlisle PA 17015

Call Sign: WA3KYS
Philip H Wittlin
541 Conodoguinet Ave
Carlisle PA 17013

Call Sign: KB3ROA

James C Mccanna
606 Copper Cir
Carlisle PA 17015

Call Sign: N3PVW
Doris M Service
35 Country Club Rd
Carlisle PA 17013

Call Sign: KB3QWT
Ricky A Bezold Jr
553 Craig Rd
Carlisle PA 17013

Call Sign: KA3VPC
Lawrence B Massey
198 Crain Dr
Carlisle PA 17013

Call Sign: WB3GRT
Judith A Showers
1050 Cranes Gap Rd
Carlisle PA 170139676

Call Sign: KB3VAX
Donald G Evans
811 Creek Rd
Carlisle PA 17015

Call Sign: N3MKJ
Paul A Ferenz
407 Crossroad School Rd
Carlisle PA 17013

Call Sign: KB3LQX
Brendan D Kearney
64 Derbyshire Dr
Carlisle PA 17013

Call Sign: KB3OVK
Christopher M Kearney
64 Derbyshire Dr
Carlisle PA 17015

Call Sign: W3AZX

Charles Cuper
250 Dorwood Dr
Carlisle PA 17013

Call Sign: KB3VII
Charles P Mcdowell
2308 Douglas Dr
Carlisle PA 17013

Call Sign: KB3NLP
Thomas C Whitmore
6 E Harmon Dr
Carlisle PA 17013

Call Sign: KB3TKW
John L Sloane
165 E Louther St
Carlisle PA 17013

Call Sign: KB3NCS
Brian T Ericson
112 E North St
Carlisle PA 17013

Call Sign: KB3PGM
Mark E Mcnutt
150 E North St
Carlisle PA 17013

Call Sign: KB3PHV
Jerome J Sodus
163 E Park St
Carlisle PA 17013

Call Sign: KM3K
Jerome J Sodus
163 E Park St
Carlisle PA 17013

Call Sign: KA3VGY
Jeffrey S Barone
35 E Ridge St
Carlisle PA 17013

Call Sign: KB3RRW

Michael D Brown
400 Eisenhower Dr
Carlisle PA 17013

Call Sign: KB3KLG
David T Bupp
149 Elm St
Carlisle PA 17013

Call Sign: KB3NLH
Andrew P Hornung
2848 Enola Rd
Carlisle PA 17013

Call Sign: KB3FOO
Mathew D Madden
9 Erin Pl
Carlisle PA 17013

Call Sign: KB3SAA
Alycia M Stokes
21 Essex Dr
Carlisle PA 17015

Call Sign: N3RGD
James M Wrightstone
1924 Esther Dr
Carlisle PA 17013

Call Sign: KB3OOJ
Samuel E Michaels
813 Factory St
Carlisle PA 17013

Call Sign: KB3STP
Michael R Gruschow
293 Fairview St
Carlisle PA 17015

Call Sign: N3CYI
Dennis P Houtz
319 Fairview St
Carlisle PA 17013

Call Sign: KB3QDF

Richard M Davies
108 Fairway Dr
Carlisle PA 17013

Call Sign: KB3LCL
Charles C Pfeiffer
185 Faith Cir
Carlisle PA 17013

Call Sign: KB3QPX
Ashley A Satterlee
113 Fieldstone Dr
Carlisle PA 17015

Call Sign: KA3LEQ
Herbert C Perlman
1104 Fleetwood Dr
Carlisle PA 17013

Call Sign: KB3DGG
Andrea L Bryer
216 Garland Dr
Carlisle PA 17013

Call Sign: KG4NYN
Scott R Bryer
216 Garland Dr
Carlisle PA 17013

Call Sign: WA3CPO
Gary L Blacksmith Jr
1215 Georgetown Cir
Carlisle PA 17013

Call Sign: WA3UFX
Samuel Ryesky
301 Glendale St
Carlisle PA 17013

Call Sign: KB3SNW
Georgeann Laughman
15 Goodyear Rd
Carlisle PA 17015

Call Sign: K3PTW

Lewis E Burgett
31 Greenfield Dr
Carlisle PA 170157611

Call Sign: KB3IZH
Patrick B Haller
704 Hamilton St
Carlisle PA 17013

Call Sign: K3GB
Gary L Bowes
10 Har John Dr
Carlisle PA 17015

Call Sign: KA3LLC
Gordon D Nell
1519 Hemlock Ave
Carlisle PA 17013

Call Sign: WB3IOA
Lance V Borden
15 Hilltop Cir
Carlisle PA 17015

Call Sign: KB3IYW
Zachary T Williams
300 Hollowbrook Dr
Carlisle PA 17013

Call Sign: N3DXZ
Emerson L Henry
5 Hoover Rd
Carlisle PA 17013

Call Sign: KB3KMM
Andrew J Laganosky
86 Hoover Rd
Carlisle PA 17013

Call Sign: KB3QDV
Catherine B Campbell
15 Irene Ct
Carlisle PA 17015

Call Sign: KB3RZH

Kerry E Campbell
15 Irene Ct
Carlisle PA 17015

Call Sign: N3XHN
David M Kletter
2 Jane Ln
Carlisle PA 170131034

Call Sign: KD3QD
Robert C Bales
41 Kelly Dr
Carlisle PA 17015

Call Sign: KB3KMZ
Mark A Rebuck
141 Ken Lin Dr
Carlisle PA 17013

Call Sign: N3VYG
Joel M Hock
1334 Kiner Blvd
Carlisle PA 170139769

Call Sign: K3IEC
Cumberland ARC
1367 Kiner Blvd
Carlisle PA 17013

Call Sign: K3LHD
David E Smith
1367 Kiner Blvd
Carlisle PA 17013

Call Sign: K3LHD
Appalachian Dx Assn
1367 Kiner Blvd
Carlisle PA 17013

Call Sign: W3SOX
David E Smith
1367 Kiner Blvd
Carlisle PA 17013

Call Sign: KB3GVI

Appalachian Dx Assn
1367 Kiner Blvd
Carlisle PA 17013

Call Sign: KV3K
Robert C Bennett
83 Ladnor Ln
Carlisle PA 17013

Call Sign: WA6LWU
Junie M Bennett
83 Ladnor Ln
Carlisle PA 17013

Call Sign: KB3KNB
Eduardo A Rodriguez
522 Limestone Rd
Carlisle PA 17013

Call Sign: KB3RYY
Elisa M Rodriguez
522 Limestone Rd
Carlisle PA 17015

Call Sign: KB3OIZ
Adam B Seifert
75 Manada Creek Cr
Carlisle PA 17013

Call Sign: KB3SIP
Michael S Dempsey
1886 Mary Ln
Carlisle PA 17013

Call Sign: KB3LQG
Siobhan C Dempsey
1886 Mary Ln
Carlisle PA 17013

Call Sign: KB3LXI
P Denis Rossiter
1888 Mary Ln
Carlisle PA 17013

Call Sign: KE4EDV

Frances K Sylvester
120 McAlliser Church Rd
Carlisle PA 170139411

Call Sign: KC4QD
Arthur F Sylvester
120 McAllister Church Rd
Carlisle PA 170139411

Call Sign: N3LPN
Donald L Emerick Jr
110 Meals Dr
Carlisle PA 17013

Call Sign: KA0POG
Ruby J Early
Mel Ron Ct
Carlisle PA 17013

Call Sign: KB3LQC
Laura L Cherchuck
434 Mill Race Rd
Carlisle PA 17013

Call Sign: W0BR
Robert G Raker
695 Mt Rock Rd
Carlisle PA 170157423

Call Sign: KB3NVC
Michael P Moyer Sr
809 N College St
Carlisle PA 17013

Call Sign: N3KEE
Scott A Feeser
159 N Hanover Apt 301
Carlisle PA 17013

Call Sign: N3LCJ
Dennis E Thomas
23 N Hanover St
Carlisle PA 17013

Call Sign: KB3NTC

Michael D Dilger
122 N Hanover St Apt 2
Carlisle PA 17013

Call Sign: KB3QXJ
Victoria J Jumper
247 N Middlesex Rd
Carlisle PA 17013

Call Sign: KB3MXF
Haley N Wallace
94 N Old Stonehouse Rd
Carlisle PA 17013

Call Sign: KB3PAH
Daniel J Marton Jr
N Old Stonehouse Rd
Carlisle PA 17015

Call Sign: KB3SNU
Carlette A Morrison
1307 N Pitt St
Carlisle PA 170131433

Call Sign: KB3HJC
Randy M Ballard
1319 N West St
Carlisle PA 17013

Call Sign: K4ITO
Curtis M Wann II
18 Nelson Dr
Carlisle PA 17013

Call Sign: WB3FZG
Marlin L Chronister
1694 Newville Rd
Carlisle PA 17013

Call Sign: KB3SNS
Michelle M Yohn
2155 Newville Rd
Carlisle PA 17015

Call Sign: KB3UBS

Julie A Ballard
1325 Northwest St
Carlisle PA 17013

Call Sign: N2LDB
James E Boggess Sr
112 Oriole Dr
Carlisle PA 170138769

Call Sign: N3TWT
Raymond H Rowand
117 Peach Ln
Carlisle PA 170137808

Call Sign: KB3RYZ
Nicholas M Schleindofer
15 Pennway Dr
Carlisle PA 17015

Call Sign: KB3RZN
Kyle T Donnelly
414 Petersburg Rd
Carlisle PA 17015

Call Sign: KA3YRP
Adam W Moschette
417 Petersburg Rd
Carlisle PA 17013

Call Sign: KB3LSE
Sarah E Wiskeman
486 Petersburg Rd
Carlisle PA 17013

Call Sign: KB3RZF
Aaron W Wiskeman
486 Petersburg Rd
Carlisle PA 17015

Call Sign: KB3YDF
Allen J Light
507 Pine Rd
Carlisle PA 17015

Call Sign: K0MB

Martin T Buinicki
440 Ponderosa Rd
Carlisle PA 17015

Call Sign: W3DAY
Kenneth S Barnhart
145 Porter Ave
Carlisle PA 17013

Call Sign: N3BXO
Richard L Griffiths
1227 Redwood Hills Cir
Carlisle PA 170159735

Call Sign: WA3WQO
Wayne L Wacker
42 Regency S
Carlisle PA 17013

Call Sign: N2AKD
Karl R Codner
17 Ridge Ave
Carlisle PA 17013

Call Sign: KB3YDO
Donald L Tice
24 Ridgeway Dr
Carlisle PA 17015

Call Sign: KB3MWF
Julie A Graham
2037 Ritner Hwy
Carlisle PA 17013

Call Sign: N3DAZ
Frank D Haslett
2140 Ritner Hwy
Carlisle PA 17013

Call Sign: KB8TQ
Robert W Camp Jr
20 Roaring Creek Ct
Carlisle PA 17013

Call Sign: KB3OVJ

Corbin A Helis
263 Royal American Cir
Carlisle PA 17013

Call Sign: N3BBL
Charles L Stoup Jr
510 S College St
Carlisle PA 17013

Call Sign: KB3FTX
Julie D Sitch
105 S East St
Carlisle PA 17013

Call Sign: W3SMS
J Paul Burkhart II
311 S Orange St
Carlisle PA 17013

Call Sign: KB3MNN
Jason W Smith
126 S West St
Carlisle PA 17013

Call Sign: KB3NLB
Benjamin C Brenner
1306 Sadler Dr
Carlisle PA 17013

Call Sign: WA3TRD
Benjamin L Freet
514 School Ave
Carlisle PA 17013

Call Sign: KB3OIS
Sarah J Engle
11 Sherwood Dr
Carlisle PA 17015

Call Sign: N3IBL
Dawn H Valentine
2 Shover Dr
Carlisle PA 17013

Call Sign: N3BV

Brett G Valentine
2 Shover Dr
Carlisle PA 17013

Call Sign: KA3CET
Gary I Shuey
1538 Shughart Rd
Carlisle PA 17015

Call Sign: N3XLI
Sean Stevenson
1369 Shuman Dr
Carlisle PA 17013

Call Sign: N3GCG
George K Orner
23 Spring Garden Est
Carlisle PA 170139257

Call Sign: W3GKO
George K Orner
23 Spring Garden Ests
Carlisle PA 17015

Call Sign: N3MMH
Daniel L McLaughlin
50 Spring Garden Ests
Carlisle PA 17013

Call Sign: WA3DLV
Elmer E Loy
1509 Spring Rd
Carlisle PA 17013

Call Sign: KA3TJC
Shirley A Shearer
2360 Spring Rd
Carlisle PA 17013

Call Sign: WB3LRG
William E Harwood Jr
2870 Spring Rd
Carlisle PA 170138732

Call Sign: WB3FNJ

Darrel R Justh Sr
3240 Spring Rd
Carlisle PA 17013

Call Sign: KB3FGZ
Todd C Raymer
3767 Spring Rd
Carlisle PA 17013

Call Sign: KB3JTK
Ryan D Sullivan
1 Stonehedge Way
Carlisle PA 17013

Call Sign: KB3STO
Brian V Gronkiewicz
1209 Stratford Dr
Carlisle PA 17013

Call Sign: KA3GAW
George A Auman
37 Strawberry Dr
Carlisle PA 17013

Call Sign: KB3RZK
Connor M Bower
32 Strayer Dr
Carlisle PA 17013

Call Sign: K3LUE
Ronald L Tregl
116 Strayer Dr
Carlisle PA 17013

Call Sign: KB3LWS
Jeffrey R Groves
9 Teaberry Dr
Carlisle PA 17013

Call Sign: KB3SAB
Kyle A Walters
10 Teaberry Dr
Carlisle PA 17015

Call Sign: WF3A

J F Quigley
18 Thornhill Ct
Carlisle PA 17013

Call Sign: W3IWF
Calvin A Hoerneman
203 Todd Cir
Carlisle PA 17013

Call Sign: KB3KLV
Lauren D Connelly
13 Todd Rd
Carlisle PA 17013

Call Sign: KB3OZI
Thomas J Connelly
13 Todd Rd
Carlisle PA 17013

Call Sign: KB3BOW
Aaron T Patterson
1679 Trindle Rd
Carlisle PA 17013

Call Sign: WA3JLV
Donald H Mowery
166 Union Hall Rd
Carlisle PA 17013

Call Sign: WB3EAH
Usaisc Carlisle Barracks
Usaisc Carlisle Barracks
Carlisle PA 17013

Call Sign: WK2P
Edwin Simoncek
23 W Eppley Dr
Carlisle PA 17015

Call Sign: KB3IYU
Chad A Fahnestock
1849 W Lisburn Rd
Carlisle PA 17013

Call Sign: KB3LQY

Nicholas S Larson
22 W Mulberry Hill Rd
Carlisle PA 17013

Call Sign: KB3LCK
Mark W Blashford
724 W North St
Carlisle PA 17013

Call Sign: KB9CSA
Patrick E Donnelly
8 W Oakwood
Carlisle PA 17015

Call Sign: KB3LRO
Mary C Nestor
31 W Oakwood Dr
Carlisle PA 17013

Call Sign: W2HYX
Mark B Rudensey
100 W Pomfret St
Carlisle PA 17013

Call Sign: N3QZC
John P Jensen
154 W South St
Carlisle PA 17013

Call Sign: KB3MXB
Maliya E Pion
835 W South St
Carlisle PA 17013

Call Sign: N3LKL
Robert E Carpenter
239 W Yell Brchs Rd
Carlisle PA 17013

Call Sign: KB3EWL
Judy M Carpenter
239 W Yellow Breeches
Rd
Carlisle PA 17015

Call Sign: KB3SNN
Carol J Barrick
2210 Waggoners Gap Rd
Carlisle PA 17013

Call Sign: KC7KEU
Ted M Giampietro
1400 Waggoners Gap Rd
Carlisle PA 17013

Call Sign: NR3B
Steven C Gray
244 Walnut Bottom Rd
Carlisle PA 17013

Call Sign: W3HE
Howard J Eich Sr
940 Walnut Bottom Rd
Carlisle PA 17013

Call Sign: N3WPW
Glenn E Love
1417 Walnut Bottom Rd
Carlisle PA 17013

Call Sign: N3RXX
Janet C McCoy
45 Walnut St
Carlisle PA 17013

Call Sign: KB3KNM
Elizabeth K Wall
234 Walnut St
Carlisle PA 17013

Call Sign: KB3NCA
Ellen C Wall
234 Walnut St
Carlisle PA 17013

Call Sign: N4NXO
Mark C Weston
70 Wedgewood Dr
Carlisle PA 170159367

Call Sign: W3BTE
Dean S Helwig
440 Wertz Run Rd
Carlisle PA 17013

Call Sign: KB3NBP
Carly A Haslam
42 Wheatfield Dr
Carlisle PA 17013

Call Sign: N3DVL
Herbert E Halliday
545 Wilson St
Carlisle PA 17013

Call Sign: KA3CEU
Ted W Horn
104 Winchester Gardens
Carlisle PA 17013

Call Sign: W3MXE
Day K Grimes Jr
317 Wolfs Bridge Rd
Carlisle PA 17013

Call Sign: KA6EBA
David J Smith
1307 Woodward Dr
Carlisle PA 170134712

Call Sign: KB3WVS
James W Connell Jr
317 York Rd
Carlisle PA 170133160

Call Sign: KC3SZ
Charles P Scott
1436 Zimmerman Rd
Carlisle PA 17013

Call Sign: K3IT
Donald G Swartz
Carlisle PA 17013

Call Sign: N3ODV

La Verne L Enck
Carlisle PA 17013

Call Sign: N3QFJ
Jason Smith
Carlisle PA 17013

FCC Amateur Radio Licenses in Carroll Valley

Call Sign: KB3NPL
Thomas C Forsythe III
3 Cross Trl
Carroll Valley PA 17320

FCC Amateur Radio Licenses in Carrolltown

Call Sign: KA3YVT
Harry C Trout
638 E Carroll St
Carrolltown PA 15722

Call Sign: KB3MFO
Daniel J Lieb
107 George Kirsh Ln
Carrolltown PA 15722

Call Sign: WA3QEV
Wilbur M Kirsch
13 Old Dutch Ln
Carrolltown PA 15722

Call Sign: KB3NMG
Donald C Leslie
Carrolltown PA 15722

Call Sign: K3RRA
Donald C Leslie
Carrolltown PA 15722

FCC Amateur Radio Licenses in Cassville

Call Sign: KA3NWG
Kenneth R Covert
45 Seminary St
Cassville PA 16623

FCC Amateur Radio Licenses in Catawissa

Call Sign: K3EAU
Harold R Dalious
184 Bethel Dr
Catawissa PA 17820

Call Sign: KB3CJR
Dennis W Hartranft
27 Deer Rd
Catawissa PA 17820

Call Sign: W3ROK
Weldie A Dent
2 Mi NW Of Slabtown On
Twp Rt 375
Catawissa PA 178209731

Call Sign: KB3LGZ
R Jesse Fetterman
4 Mt Zion Rd
Catawissa PA 17820

Call Sign: WA3HTI
Frank J Monoski
16 Mtn View Est
Catawissa PA 17820

Call Sign: KE3UL
Edmund W Minnich
1302 Numidia Dr
Catawissa PA 17820

Call Sign: N3VWK
Mary Ann Minnich
1302 Numidia Dr
Catawissa PA 17820

Call Sign: AA3PX

Lawrence J Thomas Jr
929 Old Reading Rd
Catawissa PA 17820

Call Sign: K3BOI
James A Riegel
324 Pine St
Catawissa PA 17820

Call Sign: N3PEF
Monroe R Daniels
200 S 3rd St
Catawissa PA 17820

Call Sign: N2ABE
Warren E Remig
515 W Evergreen Ln
Catawissa PA 17820

FCC Amateur Radio Licenses in Central City

Call Sign: WB3LUP
Stanley N Lenart
279 Leppert Rd
Central City PA 15926

Call Sign: KB3PLR
Jeffrey A Hunt
680 Lynn St
Central City PA 15926

Call Sign: N2SFU
Richard A Hunt
680 Lynn St
Central City PA
159261152

Call Sign: N3SPX
Michael D Miscoe
1032 Peninsula Dr
Central City PA 15926

Call Sign: N3ZEC
Michael D Kubek

465 Rock Cut Rd
Central City PA 15926

Call Sign: KB3SSF
Aaron J Emerick
626 S Shore Tr
Central City PA 15926

Call Sign: KB3FBQ
Scott B Sarver
484 Sorber Rd
Central City PA 15926

FCC Amateur Radio Licenses in Centralia

Call Sign: KE3W
Nevins A Frankel
518 W Center St
Centralia PA 17921

FCC Amateur Radio Licenses in Centre Hall

Call Sign: K3TRV
Walter T Lingle
Box 234
Centre Hall PA 16828

Call Sign: KB3OYW
David W Hege
118 Hege Ln
Centre Hall PA 16828

Call Sign: K3DWH
David W Hege
118 Hege Ln
Centre Hall PA 16828

Call Sign: N7BUQ
Richard L Ruth
135 Laurel Meadow Ln
Centre Hall PA 168287818

Call Sign: AA3R

Richard L Ruth
135 Laurel Meadow Ln
Centre Hall PA 168287818

Call Sign: KB3ESN
Stephen W Coder
133 Mountainside Trl
Centre Hall PA 16828

Call Sign: N3VHM
William F Reilly
135 N Pennsylvania Ave
Centre Hall PA 16828

Call Sign: WA3ZPW
Paul S Dimick
131 Penns Ct
Centre Hall PA 16828

Call Sign: K3PSD
Paul S Dimick
131 Penns Ct
Centre Hall PA 16828

Call Sign: KB3YEB
Charles W Horner
150 Summit Dr
Centre Hall PA 16828

Call Sign: KF4LXD
David R Salmen
Centre Hall PA 16828

Call Sign: N3YAL
David A Powell
Centre Hall PA 168280123

FCC Amateur Radio Licenses in Chalk Hill

Call Sign: AA3EE
David A Mueller
64 Old Mill Rd
Chalk Hill PA 154210421

Call Sign: KA3WRC
Cathy M Herring
Chalk Hill PA 15421

Call Sign: WS3N
Mark D Johnson
Chalk Hill PA 15421

Call Sign: N3IUG
Charles F Johnson
Chalk Hill PA 15421

Call Sign: KB3LDX
Justin M Wilson
Chalk Hill PA 15421

FCC Amateur Radio Licenses in Chambersburg

Call Sign: W3CKU
James H Doyle
2956 Adams Dr
Chambersburg PA
172018972

Call Sign: WH7USA
Robert T Godlewski
6445 Bellhurst Dr
Chambersburg PA
172028598

Call Sign: KC8OYJ
Dwight D Weidman
1216 Brandon Dr
Chambersburg PA 17201

Call Sign: K3FFJ
Henry V Betz
294 Briar Ln
Chambersburg PA
172013116

Call Sign: WB2RQA
Robert E Sullivan

398 Briar Ln
Chambersburg PA 17201

Call Sign: N3XGI
Jeffrey P Sarsfield
479 Briar Ln
Chambersburg PA 17201

Call Sign: WD8PBC
James A Dawson
505 Broad St
Chambersburg PA
172011607

Call Sign: N3LJP
William C Gray
10 Canterbury Dr
Chambersburg PA 17201

Call Sign: N3PMM
Darwyn D Gray
10 Canterbury Dr
Chambersburg PA 17201

Call Sign: KB3ONL
John P Birster
1621 Chamberlayne Dr
Chambersburg PA 17201

Call Sign: KB3PLF
Dale A Johanson
121 Chancellor Dr
Chambersburg PA 17201

Call Sign: KB3VWE
Nathan C Meyer
433 Channing Dr
Chambersburg PA 17201

Call Sign: KB3OPM
Bruce M Ericksen
2926 Constellation Dr
Chambersburg PA 17201

Call Sign: KB3OHD

Daniel A Rosenberry
2947 Country Rd
Chambersburg PA 17201

Call Sign: K3RCR
Thomas E Montgomery
3034 Country Rd
Chambersburg PA 17201

Call Sign: KB3PHQ
Larry M Miller
1391 Cove Dr
Chambersburg PA 17202

Call Sign: W3LAR
Larry M Miller
1391 Cove Dr
Chambersburg PA 17202

Call Sign: KB3KNV
Todd A Mclaughlin
630 Cumberland Ave
Chambersburg PA 17201

Call Sign: W3DWI
Edward M Brooks
4835 Cumberland Hwy
Chambersburg PA
172029655

Call Sign: W3UMY
Raymond I Leininger
5237 Cumberland Hwy
Chambersburg PA 17201

Call Sign: N3YFS
David K Grant
50 Diopside Dr
Chambersburg PA 17201

Call Sign: KB3NXK
Richard W Baughman
233 E Catherine St
Chambersburg PA 17201

Call Sign: W3HSU
Richard E Pheil
744 E Garfield St
Chambersburg PA 17201

Call Sign: KB3LNY
Brian L Umbrell
235 E King St
Chambersburg PA 17201

Call Sign: W3PDW
Brian L Umbrell
235 E King St
Chambersburg PA 17201

Call Sign: KB3WOU
Daniel W Dorman
439 E King St
Chambersburg PA 17201

Call Sign: KB3NLF
Timothy J Gorman
537 E King St
Chambersburg PA 17201

Call Sign: KB3FHN
Dane R Morris
545 E King St
Chambersburg PA 17201

Call Sign: N3IXX
Ferguson M Robinson
257 E Liberty St
Chambersburg PA 17201

Call Sign: N3UTP
Kenneth S Akehurst Jr
829 E McKinley St
Chambersburg PA
172012821

Call Sign: K3IDJ
Marlin E Gayman
2633 Edenville Rd
Chambersburg PA 17202

Call Sign: WB3DKD
Joe E Kelso Sr
1840 Edgar Ave
Chambersburg PA 17201

Call Sign: K3YWL
Barry A Martz
1554 Fairview Ave
Chambersburg PA 17201

Call Sign: AB3EV
David W Gabler
2542 Fisler Rd
Chambersburg PA 17201

Call Sign: N3BUW
Donald M Kelley
765 Franklin Sq Dr
Chambersburg PA
172011475

Call Sign: WD8KOT
Ronald K Robinson Sr
7500 Friendship Vlg Rd
Chambersburg PA 17201

Call Sign: N3GKT
Eugene L Eckenrode
366 Glen St
Chambersburg PA 17201

Call Sign: KB3YDD
Thomas A Dolan
3435 Gleneagles Dr
Chambersburg PA 17202

Call Sign: WB3CKX
Fred L Widney
3246 Grand Pnt Rd
Chambersburg PA
172018186

Call Sign: KB3QJA
Michael E Glover

3149 Grand Pt Rd
Chambersburg PA 17202

Call Sign: KD6GET
David J Dukette IV
232 Grandview Ave
Chambersburg PA 17201

Call Sign: KB3GSC
David J Dukette IV
232 Grandview Ave
Chambersburg PA 17201

Call Sign: K3ZUZ
Allan D Green
338 Grandview Ave
Chambersburg PA 17201

Call Sign: N3RTH
Charles G Landis
1029 Graystone Cir
Chambersburg PA
172012939

Call Sign: N3XYJ
Dean L Martin
3508 Guilford Spring Rd
Chambersburg PA 17202

Call Sign: WB6LLT
James K Mills
1060 Heather Dr
Chambersburg PA
172013028

Call Sign: KB3VJX
Thomas L Hollinger
144 Highland Rd
Chambersburg PA 17202

Call Sign: KA3STE
David A Hartwick
191 Highland Rd
Chambersburg PA 17201

Call Sign: WA3URR
David A Hartwick
191 Highland Rd
Chambersburg PA 17201

Call Sign: KB3MUO
Joseph E Hovetter III
1519 Hollywell Ave
Chambersburg PA 17201

Call Sign: KB3RBR
Joss C Steward
1438 Hospitality Dr
Chambersburg PA 17202

Call Sign: N3MMH
Todd A Mclaughlin
1475 Hunters Chase
Chambersburg PA 17201

Call Sign: KB3ODO
Stephen C Edney
2235 Ivan Rd
Chambersburg PA 17201

Call Sign: KB3TFG
Zachary A Fry
2919 Jefferson Dr
Chambersburg PA 17201

Call Sign: KB3KMF
Christopher J Gregorio
1151 King Dr
Chambersburg PA 17201

Call Sign: KB3LWP
Laura M Gregorio
1151 King Dr
Chambersburg PA 17201

Call Sign: KC3YC
Wallace N Mook Jr
264 Kolpark Dr
Chambersburg PA
172013006

Call Sign: KB3DYY
Diane C Karper
524 Kraiss Ave
Chambersburg PA 17201

Call Sign: KB3EOD
Jesten G Karper
524 Kraiss Ave
Chambersburg PA 17201

Call Sign: KB3DYX
Christopher S Karper
524 Kraiss Ave
Chambersburg PA 17201

Call Sign: K3SSM
James I Powers
2631 Letter Kenny Rd
Chambersburg PA
172018309

Call Sign: KO3V
John F Stenger
99 Limekiln Dr
Chambersburg PA 17201

Call Sign: W3FMK
Ralph D Gilbert
592 Lincoln Way E
Chambersburg PA 17201

Call Sign: KF5UV
William D Putman
849 Lindia Dr
Chambersburg PA 17202

Call Sign: KB3MUQ
John S Meyer
2059 Loop Rd
Chambersburg PA 17201

Call Sign: K3GOY
John S Meyer
2059 Loop Rd

Chambersburg PA 17201

Call Sign: KB3UGR
Nathaniel S Meyer
2059 Loop Rd
Chambersburg PA 17202

Call Sign: KB3TQO
Christian J Brushie
209 Macintosh Way
Chambersburg PA 17201

Call Sign: WA3RGQ
Donald E Hawbaker
1661 Malibu Dr
Chambersburg PA 17202

Call Sign: WB3EZU
Robert H Murray Jr
1128 Marvern Dr
Chambersburg PA
172019470

Call Sign: WA3WJE
Paul W Bridegam Jr
222 Meadow Ln
Chambersburg PA 17201

Call Sign: KD0FGT
Steven C Fox
224 Meadow Ln
Chambersburg PA 17202

Call Sign: W3PNI
Wilmer C Knepper
539 Mentzer Ave
Chambersburg PA
172011429

Call Sign: KA3VAX
Patrick M Bent
4859 Molly Pitcher Hwy S
Chambersburg PA 17201

Call Sign: WA3TCM

Darwin R Martin
6993 Molly Pitcher Hwy S
Chambersburg PA 17201

Call Sign: K3MUF
Theodore E Brand
620 Montgomery Ave
Chambersburg PA 17201

Call Sign: K3TNH
Theodore A Lucas
1431 Moosic Dr
Chambersburg PA
172029298

Call Sign: N3UPE
Joshua D Strickler
5805 Mountain Rd
Chambersburg PA 17201

Call Sign: K3NRK
David E Cowan
169 N 4th St
Chambersburg PA 17201

Call Sign: KB3EHT
Michael A Rider
649 N Franklin St Lot 44
Chambersburg PA 17201

Call Sign: W3PB
L Patrick Durham
2368 New Franklin Rd
Chambersburg PA 17202

Call Sign: N3VZQ
Vernon D Shank
3641 New Franklin Rd
Chambersburg PA 17201

Call Sign: K3IWU
George S Keener
1426 Oakwood Ct
Chambersburg PA 17201

Call Sign: N3UEB
Joan P Stewart
579 Overcash Rd
Chambersburg PA 17201

Call Sign: K3SJG
Robert J Palladino
2248 Philadelphia Ave
Chambersburg PA
172018931

Call Sign: WA3AIR
Stephen Demes
2321 Philadelphia Ave
Chambersburg PA 17201

Call Sign: N3XUF
Andrew C Jones
507 Philadelphia Ave 4
Chambersburg PA 17201

Call Sign: KB3MUR
David E Cowan
2004 Philadelphia Ave 6
Chambersburg PA 17201

Call Sign: KB3MYA
David E Cowan
2004 Philadelphia Ave 6
Chambersburg PA 17201

Call Sign: KB3ODS
William P Houck
282 Phoenix Dr
Chambersburg PA
172014538

Call Sign: W3WPH
William P Houck
282 Phoenix Dr
Chambersburg PA
172014538

Call Sign: N3MZJ
Robert W Piper

634 Rockview Ave
Chambersburg PA
172012910

Call Sign: KB3IVQ
Clarence L Carty Jr
4006 Rocky Spring Rd
Chambersburg PA
172018784

Call Sign: N3KI
Clarence L Carty Jr
4006 Rocky Spring Rd
Chambersburg PA
172018784

Call Sign: N8UDA
William T Blednick Jr
158 Ruby Dr
Chambersburg PA 17201

Call Sign: N8VZZ
Kathryn E Blednick
158 Ruby Dr
Chambersburg PA 17201

Call Sign: KB3VIU
Lois A Osterman
184 S 8th St
Chambersburg PA
172012724

Call Sign: KB3TFT
Robert L Martin
1065 S Main St
Chambersburg PA 17201

Call Sign: KD4HUV
Charles Probst
2672 Sarah Pl
Chambersburg PA
172017035

Call Sign: WD4RDO
Ronald K Doyle Sr

1120 Scotland Ave
Chambersburg PA
172011242

Call Sign: KB3LFF
Ronald K Doyle Sr
1120 Scotland Ave
Chambersburg PA
172011242

Call Sign: KC8GZG
Roy L Taylor
1338 Scotland Ave
Chambersburg PA 17201

Call Sign: KB3CQI
Michael R Feltman
1545 Scotland Ave
Chambersburg PA
172018933

Call Sign: KB3SNX
Charles D Berg
1715 Scotland Ave
Chambersburg PA 17201

Call Sign: W3ZIP
Albert A Evangelista
2336 Scotland Rd
Chambersburg PA 17201

Call Sign: N3UMV
Robert W Lake Jr
5560 Sheller Rd
Chambersburg PA 17201

Call Sign: K0TEN
Carl J Creswell
2503 Sherry Dr
Chambersburg PA 17201

Call Sign: WB3BAP
Robert F Caufman
739 Siloam Rd
Chambersburg PA 17201

Call Sign: N3NAY
Larry C Rosenberry
753 Siloam Rd
Chambersburg PA 17201

Call Sign: N3VGO
Rufus A Day
1509 Spring View Cir
Chambersburg PA 17201

Call Sign: WB2CQS
Herbert G Gustafsson
2676 St Paul Rd
Chambersburg PA 17202

Call Sign: N3LHI
Patricia M Curran
499 Starr Ave
Chambersburg PA 17201

Call Sign: NW3M
William E Curran
499 Starr Ave
Chambersburg PA 17201

Call Sign: K3WVU
Dwight D Weidman
16 Summer Breeze Ln
Chambersburg PA 17202

Call Sign: KE6IJG
Varna R Shrewsberry
266 Sunbrook Dr
Chambersburg PA 17201

Call Sign: WB3CTW
William Valora Jr
2220 Tanya Dr
Chambersburg PA 17201

Call Sign: N3LTF
Dominick T Pece
179 Theodore Dr
Chambersburg PA 17201

Call Sign: N3LTG
Patricia M Pece
179 Theodore Dr
Chambersburg PA 17201

Call Sign: N3HOO
Edwin K Fisher
1665 Walker Rd
Chambersburg PA 17202

Call Sign: K3DXA
William H Myers
2085 Wayne Rd
Chambersburg PA 17201

Call Sign: K3WWH
Raymond W Green
2085 Wayne Rd
Chambersburg PA 17201

Call Sign: WB2NED
Constantine G Vloutely
581 Wennington Dr
Chambersburg PA
172010669

Call Sign: AA3MK
Evans T Prieston
263 Westover Way
Chambersburg PA
172014458

Call Sign: KB3KLT
Erin M Bishop
266 Westover Way
Chambersburg PA 17201

Call Sign: WA2PIJ
Michael J Marshall
4521 White Church Rd
Chambersburg PA 17201

Call Sign: N3YZW
Rebecca A Holland

27 Woodland Way
Chambersburg PA 17201

Call Sign: W3ACH
Cumberland Valley ARC
Chambersburg PA 17201

Call Sign: KB3GBF
Gerald E Rosenberry
Chambersburg PA 17201

Call Sign: K3ZIV
William H Beyrer
Chambersburg PA 17201

Call Sign: KB3LDA
William H Beyrer
Chambersburg PA 17241

FCC Amateur Radio Licenses in Chest Springs

Call Sign: KB3LFZ
Eric L Flumerfelt
Chest Springs PA
166240108

FCC Amateur Radio Licenses in Christiana

Call Sign: KB3GAR
Michael W Mccown Jr
1512 Georgetown Rd
Christiana PA 17509

Call Sign: KB3KUE
Le Ann M McCown
1512 Georgetown Rd
Christiana PA 17509

Call Sign: N3HY
Michael W Mccown Jr
1512 Georgetown Rd
Christiana PA 17509

Call Sign: K1IZS
Donald W Moffett
207 Harrison Ave
Christiana PA 175091303

Call Sign: WB3FJH
Carl J Haag
320 Highland Rd
Christiana PA 17509

Call Sign: N3PQQ
Ralph E Joe
18 Mary St
Christiana PA 17509

Call Sign: N3MMW
C Edward Baylor Jr
24 Newport Ave
Christiana PA 17509

Call Sign: KB3UEA
Christine Simon-Wolski
24 Newport Ave
Christiana PA 17509

Call Sign: KB3HYR
James P Neely
880 Noble Rd
Christiana PA 17509

Call Sign: K3PGU
Harley M Kooker
15 Orchard Buck Rd
Christiana PA 175099631

Call Sign: KB3ECU
William J Snyder
118 Upper Valley Rd
Christiana PA 17509

Call Sign: K3ECU
William J Snyder
118 Upper Valley Rd
Christiana PA 17509

Call Sign: K3YU
William J Snyder
118 Upper Valley Rd
Christiana PA 17509

Call Sign: KB3NQM
Ben E Beiler
812 Vintage Rd
Christiana PA 17509

Call Sign: KD4CVL
Deborah K Stoltzfus
6961 White Oak Rd
Christiana PA 175099532

FCC Amateur Radio Licenses in Churchtown

Call Sign: KA3NKN
Andrew B Galligan
Narvon
Churchtown PA 17555

FCC Amateur Radio Licenses in Clarence

Call Sign: KA3YQH
Larry L Ellsworth
Clarence PA 16829

FCC Amateur Radio Licenses in Claysburg

Call Sign: N3KKX
Matthew W Lightner
1771 Beaver Dam Rd
Claysburg PA 16625

Call Sign: N3LEI
Matthew W Lightner
1771 Beaver Dam Rd
Claysburg PA 16625

Call Sign: WB3KGN
Barton B Hoover

Box 1250
Claysburg PA 166259750

Call Sign: N3MWF
Roger A Lingenfelter
Box 1287
Claysburg PA 16625

Call Sign: N3QOI
Edward L Mohney
Box 1326
Claysburg PA 16625

Call Sign: N3HCS
Clayton E Dodson
Box 727
Claysburg PA 16625

Call Sign: N3BZU
Harry A Knisely
Box 899
Claysburg PA 16625

Call Sign: N3JXY
Pete Tremmel
Box 925
Claysburg PA 16625

Call Sign: N3BFC
William R Lightner
Rd 1
Claysburg PA 16625

Call Sign: K3NQT
Walter L Knisely
2664 Schellsburg Rd
Claysburg PA 166258941

Call Sign: N3LEY
Byrle R Ritchey Jr
Claysburg PA 166250048

FCC Amateur Radio Licenses in Clearfield

Call Sign: N3PAY
John D Bennese
623 Barclay St
Clearfield PA 16830

Call Sign: N3PIW
Kathy A Bennese
623 Barclay St
Clearfield PA 16830

Call Sign: N3QET
Aaron J Bennese
623 Barclay St
Clearfield PA 16830

Call Sign: N3SPH
Dominick M Bennese
623 Barclay St
Clearfield PA 16830

Call Sign: N3PUK
Linda L Whited
Box 151
Clearfield PA 16830

Call Sign: K3JE
Edward S Morrison
31 Collins Ave
Clearfield PA 16830

Call Sign: N3PUQ
Dorothy S Morrison
31 Collins Ave
Clearfield PA 16830

Call Sign: KD3KO
Duane R Carr Jr
413 Daisy St
Clearfield PA 16830

Call Sign: N3PUF
Rebecca H Mollica
1216 Daisy St
Clearfield PA 16830

Call Sign: N2GUN
Jerry J Kovach
411 E Walnut St
Clearfield PA 16830

Call Sign: N3MUX
John R Woolridge Jr
113 Elizabeth St
Clearfield PA 16830

Call Sign: N3THC
Justin L Ogden
516 Elm Ave
Clearfield PA 16830

Call Sign: WA3JBV
Percy T Wonderling
827 Flegal Rd
Clearfield PA 16830

Call Sign: KA3SFQ
James R Whited Sr
44 Greenland St
Clearfield PA 16830

Call Sign: K3JRW
James R Whited Sr
44 Greenland St
Clearfield PA 16830

Call Sign: N3OCB
Charles T Bungo
1208 Haney St
Clearfield PA 16830

Call Sign: N3PUT
Robert E Daub
629 Indian Rd
Clearfield PA 16830

Call Sign: N3HRM
Andrea L Szejk
1976 Jerry Run Rd
Clearfield PA 168308935

Call Sign: WA3R
Robert B Szejk
1976 Jerry Run Rd
Clearfield PA 16830

Call Sign: KA3USM
Samuel L McGhee Jr
607 Martin St
Clearfield PA 16830

Call Sign: KA3YGX
Jacqueline D McGhee
607 Martin St
Clearfield PA 16830

Call Sign: KA3YGY
Steven L McGhee
607 Martin St
Clearfield PA 16830

Call Sign: KA3YGZ
Crystal A McGhee
607 Martin St
Clearfield PA 16830

Call Sign: KA3ZZO
Aaron W Fulton
708 Martin St
Clearfield PA 16830

Call Sign: W3QKP
Franklin W Wall
701 McBride St
Clearfield PA 16830

Call Sign: KB3EFX
Richard R Thomas
521 Mill St
Clearfield PA 16830

Call Sign: N3PUL
Timothy V Lumadue
2712 Mitchell Rd
Clearfield PA 16830

Call Sign: KB3WBT
Lars A Kvant
418 Mt Joy Rd
Clearfield PA 16830

Call Sign: KA2CBP
Richard L Welch Sr
542 Mt Joy Rd
Clearfield PA 16830

Call Sign: N3HTQ
James P Dillman
721 Nichols St
Clearfield PA 16830

Call Sign: KB3ABK
Janet L Lovesky
8 NW 4th Ave
Clearfield PA 16830

Call Sign: AA3AZ
John J Lovesky
8 NW 4th Ave
Clearfield PA 16830

Call Sign: N3PUP
Sarah A Lovesky
8 NW 4th Ave
Clearfield PA 16830

Call Sign: N3IZE
Richard L Hummel Jr
24 NW 4th Ave
Clearfield PA 16830

Call Sign: N3IYZ
Richard L Hummel Sr
24 NW 4th Ave
Clearfield PA 16830

Call Sign: N3IZA
Rebecca A Hummel
24 NW 4th Ave
Clearfield PA 16830

Call Sign: KB3HYL
Bernard L Mccreadie
1303 Parkview Dr
Clearfield PA 168301121

Call Sign: N3ZFW
Stephen L Putt
315 Poplar Ave
Clearfield PA 16830

Call Sign: K3HEZ
Ward W Haines
401 Poplar Ave
Clearfield PA 16830

Call Sign: WA3NRC
Harold K Miller
711 Quarry Ave
Clearfield PA 16830

Call Sign: KB3SVW
Al A Maddas
1318 S 2nd St
Clearfield PA 16830

Call Sign: N3PUO
Thomas L Berry
212 S 3rd
Clearfield PA 16830

Call Sign: WA3LDZ
Leonard A Gearhart Jr
114 S 5th St
Clearfield PA 16830

Call Sign: WA4YVZ
Wayne S Stewart
521 Spruce St Apt 5
Clearfield PA 16830

Call Sign: W3KQR
William H Boalich
608 Thompson St
Clearfield PA 16830

Call Sign: N3ZFX
Janet M Haag
4 Tpke Ave
Clearfield PA 16830

Call Sign: N3RTK
Harvey E Haag
4 Tpke Ave
Clearfield PA 168301742

Call Sign: N3VWR
Christian J W Haag
4 Tpke Ave
Clearfield PA 168301742

Call Sign: N3XHF
Elizabeth A Schmahl
4 Tpke Ave
Clearfield PA 168301742

Call Sign: N3PUN
Mary Kay Master
412 W 1st St
Clearfield PA 16830

Call Sign: N3XIW
Edward J Master III
412 W 1st St
Clearfield PA 16830

Call Sign: N3IES
Joseph B Bitner
424 W 7th Ave
Clearfield PA 168301332

Call Sign: N3PUH
Mary A Wigfield
424 W 7th Ave
Clearfield PA 168301332

Call Sign: K3UZL
Ellery D Stoughton
8 W Pauline Dr
Clearfield PA 16830

Call Sign: N3PUI
Edward L Kumm
739 Wearer St
Clearfield PA 16830

Call Sign: W3ZVK
Karl Khuen Kryk
123 Welles St
Clearfield PA 16830

Call Sign: WB3EQW
Michael J Errigo
123 Wells St
Clearfield PA 168301962

Call Sign: KB3OTX
Jonathan P Bowers
110 Williams St
Clearfield PA 16830

Call Sign: WA2TAK
Stephen G Tetorka
Clearfield PA 16830

Call Sign: N3QBP
Benjamin J Hummel
Clearfield PA 16830

FCC Amateur Radio Licenses in Clearville

Call Sign: KB3WXW
Clinton D Robosson
266 Beans Cove Rd
Clearville PA 15535

Call Sign: WA3PMQ
William D Robosson
400 Beans Cove Rd
Clearville PA 155358023

Call Sign: K3ZF
William D Robosson
400 Beans Cove Rd
Clearville PA 155358023

Call Sign: N3ZMY
Angela J Ziviello
Box 13 A
Clearville PA 15535

Call Sign: WC3G
James T ORourke
243 Jay Rd
Clearville PA 15535

Call Sign: KA3DAJ
Delores K ORourke
243 Jay Rd
Clearville PA 15535

Call Sign: KB3LTD
Aaron Tesler
221 Miller Rd
Clearville PA 155356711

Call Sign: W3DRW
Bernard F Frank
3299 Ragged Mtn Rd
Clearville PA 155358920

Call Sign: WA3PYT
Archimede Ziviello Jr
128 Short Rd
Clearville PA 15535

Call Sign: K3PYT
Archimede Ziviello Jr
128 Short Rd
Clearville PA 15535

FCC Amateur Radio Licenses in Cleona

Call Sign: WA3TIG
Carmine Izzo
415 Cleona Blvd
Cleona PA 17042

Call Sign: K3DIN

Luther F Klick
315 E Chestnut St
Cleona PA 17042

Call Sign: N3KKZ
Marylouise Zengerle
339 E Chestnut St
Cleona PA 17042

Call Sign: N3JPA
Francis D Hemler
214 E Maple St
Cleona PA 170422423

Call Sign: N3BTH
Carl A Gerber
333 E Maple St
Cleona PA 170422425

Call Sign: N3EUO
Cynthia L Brandt
501 E Maple St
Cleona PA 170422536

Call Sign: WA3GPM
David I Brandt
501 E Maple St
Cleona PA 170422536

Call Sign: KB3TOM
Robert S Kleckner
101 E Penn Ave
Cleona PA 17042

Call Sign: WA3CVN
Gregory J Lynagh
227 S Gary St
Cleona PA 170422448

Call Sign: KA3IOP
Fred K Demler
217 S Mill St
Cleona PA 17042

Call Sign: KB3GSR

Ronald L Rowe
228 S Mill St
Cleona PA 170423127

Call Sign: K3PVR
Raymond J Stima Sr
108 S Wilson St
Cleona PA 17042

Call Sign: KD3OQ
Elias R Kanoun
118 W Chestnut St
Cleona PA 17042

Call Sign: N3SSI
Kenneth L Dissinger
212 W Penn Ave
Cleona PA 17042

Call Sign: KB3TOL
Cindy A Howard
12 Walnut Mill Ln
Cleona PA 17042

Call Sign: KB3QAQ
Robert A Howard
12 Walnut Mill Ln
Cleona PA 17042

FCC Amateur Radio Licenses in Clermont

Call Sign: W3PZF
John H Yoder
11 North St
Clermont PA 16740

FCC Amateur Radio Licenses in Coal Township

Call Sign: WB3JNZ
Andrew M Latovich
1500 Mohawk St

Coal Township PA
178663904

Call Sign: KB3KWZ
John Poponiak
1333 Nelson St
Coal Township PA 17866

Call Sign: WB3DOS
James P Robel
1818 Park Ave
Coal Township PA
178661639

Call Sign: K3CPB
Charles P Barrett
1420 Pulaski Ave
Coal Township PA 17866

Call Sign: KA3DIN
Frank R Varano
1968 Stetler Dr
Coal Township PA 17866

Call Sign: N3FK
Francis J Kelley
1975 Stetler Dr
Coal Township PA
178661644

Call Sign: N3MXM
Gary E Keough
1800 Tioga St 10
Coal Township PA 17866

Call Sign: KB3JZG
Robert M Jaworski
1172 Trevorton Rd
Coal Township PA 17866

Call Sign: WA3ETR
James H Kramer
1001 W Chestnut St
Coal Township PA 17866

Call Sign: KB3JZF
Ernest L Jaworski
408 Water St
Coal Township PA 17866

FCC Amateur Radio Licenses in Coalport

Call Sign: KB0QWE
Deborah J Emond
117 Shore Ln
Coalport PA 16627

Call Sign: N3BZR
John W Zipf
16 Track Rd
Coalport PA 16627

Call Sign: N3BZS
Jane G Zipf
16 Track Rd
Coalport PA 16627

Call Sign: N3QLC
Paul N Zipf
16 Track Rd
Coalport PA 16627

Call Sign: N3UDG
Hugh B Kepple
Coalport PA 16627

FCC Amateur Radio Licenses in Coburn

Call Sign: KA3MIH
Dana C Harlan
166 Zachary Rd
Coburn PA 16832

FCC Amateur Radio Licenses in Codorus

Call Sign: KA3OTN
John R Young

Monticello Ave
Codorus PA 17311

FCC Amateur Radio Licenses in Cogan Station

Call Sign: N3MFI
Barry L McCarty
1956 Beauty Ave
Cogan Station PA 177288377

Call Sign: N3UXJ
Nan E Swift
Box 367
Cogan Station PA 17728

Call Sign: N3XUP
Michael A Albert
436 Brentwood Dr
Cogan Station PA 17728

Call Sign: WA3YQH
Eric K Albert
436 Brentwood Dr
Cogan Station PA 17728

Call Sign: AC9L
Thomas E Ask
19 Buffalo St
Cogan Station PA 17728

Call Sign: W3TO
Jack C Shaffer
223 Chaapel Mtn Rd
Cogan Station PA 17728

Call Sign: KA3JBE
Homar N Hendershot
49 Crescent Hill Rd
Cogan Station PA 17728

Call Sign: N3SZC
Melissa B Seeley

2076 Eckard Rd
Cogan Station PA 17728

Call Sign: N6TX
H Paul Shuch
121 Florence Dr
Cogan Station PA 17728

Call Sign: KC3EH
Melvin E Bennett
5065 Northway Rd
Cogan Station PA 17728

Call Sign: N3JDA
Nathan T Frymire
13 Pleasant Valley Rd
Cogan Station PA 17728

Call Sign: KE3LM
Kenneth E Horn
5747 Pleasant Valley Rd
Cogan Station PA 17728

Call Sign: KB3PEV
Michael W Rhone II
1086 Pleasent Hill Rd
Cogan Station PA 17728

Call Sign: K3NX
Stephen L Phillips
201 Reade Dr
Cogan Station PA 17728

Call Sign: W3AVK
West Branch ARA
201 Reade Dr
Cogan Station PA 17728

Call Sign: K3PFU
Robert P Eckard
592 Rt 973 E
Cogan Station PA 17728

Call Sign: N3FOS
Pamela J Hitchens

267 Sawmill Rd 22
Cogan Station PA 17728

Call Sign: W3AHS
Millionaire ARC
1876 State Rt 973 W
Cogan Station PA 17728

Call Sign: KB3LBM
Millionaire ARC
1876 State Rte 973 W
Cogan Station PA 17728

Call Sign: N3UXE
Jessica L Tobias
76 Viewpoint Rd
Cogan Station PA 17728

FCC Amateur Radio Licenses in Columbia

Call Sign: N3IKH
Teresa A Rhoads
4583 Airy View Dr
Columbia PA 17512

Call Sign: N3CRS
Scott P Rhoads
4583 Airy View Dr
Columbia PA 17512

Call Sign: K3ZEN
Brian K Miller
3947 Birchwood Ln
Columbia PA 17512

Call Sign: K3SKY
Brian K Miller
3947 Birchwood Ln
Columbia PA 17512

Call Sign: AB3HN
Brian K Miller
3947 Birchwood Ln
Columbia PA 17512

Call Sign: KB3UWP
Debra A Gingher
3948 Birchwood Ln
Columbia PA 17512

Call Sign: KB3CD
Harlan S Zimmerman
2626 Ironville Pike Rd 1
Columbia PA 17512

Call Sign: N3KYS
Jesse S Fischer
646 Manor St
Columbia PA 17512

Call Sign: KB3UVG
Robert W Wright Jr
3948 Birchwood Ln
Columbia PA 17512

Call Sign: WA8ZMI
Roger V Chastain Jr
2405 Jetty Ln
Columbia PA 175129524

Call Sign: WB2MMB
James F Muller
15 Maria Ln
Columbia PA 17512

Call Sign: N3NML
Jeffrey M Helm
1033 Central Ave
Columbia PA 17512

Call Sign: N3QZB
Carolyn S Hanusa
3654 Keen Ave
Columbia PA 17512

Call Sign: N3KKG
William J Carman
4872 Marietta Ave
Columbia PA 17512

Call Sign: N3NTM
Robert L Buzzendore Jr
1053 Central Ave
Columbia PA 17512

Call Sign: N3MPU
Thomas E Eisenberger
3657 Keen Ave
Columbia PA 17512

Call Sign: KB3BQZ
Mark D Moore
220 N 10th St
Columbia PA 17512

Call Sign: N3XPB
George F White
623 Chestnut St
Columbia PA 17512

Call Sign: KB3WKN
Kevin C Lampo
482 Lancer Dr
Columbia PA 17512

Call Sign: KB3OYT
William T Graham
228 N 2nd St
Columbia PA 17512

Call Sign: N3QFP
Parke D Dicely
148 Church St
Columbia PA 17512

Call Sign: K3LLC
Kevin C Lampo
482 Lancer Dr
Columbia PA 17512

Call Sign: KB3RSR
Edward L Montalvo
230 N 3rd St
Columbia PA 17512

Call Sign: WA3PHL
Edmond C McKenzie
1188 Habecker Rd
Columbia PA 17512

Call Sign: KA3SOM
Dale E Zimmerman
1257 Loop Rd
Columbia PA 175129631

Call Sign: KB3JXU
Daniel L Scully Sr
751 Old Chickies Hill Rd
Columbia PA 17512

Call Sign: N3UUU
Frederick J Rowe
286 Indianhead Rd
Columbia PA 17512

Call Sign: N3LOM
David L Payne Sr
1373 Malleable Rd
Columbia PA 17512

Call Sign: KB3DWH
James T Douglas Jr
86 Pine Tree Dr
Columbia PA 175129684

Call Sign: KC0GES
Denise L Mccrabb
2638 Ironville Pike
Columbia PA 17512

Call Sign: WA3YDG
Joel R Enders
194 Manor Church Rd
Columbia PA 17512

Call Sign: KB3IRV
Scott T Baer
1091 Prospect Rd
Columbia PA 17512

Call Sign: N3IOE
Charles E Hoffman
1753 Quarry Dr
Columbia PA 17512

Call Sign: KA3WHH
Scott A Rahe
660 Raintree Rd
Columbia PA 17512

Call Sign: K3HMB
P Eugene Shaiebly
1170 Ridge Ter Apt 1 A
Columbia PA 17512

Call Sign: AD3X
Harold W Hartman Jr
1371 Rock Cir Dr
Columbia PA 17512

Call Sign: WA3ZUC
Charles P Clark
625 S 14th St
Columbia PA 17512

Call Sign: N3WED
Brett W Hallacher
230 S 2nd St
Columbia PA 17512

Call Sign: N3JPF
Jason S Fisher
641 S 9th St
Columbia PA 17512

Call Sign: WB3BTH
C Rodney Burg
109 S Luther Ln
Columbia PA 17512

Call Sign: WA3PJS
Lee I Noffz
320 Sylvan Retreat Rd
Columbia PA 17512

Call Sign: N3JPC
John M Green
424 Union St
Columbia PA 17512

Call Sign: N3JPE
Andrew W Gotwols Jr
650 Walnut St
Columbia PA 17512

FCC Amateur Radio Licenses in Concord

Call Sign: KB3QEF
Christopher M Lewis
25013 Back Rd
Concord PA 17217

FCC Amateur Radio Licenses in Conemaugh

Call Sign: W3RRO
Michael Mitnik
425 Donruth Ln
Conemaugh PA 15909

FCC Amateur Radio Licenses in Conestoga

Call Sign: AF3Z
James A Goudie
335 Colemanville Church
Rd
Conestoga PA 17516

Call Sign: WA3BWM
John E McClarigan
Conestoga Blvd
Conestoga PA 175169625

Call Sign: WA2VSL
Donald W Gibb
30 Fitzkee Rd
Conestoga PA 17516

Call Sign: KB3TIU
Craig M Martelle
13 Ivy Ct
Conestoga PA 17516

Call Sign: N3WWJ
Gregory K Olena
3014 Main St
Conestoga PA 17516

Call Sign: KB3MFF
Dennis A Stewart
3237 Main St
Conestoga PA 17516

Call Sign: K3OMB
Joseph F Brackin Jr
3792 Main St
Conestoga PA 17516

Call Sign: WA3DOO
Robert H Fulton
Main St
Conestoga PA 17516

Call Sign: KB3PIH
David C Shore
32 Oak Rd
Conestoga PA 17516

Call Sign: N3DCS
David C Shore
32 Oak Rd
Conestoga PA 17516

Call Sign: KB3POW
Judy C Shore
32 Oak Rd
Conestoga PA 17516

Call Sign: AA3WL
Milton D Machalek
707 River Corner Rd
Conestoga PA 17516

Call Sign: N3BAU
David F Destafano
6995 River Rd
Conestoga PA 17516

Call Sign: ND3Y
John R Sollenberger
7368 River Rd
Conestoga PA 17516

Call Sign: W3APO
Frank H Altdoerffer II
179 Run Valley Rd
Conestoga PA 17516

Call Sign: KB3OWI
Hoyt E Roark
18 Sweetwater Dr
Conestoga PA 17516

Call Sign: N3YHN
Michael E Baker
204 Tomahawk Dr
Conestoga PA 17516

Call Sign: KA3VTS
Raymond M Bencak Jr
162 Woods Ave
Conestoga PA 17516

FCC Amateur Radio Licenses in Confluence

Call Sign: N3SQK
Julie A Custer
810 Anderson St
Confluence PA 154242408

Call Sign: KA3AHZ
Elmer E Hachman
Box 214
Confluence PA 15424

Call Sign: KA3EPD

Edna I Hachman
Box 214
Confluence PA 15424

Call Sign: K3SMT
Somerset County ARC
708 Casselman St
Confluence PA 15424

Call Sign: KC3XD
Sherman L Gary
708 Casselman St
Confluence PA 15424

Call Sign: KB3GER
Tara E Holliday
1033 Draketown Rd
Confluence PA 15424

Call Sign: W3HGT
Paul C Rakow
170 Flanigan Rd
Confluence PA 15424

Call Sign: N3UOY
Christopher J Witt
1633 Listonburg Rd
Confluence PA 15424

Call Sign: N3XMK
John R Wagner
896 Mae W Rd
Confluence PA 15424

Call Sign: KB3HQU
Bobbi S Wagner
896 Mae W Rd
Confluence PA 15424

Call Sign: K3VOO
Nancy T Hillman
1479 Mae W Rd
Confluence PA 154241905

Call Sign: W3VGF

James D Hillman
1479 Mae W Rd
Confluence PA 154241905

FCC Amateur Radio Licenses in Cornwall

Call Sign: WB3GRP
William J Biega Jr
27 Ridgeway Dr
Cornwall PA 17015

Call Sign: KB3LWH
William R Smith
Cornwall PA 17016

Call Sign: KB3EEQ
Clinton A Leroy
Cornwall PA 17016

Call Sign: AB3HX
Clinton A Leroy
Cornwall PA 17016

FCC Amateur Radio Licenses in Coudersport

Call Sign: KB3SVT
Chris L Heimel
6 Anchor Toy Ln
Coudersport PA 16915

Call Sign: KD2KB
Wayne E Stahler II
887 Black Hole Rd
Coudersport PA 16915

Call Sign: N3PC
Headwaters ARC
887 Black Hole Rd
Coudersport PA 16915

Call Sign: KB3MHK
Gail A Stahler
887 Black Hole Rd

Coudersport PA 16915

Coudersport PA 16915

Coudersport PA 16915

Call Sign: W3GSS
Gail A Stahler
887 Black Hole Rd
Coudersport PA 16915

Call Sign: N3PVI
Lonnie J Northeimer
Box 81 US Rt 6
Coudersport PA 16915

Call Sign: W2CMR
Charles M Richardson
95 Dutch Hill Rd
Coudersport PA 16915

Call Sign: WS3PC
Wayne E Stahler II
887 Black Hole Rd
Coudersport PA 16915

Call Sign: KB3DUL
Doris A Henry
1261 Cherry Springs Rd
Coudersport PA 16915

Call Sign: N2ZWG
Walter L Hinds
49 Dwight Rd
Coudersport PA 16915

Call Sign: N3JWZ
Darrel E Anthony
Box 107Aa
Coudersport PA 16915

Call Sign: KB3DUN
William B Henry
1261 Cherry Springs Rd
Coudersport PA 16915

Call Sign: KB3LSX
Robert J Weiskopff
364 E 2nd St
Coudersport PA 16915

Call Sign: AA3DT
Moises B Cruz Jr
Box 114
Coudersport PA 16915

Call Sign: N3GGC
Paul T Bednar
Cmhp Davidge St 24
Coudersport PA 16915

Call Sign: KB3AUU
Patrice S Northeimer
401 E 2nd St
Coudersport PA 16915

Call Sign: N3PVK
Ann E Long
Box 197
Coudersport PA 16915

Call Sign: KB3RGD
James P Steiner
14 Dingman Run Rd
Coudersport PA 16915

Call Sign: N2QNF
Michael Fitzpatrick
367 E 2nd St
Coudersport PA 16915

Call Sign: N3PTL
Vito A Lanzillo Jr
Box 2094
Coudersport PA 16915

Call Sign: KB3RGL
Rebecca L Steiner
14 Dingman Run Rd
Coudersport PA 16915

Call Sign: K3FHC
James T Douglas Sr
264 Green Hill Rd
Coudersport PA 16915

Call Sign: N2CSZ
Misty L Reed
Box 35A
Coudersport PA 16915

Call Sign: KB3RGB
Diana L Guilfoy
15 Dry Run Rd
Coudersport PA 16915

Call Sign: KB3VCN
Clark L Lerch
32 Hummingbird Rd
Coudersport PA 16915

Call Sign: W3ZY
Mark E Lawyer
Box 4472
Coudersport PA 16915

Call Sign: KB3WAT
Gregory L Dicesare
15 Dry Run Rd
Coudersport PA 16915

Call Sign: N3VHB
Roderick G Kinley Jr
116 Kinley Ln
Coudersport PA 16915

Call Sign: WB3LGS
Clair I Lawyer
Box 4472

Call Sign: WA3HLC
Thomas W Guilfoy
15 Dry Run Rd

Call Sign: KB3NPY
Martin E Wright
15 Middle Ln

Coudersport PA 16915

Call Sign: KB3GQL
Gayle N Anthony
13 Mockingbird Ln
Coudersport PA 16915

Call Sign: N3PVJ
Derek E Anthony
13 Mockingbird Ln
Coudersport PA 16915

Call Sign: N3BUM
Alonzo W Bunch
59 Morley Dr
Coudersport PA 16915

Call Sign: KB3CCI
Headwaters ARC
6 N East St
Coudersport PA 16915

Call Sign: KB3DUJ
Marjorie E Heimel
6 N East St
Coudersport PA 16915

Call Sign: KB3HWS
J Fred Fish
411 N East St
Coudersport PA 16915

Call Sign: W3LGL
Edwin H Scheid
692 N Hollow Rd
Coudersport PA 16915

Call Sign: AG3Z
Leo J Szczesny
705 N Hollow Rd
Coudersport PA 16915

Call Sign: K3WF
Walter R Fleet
405 N West St

Coudersport PA 16915

Call Sign: K3CC
Gilbert H Kauffman
121 Niles Hill Rd
Coudersport PA 16915

Call Sign: W2IMK
James D Centanni
257 Niles Hill Rd
Coudersport PA
169157940

Call Sign: KB3GQP
Joseph E Russell
143 Roberts Rd
Coudersport PA 16915

Call Sign: KB3VFD
Peter J Tremblay
608 S East St
Coudersport PA 16915

Call Sign: N3INR
Carl G Sprouse Jr
801 S Main St
Coudersport PA 16915

Call Sign: KB3GQQ
James Shaffer
1664 Sr 49 E
Coudersport PA 16915

Call Sign: KB3JSP
James J Hayes
34 Tennessee Ave
Coudersport PA
169158267

Call Sign: K3MLW
Mark L Williams
8 Town Line Rd Apt 7
Coudersport PA 16915

Call Sign: K3MW

Martin D Weiss
380 Vader Hill Rd
Coudersport PA 16915

Call Sign: KB3RFZ
Edward A Rinehults
601 Vine St
Coudersport PA 16915

Call Sign: KB3GQR
Althea L Matusiak
Coudersport PA 16915

Call Sign: KB3HCB
Brad A Moore
Coudersport PA 16915

FCC Amateur Radio Licenses in Covington

Call Sign: N3QNK
Nathan A Smith
Box 141A
Covington PA 16917

Call Sign: WB3GQH
Sanford E Livermore
Box 148
Covington PA 16917

Call Sign: N3VKL
Kelly J Copley II
Box 200 C
Covington PA 16917

Call Sign: NQ3R
Wilbur G Rockwell
Box 84
Covington PA 16917

Call Sign: N3BWB
H Lee Hoar
3734 Cherry Flats Rd
Covington PA 169179757

Call Sign: N3UPI
Mary E Hoar
3734 Cherry Flats Rd
Covington PA 169179757

FCC Amateur Radio Licenses in Cresson

Call Sign: KB3RJC
Daniel T Eberhart
715 5th St
Cresson PA 16630

Call Sign: N3XVU
Michael D Noland
46 Aspen Ct
Cresson PA 16630

Call Sign: N3DWM
Gregory P Norris
26 Country Club Rd
Cresson PA 16630

Call Sign: WA3ELK
Harry J Prosser Jr
228 Jackson Ave
Cresson PA 16630

Call Sign: W8CSC
Karl S Lear
1008 Old Coach Rd
Cresson PA 16630

Call Sign: K3JN
Joseph A Norris
1011 Powell Ave
Cresson PA 166301451

Call Sign: N3JXX
Rose M Norris
1011 Powell Ave
Cresson PA 166301451

Call Sign: K3RMN
Rose M Norris

1011 Powell Ave
Cresson PA 166301451

Call Sign: N3BZT
Joseph A Norris Jr
Cresson PA 16630

FCC Amateur Radio Licenses in Crystal Spring

Call Sign: W3EWO
Howard J Elmore
Box 101
Crystal Spring PA 15536

FCC Amateur Radio Licenses in Curwensville

Call Sign: K3LAY
Burton M Norris
1421 Bloomington Ave Ext
Curwensville PA 16833

Call Sign: W8MCT
Walter V Robinson
Box 536
Curwensville PA 16833

Call Sign: K3LTP
Ronald W Kuhn
Box 97 119Griffith Ave
Curwensville PA 16833

Call Sign: KD3FQ
Richard J Marton
607 Center St
Curwensville PA 16833

Call Sign: KE4BIN
Edwin G McCulley
204 Filbert St
Curwensville PA 16833

Call Sign: KB3GZU
Margaret R Mcculley
204 Filbert St
Curwensville PA 16833

Call Sign: K3BTR
John J Arnold Sr
328 High
Curwensville PA 16833

Call Sign: KB3EUO
Mary B Barr
855 Laurel Run Rd
Curwensville PA 16833

Call Sign: KB3VWX
Edward L Neeper Jr
241 McLaughlin St
Curwensville PA 16833

Call Sign: KC2RHQ
Lorie J Neeper
241 McLaughlin St
Curwensville PA 16833

Call Sign: N3YYY
Scott C Rummings
417 Meadow St 2
Curwensville PA 16833

Call Sign: W3EOD
Scott C Rummings
417 Meadow St 2
Curwensville PA 16833

Call Sign: KD3OI
Stephen D Shields
306 Park Ave Ext
Curwensville PA 16833

Call Sign: N3HJP
Laurel A Shields
306 Park Ave Ext
Curwensville PA 16833

Call Sign: KB3EDJ
Timothy A Shields
306 Park Ave Ext
Curwensville PA 16883

Call Sign: N3THB
Jared L Fink
12891 Tyrone Pike
Curwensville PA 16833

Call Sign: KB3YJM
Ian D Gerard
425 Walnut St 2
Curwensville PA 16833

Call Sign: N3SYC
Kenneth G Maines
Curwensville PA 16833

FCC Amateur Radio Licenses in Custer City

Call Sign: N3BKG
Max C Douthit
Custer City PA 16725

Call Sign: KB3ADG
James W Johnson Sr
Custer City PA 16725

Call Sign: KB3AEZ
James W Johnson Jr
Custer City PA 16725

FCC Amateur Radio Licenses in Cyclone

Call Sign: NU3K
Kenneth G Geiser
Box 96
Cyclone PA 16726

Call Sign: N3IMP
Laura A Geiser
11077 Rt 59

Cyclone PA 16726

Call Sign: N3NRL
Richard H Rabineau
Cyclone PA 16726

FCC Amateur Radio Licenses in Daisytown

Call Sign: KB3FZS
Carl R Lancaster
319 Pike Run Dr
Daisytown PA 15427

Call Sign: KD3XY
Stanley J Tyrpin
27 S California Dr
Daisytown PA 15427

FCC Amateur Radio Licenses in Dallastown

Call Sign: KK3Y
David L Gutshall
154 April Ln
Dallastown PA 17313

Call Sign: KB3PIP
Joshua J Zorbaugh
107 Blymire Rd
Dallastown PA 17313

Call Sign: N3SWS
Joanne G Gotwalt
609 Colonial Dr
Dallastown PA 17313

Call Sign: N3SWU
Clyde L Gotwalt
609 Colonial Dr
Dallastown PA 17313

Call Sign: KB3HAY
Steven P Weirich
238 E Cherry Ln Rear

Dallastown PA 17313

Call Sign: WA3HDQ
Michael D Carbaugh
13 E Frederick St
Dallastown PA 17313

Call Sign: K3OCW
Michael D Carbaugh
13 E Frederick St
Dallastown PA 17313

Call Sign: KA3OUF
Sandra L Clippinger
11 E Gay St
Dallastown PA 17313

Call Sign: K3IMR
Richard D Snyder
195 E King St
Dallastown PA 17313

Call Sign: N3GJW
Thomas W Emig
77 E Main St
Dallastown PA 17313

Call Sign: KB3SNR
Melissa M Zarfos
544 E Main St
Dallastown PA 17313

Call Sign: KB3SNP
Jeffery A Zarfos
544 E Main St
Dallastown PA 17313

Call Sign: K3GVE
Andrew J Tempel
709 E Main St
Dallastown PA 17313

Call Sign: KB3VPV
David M Herr
349 Frederick Dr

Dallastown PA 17313

Dallastown PA 17313

Dallastown PA 17313

Call Sign: W3CRL
Guy L Clippinger
11 Gay St
Dallastown PA 17313

Call Sign: W3SUD
Shawn M Cooper
360 Pulaski Pl
Dallastown PA 17313

Call Sign: K3AVF
Paul W Miller
100 W Queen St
Dallastown PA 17313

Call Sign: KB3DVW
Steven A Thornsberry
559 Green Meadows Dr
Dallastown PA 17313

Call Sign: N3DUX
Larry R Reiber
458 Ridgeford Rd
Dallastown PA 17313

Call Sign: K3GJO
Leonard Shuster Jr
225 Leaderton Dr
Dallastown PA 17313

Call Sign: WA3UDA
Johnny J Jones Sr
135 S Pleasant Ave
Dallastown PA 17313

Call Sign: WB3FHU
David A Newman
Box 528
Dalmatia PA 17017

Call Sign: KB3WJY
Donald G Mueller Jr
541 Lions Dr
Dallastown PA 17313

Call Sign: KB3FFG
Carl H Castell Jr
27 S Walnut St
Dallastown PA 17313

Call Sign: N3YHO
Paul C Nell Jr
1462 Deiblers Gap Rd
Dalmatia PA 17017

Call Sign: KB3VVI
Damon A Suskie
140 N Pleasant Ave
Dallastown PA 17313

Call Sign: KA3FOO
Charles J Maguire III
769 St Johns Pl
Dallastown PA 17313

Call Sign: KB3LHB
Todd M Mace
117 Susanna St
Dalmatia PA 17017

Call Sign: KB3VQR
Thanos Kanellakos
488 N Walnut St
Dallastown PA 17313

Call Sign: KA3CCB
George A Jamison
2857 Sunset Dr
Dallastown PA 17313

Call Sign: K3JYU
Charles T Reitz
Dalmatia PA 170170220

Call Sign: KG4CXW
Eric F Haywood Sr
113 Oak Ridge Ln
Dallastown PA 17313

Call Sign: KA4RTE
Kenneth D Barnhart
212 Troy Rd
Dallastown PA 17313

Call Sign: KA3TWD
Mark J Seibel
110 10th St
Danville PA 17821

Call Sign: KG4IYV
Donna W Haywood
113 Oak Ridge Ln
Dallastown PA 17313

Call Sign: KB3VVK
Bernell L Kohler
454 W Main St
Dallastown PA 17313

Call Sign: N3TBE
Joseph E Hauer
11 2nd St
Danville PA 17821

Call Sign: KB3IMC
Shawn M Cooper
360 Pulaski Pl

Call Sign: KB3KTR
Steven E Olphin
218 W Maple St

Call Sign: N3MGW
Miles W Bowen
800 4th St RR6

Danville PA 17821

Danville PA 17821

Danville PA 17821

Call Sign: WA3ETP
Nelson D Young
101 Ardmoor Ave
Danville PA 17821

Call Sign: WA3JRL
Ruth L Kagey
Box 277
Danville PA 17821

Call Sign: N3XXF
Edward F Pisarski
35 Cherokee Rd
Danville PA 17821

Call Sign: KA3QVH
Bruce L Krebs
102 Ardmoor Ave
Danville PA 17821

Call Sign: N3JYN
Dennis A Leighow
Box 363
Danville PA 17821

Call Sign: KB3GUG
Nolan J Dwyer
104 Cherokee Rd
Danville PA 17821

Call Sign: KA3QGQ
William J Ashman
23 Ash St
Danville PA 17821

Call Sign: KA3SJE
Brian R Achy
Box 688
Danville PA 17821

Call Sign: N3PJS
Frederick J Mahoney
18 Cherry St
Danville PA 17821

Call Sign: N3BVV
Willis C Manges Jr
505 Ave B
Danville PA 17821

Call Sign: KB3DWT
Paul E McWilliams
Box 8
Danville PA 178218703

Call Sign: N3NSO
Harry A Linker
216 Cherry St
Danville PA 17821

Call Sign: KA1OON
Lance E Kisby
989 Ave F
Danville PA 17821

Call Sign: N3ZIT
Louis R Mayan
36 Bull Run Rd
Danville PA 17821

Call Sign: N3ENC
William R Betz
4 Cricket Ln
Danville PA 17821

Call Sign: W3GY
John J McCann
11 Baldtop Hts
Danville PA 17821

Call Sign: KB3PWE
David M Torrey
205 Cameltown Hill Rd
Danville PA 17821

Call Sign: AB3MY
Lucy A Tence Corbin
114 Degreen Rd
Danville PA 17821

Call Sign: KB3SYG
Donald E Mausteller
205 Baldtop Rd
Danville PA 17821

Call Sign: KA3GLP
David O Carew
357 Cameltown Hill Rd
Danville PA 17821

Call Sign: N3PND
Bradford G Bason
12 Delwood Dr
Danville PA 17821

Call Sign: K3LRD
Donald E Mausteller
205 Baldtop Rd
Danville PA 17821

Call Sign: KB3GUB
John F Moyer Jr
29 Cashner Rd
Danville PA 17821

Call Sign: N3QWN
Scott A Davis
315 E Front St
Danville PA 17821

Call Sign: W3KRQ
James A Dewald Sr
Box 131

Call Sign: W1TAP
Richard M Phillip
1 Catherine Dr

Call Sign: N3XXI
Calvin A Nichols Jr
943 E Market St

Danville PA 17821

Call Sign: KB3LSW
Michelle L Long
203 E Mohoning St
Danville PA 17821

Call Sign: K3AKZ
Henry D Dobson
172 Frosty Valley Rd
Danville PA 17821

Call Sign: KB3COG
James R Raup II
104 Grand St
Danville PA 17821

Call Sign: WB2VFX
William C Godfrey
119 Grand St
Danville PA 178212123

Call Sign: WB8ARW
Melvin L Tracy
7 Grotto Dr
Danville PA 17821

Call Sign: N3CDL
Edward S Sudo
140 Hess Hill Rd
Danville PA 17821

Call Sign: N3JIX
William L Barnes
4 Laurel Ln
Danville PA 178218554

Call Sign: WA3LCE
Edward G Pulsifer
100 Liberty Valley Rd
Danville PA 17821

Call Sign: N3XJZ
John F Moyer
520 Liberty Valley Rd

Danville PA 17821

Call Sign: K3EGK
John E Kurtinecz Sr
8 Majestic Dr
Danville PA 17821

Call Sign: WA3EWO
John H Heller
21 Maple Ave
Danville PA 17821

Call Sign: W3HXL
Oscar A Hahn
204 Maple St
Danville PA 17821

Call Sign: WB3IPR
Ronald Smeltzer
4 Meadow Ave
Danville PA 17821

Call Sign: KB3WRP
Krimzen Rose S Haugen
61 Meadow Ln
Danville PA 17821

Call Sign: KB3WRR
Thorsen W Haugen
61 Meadow Ln
Danville PA 17821

Call Sign: KA3RZE
Keith E Brown
75 Mexico Rd
Danville PA 17821

Call Sign: KB3CB
Keith E Brown
75 Mexico Rd
Danville PA 17821

Call Sign: KB3EOV
Andrew C Poler
8 Millwood Dr

Danville PA 17821

Call Sign: KB3FHU
S Mark Poler
8 Millwood Dr
Danville PA 178218459

Call Sign: N3CNR
Stephen A Kudrick
90 Mooresburg Rd
Danville PA 17821

Call Sign: N4CXC
Paul J Moser
151 Moser Rd
Danville PA 178217713

Call Sign: KB3FGR
William J Green
203 N Crestwood Dr
Danville PA 17821

Call Sign: KB3YKZ
Brandon J Walls
205 N Crestwood Dr
Danville PA 17821

Call Sign: KE3NJ
David A Letterman
115 Nare Hood Rd
Danville PA 178216843

Call Sign: KB3GNZ
Richard H Hoover
20 Norman Rd
Danville PA 17821

Call Sign: N3ADM
Willard A Dietz
15 Patton Rd
Danville PA 178218724

Call Sign: W3SLK
Michael D Sawyer
321 Pine Swamp Rd

Danville PA 17821

Call Sign: AA3HV
Richard R Hess
439 Ppl Rd
Danville PA 17821

Call Sign: K3SDR
David M Litchard
495 Ppl Rd
Danville PA 17821

Call Sign: KB3FGQ
Daniel W Green
204 Railroad St
Danville PA 17821

Call Sign: KB3OZE
Tyler E Patterson
1208 Red Ln
Danville PA 17821

Call Sign: KB3LVV
James G Gallagher
1407 Red Ln
Danville PA 178218467

Call Sign: N3PWL
Gina M Brown
1502 Ridgevie W Lawn
Danville PA 17821

Call Sign: N3VDQ
Jeffrey S Von Blohn
1802 River Dr
Danville PA 17821

Call Sign: N3XJX
John J Lamb
6 Rushtown Rd
Danville PA 17821

Call Sign: WA3UVP
Joseph J Dozpat III
436 Rustown Rd

Danville PA 17821

Call Sign: N3TQZ
Daniel F Jenkins
42 Steltz Rd
Danville PA 17821

Call Sign: KB3GOA
Dean E McCahan
115 Sunbury Rd
Danville PA 17821

Call Sign: K3MBZ
Dean E McCahan
115 Sunbury Rd
Danville PA 17821

Call Sign: WA3GQA
Stephen M Zappe
3051 Sunbury Rd
Danville PA 17821

Call Sign: WA3OLW
John F Wolfe
86 Trump Rd
Danville PA 17821

Call Sign: N3KFI
Goven H Saienni
201 Upper St
Danville PA 178218499

Call Sign: N3ZTT
Alex R Frew
35 Valley View
Danville PA 17821

Call Sign: WA2JOC
William W Dickerson
95 Valley View Rd
Danville PA 17821

Call Sign: N3ZDD
Brandon S Harter
108 Valley View Rd

Danville PA 17821

Call Sign: KD3RN
Ray A Krohn
400 Villa St
Danville PA 17821

Call Sign: K3IBM
John R Haines Sr
219 Vine
Danville PA 17821

Call Sign: N3EUM
John V McCormick
26 Vine St
Danville PA 17821

Call Sign: W3YMY
Daniel J Lyons
111 W Mahoning St
Danville PA 17821

Call Sign: KB3LGY
Terry A Long
202 Woodside Dr
Danville PA 17821

Call Sign: WA3YJN
Robert L Honicker
Danville PA 17821

Call Sign: KB3EXE
Jeffrey W Gum
Danville PA 17821

**FCC Amateur Radio
Licenses in Dauphin**

Call Sign: KB3MIM
Kristin A Jessop
31 Affection Rd
Dauphin PA 17018

Call Sign: KB3PBD
Russell C Jessop

31 Affection Rd
Dauphin PA 17018

Call Sign: KB3MIL
Ryan J Jessop
31 Affection Rd
Dauphin PA 17018

Call Sign: W3CAS
Geoffrey A Corson
881 Allegheny St
Dauphin PA 17018

Call Sign: KB3MXI
Jennifer R Balthaser
1915 Clarks Valley Rd
Dauphin PA 17018

Call Sign: WA3IHT
Phillip C Ranck
709 Erie St
Dauphin PA 17018

Call Sign: N3BVS
Clyde B Fry Jr
1621 Fulton Rd
Dauphin PA 17018

Call Sign: KB3HCW
Kenneth L Hall
1211 Narrow Ln
Dauphin PA 17018

Call Sign: W3KLH
Kenneth L Hall
1211 Narrow Ln
Dauphin PA 17018

Call Sign: W3ARY
Charles E Ross III
1701 Pine Ln
Dauphin PA 17018

Call Sign: KB3MTO
Alan W Mertz

1205 Red Hill Rd
Dauphin PA 17018

Call Sign: KB3LRU
Alyssa M Ryan
1604 Red Hill Rd
Dauphin PA 17018

Call Sign: KC4SHK
John T Shingara II
305 Riverview Ter
Dauphin PA 17018

Call Sign: WB3HXH
Wilbert E Lawrence
415 Riverview Ter
Dauphin PA 170189103

Call Sign: N3TKQ
Alan B Corson
781 Rt 322
Dauphin PA 17018

Call Sign: N3YLD
Thomas R Kiger
700 S Maple Dr
Dauphin PA 17018

Call Sign: KA3DGW
Richard J Shaver
1301 Stone Glen Rd
Dauphin PA 17018

Call Sign: N3NAZ
Stephen L Plasic
1450 Stone Glen Rd
Dauphin PA 17018

Call Sign: KB3VNN
Richard L Smith Jr
1840 Stoney Creek Rd
Dauphin PA 17018

Call Sign: KB3VNM
Zachary M Smith

1840 Stoney Creek Rd
Dauphin PA 17018

Call Sign: W3KNK
Sherwood W Doughman
312 Vesta Dr
Dauphin PA 17018

Call Sign: K3SGE
Harvey E Knupp
Dauphin PA 17018

Call Sign: N3QWO
John H Koppenheffer
Dauphin PA 17018

**FCC Amateur Radio
Licenses in Davidsville**

Call Sign: K3BSY
John D Seibert
2863 Carpenter Park Rd
Davidsville PA 15928

Call Sign: KB3BV
Lanny L Vrooman
2979 Carpenters Park Rd
Davidsville PA 159289206

Call Sign: KB3JOC
Daniel Z Kemp
305 Crestview Dr
Davidsville PA 15928

Call Sign: WB3FBR
Wayne A Kaufman
110 Pine St
Davidsville PA 15928

Call Sign: W3CTR
Donald W Rayner
1000 Vista Dr Apt 908
Davidsville PA 15928

Call Sign: WB3FBO

Neil Kaufman
106 W Campus Ave
Davidsville PA 15928

Call Sign: N3ZED
Robert G Berkebile
Davidsville PA 15928

**FCC Amateur Radio
Licenses in Delta**

Call Sign: W3FJD
Chip Diamond
141 Ailes Rd
Delta PA 17314

Call Sign: N3MSP
Harold C Thomas
13 Birchwood Dr
Delta PA 17314

Call Sign: N3PAL
Helen H Humphrey
28 Birchwood Dr
Delta PA 17314

Call Sign: KA3WVK
Gary W Feveryear
Box 176B
Delta PA 17314

Call Sign: N3RMJ
John D Arrigo
Box 236A2
Delta PA 17314

Call Sign: KA3SUO
Martin R Hess
Box 37
Delta PA 17314

Call Sign: N3UEL
Robert L Ensley
101 Broad St
Delta PA 17314

Call Sign: WB3KDO
Kennard L Loignon
3076 Bryansville Rd
Delta PA 17314

Call Sign: KB3IJZ
James J Milwid
4541 Delta Rd
Delta PA 17314

Call Sign: KB3KDT
C Glenn Feveryear
701 Main St
Delta PA 173140305

Call Sign: WB3CGD
James W Hoffman
835 Main St
Delta PA 17314

Call Sign: KB3CQE
Susan T Agne
48 Oakwood Dr
Delta PA 17314

Call Sign: N3LTS
Melvyn L Agne
48 Oakwood Dr
Delta PA 17314

Call Sign: KB3LHP
Graham P Agne
48 Oakwood Dr
Delta PA 17314

Call Sign: KB3LHQ
Matthias Agne
48 Oakwood Dr
Delta PA 17314

Call Sign: KB3ADP
James V Presti
687 Pikes Peak Rd
Delta PA 17314

Call Sign: W4JVP
James V Presti
687 Pikes Peak Rd
Delta PA 17314

Call Sign: WA3YLX
Lorenzo Gilchriest Dr
55 Pond Rd
Delta PA 17314

Call Sign: N3NHI
Aloysius B Yucis
38 Poplar Dr
Delta PA 173149398

Call Sign: AG3D
Irwin K Welker
88 Poplar View Rd
Delta PA 17314

Call Sign: N3CXU
Ronald S Maddox
516 River Rd
Delta PA 17314

Call Sign: N3CNJ
David J Hahn
69 Roycroft Ln
Delta PA 17314

Call Sign: KB3HVO
Bruce H Simpson
24 S White Pine Trl
Delta PA 17314

Call Sign: AB3AY
Bruce H Simpson
24 S White Pine Trl
Delta PA 17314

Call Sign: K3HY
Bruce H Simpson
34 S White Pine Trl
Delta PA 17314

Call Sign: KB3JVJ
Virginia F Simpson
34 S White Pine Trl
Delta PA 17314

Call Sign: KA3SGT
David L Gosman
8 Skyview Rd
Delta PA 17314

Call Sign: KA3RVS
Donald E Foster
35 Skyview Rd
Delta PA 17314

Call Sign: WB3EFP
Leonard W Walinski
317 Slab Rd
Delta PA 17314

Call Sign: WA3YPB
Howard E Houser
420 Slab Rd
Delta PA 17314

Call Sign: N3ISZ
Arthur L Wilson
Delta PA 17314

**FCC Amateur Radio
Licenses in Denver**

Call Sign: KA3SPU
Larry P Everhart
Box 82
Denver PA 17517

Call Sign: KD3KL
Edward L Stork
7 Burkey Dr
Denver PA 17517

Call Sign: KA3ENP
Bruce F Barr

148 Country Dr
Denver PA 17517

Call Sign: N3SWG
Richard L Steffy
1037 Dry Tavern Rd
Denver PA 17517

Call Sign: N3DCU
Bruce A Kaminski
133 E Lancaster Ave
Denver PA 17517

Call Sign: WA3OHX
Bruce A Kaminski
133 E Lancaster Ave
Denver PA 17517

Call Sign: N2AQJ
Edward C Morgan
533 Fivepointville Rd
Denver PA 17517

Call Sign: K3QJ
Edward C Morgan
533 Fivepointville Rd
Denver PA 17517

Call Sign: KB3JWE
Kevin J Fleming
10 Garvin Rd
Denver PA 17517

Call Sign: KB3JWD
Susan E Fleming
10 Garvin Rd
Denver PA 17517

Call Sign: N3JHQ
Marlin W Sensenig
1380 Girl Scout Rd
Denver PA 17517

Call Sign: W3LPA
John S Lesmeister

1700 Girl Scout Rd
Denver PA 175170098

Call Sign: K3LPA
Karen H Lesmeister
1700 Girl Scout Rd
Denver PA 175170098

Call Sign: KB3QXU
Minh Nhut H Nguyen
212 Hawthorne Dr
Denver PA 17517

Call Sign: KA3ZJF
Carol L Geiger
6 Heron Dr
Denver PA 17517

Call Sign: N3TBU
Robert W Geiger
6 Heron Dr
Denver PA 17517

Call Sign: KB3AZA
Dave O Betz
26 Heron Dr
Denver PA 17517

Call Sign: N3JYD
Brian S Auker
306 Hill Rd
Denver PA 17517

Call Sign: K3BO
Barry L Halterman
1040 Holly Ln
Denver PA 17517

Call Sign: KA3TCQ
John E Coldren
1328 Horning Rd
Denver PA 17517

Call Sign: KA3TCF
Brenda J Megivern

1960 Last Run Dr
Denver PA 17517

Call Sign: N3HUC
Daniel G Megivern
1960 Last Run Dr
Denver PA 17517

Call Sign: N3FBM
Thomas D Pierce
4 Linda Ln
Denver PA 17517

Call Sign: W3DIN
Melvin L Hall
121 Millstone Dr
Denver PA 175179663

Call Sign: N3VNE
Christopher L Krafft
28 Muddy Creek Church
Rd
Denver PA 17517

Call Sign: KB3HCF
Jason E Motter
337 N 7th St
Denver PA 17517

Call Sign: KB3VPG
Daniel L Stingel
190 N Muddy Creek Rd
Denver PA 17517

Call Sign: N3VLV
Daniel L Stingel
190 N Muddy Creek Rd
Denver PA 17517

Call Sign: K3YTQ
Merrill F Arbogast
732 Reinholds Rd
Denver PA 175179170

Call Sign: KB3OFC

James M Taylor
101 S 4th St
Denver PA 17517

Call Sign: W3XP
Thomas A Youngberg
270 S Windy Mansion Rd
Denver PA 17517

Call Sign: N3ZQQ
Earl W Potts
900 Smokestown Rd
Denver PA 175178761

Call Sign: AE3P
Earl W Potts
900 Smokestown Rd
Denver PA 175178761

Call Sign: KB3BRX
Kelvin R Martin
95 Sportsman Rd
Denver PA 17517

Call Sign: KB3CKK
Marlene M Rissler
229 Spruce St
Denver PA 17517

Call Sign: N3MKN
James R Rissler
229 Spruce St
Denver PA 17517

Call Sign: KB3AJJ
Bruce F Bobiner
624 Walnut St
Denver PA 17517

Call Sign: N3WCV
Douglas E Heilman Jr
505 Weaver Rd
Denver PA 17517

Call Sign: K3DEH

Douglas E Heilman Jr
505 Weaver Rd
Denver PA 17517

Call Sign: WJ3W
Douglas E Heilman Sr
505 Weaver Rd
Denver PA 17517

Call Sign: KB3UAE
Derek E Heilman
505 Weaver Rd
Denver PA 17517

Call Sign: W3DEH
Derek E Heilman
505 Weaver Rd
Denver PA 17517

Call Sign: K3NBX
Richard S Getz
105 Wollups Hill Rd
Denver PA 17517

Call Sign: N3ZAA
Leonard E Swanger
1394 Woodland Cir
Denver PA 17517

Call Sign: N3TBI
Kerry L Brubaker
1269 Woodlyn Dr
Denver PA 17517

Call Sign: KB3GYY
Elmer G Haines
Denver PA 175170236

**FCC Amateur Radio
Licenses in Derrick City**

Call Sign: N3XQE
David M Rosswog
46 Hall Rd
Derrick City PA 16727

Call Sign: KB3GGP
Christopher S Mincemover
170 Olean Rd
Derrick City PA 16727

Call Sign: KA3WLS
Judith E Cabisca
Derrick City PA 16727

**FCC Amateur Radio
Licenses in Dillsburg**

Call Sign: WB3EHJ
Michael Koczwara
16 Ashley Dr
Dillsburg PA 17019

Call Sign: KB3BQK
Terry H Sharp
54 Aspen Rd
Dillsburg PA 17019

Call Sign: N3UZR
David G Roof
21 Audubon Pk
Dillsburg PA 17019

Call Sign: KA3YMP
Teresa S Diez
829 Baltimore Rd
Dillsburg PA 17019

Call Sign: N3XNW
Daniel S Beaver
18 Beechwood Dr
Dillsburg PA 17019

Call Sign: KB3QDQ
Shane T Seymore
120 Capitol Hill Rd
Dillsburg PA 17019

Call Sign: KB3AYZ
Nathan L Hoover

631 Capitol Hill Rd
Dillsburg PA 17019

Call Sign: N3QKY
Wendell L Hoover
631 Capitol Hill Rd
Dillsburg PA 17019

Call Sign: K4TIE
Earl V Higgins
Capitol Hill Rd
Dillsburg PA 17019

Call Sign: KB3IWZ
Sean P Mccormick
41 Central View Rd
Dillsburg PA 17019

Call Sign: N3RPL
William E OBerry
126 Cherry Ln
Dillsburg PA 17019

Call Sign: N3YAB
Debra E OBerry
126 Cherry Ln
Dillsburg PA 17019

Call Sign: N3YAM
James E OBerry
126 Cherry Ln
Dillsburg PA 17019

Call Sign: WA3QYY
James A Schaeffer
70 E Barrens Valley Rd
Dillsburg PA 170199635

Call Sign: KA3VCZ
Henry L Sollenberger
21 E Siddonsburg Rd
Dillsburg PA 17019

Call Sign: KB3OZL
Courtney N Dentler

1120 Fickes Rd
Dillsburg PA 17019

Call Sign: KB3LRL
Charles R Moore III
410 Franklin Church Rd
Dillsburg PA 17019

Call Sign: KA3PIN
Robert G Bagian
555 Garrett Rd
Dillsburg PA 17019

Call Sign: N3NZG
Matthew J Sanders
206 Gettysburg St
Dillsburg PA 17019

Call Sign: KB3NLI
Benjamin A Mumma
135 Gilbert Rd
Dillsburg PA 17019

Call Sign: KB3LRP
Daniel D Nicholson
304 Gilbert Rd
Dillsburg PA 17019

Call Sign: W3RY
David G Kratzer
3 Hall Dr
Dillsburg PA 17019

Call Sign: KB3RZP
Thomas Herstek
5 Hickory Rd
Dillsburg PA 17019

Call Sign: KA3ZNP
Edward R Cole
608 Hillcrest Dr
Dillsburg PA 17019

Call Sign: KA3ZUM
Rodney D Morgan

20 Junction Rd
Dillsburg PA 17019

Call Sign: N3TMT
Sharon E Morgan
20 Junction Rd
Dillsburg PA 170199432

Call Sign: KB3QXG
Nathan E Houck
159 Locust Grove Rd
Dillsburg PA 17019

Call Sign: KB3PO
John F Rogers
103 Locust Way
Dillsburg PA 17019

Call Sign: N3XIF
Dale E Brubaker
105 Locust Way
Dillsburg PA 17019

Call Sign: KA3YQD
J Augustus Myers
153 Logan Rd
Dillsburg PA 17019

Call Sign: KB3WIJ
Robert E Pomeroy
191 Lost Hollow Rd
Dillsburg PA 17019

Call Sign: NV3U
John S Transue Sr
106 Maple St
Dillsburg PA 17019

Call Sign: KB3MWY
Nicholas R Pease
122 Martel Cir
Dillsburg PA 17019

Call Sign: KB3RZT
Caela D Millar

149 Martel Cir
Dillsburg PA 17019

Call Sign: KB3MXD
Kevin J Smith
176 Martel Cir
Dillsburg PA 17019

Call Sign: KB3VVG
Robert L Guyer II
12 Mary Dr
Dillsburg PA 17019

Call Sign: KB3PAB
Caitlin E Laughlin
9 Montego Ct
Dillsburg PA 17019

Call Sign: N3GYO
Francis W Clarke
Mountain Rd
Dillsburg PA 17019

Call Sign: KB3SHQ
Erin T Guty
10 N Fileys Rd
Dillsburg PA 17019

Call Sign: N3UHF
William E Black Jr
493 N US Hwy 15
Dillsburg PA 17019

Call Sign: WA1HOL
Andrew J Forsyth
5 Northern Dancer Dr
Dillsburg PA 17019

Call Sign: AF3I
Andrew J Forsyth
5 Northern Dancer Dr
Dillsburg PA 17019

Call Sign: KB3MWD
Roxanne N Gieda

8 Northern Dancer Dr
Dillsburg PA 17019

Call Sign: N3WWF
Larry R Harbold
153 Old Cabin Hollow Rd
Dillsburg PA 17019

Call Sign: N3URG
Donald E Bowers
216 Old York Rd
Dillsburg PA 17019

Call Sign: KB3KNR
Gerald D Follett Jr
230 Poplar Rd
Dillsburg PA 17019

Call Sign: N3ESG
Linda A Amos
133 Quail Dr
Dillsburg PA 17019

Call Sign: KB3PHR
Ronald E Martin
708 Range End Rd
Dillsburg PA 17019

Call Sign: N3WWI
John O Hoffman
744 Range End Rd
Dillsburg PA 17019

Call Sign: KB3LSA
Stephen T Streck
4 Ruffian Cir
Dillsburg PA 17019

Call Sign: KB3LRD
Gabriella E Marchi
109 S 2nd St
Dillsburg PA 17019

Call Sign: KB3NBT
Anthony M Maro

11 S 3rd St
Dillsburg PA 17019

Call Sign: KE4UIS
Gary S Large
29 S Alydar Blvd
Dillsburg PA 17019

Call Sign: N3XNV
Conrad A Weiser
162 S Baltimore St
Dillsburg PA 17019

Call Sign: W3BJG
G David Germeyer
306 S Baltimore St
Dillsburg PA 17019

Call Sign: N3LKI
Glenn Hughes II
514 S Baltimore St
Dillsburg PA 17019

Call Sign: KB3VJP
Jeffery E Wright
721 S Baltimore St
Dillsburg PA 17019

Call Sign: N3XIG
Laurin E Fleming
928 S Mountain Rd
Dillsburg PA 17019

Call Sign: KA3FVJ
David P Belsky
15 S Seasons Dr
Dillsburg PA 17019

Call Sign: KB3KRD
Krista M Voggenreiter
850 S York Rd
Dillsburg PA 17019

Call Sign: W3BQA
Charles T Vogelsong

114 Sawmill Rd
Dillsburg PA 17019

Call Sign: N3TAP
Lon T Danley
227 Scotch Pine Rd
Dillsburg PA 17019

Call Sign: AA3JV
Craig M Martek
50 Spring Dr Rd
Dillsburg PA 17019

Call Sign: KB3SSU
Christopher B Wyman
215 Stone Head Rd
Dillsburg PA 17019

Call Sign: KB3EWJ
Robert S Getty III
17 Summit Dr
Dillsburg PA 17019

Call Sign: N3XTZ
Clyde L Bertram
123 Tuckahoe Rd
Dillsburg PA 17019

Call Sign: W3BET
Paul E De Buigne
7 W Ridge Rd
Dillsburg PA 170198939

Call Sign: N0XLL
Linda M Null
130 W Ridge Rd
Dillsburg PA 170198940

Call Sign: KA3NDR
Larry S Holmes
35 Walmar Manor
Dillsburg PA 17019

Call Sign: N3ZXD
Gardner M Rhoads

1670 Williams Rd Apt 2
Dillsburg PA 17019

Call Sign: KB3RSW
Joseph J Venzlowsky
10 Winter Dr
Dillsburg PA 17019

Call Sign: K3QQA
Perry C Bates
Dillsburg PA 17019

**FCC Amateur Radio
Licenses in Dornsife**

Call Sign: KE3VH
Ralph E French
Box 17
Dornsife PA 178239505

Call Sign: WA3VAY
Richard L Kauffman
Box C1
Dornsife PA 17823

Call Sign: N3XEF
Miriam R Hartman
Creek Rd
Dornsife PA 178230121

**FCC Amateur Radio
Licenses in Dover**

Call Sign: KC3DU
Charles J Aiello
2045 Andover Dr
Dover PA 17315

Call Sign: WA3ZVR
Robert W Brandick
2341 Belair Dr
Dover PA 17315

Call Sign: KA3IQN
Terry L Long

2417 Berkshire Ln
Dover PA 17315

Call Sign: KB3GGI
Andrew L Green
2482 Berkshire Ln
Dover PA 17315

Call Sign: KB3SST
Lorna J Miller
3135 Brookside Ave
Dover PA 17315

Call Sign: WA3MKB
David E Warnick
4755 Bull Rd
Dover PA 17315

Call Sign: WA3F
David E Warnick
4755 Bull Rd
Dover PA 17315

Call Sign: KB3SYH
Steven M Swancer
Bull Rd
Dover PA 17315

Call Sign: W3OKC
Steven M Swancer
Bull Rd
Dover PA 17315

Call Sign: KB3UYL
David M Klepper
4550 Bull Rd Lot 34
Dover PA 17315

Call Sign: KB3GGJ
Martin L Green
1220 Butter Rd
Dover PA 173152710

Call Sign: N3ONL
David L Sharp Jr

3636 Carlisle Rd
Dover PA 17315

Call Sign: W3CGG
Charles L Guise
4071 Carlisle Rd
Dover PA 17315

Call Sign: KB3ROL
Ray E Myers
990 Cherry Orchard Rd
Dover PA 17315

Call Sign: K3KTY
John A Tate Sr
3130 Claremont Rd
Dover PA 17315

Call Sign: KB3WZX
Timothy E Snook
2141 Conewago Rd
Dover PA 17315

Call Sign: WB3CQN
Ruthanna Pearson
3951 Country Dr
Donwood Ests
Dover PA 17315

Call Sign: N3EEI
Daniel J Shortencarrier
3595 Cypress Ct
Dover PA 17315

Call Sign: N3NCS
Natasha C Shortencarrier
3595 Cypress Ct
Dover PA 17315

Call Sign: KA3OCD
Edwyn A Bennett Jr
2331 Cypress Rd
Dover PA 17315

Call Sign: W2MZU

Edwyn A Bennett Jr
2331 Cypress Rd
Dover PA 17315

Call Sign: N3IEV
Dennis C Tilton
3000 Cypress Rd
Dover PA 17315

Call Sign: N3SUH
Edward W Measley
2572 Danielle Dr
Dover PA 17315

Call Sign: KA3GNJ
Peter J Dilkus
2618 Danielle Dr
Dover PA 173154619

Call Sign: KB3LZY
Joseph F Reiser
3361 Davidsburg Rd
Dover PA 17315

Call Sign: N3ZPO
Franklin K Brown Jr
3681 Davidsburg Rd
Dover PA 173154457

Call Sign: KB3VIG
Anthony R Cherone
Davidsburg Rd
Dover PA 17315

Call Sign: KA5BTU
Michael B Feldblum
1849 Deerfield Dr
Dover PA 17315

Call Sign: KB3GDA
James M Gillespie
227 Delaware Ave
Dover PA 17315

Call Sign: KD4RFV

Ricky L Brown
108 Delwood Dr
Dover PA 17315

Call Sign: K3SPD
Joseph M Lovell Sr
840 Detters Mill Rd
Dover PA 17315

Call Sign: KB3KCG
James R Detter
6797 Detters Mill Rd
Dover PA 173152923

Call Sign: KA3OBY
Charles E Gotwalt
2737 Emig Mill Rd
Dover PA 17315

Call Sign: KB3EEI
Daniel J Shortencarrier
3047 Englewood Ct
Dover PA 17315

Call Sign: KB3FQM
Joyce A Shortencarrier
3047 Englewood Ct
Dover PA 17315

Call Sign: KB3KTZ
Ray E Holtzapple
3260 Falcon Ln
Dover PA 17315

Call Sign: KB3CHC
Dennis E Hendricks
3715 Fox Chase Dr
Dover PA 173153704

Call Sign: AA3SX
Dennis E Hendricks
3715 Fox Chase Dr
Dover PA 173153704

Call Sign: KB3FHA

Wanda L Knokey
3715 Fox Chase Dr
Dover PA 173153704

Call Sign: KB3MZL
Victoria A Serrano
3675 Foxchase Dr
Dover PA 17315

Call Sign: KA3VWM
Kimberly A Iati
3198 Grenway Rd
Dover PA 17315

Call Sign: K3IWK
Charles W Byers
5120 Harmony Grove Rd
Dover PA 17315

Call Sign: WB3GQZ
Jeffrey L Edmonds
6561 Harmony Grove Rd
Dover PA 17315

Call Sign: N3XU
Arthur D Calvert Sr
4565 Hikey St
Dover PA 173153483

Call Sign: K3GXU
Sterling I Trimmer
3600 Holly Rd
Dover PA 17315

Call Sign: N3LHJ
William G Coleman
3083 Jodi Ln
Dover PA 173155400

Call Sign: KA3KWC
Emory E Lyons
4050 Jules Ln
Dover PA 173153680

Call Sign: KB3YDJ

David K Merges
5750 Kewisberry Rd
Dover PA 17315

Call Sign: N3XDM
Frank Lomenzo
4193 Leah Ave
Dover PA 17315

Call Sign: W3AXC
Raymond A Shaub
2331 Locust Rd
Dover PA 17315

Call Sign: KB3KNT
Qcwa Chapter 165
2331 Locust Rd
Dover PA 173154541

Call Sign: W3EDO
Qcwa Chapter 165
2331 Locust Rd
Dover PA 173154541

Call Sign: K3ACJ
Arthur L Jerome
214 Maplewood Dr
Dover PA 17315

Call Sign: KB3RQW
Jason E Sutherland
2570 Mill Creek Rd
Dover PA 17315

Call Sign: KE3CW
Gregory A Hagens
6059 Mountain Rd
Dover PA 17315

Call Sign: N5QNP
Lester F Stump Jr
2330 Mtn View Dr
Dover PA 173153512

Call Sign: AA3BJ

Timothy W Barefoot
3040 Muirfield Rd
Dover PA 17315

Call Sign: N3NBV
Caine C Haffner
3040 Muirfield Rd
Dover PA 17315

Call Sign: N3NCF
Sandra J Barefoot
3040 Muirfield Rd
Dover PA 17315

Call Sign: N3SUI
Adam W Barefoot
3040 Muirfield Rd
Dover PA 17315

Call Sign: W3UQJ
Adam W Barefoot
3040 Muirfield Rd
Dover PA 17315

Call Sign: W3TWB
Timothy W Barefoot
3040 Muirfield Rd
Dover PA 17315

Call Sign: K3DUL
Carlton M Gerhart Jr
4760 Nursery Rd
Dover PA 17315

Call Sign: KB3TTJ
Adam Stevens
2894 Oakland Rd
Dover PA 17315

Call Sign: KA3CST
Royal A Cannon III
527 Oakwood Dr
Dover PA 17315

Call Sign: N3ODI

Sharon S Cannon
527 Oakwood Dr
Dover PA 17315

Call Sign: KB3DHI
Russell S Seigle
6231 Old Carlisle Rd
Dover PA 17315

Call Sign: AA3QU
John C Bradley
1970 Park St
Dover PA 173153656

Call Sign: AB3EC
John C Bradley
1970 Park St
Dover PA 173153656

Call Sign: K3EDB
Eric D Blacker
142 Pawnee Ave
Dover PA 17315

Call Sign: W3LIZ
Elisabeth J Shulenski
146 Pawnee Ave
Dover PA 17315

Call Sign: WB7AUU
Robert J Carter
1320 Pleasant Dr
Dover PA 17315

Call Sign: N3ZMN
Randy E Mobley
55 S Main St
Dover PA 173151505

Call Sign: N3PWM
Robert K Wonner
4820 S Salem Church Rd
Dover PA 17315

Call Sign: WA3CSH

Steven L Dress
6171 Salem Run Rd
Dover PA 17315

Call Sign: W3IUQ
Alan G Vogt Jr
3000 School House Rd
Dover PA 17315

Call Sign: KB3KRA
Floyd B Parsons Jr
4101 Schoolhouse Rd
Dover PA 17315

Call Sign: N3LLN
Terry L Bosserman
2703 Sedgwick Ave
Dover PA 17315

Call Sign: KB3RQX
Thomas D Boyer
4424 Sherwood Dr
Dover PA 17315

Call Sign: KB3GPY
Glenn D Boyer
4424 Sherwood Dr
Dover PA 17315

Call Sign: WA3IKQ
Thomas J Conard
2630 Sky Top Trl
Dover PA 17315

Call Sign: KB3JNM
Joseph J Hainey Jr
2550 Skytop Trl
Dover PA 17315

Call Sign: KB3QOG
Alexander J Meacher
3041 Spectrum Rd
Dover PA 17315

Call Sign: WB3GRG

James B Musselman
1465 Steeple Chase Dr
Dover PA 17315

Call Sign: N3XYW
Neal E Winters
2615 Tamela Ave
Dover PA 17315

Call Sign: KB3CMV
South Mountain Vhf
Contest Team
3601 Tower Dr
Dover PA 17315

Call Sign: KC2IYS
Joseph M Larocco Sr
2956 Village Sq Dr
Dover PA 17315

Call Sign: KB3VCL
Joseph M Larocco Sr
2956 Village Sq Dr
Dover PA 17315

Call Sign: KB3RGH
Tabitha J Knaub
2063 Wyatt Cir
Dover PA 17315

Call Sign: KA3LHK
Raymond J Luster
800 York Rd Lot 122
Dover PA 17315

FCC Amateur Radio Licenses in Drifting

Call Sign: KA3KMB
Shirley R Morrison
Drifting PA 16834

FCC Amateur Radio Licenses in Driftwood

Call Sign: KA3OGC
Gertrude F Collins
Box 280
Driftwood PA 15832

FCC Amateur Radio Licenses in Drumore

Call Sign: KB3EMJ
Ethan A Demme
1378 River Rd
Drumore PA 17518

Call Sign: KB3LKH
Ronald J Hash
1710 River Rd
Drumore PA 17518

FCC Amateur Radio Licenses in DuBois

Call Sign: WA3GQU
Charles F Barr
367 Barr Rd Brady Tnsp
DuBois PA 15801

Call Sign: KA3ISM
Mildred M Gearhart
Box 208
DuBois PA 15801

Call Sign: KB3KTE
Carol A Lyons
Box 247A
DuBois PA 15801

Call Sign: KB3KTD
William J Lyons
Box 247A
DuBois PA 15801

Call Sign: KB3KTF
Theodore E Lyons
Box 249
DuBois PA 15801

Call Sign: KA3YHS
Leah M Barnett
Box 294
DuBois PA 15801

Call Sign: N3HCB
Joseph M Hook
Box 5
DuBois PA 15801

Call Sign: KA3DEO
David C Lindahl
42 Brown St
DuBois PA 15801

Call Sign: KB3MYT
Kevin C Hoynoski
515 Chestnut Ave
DuBois PA 15801

Call Sign: W3PIG
Kevin C Hoynoski
515 Chestnut Ave
DuBois PA 15801

Call Sign: K3MJT
Norris R Boucher
913 Chestnut Ave
DuBois PA 15801

Call Sign: KB3YLL
Alexander M Reasinger
206 E Logan Ave
DuBois PA 15801

Call Sign: WB3IIH
James B Swauger Sr
867 Edinger Rd
DuBois PA 15801

Call Sign: N3RYG
Jerry L Robinson
99 Keen Ct Dr
DuBois PA 15801

Call Sign: KA3OHH
John C Bishop
519 Lincoln Dr
DuBois PA 15801

Call Sign: KB3WKD
Gregory E Donahue
727 Maple Ave
DuBois PA 15801

Call Sign: N3GZT
Marc D Johnson
1173 Mtn Run Rd
DuBois PA 15801

Call Sign: KB3VWY
Marc D Johnson
1173 Mtn Run Rd
DuBois PA 15801

Call Sign: W3MDJ
Marc D Johnson
1173 Mtn Run Rd
DuBois PA 15801

Call Sign: KA3YOI
Mark R Meholick
102 N 3rd St
DuBois PA 15801

Call Sign: W3WM
Arthur F Kunst
547 Orient Ave
DuBois PA 15801

Call Sign: KB3HYV
Sylbia S Kunst
547 Orient Ave
DuBois PA 15801

Call Sign: W3DQF
Mason H Freeman
500 Rumbarger Ave
DuBois PA 15801

Call Sign: N3GSR
Kenneth A Haley
628 S Brady St
DuBois PA 15801

Call Sign: KA3TVW
Jane B Haley
628 S Brady St
DuBois PA 15801

Call Sign: N2KIK
Judith E Shirley
1231 S Brady St
DuBois PA 15801

Call Sign: WV2RJH
Patrick J Shirley
1231 S Brady St
DuBois PA 15801

Call Sign: K3LIX
Richard M Hockman
328 S Highland St
DuBois PA 15801

Call Sign: WA3UKE
Bernard A Masonis
224 S Stockdale
DuBois PA 15801

Call Sign: WA3MMG
William F Kolash Jr
522 Showers Rd
DuBois PA 15801

Call Sign: KA3TCV
Clarence P Micknis
316 South Ave
DuBois PA 15801

Call Sign: K3QEQ
William J Zavatsky
406 South Ave
DuBois PA 158011544

Call Sign: KA3MYQ
Shelly M Luchini
289 Treasure Lk
DuBois PA 15801

Call Sign: WB3GAB
Edwin A Haddow
435 Treasure Lk
DuBois PA 15801

Call Sign: N3SYB
Leland P Maines
527 Treasure Lk
DuBois PA 15801

Call Sign: KB3YJK
Devon Lorance
605 Treasure Lk
DuBois PA 15801

Call Sign: KB3YJL
Jay Lorance
605 Treasure Lk
DuBois PA 15801

Call Sign: KB3YJJ
Nicholas Lorance
605 Treasure Lk
DuBois PA 15801

Call Sign: N3KQC
Michael E Barchony
676 Treasure Lk
DuBois PA 15801

Call Sign: N3NWM
Diana G Thompson
1047 Treasure Lk
DuBois PA 15801

Call Sign: N3MZD
Richard D Dietz
1051 Treasure Lk
DuBois PA 15801

Call Sign: KA3RDR
Perry R Phillips
1128 Treasure Lk
DuBois PA 15801

Call Sign: KA2NWJ
Karen J Aravich
1160 Treasure Lk
DuBois PA 15801

Call Sign: KB3HMM
Brian M Elias
1324 Treasure Lk
DuBois PA 15801

Call Sign: N3JYL
Shirish N Shah
1383 Treasure Lk
DuBois PA 15801

Call Sign: KB3WKE
Robert B Thunberg
1442 Treasure Lk
DuBois PA 15801

Call Sign: N3DIR
Robert B Thunberg
1442 Treasure Lk
DuBois PA 15801

Call Sign: N3VFO
Bernard L Walkowiak
1465 Treasure Lk
DuBois PA 15801

Call Sign: K3WVR
James M Domitrovich
1466 Treasure Lk
DuBois PA 15801

Call Sign: W3IRY
Richard V Mulvihill
Treasure Lk 126
DuBois PA 15801

Call Sign: KA3BWA
Wilbur R Murrell
427 Treasure Lk Desirade
St
DuBois PA 15801

Call Sign: N3HAO
Bradley R Bedell
4112 W Liberty Rd
DuBois PA 15801

Call Sign: KD3RJ
George E Donahue Sr
111 W Long Ave
DuBois PA 15801

Call Sign: WB3DUF
Daniel A Bunn
111 W Long Ave Apt 6 E
DuBois PA 15801

Call Sign: N3PUG
Mark A Flanagan
28.5 W Scribner Ave
DuBois PA 15801

Call Sign: N3HBD
Allen R Muth
218 Wayne Rd
DuBois PA 15801

Call Sign: WA3BUX
Harry R Flanders
222 Wayne Rd
DuBois PA 15801

Call Sign: WA3UFN
Bryan J Simanic
9 Wild Cherry Dr
DuBois PA 15801

Call Sign: KB3YJI
Bev Hudsick
9 Wild Cherry Dr

DuBois PA 15801

Call Sign: N3ZFV
Fred G Terwilliger
317 Wood St
DuBois PA 15801

Call Sign: KB3OUG
John H Buttner
DuBois PA 15801

FCC Amateur Radio Licenses in Duboistown

Call Sign: W3LXX
Walter B Tyndall
320 Winter St
Duboistown PA 17701

FCC Amateur Radio Licenses in Duke Center

Call Sign: KA1NDY
Gary C Lewis
213 Oil Valley Rd
Duke Center PA 16729

Call Sign: KA1NDZ
Sue I Lewis
213 Oil Valley Rd
Duke Center PA 16729

FCC Amateur Radio Licenses in Ducannon

Call Sign: KB3RYU
Anna E Maciorkoski
401 Barley Dr
Duncannon PA 17020

Call Sign: N3UXF
Mark A Hollingsworth
201 Center St
Duncannon PA 17020

Call Sign: KB3SNO
Matthew Shields III
327 Faculty Rd
Duncannon PA 17020

Call Sign: WB3EEM
Russell E Marsh
307 Lincloln Sr
Duncannon PA 170201422

Call Sign: N3JRO
James D Acri
202 Montebello Farm Rd
Duncannon PA 17020

Call Sign: N3IOZ
Randon L Morgan
216 Montebello Farm Rd
Duncannon PA 17020

Call Sign: N3HVR
Douglas P Sheaffer
290 Montebello Farm Rd
Duncannon PA 17020

Call Sign: KB3LRV
Dylan J Shannon
312 Montebello Farm Rd
Duncannon PA 17020

Call Sign: KA3GZI
Floyd O Crum
60 Montebello Rd
Duncannon PA 17020

Call Sign: N3NSC
Elwood L Hoffman
407 N High St
Duncannon PA 17020

Call Sign: KB3UWG
Wayne J Ferguson
29 N Market St
Duncannon PA 170201229

Call Sign: KB3THP
Michael J Hammar
1500 Newport Rd
Duncannon PA 170208944

Call Sign: KA3ADV
Gary R Goss
11 Paradise Rd
Duncannon PA 17020

Call Sign: KB3GSS
Albert L Sites Sr
3 Schoolhouse Rd
Duncannon PA 17020

Call Sign: KB3RDA
Joseph S Stine
1037 State Rd
Duncannon PA 17020

Call Sign: KB3HIG
Catharene A Garula
2 Sulphur Springs Rd
Duncannon PA 170209662

Call Sign: KB3DNZ
Sam Garula
2 Sulphur Springs Rd
Duncannon PA 170209662

Call Sign: K3DLA
Daniel L Angstadt
23 Sulphur Springs Rd
Duncannon PA 17020

FCC Amateur Radio Licenses in Duncansville

Call Sign: N3BIQ
John B Campbell
915 6th Ave
Duncansville PA 16635

Call Sign: N3JXS
Doris M Campbell

915 6th Ave
Duncansville PA 16635

Call Sign: KB8SCK
James A Zaebst
644 Appleview Ln
Duncansville PA 16635

Call Sign: N3MHL
Sherry I Montgomery
Box 295
Duncansville PA 16635

Call Sign: N3HLF
Charles M White
Box 296
Duncansville PA 16635

Call Sign: KA3OKC
Linda J Miller
Box 407
Duncansville PA 16635

Call Sign: W3UNQ
Sherman H Ostrander Sr
Box 464 Old 6th Ave Rd
Duncansville PA 16635

Call Sign: KB3PPS
Carol A Reynolds
1182 Carson Valley Rd
Duncansville PA 16635

Call Sign: KB3PPR
John J Reynolds
1182 Carson Valley Rd
Duncansville PA 16635

Call Sign: N3CBD
Ronald W Yingling
3181 Colonial Dr
Duncansville PA
166358022

Call Sign: N3BZV

Leonard D Pacifico Jr
107 Drake Ln
Duncansville PA
166354545

Call Sign: KB4JDK
Lois A Mock
1220 Foot Of Ten Rd
Duncansville PA 16635

Call Sign: N3WMJ
Darren S Mock Jr
1220 Foot Of Ten Rd
Duncansville PA 16635

Call Sign: KB3DSW
Vincent J Mock
1220 Foot Of Ten Rd
Duncansville PA 16635

Call Sign: KB3PSG
John C Muir
641 Hillside View Dr
Duncansville PA 16635

Call Sign: KA8PUU
Francis T Hartnett III
124 Lowry Dr
Duncansville PA 16635

Call Sign: N3BZY
Beverlie L Hartnett
124 Lowry Dr
Duncansville PA 16635

Call Sign: N3NZK
Beverlie L Hartnett
124 Lowry Dr
Duncansville PA 16635

Call Sign: N3JXJ
Alan W Montgomery
275 Montgomery Ln
Duncansville PA 16635

Call Sign: N3JXZ
Jeremiah W Montgomery
275 Montgomery Ln
Duncansville PA 16635

Call Sign: KA3WJO
Frank C Hebler Jr
2060 Old 6th Ave Rd S
Duncansville PA 16635

Call Sign: WB3AVD
Theodore J Holland Jr
1172 Old Rt 22
Duncansville PA 16635

Call Sign: N3JXV
Deloras J Dean
1206 Old Rt 22
Duncansville PA 16635

Call Sign: WB3CKY
Roy G Rabenstein
2074 Old Rt 220 N
Duncansville PA 16635

Call Sign: N3SDL
John C Muir
782 Peachview Ln
Duncansville PA 16635

Call Sign: N3BZX
James J MacInnis
619 Robertdale Dr
Duncansville PA 16635

Call Sign: N3IBK
Robbie L Miller
111 Sprucedale Dr
Duncansville PA 16635

Call Sign: N3MHM
Lori L Miller
111 Sprucedale Dr
Duncansville PA 16635

Call Sign: WB3FIE
Urban J Zierer
1000 Tash Valley Ln
Duncansville PA 16635

Call Sign: N3VYD
Vaughn G Brubaker
1116 W Carson Valley Rd
Duncansville PA 16635

Call Sign: K3GCN
Jack L Chilcote
181 Willowbrook Village
Duncansville PA 16635

FCC Amateur Radio Licenses in Dunlo

Call Sign: KA3UOJ
Mark F Katrancha
Dunlo PA 15930

Call Sign: W3RSP
John Cimba
Dunlo PA 15930

FCC Amateur Radio Licenses in Dysart

Call Sign: W3MJO
James C Kensinger
851 Dysart Dr
Dysart PA 16636

Call Sign: N3VOG
Gary L Christiansen
1198 Marra Rd
Dysart PA 16636

FCC Amateur Radio Licenses in East Berlin

Call Sign: KB3RZA
Heather L Schultz
1814 Baltimore Pike

East Berlin PA 17316

Call Sign: W3AJD
Dale T Rahe
530 Conewago Dr
East Berlin PA 173169442

Call Sign: WO4L
Robert J Hess
74 Curtis Dr
East Berlin PA 17316

Call Sign: KA3UEI
Robert C Moul
209 Garden Ln
East Berlin PA 17316

Call Sign: W3JRY
John R Yupatoff
9 Grant Cove
East Berlin PA 17316

Call Sign: KB3DNY
Michael E Leas
724 Hoover School Rd
East Berlin PA 173169572

Call Sign: KB3GCZ
Jeremy T Utterback
36 Jackson Dr
East Berlin PA 17316

Call Sign: KA3YMR
Richard C Fowler
64 Lake Meade Dr
East Berlin PA 17316

Call Sign: WA2EXE
Robert Clayton
106 Lodge Ln
East Berlin PA 17316

Call Sign: N3YZS
Wesley H Obert
12 Long St Dr

East Berlin PA 17316

Call Sign: N3XTY
Charles W Krall
119 N Water St
East Berlin PA 17316

Call Sign: KB3ONH
Raymond A Stonesifer
203 Rife Rd Lot 25
East Berlin PA 17316

Call Sign: N3RML
June H Rodes
17 Sedgwick Dr
East Berlin PA 17316

Call Sign: KE3SO
Theodore B Rodes
17 Sedgwick Dr
East Berlin PA 173169348

Call Sign: KB3VVC
Donald L Rosenzweig
1534 Stoney Pt Rd
East Berlin PA 17316

Call Sign: N3XRX
Robert L Nace
29 Wadsworth Dr
East Berlin PA 17316

Call Sign: N3WWE
Nicholas J Meacher
East Berlin PA 17316

FCC Amateur Radio Licenses in East Earl

Call Sign: N3PRJ
James P Doman Jr
1932 Echo Valley Dr
East Earl PA 17519

Call Sign: NT3F

Ralph W Dixon
1956 Echo Valley Dr
East Earl PA 17519

Call Sign: K3NCY
David E Nonnemacher
1312 Edgewood Dr
East Earl PA 17519

Call Sign: N3BUV
Nancy A Diehl
345 Farm View Dr
East Earl PA 17519

Call Sign: N3LTR
Brian E Diehl
345 Farm View Dr
East Earl PA 17519

Call Sign: WA3FZK
Jay L Martin
237 Goods Store Rd
East Earl PA 175199697

Call Sign: N3FDD
John Clough
391 Linden Rd
East Earl PA 17519

Call Sign: N3RZD
Kevin H Clough
391 Linden Rd
East Earl PA 17519

Call Sign: KB3QNK
Benjamin D Rittenhouse
168 Pleasant Valley Rd
East Earl PA 17519

Call Sign: N3JHU
Elvin W Sensenig
220 Reading Rd
East Earl PA 17519

Call Sign: WB3CTD

Leland E Martin
442 Spring Grove Rd
East Earl PA 17519

Call Sign: N3NMH
Jerry L Yost Jr
7 Terrie Ln
East Earl PA 17519

Call Sign: KB3JWG
Scott H Taylor
1689 Turkey Hill Rd
East Earl PA 17519

FCC Amateur Radio Licenses in East Freedom

Call Sign: KA3SVG
Frank C Gates
Box 10
East Freedom PA 16637

Call Sign: N3VYC
Miles A Wicker Jr
Box 429
East Freedom PA 16637

Call Sign: KB3MAH
Charles J Hall
Box 734
East Freedom PA 16637

Call Sign: KB3DRJ
Michael X Hoover
Box A336
East Freedom PA 16637

Call Sign: KB3HYQ
Robert M X Hoover
Box A336
East Freedom PA 16637

Call Sign: N3IUI
Michael McCarty
101 Whistle Ln

East Freedom PA 16637

Call Sign: N3GOJ
James S Dodson Jr
East Freedom PA 16637

FCC Amateur Radio Licenses in East Petersburg

Call Sign: KB3IES
G Richard Garber Jr
5216 Brook Dr
East Petersburg PA 17520

Call Sign: W3OSA
Charles J Burket
6290 High St
East Petersburg PA 17520

Call Sign: KB3DWJ
Shawn C Hammond
6516 Hollow Dr
East Petersburg PA 17520

Call Sign: WB3ESA
Harry M Buchanan Jr
5340 Lake Dr
East Petersburg PA 17520

Call Sign: W3SUR
Fred G Hammersand
5980 Leebel Rd
East Petersburg PA 17520

Call Sign: N3HKF
William R Sell Sr
5018 Martin Dr
East Petersburg PA 17520

Call Sign: KA3UQA
Timothy M Headings
2061 Miller Rd
East Petersburg PA 17520

Call Sign: N3LZK
Ronald R Roberts Jr
2520 Miller Rd
East Petersburg PA 17520

Call Sign: KI3M
Jay E Consylman
1932 New St
East Petersburg PA 17520

Call Sign: KD8WY
Paul W Herr
5710 Pine St
East Petersburg PA
175201540

Call Sign: AA3SI
Fred S Althouse
5730 Pine St
East Petersburg PA
175201540

Call Sign: KA3TAB
Allyn R Mayer
5425 Rainbow Dr
East Petersburg PA 17520

Call Sign: N3PIL
Steven S Shenk
5950 Reeves Rd
East Petersburg PA 17520

Call Sign: WB3BZX
William F Landis
2547 Speckled Dr
East Petersburg PA 17520

Call Sign: WB3EKN
David J Cruikshank
2043 State St
East Petersburg PA 17520

Call Sign: WA3WPA
Matthew J Frey
East Petersburg PA 17520

Call Sign: KB3FGA
Christopher W Bunting
East Petersburg PA
175200142

FCC Amateur Radio Licenses in East Prospect

Call Sign: KB3DLP
Jeremy W Kiehner
11 W Maple St
East Prospect PA 17317

Call Sign: WB3AVZ
K Franklin Kiehner
11 W Maple St
East Prospect PA
173170497

FCC Amateur Radio Licenses in Ebensburg

Call Sign: KB3DMG
Troy A Bugosh
2028 Ben Franklin Hwy
Ebensburg PA 15931

Call Sign: KA3RCR
Kathy J Warzel
3482 Ben Franklin Hwy
Ebensburg PA 15931

Call Sign: ND3L
Desmond E Warzel
3482 Ben Franklin Hwy
Ebensburg PA 15931

Call Sign: KA3VXR
Blanche B Bender
533 Bovine Rd
Ebensburg PA 159315413

Call Sign: W3SYY
Richard M Bender

533 Bovine Rd
Ebensburg PA 159315413

Call Sign: N3NXU
Michael G Kokus
Box 48
Ebensburg PA 15931

Call Sign: KB3PLC
Cambria County
Department Of Emergency
Services
401 Candlelight Dr Ste 100
Ebensburg PA 159311959

Call Sign: KC3DES
Cambria County
Department Of Emergency
Services
401 Candlelight Dr Ste 100
Ebensburg PA 159311959

Call Sign: N3YIR
Larry E Davis Jr
233 Circle Dr
Ebensburg PA 15931

Call Sign: KC3HR
Bruce McCardell
Laurel Crest Manor
Ebensburg PA 15931

Call Sign: KA3ZYC
Francis C Krug
510 Lemon Drop Rd
Ebensburg PA 15931

Call Sign: KB3PCM
Brandon T Odonnell
221 Lincoln St
Ebensburg PA 15931

Call Sign: N3LC
Raymond L Cramer
173 Mtn Ests Rd

Ebensburg PA 15931

Call Sign: WB3GXI
James F Weaver
723 N Beech St
Ebensburg PA 15931

Call Sign: KF3CH
George J Letavish Sr
209 S Julian St
Ebensburg PA 15931

Call Sign: N3QLF
Chad A Cessna
1200 W High St
Ebensburg PA 15931

Call Sign: W3KFG
John D Wesley
1253 Wilmore Rd
Ebensburg PA 15931

Call Sign: KA3GWN
Charles G Hasson
Ebensburg PA 15931

FCC Amateur Radio Licenses in Edgemont

Call Sign: WA3JSE
Vincent C De Rico
Edgemont PA 19028

FCC Amateur Radio Licenses in Eldred

Call Sign: W3OCR
Delbert L Mills
Barbertown Rd
Eldred PA 16731

Call Sign: KB3FFB
Kenneth E Mostyn
219 Barden Brook Rd
Eldred PA 16731

Call Sign: KA3RAG
Dorothy J Trask
Box 152 W Eldred Rd
Eldred PA 167319647

Call Sign: KD3JD
Robert C Trask
411 E Eldred Rd
Eldred PA 16731

Call Sign: KB3DLM
David A Wood
40 Edson St
Eldred PA 167310478

Call Sign: W3OOD
David A Wood
40 Edson St
Eldred PA 167310478

Call Sign: KA3ISZ
John G Todd
11 King St
Eldred PA 16731

Call Sign: N3SFL
Curt D Priest
61 King St
Eldred PA 16731

Call Sign: KB3QNP
Paul A Mcvinney
146 Main St
Eldred PA 16731

Call Sign: KB3RNU
Paul A Mcvinney
146 Main St
Eldred PA 16731

Call Sign: N3SFL
Paul A Mcvinney
146 Main St
Eldred PA 16731

Call Sign: KI3U
Berj N Ensanian
Eldred PA 16731

**FCC Amateur Radio
Licenses in
Elizabethtown**

Call Sign: KE4MFN
Jared S Akers
642 Aberdeen Rd
Elizabethtown PA 17022

Call Sign: N3NTJ
Matthew W Steger
2133 Andrew Ave
Elizabethtown PA 17022

Call Sign: N3TUE
Catherine A Steger
2133 Andrew Ave
Elizabethtown PA 17022

Call Sign: N3NDJ
David B Sarraf
303 Arch St
Elizabethtown PA 17022

Call Sign: KB3OSX
Amber L Pickel
546 Bellaire Rd
Elizabethtown PA 17022

Call Sign: KB3LHT
Donald C Pickel Jr
546 Bellaire Rd
Elizabethtown PA 17022

Call Sign: KB3LOK
Sharon L Pickel
546 Bellaire Rd
Elizabethtown PA 17022

Call Sign: WD3X

George B Tullidge IV
4780 Bossler Rd
Elizabethtown PA 17022

Call Sign: N3MFQ
Laura S McKenzie
734 Cassell Rd
Elizabethtown PA 17022

Call Sign: N3ITQ
Christopher T Fuller
165 Ceader Manor
Elizabethtown PA 17022

Call Sign: N3PIO
Richard M Franklin
116 Cedar Manor
Elizabethtown PA 17022

Call Sign: N3QPB
Sharol Y Franklin
116 Cedar Manor
Elizabethtown PA 17022

Call Sign: N3LOO
Charles H Hafer
2492 Chestnut Rd
Elizabethtown PA 17022

Call Sign: KB3WVT
Richard J Regel
30 Chestnut Run
Elizabethtown PA 17022

Call Sign: KB3FWK
Andrew J Nightingale
205 College Ave
Elizabethtown PA 17022

Call Sign: KB3SDU
Brian R Dobslaw
525 Conoy Ave
Elizabethtown PA 17022

Call Sign: N1BRD

Brian R Dobslaw
525 Conoy Ave
Elizabethtown PA 17022

Call Sign: N3QCF
Edmund H Emery
40 Cottage Ave
Elizabethtown PA 17022

Call Sign: W3MFW
Russel E Martin
73 Creek Rd
Elizabethtown PA 17022

Call Sign: KB3CKN
Timothy M Barry
2417 Deodate Rd
Elizabethtown PA 17022

Call Sign: KA3VEE
David A Culbertson
20 E Hummelstown St
Elizabethtown PA 17022

Call Sign: AA3OE
Harold R Brandt
600 E Hummelstown St
Elizabethtown PA 17022

Call Sign: N3RXG
Jean L Brandt
600 E Hummelstown St
Elizabethtown PA 17022

Call Sign: N3XTG
Douglas S Ruth
41 E Park St
Elizabethtown PA 17022

Call Sign: N3ZKY
Eddy R Reed
50 E Wasington St
Elizabethtown PA 17022

Call Sign: W3SOK

Joseph H Loraw
136 E Willow St
Elizabethtown PA 17022

Call Sign: KA3VYG
Larry M Byron
525 E Willow St
Elizabethtown PA 17022

Call Sign: K3RYM
Gardner H Schoenly
31 Edenview Rd Apt 353
Elizabethtown PA
170223114

Call Sign: W3PWH
Roger O Colvin
42 Elm Ave
Elizabethtown PA 17022

Call Sign: KF3Y
Andrew J Bomboy
8 Farmington Ln
Elizabethtown PA 17022

Call Sign: N3JAK
Howard Kane Jr
456 Ford Dr
Elizabethtown PA 17022

Call Sign: N3MYT
John C Brown Jr
443 Foreman Rd
Elizabethtown PA 17022

Call Sign: KB3BK
James M Shellem
161 Foxchase Dr
Elizabethtown PA 17022

Call Sign: KW3E
James R Silvius
37 Franklin Dr
Elizabethtown PA 17022

Call Sign: K3HOX
Robert E Hager
100 Freemason Dr Apt
1582
Elizabethtown PA 17022

Call Sign: N3PAV
Donald G Muston
314 Furnace Hill Rd
Elizabethtown PA 17022

Call Sign: KE3LD
Joshua M Peters
180 Governer Stable Rd
Elizabethtown PA 17022

Call Sign: KB3HZV
Ronald A Kedell
7 Greenleaf Ln
Elizabethtown PA
170222882

Call Sign: KB3HZW
Derek R Kedell
7 Greenleaf Ln
Elizabethtown PA
170222882

Call Sign: KC3AB
Harold R Morris Jr
643 Hampden Rd
Elizabethtown PA 17022

Call Sign: W2LEI
George H Kraus
718 Harding Dr
Elizabethtown PA 17022

Call Sign: WA2FYC
Sally E Kraus
718 Harding Dr
Elizabethtown PA 17022

Call Sign: KB3MEX
Randy H Lightner

4318 Heather Rd
Elizabethtown PA 17022

Call Sign: WA3RRX
Thomas R Leap
85 Hillcrest Ln
Elizabethtown PA 17022

Call Sign: W3DRB
Miles G Newman
86 Hillcrest Ln
Elizabethtown PA 17022

Call Sign: N3QZE
Mark B Peters
441 Hillside Ave
Elizabethtown PA 17022

Call Sign: KB3FDT
Kristopher M Keller
1021 Hillside Ave
Elizabethtown PA 17022

Call Sign: N3KAB
Melvin D Schneider
320 Hillside Rd
Elizabethtown PA 17022

Call Sign: N3OEY
Donald L Espenshade
455 Hilltop Cir
Elizabethtown PA 17022

Call Sign: N3QWS
Penny L Espenshade
455 Hilltop Cir
Elizabethtown PA 17022

Call Sign: N3RMH
Crystal A Espenshade
455 Hilltop Cir
Elizabethtown PA 17022

Call Sign: KB3RYF
Taylor W Gilmore

467 Hilltop Cir
Elizabethtown PA 17022

Call Sign: K3WEB
Masonic Village ARC
3 Jackson Dr
Elizabethtown PA
170223137

Call Sign: K3SU
Roger L Wheeler
3 Jackson Dr
Elizabethtown PA
170223137

Call Sign: N3MKD
Michael L Morton
11 James Buchanan Dr
Elizabethtown PA 17022

Call Sign: W3LN
Abram J McClune
1114 James Buchanan Dr
Elizabethtown PA 17022

Call Sign: WA3CMS
John S Reese
1203 James Buchanan Dr
Elizabethtown PA 17022

Call Sign: N3MKF
Frederick G Perkins
2301 James Buchanan Dr
Elizabethtown PA 17022

Call Sign: W3GPH
Raymond E Wagner Jr
3301 James Buchanan Dr
Elizabethtown PA 17022

Call Sign: N3NJC
Joseph F Answine
60 Kirby Dr
Elizabethtown PA 17022

Call Sign: WA2ORG
Joseph F Answine
60 Kirby Dr
Elizabethtown PA 17022

Call Sign: KB3LKN
J Darryl Wenger
1291 Mapledale Rd
Elizabethtown PA 17022

Call Sign: N3ZKG
Ronald W Oyler
532 Mark Dr
Elizabethtown PA 17022

Call Sign: KA3AJG
Harry F Deibert Sr
1 Masonic Dr
Elizabethtown PA 17022

Call Sign: W3JWF
Irdell Gaskill
1 Masonic Dr
Elizabethtown PA 17022

Call Sign: W3VGM
Jack C Byron
1 Masonic Dr
Elizabethtown PA
170222199

Call Sign: WA3PWZ
Thomas M Joiner
1 Masonic Dr
Elizabethtown PA
170222199

Call Sign: N3IMS
Connie R Roschel
485 Maytown Rd
Elizabethtown PA 17022

Call Sign: N3JDF
Eric D Clark
485 Maytown Rd

Elizabethtown PA 17022

Call Sign: N3VRB
Adam M Clark
485 Maytown Rd
Elizabethtown PA 17022

Call Sign: KA3VEV
Teresa J Engle
529 Maytown Rd
Elizabethtown PA 17022

Call Sign: WN3U
Roger L Engle
529 Maytown Rd
Elizabethtown PA 17022

Call Sign: WA3UIP
Simon P Kraybill
860 Maytown Rd
Elizabethtown PA 17022

Call Sign: N3TSX
Andrew L Grosh
537 Miller Rd
Elizabethtown PA 17022

Call Sign: KB3HZU
Cynthia L Davidson
982 Mt Grenta Rd
Elizabethtown PA 17022

Call Sign: KB3SOO
Keith R B Wingate
836 N Deodate Rd
Elizabethtown PA 17022

Call Sign: KB3IIA
Steven M Conn
489 N Holly Rd
Elizabethtown PA 17022

Call Sign: KE4OII
Ryan P Turner
500 N Locust St

Elizabethtown PA
170221630

Call Sign: K3QAW
James P Murray
217 N Poplar St
Elizabethtown PA 17022

Call Sign: N3EUU
John M Hohenwarter
74 Old English Ln
Elizabethtown PA 17022

Call Sign: KE3CV
Curtis D Zell
218 Old Hershey Rd
Elizabethtown PA 17022

Call Sign: KZ3J
Curtis D Zell
218 Old Hershey Rd
Elizabethtown PA 17022

Call Sign: N3UAF
Susan I Young
41 Park View Dr
Elizabethtown PA 17022

Call Sign: N8WXZ
Jason J Bachman
34 Parkview Dr
Elizabethtown PA 17022

Call Sign: N3QLB
Rodney W Young
41 Parkview Dr
Elizabethtown PA 17022

Call Sign: N3RJL
Rodney W Young Jr
41 Parkview Dr
Elizabethtown PA 17022

Call Sign: KA3SQT
James G Dunbar

25 Poplar Ln
Elizabethtown PA
170229419

Call Sign: K3OET
Dale F Stough
704 Radio Rd
Elizabethtown PA 17022

Call Sign: W3FXE
Ralph P Miller
1000 Ridge Rd
Elizabethtown PA
170229797

Call Sign: KB3RKL
Richard C Downs
4956 Ridge Rd
Elizabethtown PA 17022

Call Sign: N2YBH
Bhunesh Chandra
5016 Ridge Rd
Elizabethtown PA 17022

Call Sign: KA3AJD
James E Watson
5469 Ridge Rd
Elizabethtown PA 17022

Call Sign: KB3IGQ
Walt Eby
Ridge Rd
Elizabethtown PA 17022

Call Sign: W3CNS
James R Shank
21 Rosebud Ln
Elizabethtown PA 17022

Call Sign: N3IPC
Donald R Swope
738 S Mt Joy St
Elizabethtown PA 17022

Call Sign: N3AYY
Roger C Thompson
1302 S Mt Joy St
Elizabethtown PA 17022

Call Sign: AE3RT
Roger C Thompson
1302 S Mt Joy St
Elizabethtown PA 17022

Call Sign: N3NIF
Jeffrey L Whitehead
19 Sager Rd
Elizabethtown PA 17022

Call Sign: N3TMV
James A Whitehead
19 Sager Rd
Elizabethtown PA 17022

Call Sign: WA3FFK
Harry D Bauder
4319 Snavely Rd
Elizabethtown PA 17022

Call Sign: WA3KJV
Ralph J Myers
500 Snyder Ave
Elizabethtown PA 17022

Call Sign: K3ORU
Eugene B Smith
530 Snyder Ave
Elizabethtown PA 17022

Call Sign: N3XUI
Jeff C Persinotti
564 Snyder Ave
Elizabethtown PA 17022

Call Sign: KB3NLV
William D Kozma Jr
957 Spring Garden St
Elizabethtown PA 17022

Call Sign: N3XHB
James F Wess
1496 Stone Mill Dr
Elizabethtown PA
170229422

Call Sign: KB3MPQ
Jeremy R Loos
356 Sunrise Blvd
Elizabethtown PA 17022

Call Sign: KA3KHR
Daniel E Milligan
80 Sycamore Dr Apt 215
Elizabethtown PA 17022

Call Sign: W3SQR
Richard W Zechman
13 Teakwood Cir
Elizabethtown PA 17022

Call Sign: WB3BNX
Larry E Ierley
923 Thistle Rd
Elizabethtown PA 17022

Call Sign: N3VZV
Frank E Arendt IV
82 Tower Dr
Elizabethtown PA 17022

Call Sign: KB3JHX
David R Clouser
3118 Tpke Rd
Elizabethtown PA 17022

Call Sign: W3NAP
David R Clauser
3118 Tpke Rd
Elizabethtown PA 17022

Call Sign: AB3BK
David R Clouser
3118 Tpke Rd
Elizabethtown PA 17022

Call Sign: NZ3M
David R Clouser
3118 Tpke Rd
Elizabethtown PA 17022

Call Sign: KB3CHT
Andrew B Hahn
3259 Tpke Rd
Elizabethtown PA 17011

Call Sign: W9LWY
Jerry F Edgerton
Truman Dr
Elizabethtown PA
170223125

Call Sign: KB3GNA
Bernard G Heim
108 W Harrisburg Ave
Elizabethtown PA 17022

Call Sign: KB3TEC
Thomas K Peters Jr
28 W Hummelstown St
Apt 101
Elizabethtown PA 17022

Call Sign: N3MKH
Joseph F Sollenberger Jr
423 W Ridge Rd
Elizabethtown PA 17022

Call Sign: WA3TFC
Albert Roth
35 Watercress Ln
Elizabethtown PA 17022

Call Sign: KZ3I
William M Slabonik
4447 Woodcrest Dr
Elizabethtown PA 17022

Call Sign: KB3KBM
David A Slabonik

4447 Woodcrest Dr
Elizabethtown PA 17022

Call Sign: NZ3I
David A Slabonik
4447 Woodcrest Dr
Elizabethtown PA 17022

Call Sign: KB3EYK
Thomas H Jones
4454 Woodcrest Dr
Elizabethtown PA 17022

Call Sign: KB3EYL
Kathleen A Jones
4454 Woodcrest Dr
Elizabethtown PA 17022

Call Sign: KA3YPL
Bradley D Hartzler
Elizabethtown PA 17022

Call Sign: KB3QBQ
Anthony D Brenner
Elizabethtown PA 17022

Call Sign: KB3WER
Andrew P Robertucci
292 Kocher Ln
Elizabethville PA 17023

Call Sign: KB3PAF
Keith N Miller
664 Mountain Rd
Elizabethville PA 17023

Call Sign: KB3STY
John S Miller
664 Mountain Rd
Elizabethville PA 17023

Call Sign: N3OTX
Russell E Walborn Jr
4178 Rt 209
Elizabethville PA 17023

Call Sign: KR3G
Robin E Troutman
5023 Rt 209
Elizabethville PA
170238462

Call Sign: KA3YPH
Yvonne D Troutman
5032 Rt 209
Elizabethville PA 17023

Call Sign: KA3YPG
Christine Y Troutman
1 Rumberger Ln
Elizabethville PA 17023

Call Sign: N3WEH
Jesse T Geiman
250 W Broad St
Elizabethville PA 17023

FCC Amateur Radio Licenses in Elkland

Call Sign: KA3DWS
David G Tubbs
1199 Barney Hill Rd
Elkland PA 16920

Call Sign: KA3AMS
William G Tubbs
Box 50
Elkland PA 16920

Call Sign: WB3LQX
Rose M Kimble
102 Parallel Rd
Elkland PA 16920

Call Sign: KB3NKX
Robert L Stone II
304 Parkhurst St
Elkland PA 16920

Call Sign: N3VAX
Russell G Oberther
101 Taft Ave
Elkland PA 16920

Call Sign: KC2XL
Peter Dieterich
231 W Main St
Elkland PA 16920

Call Sign: KB3KKV
Robert E Foulk
416 W Main St
Elkland PA 16920

Call Sign: WB3DDJ
Michael E Kimble
103 W Woodlawn Ave
Elkland PA 16920

Call Sign: WB3JQU
Wendy S Kimble
103 W Woodlawn Ave
Elkland PA 16920

Call Sign: N3PZG
Carl F Lawrenson
106 W Woodlawn Ave
Elkland PA 16920

Call Sign: N3PZH
Holly S Lawrenson
106 W Woodlawn Ave
Elkland PA 16920

FCC Amateur Radio Licenses in Elliottsburg

Call Sign: N3GTK
Allan S Thomas
712 Pleasant Valley Rd
Elliottsburg PA 17024

FCC Amateur Radio Licenses in Elm

Call Sign: W3EEE
Stephen H Dove
Elm PA 17521

FCC Amateur Radio Licenses in Elton

Call Sign: KB3UIY
Howard W Fry
2092 Forest Hill Dr
Elton PA 15934

Call Sign: KA3NAW
Joseph A Chon
145 Villa Rd
Elton PA 15934

FCC Amateur Radio Licenses in Elysburg

Call Sign: WA3SUZ
William F Baker
818 Bear Gap Rd
Elysburg PA 17824

Call Sign: KB3VXC
Jan M Bucanelli
763 Bear Hollow Rd
Elysburg PA 17824

Call Sign: WA3OLP
Harry H Ruman
Box 254 Reading Tpk
Elysburg PA 17824

Call Sign: KE3EG
Joseph J Bucanelli Jr
Box 571
Elysburg PA 17824

Call Sign: K3HRF
George Vacca Sr
10 Circle View Dr
Elysburg PA 17824

Call Sign: WB3DZW
Shirley L Vacca
10 Circle View Dr
Elysburg PA 17824

Call Sign: KA2HZO
Ronald J Chapman
1 Deerfield Dr
Elysburg PA 17824

Call Sign: W3LCU
Harry W Jones
75 N Market St
Elysburg PA 17824

Call Sign: W3TRM
Stephen F Sosh
Rr 1
Elysburg PA 17824

Call Sign: N3GEJ
Alvin R Cook
46 S Market St
Elysburg PA 17824

Call Sign: KB3EGS
Thomas J Petrusky
22 Wood Ave
Elysburg PA 17824

FCC Amateur Radio Licenses in Emeigh

Call Sign: N4KGH
Marilyn J Cavallaro
Tracy St
Emeigh PA 157380097

FCC Amateur Radio Licenses in Emigsville

Call Sign: WB3KPQ
Charles L Dundore
3144 N George St

Emigsville PA 17318

Call Sign: N3ZMP
Cindy L Fernsler
Emigsville PA 17318

Call Sign: N3ZMR
Andrew L Rittenhouse
Emigsville PA 17318

FCC Amateur Radio Licenses in Emporium

Call Sign: N3LVJ
Jean L Pugh
Box 263 E
Emporium PA 158349304

Call Sign: N3DEO
Evan H Boden
Box 61
Emporium PA 15834

Call Sign: WT3R
Michael J Callahan
2945 Cameron Rd
Emporium PA 15834

Call Sign: KB3RKU
Kent W Davis
150 Carson St
Emporium PA 15834

Call Sign: KD5CSA
James B Russell
345.5 E 3rd St
Emporium PA 15834

Call Sign: KA3MMN
Mary R Burgoon
29 E 5th
Emporium PA 15834

Call Sign: N3DKA
James F Burgoon

29 E 5th St
Emporium PA 15834

Call Sign: N3LBV
David L Kotula
349 E 5th St
Emporium PA 15834

Call Sign: KA8ETQ
Robert F Stampee
286 Hercules Rd
Emporium PA 15834

Call Sign: W3LJB
Charles J Schnering
43 Huckleberry Cir Sylvan
Hts
Emporium PA 15834

Call Sign: N3SNN
John E Jordan
6287 May Hollow Rd
Emporium PA 15834

Call Sign: KB3MBY
Kevin T Johnson
3083 Rich Valley Rd
Emporium PA 15834

Call Sign: N3HBE
Michael B Pugh
7150 Rt 120
Emporium PA 15834

Call Sign: N3FYD
Gregory E Jeffers
704 Sizerville Rd
Emporium PA 15834

Call Sign: N3SFM
William A Fleming
268 W 7th St
Emporium PA 15834

Call Sign: WA3WPS

Charles A Zimmer
127 Zimmer Dr
Emporium PA 15834

Call Sign: W3WPS
Charles A Zimmer
127 Zimmer Dr
Emporium PA 15834

Call Sign: N3JZD
Floyd G Keefer
Emporium PA 15834

Call Sign: W3KCJ
Durward L Vergason
Emporium PA 15834

FCC Amateur Radio Licenses in Enola

Call Sign: KB3KBL
Laurinda A Sarver
329 5th St
Enola PA 17025

Call Sign: KB3KNJ
Kyle D Thompson
6208 Brighton Ln
Enola PA 17025

Call Sign: WA3GRG
Bradley A Faesel
2105 Cedar Ln
Enola PA 170253323

Call Sign: N3PRO
Dave L Hoffman
2130 Cedar Ln
Enola PA 170253319

Call Sign: W3ND
Central PA Repeater Assn
Inc
2130 Cedar Ln
Enola PA 170253319

Call Sign: N3DVR
Scott R Ross
2180 Cedar Ln
Enola PA 17025

Call Sign: KA3TZD
Roy E Eckler
320 Center St
Enola PA 17025

Call Sign: KB3NBQ
William C Horvath
806 Charlotte Way
Enola PA 17025

Call Sign: N3WOE
Donald A Shenck
36 College Hill Rd
Enola PA 17025

Call Sign: KA3IJN
John H Potts
5 Cordial Dr
Enola PA 17025

Call Sign: KB3RYS
Kelsey S Ihman
1018 Dogwood Ln
Enola PA 17025

Call Sign: KB3OPN
Judson R Fodness
1038 Dogwood Ln
Enola PA 17025

Call Sign: KB3OPO
Benjamin R Fodness
1038 Dogwood Ln
Enola PA 17025

Call Sign: KB3RUM
Stoney Creek ARC
2136 Englewood Ct
Enola PA 17025

Call Sign: KB3TW
James M Updike
350 Fulton St
Enola PA 17025

Call Sign: KB3KMD
Raquel B Felix
62 Greenmont Dr
Enola PA 17025

Call Sign: KB3MWJ
Stephanie N Heikel
70 Greenmont Dr
Enola PA 17025

Call Sign: KB3LRS
Christina M Prudencio
523 Halyard Way
Enola PA 17025

Call Sign: N3DSA
David E Hutchison
912 Hawthorne St
Enola PA 17025

Call Sign: KA3PCX
Ray E Jacobs Jr
15 Hillcrest Rd
Enola PA 17025

Call Sign: N3DZR
Michael Matkowski
773 Lee Ln
Enola PA 17025

Call Sign: N3MUQ
Grahame C Rendell
789 Lee Ln Westwood
Village
Enola PA 17025

Call Sign: KB3DVV
Robert M Smeck
46 Logans Run

Enola PA 17025

Call Sign: KB3MQN
David W Tyson
837 Magaro Rd
Enola PA 17025

Call Sign: KB3DT
David W Tyson
837 Magaro Rd
Enola PA 17025

Call Sign: KB3WPK
Scott A Harling
931 Maplewood Ln
Enola PA 17025

Call Sign: KB3QXK
Chris J Kacyon
35 Millers Gap Rd
Enola PA 17025

Call Sign: KB3PAU
Allison F Sheely
78 Millers Gap Rd
Enola PA 17025

Call Sign: KB3RVL
Harold G Steager
625 Mountain St
Enola PA 17025

Call Sign: K3HFR
Harold G Steager
625 Mountain St
Enola PA 17025

Call Sign: N3YHF
Michael A Laughman
110 N Enola Dr
Enola PA 17025

Call Sign: KB3OJY
Jeffrey A Weaver
109 Pine Hill Rd

Enola PA 17025

Call Sign: WB3CZD
Edward F Marshall Jr
1 Randall Dr
Enola PA 17025

Call Sign: N3FWE
Steven M Hancock
1970 Randall Rd
Enola PA 17025

Call Sign: KB3GSP
Blaine R Handerhan
4 Redwood Dr
Enola PA 17025

Call Sign: WA3TKU
Norman F Shuey Jr
101 S Enola Dr
Enola PA 17025

Call Sign: N3KFJ
Mike A Thornton
135 S Enola Dr
Enola PA 17025

Call Sign: KB3HCR
Nancy Sue Bevis
231 S Enola Dr
Enola PA 17025

Call Sign: KB3RZR
Sean T Hoffecker
31 Sherwood Cir
Enola PA 17025

Call Sign: KB3TKX
Robert T Single
56 Sherwood Cir
Enola PA 17025

Call Sign: N3ACP
Robert T Single
56 Sherwood Cir

Enola PA 17025

Call Sign: KA1EEV
Elaine S Cox
Susquehanna Ave
Enola PA 17025

Call Sign: KD3LV
Donald F Taylor
1010 Teakwood Ln
Enola PA 17025

Call Sign: KB3YGO
John W Storer
28 Tory Cir
Enola PA 17025

Call Sign: KB3KRC
Kinjo Koyo
210 W Locust St
Enola PA 17025

Call Sign: WB3BXJ
Allen Lair
102 Wayne Ave
Enola PA 17025

Call Sign: KC3KN
Lemmerman C Kroh Sr
803 Wertzville Rd
Enola PA 17025

Call Sign: K5KZO
Ernest L Norton
4130 Wertzville Rd
Enola PA 17025

Call Sign: N3DJD
Cordelia A Peters
6932 Wertzville Rd
Enola PA 17025

Call Sign: WN3NIU
George N Peters
6932 Wertzville Rd

Enola PA 17025

Call Sign: KB3LWQ
Jesse P Culley
6977 Wertzville Rd
Enola PA 17025

Call Sign: KB3PAY
Meghan E Taglang
5500 Westbury Dr
Enola PA 17025

Call Sign: KB3LRM
Kevin M Mullen
5530 Westbury Dr
Enola PA 17025

Call Sign: KA3YES
Jeffery L Jackson
939 Woodridge Dr
Enola PA 170251547

Call Sign: KA3WLG
Kimela J Michael
233 Wyoming Ave
Enola PA 17025

FCC Amateur Radio Licenses in Ephrata

Call Sign: N3TJT
William M Rhoat
Acadamy Hts Ave
Ephrata PA 17522

Call Sign: WA3HXV
Michael L Brown
55 Bethany Rd
Ephrata PA 17522

Call Sign: N3XNT
Jackson R Yoder
30 Bethany Rd Apt H
Ephrata PA 17522

Call Sign: KB3QZD
Claire E Theis
41 Black Diamond Rd
Ephrata PA 17522

Call Sign: KA3TUF
Claire E Theis
41 Black Diamond Rd
Ephrata PA 17522

Call Sign: K3TUF
Philip C Theis Jr
41 Black Diamond Rd
Ephrata PA 17522

Call Sign: N3HWA
W A Davis
298 Boomerang Dr
Ephrata PA 17522

Call Sign: WA3QAZ
James M Reidenbach
174 Brian Dr
Ephrata PA 17522

Call Sign: KB3AOS
Ryan A Fegley
7 Briarwood Ln
Ephrata PA 17522

Call Sign: N3TUP
Craig T Rearich
242 Buchanan Dr
Ephrata PA 17522

Call Sign: KB3HXA
Kenneth A Brennan
155 Cedar St
Ephrata PA 17522

Call Sign: KA3CNK
David R Weaver Sr
16 Circle Dr
Ephrata PA 17522

Call Sign: N3ZKB
Dwayne M Wenger
1534 Clay Rd
Ephrata PA 17522

Call Sign: KB3RB
George R Eberly
906 Clearview Ave
Ephrata PA 17522

Call Sign: KA3SXC
Michael A Heffner
547 Cloverbrook St
Ephrata PA 17522

Call Sign: KA1OWS
Christopher J Sloane
28 Coolidge Dr
Ephrata PA 17522

Call Sign: N3UGX
Glenn E Stauffer
1534 Division Hwy
Ephrata PA 17522

Call Sign: N3UCU
Peter M Shrom
24 E Chestnut St
Ephrata PA 175222204

Call Sign: KB3ANY
Aleem N Fazal
26 E Chestnut St
Ephrata PA 17522

Call Sign: N3YEM
Dwayne L Fisher
173 E Farmersville
Ephrata PA 17522

Call Sign: AA3GS
Dean L Lutz
58 E Fulton St
Ephrata PA 17522

Call Sign: WY3J
Dean L Lutz
58 E Fulton St
Ephrata PA 17522

Call Sign: KA3TIV
Satyajit Tipirneni
E Fulton St
Ephrata PA 17522

Call Sign: KA3FPZ
Stephen E Petticoffer
529 E Hill St
Ephrata PA 17522

Call Sign: KB3MFD
Steven F Kintzler
592 E Hill St
Ephrata PA 17522

Call Sign: KB3OEK
Amanda L Kintzler
592 E Hill St
Ephrata PA 17522

Call Sign: KA3MFI
Randall J Shank
531 E Main St
Ephrata PA 17522

Call Sign: WA3HKT
L Douglas Weaver
132 E Mohler Church Rd
Ephrata PA 17522

Call Sign: KB3PEL
Walter L Hasselback
253 E Walnut St
Ephrata PA 175222530

Call Sign: W3JQY
Lester W Gehman
1202 Farm Crest Dr
Ephrata PA 17522

Call Sign: KJ4GPV
Robert L Starr
197 Fieldcrest Ln
Ephrata PA 17522

Call Sign: W3RLS
Robert L Starr
197 Fieldcrest Ln
Ephrata PA 17522

Call Sign: WA3PNS
Robert L Bensing
826 Grandview Dr
Ephrata PA 17522

Call Sign: KB3HHS
Rose Timmreck
146 Gregg Cir
Ephrata PA 17522

Call Sign: NQ3RP
John F McClun
1011 Hammon Ave
Ephrata PA 17522

Call Sign: KA3TAA
Timothy J Aument
130 Hemlock Rd
Ephrata PA 17522

Call Sign: WA3HLP
Randy B Maurer
336 Hillcrest Dr
Ephrata PA 17522

Call Sign: WA3MMS
Ronald J Bensing
385 Hillcrest Dr
Ephrata PA 17522

Call Sign: KB3OEJ
Charles W Hamberger
216 Jennifer Ln
Ephrata PA 17522

Call Sign: KB3JWF
Susan D Hamberger
216 Jennifer Ln
Ephrata PA 17522

Call Sign: N3OCK
Mark F Cohen
1142 Joann Ave
Ephrata PA 17522

Call Sign: WA3VVH
Dennis J Weidman
221 Joshua Ln
Ephrata PA 17522

Call Sign: KB3DWN
James W Hubbard
20 Kings Ct
Ephrata PA 17522

Call Sign: KF4KXE
James M Stephens
381 Lake St
Ephrata PA 17522

Call Sign: KB3IZC
John J Roth
225 Lincoln Ave
Ephrata PA 17522

Call Sign: WB3IGG
Robert J Gottlieb
993 Lincoln Hts Ave
Ephrata PA 17522

Call Sign: WY3F
Dennis B Sheaffer
1433 Lincoln Hts Ave B
Ephrata PA 17522

Call Sign: KB3WIS
Michael J Ciaio
38 Market View Dr
Ephrata PA 17522

Call Sign: W1DTH
Michael J Ciaio
38 Market View Dr
Ephrata PA 17522

Call Sign: KB3SHK
Ephrata Community
Hospital ARC
169 Martin Ave
Ephrata PA 175221002

Call Sign: K3ECH
Ephrata Community
Hospital ARC
169 Martin Ave
Ephrata PA 175221002

Call Sign: KB3RVZ
Ryan M Trella
1114 Martin Ave
Ephrata PA 17522

Call Sign: KB3TJL
Timothy E Davis
185 Mortar Ln
Ephrata PA 175222674

Call Sign: KA3MKT
Christopher S Peters
485 N Maple St
Ephrata PA 175221884

Call Sign: WA3MCV
Robert E Miller
499 N Maple St
Ephrata PA 17522

Call Sign: N3JPI
Timothy J Krauter
50 N Oak St
Ephrata PA 17522

Call Sign: KB3DXD
Herbert J Martin
151 Napierville Rd

Ephrata PA 17522

Call Sign: KB3ATY
Jere E Sweigart
20 Overlook Dr
Ephrata PA 17522

Call Sign: WA3AJU
Barry L Rupp
732 Pershing Ave
Ephrata PA 17522

Call Sign: WB3ABS
Donald Nissley
666 Pointview Ave
Ephrata PA 175222320

Call Sign: KB8YQI
David Sarker
37 Reagan Dr
Ephrata PA 17522

Call Sign: WA3RMS
Wilmer C Arms
61 Reagan Dr
Ephrata PA 17522

Call Sign: KB3LON
Ralph H Ransom
102 Ridge Ave
Ephrata PA 175222549

Call Sign: KA3KXA
Daniel E Ressler
540 Ridge Ave
Ephrata PA 17527

Call Sign: N3VUR
James D Martin
574 Ridge Ave
Ephrata PA 17522

Call Sign: N3VUS
Mary Jane Martin
574 Ridge Ave

Ephrata PA 17522

Call Sign: KA3YLV
Anthony T In
122 Ridge Ave
Ephrata PA 17522

Call Sign: K3OGY
Robert L King
112 Ringneck Dr
Ephrata PA 175229523

Call Sign: N3HCW
Dorothy L Musser
328 S Oak St
Ephrata PA 17522

Call Sign: WB3GRF
K Michael Musser
328 S Oak St
Ephrata PA 17522

Call Sign: KB3OEI
Eric C Sellers
363 S Reamstown Rd
Ephrata PA 17522

Call Sign: W3EB
D Scott Eaby
29 S State St
Ephrata PA 17522

Call Sign: W3DYT
Robert C Wenger
402 S State St
Ephrata PA 175222334

Call Sign: K3RHR
Ralph H Ransom
266 Sand Ct
Ephrata PA 175222549

Call Sign: N3KXC
Dale L Snyder
117 Schoeneck Rd

Ephrata PA 17522

Call Sign: W3HOX
Andrew J Yundt
70 Snyder Ln Lot 19
Ephrata PA 17522

Call Sign: KB3GKI
Heidi L Deremer
68 Spruce St
Ephrata PA 17522

Call Sign: KB3JDP
Anthony T In
32 Stonecreek Ct
Ephrata PA 17522

Call Sign: N3LNP
Robert G Jameson
90 Summerlny Dr
Ephrata PA 17522

Call Sign: K3TLM
Thomas L Mccurdy Jr
72 Summerlyn Dr
Ephrata PA 17522

Call Sign: N3JEK
Joseph J Lees
371 Vista Dr
Ephrata PA 17522

Call Sign: N3JJL
Joseph J Lees
371 Vista Dr
Ephrata PA 17522

Call Sign: N3MUO
Jeff S Walgren
280 W Church Rd
Ephrata PA 17522

Call Sign: KA3DPJ
David V Messner
938 W Main St

Ephrata PA 17522

Call Sign: KB3AVU
Claude F Morris
979 W Main St
Ephrata PA 17522

Call Sign: AB3NU
Claude F Morris
979 W Main St
Ephrata PA 17522

Call Sign: KB3VFA
Bradley A Morris
979 W Main St
Ephrata PA 17522

Call Sign: N4TKR
Roy A McCutcheon
1728 W Main St
Ephrata PA 17522

Call Sign: N4TLE
Barbara S McCutcheon
1728 W Main St
Ephrata PA 17522

Call Sign: KB3ERM
Timothy D Brunk
2002 W Main St 43
Ephrata PA 17522

Call Sign: KB3EXG
Megan L Rosenbaum
354 W Main St Apt B
Ephrata PA 17522

Call Sign: N3PKQ
Keith Bear
27 W Sunset Ave
Ephrata PA 17522

Call Sign: N3WSQ
Paul E Gause
115 Washington Ave

Ephrata PA 17522

Call Sign: N3NAS
Earl W Witmer
229 Washington Ave
Ephrata PA 17522

Call Sign: WO3P
George N Pappas
6 Weaver Ave
Ephrata PA 17522

Call Sign: WU8W
Aaron S Sweigart
58 Weaver Ave
Ephrata PA 17522

Call Sign: N3XAL
Philip L Herr
10 Woodcorner Rd
Ephrata PA 17522

**FCC Amateur Radio
Licenses in Etters**

Call Sign: KD3LL
Glen R Skinner
155 Bass Lake Rd
Etters PA 17319

Call Sign: KB3NLK
Kelli L Rapak
611 Beinhower Rd
Etters PA 17319

Call Sign: N3PNF
Thomas H Alsted
25 Bobby Jones Dr
Etters PA 17319

Call Sign: KB3OVY
Young Joo Yi
15 Bridle Ct
Etters PA 17319

Call Sign: WB3LJS
Robert G Ickes
385 Cameron St
Etters PA 17319

Call Sign: KA3MIS
Robert C Nemeth
375 Cartref Rd
Etters PA 17319

Call Sign: KD3EX
Robert A Nemeth
375 Cartref Rd
Etters PA 17319

Call Sign: KE3GZ
Zackery A Nemeth
375 Cartref Rd
Etters PA 17319

Call Sign: KB3KNF
Jordan A Shettle
180 Church Rd
Etters PA 17319

Call Sign: KB3NBX
Tervan J Shettle
180 Church Rd
Etters PA 17319

Call Sign: KA3GAX
Donald R Emert
80 Conley Ln
Etters PA 17319

Call Sign: KB3BHC
Dennis J Rumple
656 Diane Dr
Etters PA 17319

Call Sign: N3WJP
Sean S Burns
340 Fairway Dr
Etters PA 17319

Call Sign: AJ4ZM
Dustin J Crosby
175 Fisher Rd
Etters PA 17319

Call Sign: KJ3E
Dustin J Crosby
175 Fisher Rd
Etters PA 17319

Call Sign: KB3LEV
Christopher G Howard
201 Fisher Rd
Etters PA 17319

Call Sign: N2QDZ
York T Yuen
340 Fox Run Cir
Etters PA 17319

Call Sign: KB3DBV
Robert D Farabaugh
50 Harvest Dr
Etters PA 17319

Call Sign: KB3DHG
Robert D Farabaugh Jr
50 Harvest Dr
Etters PA 17319

Call Sign: KB3DVH
Dale L Carroll
166 Juniper Dr
Etters PA 17319

Call Sign: KB3ETR
Dale L Carroll
166 Juniper Dr
Etters PA 17319

Call Sign: N2CZX
Robert R Knuth
35 Mackenzie Ln
Etters PA 173199065

Call Sign: KB3SES
Nathan L Herr
51 Mall Rd
Etters PA 17319

Call Sign: KA3RBI
Francine H Reese
35 Maple Dr
Etters PA 17319

Call Sign: N2DPV
Richard W Reese
35 Maple Dr
Etters PA 17319

Call Sign: KR3EE
Richard M Reese
35 Maple Dr
Etters PA 17319

Call Sign: W3YXV
Robert D Shaffner Jr
100 Mtn View Dr
Etters PA 17319

Call Sign: N3TQV
Keith E Krause
135 Mulligan Dr
Etters PA 17319

Call Sign: KB3GXI
Jean M Krause
135 Mulligan Dr
Etters PA 17319

Call Sign: KA3PDQ
Steven V Gobat
1160 Old Trl Rd
Etters PA 17319

Call Sign: W3UU
Harrisburg Radio
Amateurs Club
1160 Old Trl Rd
Etters PA 17319

Call Sign: K3ZMP
Stephen P Intrieri
275 Pleasant View Dr
Etters PA 17319

Call Sign: W3PSU
Harry M Books Jr
699 Red Mill Rd
Etters PA 17319

Call Sign: KB3OVR
Viplav N Patel
70 Robinhood Dr
Etters PA 17319

Call Sign: KB3MWI
Shea A Hassett
70 Sam Snead Cir
Etters PA 17319

Call Sign: WA5OMY
Ellsworth M Jones
1285 Valley Green Rd 1
Etters PA 173199726

Call Sign: KB3TWW
Christopher P Shover
268 Valley Rd
Etters PA 17319

Call Sign: KB3CCT
Phillip R Shepherd
1930 Valley Rd
Etters PA 17319

Call Sign: W3PRS
Phillip R Shepherd
1930 Valley Rd
Etters PA 17319

Call Sign: N3OSO
Donald J Inscho
20 Vista Cir
Etters PA 17319

Call Sign: N3VQH
Michael A Stackpoole
91 White Dogwood Dr
Etters PA 17319

Call Sign: KG4EGM
Richard B Hershberger
188 White Dogwood Dr
Etters PA 17319

Call Sign: N3EOJ
Steven K Dormuth Jr
218 Willis Rd
Etters PA 17319

Call Sign: N3RMM
Angela M Treffinger
221 Willis Rd
Etters PA 17319

Call Sign: KE3IN
Bradford J Bobbitt
255 Willis Rd
Etters PA 17319

Call Sign: KB3QXE
Ronald J Gilbertson III
263 Willis Rd
Etters PA 17319

Call Sign: KB3STN
Nicole M Gilbertson
263 Willis Rd
Etters PA 17319

Call Sign: W3QCM
William A Huston
2020 York Haven Rd
Etters PA 17319

Call Sign: KB3OVU
Derek E Stump
20 York Hill Rd
Etters PA 17319

Call Sign: KB3LOW
Brian E Neihart
Etters PA 17319

FCC Amateur Radio Licenses in Everett

Call Sign: WB3KUA
Clyde C Shoemaker
Box 218
Everett PA 15537

Call Sign: KA3TCD
Thomas F Imgrund
Box 354
Everett PA 15537

Call Sign: K3DKJ
Joseph W Stewart
Box 447
Everett PA 15537

Call Sign: W1TRF
Robert M Resconsin
1330 Bunker Hill Rd
Everett PA 15537

Call Sign: N3AAH
Charles H McCormick
40 N Spring St
Everett PA 15537

Call Sign: KA3CUA
Gary N Trivelpiece
563 Perrin Rd
Everett PA 155376638

Call Sign: W3AMX
Thomas J Harclerode
223 Water St
Everett PA 15537

Call Sign: K3KYT
Lynn D Whetstone

196 Whetstone Rd
Everett PA 15537

Call Sign: N3XVN
Dennis E Brallier
Everett PA 15537

FCC Amateur Radio Licenses in Fairfield

Call Sign: W3CAR
Charles M Poore
13 Autumn Trl
Fairfield PA 17320

Call Sign: W3SVT
Barbara A Poore
13 Autumn Trl
Fairfield PA 17320

Call Sign: KB4FBK
Michael A Rhoades
12 Bonnie Trl
Fairfield PA 17320

Call Sign: WB7COW
Dominic Bonitatis Jr
1975 Bullfrog Rd
Fairfield PA 17320

Call Sign: N3GB
George W Baltz
298 Carrolls Tract Rd
Fairfield PA 17320

Call Sign: KB3VHZ
Kevin A Mcgough
30 Diane Trl
Fairfield PA 17320

Call Sign: KA3MCG
Kevin A Mcgough
30 Diane Trl
Fairfield PA 17320

Call Sign: KJ6WNB
William N Bequette
52 Diane Trl
Fairfield PA 17320

Call Sign: W3ATM
William N Bequette
52 Diane Trl
Fairfield PA 17320

Call Sign: KU3V
William N Bequette
52 Diane Trl
Fairfield PA 17320

Call Sign: N3KVD
Elliot M Hartzell
31 Eagle Trl
Fairfield PA 17320

Call Sign: KB3PZR
Beth A Hartzell
31 Eagle Trl
Fairfield PA 17320

Call Sign: N3EFC
Ronald J Gates
5155 Fairfield Rd
Fairfield PA 17320

Call Sign: KB3PEG
Richard K Maccani
14 Fox Trl
Fairfield PA 17320

Call Sign: W3DEX
Robert B Lauder Jr
40 Grasshopper Ln
Fairfield PA 173209122

Call Sign: KA3LAO
John W Sichert
14 Helen Trl
Fairfield PA 17320

Call Sign: KA3NGJ
David J Mickley
65 Lost Limb Ln
Fairfield PA 17320

Call Sign: WA3FNQ
Robert F Holmes
197 Old Waynesboro Rd
Fairfield PA 17320

Call Sign: N5RDF
Tom D Shirley
8 Snow Plow Trl
Fairfield PA 17320

Call Sign: N3FLY
Paul H Sell
450 Middle Creek Rd
Fairfield PA 17320

Call Sign: KB3QIC
Bonnie J Whitney
2 Pine Hill Trl
Fairfield PA 173208204

Call Sign: KE3TD
Dennis F Carter
13 Snowbird Trl
Fairfield PA 173208525

Call Sign: N3HRZ
Henry E Rajotte
606 Middle Creek Rd
Fairfield PA 17320

Call Sign: KB3QIE
D Phillip Moore
2 Pine Hill Trl
Fairfield PA 173208204

Call Sign: N3YJW
Rebecca J Carter
13 Snowbird Trl
Fairfield PA 173208525

Call Sign: KA3RWX
Edward R Buchheit Jr
976 Middle Creek Rd
Fairfield PA 17320

Call Sign: KB3QID
Vickie L Moore
2 Pine Hill Trl
Fairfield PA 173208204

Call Sign: KB3YLK
David P Dunaj II
120 Sour Mash Trl
Fairfield PA 17320

Call Sign: AA3ZR
Edward R Buchheit Jr
976 Middle Creek Rd
Fairfield PA 17320

Call Sign: W3MOL
Lawrence P Donnelly Jr
27 Pine Hill Trl
Fairfield PA 17320

Call Sign: N3RCJ
Timothy I Rhoads
62 Swallow Trl
Fairfield PA 17320

Call Sign: KA3THQ
Mary C Buchheit
976 Middlecreek Rd
Fairfield PA 17320

Call Sign: W3TOO
Robert G Hildenbrandt
50 Raven Trl
Fairfield PA 17320

Call Sign: KA3KDH
Peter A Boving
4 Trudy Trl
Fairfield PA 173208032

Call Sign: KB3NLY
Troy J Kump
70 Mt Hope Rd
Fairfield PA 17320

Call Sign: AD4FP
Richard W Etzel
63 Ringneck Trl
Fairfield PA 17320

Call Sign: KB3PCC
Bryon T Short
208 W Main St
Fairfield PA 17320

Call Sign: KB4IGS
George E Van Buskirk
60 N Miller St
Fairfield PA 17320

Call Sign: KA3SDI
Richard L Vitek
6 Skyline Trl
Fairfield PA 17320

Call Sign: KD3PD
Marco Aurelio
54 Walnut Trl
Fairfield PA 17320

Call Sign: KB3JPE
Jacob P Myers
11 Novice Run Trl
Fairfield PA 17320

Call Sign: N5RBF
Tom D Shirley
8 Snow Plow Trl
Fairfield PA 17320

Call Sign: KB2WEZ
Matthew P Rose
23 Water St
Fairfield PA 173200182

Call Sign: W3II
John F Clarke
1279 Waynesboro Pike
Fairfield PA 17320

Call Sign: WB3ILC
Richard F Abraham
10 Wortz Dr
Fairfield PA 17320

Call Sign: KB3TLX
Kimberly A McFerren
Fairfield PA 17320

FCC Amateur Radio Licenses in Fairhope

Call Sign: KB3NMJ
Kevin D Hillegas
156 Brush Creek Rd
Fairhope PA 15538

FCC Amateur Radio Licenses in Fallentimber

Call Sign: N3YBQ
John E Morrissey Sr
Box 44
Fallentimber PA 16639

Call Sign: KB3DXQ
Gary P Hollen
290 Executive Dr
Fallentimber PA 16639

Call Sign: W3ILT
Mark E Wilt
290 Fiske Rd
Fallentimber PA 16639

Call Sign: KB9OGE
Seth A Peasley
218 Foster Rd
Fallentimber PA 16639

Call Sign: N3TPU
Lisa C McClinsey
218 Foster Rd
Fallentimber PA 16639

FCC Amateur Radio Licenses in Fawn Grove

Call Sign: KA3OJR
Drew R Paren
Box 191H
Fawn Grove PA 17321

Call Sign: KB3DLB
Donald R Thompson
355 Deer Rd
Fawn Grove PA 17321

Call Sign: K3DRT
Donald R Thompson
355 Deer Rd
Fawn Grove PA 17321

Call Sign: N3FJN
Bryant B Shortley
787 Graceton Rd
Fawn Grove PA 17321

Call Sign: KB3EBR
Joseph M Leyhe
375 Kunkle Rd
Fawn Grove PA 17321

Call Sign: N3ZSU
Timothy J Leyhe
375 Kunkle Rd
Fawn Grove PA 17321

Call Sign: N3UOS
Scott A Heaps
33 Morris Ave
Fawn Grove PA 17321

Call Sign: KB3BCR
Lori J Knecht

606 Salt Lake Rd
Fawn Grove PA 17321

Call Sign: N3TBF
Martin J Knecht III
606 Salt Lake Rd
Fawn Grove PA 17321

Call Sign: N3WIN
Charles E Austin
915 W Main St
Fawn Grove PA 17321

FCC Amateur Radio Licenses in Fayetteville

Call Sign: KB3UEJ
Rexel P Gillespie
203 Ann Dr
Fayetteville PA 17222

Call Sign: K3BOU
Frank P Pinkl
7009 Augusta National
Fayetteville PA 172229418

Call Sign: KB3PCA
David L Dice
198 Black Gap Rd Trlr 150
Fayetteville PA 17222

Call Sign: NB2W
Raymond G Smalley
6226 Burning Tree Ln
Fayetteville PA 17222

Call Sign: AI4CH
Dixon C Barthel
6356 Burning Tree Ter
Fayetteville PA 17222

Call Sign: KB3ETI
Charles E Miller
6789 Fairway Dr E
Fayetteville PA 172229438

Call Sign: WB3FQJ
Lawrence M Roberts
7034 Fairway Oaks
Fayetteville PA 172229416

Call Sign: N3DAJ
Patrick T Kress
1343 Houser Rd
Fayetteville PA 17222

Call Sign: KB3HBM
Daniel Maldonado
224 Joyce Dr
Fayetteville PA 17222

Call Sign: KB3RDZ
Jill D Maldonado
224 Joyce Dr
Fayetteville PA 17222

Call Sign: N3FFI
Tracy L Stenger
124 Lincoln Ter
Fayetteville PA 17222

Call Sign: W3KRM
Robert M Stenger
124 Lincoln Ter
Fayetteville PA 17222

Call Sign: K3DPG
William R Schoenleber
4304 Lincoln Way E
Fayetteville PA 17222

Call Sign: W3JIE
John P Izzo Jr
5300 Lincoln Way E
Fayetteville PA 17222

Call Sign: KB3COE
Sylvia J Morris
5670 Lincoln Way E
Fayetteville PA 172221030

Call Sign: WN3DUG
Carlin W Morris
5670 Lincoln Way E
Fayetteville PA 172221030

Call Sign: N3SSF
William M De Gregorio Sr
111 Mont Alto Ro
Fayetteville PA 17222

Call Sign: WA3MDN
Gary L Strickler
6320 Saucon Valley Dr
Fayetteville PA 17222

Call Sign: KB3WRK
Jonathan E Dean
5112 Spruce Rd
Fayetteville PA 17222

Call Sign: WA3BWI
Holles E Dick
5113 Treher Rd
Fayetteville PA 17222

Call Sign: N3QKP
Thomas J Kissel
102 W Main St
Fayetteville PA 17222

Call Sign: KB3ABS
Brian R Deardorff
323 W Main St
Fayetteville PA 17222

Call Sign: WB2EUL
George F Lindley
177 Wilkson Ln
Fayetteville PA 17222

**FCC Amateur Radio
Licenses in Felton**

Call Sign: N3XRJ

David J Myers
Box 135A
Felton PA 17322

Call Sign: N3STB
John F Wurzbacher
Box 1388
Felton PA 17322

Call Sign: N3TSK
Daniel J Wurzbacher
Box 1388
Felton PA 173229766

Call Sign: N3PJR
John C Dumbrill
Box 605 Cross Mill Rd
Felton PA 17322

Call Sign: KD3HN
Michael A Hoffman
10295 Brogueville Rd
Felton PA 17322

Call Sign: N3XGW
Ethan A Poe
4947 Church Rd
Felton PA 17322

Call Sign: N3XGV
Sheldon A Sipe
4947 Church St
Felton PA 17322

Call Sign: KB3GLR
George M Mcclelland
154 Cold Stream Trl
Felton PA 17322

Call Sign: K3DCU
Cecil M Mundorff
2085 Delta Rd
Felton PA 17322

Call Sign: K3UQB

Lois J Mundorff
2085 Delta Rd
Felton PA 173227979

Call Sign: N3RDS
William A Grove
1500 Felton Rd
Felton PA 17322

Call Sign: KB3AII
Craig W Fulton
8185 Fulton School Rd
Felton PA 17322

Call Sign: KB3RWW
Jeffrey D Hersey
13106 Glessick School Rd
Felton PA 173228269

Call Sign: KB3SVQ
Jacob B Emenheiser
11384 Hill St
Felton PA 17322

Call Sign: W3SSA
Social Security
Administration Employees
ARC
2015 Jamie Ct
Felton PA 173227917

Call Sign: KB3FVR
Social Security
Administration Employees
ARC
2015 Jamie Ct
Felton PA 173227917

Call Sign: WI3K
Reid D Selby
2015 Jamie Ct
Felton PA 17322

Call Sign: KB3OYU
Timothy A Kise

37 Main St
Felton PA 17322

Call Sign: N3TAK
Timothy A Kise
37 Main St
Felton PA 17322

Call Sign: WB3HOQ
Edward V Edler Sr
12030 Mt Olivet Rd
Felton PA 173228422

Call Sign: K3YTJ
Robert R Woods
13005 Mt Olivet Rd
Felton PA 17322

Call Sign: KA7DBX
David L Wilbur
13767 Rambo Rd
Felton PA 17322

Call Sign: KB3SCX
Matthew L Collier
1778 Raub Rd
Felton PA 17322

Call Sign: KJ3K
David F Laughlin
4150 Ridgeway Dr
Felton PA 173228455

Call Sign: KB3RGS
Kimberly L Slaughter
4241 Ridgeway Dr
Felton PA 17322

Call Sign: KA3PSX
Francis X Kohlway
8281 Rock Jim Rd
Felton PA 17322

Call Sign: N3HIB
Ralph E Daughton Jr

13300 Trout School Rd
Felton PA 17322

Call Sign: KB3SBZ
Cindy L Fulton
13787 Winterstown Rd
Felton PA 17322

Call Sign: K3DGG
Dallas S Downs
Felton PA 17322

FCC Amateur Radio Licenses in Ferndale

Call Sign: KA3YIU
John S Becker
Beverly Dr
Ferndale PA 18921

FCC Amateur Radio Licenses in Fishertown

Call Sign: KB3TQJ
Paula D Pope
158 Read Hill Rd
Fishertown PA 15539

Call Sign: KB3WVH
Frederick C Wolfe Jr
544 Stone Church Rd
Fishertown PA 15539

FCC Amateur Radio Licenses in Fleming

Call Sign: N3UXG
Carolyn E Barton
Fleming PA 16835

FCC Amateur Radio Licenses in Flemington

Call Sign: K3NTR

Herbert E Baum
314 High St
Flemington PA 17745

FCC Amateur Radio Licenses in Flinton

Call Sign: WA3ILW
James D McFadden
Flinton PA 16640

Call Sign: KB3UIW
Michael P Reigh
Flinton PA 16640

FCC Amateur Radio Licenses in Fort Loudon

Call Sign: WA3ZPO
Glenn A Clever
45 Path Valley Rd
Fort Loudon PA 17224

Call Sign: KB3TKU
John A Bard
1086 Path Valley Rd
Fort Loudon PA
172249605

Call Sign: K3DP
John A Bard
1086 Path Valley Rd
Fort Loudon PA
172249605

Call Sign: WA3AIA
Richard H Blouch
118 S Baltimore St Box 75
Franklintown PA 17323

FCC Amateur Radio Licenses in Fredericksburg

Call Sign: N3PLJ

Shawn D Malone
341 Blue Mtn Rd
Fredericksburg PA 17026

Call Sign: N3TJQ
Delbert R Weaver
Box 205
Fredericksburg PA 17026

Call Sign: KA3TSE
Jeffrey L Gensemer
10 Cedar St Oakridge Ests
Fredericksburg PA
170269513

Call Sign: KA3KEQ
Wayne W Tobias
117 Hemlock Dr
Fredericksburg PA
170269200

Call Sign: KB3PMR
Robert C Campbell
137 Lions Dr
Fredericksburg PA 17026

Call Sign: KA3PYB
Kathleen A Sauder
261 Mountain Dr
Fredericksburg PA 17026

Call Sign: N3VQV
Donna M Rodkey
138 N Pine Grove St
Fredericksburg PA 17026

Call Sign: KC3OR
Thomas A Trainor
10 Pine St
Fredericksburg PA 17026

Call Sign: N3CKR
Kenneth E Blair
116 Poplar St
Fredericksburg PA 17026

FCC Amateur Radio Licenses in Freeburg

Call Sign: N9QLA
Curtis B Osborne
4 Fountain Run Rd
Freeburg PA 17827

FCC Amateur Radio Licenses in Friedens

Call Sign: N3IDN
Martha B Ackroyd
Box 45
Friedens PA 15541

Call Sign: KB3VYN
Brian E Mostoller
803 Causeway Dr
Friedens PA 15541

Call Sign: W3DLC
Dawn L Custer
1143 Coleman Station Rd
Friedens PA 15541

Call Sign: KB3HIS
Dawn L Custer
1143 Colemari Station Rd
Friedens PA 15541

Call Sign: KB3LBK
Travis J Murray
581 Day Rd
Friedens PA 15541

Call Sign: KQ3M
James F Welsh
178 Kent Ln
Friedens PA 155418322

Call Sign: N3QPA
Doris J Welsh
178 Kent Ln

Friedens PA 155418322

Call Sign: W3SRS
Stewart R Saylor
156 Sequoia Ln Apt 1
Friedens PA 15541

Call Sign: AK3J
Stewart R Saylor
156 Sequoia Ln Apt 1
Friedens PA 15541

Call Sign: N3IAT
Joseph G Thrash
1834 Stoystown Rd
Friedens PA 15541

Call Sign: KB3PYY
Peter P Bumbarger
365 Watson Ave
Friedens PA 15541

Call Sign: N3XDZ
Barry L Shaffer
103 Wells Creek Rd
Friedens PA 15541

Call Sign: N3BLS
Barry L Shaffer
103 Wells Creek Rd
Friedens PA 15541

Call Sign: KB3IDP
Tammy J Shaffer
103 Wells Creek Rd
Friedens PA 15541

Call Sign: KB3RHB
Northeastern Amateur
Radio Group
Friedens PA 15541

Call Sign: KB3JKY
Allegheny Highlands
Repeater Assn

Friedens PA 155410146

Call Sign: KB3JNW
Allegheny Highlands
Repeater Assn
Friedens PA 155410146

Call Sign: KQ3M
Allegheny Highlands
Repeater Assn
Friedens PA 155410146

Call Sign: WR3AJL
Allegheny Highlands
Repeater Assn
Friedens PA 155410146

Call Sign: KB3IAW
Allegheny Highlands
Repeater Assn
Friedens PA 155410146

Call Sign: W3WGX
Allegheny Highlands
Repeater Assn
Friedens PA 155410146

FCC Amateur Radio Licenses in Gaines

Call Sign: KB3RFY
James E Lucy
1944 Elk Run Rd
Gaines PA 16921

Call Sign: KB3DQP
Wayne B Williams
23 Geneva St
Gaines PA 16921

Call Sign: KB3DLX
Sylvia R Williams
23 Geneva St
Gaines PA 169210081

Call Sign: KB3DJK
Karl R Dietzel
93 Parker Hollow Ln
Gaines PA 16921

Call Sign: KB3NPC
Kathleen D Merkle
32 Ridge Rd
Gaines PA 16921

FCC Amateur Radio Licenses in Galeton

Call Sign: KB3GCQ
Adriaan A Arbeider
64 Alpine Ln
Galeton PA 16922

Call Sign: KB3GUE
Nancy Arbeider
64 Alpine Ln
Galeton PA 16922

Call Sign: N3LAN
David A Close
Box 187
Galeton PA 16922

Call Sign: KE3SX
Kim M Rarig
64 Club Hill Rd
Galeton PA 16922

Call Sign: KA3UBE
Michael A Johnson
27 Elm St
Galeton PA 16922

Call Sign: KB3FWV
John R Andrews
2136 Germania Rd
Galeton PA 16922

Call Sign: KB3NPD
Barbara K Andrews

2136 Germania Rd
Galeton PA 16922

Call Sign: WA3ITZ
Donald J Mrozowicz Sr
236 Gross Rd
Galeton PA 16922

Call Sign: K3RZL
Alfred R Lund
25 Poplar Ave
Galeton PA 169221109

Call Sign: N3NXB
John M Ruman
35 Prospect Ave
Galeton PA 16922

Call Sign: N3THY
Stephen J Szep Sr
14 Whispering Pines Ln
Galeton PA 16922

Call Sign: K3SIF
Richard L Wenzel Sr
Galeton PA 16922

Call Sign: N2PKC
Jeffrey L Bailey
Galeton PA 16922

**FCC Amateur Radio
Licenses in Gallitzin**

Call Sign: N3FQQ
Patrick J OMalley
828 Hemlock St
Gallitzin PA 16641

**FCC Amateur Radio
Licenses in Gap**

Call Sign: KB3SJG
David Zhang
5495 Deer Path Ln

Gap PA 17527

Call Sign: KB3GAW
Adam E Dellinger
933 Hidden Hollow Dr
Gap PA 17527

Call Sign: W4MSZ
William B Butcher
5571 Lincoln Hwy
Gap PA 175279631

Call Sign: KA3GLI
David B Gibbs
5607 Meadeville Rd
Gap PA 17527

Call Sign: KB3CDV
Robert F Hall
626 Meeting House Rd
Gap PA 17527

Call Sign: W3RFH
Robert F Hall
626 Meeting House Rd
Gap PA 17527

Call Sign: KC0KR
Alfred J Kostanoski
188 N Christiana Ave
Gap PA 17527

Call Sign: NE3EE
Alfred J Kostanoski
188 N Christiana Ave
Gap PA 17527

Call Sign: KB3DIW
Adam T Wilkes
6110 Old Philadelphia
Pike Apt 1
Gap PA 17527

Call Sign: KB3NRT
Elizabeth K Hull

40 Quarry Rd
Gap PA 17527

Call Sign: KB3TON
Jennifer A Sauter
40 Quarry Rd
Gap PA 17527

Call Sign: N3NAA
Jeffrey M Jankowiak
263 Quarry Rd
Gap PA 17527

Call Sign: N3PQS
William H Vandenberg
1167 Simmontown Rd
Gap PA 17527

Call Sign: WA3UMX
Joseph R Potts
5338 Strasburg Rd
Gap PA 17527

Call Sign: W3UMX
Joseph R Potts
5338 Strasburg Rd
Gap PA 17527

Call Sign: N3CBI
Edward G Shultz
870 Timberline Dr
Gap PA 17527

Call Sign: KB3RSP
Kimberly A Kennedy
5560 Umbletown Rd
Gap PA 17527

Call Sign: N3QNC
Joseph M Kennedy
754 Willow Ln
Gap PA 17527

Call Sign: AA3DP
Nancy E Walker

Gap PA 17527

Call Sign: KA3TSA
Michael R Smith
Box 285
Gardners PA 17324

Call Sign: KA3YTW
F Allen Frere
95 Fanus Rd
Gardners PA 17324

Call Sign: KB3JON
Cindy L Quigley
95 Fanus Rd
Gardners PA 173248918

Call Sign: KB3PED
Teague S Hurkala
1480 Goodyear Rd
Gardners PA 173249028

Call Sign: KG4CEB
Anthony Hurkala
1480 Goodyear Rd
Gardners PA 173249028

Call Sign: KB3FWG
Erick R Sotello
224 Oxford Rd
Gardners PA 17324

Call Sign: N7ZGQ
Danny Hunley
6253 Oxford Rd
Gardners PA 17324

Call Sign: N3XBO
Terry J Neth
6266 Oxford Rd
Gardners PA 17324

Call Sign: KB3BMO
Benjamin D Wenk
241 Reservoir Rd
Gardners PA 17324

Call Sign: KB3BKN
Grant T Delong
335 Reservoir Rd
Gardners PA 17324

Call Sign: N3XPU
Robert W Delong
335 Reservoir Rd
Gardners PA 17324

Call Sign: N3WCF
Michael A Fasick
56 School House Rd
Gardners PA 17324

Call Sign: WB3FBD
Donald R Younkin
138 Decker St
Garrett PA 155428402

Call Sign: N3NEC
Thomas M Kielbasinski
2311 Rockdale Rd
Garrett PA 15542

Call Sign: KB3JVC
Diana L Sharpe
1062 French Rooney Rd
Genesee PA 16923

Call Sign: KB3JVD
Charles F Sharpe III
1062 French Rooney Rd
Genesee PA 16923

Call Sign: KB3BLP
Tracey A Kiessling
345 7 Stars Rd
Gettysburg PA 17325

Call Sign: N3HQM
Robert L Alcorn III
360 7 Stars Rd
Gettysburg PA 173257388

Call Sign: K3RLA
Robert L Alcorn III
360 7 Stars Rd
Gettysburg PA 173257388

Call Sign: WA4DTE
Joni N Scheufel
4 Adams Ct
Gettysburg PA 17325

Call Sign: W3DTE
Joni N Scheufel
4 Adams Ct
Gettysburg PA 17325

Call Sign: NT3B
Jack R Ditzler
12 Autumn Dr
Gettysburg PA 17325

Call Sign: N3YCX
Paul A Kolumban
47 Baltimore St Apt 205
Gettysburg PA 17325

Call Sign: WA3RSV
Gilson C Sheffer
40 Baltimore St Apt 3
Gettysburg PA 17325

Call Sign: WC3AAD

Adams County Emergency
Management Agency
117 Baltimore St Rm 6
Gettysburg PA 173252313

Call Sign: WB1AUB
David M Birdwell
4 Banner Ct
Gettysburg PA 17325

Call Sign: AK3F
Michael B Hayden
394 Barlow Greenmount
Rd
Gettysburg PA 17325

Call Sign: KB3CTA
Lyman D Schwartz
1045 Barlow Two Taverns
Rd
Gettysburg PA 173257037

Call Sign: KB3CTB
Paul M Schwartz
1045 Barlow Two Taverns
Rd
Gettysburg PA 173257037

Call Sign: KA3SXJ
Ray B Miller
615 Belmont Rd
Gettysburg PA 17325

Call Sign: KB3ADZ
Chris W Andes
430 Bullfrog Rd
Gettysburg PA 17325

Call Sign: K3KGF
Tommy F McCraw
787 Burnside Dr
Gettysburg PA 17325

Call Sign: N3RQL
Bruce L Wagner

235 Carey Ln
Gettysburg PA 17325

Call Sign: N4DOL
Peter J Samuels
530 Carr Hill Rd
Gettysburg PA 17325

Call Sign: KA3VCL
Kristi L Sentz
257 Cashman Rd
Gettysburg PA 17325

Call Sign: KA2IIW
Madeline E Benyeda
48 Cedarfield Dr
Gettysburg PA 17325

Call Sign: K1PJB
Paul J Benyeda
48 Cedarfield Dr
Gettysburg PA 17325

Call Sign: KB3IPA
Adams County ARS
255 Chapel Rd
Gettysburg PA 17325

Call Sign: W3KGN
Adams County ARS
255 Chapel Rd
Gettysburg PA 17325

Call Sign: WB3JKT
Perry A D Wood
255 Chapel Rd
Gettysburg PA 17325

Call Sign: N3ZLD
Robert F Wark
87 Chapel Rd Ext
Gettysburg PA 17325

Call Sign: KB3VUT
David W Sisk

2 E Manover St Apt 3
Gettysburg PA 17325

Call Sign: KB3DVX
Jeffrey R Martini
34 E Stevens St
Gettysburg PA 17325

Call Sign: K3GLJ
James M Cole
51 E Stevens St
Gettysburg PA 17325

Call Sign: KB3AON
Jonathan C Bumbaugh
174 Early Ave
Gettysburg PA 173253127

Call Sign: W1LRZ
Raymond M Drew
563 Elm St
Gettysburg PA 17325

Call Sign: KB3NPJ
David C Reck
2190 Emmitsburg Rd
Gettysburg PA 17325

Call Sign: WA3SEE
Carl C Olson
2235 Emmitsburg Rd
Gettysburg PA 17325

Call Sign: KB3TWC
Lucas W Currens
2313 Emmitsburg Rd
Gettysburg PA 17325

Call Sign: KB3JZX
Warren E Brockett
620 Fairview Ave
Gettysburg PA 17325

Call Sign: KA6YWM
Jeffery D Robeson

650 Fairview Ave
Gettysburg PA 17325

Call Sign: W4FV
Kenneth J Lovelace
321 Forrest Dr
Gettysburg PA 17325

Call Sign: KE3RZ
John M Hartzell
174 Gordon Ave
Gettysburg PA 17325

Call Sign: KB3EEY
James A Hartzell
174 Gordon Ave
Gettysburg PA 17325

Call Sign: W3HN
John M Hartzell
174 Gordon Ave
Gettysburg PA 17325

Call Sign: K3QAC
Bob V Clow
755 Goulden Rd
Gettysburg PA 17325

Call Sign: KA3ESM
Linda L Plank
1701 Granite Station Rd
Gettysburg PA 17325

Call Sign: N3SGF
Richard W Hutchison
1370 Hanover Rd
Gettysburg PA 17325

Call Sign: KB3EUA
Craig R Hutchison
1370 Hanover Rd
Gettysburg PA 17325

Call Sign: KB3IIU
John W Wynegar

1540 Hanover Rd
Gettysburg PA 17325

Call Sign: K3ONW
Kenneth R Eshleman
27 Hanover St
Gettysburg PA 17325

Call Sign: N3ECL
Ronald E Paull
2449 Heidlersburg Rd
Gettysburg PA 17325

Call Sign: KA3NRA
Marcia D Paull
2449 Heidlersburg Rd
Gettysburg PA 173257683

Call Sign: KB1GOA
Darius P Estavillo
1047 Heritage Dr
Gettysburg PA 17325

Call Sign: KB1GOB
Paul Estavillo
1047 Heritage Dr
Gettysburg PA 17325

Call Sign: K4ZDH
William R Hollingsworth
580 Herrs Ridge Rd
Gettysburg PA 173258498

Call Sign: K3KS
Kenneth E Sease
1619 Herrs Ridge Rd Apt
A
Gettysburg PA 173258406

Call Sign: KB3MOH
Darrin S Brown
16 Hickory Ave
Gettysburg PA 17325

Call Sign: KA3HNN

Donald G Hubbard Jr
1919 Highland Ave Rd
Gettysburg PA 17325

Call Sign: WB3BQC
Graham S Bugbee
526 Hillcrest Pl
Gettysburg PA 173252614

Call Sign: N1EON
Todd W Neller
475 Hilltown Rd
Gettysburg PA 17325

Call Sign: N2PDJ
Keith D De Mell
235 Hoffman Home Rd
Gettysburg PA 17325

Call Sign: N3ZRB
Tito L Nakpil
131 Hoffman Rd
Gettysburg PA 17325

Call Sign: KC8RWD
Kurt W Keilhofer
4 Hounds Run
Gettysburg PA 17325

Call Sign: N3BVA
Steven S Myers
505 Hunterstown Rd
Gettysburg PA 17325

Call Sign: KB3ONO
Raymond E Wegley Jr
143 Jackson Dr
Gettysburg PA 173258914

Call Sign: K3BL
Raymond E Wegley Jr
143 Jackson Dr
Gettysburg PA 173258914

Call Sign: K3JHB

Earnest E Long Jr
975 Johnson Dr Lake
Heritage
Gettysburg PA 17325

Call Sign: KA3HSR
Joan B Long
975 Johnson Dr Lake
Heritage
Gettysburg PA 17325

Call Sign: WA3RXL
Richard R Golden
1670 Knoxlyn Rd
Gettysburg PA 17325

Call Sign: KB3VGK
Robert A Tavenner
716 Lee Dr
Gettysburg PA 17325

Call Sign: KA3CAC
William J Hinrichs
31 Liberty St
Gettysburg PA 17325

Call Sign: KB3ITW
Philip G Plotica
600 Long Rd
Gettysburg PA 17325

Call Sign: KB3GCY
Donald C Schmitt
500 McMillan St
Gettysburg PA 17325

Call Sign: K3DCS
Donald C Schmitt
500 McMillan St
Gettysburg PA 17325

Call Sign: KB3JXW
Carolann W Schmitt
500 McMillan St
Gettysburg PA 173252422

Call Sign: WA3DBZ
Nathan J Atwood
2737 Meadow Dr
Gettysburg PA 173257882

Call Sign: KB3VMJ
Gregory S Thomas
320 Montclair Rd
Gettysburg PA 173257772

Call Sign: KG8TM
Brock A Fekken
355 Montclair Rd
Gettysburg PA 17325

Call Sign: KB3SNI
John C Eline
240 N 4th Sts
Gettysburg PA 17325

Call Sign: KB3ONP
Nathan A Light
135 N Straton St
Gettysburg PA 17325

Call Sign: N3WQS
Jeremy J Mitchel
3005 Old Harrisburg Rd
Gettysburg PA 17325

Call Sign: KA3IXD
Milford E Rouse
1075 Old Harrisburg Rd
Lot 192 Luth
Gettysburg PA 17325

Call Sign: W1BBZ
Albert R May
203 Pegram St
Gettysburg PA 17325

Call Sign: WB8CPY
William B Bugert
1230 Red Rock Rd

Gettysburg PA 173256927

Call Sign: KB3JDJ
Elizabeth T Wood
1049 Ridge Rd
Gettysburg PA 17325

Call Sign: N3QPV
John F Kaczorowski
1091 Ridge Rd
Gettysburg PA 17325

Call Sign: N3RXY
Mycala S Kaczorowski
1091 Ridge Rd
Gettysburg PA 17325

Call Sign: WB3CVM
James D Fox
20 Ridgewood Dr Rd 8
Gettysburg PA 17325

Call Sign: K3GIS
William H Lane
1420 Russell Tavern Rd
Gettysburg PA 17325

Call Sign: KB3JHV
William D Clark
347 S Washington St
Gettysburg PA 17325

Call Sign: KB3OQI
Mark W Clinger
340 Shrivers Corner Rd
Gettysburg PA 17325

Call Sign: KB3ASA
Albert G Albanowski
226 Solomon Rd
Gettysburg PA 17325

Call Sign: NQ1M
Dennis R Mcgough
225 Springs Ave

Gettysburg PA 17325

Call Sign: W4FDP
Gary L Stanford
69 Spruce Dr
Gettysburg PA 17325

Call Sign: N4XR
Victor W Paounoff
700 Sunset Ave
Gettysburg PA 17325

Call Sign: KA3KXO
Ralph N Hall
1917 Taneytown Rd
Gettysburg PA 17325

Call Sign: KB3EWK
Pamela F Sparks
315 Village Dr
Gettysburg PA 17325

Call Sign: KB3UYG
Kyle P Miller
23 Vista Larga Dr
Gettysburg PA 173257883

Call Sign: N3EBM
Michael J Hutchison
102 W Middle St
Gettysburg PA 17325

Call Sign: KA3LCI
Thomas J Gibbons Jr
155 White Church Rd
Gettysburg PA 17325

Call Sign: KB3TOZ
Alan N Fleckner
22 Winding Dr
Gettysburg PA 17325

Call Sign: KN7ITZ
John A Messeder Jr
60 Woodcrest Dr

Gettysburg PA 17325

Call Sign: KA3MGU
Richard L Ketterman
2370 York Rd
Gettysburg PA 17325

Call Sign: KA3NBG
Paul E Karchner
2990 York Rd
Gettysburg PA 17325

Call Sign: WB6JKQ
John P Le May
Gettysburg PA 17325

Call Sign: KB3FWH
Richard K Wood
Gettysburg PA 17325

Call Sign: KB3NAQ
Donald L Redman
Gettysburg PA 17325

Call Sign: KB3TUH
Ryan W Laughman
Gettysburg PA 17325

Call Sign: KB3HRS
Richard B Le May
Gettysburg PA 173254241

Call Sign: K3RR
Joseph M Johnson
Gettysburg PA 173254807

**FCC Amateur Radio
Licenses in Glen Rock**

Call Sign: KA3UCQ
Howard C Yarbrough
18 Argyle Ave
Glen Rock PA 17327

Call Sign: N1VXD

Noel A Pierce
3409 Boose Rd
Glen Rock PA 173278347

Call Sign: N3LZR
Suzanne T Shoul
Box 189A2
Glen Rock PA 17327

Call Sign: N3RJM
Daniel O Plaine
Box 34
Glen Rock PA 17327

Call Sign: N3ZOZ
Joseph G Dzwonczyk
Box 4034
Glen Rock PA 173279502

Call Sign: KB3AQX
Patricia A Brewer
Box 451
Glen Rock PA 17327

Call Sign: KE3GU
Wayne L Smith
Box 451
Glen Rock PA 17327

Call Sign: KB3CHU
Mark A Cramer
Box 4918
Glen Rock PA 17327

Call Sign: KB3TEG
David L Crowl
6431 Brodbeck Rd
Glen Rock PA 17329

Call Sign: N3XMP
John D Magaha Jr
3243 Catholic Valley Rd
Glen Rock PA 173277657

Call Sign: KB3IMD

Thurman L Lynch
21 Church St
Glen Rock PA 17327

Nevin L McCann
201 Hanover St
Glen Rock PA 173271009

William V Kirby
5 Ridgewood Rd
Glen Rock PA 17327

Call Sign: N3VQJ
Donald B McGonigle
2593 Club House Rd
Glen Rock PA 17327

Call Sign: KB3IGH
Jonathan M Abbott
26 High St
Glen Rock PA 17327

Call Sign: W3PN
William V Kirby
5 Ridgewood Rd
Glen Rock PA 17327

Call Sign: N3ZNX
Elizabeth L McGonigle
2593 Club House Rd
Glen Rock PA 17327

Call Sign: W3CAL
James I Alban
3883 Jefferson Rd
Glen Rock PA 17327

Call Sign: KB3HZO
Rita Y Buschman
11409 Rockville Rd
Glen Rock PA 17327

Call Sign: KB3GLN
James P Mcgonigle
2593 Club House Rd
Glen Rock PA 17327

Call Sign: NY3A
Steve E Sluz
7250 Lineboro Rd
Glen Rock PA 17327

Call Sign: KB3IGF
Patricia A Bilous
4288 Shaffers Church Rd
Glen Rock PA 17327

Call Sign: KK3G
Donald B Mcgonigle
2593 Club House Rd
Glen Rock PA 17327

Call Sign: KB3GLU
Timothy W Moran
7408 Lineboro Rd
Glen Rock PA 17327

Call Sign: KB3MOF
Jonathan W Bilous
4288 Shaffers Church Rd
Glen Rock PA 17327

Call Sign: KB3PIF
Colleen E Mcgonigle
2593 Club House Rd
Glen Rock PA 17327

Call Sign: N3UDD
Ronald C Butz
4147 Pierceville Rd
Glen Rock PA 17327

Call Sign: K3DQB
Walter Bilous
4288 Shaffers Church Rd
Glen Rock PA 173279595

Call Sign: W1NPS
Hugh H Quackenbush Jr
97 Edgehill Rd
Glen Rock PA 17327

Call Sign: KA3GDI
Henry L Ziegler
178 Pine St
Glen Rock PA 17327

Call Sign: KB3IGG
Michael A Davis
11203 Susquehanna Trl
Glen Rock PA 173278600

Call Sign: W3CAK
Wilbur H Humphrey Jr
6364 Grave Run Rd
Glen Rock PA 173278752

Call Sign: KB3JSL
Mark A Koski
12294 Pleasant Valley Rd
Glen Rock PA 17327

Call Sign: N3SID
Martin J Pokrivka
33 Valley St
Glen Rock PA 17327

Call Sign: N3IKB
Nevin L McCann
201 Hanover St
Glen Rock PA 17327

Call Sign: KB3GLM
Catherine J Kirby
5 Ridge Wood Rd
Glen Rock PA 17327

Call Sign: KA3EPR
Bradley W Buchar
795 W Forrest Ave
Glen Rock PA 173277914

Call Sign: K3NLM

Call Sign: WA3PQN

Call Sign: WB3BUP

Robert P Ruby
13 West
Glen Rock PA 17327

FCC Amateur Radio Licenses in Glencoe

Call Sign: N3LIG
Harold D Nicholson
2278 Glencoe Rd
Glencoe PA 15538

Call Sign: N3MZN
Theresa A Nicholson
2278 Glencoe Rd
Glencoe PA 155382711

Call Sign: N3NDD
Stephen C Nicholson
2278 Glencoe Rd
Glencoe PA 155382711

FCC Amateur Radio Licenses in Glenville

Call Sign: KA3PNM
Larry L Rummel Sr
4964 Blue Hill Rd
Glenville PA 17329

Call Sign: KB3NRY
Steven R Kirkpatrick
5173 Rocky Rd
Glenville PA 17329

Call Sign: KB3KJO
John C Chase
4639 Shaffers Church Rd
Glenville PA 17329

Call Sign: KA3GCM
John H Cooper II
4054 Skyview Dr
Glenville PA 173299221

Call Sign: KB3PHU
Daniel I Enig
4235 Skyview Dr
Glenville PA 17329

FCC Amateur Radio Licenses in Goodville

Call Sign: N3LEB
John J Pinkas Jr
1586 Main St
Goodville PA 175280145

FCC Amateur Radio Licenses in Gordonville

Call Sign: K4GXI
Joan E Goodman
6 Boxwood Ln
Gordonville PA 17529

Call Sign: K4GXJ
Stanley F Goodman
6 Boxwood Ln
Gordonville PA 17529

Call Sign: KB3VKN
John S Dienner
74 Evergreen St
Gordonville PA 17529

Call Sign: KA3TAL
Lynn H Cole
2939 Lincoln Hwy E
Gordonville PA 17529

Call Sign: KA3TKV
William E Yelk
3714 Yost Rd
Gordonville PA
175299671

Call Sign: K3TKV
William E Yelk
3714 Yost Rd

Gordonville PA
175299671

Call Sign: N3XCV
Kevin Yost
Gordonville PA
175290061

FCC Amateur Radio Licenses in Grampian

Call Sign: WB3DVR
Cheryl A Cain
Box 357
Grampian PA 16838

Call Sign: KG4ZXC
Jesse T Tucker
5376 Chestnut Grove Hwy
Grampian PA 16838

Call Sign: KB3QKQ
Paul R Lowes
1106 Curwensville
Grampian Hwy
Grampian PA 16838

Call Sign: KB3GWP
Brian E Madera
4463 Splash Dam Rd
Grampian PA 16838

Call Sign: N3MOU
Ronald C Westover
69 W Hepburnia Rd
Grampian PA 16838

Call Sign: N3PAX
Sherryetta M Westover
69 W Hepburnia Rd
Grampian PA 16838

Call Sign: K3RCW
Ronald C Westover
69 W Hepburnia Rd

Grampian PA 16838

Call Sign: WB3DDA
Ocie P Cain
Grampian PA 16838

Call Sign: KA3KNJ
Brian D Gayan
Grampian PA 16838

FCC Amateur Radio Licenses in Grantham

Call Sign: KB3SQY
Evan E Liem
1 College Ave Box 5699
Grantham PA 17027

Call Sign: KB3RCU
Adelani E Osunsakin
Messiah College
Grantham PA 17027

Call Sign: KB3VXO
Benjamin R Clouser
1 S College Ave Box 5224
Grantham PA 17027

FCC Amateur Radio Licenses in Grantville

Call Sign: WB3FWP
Ronald J Via
512 County Line Rd
Grantville PA 17028

Call Sign: N3VOR
Gerarda A Staruch
157 Houston Dr
Grantville PA 17028

Call Sign: KC2JCD
Edward J Koster
8221 Jonestown Rd
Grantville PA 17028

Call Sign: N3ILL
Donald H Yorty
Jonestown Rd
Grantville PA 17028

Call Sign: WB3CKW
Gerard R Whisler
9000 Mountain Rd
Grantville PA 17028

Call Sign: KE3XH
Michael J Wachter
9642 Mountain Rd
Grantville PA 17028

Call Sign: NN3P
Michael J Wachter
9642 Mountain Rd
Grantville PA 17028

Call Sign: N3MLD
James K McHenry II
31 Webster School Rd
Grantville PA 17028

Call Sign: KB3RMO
Rodney J Underkoffler
Grantville PA 17028

Call Sign: W3DUS
James E Wagner
Grantville PA 17029

FCC Amateur Radio Licenses in Grassflat

Call Sign: KB3QKR
Richard A Brnik Jr
830 Cooper Ave
Grassflat PA 16839

FCC Amateur Radio Licenses in Gratz

Call Sign: KA3WYB
Grant F Beitler
Box 30
Gratz PA 17030

Call Sign: KB3CDY
Paul E Rudy Sr
213 W Market St
Gratz PA 17030

Call Sign: KA3ZFR
Leslie A Fralick
Gratz PA 17030

Call Sign: KB3ACL
Frances L Fralick
Gratz PA 17030

FCC Amateur Radio Licenses in Gray

Call Sign: K3VL
Ralph M Geiyer
120 Main St
Gray PA 15544

Call Sign: N3UVC
Lorraine E Ott
140 W 3rd St
Gray PA 15544

Call Sign: N3VHR
Bradley L Ott
W 3rd St
Gray PA 15544

Call Sign: KD3NO
Ralph A Geiyer
1071 W St Box 1416
Gray PA 15544

FCC Amateur Radio Licenses in Greencastle

Call Sign: K3ONE

Robert J French
2795 Anna Ct
Greencastle PA 17225

Call Sign: N3JDR
William A Mccarrey
9694 Antrim Church Rd
Greencastle PA 17225

Call Sign: N3ZGT
Patrick A Frederick
805 Antrim Ln
Greencastle PA 17225

Call Sign: KA3ZKU
Eldon S Geiman
11510 Burkett Ln
Greencastle PA 17225

Call Sign: N3ZAI
Terry L Yoder
12321 Carol Ave
Greencastle PA 17225

Call Sign: KB3EJL
Kristina R Yoder
12321 Carol Ave
Greencastle PA 17225

Call Sign: N3VZR
Regina E Rosenberry
3412 Conococheague Ln
Greencastle PA 17225

Call Sign: N3XUH
Darwin L Rosenberry
3412 Conococheague Ln
Greencastle PA 17225

Call Sign: N3RBV
Stephen L Fetterhoff
4192 Coseytown Rd
Greencastle PA 17225

Call Sign: KB3PJK

Douglas G Ott
12040 Crestview Dr
Greencastle PA 17225

Call Sign: N3TGT
Bryan N Crider
2208 E Weaver Rd
Greencastle PA 17225

Call Sign: N3VGT
Ronald L Kennedy Sr
3826 Filer Rd
Greencastle PA 17225

Call Sign: KB3UCS
Richard T Mcclain
4225 Fletcher Dr
Greencastle PA 17225

Call Sign: N3YSS
Jason T Long
4251 Fletcher Dr
Greencastle PA 17225

Call Sign: KB3FJN
Phillip E Bowser
12278 Grant Shook Rd
Greencastle PA 17225

Call Sign: N3WGN
Herbert T Behrens
43 Hearthside Ln
Greencastle PA 17225

Call Sign: W8JYN
Donald C Myers
48 N Jefferson St
Greencastle PA 17225

Call Sign: WA3SSC
Lee E Martin
120 Pine Dr
Greencastle PA 17225

Call Sign: KD3XO

David L Kipp
11500 Rhapsody Rd
Greencastle PA 17225

Call Sign: K3YNO
John V Stockslager
706 Ryan Ln
Greencastle PA 17225

Call Sign: KA3ZLQ
Rahn A Leitzel
572 Tall Cedar Ln
Greencastle PA 17225

Call Sign: KB3VJW
Charles A Daniels
W Baltimore St
Greencastle PA 17225

Call Sign: KA3JYG
Michael E Hunt
3416 W View Cir
Greencastle PA 17225

Call Sign: WA3AAT
Theodore E Lawhead Jr
14432 Walnut Loop
Greencastle PA 17225

Call Sign: KD3IF
William Troskoski
2730 Weaver Rd
Greencastle PA 17225

Call Sign: KB3CXH
Barry L Bland
11074 Welsh Run Rd
Greencastle PA 17225

Call Sign: KB3CXJ
Rebecca C Bland
11074 Welsh Run Rd
Greencastle PA 172259327

Call Sign: KA3LIX

Barry C Hunt
3416 Westview Cir
Greencastle PA 17225

Call Sign: KE3TB
Cliff A Nunemaker
228 Williamson Ave
Greencastle PA 17225

Call Sign: KA3RJL
Jack Sharkey III
304 Williamson Ave
Greencastle PA 17225

FCC Amateur Radio Licenses in Greenfield Township

Call Sign: N3IPR
Thomas J Drennan
221 Shadyside Dr
Greenfield Township PA 18407

FCC Amateur Radio Licenses in Halifax

Call Sign: WB3ECC
Randall M Hull
134 Armstrong St Box 501
Halifax PA 17032

Call Sign: KA3CCM
Madeline D Fulkrod
3160 Armstrong Valley Rd
Halifax PA 17032

Call Sign: KA3GRA
Randy S Macko
Back Rd
Halifax PA 17032

Call Sign: W3TS
Dana A Michael
129 Church Ln

Halifax PA 170328372

Call Sign: KA3ALL
Michael E Reedich
991 Deitrich Rd
Halifax PA 17032

Call Sign: KB3NFX
Sharon D Nissel
10 Dietrich Rd
Halifax PA 17032

Call Sign: KB3PFC
Charles R Sharp
921 Enders Rd
Halifax PA 17032

Call Sign: KD4NAP
Charles R Sharp
921 Enders Rd
Halifax PA 17032

Call Sign: N3KOM
Patrick E Castellani
60 Hill Top Rd
Halifax PA 170329405

Call Sign: WU3X
Thomas B Hale
31 Kinsinger Rd
Halifax PA 17032

Call Sign: KB3RYI
Justin I Kabonick
91 Lauren Ln
Halifax PA 17032

Call Sign: KA3GHV
Charles A Kembring Jr
Matamoras Rd
Halifax PA 17032

Call Sign: KB3BWM
Terry L Long
2778 Peters Mtn Rd

Halifax PA 17032

Call Sign: N3ZUJ
James R Funck
3000 Powells Valley Rd
121
Halifax PA 170329625

Call Sign: WB8HIA
Jeffery S Riling
32 S 2nd St
Halifax PA 17032

Call Sign: KB3EO
Richard L Wolfgang
641 Wolf Hole Rd
Halifax PA 170329213

Call Sign: KB3YIU
Halifax Radio Club
Halifax PA 17032

Call Sign: WB3BKN
Terry E Snyder
Halifax PA 170320355

FCC Amateur Radio Licenses in Hallam

Call Sign: KA3SVW
Jeffrey V Salzman
68 Artman Ave E2
Hallam PA 174061134

Call Sign: KB3VIK
Jesse O Sheeder
Friendship Ave
Hallam PA 17406

FCC Amateur Radio Licenses in Hamlin

Call Sign: N3XXE
Albert L Pike
Hamlin PA 18427

Call Sign: WX3A
Raymond A Collins
Hamlin PA 18427

**FCC Amateur Radio
Licenses in Hanover**

Call Sign: N3GVQ
Jay A Elder
628 3rd St
Hanover PA 17331

Call Sign: KB3NCT
Christian E Riley
605 3rd St Apt 4
Hanover PA 17331

Call Sign: KA3QDZ
Cecil D Baber
26 5th St
Hanover PA 17331

Call Sign: K3GKC
Thomas H Walmer
1385 Abbottstown Pike
Hanover PA 17331

Call Sign: N3TQW
Rudolph E Mullar Jr
160 Albright Dr
Hanover PA 17331

Call Sign: W3MUM
Penn Mar Radio Club
160 Albright Dr
Hanover PA 17331

Call Sign: KA3SSQ
Shawn T Marchio
29 Allegheny Ave
Hanover PA 17331

Call Sign: KB3PZS
Danny L Tesch

31 Arlene Ct
Hanover PA 17331

Call Sign: KB3TDC
John P Henrich
1637 Baltimore Pike
Hanover PA 173318439

Call Sign: N3PNO
Mary C Brown
436 Baltimore St
Hanover PA 17331

Call Sign: N3OKF
Richard E Brown
436 Baltimore St
Hanover PA 173313309

Call Sign: NT3C
Donald L Luckabaugh
888 Baltimore St
Hanover PA 17331

Call Sign: KA3RAI
Kenneth M Parvis
1054 Baltimore St
Hanover PA 17331

Call Sign: N3IRF
Mary L Dorffner
1036 Beck Mill Rd
Hanover PA 17331

Call Sign: WW3U
Patton C Stump
20 Beckmill Rd
Hanover PA 17331

Call Sign: WB3GSO
Bert B Brooks
460 Beckmill Rd
Hanover PA 17331

Call Sign: WA3GLL
Arthur N Miller Jr

35 Bee Jay Ln
Hanover PA 173319041

Call Sign: KB3BZC
Robert Sprovieri
105 Bee Jay Ln
Hanover PA 17331

Call Sign: KA3WQE
Joseph C Dorffner Sr
1940 Black Rock Rd
Hanover PA 17331

Call Sign: N3JEJ
Kerry A Dorffner
1940 Black Rock Rd
Hanover PA 17331

Call Sign: N3QYD
Erin M Dorffner
1940 Black Rock Rd
Hanover PA 17331

Call Sign: WB3HYN
Catherine M Snyder
217 Blooming Grove
Hanover PA 17331

Call Sign: N3IXF
Randy L Bechtel
484 Blooming Grove Rd
Hanover PA 17331

Call Sign: KB8ABL
David W Brooks
329 Boundary Ave
Hanover PA 17331

Call Sign: N8HQX
Edna B Brooks
329 Boundary Ave
Hanover PA 17331

Call Sign: N3MKE
Joseph W Clingan Jr

501 Boundary Ave
Hanover PA 17331

66 Cardinal Dr
Hanover PA 17331

8 Charles Ave
Hanover PA 17331

Call Sign: N3PJC
Ricky J Clingan
501 Boundary Ave
Hanover PA 17331

Call Sign: KC5EDV
Jerome Pritchett
2 Caribou St
Hanover PA 17331

Call Sign: N3HDC
Robert I Garman III
8 Charles Ave
Hanover PA 17331

Call Sign: KA3PNR
Djan L Brooks
Box 421
Hanover PA 17331

Call Sign: KB3NRX
Gary W Nalavany
1603 Carlisle Pike
Hanover PA 17331

Call Sign: N3HOA
Louanne M Garman
8 Charles Ave
Hanover PA 17331

Call Sign: W3WJZ
Kenneth W Starck
Box 451I Glatco Rd
Hanover PA 17331

Call Sign: KA3SNV
Eric C Baker
453 Carlisle St
Hanover PA 17331

Call Sign: N3YHK
Christopher M Jacobs
10 Charles Ave
Hanover PA 17331

Call Sign: WA3UNJ
Wilbur A Gilbert
151 Breezewood Dr
Hanover PA 17331

Call Sign: N3UQF
David W Barrett
30 Carlisle St 1
Hanover PA 17331

Call Sign: KB3WLS
Christopher M Jacobs
10 Charles Ave
Hanover PA 17331

Call Sign: KA3SSB
Tara Dawn Rummel
204 Broadway
Hanover PA 17331

Call Sign: N3UXM
Robert D Reib
1150 Carlisle St 463
Hanover PA 17331

Call Sign: N3NAJ
Cyril D Hockensmith
17 Charles Ave
Hanover PA 17331

Call Sign: WB3GCQ
Ned W Thoman
583 Broadway
Hanover PA 17331

Call Sign: N1JCR
John C Reynolds
1150 Carlisle St Pmb 139
Hanover PA 173311100

Call Sign: NN0W
Daryl E Duckworth
55 Cheetah Dr
Hanover PA 17331

Call Sign: KB3MCS
Mark A Zier Sr
3 Cardinal Dr
Hanover PA 17331

Call Sign: KA3UJS
Scott L Snyder
202 Centennial Ave
Hanover PA 17331

Call Sign: N3NSA
Michael E Livingston
86 Collins Cir
Hanover PA 17331

Call Sign: N3TOH
Tabitha A Zier
3 Cardinal Dr
Hanover PA 17331

Call Sign: KB3QLO
Ian W Stump
355 Centennial Ave
Hanover PA 17331

Call Sign: KB3PJD
Jill M Masenheimer
23 Colonial Ct
Hanover PA 17331

Call Sign: N3YCW
Benjamin T Munion

Call Sign: KA3VIF
Melissa A Garman

Call Sign: N3ZQO
Douglas L Kibler

12 Colonial Dr
Hanover PA 17331

Call Sign: N3HDK
William H Dukes Jr
21 Colonial Dr
Hanover PA 17331

Call Sign: N3MCT
Walter Jaworskyj
44 Colonial Dr
Hanover PA 17331

Call Sign: WA2EIQ
Jon E Stroberg
7 Cornell Dr
Hanover PA 17331

Call Sign: WB3LDI
Jad S Sneeringer
355 Dart Dr
Hanover PA 17331

Call Sign: K3JAD
Jad S Sneeringer
355 Dart Dr
Hanover PA 17331

Call Sign: W3PWW
Theodore W Young
601 Deagen Rd
Hanover PA 17331

Call Sign: KA3WXQ
Lewis D McAnall
50 Deer Dr
Hanover PA 17331

Call Sign: KB3WSK
Kyle M OKeeffe
30 Diana Ct
Hanover PA 17331

Call Sign: KB3FYK
Casimir J Stankovitz

82 Dickinson Dr
Hanover PA 173317754

Call Sign: KB3DDH
Richard E Haugh Sr
88 Dickinson Dr
Hanover PA 17331

Call Sign: N3SWT
Timothy R Gude
14 Dove Cir
Hanover PA 17331

Call Sign: N3YAN
Margaret E Gude
14 Dove Cir
Hanover PA 17331

Call Sign: W3FDA
Millard H Klunk
118 E Hanover St
Hanover PA 17331

Call Sign: NU3X
Richard E Hershey
634 E Middle St
Hanover PA 17331

Call Sign: WW4BS
West W B Seachrist
35 Eagle Dr
Hanover PA 173318110

Call Sign: KB3ISR
James E Fisher Jr
239 El Vista Dr
Hanover PA 173318402

Call Sign: N3NVG
Richard J Utz
296 El Vista Dr
Hanover PA 17331

Call Sign: KB3LLS
Michele S Mitroff

383 El Vista Dr
Hanover PA 17331

Call Sign: KD7AHN
William M Street
34 Elk Dr
Hanover PA 17331

Call Sign: N3LKR
Gregory S Hagan Sr
79 Fox Run Rd
Hanover PA 17331

Call Sign: W1RRL
Robert R Lowery Jr
1110 Fox Run Ter
Hanover PA 17331

Call Sign: KA3SSN
Timothy R Rohrbaugh
272 Frederick St
Hanover PA 17331

Call Sign: KB3VWT
Joseph M Sheldon Jr
30 Frock Dr
Hanover PA 17331

Call Sign: KB3MQK
Joseph M Sheldon Sr
30 Frock Dr
Hanover PA 173319155

Call Sign: K3CAR
Joseph M Sheldon Sr
30 Frock Dr
Hanover PA 173319155

Call Sign: KA3ZKF
Lois M Wherley
514 Fulton St
Hanover PA 17331

Call Sign: KA3ZKP
Mark A Wherley

514 Fulton St
Hanover PA 17331

Greensprings Rd
Hanover PA 17331

18 Heights Ave
Hanover PA 17331

Call Sign: W3KAZ
Joseph J Edwards
36 George St
Hanover PA 173311911

Call Sign: N3YWK
Amanda L Hoffman
Greensprings Rd
Hanover PA 17331

Call Sign: KA3TDI
Anne M Einhorn
208 Hobart Rd
Hanover PA 17331

Call Sign: N3LJV
Bonnie J Starck
1238 Glatco Lodge Rd
Hanover PA 17331

Call Sign: N3RAM
John E Hoffman
Greensprings Rd
Hanover PA 17331

Call Sign: KA3SVE
David M Einhorn
208 Hobart Rd
Hanover PA 173318105

Call Sign: N3IOV
Scott W Starck
1238 Glatco Lodge Rd
Hanover PA 17331

Call Sign: N2KAG
Patricia T Collamer
223 Hall Dr
Hanover PA 17331

Call Sign: KA3NBS
Douglas E Wagner
932 Hobart Rd
Hanover PA 17331

Call Sign: N3ZDH
David L Hess
7719 Gnatstown Rd
Hanover PA 17331

Call Sign: N3QGD
Nathan A Little
1999 Hanover Pike
Hanover PA 17331

Call Sign: N3PPL
Todd A Comstock Sr
1243 Hoff Rd
Hanover PA 17331

Call Sign: K3REE
Lester W Kerchner
Grandview Rd
Hanover PA 17331

Call Sign: KA3TLJ
Scott C Decker
5534 Hanover Rd
Hanover PA 17331

Call Sign: N3HZM
Craig E Chandler
202 Honeysuckle Ct
Hanover PA 173311318

Call Sign: KA3SSO
Neil M Johnson
26 Grant Dr
Hanover PA 17331

Call Sign: KB3KYU
Douglas L Kincaid Jr
3436 Harbor Ct
Hanover PA 17331

Call Sign: KA3SSL
Vijai S Tivakaran
206 Honeysuckle Ct
Hanover PA 17331

Call Sign: N3YCY
Rosemary Hoffman
Green Springs Rd
Hanover PA 17331

Call Sign: K3DLK
Douglas L Kincaid Jr
3436 Harbor Ct
Hanover PA 17331

Call Sign: KA3SNU
Douglas F Lieb
207 Honeysuckle Ct
Hanover PA 17331

Call Sign: N3YEF
David M Forck
Green Springs Rd
Hanover PA 17331

Call Sign: K3JUC
Jerome J Schoolden
657 Hartman Ave
Hanover PA 173313710

Call Sign: N3XSC
Scott E Forney Sr
105 Hufnagle Dr
Hanover PA 17331

Call Sign: N3QHX
Adam A Hoffman

Call Sign: KA3SQY
Nelson J Myers

Call Sign: KB3CLT
Edward M Calvert Jr

201 Jasmine Dr
Hanover PA 173313462

101 Linden Ave
Hanover PA 17331

37 Meade Ave
Hanover PA 17331

Call Sign: KB3QVW
Todd B Packer
221 Jasmine Dr
Hanover PA 17331

Call Sign: N3NPB
Albert T Crigger II
330 Linden Ave
Hanover PA 17331

Call Sign: KB3QLP
Jesse M Lucabaugh
217 Meade Ave
Hanover PA 17331

Call Sign: N3EOT
Todd B Packer
221 Jasmine Dr
Hanover PA 17331

Call Sign: KB3RGJ
Gary L Shoemaker Jr
8 Loop Dr
Hanover PA 17331

Call Sign: KB3MVB
Marty G Burton
414 Meade Ave
Hanover PA 17331

Call Sign: W2BOW
Joseph E Bright Sr
349 Jasmine Dr
Hanover PA 17331

Call Sign: WB3EME
Hubert T Adkins
110 Los Alamitos Cir
Hanover PA 173317830

Call Sign: KB3RGP
Teresa M Burton
414 Meade Ave
Hanover PA 17331

Call Sign: W2QPI
Martha O Bright
349 Jasmine Dr
Hanover PA 17331

Call Sign: N3LRJ
James T Scharf
25 McAllister St
Hanover PA 17331

Call Sign: KA3TQH
William K Mixter
44 Misty Ct
Hanover PA 17331

Call Sign: W3KA
James G Weisz
369 Joshua Ct
Hanover PA 17331

Call Sign: KA3SDR
William H Fissel IV
843 McAllister St
Hanover PA 17331

Call Sign: W3WVQ
Donald F Staub
71 Monroe St
Hanover PA 17331

Call Sign: KB3VWR
Charles R Mackley
1125 Krentler Dr
Hanover PA 17331

Call Sign: K3SFK
William E Bartholomew Jr
100 McClellan Ln
Hanover PA 17331

Call Sign: N3CST
Robert J Scott
609 Morning Glory Dr
Hanover PA 17331

Call Sign: AB6PO
James L Hamlin
15 Laurel Dr
Hanover PA 17331

Call Sign: KA3SNW
Mark A Bittinger
508 McCosh St
Hanover PA 17331

Call Sign: W3CQB
Charles R Strong
1198 Moulstown Rd N
Hanover PA 173316853

Call Sign: KE3YT
Daniel R Simmonds
862 Laurel Woods Ln
Hanover PA 17331

Call Sign: K3SUN
Joel M Ruths
833 McCosh St
Hanover PA 17331

Call Sign: KA3SQQ
Bruce P Bouchard
430 N Franklin St
Hanover PA 17331

Call Sign: N0NYY
Kenneth B Schmidt

Call Sign: KB3OYI
Joel M Ruths

Call Sign: KA3SQR
Matthew P Bouchard

430 N Franklin St
Hanover PA 17331

Call Sign: W3JNT
Clyde D Coulson
235 N Stephen Pl
Hanover PA 17331

Call Sign: KB3TVG
John C Reynolds
45 Northview Dr
Hanover PA 173314520

Call Sign: WA3ZGK
Dorothy R Wise
18 O Neill
Hanover PA 17331

Call Sign: WB3FNP
Wayne C Reindollar
118 Paul St
Hanover PA 173311411

Call Sign: KB3ITR
James M OConnor
322 Penn St
Hanover PA 17331

Call Sign: KB3MCP
Brandee W Markle
148 Pheasant Run Ln
Hanover PA 17331

Call Sign: KB3MCI
Frederick N Markle III
148 Pheasant Run Ln
Hanover PA 17331

Call Sign: N3OZS
Frederick N Markle III
148 Pheasant Run Ln
Hanover PA 17331

Call Sign: K3ZXW
Henry J Hoffacker Jr

9 Rebecca Ln
Hanover PA 17331

Call Sign: KA3SRQ
Philip E Bealing
205 Ruth Ave
Hanover PA 17331

Call Sign: KB3FUW
Shawn A Shaffer
44 S Allwood Dr
Hanover PA 17331

Call Sign: KB3ETX
Robert A Shaffer Jr
44 S Allwood Rd
Hanover PA 17331

Call Sign: W3TRW
Robert A Shaffer Jr
44 S Allwood Rd
Hanover PA 17331

Call Sign: N3VNX
Brian E Barnhart
415 S High St
Hanover PA 17331

Call Sign: N3XTP
Bobbie S Barnhart
415 S High St
Hanover PA 17331

Call Sign: N3VN
Brian E Barnhart
415 S High St
Hanover PA 17331

Call Sign: KB3EE
Philip L Braun
55 Sandy Ct
Hanover PA 17331

Call Sign: KB3AOA
Ryan J Sexton

56 Sara Ln
Hanover PA 17331

Call Sign: KA3SQP
Troy L Bolin
1011 Shafer Dr
Hanover PA 17331

Call Sign: KA3SSM
Daniel C Frey
140 Sheppard Rd
Hanover PA 17331

Call Sign: KC8RHC
Michael W Kipps
263 Smeach Dr
Hanover PA 17331

Call Sign: KA3ORO
Dale R Martin
54 South St
Hanover PA 17331

Call Sign: KG3N
Randy E Shriver
209 South St
Hanover PA 17331

Call Sign: KA3WKO
Ralph S Green Sr
305 South St
Hanover PA 17331

Call Sign: W3LPW
Theron B Unger
35 Sprenkle Ave
Hanover PA 17331

Call Sign: KQ4KZ
Jeffrey D Wise
612 Spring Ave
Hanover PA 17331

Call Sign: KA3PST
Gerald A Applefeld

236 St Bartholomew Rd
Hanover PA 17331

Call Sign: KC3UZ
Harold A Nixon
80 St Michaels Way
Hanover PA 17331

Call Sign: N3EZO
Richard T Oberlander Jr
158 Sunset Dr
Hanover PA 173319736

Call Sign: KB3LUO
Kenneth I Keeling
45 Timber Ln
Hanover PA 17331

Call Sign: KB3SZY
Christopher J Flynn
116 Timber Ln
Hanover PA 17331

Call Sign: KB3PZQ
Kate E Lambert
11 Toll Gate Rd
Hanover PA 17331

Call Sign: KB3DSR
Joseph D Lambert
11 Tollgate Rd
Hanover PA 17331

Call Sign: WB3IKC
Haley W Hobbs Jr
5 Utz Dr
Hanover PA 17331

Call Sign: N0AA
Moody C Thompson
1700 Utz Ter 309
Hanover PA 17331

Call Sign: N0KYZ
Virginia R Thompson

1700 Utz Ter 309
Hanover PA 17331

Call Sign: KA3SSP
Mitchell D Lehigh
116 W Elm Ave
Hanover PA 17331

Call Sign: KB3KAU
Rodney B Messinger
122 W Granger St
Hanover PA 17331

Call Sign: N3XSD
Galen W Eline
322 W Walnut St
Hanover PA 17331

Call Sign: N3NFG
Janet N Weir
213 West Ave
Hanover PA 17331

Call Sign: KD3GI
Robert W Weir
213 West Ave
Hanover PA 173311858

Call Sign: N3OTK
Nathan A Weir
213 West Ave
Hanover PA 173311858

Call Sign: W3BCS
Howard E Narkates
222 West Ave
Hanover PA 17331

Call Sign: N3OKE
Mark A Hockensmith
1230 Westminster Ave
Hanover PA 17331

Call Sign: KA3SLM
George A Moll

425 Westminster Ave 136
Hanover PA 173319141

Call Sign: KI4IH
Frank J Paskowski
425 Westminster Ave 165
Hanover PA 17331

Call Sign: K3DNC
Richard S Klunk
Hanover PA 17331

Call Sign: K3DUP
Pearl M Klunk
Hanover PA 17331

Call Sign: KE3WE
Christopher L Fedor
Hanover PA 17331

Call Sign: K3QO
Christopher L Fedor
Hanover PA 17331

**FCC Amateur Radio
Licenses in Harrisburg**

Call Sign: KB3YDS
Francis Quigley
2317 Abbey Ln
Harrisburg PA 17112

Call Sign: KB3YDR
Mary Marie Quigley
2317 Abbey Ln
Harrisburg PA 17112

Call Sign: W3UTD
Fraser Bonnett
2340 Abbey Ln
Harrisburg PA 17112

Call Sign: K3WKK
Brian R Greenway
2545 Alessandro Blvd

Harrisburg PA 17110   Harrisburg PA 17112   Harrisburg PA 171093443

Call Sign: KB3VM   Call Sign: K3BHZ   Call Sign: KB3AGR
Brian R Greenway   Robert W Horvath   Kathleen L Marzari
2545 Alessandro Blvd   5027 Bass Lake Dr   2709 Birch St
Harrisburg PA 17110   Harrisburg PA 17111   Harrisburg PA 17109

Call Sign: N2NZA   Call Sign: N3PVX   Call Sign: N3IRD
Lew Lloyd   Mark D Spoonhour   James B Kirk
2615 Alessandro Blvd   6540 Baywood Dr   533 Blanchester Rd
Harrisburg PA 171109351   Harrisburg PA 17111   Harrisburg PA 17112

Call Sign: WA3LWM   Call Sign: WA3WEO   Call Sign: KB3MCK
Albert A Oberheim   John H Gamber   Barry W Ernest
7953 Appalachian Trl E   3400 Beaucrest St   542 Blanchester Rd
Harrisburg PA 17112   Harrisburg PA 17111   Harrisburg PA 171122206

Call Sign: KJ4RVF   Call Sign: KA3UFO   Call Sign: K3NVO
Henry Scherrer   William E C Fuller IV   Ronald L Kaullen
7633 Appleby Rd   425 Berryhill Rd   6326 Blue Flag Ave
Harrisburg PA 17112   Harrisburg PA 17109   Harrisburg PA 171122323

Call Sign: KA3ACF   Call Sign: KA3ZLC   Call Sign: N3OAH
Jasper P Buela   Paul C Mauger   Henry W Demler Jr
4815 Arney Rd   1320 Berryhill St   808 Blue Jay Rd
Harrisburg PA 17111   Harrisburg PA 17104   Harrisburg PA 17111

Call Sign: KB3IIC   Call Sign: KA3ZLD   Call Sign: KB3QPS
Yuri A Topolnicki   Nancy R Mauger   Hu Young Kim
2313 Aspen Way   1320 Berryhill St   913 Blue Jay Rd
Harrisburg PA 17110   Harrisburg PA 17104   Harrisburg PA 17111

Call Sign: KB3HOX   Call Sign: KC3MS   Call Sign: KA3AAQ
Aaron M Zeiset   Jack M Gussman   John K Nally
36 Balm St   2146 Berryhill St   2451 Blue Mtn Pky
Harrisburg PA 17103   Harrisburg PA 17104   Harrisburg PA 17112

Call Sign: N3YCL   Call Sign: N3KZK   Call Sign: KB3TWX
John H Stillwagon Jr   Todd A De Angelis   Kief T Sherow
1346 Bamberger Rd   2158 Berryhill St   6119 Blue Stone Ave
Harrisburg PA 17110   Harrisburg PA 17104   Harrisburg PA 17112

Call Sign: K3SPK   Call Sign: W3BZS   Call Sign: W9PEP
John J Hrabovsky   James E Thomas   Kief T Sherow
5590 Banbridge Dr   2600 Birch St   6119 Blue Stone Ave

Harrisburg PA 17112

Harrisburg PA 17112

Harrisburg PA 17111

Call Sign: W3KST
Kief T Sherow
6119 Blue Stone Ave
Harrisburg PA 17112

Call Sign: KB3RWB
Greg S Brulo
6251 Bridle Ct
Harrisburg PA 17111

Call Sign: N3GSZ
Gary F Torcaso
906 Cardinal Dr
Harrisburg PA 17111

Call Sign: N3PHQ
Rick A Walter
6112 Bluebird Ave
Harrisburg PA 17112

Call Sign: KB3RRV
Michael S Brulo
6251 Bridle Ct
Harrisburg PA 17111

Call Sign: N3GTA
Barbara J Torcaso
906 Cardinal Dr
Harrisburg PA 17111

Call Sign: N3BVO
Richard E Dare
6312 Bluestone Ave
Harrisburg PA 17112

Call Sign: KB3KBN
Rachel A Lambdin
218 Briggs St
Harrisburg PA 17102

Call Sign: KA3SHU
Walter G Hurliman
4217 Catalina Ln
Harrisburg PA 17109

Call Sign: N3PEE
Paul J Troiani III
660 Boas St
Harrisburg PA 17102

Call Sign: N3KXZ
J Keith Ostertag
3619 Brisban St
Harrisburg PA 17111

Call Sign: N3DKB
Robert O Thompson
6211 Catherine St
Harrisburg PA 171121815

Call Sign: W3ADE
Lewis E Elicker Jr
2260 Boas St
Harrisburg PA 17103

Call Sign: N3WEC
John A Jones
3864 Brisban St
Harrisburg PA 17111

Call Sign: KB3GKR
David J Miceli
6040 Chamber Hill Rd
Harrisburg PA 17111

Call Sign: N2XHD
Howard E Corsnitz
2618 Boas St
Harrisburg PA 17103

Call Sign: KB3SNZ
Jacob J Richards
3826 Brytton Ln
Harrisburg PA 17110

Call Sign: KB3JHY
Ronald L Stahl
5860 Chambers Hill Rd
Harrisburg PA 171113305

Call Sign: KA3ZZN
Dace L Edwards
660 Boas St Apt 708
Harrisburg PA 17102

Call Sign: W3IGH
Harry B Schaefer
3251 Butler St
Harrisburg PA 17103

Call Sign: WB3DNA
Timothy R Fanus
6140 Chambers Hill Rd
Harrisburg PA 17111

Call Sign: KB3EMQ
Tsr Wireless ARC
1649 Bobali Dr
Harrisburg PA 17104

Call Sign: KC3JG
John F Booker
1021 Buttonwood Dr
Harrisburg PA 17109

Call Sign: K3LWP
John D Scheib
7341 Chambers Hill Rd
Harrisburg PA 17111

Call Sign: WA3AUW
Cary O Johnson Sr
421 Bolton Dr

Call Sign: KB3MVN
Donald C Alfano II
1025 Canter Ct

Call Sign: KP4XY
Miguel I Cupeles
7450 Chambers Hill Rd

Harrisburg PA 171115115

Harrisburg PA 17112

Harrisburg PA 171121405

Call Sign: N3YKJ
Mary R Cupeles
7450 Chambers Hill Rd
Harrisburg PA 171115115

Call Sign: N3TKP
Jacob L Raynes Jr
6361 Clearfield St
Harrisburg PA 17111

Call Sign: KS4W
Mark A Frank
1903 Colonial Rd
Harrisburg PA 17112

Call Sign: WB3M
Miguel I Cupeles
7450 Chambers Hill Rd
Harrisburg PA 171115115

Call Sign: N3VLU
Mona B Raynes
6361 Clearfield St
Harrisburg PA 17111

Call Sign: N3JJG
Robert I Boyer
4917 Colorado Ave
Harrisburg PA 17109

Call Sign: N3BCT
Michael Tracz
7671 Chambers Hill Rd
Harrisburg PA 171115120

Call Sign: N3UJS
David E Clouser
6400 Clearfield St
Harrisburg PA 17111

Call Sign: KB3TGZ
Patricia A Shaver
5008 Colorado Ave
Harrisburg PA 17109

Call Sign: WS3Y
Paul B Moyer
8111 Chambers Hill Rd
Harrisburg PA 17111

Call Sign: WB3JFA
John C Frye II
7015 Clearfield St
Harrisburg PA 171110122

Call Sign: KA3DXW
John R Shaver
5008 Colorado Ave
Harrisburg PA 171095555

Call Sign: N3KYP
Richard S Aurand
6396 Chelton Ave
Harrisburg PA 17112

Call Sign: KA3VRD
Stephen D Gherardini
532 Clermont Dr
Harrisburg PA 17112

Call Sign: N3YCK
David J Long
4029 Concord St
Harrisburg PA 17109

Call Sign: K3ETZ
James C Cooper
6021 Cherry Hill Rd
Harrisburg PA 171114720

Call Sign: N3ZHV
Frank J Nestler
3613 Cloverfield Rd
Harrisburg PA 17109

Call Sign: WA4TVA
Robert G Bodenheimer
1547 Creek Bed Dr
Harrisburg PA 17110

Call Sign: WB3CAW
Clifford P Miller
301 Chestnut St Apt 2114
Harrisburg PA 17101

Call Sign: KB3RKN
Dimitri G Ressetar
3620 Cloverfield Rd
Harrisburg PA 171092540

Call Sign: KA3CCL
Herman J Egresitz
343 Crescent St
Harrisburg PA 171041713

Call Sign: KB3WGU
Amy S Withrow
1610 Churchill Rd
Harrisburg PA 171114898

Call Sign: N3VYF
Nicholas G Megoulas
696 Colleen Dr
Harrisburg PA 17109

Call Sign: K3SZX
Alan A Abt
4310 Crestview Rd
Harrisburg PA 17112

Call Sign: N3WWG
Ernest F Laurich
5017 Circle Dr

Call Sign: K3KJS
Samuel P Lanza
1802 Colonial Rd

Call Sign: KB3KLE
Martin P Gutekunst
5705 Crickett Ln

Harrisburg PA 171123112

Call Sign: KB3BAA
Martin P Gutekunst
5705 Crickett Ln
Harrisburg PA 171123112

Call Sign: KB3NSX
David C Posavec
1039 Custan Dr
Harrisburg PA 171102804

Call Sign: N6CAZ
James E Irish
4105 Cypress Rd Apt L
Harrisburg PA 17112

Call Sign: N3XDI
Jared R Miller
7691 Daniel Dr
Harrisburg PA 17112

Call Sign: KE3WL
Gregory A Shawley
324 Deaven Rd
Harrisburg PA 17111

Call Sign: KB3PXV
Timothy R Wallace
16 Deckert Rd
Harrisburg PA 17109

Call Sign: W3SRV
Scott W Yerger
3524 Derry St
Harrisburg PA 17111

Call Sign: N3DSQ
Randy H Heckard Jr
4605 Derry St
Harrisburg PA 17111

Call Sign: KB3QNM
Cory P Mcnamara
6202 Devonshire Hts Rd

Harrisburg PA 17112

Call Sign: KB3SNJ
Howard J Himes
5580 Devonshire Rd
Harrisburg PA 171123909

Call Sign: KB3TWV
Richard B Taylor II
6012 Devonshire Rd
Harrisburg PA 17112

Call Sign: K2RBT
Richard B Taylor II
6012 Devonshire Rd
Harrisburg PA 17112

Call Sign: KB3QDP
Eric M Pochak
2824 Dochne Rd
Harrisburg PA 17110

Call Sign: AA4GB
George H Britton Jr
1532 Dogwood Dr
Harrisburg PA 17110

Call Sign: N3HSH
Charles E Hursh
1004 Donald Dr
Harrisburg PA 171114613

Call Sign: WB3DRT
Leander R Schwan
2066 Doral Dr
Harrisburg PA 171121520

Call Sign: KA3VDA
Wayne E Kisner
509 Drexel Rd
Harrisburg PA 17109

Call Sign: N3SFV
Harold Hassman
3825 Durham Rd

Harrisburg PA 17110

Call Sign: W3HUP
Roger H Urban
4004 Eastbrook Rd
Harrisburg PA 17109

Call Sign: AA3CK
William H Ruddy
5548 Edsel St
Harrisburg PA 17109

Call Sign: WA3JPX
Richard H Fogarty
5549 Edsel St
Harrisburg PA 17109

Call Sign: N3WWH
William R Dimeler
6205 Elaine Ave
Harrisburg PA 17112

Call Sign: KA3PQJ
Teresa A Dermes
3897 Elder Rd
Harrisburg PA 17111

Call Sign: KB3KNQ
Scott W Gardner
3211 Elm St
Harrisburg PA 17109

Call Sign: WA3VDQ
William F Bostic
6204 Elmer Ave
Harrisburg PA 171121732

Call Sign: KB3CDD
Sean E Sangree
4141 Elmerton Ave
Harrisburg PA 17109

Call Sign: N3FKC
Robert J Engle
917 Emerald Ln

Harrisburg PA 17112

Call Sign: KA3WPK
Karl Karpa
Evans Ave
Harrisburg PA 17109

Call Sign: N3OUO
James N Correll Jr
6336 Evelyn St
Harrisburg PA 17111

Call Sign: K3ECD
Lee M Frank Sr
6337 Evelyn St
Harrisburg PA 17111

Call Sign: N3QWU
John C Frye III
7926 Evening Star Dr
Harrisburg PA 171129305

Call Sign: W3DAR
Dennis A Rayfield
6407 Farmcrest Ln
Harrisburg PA 17111

Call Sign: KI3F
Dennis A Rayfield
6407 Farmcrest Ln
Harrisburg PA 17111

Call Sign: N3QWT
John F Shinkowsky
316 Fawn Ridge N
Harrisburg PA 17110

Call Sign: KA3GEQ
Merle L Thomas
125 Ferree St
Harrisburg PA 17109

Call Sign: KB3OIY
Christian W Ribec

3421 Fishing Creek Valley Rd
Harrisburg PA 17112

Call Sign: KB3EUU
Gregory R Whisler
179 Florence Dr
Harrisburg PA 17112

Call Sign: KB3MWK
Christopher M Hennessy
6480 Gallop Rd
Harrisburg PA 17111

Call Sign: KB3STR
Gregory R Hennessy
6480 Gallop Rd
Harrisburg PA 17111

Call Sign: KB3OJB
Jonathan R Wilson
216 Glenview Ave
Harrisburg PA 17112

Call Sign: N3QCD
Robert M Hinkelman
4 Gloucester St
Harrisburg PA 17109

Call Sign: KB3LRR
Thurgood A Powell
4701 Great Oak Ln
Harrisburg PA 17110

Call Sign: KB3SNT
Lauren Mills
1927 Green St
Harrisburg PA 17102

Call Sign: WB3AMB
Gregory V Gross
3122 Green St
Harrisburg PA 17110

Call Sign: KA3TZE

Ira Silverman
3495 Green St
Harrisburg PA 17110

Call Sign: W3HJA
David Feinberg
3624 Green St
Harrisburg PA 171101538

Call Sign: W3SAV
Donald Vaninwegen
1731 Green St Apt 3
Harrisburg PA 17102

Call Sign: KB3KNP
David J Mitsky
685 Gregs Dr Apt 73
Harrisburg PA 17111

Call Sign: W3ILQ
Joseph K Goldsmith
4043 Greystone Dr
Harrisburg PA 17112

Call Sign: K3LG
Bernard Schmidt
4055 Greystone Dr
Harrisburg PA 17112

Call Sign: N3MFV
Wallis E Bluhm
3015 Guineveers Dr Apt A2
Harrisburg PA 171103511

Call Sign: WA1VCL
Robert E Masoero
300 Harford Ave
Harrisburg PA 17111

Call Sign: K3GCR
Norman A Diefenderfer Sr
4923 Harman Dr
Harrisburg PA 17112

Call Sign: W3AIL
Terry L Guerrant Sr
647 Harris St
Harrisburg PA 171021126

Call Sign: N3ZZD
Daniel A Hodge
560 Harvest Dr
Harrisburg PA 17111

Call Sign: N3WEG
Michael J Orris
6296 Harvest Field Ln
Harrisburg PA 171117062

Call Sign: WB3IDG
Matthew M Douglas Jr
610 Hastings Dr
Harrisburg PA 17109

Call Sign: AB0PB
Jeffrey T Sanford
6499 Heatherfield Way
Harrisburg PA 17112

Call Sign: N3LOP
Craig A Telesha
Heathrow Ct
Harrisburg PA 17109

Call Sign: KE7GTK
John J Perez
1136 Hedgerow Ln
Harrisburg PA 17111

Call Sign: N3RXZ
Philip D Dullen
5 Hereford St
Harrisburg PA 17109

Call Sign: K3ELJ
Ezell L Jackson
1513 Herr St
Harrisburg PA 17103

Call Sign: WA3NAP
Ezell L Jackson
1513 Herr St
Harrisburg PA 17403

Call Sign: WA3UEG
Thomas C Garvie
159 Hiddenwood Dr
Harrisburg PA 17110

Call Sign: KB3PKC
Mark E Adams
562 Highland St
Harrisburg PA 17113

Call Sign: KW3V
Mark E Adams
562 Highland St
Harrisburg PA 17113

Call Sign: KB3YDL
Craig E Powers
4920 Hill Top Rd
Harrisburg PA 171113457

Call Sign: K3URT
Curtis D Sanders
4707 Hillside Rd
Harrisburg PA 171095203

Call Sign: K3CES
Joseph J Hinkelman
4708 Hillside Rd
Harrisburg PA 17109

Call Sign: KB2EBT
Brad C Hinkelman
4708 Hillside Rd
Harrisburg PA 17109

Call Sign: KB3WOW
Ronald M Higley
825 Hilltop Dr
Harrisburg PA 171111716

Call Sign: KA3JEZ
Glen E Heise
1906 Holly St
Harrisburg PA 17104

Call Sign: N3BVP
James W Musser
3 Hollywood Dr
Harrisburg PA 171095563

Call Sign: N3QZH
Albert L Davis Jr
1345 Howard St
Harrisburg PA 17104

Call Sign: N3JOR
Harold G Harlan
1135 Hudson St
Harrisburg PA 17104

Call Sign: KD3LS
Rodney S Panian
1613 Hunter St
Harrisburg PA 17104

Call Sign: KF3AR
Walter L Spohn Jr
6200 Huntingdon St
Harrisburg PA 17111

Call Sign: AA3UT
Richard Lindway
6751 Huntingdos St
Harrisburg PA 17111

Call Sign: KA3OUB
Mervin W Scott Sr
1089 Huron Dr Apt A
Harrisburg PA 171108015

Call Sign: KB3NIA
PA Emergency
Management Agency
2605 Interstate Dr
Harrisburg PA 17110

Call Sign: KB3OVP
Alejandro M Negrete
2232 Ionoff Rd
Harrisburg PA 17110

Call Sign: KA3CMG
David W De Moss
7330 Jonestown Rd
Harrisburg PA 17112

Call Sign: K3DOL
Thomas J Dimeo
3826 Kramer St
Harrisburg PA 17109

Call Sign: W3JMH
Daniel C Irving
5036 Irene Dr
Harrisburg PA 17112

Call Sign: KE3KW
Peter J Grabko
1405 Karen Dr
Harrisburg PA 17109

Call Sign: W3IRH
Barbara L Soester
1200 La Porte St
Harrisburg PA 17112

Call Sign: KA3NCT
Edythe L Guerrant
647 Itarris
Harrisburg PA 17102

Call Sign: N3NMD
Peter J Grabko III
1405 Karen Dr
Harrisburg PA 17109

Call Sign: N2IDN
John J Cosgrove
641 Lancaster Ave
Harrisburg PA 17112

Call Sign: KA3UNY
Fernando Verones Jr
7100 Jefferson St
Harrisburg PA 17111

Call Sign: K3IBN
John A Bosak
850 Keckler Rd
Harrisburg PA 17111

Call Sign: N6TAF
Frank W Collins III
Lancaster St
Harrisburg PA 17111

Call Sign: KC6UCR
Baron L Stare
7151 Jefferson St
Harrisburg PA 171115245

Call Sign: KB3UID
Matthew F Ryan
2404 Kensington Way
Harrisburg PA 17112

Call Sign: K3WKK
Brian R Greenway
421 Larry Dr
Harrisburg PA 17109

Call Sign: KB3MHD
Veronica G Connor
2436 Jericho Dr
Harrisburg PA 17110

Call Sign: N3NZI
Martin L Ginter
318 Kent Dr
Harrisburg PA 17111

Call Sign: N3KVV
Frederic W Richter
5205 Laurel Ln
Harrisburg PA 17109

Call Sign: KB3YJC
Robert L Miller
6211 Jerome Blvd
Harrisburg PA 17112

Call Sign: KA3TDR
Jeffry A Smith
2723 Keystone Dr
Harrisburg PA 17112

Call Sign: W8RSO
William N Genematas
4505 Laurelwood Dr
Harrisburg PA 17110

Call Sign: WA3PUN
James E Bolton
4212 Jonestown Rd
Harrisburg PA 17109

Call Sign: N3CNI
Harry M Capper
153 Kingswood Dr
Harrisburg PA 17112

Call Sign: N3QZJ
Ronald G Krosnar
301 Lenker Rd
Harrisburg PA 17111

Call Sign: W3HQA
Joseph A Macko Sr
7307 Jonestown Rd
Harrisburg PA 171123654

Call Sign: N3YCM
Seth Wolpert
1433 Kirkwood Rd
Harrisburg PA 17110

Call Sign: N3NIH
Elizabeth A Sipe
4004 Lexington St
Harrisburg PA 17109

Harrisburg PA 17112

Call Sign: KA3RSE
William D Sipe
4004 Lexington St
Harrisburg PA 171092620

Call Sign: W3EUC
Joseph R Hoeflich
4209 Lexington St
Harrisburg PA 17109

Call Sign: KB3TUV
David M Ravegum
326 Lincoln Ave
Harrisburg PA 17111

Call Sign: KE3OY
Edward G Nettling
4103 Linden St
Harrisburg PA 17109

Call Sign: WA3DRK
Morton A Friedman
3941 Linglestown Rd
Harrisburg PA 17110

Call Sign: KB3JIB
James R Morgan
117 Litchfield Rd
Harrisburg PA 17112

Call Sign: WB3ADJ
James A Walsh
3828 Locust Ln
Harrisburg PA 17109

Call Sign: KR3Z
Paul H Bauserman Sr
5201 Locust Ln
Harrisburg PA 17109

Call Sign: KE3YR
Joseph L Mclaughlin Sr
5205 Locust Ln
Harrisburg PA 17109

Call Sign: KA3ZLP
Mary A Poleshuk
5828 Locust Ln
Harrisburg PA 17109

Call Sign: KB3FYD
Scott M Lyter
5609 Locust Ln
Harrisburg PA 17109

Call Sign: N1KPU
David S Keller
4570 Londonderry Rd Apt
88A
Harrisburg PA 17109

Call Sign: WA3KAL
James H Chamberlin
2740 Ludwig
Harrisburg PA 17103

Call Sign: KB3KGH
Kirk L Barbour
321 Luther Rd
Harrisburg PA 171111930

Call Sign: K3SZH
Josef Spandler
821 MacArthur Dr
Harrisburg PA 17111

Call Sign: N3UVS
Glenn C Hess Jr
8028 Manada View Dr
Harrisburg PA 17112

Call Sign: K3YG
Glenn C Hess Jr
8028 Manada View Dr
Harrisburg PA 17112

Call Sign: N3UGW
Richard L Wenner
8056 Manada View Dr

Call Sign: KA3AJE
Robert G Yottey
510 Manor Ter
Harrisburg PA 17101

Call Sign: WA3ZHI
Clinton E Stricker
Marble Head
Harrisburg PA 17109

Call Sign: K3JJK
Le Roy S Ash
1430 Marene Dr
Harrisburg PA 17109

Call Sign: KB3YDC
Jayanth K Devasundaram
4803 Margaret Ln
Harrisburg PA 17110

Call Sign: KB3PIM
Marcia W Shore
6006 Meade Ct
Harrisburg PA 17112

Call Sign: N3KZL
Curtis L Smith
5736 Meadowbrook Dr
Harrisburg PA 17112

Call Sign: KB3ENV
Betsy S Smith
5736 Meadowbrook Dr
Harrisburg PA 17112

Call Sign: K3ZBP
W Donaven Allen
6195 Mifflin Ave
Harrisburg PA 17111

Call Sign: WB2VLM
Paul E Rokoff
104 Millwood Dr

Harrisburg PA 17110

Call Sign: KB3QWZ
Christopher J Disanto
6122 Minglewood Rd
Harrisburg PA 17112

Call Sign: KA3RMP
Danny L Cullison
7615 Morningstar Ave
Harrisburg PA 17112

Call Sign: AA3ES
Gerardus H Geurts
Ms520
Harrisburg PA 17105

Call Sign: N3SV
Spyridon N Varnalis
1801 Mulberry St
Harrisburg PA 17104

Call Sign: N3JQM
Neil R Shatto Jr
1452 Mumma Rd
Harrisburg PA 17112

Call Sign: N3NIJ
William P Kamarer
121 N 18th St
Harrisburg PA 17103

Call Sign: N3PYZ
Richard Lindway
904 N 21st St
Harrisburg PA 17103

Call Sign: N3ZVE
Michael C Badger
3 N 28 St
Harrisburg PA 17103

Call Sign: KB3SUG
Ethan A Solomon
1007 N 2nd St

Harrisburg PA 17102

Call Sign: KB3UYQ
Dustin Ventresca
2644 N 2nd St
Harrisburg PA 17110

Call Sign: N3NZJ
George J Warlow
2735 N 2nd St
Harrisburg PA 17110

Call Sign: KB3QPW
Timothy R Pianka
2811 N 2nd St
Harrisburg PA 17110

Call Sign: KB3UWD
Mary M Johnson
3103 N 2nd St
Harrisburg PA 17110

Call Sign: N3HFS
Franz Niedermeyer
3107 N 2nd St
Harrisburg PA 17110

Call Sign: KB3GZE
Astro-American Radio
Guild
3107 N 2nd St
Harrisburg PA 17110

Call Sign: NK3E
Astro American Radio
Guild
3107 N 2nd St
Harrisburg PA 17110

Call Sign: WB3IDE
William C Pool
207 N 38th St
Harrisburg PA 17109

Call Sign: KB3TCN

Matthew R Gillespie
1703 N 3rd St
Harrisburg PA 17102

Call Sign: N3URH
Patricia L Fawber
2252 N 3rd St
Harrisburg PA 17110

Call Sign: KB3VOE
Justin A Sallusti
361 N 48th St
Harrisburg PA 17111

Call Sign: KA3TXN
Joseph Harfmann
3419 N 4th St
Harrisburg PA 17110

Call Sign: KA3TXO
Kathleen M Wagner
3419 N 4th St
Harrisburg PA 17110

Call Sign: KB3LMU
Garth M Hess Jr
365 N 50th St
Harrisburg PA 171113413

Call Sign: KC3BN
Robert L Marzari
621 N 66th St
Harrisburg PA 17111

Call Sign: WA3KXG
Central PA Repeater Assn
Inc
621 N 66th St
Harrisburg PA 171114508

Call Sign: W3PT
Robert L Marzari
621 N 66th St
Harrisburg PA 171114508

Call Sign: KY3Y
Richard C Hill
4307 N Carolina Ct
Harrisburg PA 17112

Call Sign: W3ABF
Frank M Masters Jr
5501 N Front St
Harrisburg PA 17110

Call Sign: KB3IUP
Lenore R Brown
5529 N Front St
Harrisburg PA 17110

Call Sign: KA3OBA
Elizabeth S Gault
377 N Hoernerstown Rd
Harrisburg PA 17111

Call Sign: N3UJ
Yoshinobu Suwabe
56 N Madison St
Harrisburg PA 17109

Call Sign: KB3PLB
Yoshinobu Suwabe
56 N Madison St
Harrisburg PA 17109

Call Sign: KB3PXU
Naoko Suwabe
56 N Madison St
Harrisburg PA 17109

Call Sign: N3UJA
Naoko Suwabe
56 N Madison St
Harrisburg PA 17109

Call Sign: KA3HAB
Kevin A Beam
1052 N Mountain Rd
Harrisburg PA 17112

Call Sign: KB3GCD
Steven R Donbach
3620 N Progress Ave
Harrisburg PA 17110

Call Sign: KB3GKQ
Waitus A Reaves
3213 N Scenic Rd
Harrisburg PA 17109

Call Sign: KD4FSB
Marie J Repetti
409 N Star Dr
Harrisburg PA 17112

Call Sign: NT1C
Daniel A Repetti
409 N Star Dr
Harrisburg PA 17112

Call Sign: N3MJY
Francis W Weges
4317 New Hampshire Dr
Harrisburg PA 17112

Call Sign: N3ZSI
Ayesha L Gray
237 North St 4
Harrisburg PA 17101

Call Sign: KA3FKL
Philip J Pishney
6613 Northampton Ct
Harrisburg PA 17111

Call Sign: W3RB
Robert L Bomboy
229 Oak Park Rd
Harrisburg PA 17109

Call Sign: N4HNW
David Nelson
4500 Oakhurst Blvd Apt
123
Harrisburg PA 17110

Call Sign: KB8ZQE
Rouletta A Blowers
1 Oakmont Rd
Harrisburg PA 17109

Call Sign: KB3UVJ
Adam M Walter
5005 Ohio Ave
Harrisburg PA 17109

Call Sign: K3AMW
Adam M Walter
5005 Ohio Ave
Harrisburg PA 17109

Call Sign: KA3EMH
Terrance M Shingara
5007 Ohio Ave
Harrisburg PA 17109

Call Sign: K3IQ
Donald J Shenck
1113 Old Pond Rd
Harrisburg PA 171123526

Call Sign: KB3KMJ
Chien-Ying Huang
4808 Orchard
Harrisburg PA 17109

Call Sign: NM3F
Richard H Smith
4501 Oxford Rd
Harrisburg PA 17109

Call Sign: KA3SPY
Maurey B Katz
5907 Palmer Dr
Harrisburg PA 17112

Call Sign: KB3WSR
Ben L Brown
6675 Parkway E
Harrisburg PA 17112

Call Sign: WA3GSI
Charles R Sayers
6130 Parson Dr
Harrisburg PA 17111

Call Sign: NZ3U
William E C Fuller
841 Pheasant Rd
Harrisburg PA 17112

Call Sign: KB3IZD
Gary S Abbondanza
7086 Red Top Rd
Harrisburg PA 17111

Call Sign: K3ETD
Charles R Sayers
6130 Parson Dr
Harrisburg PA 17111

Call Sign: KB3FSY
Joseph E Dettinger Jr
656 Piketown Rd
Harrisburg PA 171129068

Call Sign: K3AIK
Eugene P Maley
1414 Regina
Harrisburg PA 17103

Call Sign: N3ESH
Bryson L Leidich
7644 Patterson Cir S
Harrisburg PA 17112

Call Sign: KB3IZF
Robert A Book
731 Piketown Rd
Harrisburg PA 17112

Call Sign: N3JFR
Gordon T Humbert
5219 Ridgeview Dr
Harrisburg PA 17112

Call Sign: KQ3F
Joseph M Stepansky
7648 Patterson Dr
Harrisburg PA 17112

Call Sign: KA3UIJ
John T Miller
830 Piketown Rd
Harrisburg PA 17112

Call Sign: N3ZFP
Sally P Humbert
5219 Ridgeview Dr
Harrisburg PA 17112

Call Sign: N3WQU
David W Kaprocki
2760 Patton Rd
Harrisburg PA 17112

Call Sign: N3CES
Thomas E Dawson
1365 Piketown Rd
Harrisburg PA 17112

Call Sign: KB3HCS
Nicholas Stanziola
5329 Ridgeview Dr
Harrisburg PA 17112

Call Sign: N3XBN
David J Gaiski
1628 Paxton St
Harrisburg PA 17104

Call Sign: KB9LUO
Kyle J Kasten
5908 Pine Hollow Ct
Harrisburg PA 17109

Call Sign: KB3PAI
Kristen M Murray
4135 Ridgeview Rd
Harrisburg PA 17112

Call Sign: KB3THZ
William J Greene
2001 Paxton St
Harrisburg PA 17111

Call Sign: N3NMA
Jeffrey A Williams
5630 Plainview Rd
Harrisburg PA 17111

Call Sign: KB3LRN
Katelyn E Murray
4135 Ridgeview Rd
Harrisburg PA 17112

Call Sign: N3TEX
Kurt A Eby
1061 Pennsylvania Ave
Harrisburg PA 17111

Call Sign: KA3RRU
Gerald D Campbell
4301 Plymouth St
Harrisburg PA 17109

Call Sign: AC3H
John H Booker
3403 Ridgeway Rd
Harrisburg PA 171091123

Call Sign: WA3MWT
William E C Fuller
841 Pheasant Rd
Harrisburg PA 17112

Call Sign: KB3EZX
Samuel Maldonado
2130 Queens Dr Apt A3
Harrisburg PA 17110

Call Sign: N3ZVL
Andrew W Schwilk
24 Ringneck Dr
Harrisburg PA 17112

Call Sign: W3GZT
Everett C Waltman
525 Robewood Ln
Harrisburg PA 17111

Call Sign: W3VPI
Dominick E Falvo
1438 S 13th St
Harrisburg PA 17104

Call Sign: K3AM
Richard A Kerlin
1021 S Progress
Harrisburg PA 171112051

Call Sign: KA3ECQ
Terrance L Ash
4335 Rodkey Rd
Harrisburg PA 17110

Call Sign: KB3OZN
Chelsea A Doub
8 S 20th St
Harrisburg PA 17104

Call Sign: WA3NGD
Edmund G Good III
640 Sandra Ave
Harrisburg PA 171095816

Call Sign: N3SDG
Clifford H Tooker Jr
Rolling Glen Dr
Harrisburg PA 171094922

Call Sign: N3CYD
David A Fisher
610 S 20th St
Harrisburg PA 17104

Call Sign: KB3OZJ
Allison J Daly
6502 Sanibel Dr
Harrisburg PA 17111

Call Sign: KA3FYD
Sara T Rappolt
2832 Rose Hill Rd
Harrisburg PA 17110

Call Sign: KA3JKA
Wanda L Heise
2 S 21st St
Harrisburg PA 171041314

Call Sign: KB3KLY
Kristen L Daly
6502 Sanibel Dr
Harrisburg PA 17111

Call Sign: WB3KBU
James A Rappolt
2832 Rose Hill Rd
Harrisburg PA 171109562

Call Sign: N3NZE
Charles M Roy Jr
56 S 39th St
Harrisburg PA 17109

Call Sign: KA3OLZ
Paul V Dominick
100 Sarkoni Ave
Harrisburg PA 17110

Call Sign: KA3YII
Nancy J Allgyer
3026 Rose Hill Rd
Harrisburg PA 17110

Call Sign: W3YFT
Robert J Heineman
130 S 3rd St Apt 1015
Harrisburg PA 17101

Call Sign: KB3NLN
Armen D Vartan
104 Sarkuni Ave
Harrisburg PA 17110

Call Sign: N3BAP
William A Smith
4075 Rosewall Ct
Harrisburg PA 17112

Call Sign: N3NLZ
Douglas M Spoonhour
595 S 60th St
Harrisburg PA 17111

Call Sign: KB3WPL
Jonathan T Trexler
108 Sarkuni Ave
Harrisburg PA 17110

Call Sign: WA3WLB
Edgar H Cohen Jr
1902 Rudy Rd
Harrisburg PA 17104

Call Sign: W3ESW
James G Megoulas
606 S Arlington Ave
Harrisburg PA 17109

Call Sign: KB3JYZ
Steven P Bosak
259 Sasafras St
Harrisburg PA 17102

Call Sign: KA3PNV
David J Costanza
585 Rupp Hill Rd
Harrisburg PA 17111

Call Sign: KB3NBZ
Mary-Alys Turner
4289 S Carolina Dr
Harrisburg PA 17112

Call Sign: N3HKC
John L Hill
4429 Saybrook Ln
Harrisburg PA 171103479

Call Sign: KB3DRA
George H Burkett
5888 Shope Pl
Harrisburg PA 17109

Call Sign: N3YB
George H Burkett
5888 Shope Pl
Harrisburg PA 17109

Call Sign: N3BWD
Stephen E Nock
605 Showers St
Harrisburg PA 17104

Call Sign: KB3IKI
Beverly A Mack
718 Showers St
Harrisburg PA 17104

Call Sign: KB3STW
Di T Le
5831 Simsbury Dr
Harrisburg PA 17111

Call Sign: KB3OVL
Nhan T Lieu
5835 Simsbury Dr
Harrisburg PA 17111

Call Sign: N3OSM
Robert W Baer
2130 Sir Lancelot Dr Apt A3
Harrisburg PA 17110

Call Sign: K3AUT
Joseph A Malesic Jr
Skyview Cir
Harrisburg PA 17110

Call Sign: N3OYB
Paul F OConnor
1405 Smokehouse Ln
Harrisburg PA 17110

Call Sign: N3ZAG
Andrew R Szekely
1417 Smokehouse Ln
Harrisburg PA 17110

Call Sign: WA1WPA
Leonard F Bendiksen
5801 Snell Dr
Harrisburg PA 17109

Call Sign: KA3ADU
Robert E Lester
6330 Somerset St
Harrisburg PA 17111

Call Sign: KA3TRJ
William H May
4604 South Rd
Harrisburg PA 17109

Call Sign: N3NIK
Ronald C Wilt Jr
4141 Spring Valley Rd C23
Harrisburg PA 17109

Call Sign: KB3QYD
Mary K West
6111 Springford Dr
Harrisburg PA 17111

Call Sign: K3EQN
Harold P Hollenbach
8146 Spruce Dr
Harrisburg PA 17111

Call Sign: KB3QHT
Kyle T Boran
4389 St Andrews Way
Harrisburg PA 17112

Call Sign: AB3LS
Geoffrey R Wolf

6260 Stirrup Ct
Harrisburg PA 17111

Call Sign: KB3YDE
John C Harlacker
900 Sunny Hill Ln
Harrisburg PA 17111

Call Sign: K1HBG
John C Harlacker
900 Sunny Hill Ln
Harrisburg PA 17111

Call Sign: WA3IJC
Robert K McCutcheon
4605 Surrey Rd
Harrisburg PA 17109

Call Sign: N3JPH
Robert W Dixon
498 Sweetbriar Dr
Harrisburg PA 17111

Call Sign: KB3KRB
Jason M Milletics
533 Sweetbriar Dr
Harrisburg PA 171115654

Call Sign: K3ZYZ
Jason M Milletics
533 Sweetbriar Dr
Harrisburg PA 171115654

Call Sign: N3YHJ
Ronald M Lawson
4838 Sweetbrier Dr
Harrisburg PA 17111

Call Sign: KA3WWR
Theresa A McKechnie
4818 Tamar Dr
Harrisburg PA 17111

Call Sign: KA3IMC
Marla J Smith

38 Taylor Blvd
Harrisburg PA 17103

7700 Valleyview Ave
Harrisburg PA 17112

6248 Warren Ave
Harrisburg PA 17112

Call Sign: KB3OL
R Frank Shaffner III
38 Taylor Blvd
Harrisburg PA 17103

Call Sign: KB3OYN
Matthew L Senft
7741 Valleyview Ave
Harrisburg PA 171123864

Call Sign: KB3OZT
Aaron E Hester
2113 Washington Ave
Harrisburg PA 17109

Call Sign: KB0ZNW
Frederick C Novello Jr
Terrace Way
Harrisburg PA 17111

Call Sign: N3URE
Margaret E Gleason
4322 Valleyview Rd
Harrisburg PA 171122028

Call Sign: KB3CDZ
Michael C Wolfe
1720 Waune St
Harrisburg PA 17104

Call Sign: KB3OZB
Todd Criste
7044 Terrann Dr
Harrisburg PA 17112

Call Sign: WA3HDP
Kenneth A Sutton
4322 Valleyview Rd
Harrisburg PA 171122028

Call Sign: KB3EGM
Joachim J Alfieri
6825 Wesley Dr
Harrisburg PA 171122762

Call Sign: KB3STV
Audrey B Latimore
4004 Thicket Ln
Harrisburg PA 17110

Call Sign: KB3KMI
Eric G Horton
313 Verbeke St
Harrisburg PA 17102

Call Sign: K3EGM
Joachim J Alfieri
6825 Wesley Dr
Harrisburg PA 171122762

Call Sign: N3JJH
David A Shingara
28 Thornwood Rd
Harrisburg PA 17112

Call Sign: N3URQ
James K Maley
Vintage Ct
Harrisburg PA 17109

Call Sign: W3JMT
George L Feehrer
611 West Dr
Harrisburg PA 17111

Call Sign: WE3G
Edward H Chubb
1308 Upton Dr
Harrisburg PA 17110

Call Sign: KA3LHX
Wilbur B Lupton
5006 Virginia Ave
Harrisburg PA 17109

Call Sign: K3DJH
John L Guerrisi
6426 Whisper Wood Ln
Harrisburg PA 17112

Call Sign: N3HDV
Clarence A Croft
4211 Valley Rd
Harrisburg PA 171122888

Call Sign: KR3K
Joseph R Keller
2406 Walker Mill Rd
Harrisburg PA 17110

Call Sign: N3QCB
William M Haken
2301 Williams View Dr
Harrisburg PA 17112

Call Sign: KA3AJR
Linda J Blough
7700 Valleyview Ave
Harrisburg PA 17112

Call Sign: WB3EYB
John T Shingara
1431 Wanda Ln
Harrisburg PA 17109

Call Sign: N3YHG
William B Webster
Williamsburg Dr
Harrisburg PA 17109

Call Sign: N3IUS
Harold B Blough

Call Sign: KA3TKW
Thomas B Shingara

Call Sign: N3BCH
Bernard G Caron

4330 Winthrop Dr
Harrisburg PA 17112

Call Sign: WB3JNX
George L Grimes Jr
5220 Woodlawn Dr
Harrisburg PA 171095544

Call Sign: WA2NQC
Jerome B Klatskin
417 Woodruff Way
Harrisburg PA 17112

Call Sign: WB3CBF
William J Farkas
391 Wyatt Rd
Harrisburg PA 17104

Call Sign: W3VKQ
Samuel H Settino
Harrisburg PA 17105

Call Sign: WP4HHS
Victor M Cruz
Harrisburg PA 17105

Call Sign: KB3WIG
Andy T Lehman
Harrisburg PA 17108

Call Sign: KB3WIH
Pete T Lehman
Harrisburg PA 17108

Call Sign: KK7IC
Jeremy L Utley
Harrisburg PA 171062311

Call Sign: KB3RCY
Linda A Lehman
Harrisburg PA 171080453

Call Sign: KB3OZA
Timothy J Lehman
Harrisburg PA 171080453

FCC Amateur Radio Licenses in Harrison Valley

Call Sign: KB3EWU
Carl J Hoppe
288 Dodge Hollow Rd
Harrison Valley PA 16927

Call Sign: K3QBU
Basil J McCutcheon
120 W Main St
Harrison Valley PA 16927

FCC Amateur Radio Licenses in Hartleton

Call Sign: KA3UMU
John L Gabel Jr
Hartleton PA 17829

Call Sign: KB3HBL
Stephen Uncapher
Hartleton PA 17829

Call Sign: KB3ICJ
Tiffany F Uncapher
Hartleton PA 17829

FCC Amateur Radio Licenses in Hastings

Call Sign: N3WZB
Jon R Soltis
110 1st St
Hastings PA 16646

Call Sign: N3VRK
Michael A Anna
4th Ave
Hastings PA 16646

Call Sign: N3UND
Kevin P Griffiths

650 Griffiths Rd
Hastings PA 16646

Call Sign: N3WZC
Paul M Dolges
144 Middle St
Hastings PA 16646

Call Sign: KB3OTA
Cambria County ARA
Hastings PA 16646

FCC Amateur Radio Licenses in Hellam

Call Sign: N3BUZ
Brian E Myers
487 E Market St
Hellam PA 17406

FCC Amateur Radio Licenses in Herndon

Call Sign: N3SHN
Mark A Letterman
Box 101
Herndon PA 17830

Call Sign: KB0LNL
Louis P Toenjes
Box 609
Herndon PA 17830

Call Sign: WB3FHT
Andrew P Bobb
1 S Center St
Herndon PA 17830

Call Sign: N3JIW
Marvin A Paul Jr
5094 State Rt 147
Herndon PA 17830

Call Sign: KA3BVJ
Dennis L Williard Sr

Herndon PA 17830

Call Sign: WA3QNK
David E Lilly
125 Apple Ln
Hershey PA 17033

Call Sign: K8ZTG
Richard P Horn
1071 Beech Ave
Hershey PA 17033

Call Sign: KB3TMW
Andrew J Kirk
255 Bittersweet Dr
Hershey PA 17033

Call Sign: KA3HEN
Laura Jean Shaffer
Box 142 Gates Rd
Hershey PA 17033

Call Sign: KB3IOV
John J Talaber Esq
226 Canal St
Hershey PA 17033

Call Sign: KB3WSS
Michael S Lalli
519 Cedar Ave
Hershey PA 17033

Call Sign: K3MIK
Richard E Wise
208 Clark Rd
Hershey PA 17033

Call Sign: N3HDW
Franklin N Graybill Jr
4871 Colebrook Rd
Hershey PA 17033

Call Sign: KB3GSE
Daniel J Graybill
4871 Colebrook Rd
Hershey PA 17033

Call Sign: KB3TPY
Todd K Pagliarulo
321 Concord Ct
Hershey PA 17033

Call Sign: KB3QPY
Alexander J Shope
326 Dogwood Dr
Hershey PA 17033

Call Sign: K3BLD
Elwood D Sipe Sr
50 E Canal
Hershey PA 17033

Call Sign: N3JY
Joseph P Joynes
1418 E Chocolate Ave
Hershey PA 17033

Call Sign: K3CYN
James C Buck
583 E Derry Rd
Hershey PA 170332716

Call Sign: K4SHE
Virginia B Mahoney
143 E Glenn Rd
Hershey PA 17033

Call Sign: KB3ULM
Mark E Neumeister
625 Fishburn Rd
Hershey PA 17033

Call Sign: N3YIZ
Shirley S Glantz
1506 Fishburn Rd
Hershey PA 17033

Call Sign: KA3IRB
John H Dowd
7 Fox Chase Dr
Hershey PA 17033

Call Sign: W3HPA
Philip P Shkuda
11 Foxanna Dr
Hershey PA 17033

Call Sign: KA3ISS
Mary Ann L Dowd
7 Foxchase Dr
Hershey PA 17033

Call Sign: KB3OZV
Shohin Hodizoda Vance
1917 Grist Mill Cir
Hershey PA 17033

Call Sign: KC5DRI
John A Zilavy
411 High Dr
Hershey PA 170339417

Call Sign: N3YRG
Nancy A Zilavy
411 High Dr
Hershey PA 170339417

Call Sign: W2CNN
Frank J Chiofaro
1044 Hillview Ln
Hershey PA 17033

Call Sign: N9DMO
Steven A Goldman
809 Lexington Ave
Hershey PA 17033

Call Sign: W8QII
John N Goldman
809 Lexington Ave
Hershey PA 17033

Call Sign: KB3NYC
Philip A Masters
106 Maple Ave
Hershey PA 17033

Call Sign: KB3MCD
Mark D Peffley
412 Sand Hill Rd
Hershey PA 17033

Call Sign: KA3JOA
Kathy A Skiles
1914 Sand Hill Rd
Hershey PA 17033

Call Sign: N3KZX
Randolph H Coleman
7038 School House Rd
Hershey PA 17033

Call Sign: WB3HEC
Paul J Felty Jr
17 Sunny Ln
Hershey PA 170332445

Call Sign: WB3CDI
Don W Stauffer
229 University Manor E
Hershey PA 17033

Call Sign: KC2HSA
Timothy P Gilmour
25 University Mnr E
Hershey PA 17033

Call Sign: KA3KUA
Harry Gardner
457 W Granada Ave
Hershey PA 17033

Call Sign: KA3USZ
Gary J Di Clemente
542 W Granada Ave
Hershey PA 17033

Call Sign: N0OEP
Sean R Conard
Hershey PA 17033

FCC Amateur Radio Licenses in Hesston

Call Sign: WA3SFO
Dam Operators At
Raystown Dam
Box 222 Raystown Lk
Hesston PA 16647

Call Sign: N3YZI
Craig A Bloom
Box 241
Hesston PA 166479218

Call Sign: AC2HG
Robert F Kurz Jr
13014 Huckleberry Ln
Hesston PA 16647

FCC Amateur Radio Licenses in Highland Park

Call Sign: N3KGG
David P Witkowski
7924 Westview Ave
Highland Park PA 19082

FCC Amateur Radio Licenses in Highspire

Call Sign: KB3DJS
Stephen C Molnar
28 Charles St
Highspire PA 17034

Call Sign: N3EIW
Bertran D Walton III
415 Eshelman St
Highspire PA 17034

Call Sign: N3RMR
Mark A Wingard
697 Eshleman St
Highspire PA 17034

Call Sign: N1JVO
Thomas T Green
210 Frederick St
Highspire PA 17034

Call Sign: KB3EAY
John L Pantaloni
56 Jury St
Highspire PA 17034

Call Sign: KA3MIN
Mary V Lerch
201 Market St
Highspire PA 170341216

Call Sign: KC3GV
Joseph E Lerch Jr
201 Market St
Highspire PA 170341216

Call Sign: KA3VEI
David M Arendt
79 Paxton St
Highspire PA 17034

Call Sign: WB3N
Henry C Tamanini
78 Roop St
Highspire PA 17034

Call Sign: KA3MKA
Dennis J Reigle
Willow St
Highspire PA 17034

Call Sign: KB3IIB
Dennis J Reigle
Willow St
Highspire PA 17034

Call Sign: N1QQN
Matt V Sabattini
507 Willow St
Highspire PA 17034

Call Sign: K1WKH
William F Baker
Highspire PA 17034

Call Sign: KA3RXE
Jeffrey L Kauffman
Highspire PA 170340071

FCC Amateur Radio Licenses in Hollidaysburg

Call Sign: K3YBS
Julianne M Graboski
508 Alleghent St
Hollidaysburg PA 16648

Call Sign: K3TJ
Edward T J Graboski
508 Allegheny St
Hollidaysburg PA 16648

Call Sign: N3JXW
Jesse N Mengel
1203 Allegheny St
Hollidaysburg PA 16648

Call Sign: KA3WCD
David C Goldenberg
812 Allegheny St Apt 1
Hollidaysburg PA 16648

Call Sign: KA3GZC
Guy E Forshey
260 Bel St
Hollidaysburg PA 16648

Call Sign: N3VJX
Terry L Holsinger
504 Betts St

Hollidaysburg PA 16648

Call Sign: WB3FLT
John G Bice
Box 15C
Hollidaysburg PA 16648

Call Sign: KB3HYP
Joseph F Moxin Jr
Box 202
Hollidaysburg PA 16648

Call Sign: KB3FLC
PA Military Affiliate
Radio System ARC
Box 369
Hollidaysburg PA
166489749

Call Sign: N3HDH
David L White
Box 426
Hollidaysburg PA 16648

Call Sign: KA3IIV
Edward G Marks Jr
Box 451
Hollidaysburg PA 16648

Call Sign: W9NET
John D Littlejohn
287 Brushmeade
Hollidaysburg PA 16648

Call Sign: KB3YHL
Simon M Littlejohn
287 Brushmeade
Hollidaysburg PA 16648

Call Sign: W3WES
Harry B Thompson
417 Cedar Blvd
Hollidaysburg PA 16648

Call Sign: KA3EGE

Anna M Reynolds
230 Chris St
Hollidaysburg PA
166489656

Call Sign: N3VJY
Richard Joseph Reynolds
230 Chris St
Hollidaysburg PA
166489656

Call Sign: KB3RAQ
Timothy P Ajay
905 Church St
Hollidaysburg PA 16648

Call Sign: W3TPA
Timothy P Ajay
905 Church St
Hollidaysburg PA 16648

Call Sign: KE6PDO
David E Field
512 Clark St
Hollidaysburg PA 16648

Call Sign: N3VJT
Mark D Leberfinger
522 Clark St
Hollidaysburg PA
166482124

Call Sign: WI3E
Mark D Leberfinger
522 Clark St
Hollidaysburg PA
166482124

Call Sign: KB3ESQ
Todd S Shope
711 Clark St
Hollidaysburg PA 16648

Call Sign: WA3WED
Michael A Mauk

19 Clover Dr
Hollidaysburg PA
166482506

Call Sign: N1FFV
Daniel A Martino Jr
77 Clover Dr
Hollidaysburg PA 16648

Call Sign: KB3RRZ
Daniel A Martino Jr
77 Clover Dr
Hollidaysburg PA 16648

Call Sign: N3BZZ
Alden P Zwerling
302 Coventry Ct
Hollidaysburg PA 16648

Call Sign: N2ZXH
John M Lavoie
264 Donna St
Hollidaysburg PA
166489630

Call Sign: KB3HBJ
Deborah J Conrad
241 Fay Dr
Hollidaysburg PA 16648

Call Sign: KB3IKJ
Jordan A Conrad
241 Fay Dr
Hollidaysburg PA 16648

Call Sign: KB3FKC
Adam C Conrad Jr
241 Fay Dr
Hollidaysburg PA 16648

Call Sign: N3OZ
Adam C Conrad Jr
241 Fay Dr
Hollidaysburg PA 16648

Call Sign: KB3IOH
Jeffrey E Fleck
105 Fiore Ln
Hollidaysburg PA 16648

Call Sign: N3JEF
Jeffrey E Fleck
105 Fiore Ln
Hollidaysburg PA 16648

Call Sign: N3WSN
Marcos A Manon
803 Holliday Hills Dr
Hollidaysburg PA
166483202

Call Sign: KD3LE
George M Long
100 Houndstooth Way Apt
100
Hollidaysburg PA 16648

Call Sign: N3KMY
Robert L Irwin
322 Klein Dr
Hollidaysburg PA 16648

Call Sign: KB3CKE
Mark A Kunselman
131 Lower Donna St
Hollidaysburg PA 16648

Call Sign: KD3YT
Eugene B Hinton
2570 Manor Dr
Hollidaysburg PA 16648

Call Sign: N3PTZ
Luis O Araneda
162 Mtn View Dr
Hollidaysburg PA 16648

Call Sign: KA3PUN
Suzanne R McGaffin
1107 N Juniata St Apt 6

Hollidaysburg PA 16648

Call Sign: N7FOX
Francis J Citro Jr
6 Oak St
Hollidaysburg PA 16648

Call Sign: N3IBT
Irvin E Lilly
202 Penn St
Hollidaysburg PA 16648

Call Sign: KC3MG
David D Dormer Jr
512 Pine St
Hollidaysburg PA
166481510

Call Sign: KC3JQ
Edward W Hughes
Rd 2
Hollidaysburg PA
166489722

Call Sign: KA3ZJZ
Adam B Schmouder
251 Richards Dr
Hollidaysburg PA 16648

Call Sign: KB3BMZ
Mark E Lipitz
311 Robin Ln
Hollidaysburg PA 16648

Call Sign: N3JXT
Lucille M Lilly
1010 Spruce St Apt 406
Hollidaysburg PA 16648

Call Sign: KL7RB
Steven L Diehl
112 Sylvan Oakes Dr
Hollidaysburg PA 16648

Call Sign: KB3DJR

Charles L Ferrell
361 Teal Dr
Hollidaysburg PA 16648

Call Sign: KB3LGU
Peter V Krzewski
1115 Walnut St
Hollidaysburg PA 16648

Call Sign: N3VJV
Gordon R Spessard
150 Woodlawn Ter
Hollidaysburg PA 16648

Call Sign: NR3T
Jerry L Cox
548 Woodlawn Ter
Hollidaysburg PA 16648

Call Sign: K3DOD
PA Military Affiliate
Radio System ARC
Hollidaysburg PA
166480443

FCC Amateur Radio Licenses in Hollsopple

Call Sign: N3WHS
Andrew H Hansen
111 Border St
Hollsopple PA 15935

Call Sign: KB3PCL
Alexander S Shroyer
404 Old Hershberger Rd
Hollsopple PA 15935

Call Sign: KE3BH
Nancy E Coleman
309 Plank Rd
Hollsopple PA 15935

Call Sign: NA3N
Nancy E Coleman

309 Plank Rd
Hollsopple PA 159356415

Call Sign: KB3MGA
Shalyn P Grindlesperger
5253 Somerset Pike
Hollsopple PA 15935

FCC Amateur Radio Licenses in Holtwood

Call Sign: WA3IAG
Joseph F Duff III
Box 1740
Holtwood PA 17532

Call Sign: N3XOV
Justin M Spearing
34 Den Mar Dr
Holtwood PA 17532

Call Sign: KB3TWG
Troy A Hatfield
50 Den Mar Dr
Holtwood PA 17532

Call Sign: K3IB
Philip M Lanese Sr
560 Drytown Rd
Holtwood PA 17532

Call Sign: KB3EIT
Michael S Schneider
389 Hilldale Rd
Holtwood PA 17532

Call Sign: KB3EIU
Jennifer B Schneider
389 Hilldale Rd
Holtwood PA 17532

Call Sign: KE3GE
Robert L Brazee
1213 Holtwood Rd
Holtwood PA 17532

Call Sign: N3NMI
Brenda L Brazee
1213 Holtwood Rd
Holtwood PA 17532

Call Sign: KB3CTW
Arthur D Welling
66 Martic Hts Dr
Holtwood PA 17532

Call Sign: N2NQA
Timothy S Roop
5 Pinnacle Rd W
Holtwood PA 175329641

Call Sign: KB3CTY
Holly M Dissinger
1107 River Rd
Holtwood PA 175329640

Call Sign: N3LXP
Thomas J Dissinger
1107 River Rd
Holtwood PA 175329640

Call Sign: AA3CT
Matthew R Kilby
35 St Francis Way
Holtwood PA 17532

Call Sign: WB3DSY
Daniel R Loraw Sr
882 Truce Rd
Holtwood PA 17532

FCC Amateur Radio Licenses in Honey Grove

Call Sign: N3GLY
Jeffrey R Henry
Box 35
Honey Grove PA 17035

FCC Amateur Radio Licenses in Hooversville

Call Sign: N3FOZ
Edward F Waltos
981 Barn St
Hooversville PA 15936

Call Sign: N3VFG
Richard B Lohr
1025 Barn St
Hooversville PA 15936

Call Sign: KB3GDU
Janet G Moyer
148 Crestwood Dr
Hooversville PA 15936

Call Sign: KB3GDV
Jack A Moyer
148 Crestwood Dr
Hooversville PA 15936

Call Sign: N3YZP
George C Tedrow
Hooversville PA 15936

FCC Amateur Radio Licenses in Hopeland

Call Sign: KA3YLW
Jared J Rabold
766 Maple St
Hopeland PA 17533

Call Sign: KA3ZPV
Tracy E Darlington
Hopeland PA 17533

Call Sign: KA3ZPW
Carrie J Darlington
Hopeland PA 17533

Call Sign: KA3ZPX
Carol K Darlington

Hopeland PA 17533

Call Sign: KA3ZPY
C Bullitt Darlington
Hopeland PA 17533

Call Sign: KB3KIJ
Michael R Thompson
Hopeland PA 17533

FCC Amateur Radio Licenses in Hopewell

Call Sign: KA3DTC
Richard A Weaver
Box 167
Hopewell PA 16650

Call Sign: K3VTQ
Kenneth F Henry
Box 194
Hopewell PA 16650

Call Sign: N3NXO
Kerry C Smith
340 Mifflin St
Hopewell PA 16650

FCC Amateur Radio Licenses in Houtzdale

Call Sign: W2CKG
Harry M Hawkins
945 Brisbin St
Houtzdale PA 16651

Call Sign: KC2SKR
Albert A Seaman
5932 Green Acre Rd
Houtzdale PA 16651

FCC Amateur Radio Licenses in Howard

Call Sign: W3SWK

Stephen W Kinley
1858 Marsh Creek Rd
Howard PA 16841

Call Sign: N3BEA
Bald Eagle ARS
1858 Marsh Creek Rd
Howard PA 16841

Call Sign: KB3GFP
Bald Eagle ARS
Marsh Creek Rd
Howard PA 16841

Call Sign: N3YUP
Milford E Lucas
2050 Old 220 Rd
Howard PA 168414820

Call Sign: K3SEW
Ronald R Klock
150 Sayers Hill Rd
Howard PA 168412018

FCC Amateur Radio Licenses in Hudson

Call Sign: KA3VRT
Gabriel Homick
50 Cleveland St
Hudson PA 18705

Call Sign: N3HXJ
Nicholas J Kozich
57 Cleveland St
Hudson PA 18705

Call Sign: KB3QI
George E Wiencek
24 Union St
Hudson PA 187053919

Call Sign: N3WV
George E Wiencek
24 Union St

Hudson PA 187053919

Call Sign: KB3GGG
Howard L Walburn
152 Boak Ave Lot 44
Hughesville PA 17737

Call Sign: KA3EEZ
Lewis C Jones
Box 121
Hughesville PA 17737

Call Sign: KA3BJP
Roy C Charles
Box 68
Hughesville PA 17737

Call Sign: KB3GNX
Jacob D Roberts
86 Cottage St
Hughesville PA 17737

Call Sign: KB3GOC
Richard T Welsh
208 E Water
Hughesville PA 17737

Call Sign: KB3GNS
Colin-Kirk B Hodge
457 E Water St
Hughesville PA 17737

Call Sign: N3NUV
Kenneth H Krah
195 Election House Hill
Rd
Hughesville PA 17737

Call Sign: KB3GNW
Eli Q Roberts
307 Elm Dr
Hughesville PA 17737

Call Sign: N3AFX
Robert C Shearer
552 Elm Dr
Hughesville PA 17737

Call Sign: N3PFE
Margaret F Shearer
552 Elm Dr
Hughesville PA 17737

Call Sign: KB3GNR
Jason E Feigles
679 Elm Dr
Hughesville PA 17737

Call Sign: WA4GPM
Joseph P Miklos
1688 Heidi Grey Rd
Hughesville PA 17737

Call Sign: KB3LEB
Martin L Golder
1405 Holmes Hollow Rd
Hughesville PA 17737

Call Sign: WA4LPD
Cecil J Tucker
196 N 2nd St
Hughesville PA 17737

Call Sign: W3CJT
Cecil J Tucker
196 N 2nd St
Hughesville PA 17737

Call Sign: N3ZJC
Michael J Callahan
264 Newhard Rd
Hughesville PA 17737

Call Sign: KA3EHB
Ruth E Jones
665 Rt 405 Hwy
Hughesville PA 17737

Call Sign: KB3GNV
Travis F Perry
360 S 2nd St
Hughesville PA 17737

Call Sign: W3EW
Anthony H Visco Jr
200 Taylor Hill Rd
Hughesville PA 17737

Call Sign: W3WNT
Robert H Wert
Hummels Wharf PA 17831

Call Sign: N3ZHD
Carl R Kready
Hummels Wharf PA 17831

Call Sign: W3VPJ
Susquehanna Valley Amat
Rad Club Inc
Hummels Wharf PA 17831

Call Sign: N3MJX
Donna M Stockley
561 Alison Dr Apt 2
Hummelstown PA 17036

Call Sign: KB3GGT
William W Williams Jr
555 Allison Dr 6
Hummelstown PA 17036

Call Sign: AA3CB
William J McConnell
14 Banbury Sq

Hummelstown PA 17036

Call Sign: N3KPF
Mark C McConnell
14 Banbury Sq
Hummelstown PA 17036

Call Sign: KB3VJG
Wayne C Hite
16 Banbury Sq
Hummelstown PA 17036

Call Sign: N3SAN
Michael J Sanchez
Box 18
Hummelstown PA 17036

Call Sign: N3SAO
Susan J Murphy
Box 18
Hummelstown PA 17036

Call Sign: KA3CAM
Martin W Kulp Sr
102 Brunner St
Hummelstown PA
170361203

Call Sign: KC3NJ
Barry B Barnhart
121 Circle Dr
Hummelstown PA 17036

Call Sign: WB3KSG
Harry W Jockers Jr
906 Clifton Hts Rd
Hummelstown PA 17036

Call Sign: W3KSG
Harry W Jockers Jr
906 Clifton Hts Rd
Hummelstown PA 17036

Call Sign: N3MKA
Ali A Behagi

2009 Colonial Way
Hummelstown PA 17036

Call Sign: N3BY
Dana C Seidl
595 Cook Ct
Hummelstown PA 17036

Call Sign: KB3SUB
Bohdana Pysarenko
137 Cooper Rd
Hummelstown PA 17036

Call Sign: KB3BZN
Brian D Feathers
1160 Cornell Dr
Hummelstown PA 17036

Call Sign: K3VBM
Donna B Rebman
1851 Deer Run Dr
Hummelstown PA 17036

Call Sign: N3BUE
Carlos M Inacio Jr
117 Dove Ct
Hummelstown PA 17036

Call Sign: N3PNM
Jennifer E Inacio
117 Dove Ct
Hummelstown PA 17036

Call Sign: WA3MIF
Byron H Timmins
208 E Canal St
Hummelstown PA
170369225

Call Sign: N3BLJ
George M Pintarch
27 E High St
Hummelstown PA
170362213

Call Sign: WA4BXY
Joseph A Gascho
563 Farmhouse Ln
Hummelstown PA 17036

Call Sign: N3BED
Joseph P Lippincott
1366 Fox Glenn Dr
Hummelstown PA 17036

Call Sign: KB3LEU
Anthony J Wert
6 Glendore Cir
Hummelstown PA 17036

Call Sign: N3LJZ
Stephen D Pearl
2040 Gramercy Pl
Hummelstown PA 17036

Call Sign: KI0EH
N Peter Fleszar
1075 Greenhill Dr
Hummelstown PA 17036

Call Sign: KB3UEV
Michael R Hauer
521 Hershey Rd
Hummelstown PA 17036

Call Sign: W3BDG
Robert E Shaffer
545 Hill Church Rd
Hummelstown PA 17036

Call Sign: N3CMQ
Paul G Hamilla Jr
7841 Jefferson St
Hummelstown PA 17036

Call Sign: W3OBU
Lloyd Maffett Jr
1421 Jill Dr
Hummelstown PA 17036

Call Sign: W3HLP
June F Johnson
1473 Jill Dr
Hummelstown PA
170369005

Call Sign: W3HLS
Alan F Johnson
1473 Jill Dr
Hummelstown PA
170369005

Call Sign: WB5URY
Rene A Martinez
2325 Joann Ave
Hummelstown PA 17036

Call Sign: K3HFJ
Warren M Cassel
343 Jonathan Ct
Hummelstown PA 17036

Call Sign: KB3MYM
Joel N Meyers
1781 Kaylor Rd
Hummelstown PA 17036

Call Sign: KA3BJR
Eric D Keller
23 Kellocks Run Rd
Hummelstown PA 17036

Call Sign: KC7JFX
Charles J Pulaski
20 Kokomo Ave
Hummelstown PA
170361113

Call Sign: KB3VAB
Ryan Campbell
314 Laurie Ave
Hummelstown PA 17036

Call Sign: N3PHP
John R Saunders

447 Lovell Ct
Hummelstown PA 17036

Call Sign: KB3OZM
Stephen M Doll
916 Merion Ct
Hummelstown PA 17036

Call Sign: KA3WXO
Richard W Strelick
18 Merion Ln
Hummelstown PA 17036

Call Sign: N3YRC
Christopher L Schwilk
491 Middletown Rd
Hummelstown PA 17036

Call Sign: N3DMR
Roxanne R Robinson
1235 Middletown Rd
Hummelstown PA 17036

Call Sign: WB3JIS
Donald M Robinson
1235 Middletown Rd
Hummelstown PA 17036

Call Sign: KB3MNR
Sandra M Robinson
1235 Middletown Rd
Hummelstown PA 17036

Call Sign: KB3SMR
Sandra M Robinson
1235 Middletown Rd
Hummelstown PA 17036

Call Sign: KA3HKN
Terry L Miller
16 Mondale Cir
Hummelstown PA 17036

Call Sign: K3MGJ
William C Henry

201 N Walnut St
Hummelstown PA 17036

Call Sign: KA3JGM
Thomas L Duck
201 N Walnut St
Hummelstown PA 17036

Call Sign: W3QN
Harold P Hollenbach
104 Penegrine Ln
Hummelstown PA 17036

Call Sign: KA3ACK
Grover B Gourley
303 Pine
Hummelstown PA 17036

Call Sign: W3ASW
Richard E Long
412 Pine Hill Rd
Hummelstown PA 17036

Call Sign: KB2GGN
Andrew Torchia
286 Pine St
Hummelstown PA 17036

Call Sign: KF3CM
David W Curtis
152 Pleasant View Rd
Hummelstown PA 17036

Call Sign: KB3UYM
Jamie F Kopinetz
494 Pleasant View Rd
Hummelstown PA 17036

Call Sign: KF3EM
Frank W Collins
152 Pleasantview Rd
Hummelstown PA 17036

Call Sign: KA3TCS
John R Detweiler

202 Poplar Ave
Hummelstown PA 17036

Call Sign: N3HJC
David W Ruhl
116 Quail Ct
Hummelstown PA
170368851

Call Sign: KB3QWW
Christopher T Carson
1126 Quail Hollow Rd
Hummelstown PA 17036

Call Sign: N3ZBA
Theodore E Hall
Raleigh Rd
Hummelstown PA 17036

Call Sign: WB3GWO
Simon W Rhoads
253 Redwood St
Hummelstown PA 17036

Call Sign: N3UZV
Mark A Wojcicki
35 Ridgeview Rd
Hummelstown PA 17036

Call Sign: KR3B
John E Nelligan Jr
293 S Meadow Ln
Hummelstown PA 17036

Call Sign: N2NYO
Jerome F Pumo
207 S Mill Rd
Hummelstown PA 17036

Call Sign: KE6BYT
Carey A Crutchfield
207 S Mill Rd
Hummelstown PA 17036

Call Sign: KA3JXT

Paul Lutzkanin
110 S Railroad St
Hummelstown PA 17036

Call Sign: N3LTO
Michael J Knarr
203 S Railroad St
Hummelstown PA 17036

Call Sign: N3NII
Stacey L Knarr
203 S Railroad St
Hummelstown PA 17036

Call Sign: KB3CHL
Ronald M Hetrick III
392 Scout Ln
Hummelstown PA
170368697

Call Sign: WB3LHZ
George F Goodeluinas
25 Shetland Dr
Hummelstown PA 17036

Call Sign: KB3PAX
Sarah M Sweitzer
2082 Southpoint Dr
Hummelstown PA 17036

Call Sign: KB3CJL
Christopher S Barrett
2130 Southpoint Dr
Hummelstown PA 17036

Call Sign: K3YYF
Samuel B Aurand
630 Stover Ct
Hummelstown PA 17036

Call Sign: N3ZKZ
Kevan S Zell
2181 Swatara Creek Rd
Hummelstown PA 17036

Call Sign: WA3PTY
Albert W First Jr
480 Trail Rd
Hummelstown PA 17036

Call Sign: N3THK
Clyde S Felker
614 W 2nd St
Hummelstown PA 17036

Call Sign: KE3TM
Harold R Baer
619 W 2nd St
Hummelstown PA 17036

Call Sign: KB3LTC
Douglas R Evans
618 W High St
Hummelstown PA 17036

Call Sign: K3DRE
Douglas R Evans
618 W High St
Hummelstown PA 17036

Call Sign: W3KUF
Henry M Spangler
1 Wagner Ave
Hummelstown PA 17036

Call Sign: W3MW
Donald R Appleby Jr
1598 Woodhaven Dr
Hummelstown PA 17036

Call Sign: K3ME
Allentown Works Amat
Rad Clb
1625 Woodhaven Dr
Hummelstown PA
170368905

Call Sign: N3VGL
David L Smith
1625 Woodhaven Dr

Hummelstown PA
170368905

Call Sign: KB3QDI
Vanessa A Hanger
637 Zurich Dr
Hummelstown PA 17036

**FCC Amateur Radio
Licenses in Huntingdon**

Call Sign: KR3C
Timothy W Clapper
512 14th St Apt 1
Huntingdon PA 16652

Call Sign: W3WIV
Joseph P Meyash
310 15th St
Huntingdon PA 16652

Call Sign: KA3WEF
Wanda M Meyash
310 15th St
Huntingdon PA 16652

Call Sign: N3FXY
Harold D Holland
30 30th St
Huntingdon PA 16652

Call Sign: N3VHO
Jeffrey L Stolkovich
30 30th St
Huntingdon PA 16652

Call Sign: K3GOM
John C Garner
712 7th St
Huntingdon PA 16652

Call Sign: K3OVY
Ronald R Yoder
6435 Birch Ln
Huntingdon PA 16652

Call Sign: KA3DTR
John J Grimes
Box 124
Huntingdon PA 16652

Call Sign: W3ITE
John R Van Sciver
Box 139
Huntingdon PA 16652

Call Sign: N3YZH
Donald A Heaton
Box 172 B
Huntingdon PA 16652

Call Sign: N3VVB
Christopher F Fleck
Box 181
Huntingdon PA 16652

Call Sign: N3YZL
Zachary D Bowser
Box 313
Huntingdon PA 16652

Call Sign: KB3BSH
Charles L Stevens
Box 313
Huntingdon PA 16652

Call Sign: N3HIQ
Leonard W Parson
Box 347C
Huntingdon PA 16652

Call Sign: WA3NDW
Jack S Cooper
Box 358
Huntingdon PA 16652

Call Sign: KA3GGJ
Janet L Garner
Box 37
Huntingdon PA 16652

Call Sign: N3OSB
William E Bush
Box 377
Huntingdon PA 16652

Call Sign: N3MIA
James F Stuller
Box 387
Huntingdon PA 16652

Call Sign: WA3DBW
Walter H Eichensehr
Box 429A
Huntingdon PA 16652

Call Sign: WB3HBB
Edward L Price
Box 51 Piney Ridge Rd Rd
3
Huntingdon PA 16652

Call Sign: W3TEN
Annabelle R Krepps
711 Church St Apt 510
Huntingdon PA 16652

Call Sign: N3HIR
Larry A Price
4724 Cold Springs Rd
Huntingdon PA 16652

Call Sign: N3YZC
Caterina P Dell
7326 Country Hills Dr
Huntingdon PA 16652

Call Sign: K2BNS
John R Van Sciver
13282 Greenwood Rd
Huntingdon PA 16652

Call Sign: NA3F
John R Van Sciver
13282 Greenwood Rd

Huntingdon PA 16652

Call Sign: N3QZI
Samuel L Heaster
9738 Hartslog Valley Rd
Huntingdon PA 16652

Call Sign: WB3CJB
Donald L Speck
5105 Iron Ore Rd
Huntingdon PA 16652

Call Sign: KB3JYF
Michael R Larcombe
250 Jennifer Dr
Huntingdon PA 16652

Call Sign: WB3FPS
Robert B Hall
824 Juniata Ave
Huntingdon PA 16652

Call Sign: N3MIB
Martin H Perk
Juniata College
Huntingdon PA 16652

Call Sign: N3HII
Robert G Snare
6183 Larkin Dr
Huntingdon PA 16652

Call Sign: N3JOJ
Allen B Moore
Lot 9
Huntingdon PA 16652

Call Sign: KA3HOZ
John D Clark Jr
819 Mifflin St
Huntingdon PA 16652

Call Sign: K3CQU
Bernard F Swartz
901 Mifflin St

Huntingdon PA 16652

Call Sign: N3IHT
Angela K Buchanan Bloch
1631 Mifflin St Apt 2
Huntingdon PA 16652

Call Sign: NA3V
James L Gooch
2475 Miller Ave
Huntingdon PA 16652

Call Sign: N3BXN
Richard A Smucker
2440 Moore St
Huntingdon PA 16652

Call Sign: KB3PLG
Brandon D Williams
911 Moore St Apt 2
Huntingdon PA 16652

Call Sign: WA3ZGM
Herbert E Gilliland
1210 Mt Vernon Ave
Huntingdon PA 16652

Call Sign: NJ3N
Barry L Kline
309 Penn St
Huntingdon PA
166521445

Call Sign: KA3RFY
Jennifer A Murray
1908 Penn St
Huntingdon PA 16652

Call Sign: KB3HQM
Chad B Little
10182 Petersburg Pike
Huntingdon PA 16652

Call Sign: WB3FOX
John B Jacobs

9091 Ponderosa Rd
Huntingdon PA 16652

Call Sign: K3IGF
Chester P Isett
2151 Prospect Ave
Huntingdon PA 16652

Call Sign: K3DXJ
Henry A Theys
10192 Raystown Rd
Huntingdon PA
166529425

Call Sign: KA3REV
Christopher L Carper
6958 Rupert Ln
Huntingdon PA 16652

Call Sign: KD3CB
Cloyd A Rupert
6959 Rupert Ln
Huntingdon PA 16652

Call Sign: W3XS
William M Blazina Jr
10180 School House
Hollow Rd
Huntingdon PA 16652

Call Sign: W3XB
David G Garner
7816 Shively Rd
Huntingdon PA 16652

Call Sign: KA3NUF
Robert A Jessell Jr
267 Standing Stone Ave
Huntingdon PA 16652

Call Sign: KA3UPK
Martha A Jessell
267 Standing Stone Ave
Huntingdon PA 16652

Call Sign: KB3VDF
Matthew E Hefright
10443 Sugar Grove Rd
Huntingdon PA 16652

Call Sign: N3ELE
Robert W Hearn
1617 Washington St
Huntingdon PA 16652

Call Sign: W3ISE
Warren T Shreve
360 Westminster Dr Rm
111
Huntingdon PA 16652

Call Sign: N3IKV
Mac Kinlay S Himes
Wyncrest
Huntingdon PA 16652

Call Sign: K3CKY
Ralph J Cramer
Huntingdon PA 16652

Call Sign: KB3ON
Wayne F Berlin
Huntingdon PA 16652

FCC Amateur Radio Licenses in Hyde

Call Sign: KE6ECY
Howard F Veihdeffer Jr
1619 Lawrence Ave
Hyde PA 168430248

Call Sign: N3PUY
Joseph T Welch
Hyde PA 16843

FCC Amateur Radio Licenses in Hyndman

Call Sign: KB3MHH

Sally A Byerley
166 5th Ave
Hyndman PA 15545

Call Sign: N3PET
John L Robinette
Box 458
Hyndman PA 15545

Call Sign: W3KDC
Albert F Hast
213 Clarence St
Hyndman PA 155450099

Call Sign: N3VZX
John L Hast
220 Clarence St
Hyndman PA 15545

Call Sign: WA3UBP
Edward W Evans Jr
Cunningham Dr
Hyndman PA 15545

Call Sign: WA3UQQ
Elizabeth A Evans
Cunningham Dr
Hyndman PA 15545

Call Sign: K3WWW
Edward W Evans Jr
Cunningham Dr
Hyndman PA 15545

Call Sign: K2WWW
Elizabeth A Evans
Cunningham Dr
Hyndman PA 15545

Call Sign: KB3LHN
Russell W Byerley
191 Farm Ln
Hyndman PA 15545

Call Sign: WB3CNW

Steven E Leydig Sr
195 Hite Hollow Rd
Hyndman PA 15545

Call Sign: N3NKE
Verle K Blankenship
5763 Kennells Mill Rd
Hyndman PA 15545

Call Sign: N3WMS
David L Christner
124 Kings Grove Rd
Hyndman PA 15545

Call Sign: N3KMH
Gary E Christner
Rd 1
Hyndman PA 15545

Call Sign: N3MZO
Glenn E Divelbiss
Hyndman PA 15545

Call Sign: N3JFI
Herman W Rawlings
Hyndman PA 15545

Call Sign: N3RVV
Bernard L Jackson
Hyndman PA 15545

FCC Amateur Radio Licenses in Ickesburg

Call Sign: WB3FQB
David A Smith Sr
Box 81
Ickesburg PA 17037

FCC Amateur Radio Licenses in Imler

Call Sign: N3CTX
Harold E Stufft
722 Fickes Rd

Imler PA 166559016

Call Sign: N3DFN
Dorothy A Young
722 Fickes Rd
Imler PA 166559016

Call Sign: KA3KIG
David R Fickes
257 N Imler Valley Rd
Imler PA 16655

Call Sign: N3MWG
Leslie B Fickes
257 N Imler Valley Rd
Imler PA 16655

Call Sign: KA3KIH
Sidney K Fickes
136 Stone Barn Ln
Imler PA 16655

FCC Amateur Radio Licenses in Intercourse

Call Sign: N3PYY
Angela S Howe
16 S Westview Dr
Intercourse PA 17534

Call Sign: KB3LMW
Joseph A Plunkett
Intercourse PA 17534

FCC Amateur Radio Licenses in Irvona

Call Sign: N3PAW
Craig C Westover
70 Strongs Rd
Irvona PA 16656

FCC Amateur Radio Licenses in Jacobus

Call Sign: N3RAW
Michael J La Martina
28 Hillside Dr
Jacobus PA 17407

Call Sign: KB3HSI
Michael C Colflesh I
109 N Main
Jacobus PA 17407

Call Sign: N3PRI
Mark S Fullerton
N Main St
Jacobus PA 17407

Call Sign: K6LAP
Lewis A Prince
17 Woodland Dr
Jacobus PA 174071228

Call Sign: KA3PQK
Kevin F Druck
204 York Rd
Jacobus PA 17407

Call Sign: WA3MEM
Dale A Druck
204 York Rd
Jacobus PA 17407

FCC Amateur Radio Licenses in James City

Call Sign: KA3EAT
Judy L Orzetti
256 Ohio Ave
James City PA 16734

Call Sign: KA3EAU
Guy R Wolfe
James City PA 16734

Call Sign: WB3IGM
Thomas J Orzetti
James City PA 16734

FCC Amateur Radio Licenses in James Creek

Call Sign: KB4KFU
Timothy F T Brookins
Box 180Aa
James Creek PA 16657

Call Sign: KB3LGX
Jimmie L Wills
Box 68 J
James Creek PA 16657

Call Sign: KB3ONK
David M Launtz
2318 Entriken Rd
James Creek PA 16657

Call Sign: KB3YG
Richard M Andreas
3524 Holly Dr
James Creek PA 16657

Call Sign: KB3RES
Michael J Bartos
4117 Todd Pass Rd
James Creek PA 16657

Call Sign: KK3DLN
Donald L Nicewonger
James Creek PA 16657

Call Sign: KB3EAD
Susan L Nicewonger
James Creek PA
166570063

FCC Amateur Radio Licenses in Jerome

Call Sign: WB3IMU
John Dohoda Jr
106 Conemaugh Ave
Jerome PA 15937

Call Sign: KB3GYD
Deborah A Mishler
Jerome PA 15937

Call Sign: KB3IGZ
Mary E Schmidt
Jerome PA 15937

Call Sign: WB3FBI
Daniel L Mishler
Jerome PA 159370411

**FCC Amateur Radio
Licenses in Jersey Shore**

Call Sign: KB3JPN
Sarina M Smith
87 8th St
Jersey Shore PA 17740

Call Sign: KA3SXD
Patrick W Ward
1310.5 Allegheny St
Jersey Shore PA 17740

Call Sign: WB3CVB
Jasper H Bay
Bardo Ave
Jersey Shore PA 17740

Call Sign: K3DPA
Gary L Emory
Box 220D
Jersey Shore PA 17740

Call Sign: N3SZB
Crist O Bardell
151 Brickley Ln
Jersey Shore PA 17740

Call Sign: KA3TZJ
Nathan T Meredith
346 Cemetery St
Jersey Shore PA 17740

Call Sign: KB3YET
Paul E Garrett
226 Front St
Jersey Shore PA 17740

Call Sign: KB3YES
Paul A Stitzer Jr
910 Furnance Run Rd
Jersey Shore PA 17740

Call Sign: N2ZWU
Keith Balogh
2145 Nices Hollow Rd
Jersey Shore PA 17740

Call Sign: KB3RDN
Richard R Munro
290 Nippenose Rd Apt 2
Jersey Shore PA 17740

Call Sign: KB3DVR
Jamie E Miller
241 Old Forge Hill Rd
Jersey Shore PA 17740

Call Sign: KE4PLM
Doug R Shaylor
241 Old Forge Hill Rd
Jersey Shore PA 17740

Call Sign: KB3LCF
Robert H Grossman
894 Pearson Rd
Jersey Shore PA 17740

Call Sign: W2RF
Edward H Russell Jr
845 Quarry Rd
Jersey Shore PA 17740

Call Sign: K2WRF
Cynthia R Russell
845 Quarry Rd
Jersey Shore PA 17740

Call Sign: N8AYN
Jerry L Eischeid
3143 Rauchtown Rd
Jersey Shore PA 17740

Call Sign: KB3DTG
Rita M Almasy
52 Shadle Rd
Jersey Shore PA 17740

Call Sign: KE3HL
Edward J Almasy Jr
52 Shadle Rd
Jersey Shore PA 17740

Call Sign: WB3AHB
Kenneth C Thompson
328 Spruce St
Jersey Shore PA 17740

Call Sign: KB3LCE
James R Passetti
2236 Sulphur Run Rd
Jersey Shore PA 17740

Call Sign: KB3GNQ
Thomas L Dutton
1401 Walnut St
Jersey Shore PA 17740

Call Sign: KB3QLH
Travis M Best
414 Washington Ave
Jersey Shore PA 17740

Call Sign: W3TMB
Travis M Best
414 Washington Ave
Jersey Shore PA 17740

Call Sign: KA1RXV
Norman W Lavallee
265 Wentworth Ln
Jersey Shore PA 17740

Call Sign: KA3TUG
William B Waddell
424 Wilson St
Jersey Shore PA 17740

FCC Amateur Radio Licenses in Johnsonburg

Call Sign: KB3TVY
Mattie A Maletto
302 1st Ave
Johnsonburg PA 15845

Call Sign: KB3MGW
Patricia A Frantz
507 2nd Ave
Johnsonburg PA 15845

Call Sign: K3TMD
John A Frantz
507 2nd Ave
Johnsonburg PA
158451116

Call Sign: KB3CQT
Valerie M Biel
218 Blaine Ave
Johnsonburg PA 15845

Call Sign: W6LAC
Robert W Plumskey
200 Clarion Rd
Johnsonburg PA
158451606

Call Sign: KB3OUH
Richard E Hetrick
151 Harrison Ave
Johnsonburg PA 15845

Call Sign: N3UFY
Antonella V Chirillo
Market St
Johnsonburg PA 15845

Call Sign: KB3IAA
Roger Plumsky
311 Water St
Johnsonburg PA 15845

Call Sign: KB3IBX
Ryan P Gapinski
423 Water St
Johnsonburg PA 15845

Call Sign: N3OCE
Joseph E King
Water St Ext
Johnsonburg PA 15845

Call Sign: N3PQI
Lawrence A Schlimm
2720 Wilcox Rd
Johnsonburg PA 15845

Call Sign: KB3MBX
James E Reinsburrow
302 Willow St
Johnsonburg PA 15845

FCC Amateur Radio Licenses in Johnstown

Call Sign: N3NTY
John E Barsda
51 Akeas Apt 209
Johnstown PA 15905

Call Sign: KB3VWH
James A Dodson
220 Alois St
Johnstown PA 15904

Call Sign: K3FHK
Edward B Kozuch
109 Arbutus Ave
Johnstown PA 15904

Call Sign: W3POR

Robert A Gorden
403 Arbutus Village Apt D
11
Johnstown PA 15904

Call Sign: KB3FBP
Kelly E Lester
221 Atiee St
Johnstown PA 15905

Call Sign: KB3REA
Herbert E Enos
196 Barron Ave
Johnstown PA 15906

Call Sign: KB3LBE
Stephen F Feist
1212 Bartlett Ave
Johnstown PA 15909

Call Sign: WB3HHQ
Bert G J Barkhymer
401 Beatrice Ave
Johnstown PA 159061421

Call Sign: N3ERS
Angie L Platco
1702 Bedford St
Johnstown PA 15902

Call Sign: NA3Y
George T Platco Jr
1702 Bedford St
Johnstown PA 15902

Call Sign: K3SPI
Richard W Davies
2829 Bedford St
Johnstown PA 15904

Call Sign: KB3HZG
Charles J Smith
231 Beechwood St
Johnstown PA 15904

Call Sign: KB3HZH
Charles J Smith
231 Beechwood St
Johnstown PA 15904

Call Sign: KA3AWQ
Ralph J Michaels
395 Bel Air Dr
Johnstown PA 15904

Call Sign: N3GVZ
Bruce F Klepack
428 Bella Vista Dr
Johnstown PA 15904

Call Sign: KB3HYM
Erin P Kabler
907 Belmont St
Johnstown PA 15904

Call Sign: KB3FU
Thomas R Bach
2218 Benchmark Ln
Johnstown PA 15905

Call Sign: WA3CLF
Anthony Morihlatko
652 Benshoff Hill Rd
Johnstown PA 15906

Call Sign: KB3HYK
Richard A Bodnar
1152 Benshoff Hill Rd
Johnstown PA 15906

Call Sign: WA2LYV
Rodger W Walls
2650 Benshoff Hill Rd
Johnstown PA 15909

Call Sign: N3LAG
John E Barsda
730 Bloom St Apt 4 B
Johnstown PA 159021812

Call Sign: KB3PCP
Jessica L Johnston
335 Bloomfield St Apt 20
Johnstown PA 15904

Call Sign: W3ICU
Robert E Johnston
212 Blue Diamond St
Johnstown PA 15902

Call Sign: KE3UC
Daniel J Ruhe
614 Bobwhite St
Johnstown PA 159041624

Call Sign: K4HYN
David A Killen
Box 351
Johnstown PA 15909

Call Sign: KD3LX
Robert Andrade
Box 404
Johnstown PA 15906

Call Sign: K3JS
James J Sedlmeyer
425 Braddock St
Johnstown PA 15905

Call Sign: N7DUP
Philip A Campanella
138 Brandle St
Johnstown PA 159041708

Call Sign: WB3FCC
Darlene L Carstensen
1425 Brier Ave
Johnstown PA 15902

Call Sign: WB3FCB
Thomas C Carstensen
1425 Brier Ave
Johnstown PA 159023622

Call Sign: KB3NCZ
City Of Johnstown
Department Of Emergency
Management
1003 Broad St Bldg B Ste
200
Johnstown PA 15906

Call Sign: K3JST
City Of Johnstown
Department Of Emergency
Management
1003 Broad St Bldg B Ste
200
Johnstown PA 15906

Call Sign: N3VFX
Robert J Johnston
535 Carnation St
Johnstown PA 15902

Call Sign: N3LZX
Jamie R Krall
Central Ave
Johnstown PA 15902

Call Sign: KB3AGW
Lyle N Alexander
401 Chancellor St
Johnstown PA 15904

Call Sign: KB3AGY
Brian L Alexander
401 Chancellor St
Johnstown PA 15904

Call Sign: KA3SZG
Joseph Kutchma
610 Chestnut St
Johnstown PA 15906

Call Sign: N1SRH
James W Rice
711 Chestnut St Rear
Johnstown PA 159062535

Call Sign: WB3FBJ
Harold B Wilson Jr
1238 Claythorne Dr
Johnstown PA 159043504

Call Sign: W3SNN
Francis L Sutton
1018 Club Dr
Johnstown PA 159051912

Call Sign: WB3FBN
Elder M Kerr Jr
85 Colgate Ave
Johnstown PA 15905

Call Sign: KB3MZT
Roger J Crowley
340 Columbia St
Johnstown PA 15905

Call Sign: WB3HZN
John J Shultz
750 Coon Ridge Rd
Johnstown PA 15905

Call Sign: AA3SM
Barry P Rummel Mim
735 Cooper Ave
Johnstown PA 159061030

Call Sign: N3PIC
Roger C Elkin
Cooper Ave
Johnstown PA 15906

Call Sign: KA3UVL
Thomas J McMillen Jr
367 Corinne St
Johnstown PA 15906

Call Sign: WB3HGW
Thomas J McMillen Sr
367 Corinne St
Johnstown PA 15906

Call Sign: KB3WMY
Steven P Kordell
657 Country Club Rd
Johnstown PA 15905

Call Sign: K3UYD
Steve J Cherney
119 Cub St
Johnstown PA 159064109

Call Sign: KB3JXK
Mark A Renowden
991 Cushon St
Johnstown PA 15902

Call Sign: K3EDN
Edward Walat
121 D St
Johnstown PA 15906

Call Sign: KB3WGZ
Ronald S Spokovich
194 D St
Johnstown PA 15906

Call Sign: KB3NLU
David R Luprek
428 Danner St
Johnstown PA 15904

Call Sign: KB3FBR
Joseph H Carney
241 Darr St
Johnstown PA 15904

Call Sign: KB3PCJ
Michael R Bischof
216 David St
Johnstown PA 15902

Call Sign: KB3LBF
Catherine J Muchesko
264 Derby St
Johnstown PA 15905

Call Sign: KB3HNV
Paul E Munshower
208 Devon Dr
Johnstown PA 15904

Call Sign: KB3HYO
Ronald G Gilbert
860 Dreyel Ave
Johnstown PA 15905

Call Sign: WB3ALQ
Stanley A Ryba
242 Dupont St
Johnstown PA 15902

Call Sign: N3SSD
Michael E Sakmar
332 Durant St
Johnstown PA 159061802

Call Sign: KA0TFQ
Michael S Lichtwardt
724 E Oakmont Blvd Apt
D
Johnstown PA 15904

Call Sign: KA3SWE
David P Engle
573 Edward St
Johnstown PA 159052634

Call Sign: KD3JO
Nancy L Engle
573 Edward St
Johnstown PA 159052634

Call Sign: NR3N
Dana R Engle
573 Edward St
Johnstown PA 159052634

Call Sign: KB3CZF
Patrick E Wess
117 Elbert St

Johnstown PA 15904

Call Sign: KB3UUS
Joshua M Miller
212 Elim St
Johnstown PA 15905

Call Sign: WA3IMX
Donald L Walker
4049 Elton Rd
Johnstown PA 15904

Call Sign: KA3SZD
Richard J Kime Sr
206 Emerald St
Johnstown PA 15902

Call Sign: WA3YOL
James B Thompson
148 Euclid Ave
Johnstown PA 15904

Call Sign: WC3AAO
Cambria County Dept Of
Emer Services
607 Evergreen St
Johnstown PA 159041610

Call Sign: N3WUQ
Walter H Wadsworth
368 Fairfield Ave
Johnstown PA 15906

Call Sign: W3NCG
Nathan C Jones
731 Ferndale Ave
Johnstown PA 15905

Call Sign: KA1QEQ
Ronald R Golby
130 Fieldstone Ave
Johnstown PA 15904

Call Sign: KB3DUC
Ryan S Eash

439 Fifty Acre Rd
Johnstown PA 15904

Call Sign: N3HTF
Barbara A Leeper
453 Fifty Acre Rd
Johnstown PA 15904

Call Sign: KA3TQS
Paul A Kurvzovich
27 Fordhook Ave
Johnstown PA 15904

Call Sign: N3GXX
Robert J Miller Jr
746 Forest Ave
Johnstown PA 15902

Call Sign: KB3PSI
Robert A Senft
1820 Frieda Ave
Johnstown PA 15902

Call Sign: K3PYL
Samuel J Marcks
230 Furnari Ave
Johnstown PA 15905

Call Sign: KB3JOW
David J Long
100 Gap Ave
Johnstown PA 159042607

Call Sign: KA3SZI
John Chanda Sr
109 Gilbert St
Johnstown PA 15906

Call Sign: WB3HHN
Herschel E Booth
536 Glenwood Ave
Johnstown PA 15905

Call Sign: KG4JGB
John E Mead

901 Goucher St
Johnstown PA 15905

Call Sign: WB3HHW
Charles A Babal
1610 Goucher St
Johnstown PA 15905

Call Sign: KB3TOB
Thomas F Brown
903 Greenich St
Johnstown PA 15902

Call Sign: KA3RKA
Stephen C Kauffman
335 Griffith Ave
Johnstown PA 15909

Call Sign: WB3FBM
John S Molchany
115 Gurth Ln
Johnstown PA 15905

Call Sign: KB3YIT
Paul E Wiand
217 Hawthorne St
Johnstown PA 15904

Call Sign: K3SEA
Jay L Gross
237 Hereford Ln
Johnstown PA 159051133

Call Sign: WA3MCA
John W Sumrada
236 Hipp St
Johnstown PA 15902

Call Sign: KB3AGS
Craig E Mills
132 Hoffman Dr
Johnstown PA 15904

Call Sign: N3XIZ
Paul W Szewczyk

304 Honan Ave
Johnstown PA 15906

1309 Kegg Ave Apt 142
Johnstown PA 15904

372 Linkville Rd
Johnstown PA 15906

Call Sign: AB3NF
John S Gnesda Jr
112 Hunsinger Rd
Johnstown PA 15904

Call Sign: W3ZKO
Spurgeon W Adams
17 Knox St
Johnstown PA 15906

Call Sign: W3RNT
Richard D Thompson
1208 Linwood Ave
Johnstown PA 15902

Call Sign: AB3J
Francis M Duffy
403 Hystone Ave
Johnstown PA 15905

Call Sign: AB3JH
Benjamin K Watkins
2235 Kring St
Johnstown PA 15905

Call Sign: KA3RHR
William J Boltz
207 Lion St
Johnstown PA 15904

Call Sign: KB3OUY
John E Mead
525 Hystone Ave
Johnstown PA 15905

Call Sign: KB3NMC
Russell J Profaizer
104 Krings St
Johnstown PA 15904

Call Sign: W3PAE
Wallace F Orlidge
208 Little John Ln
Johnstown PA 15905

Call Sign: KA3SZH
William Bloom
252 Iron St
Johnstown PA 15906

Call Sign: N3ZQX
Joseph M Sernell
706 Lawrence St
Johnstown PA 159041645

Call Sign: KB3VYM
James T Burkett
236 Lower Newtown Rd
Johnstown PA 15904

Call Sign: K3TLJ
James Piljay
598 Iron St
Johnstown PA 15906

Call Sign: N3ZTU
Joseph J Sernell
706 Lawrence St
Johnstown PA 159041645

Call Sign: K3DNS
Herold E Romesburg
237 Ludwig St
Johnstown PA 15904

Call Sign: KA3LDB
Raymond D Schuster
106 Ivy Rd
Johnstown PA 15905

Call Sign: N3ZVY
Rachel M Sernell
706 Lawrence St
Johnstown PA 159041645

Call Sign: KB3GHN
Luther A Gotwald Jr
432 Luther Rd
Johnstown PA 15904

Call Sign: KA3UOG
John G Baldwin
231 Judith Dr
Johnstown PA 15905

Call Sign: KB3WSF
Cody R Way
128 Layton Ln
Johnstown PA 15904

Call Sign: KB3DR
Thomas P Wolff
626 Luzerne St
Johnstown PA 15905

Call Sign: K3OYB
Philip A Marcinek
243 Judith Dr
Johnstown PA 159051236

Call Sign: KB3OFQ
Adam C Munko
750 Linden Ave
Johnstown PA 15902

Call Sign: W3QIZ
Lynn Faust
1235 Lydia St
Johnstown PA 15904

Call Sign: KB3VTX
Anthony J Felan

Call Sign: WB3JSW
David A Babal

Call Sign: W3LSE
Kenneth D Klenk

216 Main St Room 103A
Johnstown PA 15901

Call Sign: KA3NZN
Keith R Swaltek
121 Marcedas St
Johnstown PA 15904

Call Sign: KI6VOL
Richard E Schween
305 Marilyn Way
Johnstown PA 15904

Call Sign: N3TPA
Clair W Ross
537 Marsh Ave
Johnstown PA 15902

Call Sign: KB3PCR
Justin W Fyock
227 Martin Rd
Johnstown PA 15904

Call Sign: WB3HGZ
James L Schuster
Maryland Ave
Johnstown PA 15906

Call Sign: KB3HYN
Thomas P Coyle
104 Maxwell Ave
Johnstown PA 15904

Call Sign: WB3CIK
Richard J Boxler
192 Mayluth Rd
Johnstown PA 15904

Call Sign: WB3GXF
Thomas E Day Jr
197 Mayluth Rd
Johnstown PA 15904

Call Sign: N3AGW
David C Stiver

213 Meadow Dr
Johnstown PA 15905

Call Sign: KB3PZG
Christopher K Schultz
304 Meadow Dr
Johnstown PA 15905

Call Sign: N3ZDW
Daniel E Sprague
1044 Menoher Blvd
Johnstown PA 15905

Call Sign: N3TGY
Lon A Shaffer
218 Mifflin St
Johnstown PA 15905

Call Sign: K3JTN
Robert G Kime
1925 Minno Dr
Johnstown PA 159051137

Call Sign: N3VQT
Robert L Foster
756 Mt Airy Dr
Johnstown PA 15904

Call Sign: K3RLF
Robert L Foster
756 Mt Airy Dr
Johnstown PA 15904

Call Sign: AB3JG
Andrew A Krawczyk
1090 Norwood St
Johnstown PA 15904

Call Sign: N3BMS
Donald R Pudliner
1128 Norwood St
Johnstown PA 159043028

Call Sign: N3UDI
Ralph M Timblin Jr

378 Ohio St
Johnstown PA 15902

Call Sign: WA3HMC
Ronald W Lorence
858 Olim St
Johnstown PA 15904

Call Sign: W3BJQ
J Lester Lambert
215 Ottawa St Bldg B Rm
08
Johnstown PA 15904

Call Sign: WB3COX
Douglas B Gregory
132 Palliser St
Johnstown PA 15905

Call Sign: WB3COS
Robert S Baum
202 Palliser St
Johnstown PA 159052557

Call Sign: W3VNI
John Martich
107 Palm Ave
Johnstown PA 15905

Call Sign: KA3HEL
Michael L Popovich
140 Palm Ave
Johnstown PA 15905

Call Sign: KA3UOH
Mark A Balak
618 Park Ave
Johnstown PA 15902

Call Sign: WB3HXS
John E Bechtold
1341 Paulton St
Johnstown PA 15905

Call Sign: WB3HXT

Constance K Bechtold
1341 Paulton St
Johnstown PA 15905

Call Sign: KB3TKV
Rodney E Waehner
112 Peden Ln
Johnstown PA 15905

Call Sign: KB3HZK
Thomas J May
114 Penrod St
Johnstown PA 159023323

Call Sign: WB3ADF
Dennis C Koss
126 Penrod St
Johnstown PA 15902

Call Sign: K3RBK
Edward F Hilbrecht
302 Phillip
Johnstown PA 15904

Call Sign: N3GRT
Matthew B Patti
2239 Pitt Ave Ext
Johnstown PA 15905

Call Sign: WA3QKM
Ralph A Carbone
1104 Rachel St
Johnstown PA 15904

Call Sign: KB3PCO
Paul E Pentz
207 Rainbow Dr
Johnstown PA 15904

Call Sign: N3QBS
Thomas J Lonergan Jr
Rd 6
Johnstown PA 15909

Call Sign: KB3CNA

Joan Hunter
204 Rean St
Johnstown PA 15904

Call Sign: N3YFO
David A Hunter
204 Rean St
Johnstown PA 15904

Call Sign: WA3BIX
John H Lenz
117 Rockwell Ave
Johnstown PA 159059555

Call Sign: WA3CPH
Thomas G Varmecky
119 Royal Ave
Johnstown PA 15905

Call Sign: WA3WAL
Harry F Cauffield
425 Russell Ave
Johnstown PA 159022548

Call Sign: KB3CNL
Eric D Ferpas
271 Saintz St
Johnstown PA 15906

Call Sign: KA3WIC
Sanford Q Gunby
310 Salmon Ave
Johnstown PA 15902

Call Sign: KB1CU
Richard A Vince
401 Salmon Ave
Johnstown PA 15904

Call Sign: KB3WMT
John N Geiser
379 Sam St
Johnstown PA 15902

Call Sign: AB3OV

John N Geiser
379 Sam St
Johnstown PA 15902

Call Sign: KB3WUD
Leann M Geiser
379 Sam St
Johnstown PA 15902

Call Sign: KB3AGX
John B Kohan
132 School St
Johnstown PA 15906

Call Sign: KB3YBJ
Ieee Upj Mountain Cat
ARC
450 Schoolhouse Rd
Johnstown PA 15904

Call Sign: W3SNN
Ieee Upj Mountain Cat
ARC
450 Schoolhouse Rd
Johnstown PA 15904

Call Sign: AB3NG
Ulric Meffert
450 Schoolhouse Rd
Johnstown PA 15904

Call Sign: WB3FCA
Gilbert D Slagle
145 Sell St
Johnstown PA 15905

Call Sign: KA3BJA
Michael Matolyak Jr
308 Sherwood Dr
Johnstown PA 159051225

Call Sign: KB3OKF
Matthew R Stahl
1085 Soap Hollow Rd
Johnstown PA 15905

Call Sign: K3JRS
James R Salvaggio Jr
1359 Solomon Run Rd
Johnstown PA 15904

Call Sign: KB3PCH
Aaron W Roberts
325 Theatre Dr Apt 3A21
Johnstown PA 15904

Call Sign: N3AGK
Mark P Williams
1307 Virginia Ave
Johnstown PA 15906

Call Sign: KB3AYU
Jeffrey P Masterson
322 Southmont Blvd
Johnstown PA 15905

Call Sign: KB3IAU
Terry A Berkebile
88 Thoburn St
Johnstown PA 15905

Call Sign: N3HEZ
Douglas G Zimmer
109 Vivian Dr
Johnstown PA 15904

Call Sign: N3RVQ
Pamela J Masterson
322 Southmont Blvd
Johnstown PA 15905

Call Sign: KA3RHU
Caleb G Butler
115 Thora St
Johnstown PA 15904

Call Sign: KB3AGT
Clifford P Miller
110 Vivian Dr
Johnstown PA 15904

Call Sign: N3ZEE
Eric J Farabaugh
387 Southmont Blvd
Johnstown PA 15905

Call Sign: W3ZMP
John Rusnak
115 Timothy St
Johnstown PA 15904

Call Sign: KA3IUV
Todd A Gorden
928 Von Lunen Rd
Johnstown PA 159021850

Call Sign: K3BLH
Robert Sumrada
1235 Spruce St Rear
Johnstown PA 15909

Call Sign: N3BDI
Joachim W Figge
345 Tioga St
Johnstown PA 15905

Call Sign: N3IBU
Darren S Mock
558 W Howard St
Johnstown PA 15906

Call Sign: N3LEL
Dwayne W Rosko
Stackhouse St
Johnstown PA 15906

Call Sign: KA3SFL
Magnus L Rogers
538 Tioga St
Johnstown PA 15905

Call Sign: KA3TDU
Franklin D Reffner
209 W Oakmont Blvd
Johnstown PA 15904

Call Sign: N3MAS
Dwight B Blue Jr
118 Stephens St
Johnstown PA 159054640

Call Sign: W3IW
John L Rogers
538 Tioga St
Johnstown PA 15905

Call Sign: KB3DFN
Kenneth L Downer
120 Whysong Ln
Johnstown PA 15906

Call Sign: N3JCV
Fred E Raco Jr
212 Sunapee Dr
Johnstown PA 15904

Call Sign: WB8QKM
Paul R Hyman
633 Tioga St
Johnstown PA 159052853

Call Sign: KA3HUR
Larry W Bracken
61 Wildcat Rd
Johnstown PA 15906

Call Sign: W3MU
John R Grumling
201 Terlyn Dr
Johnstown PA 15904

Call Sign: N3ZDV
Stephen E Laslo
315 Vaughn St
Johnstown PA 15906

Call Sign: KA3RJY
Barbara A Bracken
61 Wildcat Rd
Johnstown PA 15906

Call Sign: KA3IUJ
Edward T Ocipa
1181 William Penn Ave
Johnstown PA 15906

Call Sign: WB3IXE
Larry E Wainwright
1759 William Penn Ave
Johnstown PA 15909

Call Sign: W3ZHU
Clarence Good Jr
3728 William Penn Ave
Johnstown PA 15909

Call Sign: KB3JOX
Kevin A Weaver
324 Wilson St
Johnstown PA 15906

Call Sign: KB3DUE
Scott A Mahan
1717 Winter St
Johnstown PA 159023417

Call Sign: N3HBB
Charles R Mackel Sr
1664 Wm Penn Ave
Johnstown PA 15909

Call Sign: KB3NSZ
Stephen J Riley
141 Wonder St
Johnstown PA 15905

Call Sign: WB3Q
John E Gritzer
2192 Woodcrest Dr
Johnstown PA 15905

Call Sign: W3DB
David J Bechtold
2406 Woodcrest Dr
Johnstown PA 159051544

Call Sign: N3MZR
Alan B Carr Sr
101 Woodhaven Ln
Johnstown PA 15905

Call Sign: WA3IWF
Robert L Maslak
145 Work Dr
Johnstown PA 15904

Call Sign: KB3MBI
Jeffrey G Lowry
1189 Zucco Ln
Johnstown PA 15905

Call Sign: N3WUR
Stephen G Tondora
Johnstown PA 15907

Call Sign: KB3PSJ
Thomas Gallo
Johnstown PA 15907

FCC Amateur Radio Licenses in Jonestown

Call Sign: N3XIB
Charles W Hendrick Jr
10680 Allentown Blvd
Jonestown PA 17038

Call Sign: N3XIC
Linda J Hendrick
10680 Allentown Blvd
Jonestown PA 17038

Call Sign: AA3WH
Gary R Sweigert
289 Awol Rd
Jonestown PA 17038

Call Sign: KE3MZ
Robert M Kreider
Box 2180

Jonestown PA 17038

Call Sign: N3OGN
Curtis S Leister
Box 2519 Greble Rd
Jonestown PA 17038

Call Sign: KB3CKL
Scott A Kline
Box 4450
Jonestown PA 17038

Call Sign: KB3CKP
Gary R Sweigert
Box 5000
Jonestown PA 17038

Call Sign: N3OBE
Keith W Kreider
Box 5620
Jonestown PA 17038

Call Sign: WB3CAR
James E Miller
Box 7130
Jonestown PA 17038

Call Sign: N3DGI
Robert E Buckingham II
22 Colonial Dr
Jonestown PA 17038

Call Sign: KA3SET
Joseph C Colaguori
27 Colonial Dr
Jonestown PA 17038

Call Sign: KB3TKL
Mike S Carnegie
132 Deer Dr
Jonestown PA 17038

Call Sign: KB3OYO
Roger A Soliday
57 Greble Rd

Jonestown PA 17038

Call Sign: N3DWB
Jeffrey S Dolph
67 Greble Rd
Jonestown PA 17038

Call Sign: KA3FPR
Rollin R Rheinheimer
135 Greble Rd
Jonestown PA 17038

Call Sign: KB3EGN
William Major
201 Greble Rd
Jonestown PA 17038

Call Sign: N3ICS
Gary L Wolfe
219 Highland Dr Box 493
Jonestown PA 17038

Call Sign: N3EDF
Edward D Fry
183 Monroe Valley Dr
Jonestown PA 170389705

Call Sign: WB3HBX
Timothy D Zimmerman Sr
220 Moonshine Rd
Jonestown PA 17038

Call Sign: KA3BAB
Kevin L Broughton
119 N Lancaster St
Jonestown PA 17038

Call Sign: N3PTX
Anthony R Kreider
245 Old Rt 22
Jonestown PA 17038

Call Sign: N3BHN
Arthur A Miller
831 Ono Rd

Jonestown PA 170388312

Call Sign: N3OGR
Marie E Brady
20 Orchard Dr
Jonestown PA 17038

Call Sign: WA3TOJ
Robert D Sweigert
15 Plymouth Dr
Jonestown PA 17038

Call Sign: W3NEW
Robert D Sweigert
15 Plymouth Dr
Jonestown PA 170389252

Call Sign: W3TOY
Robert D Sweigert
15 Plymouth Dr
Jonestown PA 170389252

Call Sign: W3GJX
Patrick A Dunne Jr
25 Plymouth Dr
Jonestown PA 17038

Call Sign: KB3UJO
John W Hess
688 Shirksville Rd
Jonestown PA 17038

Call Sign: KA3CLI
Constance J Dorula
964 Thompson Ave
Jonestown PA 170388403

Call Sign: N3OAJ
Michael S Hopkins
127 W Market St
Jonestown PA 17038

**FCC Amateur Radio
Licenses in Julian**

Call Sign: KB3JNH
Charles L Carroll
151 Janet Ln
Julian PA 16844

Call Sign: KB3IOI
Christopher W Deppe
1741 Rattlesnake Pike
Julian PA 16844

Call Sign: KF3BP
Joseph J Barton
2175 S Eagle Valley Rd
Julian PA 16844

Call Sign: WB3EOG
William E Drosnes
225 Sengle Ln
Julian PA 16844

Call Sign: KB3DTA
James G Stewart Sr
998 Spotts Rd
Julian PA 168449208

**FCC Amateur Radio
Licenses in Juniata**

Call Sign: WB3FLX
M Virginia Huss
709 6th Ave
Juniata PA 16601

**FCC Amateur Radio
Licenses in Kane**

Call Sign: N3XQC
Alan L Kohut
310 Bayard St
Kane PA 16735

Call Sign: KA3WJD
Ronald E Swanson
633 Biddle St
Kane PA 16735

Call Sign: KB3TVZ
William J Campbell
318 Birch St
Kane PA 16735

Call Sign: N3UDH
Clyde S Asel
Box 162 A
Kane PA 16735

Call Sign: N3UDO
Joseph J Szymanski III
Box 58
Kane PA 16735

Call Sign: N3PQB
Nancy T Harris
Box 95
Kane PA 16735

Call Sign: N3RJI
Betty J Larson
118 Clay St
Kane PA 16735

Call Sign: KB3VPP
Sandra G Weed
118 Clay St
Kane PA 16735

Call Sign: W3LQA
Edward C Zettle
16 Edgar St
Kane PA 16735

Call Sign: KB3EGW
Matthew R Bressler
387 Flickerwood Rd
Kane PA 16735

Call Sign: KA3UVC
Fred T Siggins
302 Glenwood St
Kane PA 16735

Call Sign: N3KCW
Donna M Siggins
302 Glenwood St
Kane PA 16735

Call Sign: KA3WLU
Anthony S Giordano
Greendale Rd Rd 1
Kane PA 16735

Call Sign: KB3EFF
John M Odonish
410 Greeves St
Kane PA 16735

Call Sign: KB3JXL
Adam E Odonish
410 Greeves St
Kane PA 16735

Call Sign: W3LZK
Edward R Weidow
2 Greeves St Apt 201
Kane PA 16735

Call Sign: N3MHR
Robert D Larson
19 Hemlock Ave
Kane PA 16735

Call Sign: KB3KRI
James E Anderson
104 Hemlock Ave
Kane PA 16735

Call Sign: KB3LMY
Stephen G Nuhfer
108 Hemlock Ave
Kane PA 16735

Call Sign: KB3QFU
Jena L Springer
7045 Highland Rd
Kane PA 16735

Call Sign: KB3TWA
Robert B Swanson Jr
1000 Jojo Rd
Kane PA 16735

Call Sign: KB3TWB
Selene N Swanson
1000 Jojo Rd
Kane PA 16735

Call Sign: KB6SNB
Joanne L Benjamin
112 N Fraley St Apt 3
Kane PA 16735

Call Sign: N3AQM
Michael S Swanson Sr
128 Oak St
Kane PA 16735

Call Sign: N3PQE
Kenneth E Miller
312 Poplar St
Kane PA 16735

Call Sign: N3AQN
Stanley L Swanson
2 Reigel Rd
Kane PA 16735

Call Sign: KB3TVX
Clifford E Weiss Jr
7830 Rt 6
Kane PA 16735

Call Sign: KB3TVW
Patricia A Weiss
7830 Rt 6
Kane PA 16735

Call Sign: KB3MZH
Scott K Sanders
9533 Rt 6
Kane PA 16735

Call Sign: KB3SYJ
Timothy S Bond
6126 Rt 66
Kane PA 16735

Call Sign: N3PQC
Mary J Lutton
110 S Fraley St
Kane PA 16735

Call Sign: KA3CQM
Gary A Olson
353 Spring St
Kane PA 16735

Call Sign: N3OCC
Carol A Olson
353 Spring St
Kane PA 16735

Call Sign: KB3BAQ
Regina M Kennedy
21 Spruce Ave
Kane PA 16735

Call Sign: N3RIU
Michael J Kennedy
21 Spruce Ave
Kane PA 16735

Call Sign: K3JCK
Frank R Muisiner Jr
309 W Pine Ave
Kane PA 167351632

Call Sign: KB3BAP
Sally L Menteer
218 Walnut St
Kane PA 16735

Call Sign: KB3ADF
James W Heckman
407 Walnut St
Kane PA 16735

Call Sign: KA3YKK
Susan M Kline
130 Yarnell St Apt 2
Kane PA 16735

Call Sign: KA3CQN
Gale A Olson
Kane PA 16735

FCC Amateur Radio Licenses in Karthaus

Call Sign: WB3AFO
William T Paul
3632 Main
Karthaus PA 16845

Call Sign: KB3FBA
Richard K Peters
133 Meadow Dr
Karthaus PA 16845

FCC Amateur Radio Licenses in Kersey

Call Sign: N3LBN
Keith R Rogers
109 Fairview Rd
Kersey PA 15846

Call Sign: KB3GNE
John J Hand Jr
130 Hemlock Ln
Kersey PA 15846

Call Sign: KA3FKQ
Thomas L Wilhelm
197 Irishtown Rd
Kersey PA 15846

Call Sign: N3ZFL
Phillip G Hand
118 Krise Rd
Kersey PA 15846

Call Sign: N3UDP
Michael J Matangelo
102 Mark Ln
Kersey PA 15846

Call Sign: N3YJB
Robert A Bolt
271 Old Kersey Rd
Kersey PA 15846

Call Sign: N3YWS
Joseph P Bowser
100 Pontzer Rd
Kersey PA 15846

Call Sign: KB3NMI
Andrew D Kunes
152 Ridge Rd
Kersey PA 15846

Call Sign: KB3FEY
Delores E Keech
122 Thompson Rd
Kersey PA 15846

Call Sign: KB3FEZ
Robert W Keech
122 Thompson Rd
Kersey PA 15846

Call Sign: WA3GCM
William J Fernan
648 Toby Rd
Kersey PA 15846

FCC Amateur Radio Licenses in Kinzers

Call Sign: KB3TDG
Carl E Tracy
5005 Lincoln Hwy
Kinzers PA 17535

Call Sign: K3XF

Carl E Tracy
5005 Lincoln Hwy
Kinzers PA 17535

Call Sign: KB3TJJ
Judy A Caskey
3555 Lincoln Hwy E
Kinzers PA 17535

Call Sign: KB3TJK
Marvin J Caskey Jr
3555 Lincoln Hwy E
Kinzers PA 17535

FCC Amateur Radio Licenses in Kirkwood

Call Sign: KE3HC
Gerald G Ferguson
691 Academy Rd
Kirkwood PA 17536

Call Sign: N3HQW
Robert J Devlin
764 King Pen Rd
Kirkwood PA 17536

Call Sign: KB3MEV
Stephen C Holup
886 King Pen Rd
Kirkwood PA 17536

Call Sign: KD4OCR
Maryann Mahan
404 Liberty Ln
Kirkwood PA 17536

Call Sign: N2ALU
Philip D Mahan
404 Liberty Ln
Kirkwood PA 17536

Call Sign: W3YCE
James E Peron
48 Long Ln

Kirkwood PA 17536

Call Sign: N3NIC
Kenneth S Peron
48 Long Ln
Kirkwood PA 175369531

Call Sign: KB3VRP
Ed D Thayer
281 Mt Eden Rd
Kirkwood PA 175369560

Call Sign: K9SRD
Ed D Thayer
281 Mt Eden Rd
Kirkwood PA 175369560

Call Sign: K3MTG
Donald W Gibbs
56 Pine Dr
Kirkwood PA 175369535

Call Sign: KB3CUU
John F Pierce
101 Railway Dr
Kirkwood PA 17536

Call Sign: N3PTT
Larry K Billings
361 Sproul Rd
Kirkwood PA 175369731

FCC Amateur Radio Licenses in Knoxville

Call Sign: KB3CRM
John R Murdock
Box 472
Knoxville PA 169289742

Call Sign: KB3AZD
Tori K Wood
Box 818
Knoxville PA 16928

Call Sign: K3QHJ
Duane A Doan
242 Doan Rd
Knoxville PA 16928

Call Sign: N3ZXK
Sylvia D Wood
2268 Locey Creek Rd
Knoxville PA 16928

Call Sign: W3SME
Lincoln G Chase
105 Rr Ave Box 116
Knoxville PA 16928

Call Sign: KC2IWI
Sheldon J Wood
6187 Rt 49
Knoxville PA 16928

Call Sign: N3PDW
Philip M Weaver
Knoxville PA 16928

FCC Amateur Radio Licenses in Kreamer

Call Sign: NG3F
Christopher E Snyder
140 Kreamer Ave
Kreamer PA 17833

FCC Amateur Radio Licenses in Kulpmont

Call Sign: N3TWY
Donald L Gordner
1001 Chestnut St Apt B
Kulpmont PA 17834

Call Sign: KB4CJB
Dennis J Holleran
4 Colorado Cir
Kulpmont PA 17834

Call Sign: WA3CJL
Robert J Thomas
1100 Poplar St
Kulpmont PA 17834

Call Sign: KB3MSU
Leroy A Griffiths
12 S 13th St
Kulpmont PA 17834

Call Sign: KB3HQH
John A Klokis
832 Scott St
Kulpmont PA 178341812

Call Sign: K3JK
John A Klokis
832 Scott St
Kulpmont PA 178341812

Call Sign: KB3SZS
Keith P Tamborelli
369 Spruce St
Kulpmont PA 17834

Call Sign: N3IHV
Raymond J Miller
900 Spruce St
Kulpmont PA 17834

Call Sign: K3HOF
James W Hoffman
296 Virginia Ln
Kulpmont PA 17834

Call Sign: WA1QPU
Johannes H B Bloemen
153 Washington Dr
Kulpmont PA 17834

FCC Amateur Radio Licenses in Kylertown

Call Sign: N3SPW
John S Szwarc

417 2nd St
Kylertown PA 16847

FCC Amateur Radio Licenses in Lakemont Altoona

Call Sign: KB3LGR
Peter - John F Cain
319 Howard Ave
Lakemont Altoona PA 16602

FCC Amateur Radio Licenses in Lamar

Call Sign: KB3PVQ
Matthew J Farringer
5051 Nittany Valley Dr
Lamar PA 16848

Call Sign: KD3LG
Galen D Castlebury Jr
Lamar PA 16848

FCC Amateur Radio Licenses in Lampeter

Call Sign: KA3QON
Patrick J McDonnell
923 Village Rd
Lampeter PA 17537

Call Sign: KB3BHQ
Martin Meylin Middle
School
1007 Village Rd
Lampeter PA 17537

FCC Amateur Radio Licenses in Lancaster

Call Sign: WB2OOB
Ronald T Small

140 2nd Lock Rd
Lancaster PA 17603

Call Sign: KB3JVZ
Norma J Small
140 2nd Lock Rd
Lancaster PA 17603

Call Sign: KB3UJX
Carlos A Noguera
590 3rd St
Lancaster PA 17603

Call Sign: KB3MHE
Peter J Stockbauer
615 3rd St
Lancaster PA 17603

Call Sign: KB3MFE
Marilyn R Lieber
542 Abbeyville Rd
Lancaster PA 17603

Call Sign: KF4PPE
Robert M Olson Jr
7 Acorn Blvd
Lancaster PA 17602

Call Sign: N3ITU
Judith A Murphy
304 Ashford Dr
Lancaster PA 17601

Call Sign: N3IWA
Wayne D Murphy
304 Ashford Dr
Lancaster PA 17601

Call Sign: K1CWB
Christopher W Bunting
346 Atkins Ave
Lancaster PA 17603

Call Sign: N3FYI
Christopher W Bunting

346 Atkins Ave
Lancaster PA 17603

Call Sign: KB3GHO
Michael R Toriello
743 Barrcrest Ln
Lancaster PA 17603

Call Sign: KB3RPJ
Austin K Wood
75 Barre Dr
Lancaster PA 17601

Call Sign: WB2YNF
Robert Ruder
1331 Beaconfield Ln
Lancaster PA 17601

Call Sign: KB3ALV
James M Kreider Jr
513 Beaver St
Lancaster PA 17603

Call Sign: KB3HZX
Timothy Hoenninger
108 Bender Mill Rd
Lancaster PA 17603

Call Sign: W3TLH
Timothy Hoenninger
108 Bender Mill Rd
Lancaster PA 17603

Call Sign: AI3O
Timothy Hoenninger
108 Bender Mill Rd
Lancaster PA 17603

Call Sign: N3SMX
Anthony J Wasong
18 Bentley Ln
Lancaster PA 17603

Call Sign: WA3MNX
Francis C Wilson

1604 Bentley Ridge Blvd
Lancaster PA 17602

Call Sign: WB3BON
Cloyd R Smith
2100 Birchwood Rd
Lancaster PA 17603

Call Sign: KE3WY
Christopher P Harewood
228 Black Oak Dr
Lancaster PA 176023466

Call Sign: N3NTK
Garry R Braughler
2810 Blacksmith Way
Lancaster PA 17601

Call Sign: N3YIW
Lois D Boose
86 Block Oak Dr
Lancaster PA 17602

Call Sign: WB3HJN
Richard D Nuss
2250 Blossom Valley Rd
Lancaster PA 17601

Call Sign: N3XXK
Shane D Reichenbach
2251 Blossom Valley Rd
Lancaster PA 17601

Call Sign: N3VDV
Paul R Hess
1360 Blue Jay Dr
Lancaster PA 17601

Call Sign: K3MIX
Michael J Fiorill
3433 Blue Rock Rd
Lancaster PA 176039775

Call Sign: N3CDZ
James E Horst Jr

222 Bluff View Dr
Lancaster PA 17601

Call Sign: KB3UFW
Dustin A Groff
2249 Bob White Ln
Lancaster PA 17601

Call Sign: KB3DOT
Martin J Herskowitz
2296 Bob White Ln
Lancaster PA 17601

Call Sign: KB3JOI
William E Herskowitz
2296 Bob White Ln
Lancaster PA 17601

Call Sign: N3AMW
Antoni Wortel
62 Bowman Rd
Lancaster PA 17602

Call Sign: KA3RSW
Karen H Lesmeister
1552 Braxton Dr
Lancaster PA 17602

Call Sign: KB3EQX
John S Lesmeister
1552 Braxton Dr
Lancaster PA 17602

Call Sign: KA3TKL
Merlin J Brenneman
290 Brenneman Rd
Lancaster PA 17603

Call Sign: KB3LHU
Terry A Stimpson
2191 Butter Rd
Lancaster PA 176014943

Call Sign: N3ZQF
Barry H Penchansky

2444 Butter Rd
Lancaster PA 176015302

2741 Chapel Rd
Lancaster PA 17603

1933 Creek Hill Rd
Lancaster PA 17601

Call Sign: N3JXN
Steven R Plantholt
1617 Buttercup Rd
Lancaster PA 17602

Call Sign: K3BLC
John M Butzer
2521 Chestnut Ridge Dr
Lancaster PA 176011936

Call Sign: N2JPX
Dorothy M Salvaggio
2127 Creek Hill Rd
Lancaster PA 176015749

Call Sign: N3UEE
Douglas Y Flick
628 Candlewyck Rd
Lancaster PA 17601

Call Sign: K3IDY
James D Roshon
2600 Chestnut Valley Dr
Lancaster PA 17601

Call Sign: W2AND
Frank M Salvaggio
2127 Creek Hill Rd
Lancaster PA 176015749

Call Sign: KB3CNG
Joseph R Zikmund IV
910 Cardinal Rd
Lancaster PA 17601

Call Sign: KD3FK
Beth L Weaver
1645 Clearview Ave
Lancaster PA 17601

Call Sign: N3HTW
Robert F Stefanow
1 Creekwood Dr
Lancaster PA 17602

Call Sign: KA3TAC
William L Salmon III
1915 Carlton Pl
Lancaster PA 17601

Call Sign: N4QDX
Jay R Weaver
1645 Clearview Ave
Lancaster PA 17601

Call Sign: N3CWL
Kathleen M Waters
15 Crest Ave
Lancaster PA 17602

Call Sign: N3XDJ
Ronald T Stoltzfus
6 Caroline St
Lancaster PA 17603

Call Sign: W3ZAA
Frank W Bostick
313 College Ave
Lancaster PA 17603

Call Sign: KB3EYJ
Michael F Pickard
1708 Crossfield Dr
Lancaster PA 17603

Call Sign: K2HU
Paul D Lionardo
823 Carrie Ct
Lancaster PA 17601

Call Sign: K3QAF
Leland W Aurick II
204 Colonial Crest Dr
Lancaster PA 176016126

Call Sign: W3IPX
John P Weaver
130 Dartmouth Ave
Lancaster PA 17603

Call Sign: WA3NAO
Horace E Doggett
Center Dr
Lancaster PA 176013450

Call Sign: KB3VVF
William N Page
607 Country Pl Dr
Lancaster PA 17601

Call Sign: N3CC
William H Balabanow
74 Delp Rd
Lancaster PA 17601

Call Sign: K3UGI
James N Keperling
715 Central Manor Rd
Lancaster PA 17603

Call Sign: W3JPS
Richard C Harclerode
1933 Creek Hill Rd
Lancaster PA 17601

Call Sign: WA3JBJ
Betty A Balabanow
74 Delp Rd
Lancaster PA 17601

Call Sign: KC3BH
George W Troxell

Call Sign: WA3JKJ
Hempfield Radio Club

Call Sign: WB2ZZK
Barton L Halpern

175 Delp Rd
Lancaster PA 17601

Call Sign: WB3EAD
Otto J Funke Jr
427 Delp Rd
Lancaster PA 17601

Call Sign: KA3SZZ
Thomas C Kile
2776 Den Mil Dr
Lancaster PA 17601

Call Sign: WA3TNO
Robert E McHose
1806 Divot Ct
Lancaster PA 17602

Call Sign: N3EIZ
Philip F Stumpf
2010 Drexel Ave
Lancaster PA 17602

Call Sign: N3IRQ
Charles E Shenk
42 Duncan St
Lancaster PA 17602

Call Sign: K3OEP
Gregory G Xakellis
318 E Chestnut St
Lancaster PA 17602

Call Sign: KA3ROB
Carl E Burkholder
436 E Chestnut St
Lancaster PA 17602

Call Sign: N3EVR
Jerris A Stankus
6 E Foal Ct
Lancaster PA 176023443

Call Sign: N3RCI
Sharon L Weiler

618 E Frederick St
Lancaster PA 17602

Call Sign: KB3JAY
Steven Rios
348 E Frederick St Apt 1
Lancaster PA 17602

Call Sign: KA3UOA
Todd C Olson
632 E Fulton St
Lancaster PA 17602

Call Sign: KB3IHR
William Allen Stockbauer
Jr
625 E King St
Lancaster PA 176023111

Call Sign: K3LYR
John W Woestman
1300 E King St
Lancaster PA 17602

Call Sign: N3RCE
Jeffrey M Zankey
224 E King St 217
Lancaster PA 17602

Call Sign: KB3KGJ
Ronald S Lindhurst
729 E Madison St
Lancaster PA 176022421

Call Sign: N3VNB
Barry S Breslow
355 E Marion St
Lancaster PA 17602

Call Sign: N2RNL
Paul D Lionardo
808 E Marion St
Lancaster PA 17602

Call Sign: W3SED

Kearney A Snyder
141 E Orange St
Lancaster PA 17602

Call Sign: WA3WCR
Glenn E Brown
322 E Ross St
Lancaster PA 17602

Call Sign: KB3PBW
Leonard R Borkon
809 Eden Rd
Lancaster PA 17601

Call Sign: W3LRB
Leonard R Borkon
809 Eden Rd
Lancaster PA 17601

Call Sign: N3JBD
Michael W Keller
1615 Eden Rd
Lancaster PA 17601

Call Sign: N3KCT
Michael A Eagan
401 Eden Rd Apt C6
Lancaster PA 17601

Call Sign: KB9VBZ
Kristi M Ratliff
401 Eden Rd Apt E6
Lancaster PA 17601

Call Sign: WG3E
Allen S Huber
401 Eden Rd Apt F5
Lancaster PA 17601

Call Sign: WB3BTL
Ruth E Lasof
401 Eden Rd Apt N1
Lancaster PA 176014250

Call Sign: WA3FTJ

L Larry Wenger
1036 Edgemoor Ct
Lancaster PA 17601

Call Sign: W3EOD
Vernon A Bell
502 Elizabeth Dr
Lancaster PA 176014406

Call Sign: KB3HIH
Henry L Bachofer
502 Elizabeth Dr Hamilton
224
Lancaster PA 17601

Call Sign: W3LPM
George L Branch
2478 Ellendale Dr
Lancaster PA 17602

Call Sign: N3DHV
John W Proctor
145 Elmwood Rd
Lancaster PA 17602

Call Sign: N3FBL
Thomas M Grab
617 Euclid Ave
Lancaster PA 17603

Call Sign: KB3QJF
Carlos M Agosto
440 Euclid Ave Apt I
Lancaster PA 17602

Call Sign: W3ASE
George H Francis
101 Falcon Ct
Lancaster PA 17603

Call Sign: N3OST
Michael A Weiler
706 Fallon Dr
Lancaster PA 17601

Call Sign: KB3SZF
Thomas J Mellinger
725 Farmingdale Rd
Lancaster PA 176032310

Call Sign: N3RXV
Steven S Shearer
1342 Fieldstead Ln
Lancaster PA 17603

Call Sign: KB3KPU
Thomas P Bell
1009 Fieldstone Ct
Lancaster PA 17603

Call Sign: N3EPT
Mary M Stover
2208 Forry Rd
Lancaster PA 176015908

Call Sign: K3HEC
Bertram H Flick
831 Fremont St Apt 15
Lancaster PA 17603

Call Sign: N3MLJ
Robert F Keller
32 Fresh Meadow Dr
Lancaster PA 17603

Call Sign: N2EQB
Bradley L Hopkins
41 Fresh Meadow Dr
Lancaster PA 17603

Call Sign: N3OLT
William G McLain
314 Garden Park Cir
Lancaster PA 17601

Call Sign: KC3IM
Terry L Miller
1371 Glen Moore Cir
Lancaster PA 17601

Call Sign: N3MKM
Eduardo Rosado
1438 Glen Moore Cir
Lancaster PA 17601

Call Sign: KA3RPL
Gregory L Miller
61 Glen Oaks Dr
Lancaster PA 17603

Call Sign: KA3RPM
Raymond W Miller Jr
61 Glen Oaks Dr
Lancaster PA 17603

Call Sign: N3BCZ
Paul S Hilton
1609 Glenn Rd
Lancaster PA 17601

Call Sign: KA3OTG
Chester L Gontner
945 Grandview Blvd
Lancaster PA 17601

Call Sign: N3GBO
James R Waters Jr
204 Great Lawn Cir
Lancaster PA 17602

Call Sign: KA3YJC
Robert T Millard
964 Green Ter
Lancaster PA 17601

Call Sign: N3HPJ
Richard J Kirchner Jr
201 Greenbriar Cir
Lancaster PA 17603

Call Sign: N3LZJ
Mary J Kirchner
201 Greenbriar Cir
Lancaster PA 17603

Call Sign: KB3IRU
James R Pursel
3178 Greenridge Dr
Lancaster PA 176011344

Call Sign: KA3LFF
Kathryn K Hemlick
3190 Greentree Dr
Lancaster PA 17601

Call Sign: KA3LFG
Mark A Hemlick
3190 Greentree Dr
Lancaster PA 17601

Call Sign: N3RAX
Mark A Hemlick
3190 Greentree Dr
Lancaster PA 17601

Call Sign: KA3UTX
Daniel Zenzel III
312 Greenview Dr
Lancaster PA 176011004

Call Sign: N3ZKU
Dennis C Kaiser
62 Greenwood Ave
Lancaster PA 17603

Call Sign: N3UDC
Richard H Barr Jr
1004 Hamilton Park Dr
Lancaster PA 176034916

Call Sign: N3MUN
John J Fritz
736 Harper Ave
Lancaster PA 17601

Call Sign: W3OLV
Floyd R Jury
2730 Harrisburg Pike
Lancaster PA 17601

Call Sign: KO3D
James Pentland
2001 Harrisburg Pike Apt
113
Lancaster PA 17601

Call Sign: N3HGT
Charles R Keller
2001 Harrisburg Pike Apt
423
Lancaster PA 176012641

Call Sign: W3IDK
Walter D Hoskinson
2001 Harrisburg Pike Apt
B506
Lancaster PA 17601

Call Sign: KB2YTM
Charles W Williams
48 Harvest Rd Unit 1
Lancaster PA 17602

Call Sign: KB3QYZ
Joshua J Reheard
2507 Helena Rd
Lancaster PA 17603

Call Sign: KB3RSS
Connie A Ream
38 Hershey Ave
Lancaster PA 17603

Call Sign: KA3JJC
Paul P Sexton
240 Hershey Ave
Lancaster PA 17603

Call Sign: KB3YBU
Bryan S Martin
23 Hess Blvd
Lancaster PA 17601

Call Sign: KJ3U
Raymond F Molkenthin Sr

1701 Hidden Ln
Lancaster PA 17603

Call Sign: N3XPD
Michael D Warner
804 Hillaire Rd
Lancaster PA 17601

Call Sign: KB3DNX
Theresa A Warner
804 Hillaire Rd
Lancaster PA 176012221

Call Sign: AA3ZS
Theresa A Warner
804 Hillaire Rd
Lancaster PA 176012221

Call Sign: N3SMY
Robert D Wilcox
809 Hillaire Rd
Lancaster PA 17601

Call Sign: WA3OWD
Donald L House
832 Hillaire Rd
Lancaster PA 17601

Call Sign: NI3QM
Donald L House
832 Hillaire Rd
Lancaster PA 17601

Call Sign: K3VRE
J Elvin Kraybill
1404 Hillcrest Rd
Lancaster PA 17603

Call Sign: N2OST
Juan C Rivera
840 Hilton Dr
Lancaster PA 17603

Call Sign: NB3A
Anthony Mastriania Jr

2293 Hobson Rd
Lancaster PA 17602

Call Sign: WD8KGK
Gregory V Pencheff
3550 Horizon Dr
Lancaster PA 17601

Call Sign: W3GVP
Gregory V Pencheff
3550 Horizon Dr
Lancaster PA 17601

Call Sign: W3LMF
Wayne Seacat
163 Hostetter Ln
Lancaster PA 17602

Call Sign: KA3DZB
Robert G Zook
223 Howard Ave
Lancaster PA 17602

Call Sign: N3MKI
Harold Potts
755 Huntington Pl
Lancaster PA 17601

Call Sign: K4QYV
Gary W Jacobs
824 Imperial Dr
Lancaster PA 17601

Call Sign: KB3CHP
Matthew C Leader
937 Indian Springs Dr
Lancaster PA 17601

Call Sign: N3AKG
Werner Rueggeberg
102 Jackson Dr
Lancaster PA 176034744

Call Sign: N3NDI
Daniel T Fritsch Jr

1035 Janet Ave
Lancaster PA 17601

Call Sign: KB3EYO
Felix R Cobian
1360 Jasmine Ln
Lancaster PA 176017139

Call Sign: KB3TSY
Linda C Dwyer
Judie Ln
Lancaster PA 17603

Call Sign: WA3EON
James W Burton
104 Kent Rd
Lancaster PA 17603

Call Sign: W3LZE
William G Masho
2006 Kestrel Ct
Lancaster PA 17603

Call Sign: K3QOH
Jay W Dunwoody
7 Kimberly Ct
Lancaster PA 17602

Call Sign: KB3FHH
Julie D Keim
2632 Kimberly Rd Apt 4
Lancaster PA 17603

Call Sign: N3TUQ
Kurt M Harnish
Kloss Dr
Lancaster PA 17603

Call Sign: N3UED
Joseph W Smith Jr
83 Knollwood Dr
Lancaster PA 176015659

Call Sign: W3LEP
Joseph De Mott

2185 Kolb Dr
Lancaster PA 17601

Call Sign: KB3OHG
Timothy K Su
1841 Krystle Dr
Lancaster PA 17602

Call Sign: N3FFT
James L Linville
399 Lampeter Rd
Lancaster PA 17602

Call Sign: N3CFS
Robert M Landis
428 Lampeter Rd
Lancaster PA 17602

Call Sign: N3FQV
Thomas P Kochenberger
2100 Landis Valley Rd
Lancaster PA 17601

Call Sign: W3OID
William E Riggs
1837 Larchmont Ln
Lancaster PA 176015022

Call Sign: KB3NED
Frank Cruz
707 Lawrence Blvd
Lancaster PA 17601

Call Sign: K3JTA
James T Altieri
1051 Lehigh Ave
Lancaster PA 17602

Call Sign: N3PTP
Daniel C Lehman
826 Lightfoot Ave
Lancaster PA 17602

Call Sign: KA3SQH
Teresa E Long

1861 Lincoln Hwy E
Lancaster PA 176023357

Call Sign: KC3VW
Ray A Long
1861 Lincoln Hwy E
Lancaster PA 176023357

Call Sign: N3GOA
Matthew D Long
1861 Lincoln Hwy E
Lancaster PA 176023357

Call Sign: KB3CSM
Glenn R Kreider
1608 Linden Ave
Lancaster PA 17601

Call Sign: N3ZKT
Frederick W Lane
1045 Lititz Ave
Lancaster PA 17602

Call Sign: KB3JBA
Terrance W Lane
1045 Lititz Ave
Lancaster PA 17602

Call Sign: K3NXZ
Robert E Houck
3001 Lititz Pike
Lancaster PA 17606

Call Sign: KB3DLH
Frank J Ammerman
261 Little Creek Rd
Lancaster PA 17601

Call Sign: KA3GYM
Sean P Griggs
2828 Long Farm Ln
Lancaster PA 17601

Call Sign: WB3FFF
Terry C Griggs

2828 Long Farm Ln
Lancaster PA 17601

Call Sign: KA3TAG
Jane E Myers
159 Long Ln
Lancaster PA 17603

Call Sign: KB3FGB
Christian A Larrick
508 Long Ln
Lancaster PA 17603

Call Sign: WB3CTC
Michael M Oxenreider
1107 Manheim Pk
Lancaster PA 176013119

Call Sign: N3BUS
Robert K Meck
1610 Manor Blvd
Lancaster PA 17603

Call Sign: KB3DHK
Jeffrey W Capwell Sr
633 Manor St 1st Fl
Lancaster PA 17603

Call Sign: W3FEY
George S Gadbois
141 Maple Ln
Lancaster PA 17601

Call Sign: W3RCA
Radio Communications
Amateur Transmitting
Society
141 Maple Ln
Lancaster PA 176014013

Call Sign: KB3RKK
Matthew B Hawkins
950 Marietta Ave
Lancaster PA 17603

Call Sign: KB3RKJ
Daniel S Rifkin
950 Marietta Ave
Lancaster PA 176033105

Call Sign: KB3RST
Rita M Ream
2307 Marietta Ave
Lancaster PA 17603

Call Sign: N3QJX
H Michael Williams
2731 Marietta Ave
Lancaster PA 176012256

Call Sign: N3QKA
Nathan R Charles
3033 Marietta Ave
Lancaster PA 17601

Call Sign: NB3I
Jonathan E Charles
3033 Marietta Ave
Lancaster PA 17601

Call Sign: N3WGX
Michael W Sauder
3260 Marietta Ave
Lancaster PA 17601

Call Sign: N3WGW
Jonathan S Sauder
3260 Marietta Ave
Lancaster PA 176011224

Call Sign: N3XII
Myron K Sauder
3260 Marietta Ave
Lancaster PA 176011224

Call Sign: WB3FRC
Samuel G McCracken
1707 Marietta Ave Apt 1A
Lancaster PA 17603

Call Sign: KI4PH
Michael S McCarley Sr
2236 Marietta Pike
Lancaster PA 17603

Call Sign: KB3SCU
Nancy M Shaub
3 Middle Green
Lancaster PA 17602

Call Sign: W3JRD
Dominic A Sagolla
Millersville Pike
Lancaster PA 17603

Call Sign: W3MSM
Michael S McCarley Sr
2236 Marietta Pike
Lancaster PA 17603

Call Sign: KB3SCV
John F Knight
3 Middle Grn
Lancaster PA 176021573

Call Sign: KA3SZY
Robert F Shenton
612 Millersville Rd
Lancaster PA 17603

Call Sign: W3KAI
Richard J Stauffer
1034 Marshall Ave
Lancaster PA 17601

Call Sign: K4NET
Jeffrey R Kuhlmann
2303 Middlegreen Ct
Lancaster PA 17601

Call Sign: KB3CQF
Frank M Koch
203 Millwood Rd
Lancaster PA 17602

Call Sign: N3XJK
Elmer E Binkley
242 Marticville Rd
Lancaster PA 17603

Call Sign: KA3WGE
John H Arnold
2129 Mill Creek Rd
Lancaster PA 17602

Call Sign: KB3EDM
Daniel Koch
203 Millwood Rd
Lancaster PA 17602

Call Sign: WB3CZL
James Tim Altieri
McCaskey E High School
Lancaster PA 176080150

Call Sign: WA3JJM
Fred F Pickard
1105 Mill Mar Rd
Lancaster PA 17601

Call Sign: KB3PYI
Diane R Creme
1454 Mission Rd
Lancaster PA 17601

Call Sign: KB3IIX
Edward R Garrity Jr
704 McGrann Blvd
Lancaster PA 17601

Call Sign: KB3TTC
Stephen K Holden
59 Mill Pond Dr
Lancaster PA 17603

Call Sign: KG6LNP
Steven D Brandvold
109 Mitric Ln
Lancaster PA 17601

Call Sign: W3NOI
Robert B Carvell
929 McGrann Blvd
Lancaster PA 17601

Call Sign: WA3FBJ
Noah G Good
2180 Mill Stream Rd
Lancaster PA 17602

Call Sign: N2DYK
Kenneth H Wiggins
1052 Monticello Ln
Lancaster PA 17603

Call Sign: W3SNK
Joseph S Kambic
1350 Meadowcreek Ln
Lancaster PA 17603

Call Sign: WA3YES
G Gary Kirchner
610 Millcross Rd
Lancaster PA 17601

Call Sign: KB3VJT
Jack L Reed
135 Montrose Ave
Lancaster PA 17603

Call Sign: W2BTW
Henry M Wales
4 Michelle Lynn Dr
Lancaster PA 17602

Call Sign: KB3TRH
Neil S Kline
1935 Millersville Pike
Lancaster PA 17603

Call Sign: N3BBC
Jack L Reed
135 Montrose Ave
Lancaster PA 17603

Call Sign: KA3TAK
James M Kauffman
475 Mt Sidney Rd
Lancaster PA 17602

Call Sign: KB4NCP
Clive R Buttemere
101 Murry Hill Dr
Lancaster PA 176014109

Call Sign: KB3APG
Thomas S Lewis
420 N Concord St
Lancaster PA 17603

Call Sign: KD7YRZ
Richard K Williams
811 N Duke St
Lancaster PA 17602

Call Sign: KA3TAF
Tina L Harrison
731 N Duke St 3rd Fl
Lancaster PA 17602

Call Sign: KB3IRS
Henry R Kieffer
714 N Franklin St
Lancaster PA 17602

Call Sign: N3VQR
Richard G Weiss
737 N Franklin St
Lancaster PA 17602

Call Sign: N3BVC
Theodore Smith
755 N Franklin St
Lancaster PA 17602

Call Sign: KB3DRQ
Matt A Henderson
241 N Franklin St
Lancaster PA 17602

Call Sign: KB2IHG
Ronald C Cirino Jr
832 N Lime St
Lancaster PA 17602

Call Sign: KA3JGG
David N Shoff
1029 N Lime St
Lancaster PA 176021916

Call Sign: KA3GRZ
Richard R McCullough
322 N Mulberry St
Lancaster PA 17603

Call Sign: N1CYB
Jason R Benedick
408 N Pine St
Lancaster PA 176033312

Call Sign: KB3CTZ
John D Francer
706 N Pine St
Lancaster PA 17623

Call Sign: N3HUA
Ralph S Rineer
210 N Plum St
Lancaster PA 17602

Call Sign: N3TRL
Darryll J Purnell Sr
807 N Shippen St
Lancaster PA 17602

Call Sign: N3FOR
Anthony J Galletta
104 N Yale Ave
Lancaster PA 17603

Call Sign: N3JDX
Arthur H Shepherd
104 N Yale Ave
Lancaster PA 17603

Call Sign: WF3U
Anthony J Galletta
104 N Yale Ave
Lancaster PA 17603

Call Sign: N3MKL
Robert E Clayton
772 Nancy Ln
Lancaster PA 17601

Call Sign: KL7K
David B Olson
1824 Nevin Cir
Lancaster PA 17603

Call Sign: KQ3K
David B Olson
1824 Nevin Cir
Lancaster PA 17603

Call Sign: W3EAI
David B Olson
1824 Nevin Cir
Lancaster PA 17603

Call Sign: W3KO
Patricia E Olson
1824 Nevin Cir
Lancaster PA 17603

Call Sign: KL7L
Patricia E Olson
1824 Nevin Cir
Lancaster PA 17604

Call Sign: KX3P
Patricia E Olson
1824 Nevin Cir
Lancaster PA 17604

Call Sign: K3NJE
William F Rosskob
1439 New Holland Pike
Lancaster PA 17601

Call Sign: K3JD
James P Dux
2152 New Holland Pike
Lancaster PA 17601

Call Sign: W1GGI
Edward L Christie
2169 New Holland Pike
Lancaster PA 17601

Call Sign: WB3KSM
William G Henderson
994 Nissley Rd
Lancaster PA 17601

Call Sign: KA3ABE
Anthony E Griffith
3319 Nolt Rd
Lancaster PA 17601

Call Sign: N3GPP
Robert H Hoffman
2038 Northbrook Dr
Lancaster PA 176014918

Call Sign: KB3DHM
Donald C Bragg
55 Northview Dr
Lancaster PA 17601

Call Sign: KB3WOV
Christina M Swift
Old Blue Rock Rd
Lancaster PA 17603

Call Sign: KB3GMV
Gregg A Martell
1120 Old Eagle Rd
Lancaster PA 17601

Call Sign: KI3G
Gregg A Martell
1120 Old Eagle Rd
Lancaster PA 17601

Call Sign: WA3NZR
John J Lamparter III
2165 Old Phila Pike Apt
16
Lancaster PA 176023458

Call Sign: KI3T
John K Bryson Jr
1933 Oregon Pike Apt I 3
Lancaster PA 17601

Call Sign: NJ4J
Robert W Clark Jr
804 Paddington Dr
Lancaster PA 17601

Call Sign: KA3RST
Adam L Witkonis
81 Peach Ln
Lancaster PA 17601

Call Sign: KB3BUZ
Timothy P Fichtner
59 Peacock Dr
Lancaster PA 17601

Call Sign: W3IPW
David L Miller
106 Pearl St
Lancaster PA 17603

Call Sign: W3NDI
J Edward Brenneman
914 Penn Grant Rd
Lancaster PA 17602

Call Sign: WB7NIV
Philip De Vries
1217 Penn Grant Rd
Lancaster PA 176021828

Call Sign: KA3ABZ
Samuel R Spearing
1233 Penn Grant Rd
Lancaster PA 17602

Call Sign: N3LUT
John J Donati
106 Petersburg Rd
Lancaster PA 17601

Call Sign: N3LUS
Connie L Rivera
112 Petersburg Rd
Lancaster PA 17601

Call Sign: WV3Y
Carlos M Rivera
112 Petersburg Rd
Lancaster PA 17601

Call Sign: KA3MGW
James C Smith
24 Pickford Dr
Lancaster PA 17603

Call Sign: N3GTS
George R Warfel
55 Pilgrim Dr
Lancaster PA 17603

Call Sign: K3ZIQ
Paul E Murr
62 Pilgrim Dr
Lancaster PA 17603

Call Sign: KY3C
Charles Golin
1954 Pine Dr
Lancaster PA 17601

Call Sign: WB3CSY
Richard C Walter Jr
909 Pinetree Way
Lancaster PA 17601

Call Sign: KB3ADJ
Scott M Weaver
2659 Pinewood Rd
Lancaster PA 17601

Call Sign: W2JYW
Norman H Thompson
3210 Pinewyn Cir
Lancaster PA 17601

Call Sign: KB3CYJ
Mary Webb
230 Pulte Rd
Lancaster PA 17601

Call Sign: KA3JHR
Elaine J Spangler
331 Richland Dr
Lancaster PA 176013631

Call Sign: KB3LHV
Frank Sanocki
136 Pinnacle Pt Dr
Lancaster PA 17601

Call Sign: KI6NJ
Emanuel P Peters
211 Pyrus Pl
Lancaster PA 176012673

Call Sign: KC3IS
Dennis E Spangler
331 Richland Dr
Lancaster PA 176013631

Call Sign: WB2FPG
Barry N Shiffrin
1858 Pool Forge
Lancaster PA 17601

Call Sign: KB3IGK
Thomas A Baran
1310 Quarry Ln
Lancaster PA 17603

Call Sign: N3RNL
Pablo Gomez
1103 Richmond Rd
Lancaster PA 17603

Call Sign: KA3UOF
Andrew C Terrell
327 Powell Dr
Lancaster PA 17601

Call Sign: KB3KPY
Joseph Appleyard
1405 Quarry Ln
Lancaster PA 17603

Call Sign: KB3DCQ
Theodore F Simpson
461 Ringneck Ln
Lancaster PA 176012846

Call Sign: KB3PBP
Jacob M Vreeland
102 President Ave
Lancaster PA 17603

Call Sign: KB3ENQ
David H Drybred
432 Rabbit Hill Ln
Lancaster PA 17603

Call Sign: AB3FW
Walter L Hasselback
77 River Bend Park
Lancaster PA 17602

Call Sign: KA3BKL
Robert L Myers
301 Primrose Ave
Lancaster PA 17601

Call Sign: KB3VEM
Michael P Toner
2509 Raleigh Dr
Lancaster PA 17601

Call Sign: KB3LDD
Haskell C Royer
78 River Bend Park
Lancaster PA 17602

Call Sign: KB3ACF
Nelson Pacheco
412 Prospect St
Lancaster PA 17603

Call Sign: KB3QYT
Timothy S Klopp Jr
1102 Ranck Mill Rd
Lancaster PA 17602

Call Sign: KB3LKO
Ross B Kauffman
600 River Dr
Lancaster PA 17603

Call Sign: KB3EYH
Richard A Rivera
508 Prospect St
Lancaster PA 17603

Call Sign: KB3OQC
Zach R Hughes
465 Revere St
Lancaster PA 17601

Call Sign: KB3DCF
Samuel R Willcox
1623 Robert Rd
Lancaster PA 176015634

Call Sign: AA3Y
Wayne A Webb
230 Pulte Rd
Lancaster PA 17601

Call Sign: WB9BFC
Thomas E Kreider
318 Rhoda Dr
Lancaster PA 176013630

Call Sign: N3SWF
Ben T Eisemann
1640 Robert Rd
Lancaster PA 17603

Call Sign: KA3WGB
Bradley K Stick
815 Robin Rd
Lancaster PA 17601

Call Sign: KB3BBP
Wilfred P Gerena
309 S Marshall St
Lancaster PA 17602

Call Sign: N3WMG
Larry C Dillon
2506 Saddle Dr
Lancaster PA 17601

Call Sign: N3IGP
Chris A Kauffman
419 Rohrerstown Rd
Lancaster PA 17603

Call Sign: N3YMV
Louatha C Lawson
633 S Marshall St
Lancaster PA 17602

Call Sign: N3VOS
Christopher N Pham
2540 Saddle Dr
Lancaster PA 17601

Call Sign: KB3NCH
Janice R Vreeland
716 Rohrerstown Rd
Lancaster PA 17603

Call Sign: KB3RSO
Craig M Jordan
820 S Pearl St
Lancaster PA 17603

Call Sign: K3PSU
William E Junius
2571 Saddle Dr
Lancaster PA 17601

Call Sign: KB3NCJ
Mark E Vreeland
716 Rohrerstown Rd
Lancaster PA 17603

Call Sign: KB3NCI
Zechariah D Vreeland
102 S President Ave
Lancaster PA 17603

Call Sign: N3KSG
Roberta M Bouder
2085 Shaaron Dr
Lancaster PA 176012626

Call Sign: W1WJG
Peter G Bedrosian
63 Roosevelt Blvd
Lancaster PA 17601

Call Sign: N3CII
Paul W Kilp
212 S President Ave
Lancaster PA 17603

Call Sign: KB3RVW
Matthew R Loy
1024 Shadow Stone Dr
Lancaster PA 17603

Call Sign: N3ABC
E Kenneth Manning
2718 Royal Rd
Lancaster PA 176037012

Call Sign: N3OTW
Jonathan B Stigelman
341 S President Ave
Lancaster PA 17603

Call Sign: N2NY
Laurent N Horne
900 Sheaffer Rd
Lancaster PA 176021320

Call Sign: KB3TTK
Sarah K Troutman
218 Ruby St
Lancaster PA 17603

Call Sign: N3NCX
Kerry L Loose
629 S Prince St
Lancaster PA 17603

Call Sign: N3KYR
Harry F De Verter Jr
303 Shultz Rd
Lancaster PA 17603

Call Sign: KA3ZCX
Victor C Hugo
343 Ruth Ridge Dr
Lancaster PA 17601

Call Sign: KB3SSY
Brenda Pittman
10 S Prince St 304
Lancaster PA 17603

Call Sign: WW3D
Noel Rivera
1739 Southport Dr
Lancaster PA 17603

Call Sign: KA3ZAD
Wayland G Gillingham Jr
420 Rutledge Ave
Lancaster PA 17601

Call Sign: W3AAL
Godfrey S Summers
437 S Shippen St
Lancaster PA 17602

Call Sign: KB3EAK
G Yale Eastman
51 Spring Dell Rd
Lancaster PA 176015531

Call Sign: KB3KST
Craig A Shaubach
2904 Spring Valley Rd
Lancaster PA 17601

Call Sign: W3EUP
George W Banzhoff III
1137 St Joseph St
Lancaster PA 17603

Call Sign: KB3BGS
Vernon V Kiehl
1919 St Regis Ln
Lancaster PA 17603

Call Sign: N3VK
Vernon V Kiehl
1919 St Regis Ln
Lancaster PA 176036460

Call Sign: KB3PBQ
Jeffrey S Walls
110 St Thomas Rd
Lancaster PA 17601

Call Sign: N3TJK
Anderw J Schrock
211 Stehmans Rd
Lancaster PA 17603

Call Sign: WB4BVB
Joseph W Mast
678 Steinman Ct
Lancaster PA 17603

Call Sign: AA3DH
Robert A Washick Sr
696 Steinman Dr
Lancaster PA 17603

Call Sign: KB3GDW
Justin M Brian
1076 Sterling Pl
Lancaster PA 17603

Call Sign: AF3U
Gary J Giering
1945 Sterling Pl
Lancaster PA 17601

Call Sign: KB3QYX
Robert M Murphy
1352 Stillwater Rd
Lancaster PA 17601

Call Sign: KB3RSU
Alice A Sensenig
162 Stone Creek Rd
Lancaster PA 17603

Call Sign: WB3FQY
James E Bear
209 Stone Creek Rd
Lancaster PA 17603

Call Sign: AI3L
Charles H Rahe II
2025 Stone Mill Rd
Lancaster PA 17603

Call Sign: KA3WKT
Douglas R Rahe
2025 Stone Mill Rd
Lancaster PA 17603

Call Sign: N3JLA
Wade T Mackey
1930 Stonemill Rd
Lancaster PA 17603

Call Sign: AA3LW
W Mark Walton
221 Sunglo Rd
Lancaster PA 17601

Call Sign: K3MRK
W Mark Walton
221 Sunglo Rd
Lancaster PA 17601

Call Sign: N3XOY
Florence M Freedman
461 Surrey Dr
Lancaster PA 17601

Call Sign: K3KSA
Theodore M Freedman
461 Surrey Dr
Lancaster PA 176012842

Call Sign: KD3TA
Robert C Minsek
2641 Sutton Pl
Lancaster PA 17601

Call Sign: W9AEU
Elizabeth D Minsek
2641 Sutton Pl
Lancaster PA 17601

Call Sign: N3UDZ
Richard P Frescatore Jr
798 Sylvan Rd
Lancaster PA 17601

Call Sign: W3EOB
Fred P Koeng
1620 Temple Ave
Lancaster PA 17603

Call Sign: W3AD
Lancaster Radio
Transmitting Society
2045 Temple Ave
Lancaster PA 176034407

Call Sign: N3TJJ
Troy M Hess
2045 Temple Ave
Lancaster PA 17603

Call Sign: N3WSV
Pieter E Hegeman II
20 Tennyson Dr

Lancaster PA 17602

Lancaster PA 17603

Lancaster PA 17603

Call Sign: WA3JLN
Robert C Storck Jr
4 Thomas Rd
Lancaster PA 17602

Call Sign: KB3MEU
James L Hymes
231 Valley Rd
Lancaster PA 17601

Call Sign: KB3CWS
Mark R Gamber
18 Village Dr
Lancaster PA 17601

Call Sign: KG4THE
Kenneth A Weaver
2052 Thoroughbred Ln
Lancaster PA 17601

Call Sign: W3CMP
Christopher M Patterson
590 Valley Rd
Lancaster PA 17601

Call Sign: WA3SIX
Mark R Gamber
18 Village Dr
Lancaster PA 17601

Call Sign: N2CRU
Thomas F Watson III
111 Townhouse Ln
Lancaster PA 17603

Call Sign: KB3SIJ
Timothy R Patterson
590 Valley Rd
Lancaster PA 17601

Call Sign: KB3HWO
Mark Gamber
18 Village Dr
Lancaster PA 17601

Call Sign: N3QJV
David F Eastburn
3 Townsend Ct
Lancaster PA 17603

Call Sign: N3AKL
Craig R Sherman
1211 Valley Rd
Lancaster PA 17603

Call Sign: WA3HMJ
Clyde E Jones
340 W Chestnut
Lancaster PA 17603

Call Sign: KB3PYM
Roger G Kimber Jr
1013 Tracy Rd
Lancaster PA 176014854

Call Sign: W3APO
Frank H Altdoerffer
1414 Valley Rd
Lancaster PA 17603

Call Sign: KA9RFK
Oscar H Cardozo
19 W Frederick St
Lancaster PA 17603

Call Sign: KI4PNG
Dickson Otero
619 Union St
Lancaster PA 17603

Call Sign: KB3SYI
Nancy Ellen Walker
Valley Rd
Lancaster PA 17601

Call Sign: KB3DGB
Robert J Douglas
339 W Grant St
Lancaster PA 17603

Call Sign: KB3OSZ
Dickson Otero
619 Union St
Lancaster PA 17603

Call Sign: K3EM
David C Ballard
52 Valleybrook Dr
Lancaster PA 176014617

Call Sign: WB3JGU
Robert F Nichols
920 W Hager St
Lancaster PA 17603

Call Sign: KB3KPX
Nicholas J Elinski
1734 Valette Dr
Lancaster PA 17602

Call Sign: WA3TNX
Anna B Porter
168 Valleybrook Dr
Lancaster PA 17601

Call Sign: KA3TAJ
Harry J Hess Sr
443 W Lemon St
Lancaster PA 17603

Call Sign: KA3WHG
Jason R Ernst
2554 Valley Dr

Call Sign: W3CPF
Albert B Johnson
1800 Village Cir

Call Sign: N3QPT
David L Getchell
2153 W Ridge Dr

Lancaster PA 17603

Call Sign: K3QKU
Richard R Handel
8 W Roseville Rd
Lancaster PA 17601

Call Sign: N2YHD
Leyla A Rivera
540 W Vine St
Lancaster PA 17603

Call Sign: KB3QYS
Linus Hughes
463.5 W Wine St
Lancaster PA 17603

Call Sign: N1UUV
Scott A Grillo
2425 Water Valley Rd
Lancaster PA 17603

Call Sign: K3QVX
John H Bowman
824 Waterfront Dr
Lancaster PA 17602

Call Sign: N3CCN
A Joanne Bowman
824 Waterfront Dr
Lancaster PA 17602

Call Sign: N3NHB
Christopher M Castagna
2947 Weaver Rd
Lancaster PA 17601

Call Sign: KA3WHL
Christopher C Rahe
108 Wellington Rd
Lancaster PA 17603

Call Sign: KB3GHL
Christopher C Rahe
108 Wellington Rd

Lancaster PA 17603

Call Sign: KB0ROD
Mary M Angell
104 Wellington Rd 5
Lancaster PA 17603

Call Sign: KA3RSH
Allen J Showalter
100 Westmore Way
Lancaster PA 17603

Call Sign: AB3NE
Allen J Showalter
100 Westmore Way
Lancaster PA 17603

Call Sign: K3RAF
Abram L Leaman
1117 Wheatland Ave Apt
H2
Lancaster PA 17603

Call Sign: WA3PPC
Jess Czetli Jr
1826 Wilderness Rd
Lancaster PA 17603

Call Sign: KB3QBP
Scott M Warner
1964 Wilderness Rd
Lancaster PA 17603

Call Sign: N3SMW
Scott M Warner
1964 Wilderness Rd
Lancaster PA 17603

Call Sign: KB3FKM
Mark S Shenk
2201 William Penn Way
Lancaster PA 17601

Call Sign: K3IPI
Mark Shenk

2201 William Penn Way
Lancaster PA 17601

Call Sign: K0SO
Bradley A Farrell
2239 William Penn Way
Lancaster PA 17601

Call Sign: W3LW
Bradley A Farrell
2239 William Penn Way
Lancaster PA 17601

Call Sign: KB3GWQ
Frank S Giuffrida III
1031 Williamsburg Rd
Lancaster PA 17603

Call Sign: KB3IRT
Shaun D Meaney
1071 Williamsburg Rd
Lancaster PA 17603

Call Sign: N3DJA
John W Brubaker
12 Willis Ln
Lancaster PA 17602

Call Sign: KB3FGC
Craig S Peck
837 Willow Rd
Lancaster PA 17601

Call Sign: KB3JAZ
Melody J Peck
837 Willow Rd
Lancaster PA 17601

Call Sign: W3KKG
James F Doering
211 Willow Valley Sq Apt
C207
Lancaster PA 17602

Call Sign: KC2OG

Pauline E Pike
400 Willow Valley Sq Apt
Ga 301
Lancaster PA 17602

Call Sign: KT2C
Russell E Pike
400 Willow Valley Sq Apt
Ga 301
Lancaster PA 17602

Call Sign: K3OU
Daniel F Toner Sr
655 Willow Valley Sq Apt
L507
Lancaster PA 176024873

Call Sign: WD4EYJ
Albert H Niebaum
211 Willow Valley Sq
B116
Lancaster PA 176024893

Call Sign: KA3YJN
Harry H Breneman Jr
625 Willow Valley Sq
F106
Lancaster PA 176024867

Call Sign: W3FAG
Harvey L Heller
630 Willow Valley Sq
G006
Lancaster PA 176024868

Call Sign: K2WM
Albert T Williams
400 Willow Valley Sq
Ga204
Lancaster PA 17602

Call Sign: W3GGM
Theodore H Supplee
650 Willow Valley Sq
K108

Lancaster PA 176024872

Call Sign: KB2OGW
Carl W Illenberger
650 Willow Valley Sq
K208
Lancaster PA 176024872

Call Sign: W3HBB
Arthur H Silvers
655 Willow Valley Sq
L502
Lancaster PA 176024873

Call Sign: KB3DEK
Dolores B Conroy
660 Willow Valley Sq M
310
Lancaster PA 176024874

Call Sign: KA3LOZ
Harold L Gotwald III
2492 Willowhill Dr
Lancaster PA 17602

Call Sign: N3WWP
Vernon E Boyer
216 Winding Hill Dr
Lancaster PA 176011768

Call Sign: WA3PSA
Michael W Fecik
140 Windover Turn
Lancaster PA 176015332

Call Sign: N3CSL
Frederick C Wolf
1805 Windsong Ln
Lancaster PA 176027002

Call Sign: W3VOP
Timothy E Benner
2216 Wood St
Lancaster PA 17603

Call Sign: KC2MMV
Anne P Morett
116 Woodcrest Dr
Lancaster PA 17602

Call Sign: KA3BOU
N Stanley Ginder
701 Wyncroft Ter
Lancaster PA 176036970

Call Sign: N3NTL
Erik G Fromen
Lancaster PA 17604

Call Sign: N3YHM
Gerald M Konjura
Lancaster PA 17604

Call Sign: KK7GP
Jacob R Lauser
Lancaster PA 17607

Call Sign: KB3WVE
Matthew Greenberg
Lancaster PA 17608

Call Sign: KB3LOJ
Richard F Hess
Lancaster PA 17608

Call Sign: W3RRR
Red Rose Repeater Assn
Inc
Lancaster PA 176048316

Call Sign: KB3BVL
Red Rose Repeater Assn
Inc
Lancaster PA 176048316

Call Sign: K3IR
Southern PA ARC Inc
Lancaster PA 176081033

FCC Amateur Radio Licenses in Landisburg

Call Sign: WC3R
William N Fosselman
546 Bridgeport Rd
Landisburg PA 17040

Call Sign: KB3OCC
Kenneth W Morrison Jr
101 E High St
Landisburg PA 17040

Call Sign: KB3PSN
Matthew E Morrison
101 E High St
Landisburg PA 170400015

Call Sign: KA3FHA
Howard W Rheam
211 E Main St
Landisburg PA 170409710

Call Sign: KD4WMI
Robert B Woolever
571 Landisburg Rd
Landisburg PA 170409731

Call Sign: KE4VCJ
Krislyn K Woolever
571 Landisburg Rd
Landisburg PA 170409731

Call Sign: KB3KZW
Michael G Lyons
2020 Landisburg Rd
Landisburg PA 17040

Call Sign: WA3GDV
Charles D Steiner
1545 Pisgah Rd
Landisburg PA 17040

Call Sign: K3DD
Lloyd G Martyn

Rd 2
Landisburg PA 17040

FCC Amateur Radio Licenses in Landisville

Call Sign: KB3WKO
Dale C White
190 Broad St
Landisville PA 17538

Call Sign: KA3HYW
Ronald J Miller
584 Church St
Landisville PA 17538

Call Sign: KB3EMA
Todd A Hay
34 Country Ln
Landisville PA 17538

Call Sign: N3CEC
James R Dowell Sr
927 Drr Ave
Landisville PA 17538

Call Sign: W1GJK
Raymond J Harshman
632 Eastside Dr
Landisville PA 17538

Call Sign: N3PIN
A Michael Lowe Jr
104 Elizabeth St
Landisville PA 17538

Call Sign: KB3TLT
Mary Senft
80 Farmington Pl
Landisville PA 17538

Call Sign: KB3AX
John G Berger
86 Farmington Pl
Landisville PA 175381917

Call Sign: AA3C
James L Ibaugh
325 Lania Dr
Landisville PA 175381729

Call Sign: N3CXY
Sharon G Ibaugh
325 Lania Dr
Landisville PA 175381729

Call Sign: N3VZP
David M Buchanan
304 N Homestead Dr
Landisville PA 17538

Call Sign: KL7OQ
Leanne E Spurlin
266 Northridge Dr
Landisville PA 17538

Call Sign: KB3QKD
Richard G Mercer
85 Silver Spring Rd
Landisville PA 175381014

Call Sign: AB3HQ
Richard G Mercer
85 Silver Spring Rd
Landisville PA 175381014

Call Sign: KA3JHD
Gerald J Bertoli
1119 Snapper Dam Rd
Landisville PA 17538

Call Sign: KA3WRT
Glenn L Stoltzfus
715 Southview Dr
Landisville PA 17538

Call Sign: KA3YRC
Thomas M Otto Sr
740 Stoney Battery Rd
Landisville PA 17538

Call Sign: KB3JKN
David M Warner
1305 Timothy Dr
Landisville PA 17538

Call Sign: KD6PLK
John H Grosh Jr
160 W Main St
Landisville PA 175381129

Call Sign: N3ENR
Richard A Mowery Jr
3008 Wood Ridge Dr
Landisville PA 175381345

FCC Amateur Radio Licenses in Lawn

Call Sign: N3OFJ
James M Kline
5569 Elizabethtown Rd
Lawn PA 17041

Call Sign: N3ICQ
Patrica S Kline
Lawn PA 17041

FCC Amateur Radio Licenses in Lawrenceville

Call Sign: KB3AEL
Joanna D Stickler
Box 307 E Lawrence Rd
Lawrenceville PA
169299738

Call Sign: KA3VFE
Samuel D Brennan
Box 333D
Lawrenceville PA 16929

Call Sign: KA3SAE
Victor J Jones Sr
Box 335

Lawrenceville PA 16929

Call Sign: KB3CYI
Samuel L Fay
Box 777 B
Lawrenceville PA 16929

Call Sign: N3VHC
Roger D Fisher
1590 Buckwheat Hollow
Rd
Lawrenceville PA 16929

Call Sign: KB3TLB
Jon M Hoffer
939 Croft Hill Rd
Lawrenceville PA 16929

Call Sign: KB3TLK
Louise A Holder
939 Croft Hill Rd
Lawrenceville PA 16929

Call Sign: W3QBZ
Adda M Gontarz
50 Main St
Lawrenceville PA 16929

Call Sign: KB3HBP
John S Ripic
6 Mechanic St
Lawrenceville PA 16929

FCC Amateur Radio Licenses in Lebanon

Call Sign: K3KEK
John L Bruner Jr
201 Adam Dr
Lebanon PA 17042

Call Sign: N3CIP
Robert J Balogh Jr
1200 Ash Ln
Lebanon PA 17042

Call Sign: N3EDN
Karla K Balogh
1200 Ash Ln
Lebanon PA 17042

Call Sign: KB3IZE
Christopher M Balogh
1200 Ash Ln
Lebanon PA 17042

Call Sign: W3HVR
Harold E Kraybill
1257 Ash Ln
Lebanon PA 17042

Call Sign: W3EVU
Herman Jankowski
620 Aspen Ln
Lebanon PA 17042

Call Sign: N3LTT
Mary Jane Books
627 Aspen Ln
Lebanon PA 170429002

Call Sign: N3RJ
Ralph A Juliano Jr
737 Aspen Ln
Lebanon PA 17042

Call Sign: KB3YJD
Chris M Witmeyer
3 Aspen Way
Lebanon PA 17046

Call Sign: N3YTK
Curvin L Swartzentruber
345 Auburn Dr
Lebanon PA 17042

Call Sign: KB3FVN
Russell S Wolfe Jr
345 Birch Rd
Lebanon PA 17042

Call Sign: N3CYJ
Warren F Wampler
Box 2315
Lebanon PA 17042

Call Sign: KB3WQY
Akira Nakazawa
1 Brandthaven Dr
Lebanon PA 17046

Call Sign: W3ANA
Akira Nakazawa
1 Brandthaven Dr
Lebanon PA 17046

Call Sign: KB3KOE
James C Arnold
100 Bricker Ln
Lebanon PA 17042

Call Sign: N3MJJ
James W Talley
2075 Brook Dr
Lebanon PA 17042

Call Sign: N4YRK
Audra J Tawes
1028 Challenge Dr
Lebanon PA 17042

Call Sign: N4YRL
Lawrence E Tawes Sr
1028 Challenge Dr
Lebanon PA 17042

Call Sign: N3HSJ
Rick J Buffenmeyer
705 Charles St
Lebanon PA 17042

Call Sign: W3HD
Anthony J Walker
1116 Chestnut St
Lebanon PA 17042

Call Sign: KB3CKQ
David M Skettini
1237 Colebrook Rd
Lebanon PA 170426912

Call Sign: KA4FWU
Vincent S Conley
1205 Colony Ct Apt 119
Lebanon PA 17042

Call Sign: N3WRZ
Leonard M Oberholtzer
316 Crest Rd
Lebanon PA 17042

Call Sign: N3WSR
Elva M Oberholtzer
316 Crest Rd
Lebanon PA 17042

Call Sign: N3DZD
Ivan R Sensenig
415 Crest Rd
Lebanon PA 17042

Call Sign: N3GJJ
Lois E Sensenig
415 Crest Rd
Lebanon PA 17042

Call Sign: W3AQT
Alexander Stoffer Jr
568 Doris Dr
Lebanon PA 170464219

Call Sign: N1BKR
Christopher R Wincey
803 E Canal St
Lebanon PA 17046

Call Sign: KB3DOU
Barry A Lerch
1217 E Chestnut St
Lebanon PA 17042

Call Sign: KB3EDN
Scott A Weidman
1013 E Cumberland St
Lebanon PA 17042

Call Sign: K7CDJ
Russell L Murphy
433 E Elm St
Lebanon PA 170427629

Call Sign: KB3JZI
Rusty E Plush
8 E High St
Lebanon PA 17042

Call Sign: K1BIX
Rusty E Plush
8 E High St
Lebanon PA 17042

Call Sign: KB3TPI
Cornwall Ranger Station
ARC
8 E High St
Lebanon PA 17042

Call Sign: W3CRS
Cornwall Ranger Station
ARC
8 E High St
Lebanon PA 17042

Call Sign: KB3TRI
Samuel F Paterniti
12 E High St
Lebanon PA 17042

Call Sign: KA3RBR
William S Harris
19 E High St
Lebanon PA 170425455

Call Sign: W3DPK
William S Harris

19 E High St
Lebanon PA 170425455

54 Eastfield Dr
Lebanon PA 17042

819 Holly Ln
Lebanon PA 170429029

Call Sign: KB3TCG
Nathan M Fancovic
520 E High St
Lebanon PA 17042

Call Sign: N3FOT
Charles E Boyd Jr
1515 Fonderwhite Rd
Lebanon PA 17042

Call Sign: KB3FCQ
Olga Piergrossi
539 Horseshoe Trl Dr
Lebanon PA 17042

Call Sign: KB3GKD
Dene Light
625 E Kercher Ave
Lebanon PA 170469268

Call Sign: K3JGC
Ned F Williamson
815 Grant St
Lebanon PA 17046

Call Sign: W3WKO
G William Ruhl
630 Horseshoe Trl Dr
Lebanon PA 170428956

Call Sign: KB3WAJ
Thomas C Felty
807 E Lehman St
Lebanon PA 17046

Call Sign: N3WSW
Nolan G Martin
643 Greble Rd
Lebanon PA 17046

Call Sign: N3ICT
Sandra L White
1324 Jill Ann Dr
Lebanon PA 17042

Call Sign: N3RXH
William L Wunderlich
737 E Maple St
Lebanon PA 17042

Call Sign: N3HRS
James E Pond Jr
313 Greentree Village
Lebanon PA 17042

Call Sign: W3RE
Walter R White Jr
1324 Jill Ann Dr
Lebanon PA 17042

Call Sign: KB3CBS
Larry L Shaud Jr
224 E Weidman St
Lebanon PA 17046

Call Sign: KB3PVD
Michael J Sanger
1117 Greiner St
Lebanon PA 17042

Call Sign: KA3RIB
Woodrow E Heffelfinger
1632 Josephine Ann Dr
Lebanon PA 17042

Call Sign: KB3OIM
Christopher L Shaud
224 E Weidman St
Lebanon PA 17046

Call Sign: KB3LIZ
Bobby E Clements
934 Hauck St
Lebanon PA 17042

Call Sign: KA3VBX
Larry S Harman
3014 Joyce St
Lebanon PA 170462668

Call Sign: W3BZ
Christopher L Shaud
224 E Weidman St
Lebanon PA 17046

Call Sign: N3SJS
Laura J Cochran
1217 Heritage Ln Apt 261
Lebanon PA 17042

Call Sign: KA2HZU
Mark F Rajchel
134 Julia Ln
Lebanon PA 17042

Call Sign: KB3MGK
Dustin J Zellers
50 Eastfield Dr
Lebanon PA 17042

Call Sign: N3NWB
Bruce R Markey
819 Holly Ln
Lebanon PA 17042

Call Sign: AB3AI
Christopher J Halinar
219 Karinch St
Lebanon PA 17042

Call Sign: N3BSH
John T Manos

Call Sign: KN3C
Richard P Markey Jr

Call Sign: W3LWH
William R Smith

223 Karinch St
Lebanon PA 17042

Call Sign: KB3DJV
Jason L Sensenig
1888 Kenbrook Rd
Lebanon PA 17046

Call Sign: KE3AM
Bruce E Blessing
743 Kiner Ave
Lebanon PA 17042

Call Sign: N3SDJ
Kenneth L Snyder Jr
1428 King St
Lebanon PA 17042

Call Sign: KB3UJN
Leon F Earhart
3640 Kings Dr
Lebanon PA 17046

Call Sign: N3UDA
Mark P Doeing
2120 Kline St
Lebanon PA 17042

Call Sign: KB3FVQ
John C Tobias
1235 Lafayette St
Lebanon PA 17042

Call Sign: KB3NHJ
Ryan A Torres
1111 Lehman St
Lebanon PA 17046

Call Sign: KB3NFN
Wilson A Ballester
1111 Lehman St
Lebanon PA 17046

Call Sign: WA3LAH
Philip V Vance Jr

2 Light St
Lebanon PA 17042

Call Sign: N3EHW
James G Speck
19 Linda Ln
Lebanon PA 17042

Call Sign: WA3JIG
Charles H Noll
1016 Linden Ave
Lebanon PA 17042

Call Sign: NO3L
Charles H Noll
1016 Linden Ave
Lebanon PA 17042

Call Sign: NO3L
Charles H Noll
1016 Linden Ave
Lebanon PA 17042

Call Sign: NO3LL
Charles H Noll
1016 Linden St
Lebanon PA 17046

Call Sign: KE3PC
John B Hunt
2145 Long Ln
Lebanon PA 170461850

Call Sign: W3IMJ
John B Hunt
2145 Long Ln
Lebanon PA 170461850

Call Sign: N3UWS
Thomas J Wiest
870 Lovers Ln
Lebanon PA 17046

Call Sign: N3MSR
Marc R Miller

22 Maple St
Lebanon PA 17046

Call Sign: N3OGK
Patricia L Doll
22 Maple St
Lebanon PA 17046

Call Sign: AA3RG
Appalachian Amateur
Radio Group
34 Maple St
Lebanon PA 170463034

Call Sign: N3JOX
Edward H McGowan
517 Maple St
Lebanon PA 17046

Call Sign: WB3IHQ
Eric R Wolfe
607 Maple St
Lebanon PA 170462965

Call Sign: N3BMM
John E Blouch
509 Margin Rd
Lebanon PA 17042

Call Sign: N3GKU
David L Centini
751 Mechanic St
Lebanon PA 17046

Call Sign: N1KHS
Thomas N Rose
5 Mifflin St
Lebanon PA 17046

Call Sign: K3BFD
Bill F Daub
62 Moravian St
Lebanon PA 170425643

Call Sign: W3BFD

Bill F Daub
62 Moravian St
Lebanon PA 170425643

Call Sign: N3BVZ
John G Zimmerman
1281 Mt Wilson Rd
Lebanon PA 17042

Call Sign: KB3HKM
John G Zimmerman
1281 Mt Wilson Rd
Lebanon PA 17042

Call Sign: KB3OJG
Henry H Emrich
441 N 11th St
Lebanon PA 17046

Call Sign: KD3TS
Lanny E Hoffman
337 N 19th St
Lebanon PA 17042

Call Sign: N3MLG
Carl E Kohr Jr
303 N 21st St
Lebanon PA 17046

Call Sign: KN3H
Roy A Kleinfelter
765 N 32nd St
Lebanon PA 17046

Call Sign: KB3UZZ
Roy E Brewster II
448 N 5th St
Lebanon PA 17046

Call Sign: KB3VIF
Sherry A Brewster
448 N 5th St
Lebanon PA 17046

Call Sign: WA3ZRS

James S Zengerle
802 N 7th St
Lebanon PA 170462914

Call Sign: W3ZRS
James S Zengerle
802 N 7th St
Lebanon PA 170462914

Call Sign: KB3TLR
Linda M Jones
1007 N 8th Ave
Lebanon PA 17046

Call Sign: K3LEB
Robert B Sanborn
1007 N 8th Ave
Lebanon PA 17046

Call Sign: K3RBS
Robert B Sanborn
1007 N 8th Ave
Lebanon PA 17046

Call Sign: AB3GF
Robert B Sanborn
1007 N 8th Ave
Lebanon PA 17046

Call Sign: KB3PQJ
Deanna N Sanborn
1007 N 8th Ave
Lebanon PA 17046

Call Sign: KB3PXT
Lebanon Veterans
Amateur Assn
1007 N 8th Ave
Lebanon PA 170462135

Call Sign: K3LVA
Lebanon Veterans
Amateur Assn
1007 N 8th Ave
Lebanon PA 170462135

Call Sign: NB3Z
Allen E Sauder
1662 N 8th Ave
Lebanon PA 17046

Call Sign: N3OGQ
Adrien A Markey
1001 N 8th St
Lebanon PA 17042

Call Sign: N3OXU
Jonathan A Markey
1001 N 8th St
Lebanon PA 17042

Call Sign: N3MJK
Robert E Hockley Jr
1400 N 8th St
Lebanon PA 17046

Call Sign: N3MLB
Ronald L Lookenbill
1015 N Mill St
Lebanon PA 17042

Call Sign: N3UEH
Deborah M Vail
102 N Mine Rd
Lebanon PA 17042

Call Sign: KB3RBM
Randy L Stamm
1535 Nowlen St
Lebanon PA 17042

Call Sign: N3VMX
George W Houtz
2143 Oak
Lebanon PA 17042

Call Sign: KA3VDX
Betty Jo Wick
34 Palm Ln
Lebanon PA 170429114

Call Sign: N3XNP
Fred G Gassert
843 Patmar Dr
Lebanon PA 170462133

Call Sign: N3IDM
Matthew C Witters
2150 Quarry Rd
Lebanon PA 17046

Call Sign: K3QS
Doug Lefever
1004 S 3rd Ave
Lebanon PA 17042

Call Sign: KB3TBS
Carl J Thomas
20 Penny Ln
Lebanon PA 17046

Call Sign: KB3TTH
Shannan M Serra
2122 Quentin Rd
Lebanon PA 17042

Call Sign: KB3VWZ
Richard L Mase Sr
109 S 3rd St
Lebanon PA 17042

Call Sign: KB3GYZ
Cory L Hostetter
110 Pershing Ave
Lebanon PA 17042

Call Sign: KB3WDY
Ralph E Kaylor
187 Race St
Lebanon PA 170429043

Call Sign: WA3QWW
Christopher J Coyle
306 S 4th St
Lebanon PA 17042

Call Sign: KB3GKF
Roger L Hostetter
110 Pershing Ave
Lebanon PA 17042

Call Sign: KB3CFF
Ted Keith
1 Richard Ave
Lebanon PA 17042

Call Sign: KB3DRB
Mervin H Sensenig
2418 S 5th Ave
Lebanon PA 17042

Call Sign: NO3J
Dale R Merkey
411 Plaza Apts
Lebanon PA 17042

Call Sign: N3MGL
Timothy W Kreider
1980 Rt 72n
Lebanon PA 17046

Call Sign: KB3VIJ
Joseph F Rider
235 S 5th St
Lebanon PA 17042

Call Sign: WJ3G
Wilson G Hein
650 Poplar St
Lebanon PA 17046

Call Sign: KB3GBA
Richard J Long
326 S 13th St
Lebanon PA 17042

Call Sign: W3GTO
Nicholas J Di Nunzio
118 S 8th St
Lebanon PA 17042

Call Sign: KB3RYP
Kasey J Heberling
1752 Quarry Rd
Lebanon PA 17046

Call Sign: AA3YD
Richard J Long
326 S 13th St
Lebanon PA 17042

Call Sign: N3YSJ
Robert L Donley
710 S Lincoln Ave
Lebanon PA 17042

Call Sign: N3RBD
Bonny L Redinger
1765 Quarry Rd
Lebanon PA 17046

Call Sign: KB3KOD
Charles A Fenner Jr
504 S 2nd Ave
Lebanon PA 17042

Call Sign: N3YSK
Reba D Donley
710 S Lincoln Ave
Lebanon PA 17042

Call Sign: N3OUQ
Russell E Bender Jr
1769 Quarry Rd
Lebanon PA 17046

Call Sign: KM3K
Doug Lefever
1004 S 3rd Ave
Lebanon PA 17042

Call Sign: N3KNH
Philip L Keller
1641 S Lincoln Ave
Lebanon PA 17042

Call Sign: N3KYU
Cindy L Keller
1641 S Lincoln Ave
Lebanon PA 17042

Call Sign: WB3IGT
Larry R Deck
351 S Ramona Rd
Lebanon PA 17042

Call Sign: WA3QLR
Kenneth H Franklin
2077 S White Oak St
Lebanon PA 17042

Call Sign: WA3WXP
Craig A Eberly
1526 Sandhill Rd
Lebanon PA 170461949

Call Sign: KB2NCL
James T Powell Jr
543 Sassafras Dr
Lebanon PA 170428718

Call Sign: N3GTC
John B Moyer
909 Smith Ave
Lebanon PA 17042

Call Sign: KB3VJF
John R Brydle
314 Spring Hill Ln
Lebanon PA 17042

Call Sign: N3BP
Brandon M Peiffer
316 Spring Hill Ln
Lebanon PA 17042

Call Sign: K3GRS
Kenneth J Bates
8 Spruce Ln
Lebanon PA 17046

Call Sign: N3ICR
Ricky W Bates Sgt
8 Spruce Ln
Lebanon PA 17046

Call Sign: KB3QAP
Harold G Heverling
996 Stracks Dam Rd
Lebanon PA 17046

Call Sign: KB3PMS
Brandon M Peiffer
1123 Sun Dr
Lebanon PA 17046

Call Sign: KB3SU
Timothy W Jones
17 Sunrise Dr
Lebanon PA 17042

Call Sign: KA3RBZ
David J Auman
24 Sunrise Dr
Lebanon PA 17042

Call Sign: KB3POX
William H Hoffman Jr
25 Sunrise Dr
Lebanon PA 17042

Call Sign: KC2DUY
Manny Fernandez
921 Sycamore Ln
Lebanon PA 17046

Call Sign: WA3CUJ
Robert G Bonneville
186 Tice Ln
Lebanon PA 17042

Call Sign: KA3ULK
Stephen M Druckman
830 Tudor Ln
Lebanon PA 17042

Call Sign: K3LV
Lebanon Valley Society Of
Radio Amateurs
303 W Cumberland St
Lebanon PA 170424469

Call Sign: N3RM
Theodore R Miller
1927 W Cumberland St
Lebanon PA 17042

Call Sign: N3FOG
Lebanon Valley Dx Assn
1927 W Cumberland St
Lebanon PA 170424469

Call Sign: KA3IOL
Harry J Wright
1200 W Kercher Ave
Lebanon PA 17046

Call Sign: N3XIE
James L Shoemaker Jr
44 Walnut St
Lebanon PA 17042

Call Sign: N3KPX
Rodney L Watson
Walnut St
Lebanon PA 17042

Call Sign: N3GGO
Richard B Allwein
2045 Weavertown Rd
Lebanon PA 17046

Call Sign: N3IDA
George K Belicka Sr
515 Wedgewood Dr
Lebanon PA 17042

Call Sign: KB2DKX
Daniel J Buckley
1531 Wheatfield Ln

Lebanon PA 170426444

Call Sign: N3MSQ
Eugene J Migliorato
24 Woodland Ests
Lebanon PA 17042

Call Sign: N3MLC
Spencer W Folau
Lebanon PA 17042

Call Sign: KB3PYX
Lebanon Good Samaritan
Radio Amateurs
Lebanon PA 17042

Call Sign: K3LGS
Lebanon Good Samaritan
Radio Amateurs
Lebanon PA 17042

Call Sign: N3YLF
Thomas C Santiago Jr
Lebanon PA 17042

FCC Amateur Radio Licenses in Lemont

Call Sign: W3JAW
John A Walters
237 1st Ave
Lemont PA 16851

Call Sign: WB0RLN
Wayne R Pauley
380 Mt Nittany Rd
Lemont PA 16851

Call Sign: W3RLN
Wayne R Pauley
380 Mt Nittany Rd
Lemont PA 16851

Call Sign: WA2LHV
Peter B Trippett

225 Whitehill St Box 375
Lemont PA 168510375

Call Sign: WA3EBL
George C Williams
Lemont PA 16851

Call Sign: AD3K
Robert L Spooner
Lemont PA 16851

Call Sign: KA3HRV
Nancy E Spooner
Lemont PA 16851

Call Sign: N3NCE
William E Murphy
Lemont PA 16851

Call Sign: KB3EMF
Stanley L Peterson
Lemont PA 168510344

FCC Amateur Radio Licenses in Lemoyne

Call Sign: KB3DCI
Charles J Allen III
720 Bosler Ave
Lemoyne PA 17043

Call Sign: WA3SEU
Alex M Burba
825 Bosler Ave
Lemoyne PA 170431821

Call Sign: WA0ECV
Jeremy T Utterback
638 Bosler Ave
Lemoyne PA 17043

Call Sign: KB3LQJ
Joseph K Diminick
1057 Brandt Ave
Lemoyne PA 17043

Call Sign: KB3RYO
Brandon A Claypool
265 Clark St
Lemoyne PA 17043

Call Sign: KB3OZH
Daniel J Claypool
265 Clark St
Lemoyne PA 17043

Call Sign: N3TTC
Alfred N Muoio
280 Clark St
Lemoyne PA 17043

Call Sign: KB3JIA
Bradley W Huntingdon
407 Herman Ave
Lemoyne PA 17043

Call Sign: KB3LPY
Amber C Breski
933 Hummel Ave
Lemoyne PA 17043

Call Sign: N3WER
Chris E Wissler
707 Hummel Ave 1st Fl
Lemoyne PA 17043

Call Sign: K3KMC
John L Contino
841 Kiehl Dr
Lemoyne PA 170191201

Call Sign: KB3ELJ
Tsr Wireless ARC
717 Market St Ste 104
Lemoyne PA 17042

Call Sign: N3TAI
Diederik De Haes
401 N 5th St
Lemoyne PA 17043

Call Sign: WA3MWS
Michael W Fuller
55 N 9th St
Lemoyne PA 17043

Call Sign: N3KPV
Richard P Busler
61 N 9th St
Lemoyne PA 17043

Call Sign: KB3QYC
Brooks R Watts
700 Ohio Ave
Lemoyne PA 17043

Call Sign: WA3OWR
Robert L Fodness
State St
Lemoyne PA 17043

Call Sign: N3LKK
Bernard R Wojciechowski
316 Walnut St
Lemoyne PA 17043

Call Sign: KB3KMC
Kevin S Farrell
25 Westwind Dr
Lemoyne PA 17043

FCC Amateur Radio
Licenses in Leola

Call Sign: KA3PWW
Joseph L Castronova
36 Apricot Ave
Leola PA 17540

Call Sign: WB3GCX
Michael J Omensetter
52 Battens Cir
Leola PA 17540

Call Sign: N3KYW

Edwin P Hirsch
27 Blaine Ave
Leola PA 17540

Call Sign: KG2ML
Ronald Slota
33 Blaine Ave
Leola PA 17540

Call Sign: K3HQC
Allen R McQuate
14 Farmersville Rd
Leola PA 17540

Call Sign: WA3NOF
Sercom Inc
14 Farmersville Rd
Leola PA 17540

Call Sign: KB3VUZ
Gregory R Fritz Jr
70 Glenbrook Rd
Leola PA 17540

Call Sign: KB3UYR
Samson Xiong
84 Glenbrook Rd
Leola PA 17540

Call Sign: N3WGV
Charles Hawkins
59 Hellers Church Rd
Leola PA 17540

Call Sign: N3LUR
Chris W Ebert
343 Hilltop Dr
Leola PA 17540

Call Sign: K3AW
Arthur R Westman
17 Locust Ln
Leola PA 17540

Call Sign: N3YCB

Aaron R Rissler
121 N Maple Ave
Leola PA 17540

Call Sign: KC0VDM
Jeffery S Clark
3851 Oregon Pike
Leola PA 17540

Call Sign: KB3NCR
Jeffery S Clark
3851 Oregon Pike
Leola PA 17540

Call Sign: KB3GNB
Gerald E Wilson Jr
178 Pinetown Rd
Leola PA 17540

Call Sign: N3CTU
Donald G Kranch
64 Quarry Rd
Leola PA 17540

Call Sign: W3NOK
Charles F Nesslage
69 Ridgeview Dr
Leola PA 17540

Call Sign: KC2ASR
Thao H Vu
298 Rolling Ter
Leola PA 17540

Call Sign: WB3ART
Hallowell Dunlap
53 Timberline Dr
Leola PA 17540

Call Sign: KB3PYP
Scott L Marks
23 Village Dr
Leola PA 17540

Call Sign: KA3YWM

Sherry M Harman
Leola PA 17540

**FCC Amateur Radio
Licenses in Lewis Run**

Call Sign: N3PKL
Michael R Walter
Box 59
Lewis Run PA 16738

Call Sign: WB3FEL
Raymond J Zamiska
203 Collins Rd
Lewis Run PA 16738

Call Sign: N3OJS
James E Shields Sr
15 Irvine St
Lewis Run PA 16738

Call Sign: KB3SVK
Elaine S Summerday
123 Lineman Rd
Lewis Run PA 16738

Call Sign: N3UFZ
Kirk A Zandy
1452 S Ave
Lewis Run PA 16738

Call Sign: K3JAM
Alma S Sorokes
16 W Irvine St
Lewis Run PA 16738

Call Sign: KB3FNR
Michael P Sorokes
16 W Irvine St
Lewis Run PA 167380065

Call Sign: K3MPS
Michael P Sorokes
16 W Irvine St
Lewis Run PA 167380065

Call Sign: WA3PS
Paul M Sorokes
16 W Irvine St
Lewis Run PA 167380065

Call Sign: K3VIP
Paul M Sorokes
16 W Irvine St
Lewis Run PA 167380065

Call Sign: N3CEH
Alma S Sorokes
Lewis Run PA 16738

Call Sign: N3LAF
Stacy M Sorokes
Lewis Run PA 16738

Call Sign: WA3ZZR
Paul M Sorokes
Lewis Run PA 16738

Call Sign: WB3BUT
Duane M Clark
Lewis Run PA 16738

**FCC Amateur Radio
Licenses in Lewisberry**

Call Sign: KB3LRW
Joseph A Santa Maria
110 Bramblewood Ln
Lewisberry PA 17339

Call Sign: K3GPS
James G Binkley
117 Bramblewood Ln
Lewisberry PA 17339

Call Sign: KB3QDL
Dennis L Martin
594 Brenneman Dr
Lewisberry PA 17339

Call Sign: N3XLH
James L Formey
607 Brenneman Dr
Lewisberry PA 17339

Call Sign: KB3RCS
Theodore J Mackley
846 Cardinal Ln
Lewisberry PA 17339

Call Sign: N3LLS
Ann M Updegraff
944 Cedars Rd
Lewisberry PA 17339

Call Sign: KB3RYX
Abigail S Portwood
610 Copper Cir
Lewisberry PA 17339

Call Sign: KB3QPU
Richard A Merluzzi III
71 Foxfire Ln
Lewisberry PA 17339

Call Sign: K2ME
Jack E Scott
81 Foxfire Ln
Lewisberry PA 17339

Call Sign: KB3KMP
Christopher J Mann
113 Foxfire Ln
Lewisberry PA 17339

Call Sign: KB3RZG
John X Zornosa
127 Foxfire Ln
Lewisberry PA 17339

Call Sign: KB2NSK
Steven D Portale
687 Gap Rd
Lewisberry PA 17339

Call Sign: N3SOZ
Matthew A Kiner
305 Lewisberry Ct
Lewisberry PA 17339

Call Sign: KC9ING
Michael E Mullen
755 Lewisberry Rd
Lewisberry PA 17339

Call Sign: WA3TIZ
Ronald A Bozis
1216 Lewisberry Rd
Lewisberry PA 17339

Call Sign: N3JXE
Fred R De Camp
858 Moores Mt Rd
Lewisberry PA 17339

Call Sign: N3SWI
Doris J De Camp
858 Moores Mtn Rd
Lewisberry PA 17339

Call Sign: W3BSN
Ralph A Ditlow
531 Nauvoo Rd
Lewisberry PA 17339

Call Sign: KB6BJJ
Susan J Lumnitzer
994 Oak Hill Rd
Lewisberry PA 17339

Call Sign: N6CQ
William B Lumnitzer
994 Oak Hill Rd
Lewisberry PA 173399414

Call Sign: AA3GR
Barbara A Faletti
645 Observatory Dr
Lewisberry PA 17339

Call Sign: WM3A
John E Faletti
645 Observatory Dr
Lewisberry PA 173399549

Call Sign: KB3QWU
Petr F Boshinski
363 Old Stage Rd
Lewisberry PA 17339

Call Sign: KB3LPX
Christine L Boshinski
363 Old Stage Rd
Lewisberry PA 17339

Call Sign: KA3QPO
Robert K Park
515 Paul Ave
Lewisberry PA 17339

Call Sign: AA3PI
Louis E Skamangas
684 Potts Hill Rd
Lewisberry PA 17339

Call Sign: N3XUB
Robert C Sincavage Jr
708 Quaker Cir Apt 6
Lewisberry PA 17339

Call Sign: N3NOC
Philip W Amos
45 Rocky Wood Ln
Lewisberry PA 17339

Call Sign: N3GHN
Scott H Burkett
1375 Roundtop Rd
Lewisberry PA 17339

Call Sign: N3MMZ
Deborah J Burkett
1375 Roundtop Rd
Lewisberry PA 17339

Call Sign: N3AJB
Jonathan W Kohn
855 Seitz Dr
Lewisberry PA 17339

Call Sign: KB3SNY
Christiana V Longey
853 Silver Lake Rd
Lewisberry PA 17339

Call Sign: KB3QDE
Mathew M Bates
993 Silver Lake Rd
Lewisberry PA 17339

Call Sign: KB3QYA
Christopher H Tilley
1020 Silver Lake Rd
Lewisberry PA 17339

Call Sign: KB3RZD
Ryan D Tilley
1020 Silver Lake Rd
Lewisberry PA 17339

Call Sign: KA3RLM
Rita M Sarik
495 Stone Jug Rd
Lewisberry PA 17339

Call Sign: WB3BDB
Charles J Intrieri Jr
495 Stone Jug Rd
Lewisberry PA 17339

Call Sign: N3NZH
Robert A Kostosky
112 Turtle Hollow Dr
Lewisberry PA 17339

Call Sign: KB3QDX
Hyun-Soo Yu
210 W Front St
Lewisberry PA 17339

Call Sign: KB3MWB
Christina M Forster
690 Woodburne Rd
Lewisberry PA 17339

Call Sign: N3EBH
Thomas C Dow
1370 Beagle Rd
Lewisburg PA 178377218

Call Sign: KB3DFJ
Samuel R Alcorn
128 Beth Ellen Dr
Lewisburg PA 17837

Call Sign: K3GYF
Rodney A Dewald
Box 366
Lewisburg PA 17837

Call Sign: KA3GCA
Thomas C Smith Jr
Box 406
Lewisburg PA 17837

Call Sign: N3QPN
James D Hepler
Box 407
Lewisburg PA 17837

Call Sign: WA1YFS
Royden H Gilleo
Box 464E
Lewisburg PA 17837

Call Sign: WB3DFT
Joseph B Gallagher
91 Country Hill Rd
Lewisburg PA 17837

Call Sign: KB3TWE
Ernest R Ritter III

3441 Crossroad Dr
Lewisburg PA 17837

Call Sign: W3KRQ
Rodney A Dewald
2256 Crossroads Dr
Lewisburg PA 17837

Call Sign: N2BLF
Bernard S Huff
97 Dogwood Ln
Lewisburg PA 17837

Call Sign: KB3MSR
Jason J Hollenbach
568 Essex Pl
Lewisburg PA 17837

Call Sign: WP4DQB
Ivan T Navarro
212 Fairview Dr
Lewisburg PA 17837

Call Sign: KB3PWS
Amber R Lind
2 Field Of Dreams Ln
Lewisburg PA 17837

Call Sign: NB4J
David F Kelley
171 James Rd
Lewisburg PA 17837

Call Sign: ND3K
David F Kelley
171 James Rd
Lewisburg PA 17837

Call Sign: KB3JEV
Sara P Kelley
171 James Rd
Lewisburg PA 17837

Call Sign: KA3VXU
Matthew L Barr

614 Maclay Ave
Lewisburg PA 17837

Call Sign: W3LXN
Paul O Mitch
27 Meadow Ln
Lewisburg PA 17837

Call Sign: KC4SYX
John D Wilkins
231 Melmar Dr
Lewisburg PA 17837

Call Sign: KC4SYY
Valeria A Wilkins
231 Melmar Dr
Lewisburg PA 17837

Call Sign: KB3LRI
Matthew J Miles
326 Melmar Dr
Lewisburg PA 17837

Call Sign: WB3IGN
Raymond S Pastore
1401 Monroe Ave
Lewisburg PA 17837

Call Sign: KB3OKQ
Raymond S Pastore
1401 Monroe Ave
Lewisburg PA 17837

Call Sign: WB3IGN
Raymond S Pastore
1401 Monroe Ave
Lewisburg PA 17837

Call Sign: W3MAT
Marlin "Loon" A Troup
2010 Moores School Rd
Lewisburg PA 17837

Call Sign: W3MFV
Clair F Snyder

134 N 10th St
Lewisburg PA 17837

Call Sign: KB3LDZ
Brock H Landi
103 N 15th St
Lewisburg PA 17837

Call Sign: KB3QHF
Richard K Collins
139 N 2nd Apt 1
Lewisburg PA 17837

Call Sign: KC4AGV
Arvie Charlene P Clement
50 N 2Rd St Apt 212
Lewisburg PA 17837

Call Sign: N3LEN
Craig L Lenig
50 N 3rd St Apt 410
Lewisburg PA 17837

Call Sign: W3LZU
David R Broadt
519 N 4th St
Lewisburg PA 178371107

Call Sign: KB3QEA
Glenn A Larson
10 N Meadow Ct
Lewisburg PA 17837

Call Sign: W2OSB
Edwin S Gernant
270 Ridgecrest Cir Apt
216
Lewisburg PA 17837

Call Sign: KB3YCC
David M Gutenkauf
5 S 12th St
Lewisburg PA 17837

Call Sign: KA3RAT

Kirk P Doran
219 S 14th St
Lewisburg PA 17837

Call Sign: KJ3Z
Bruce R Long
304 S 15th St
Lewisburg PA 17837

Call Sign: KB3YCE
Mark J Mossel
488 S 19th St
Lewisburg PA 17837

Call Sign: KB3YCD
Cole J Mossel
488 S 19th St
Lewisburg PA 17837

Call Sign: KD8MKF
Alan M Amthor
134 S 3rd St Apt 1
Lewisburg PA 17837

Call Sign: KF3DF
Robert L Zorn Jr
60 S 8th St
Lewisburg PA 178371887

Call Sign: N3XZZ
Donald L Reichenbach
417 Smoketown Rd
Lewisburg PA 17837

Call Sign: N1MAM
Joshua E Steinhurst
875 St Louis St
Lewisburg PA 17837

Call Sign: KB3VFU
Spencer L Brought
748 Swanger Rd
Lewisburg PA 17837

Call Sign: N3IDQ

Ronald S Boyer Jr
218 Timberhaven Dr
Lewisburg PA 17837

Call Sign: KB3MSN
Dylan R Kalin
150 Verna Rd
Lewisburg PA 17837

Call Sign: KB3MSM
Michael P Kalin
150 Verna Rd
Lewisburg PA 17837

Call Sign: N3WEV
Miguel A Echenique
182 Wedgewood Gardens
Lewisburg PA 17837

Call Sign: N3CFD
John A Kelchner
1007 Wending Way
Lewisburg PA 17837

Call Sign: W3PBY
John W Ranck
1028 William Penn Dr
Lewisburg PA 17837

Call Sign: W3PR
Giles M Crabtree
Lewisburg PA 17837

Call Sign: N3WGE
Sarah J Berryman
Lewisburg PA 17837

Call Sign: N3WBT
Mark S Berryman
Lewisburg PA 17837

**FCC Amateur Radio
Licenses in Lewistown**

Call Sign: WA3TRG

Max K Showers
407 3rd St
Lewistown PA 17044

Call Sign: W9PEX
Rosanna E Kasdorf
41 Alfarata Rd
Lewistown PA 170449218

Call Sign: K3QLZ
Gene M Long
1346 Back Maitland Rd
Lewistown PA 17044

Call Sign: KB3PZJ
Matthew D Sunderland
166 Birch Dr
Lewistown PA 17044

Call Sign: KA3ZZC
Ryan R Ritchey
Box 255H
Lewistown PA 17044

Call Sign: KA3TGV
Douglas B Burlew
43 Cedar Dr
Lewistown PA 17044

Call Sign: W3DBB
Douglas B Burlew
43 Cedar Dr
Lewistown PA 17044

Call Sign: KB3OUJ
George F Evans
29 Central Ave
Lewistown PA 17044

Call Sign: WB3JCF
Dean A Sipe
9 Char Will Ln
Lewistown PA 170443505

Call Sign: KB3HOD

Mifflin County ARC
14 Chestnut St
Lewistown PA 17044

Call Sign: N3YPX
Blair P Hannon
671 Ewardtown Rd
Lewistown PA 17044

Call Sign: N3MKK
George J Ferenz
40 French Dr
Lewistown PA 17044

Call Sign: KB3GDF
Kristopher B Miller
30 Gray Squirrel Ln
Lewistown PA 17044

Call Sign: KB3GDG
Andrew D Miller
30 Gray Squirrel Ln
Lewistown PA 17044

Call Sign: KB3RTO
Kathy M Miller
30 Gray Squirrel Ln
Lewistown PA 17044

Call Sign: W3TBX
Kathy M Miller
30 Gray Squirrel Ln
Lewistown PA 17044

Call Sign: N3IAB
Michael F Amick
701 Highland Ave
Lewistown PA 17044

Call Sign: KE3JL
Mildred B Middlesworth
349 Holiday Ln
Lewistown PA 17044

Call Sign: WS3K

Donald L Middlesworth
349 Holiday Ln
Lewistown PA 17044

Call Sign: KA3NEV
James D Potter
76 Logan Ave
Lewistown PA 17044

Call Sign: N3TRU
Jason M Van Scyoc
512 Maple Ave
Lewistown PA 17044

Call Sign: N3TRT
Duane V Van Scyoc
512 Maple Ave
Lewistown PA 170441137

Call Sign: KB3SHY
Ryan M Manning
631 Maple Ave
Lewistown PA 17044

Call Sign: WB3ISF
Allen J Levin
9 N Grand St
Lewistown PA 170442040

Call Sign: W3LS
William C McNally
21 N Grand St
Lewistown PA 17044

Call Sign: K3JXP
Harry J Hain
136 Oak Ridge Rd
Lewistown PA 17044

Call Sign: KD3VN
Arthur R Moore
154 Ort Valley Rd
Lewistown PA 17044

Call Sign: KB3TTL

Richard W Wilcher
147 Peace Dr
Lewistown PA 170449468

Call Sign: WA3TTB
Dennis A Bishop Sr
Rd 1
Lewistown PA 17044

Call Sign: WA3WBD
Barbara K Hayes
507 S Grand St
Lewistown PA 17044

Call Sign: N1HEF
Donald B Allen Jr
205 S Main St
Lewistown PA 170442122

Call Sign: KB3WYZ
Gary T Lane
730 S Main St
Lewistown PA 17044

Call Sign: WB3KHT
Frederick A McCallips Jr
10 S Pine St
Lewistown PA 17044

Call Sign: N3OJU
Jeffrey G Burkhart
700 S Wayne St
Lewistown PA 17044

Call Sign: WA3RNC
John C Dillon
21 Somar Dr
Lewistown PA 17044

Call Sign: WA3VGD
Stephanie L Diehl
5 Spangle Ave 2nd Fl
Lewistown PA 17044

Call Sign: KB3JEP

Stephanie L Diehl
5 Spanogle Ave 2nd Fl
Lewistown PA 17044

Call Sign: KB3TU
Robert A Clouser
580 Summit Dr
Lewistown PA 17044

Call Sign: W3TBX
William H Grumbine
3936 US Hwy 522 N
Lewistown PA 17044

Call Sign: KF4TEW
Joseph B Torres
517 W 4th St
Lewistown PA 17044

Call Sign: N3KFY
Fredrick L Hess
532 W 4th St
Lewistown PA 17044

Call Sign: WA3TLJ
James C Edmiston Jr
715 W 4th St
Lewistown PA 17044

Call Sign: N3GOL
Robert F Espigh
806 W 5th St
Lewistown PA 17044

Call Sign: K3LPH
Robert T McCaa
820 W 5th St
Lewistown PA 17044

Call Sign: WB3IVX
Clifton H Bell Jr
107 Washington Ave
Lewistown PA 17044

Call Sign: KA3YBC

Luther P Waring
130 Windy Ridge Ln
Lewistown PA 17044

Call Sign: AA3KI
Lawrence S Fultz Sr
Lewistown PA 17044

FCC Amateur Radio Licenses in Liberty

Call Sign: WB3CAF
David C Johnson
1254 Blacks Creek Rd
Liberty PA 16930

Call Sign: KB3IEF
Chad W Nickerson
Box 131 B
Liberty PA 16930

Call Sign: KA3EFB
Glenn C Shaffer
Box 152G
Liberty PA 16930

Call Sign: N3OTG
Lawrence F Mase
Liberty PA 16930

FCC Amateur Radio Licenses in Lilly

Call Sign: N3KMT
Herman F Behe
176 Blueberry Rd
Lilly PA 159389639

Call Sign: N3TUZ
John G Holsberger
301 Harris St
Lilly PA 15938

Call Sign: N3PUB
Roy C Glessner

135 Ryan St
Lilly PA 15938

FCC Amateur Radio Licenses in Linden

Call Sign: KB3FUP
Terry L Weaver
1651 Daugherty Run Rd
Linden PA 17744

Call Sign: KB3ITO
Timothy A Yates
42 Harvest Moon Park
Linden PA 17744

Call Sign: KB3QAR
Timothy A Yates
42 Harvest Moon Park
Linden PA 17744

Call Sign: KA3ACU
Harry E Goodwin
183 Mtn View Rd
Linden PA 17744

Call Sign: K3QDA
Richard C Sheasley
639 N Way Rd
Linden PA 17744

Call Sign: N3NOH
Brian J Dockey
5838 Rt 220 Hwy
Linden PA 17741

Call Sign: KA3YVS
Christopher Kerns
542 S Pine Run Rd
Linden PA 17744

Call Sign: N3NNJ
Renee E Kerns
542 S Pine Run Rd
Linden PA 17744

Call Sign: KB3TIH
Katherine B Mutz
542 S Pine Run Rd
Linden PA 17744

Call Sign: KB3GID
Harold T Chubb
200 Smith Ct Cir
Linden PA 17744

Call Sign: WN3UUS
Louis M Yerger Jr
66 Yerger Rd
Linden PA 17744

Call Sign: WB3EMH
Louis M Yerger III
70 Yerger Rd
Linden PA 17744

Call Sign: W3QDO
Robert B Staver
Linden PA 17744

FCC Amateur Radio Licenses in Linglestown

Call Sign: KA3IIP
Daniel E McClure
1250 Pennsylvania Ave
Linglestown PA 17112

FCC Amateur Radio Licenses in Lititz

Call Sign: KA3MMO
Cindy K Hopkins
213 Andrea Dr
Lititz PA 17543

Call Sign: K3DHV
Glenn K Metzler
218 Andrea Dr
Lititz PA 175438724

Call Sign: N3UDV
Chad M Eichfeld
121 Apple Blossom Cir
Lititz PA 17543

Call Sign: WA4VIQ
Gary L Musser
156 April Ln
Lititz PA 17543

Call Sign: N3VLY
William English
515 Artic Tern
Lititz PA 17543

Call Sign: KB3EQY
Michael B Arbenz
326 Balmer Rd
Lititz PA 17543

Call Sign: W0NWL
John L Cardos
7 Barbara Ln
Lititz PA 175437903

Call Sign: KB3ITC
John L Cardos
7 Barbara Ln
Lititz PA 175437903

Call Sign: KB3PYQ
Matthew E Midcap
1020 Bluestone Dr
Lititz PA 17543

Call Sign: KB3VIA
Robert M Shaubach
1104 Brunnerville Rd
Lititz PA 17543

Call Sign: KB3DWK
Robert O Brown
1521 Brunnerville Rd
Lititz PA 17543

Call Sign: WB2KIN
David R Ellis
204 Cardinal Rd
Lititz PA 17543

Call Sign: N3NRO
Renaldo A Angelini Jr
420 Cardinal Rd
Lititz PA 17543

Call Sign: N3QOY
Merlin G Girder
114 Chestnut St
Lititz PA 17543

Call Sign: N3RZB
Anthony R Martin
261 Cocalico Rd
Lititz PA 17543

Call Sign: N1GCR
Mark Hochman
18 Countryside Ln
Lititz PA 17543

Call Sign: KB3KIE
Jason M Sperduto
107 Crest Rd
Lititz PA 17543

Call Sign: N3UCY
Joan E Barr
323 Crosswinds Dr
Lititz PA 17543

Call Sign: KA3BHQ
Jesse T Genevish Jr
484 Crosswinds Dr
Lititz PA 17543

Call Sign: KB3ACQ
Vivian K Eberly
300 Dead End Rd
Lititz PA 17543

Call Sign: KB3JDR
Marsha L Carter
213 E 28th Division Hwy
Lititz PA 17543

Call Sign: AA3VN
Victor E Brubacker
E 28th Division Hwy
Lititz PA 17543

Call Sign: WB3BOZ
Arthur C Kuch
417 E Main St
Lititz PA 17543

Call Sign: N3NPP
Todd A Wardell
528 E Main St
Lititz PA 17543

Call Sign: N3MDN
Beverly S Milanowicz
711 E Millport Rd
Lititz PA 17543

Call Sign: N3BUC
Harold L Capwell Jr
16 E Orange St
Lititz PA 17543

Call Sign: N3YEL
Wanda K Fahnestock
198 Fairview Rd
Lititz PA 17543

Call Sign: W3ELM
James M Stephens
755 Farnum Rd
Lititz PA 17543

Call Sign: KA3TRG
Stephen P Morris II
434 Fort Ross Ave
Lititz PA 17543

Call Sign: KA3TNT
Randall O Williams
445 Fort Ross Ave
Lititz PA 17543

Call Sign: KB3MFC
Larry C Fox
20 Fox Run Ter
Lititz PA 17543

Call Sign: KB3KIL
Milton W Pickering
54 Front St
Lititz PA 175431516

Call Sign: KB3VYK
Wesler D Kehler
314 Glen View Cir
Lititz PA 17543

Call Sign: W3QQQ
Glenn W Forman
748 Goose Neck Dr
Lititz PA 17543

Call Sign: WA3GF
Glenn W Forman
748 Goose Neck Dr
Lititz PA 17543

Call Sign: KA3ZFT
Paul M Rhineer III
101 Hershey Rd
Lititz PA 17543

Call Sign: WA3MHP
Martin Bloomberg
578 Hi View Dr
Lititz PA 175438725

Call Sign: KA3MHT
J Kyle Harris
711 Hopeland Rd
Lititz PA 17543

Call Sign: N3HIS
John A Shoultz
509 Hummingbird Dr
Lititz PA 17543

Call Sign: KA3JUT
H Robert Kulp
8 Irish Pl
Lititz PA 17543

Call Sign: W3PAT
Robert J Key Sr
5 Irvin Dr
Lititz PA 17543

Call Sign: K3TBQ
Robert J Key Sr
5 Irvin Dr
Lititz PA 17543

Call Sign: N6CFQ
Charles E Carpenter
5 Japonica Dr
Lititz PA 17543

Call Sign: W3FKF
Edward L Rogers
2601 Kissel Hill Rd
Lititz PA 175439227

Call Sign: KB3IET
Elisha T Bomberger
851 Kreider Rd
Lititz PA 17543

Call Sign: KB3BQL
Rebecca A Watson
12 Lakeview Dr
Lititz PA 17543

Call Sign: N3CGL
Glenn H Landis
711 Laurel Ave
Lititz PA 17540

Call Sign: N3OHK
Chad M Ochs
119 Laurie Ln
Lititz PA 17543

Call Sign: N3NAW
Daniel J Hugo
134 Liberty St
Lititz PA 17543

Call Sign: N3GZP
Daniel L Martin
801 Lincoln Rd
Lititz PA 17543

Call Sign: N3IRK
Jerilyn K Martin
801 Lincoln Rd
Lititz PA 17543

Call Sign: N3RDN
Kyle J Martin
801 Lincoln Rd
Lititz PA 17543

Call Sign: N3TGA
Dane M Martin
801 Lincoln Rd
Lititz PA 17543

Call Sign: N3XYX
Trent D Martin
801 Lincoln Rd
Lititz PA 17543

Call Sign: KB3NHI
Josh I Miller
803 Lititz Pike
Lititz PA 17543

Call Sign: K3III
PA Dutch Dx Club
Long Ln
Lititz PA 17543

Call Sign: N3BNA
Dale E Long
Long Ln
Lititz PA 17543

Call Sign: KB3PBS
Adam C Gardner
214 Lyndam Ln
Lititz PA 17543

Call Sign: N3VKH
Russell E Campbell
2052 Main St
Lititz PA 17543

Call Sign: WB3GRK
Kerry L Stauffer
6 Meadow Brook Ln
Lititz PA 17543

Call Sign: KB3DXF
Max K Hughes
173 Middle Creek Rd
Lititz PA 17543

Call Sign: N3VDZ
Vicky L Martin
850 Middle Creek Rd
Lititz PA 17543

Call Sign: AA3OO
Galen W Martin
850 Middlecreek Rd
Lititz PA 17543

Call Sign: KB3PYJ
Annette M Hughes
830 Millway Rd
Lititz PA 17543

Call Sign: N3YS
Daniel A Rutherford
135 Moorland Ct
Lititz PA 17543

Call Sign: KD3SK
William A Clark Jr
410 N Elm St
Lititz PA 17543

Call Sign: K4NNL
James D Miller Jr
342 N Farm Dr
Lititz PA 17543

Call Sign: KA3HGG
Bryan L Harmes
324 N New St
Lititz PA 17543

Call Sign: N3RZ
Frank G Renz
11 N New St Rear
Lititz PA 17543

Call Sign: WA2WSH
Carl K Metzler
105 Northview Rd
Lititz PA 17543

Call Sign: N6DMR
Duane M Reese
531 Oak Ln
Lititz PA 17543

Call Sign: N3DSU
George D Fox
1721 Old Rothsville Rd
Lititz PA 175439036

Call Sign: KB3KIK
William H Lau
321 Owl Hill Rd
Lititz PA 17543

Call Sign: W3KFI
George H Hockenbrocht
23 Pebble Creek Dr
Lititz PA 17543

Call Sign: KE3BW
Barth B Bailey Jr
23 Pennwick Dr
Lititz PA 17543

Call Sign: N3WNH
Edward Coyle
130 Pepperton Ct
Lititz PA 17543

Call Sign: KB3JQD
Arthur G Kolgen
16 Picnic Woods Cir
Lititz PA 17543

Call Sign: KA3DDA
Philip L Martin
1011 Pine Hill Rd
Lititz PA 17543

Call Sign: KB3KIN
Grant K Beauchamp
2909 Pointe Blvd
Lititz PA 17543

Call Sign: KA3FGH
Florence P Bouder
910 Rabbit Hill Rd
Lititz PA 17543

Call Sign: KA3CNT
Ronald T Bouder Sr
910 Rabbit Hill Rd
Lititz PA 175439112

Call Sign: KB3UQN
Christian A Reese
83 Robinhill Dr
Lititz PA 175437504

Call Sign: N6CAR
Christian A Reese
83 Robinhill Dr
Lititz PA 175437504

Call Sign: WB3CTA
Allen D Rojahn
119 Rothsville Station Rd
Lititz PA 17543

Call Sign: N3KCU
Isaac S Martin
1921 Routhsville Rd
Lititz PA 17543

Call Sign: KB3LHR
George A Kervin
330 Rumford Rd
Lititz PA 17543

Call Sign: KA3JGF
John H Himmelberger
23 S Cedar St
Lititz PA 17543

Call Sign: KU3G
John M Votano
790 S Cedar St
Lititz PA 17543

Call Sign: KB3EYG
David R Toews
118 S Oak St
Lititz PA 17543

Call Sign: N3AY
Willis E Cole
222 S Spruce St
Lititz PA 175432316

Call Sign: N3JOW
Carlton B Walls III
625 S Spruce St
Lititz PA 17543

Call Sign: N3VRA
Steven L Heffley
31 Santa Fe Dr
Lititz PA 17543

Call Sign: KB3DRC
Charles J Vance
101 Saybrooke Dr
Lititz PA 17543

Call Sign: KB3KIM
Bruce R Sheaffer Jr
8 Strawberry Ln
Lititz PA 17543

Call Sign: N3YCE
Ann L Watson
126 W Newport Rd
Lititz PA 17543

Call Sign: KB3MFA
Daryl Waraksa
616 Shelley Ct
Lititz PA 17543

Call Sign: WB3HCZ
George T Warner
461 Sturbridge Dr
Lititz PA 17543

Call Sign: N3YZY
Kurt N Lauderman
214 W Newport Rd
Lititz PA 17543

Call Sign: KA3QPC
Harold H Hoover
38 Skyview
Lititz PA 17543

Call Sign: WA3NXO
David W Hirneisen
21 Sunset Ln
Lititz PA 17543

Call Sign: K3KJK
Herbert L Rogers
394 W Newport Rd
Lititz PA 175439433

Call Sign: KD7LZA
Philip E Norris
205 Snavely Mill Rd
Lititz PA 175438913

Call Sign: KB3YDK
Patrick J Osborne
607 Thornberry Ln
Lititz PA 17543

Call Sign: W3MRG
Mark R Gamber
741 Wallingford Rd
Lititz PA 17543

Call Sign: W3PL
J Paul Lyet
4 Southview Ln
Lititz PA 17543

Call Sign: W3GJA
Darlene J Lehman
225 W 28th Div Hwy
Lititz PA 175439563

Call Sign: KB3SBM
David A Bjanes
730 Webster Hill Rd
Lititz PA 17543

Call Sign: K3SZY
Ronald L Sandhaus
533 Spring Ave
Lititz PA 17543

Call Sign: N3VTC
Stephen K Pfaff Jr
732 W Brubaker Valley Rd
Lititz PA 17543

Call Sign: N3QIF
Harry C Eastburn
5 Wicker Dr
Lititz PA 17543

Call Sign: W3AJJ
Ronald L Sandhaus
533 Spring Ave
Lititz PA 17543

Call Sign: KB3PBR
David A Shaffer Jr
16 W Lemon St Apt 3
Lititz PA 17543

Call Sign: KB3VCY
Terence S Young
603 Wickshire Cir
Lititz PA 17543

Call Sign: KD3NS
Frederick T Vander Poel
300 St Mark Ave 2232
Lititz PA 17543

Call Sign: N3SWJ
Richard E Watson
126 W Newport Rd
Lititz PA 17543

Call Sign: KB3WTZ
Ronald J Angle
117 Winterhill Rd
Lititz PA 17543

Call Sign: W1PEQ
William A Drebert
300 St Mark Ave Apt 2242
Lititz PA 17543

Call Sign: N3XRK
Andrew D Watson
126 W Newport Rd
Lititz PA 17543

Call Sign: N3HQN
Thomas A Ridder Jr
508 Woodcrest Ave
Lititz PA 17543

Call Sign: WA3AUE
Harry R Neidermyer
748 Woodfield Dr
Lititz PA 17543

Call Sign: K3UGH
William S Muehling
440 Yummerdall Rd
Lititz PA 17543

Call Sign: KB3ZV
Stephen R Bartle
Lititz PA 175430185

FCC Amateur Radio Licenses in Little Marsh

Call Sign: WB3EUE
Carl E Kimble
Box 928
Little Marsh PA 16931

Call Sign: WB3KER
Donald E Gilman
Mosher Rd
Little Marsh PA 16950

FCC Amateur Radio Licenses in Littlestown

Call Sign: KB3TIN
Jakob W Hensley
30 Babylon Rd
Littlestown PA 17340

Call Sign: W3GMZ
Charles A Little
5061 Baltimore Pike
Littlestown PA 17340

Call Sign: KB3EMY
Michael J Cahill
6060 Baltimore Pike
Littlestown PA 173409504

Call Sign: KO4A
Harold J Kohl Jr
6630 Baltimore Pike
Littlestown PA 17340

Call Sign: N3BYT
Annis J Kohl
6630 Baltimore Pike
Littlestown PA 17340

Call Sign: KB2VST
Simon J Reid
1145 Bollinger Rd
Littlestown PA 17340

Call Sign: KE3WB
Colin Mackay
1145 Bollinger Rd
Littlestown PA 17340

Call Sign: KF2SD
Thomas A Reid
1145 Bollinger Rd
Littlestown PA 17340

Call Sign: KF3T
Thomas A Reid
1145 Bollinger Rd
Littlestown PA 17340

Call Sign: N3XQF
Edward G Hook
190 Feeser Rd
Littlestown PA 17340

Call Sign: N3ST
Bryan K Dorbert
99 Feeser Rd
Littlestown PA 17340

Call Sign: WA3ZVY
Stanley B Wharton
11 Fieldcrest Dr
Littlestown PA 17340

Call Sign: WA3PIQ
Terry J Scholle
586 Fish Game Rd
Littlestown PA 17340

Call Sign: N3KBM
Robert W Shank Jr
Georgetown Rd
Littlestown PA 17340

Call Sign: NE3P
Page K Evans
798 Gettysburg Rd
Littlestown PA 17340

Call Sign: K2ATH
Edward V Migdalski
949 Gettysburg Rd
Littlestown PA 17340

Call Sign: K3QKF
Carroll C Crum
111 Harney Rd
Littlestown PA 17340

Call Sign: N3HPO
Mary Jane Wolfgang
9 Kensington Dr
Littlestown PA 17340

Call Sign: NZ3J
William M Wolfgang
9 Kensington Dr
Littlestown PA 17340

Call Sign: KX3Z
Fred T Erskine III
135 Kensington Dr
Littlestown PA 173409767

Call Sign: N3TBZ
Dolores A Erskine
135 Kensington Dr
Littlestown PA 173409767

Call Sign: KB3DDG
John R Bynaker Jr
149 Lumber St
Littlestown PA 17340

Call Sign: K7YW
Leonard J Kersheskey
420 Mathias Rd
Littlestown PA 17340

Call Sign: W3QLP
Harold D Camlin
109 Mt Carmel Dr
Littlestown PA 173401545

Call Sign: WB3JCK
Ronald C Duck
228 N Queen
Littlestown PA 17340

Call Sign: AA3RJ
John F Fischbach Sr
6 Newark St
Littlestown PA 17340

Call Sign: N2TKP
Henry M Seamon
1090 Orphanage Rd
Littlestown PA 17340

Call Sign: WB3EWB
Wilbur S Reindollar
72 Patrick Ave
Littlestown PA 173401128

Call Sign: KM6VX
Jay A Beamer
87 Prince St
Littlestown PA 17340

Call Sign: AA3IB
Phillip D Buckner II
436 S Columbus Ave
Littlestown PA 17340

Call Sign: KB3WVB
Ryan J Ruby
448 S Columbus Ave
Littlestown PA 17340

Call Sign: N3NKA
Douglas D Engelhardt
302 Shottie Rd
Littlestown PA 17340

Call Sign: KD3ZQ
Eugene R Adams
45 Stayman Way
Littlestown PA 17340

Call Sign: KA3HCO
Richard A Wisotzkey
206 W King St
Littlestown PA 17340

Call Sign: K3TNM
William J Bennett
102 Wheaton Dr
Littlestown PA 17340

FCC Amateur Radio Licenses in Liverpool

Call Sign: WB3FOE
Ralph F De Prisco
Box 107
Liverpool PA 17045

Call Sign: N3SPB
Clint A Heiser
Box 243 H
Liverpool PA 17045

Call Sign: N3ODU
Robert A Doren Jr
Box 341
Liverpool PA 17045

Call Sign: NO3O

Earl Blangger
Box 55B
Liverpool PA 17045

Call Sign: K3GLK
Larry Winemiller
350 Mountain Rd
Liverpool PA 170459250

Call Sign: WN3V
John R Miller
228 Wildcat Trl
Liverpool PA 17045

Call Sign: KB3LTB
Toshimitsu Sonobe
228 Wildcat Trl
Liverpool PA 17045

FCC Amateur Radio Licenses in Lock Haven

Call Sign: N3EBA
Frank J Whitecavage
16 Blackforest Acres
Lock Haven PA 17769

Call Sign: W3DR
Carl E Johnson
Box 114
Lock Haven PA
177459524

Call Sign: KB3FUO
Dwayne L Davis Sr
Box 52
Lock Haven PA 17745

Call Sign: KB3FZG
Kelli J Davis
Box 52
Lock Haven PA 17745

Call Sign: KB3EFB
Wayne M Royer

Box 9A
Lock Haven PA 17745

Call Sign: KB3FNO
Susan M Royer
Box 9A
Lock Haven PA 17745

Call Sign: N3JCG
Robert A Edmonston
315 Center St
Lock Haven PA 17745

Call Sign: N4CSM
Robert A Edmonston
315 Center St
Lock Haven PA 17745

Call Sign: WC3AAA
Clinton County Pa Civil
Defense
22 Cree Dr Clinton Co
Comm Cntr
Lock Haven PA 17745

Call Sign: KB3POL
Clinton County Pa Civil
Defense
22 Cree Dr Comm Cntr
Lock Haven PA 17745

Call Sign: KA3EWS
Willis B Merrifield
443 Derr Hill Rd
Lock Haven PA 17745

Call Sign: N3HTC
Harold T Chubb
418 E Bald Eagle St
Lock Haven PA 17745

Call Sign: KB3TSB
Jon A Gray
806 E Water St
Lock Haven PA 17745

Call Sign: K3WMR
Wayne M Royer
E Water St
Lock Haven PA 17745

Call Sign: KB3SMG
Susan M Royer
E Water St
Lock Haven PA 17745

Call Sign: N3ZQI
Shawn D Eyer
783 Gravel Hill Rd
Lock Haven PA 17745

Call Sign: K3KR
John B Kruk
408 Irwin St
Lock Haven PA 17745

Call Sign: KB3TSM
Tyler R Wooding
27 Linnet Ln
Lock Haven PA 17745

Call Sign: W3WSM
Earl L Lentz Jr
119 N Summit
Lock Haven PA 17745

Call Sign: WA3D
Timothy P Yoho
25 Pond Dr
Lock Haven PA 17745

Call Sign: N3YMN
Lester C Patterson
Rr 2
Lock Haven PA 17745

Call Sign: KB3EIC
Troy A Smith
119 S Fairview St
Lock Haven PA 17745

Call Sign: KB3EPH
Bobbie J Smith
119 S Fairview St
Lock Haven PA 17745

Call Sign: KB3ACS
Gerald Cierpilowski
224 Susquehanna Ave
Lock Haven PA 17745

Call Sign: KB3NUU
Steven Katz
2225 Teaberry Ln
Lock Haven PA 17745

Call Sign: KB3HPZ
Chris S Newberry
1017 W 4th St
Lock Haven PA 17745

Call Sign: KB3EPF
Floyd W Newberry III
1017 W 4th St
Lock Haven PA 17745

Call Sign: KB3EPG
Floyd W Newberry IV
1017 W 4th St
Lock Haven PA
177452601

Call Sign: KB3FZJ
Jason J Smith
38 W Cardinal Dr
Lock Haven PA 17745

Call Sign: K3WHO
Jason J Smith
38 W Cardinal Dr
Lock Haven PA 17745

Call Sign: KB3VTW
Ryhor Harbacheuski
419 W Main St

Lock Haven PA 17745

Call Sign: NI3N
Ryhor Harbacheuski
419 W Main St
Lock Haven PA 17745

Call Sign: W3NW
Ryhor Harbacheuski
419 W Main St
Lock Haven PA 17745

Call Sign: W3EAY
Leo E Ritter
710 W Walnut St
Lock Haven PA 17745

Call Sign: N3LS
Larry D Sonnie Jr
210 Walton Rd
Lock Haven PA 17745

Call Sign: KB3TII
Scott D Vairo
806 Water St
Lock Haven PA 17745

Call Sign: KB3HET
David A Ammerman
699 Woods Ave
Lock Haven PA 17745

Call Sign: KB3JPO
Roberta L Maxson
699 Woods Ave
Lock Haven PA 17745

Call Sign: N3VTB
Stephen K Pfaff
132 Woodward Ave
Lock Haven PA 17745

Call Sign: W3SKP
Stephen K Pfaff
132 Woodward Ave

Lock Haven PA 17745

Call Sign: KB3FCC
Bruce J Porritt
208 Young Ave
Lock Haven PA 17745

FCC Amateur Radio Licenses in Locustdale

Call Sign: N3LMA
Lori A Wetzel
3118 Main St
Locustdale PA 17945

FCC Amateur Radio Licenses in Loganton

Call Sign: WA2JLE
Arnold M Majerle
2407 E Winter Rd
Loganton PA 17747

Call Sign: N3AIX
James P Breon
1133 Summer Mtn Rd
Loganton PA 17747

Call Sign: N3NCD
Dean C Karstetter
36 Wolfe Ln
Loganton PA 17747

FCC Amateur Radio Licenses in Loganville

Call Sign: WB3AWJ
Robert A Poff
3 N Main St
Loganville PA 17342

Call Sign: KB3AVI
Linda J Kiser
13 S Main
Loganville PA 17342

Call Sign: W3SBA
Susquehanna Radio Club
Loganville PA 17342

FCC Amateur Radio Licenses in Loretto

Call Sign: KB3DRH
Raymond J Bradley
156 Kelly Dr
Loretto PA 15940

FCC Amateur Radio Licenses in Loysville

Call Sign: N3LUV
H Matt Johnson
Box 107M
Loysville PA 17047

Call Sign: KB3BVM
David L Mcmillen
Box 22B
Loysville PA 17047

Call Sign: KB3FNB
Gloria K Miller
Box 66
Loysville PA 17047

Call Sign: N3KNY
Charles P McGarvey
Rt 17 Rd 1
Loysville PA 17047

Call Sign: KB3CVO
Thomas A Miller
5038 Shermans Valley Rd
Loysville PA 17047

FCC Amateur Radio Licenses in Luthersburg

Call Sign: KB3YJF

James B Withers
9177 Coal Hill Rd
Luthersburg PA 15848

Call Sign: KD3BD
Mark I Gearhart
744 Evergreen Rd
Luthersburg PA 15848

Call Sign: KC8COZ
Robert D Glaze Jr
419 Ridge Rd
Luthersburg PA 15848

Call Sign: KC8DCC
Russell R Glaze
419 Ridge Rd
Luthersburg PA 15848

FCC Amateur Radio Licenses in Lykens

Call Sign: N3YAA
Casey V Geiman
199 Center St
Lykens PA 17048

Call Sign: KB3HJS
Donald R Kunst
547 Luxemburg Rd
Lykens PA 17048

Call Sign: W3LNE
Donald R Kunst
547 Luxemburg Rd
Lykens PA 17048

Call Sign: KB3LEZ
Garrison T Kunst
547 Luxemburg Rd
Lykens PA 17048

Call Sign: KA3UJE
Terry L Sherman
665 Main St

Lykens PA 17048

Call Sign: N3NDH
David R Waters
768 Main St
Lykens PA 17048

Call Sign: AB3MZ
David R Waters
768 Main St
Lykens PA 17048

Call Sign: KB3UJF
James E Hoffman
226 Market St
Lykens PA 17048

Call Sign: N3RCL
Larry S Bingaman
636 N 2nd St
Lykens PA 17048

Call Sign: WA3YMQ
Karl B Dietrich
1160 N 2nd St
Lykens PA 17048

Call Sign: KC3RZ
Ralph E Lebo Jr
1205 N 2nd St
Lykens PA 17048

Call Sign: KE6KKI
Robert L Witmer Sr
704 Parkview Rd
Lykens PA 170481517

Call Sign: K3SPU
Harl H Heckert
540 S 2nd St
Lykens PA 17048

Call Sign: WA3URX
Thomas L Buffington
5624 State Rt 209

Lykens PA 170488412

Call Sign: KE4DWV
Paula J McDaniels
457 W Middle Rd
Lykens PA 170488827

Call Sign: W4BIX
Jeffrey M Bixby
457 W Middle Rd
Lykens PA 170488827

Call Sign: KB3UJG
Andrew G Reiner
Lykens PA 17048

FCC Amateur Radio Licenses in Mackeyville

Call Sign: N3WGR
Joseph M Kitchen
74 Rag Valley Rd
Mackeyville PA 17750

FCC Amateur Radio Licenses in Madera

Call Sign: K3AAA
Jan C Hubler
52 Hickory Alley
Madera PA 16661

Call Sign: KI4DSA
Sonja M Melander
424 Spruce St
Madera PA 16661

Call Sign: KG4CXJ
Davita C Melander
424 Spruce St
Madera PA 16661

Call Sign: KA6HQJ
Dolores A Gilbert
231 Substation Rd

Madera PA 166619711

Call Sign: KB6GBP
Donald E Gilbert
Substation Rd Hc 1
Madera PA 166619711

Call Sign: N3ODQ
Kenneth W Shick
Madera PA 16661

Call Sign: W3NFH
William H Knoedler
Madera PA 16661

FCC Amateur Radio Licenses in Madisonburg

Call Sign: N3PIV
James M Abbott
Madisonburg PA 16852

FCC Amateur Radio Licenses in Mahaffey

Call Sign: KA3UKB
Thomas R Hoch
Box 304
Mahaffey PA 15757

Call Sign: KA3UKC
Mark E Hoch
Box 304
Mahaffey PA 15757

Call Sign: KA3UKD
Daniel E Hoch
Box 304
Mahaffey PA 15757

Call Sign: W3SJK
Earl L Fowkes
Box 407
Mahaffey PA 15757

Call Sign: N3VRM
C Thomas Robinson
Box 742
Mahaffey PA 15757

Call Sign: W3KWT
C Thomas Robinson
2856 Cecil Hurd Hwy
Mahaffey PA 15757

Call Sign: K3VFW
C Thomas Robinson
2856 Cecil Hurd Hwy
Mahaffey PA 15757

Call Sign: W3HT
Don E Dimmick
9754 Ridge Rd
Mahaffey PA 15757

FCC Amateur Radio Licenses in Mainesburg

Call Sign: N3XJE
Nicholas Lalic
212 Old Mill Rd
Mainesburg PA 16932

Call Sign: WB3DXW
Philip H Zagozewski
285 Tice Rd
Mainesburg PA 16932

Call Sign: N3QNI
Gary D Pelton
Mainesburg PA 16932

FCC Amateur Radio Licenses in Manchester

Call Sign: N3MVP
Donald M Huppman Jr
660 Bowers Bridge Rd
Manchester PA 17345

Call Sign: N3NSB
Nancy J Huppman
660 Bowers Bridge Rd
Manchester PA 17345

Call Sign: KA3VDD
Raymond C Orendorff
1690 Canal Rd Ext
Manchester PA 17345

Call Sign: N3FDJ
Andrew H Seville
565 Cassel Rd
Manchester PA 17345

Call Sign: KB3LHY
Mark E Baier
75 Cold Springs Dr
Manchester PA 17345

Call Sign: KC8GUW
Therlda K Chronister
114 Cooper St
Manchester PA 17345

Call Sign: N3SUG
Kathy L Ness
81 Dogwood Ct
Manchester PA 17345

Call Sign: KB3CHB
Dan B Blair
45 Evergreen Ter
Manchester PA 17345

Call Sign: KA3TFH
Dorsey M Lombardo
83 Greenfield St
Manchester PA 173459525

Call Sign: N3BSL
Lisa M Martin
35 Hickory Dr
Manchester PA 17345

Call Sign: WB3BZA
Clarence E Stambaugh
54 N Main St
Manchester PA 17345

Call Sign: N3BNQ
William A Ribblett
72 Pinetree Rd
Manchester PA 17345

Call Sign: WA3IVP
Charles W Bowers
19 S Main St
Manchester PA 17345

Call Sign: KA3PXC
Dale E Miller
5780 Susquehanna Trl
Manchester PA 17345

Call Sign: K3PXC
Dale E Miller
5780 Susquehanna Trl
Manchester PA 17345

Call Sign: K3MTD
Madeleine L Strong
910 Woodland Ave
Manchester PA 17345

Call Sign: K3QLA
Silvion B Freeman
222 York St
Manchester PA 173451198

**FCC Amateur Radio
Licenses in Manheim**

Call Sign: N3ROF
John S Drager
1734 Becker Rd
Manheim PA 17545

Call Sign: KB3AKV
David B Wilson

Box 505 Cornell Ave
Manheim PA 17545

Call Sign: WB3BJG
Dennis R Kready
Box 85
Manheim PA 17545

Call Sign: KB3VVO
Michael P Votano
2646 Camp Rd
Manheim PA 17545

Call Sign: WA3SXQ
Jerry Williamson
396 Church Rd
Manheim PA 17545

Call Sign: WB3DDZ
Mark A Spangler
484 Cider Press Rd
Manheim PA 175459527

Call Sign: KB3OOK
Colleen G Mcmonigal
122 E Logan Ave
Manheim PA 17545

Call Sign: KB3TOO
Levi A Stoltzfus
524 E Pleasant View Rd
Manheim PA 17545

Call Sign: NI3Y
Kenneth J Hartzler
639 E Pleasant View Rd
Manheim PA 17545

Call Sign: KB3PSK
Andrew J Wills
7069 Elizabethtown Rd
Manheim PA 17545

Call Sign: KB3YDQ
Jonathan R Wills

7069 Elizabethtown Rd
Manheim PA 17545

Call Sign: KB3YDH
Maria E Moll
7069 Elizabethtown Rd
Manheim PA 17545

Call Sign: KB3YDG
Elizabeth A Loverso
7071 Elizabethtown Rd
Manheim PA 17545

Call Sign: WA3FPN
Michael D Breneman
3961 Elizabethtown Rd
Manheim PA 17545

Call Sign: N3ZZB
Michael H Wills
7069 Elizabethtown Rd
Manheim PA 17545

Call Sign: WB3CTK
Claude H Hess
458 Fruitville Pike
Manheim PA 17545

Call Sign: N3ZKX
John W Reed
260 Grandview Dr
Manheim PA 17545

Call Sign: KB3VKD
Tobias J Ahnert
673 Green Ridge Dr
Manheim PA 17545

Call Sign: KB3JOH
Harry S Strother
1052 Hemlock Cir
Manheim PA 17545

Call Sign: KB3NRP
Solomon J Rudy

891 Hossler Rd
Manheim PA 17545

1414 Mountain Rd
Manheim PA 17545

1357 Newport Rd
Manheim PA 17545

Call Sign: WB3DQD
Conrad E Nasatka
1904 Hossler Rd
Manheim PA 17545

Call Sign: WB3HLG
Peter D Weiss
123 N Clay St
Manheim PA 17545

Call Sign: KB3QBS
Nathan C Horst
1640 Newport Rd
Manheim PA 17545

Call Sign: KA3WBH
Shannon Brown
1419 Jerry Ln
Manheim PA 17545

Call Sign: KE4SUR
James R Silvius
165 N Grant St
Manheim PA 17545

Call Sign: NR3J
Stephen P Morris Sr
1986 Oak Ln
Manheim PA 17545

Call Sign: KC3PB
Gary Hopkins
2184 Kilmer Rd
Manheim PA 17545

Call Sign: KB3FVO
Douglas D Goss
16 N Hazel St
Manheim PA 17545

Call Sign: KB3LCG
Michael S Sobeck
626 Oak Tree Rd
Manheim PA 17545

Call Sign: KB3RSV
Heidi L Testa
1167 Lebabon Rd
Manheim PA 17545

Call Sign: KD3YW
Peter H Schilling
1230 N Penryn Rd
Manheim PA 175457245

Call Sign: KA3RSJ
Larry S Steffy
940 Orchard Rd
Manheim PA 17545

Call Sign: WA3KQX
Kenneth E Harnly
1321 Lititz Rd
Manheim PA 17545

Call Sign: N3VDX
Eugene M Phillips
45 N Wolf St Apt 1
Manheim PA 17545

Call Sign: KA3DJK
Larry J Zook
816 Park Hill Dr
Manheim PA 17545

Call Sign: W3KBK
James L Grant
208 Maple Ave
Manheim PA 17545

Call Sign: W3DL
Doug Lefever
1316 Newport Rd
Manheim PA 17545

Call Sign: K3GZX
Michael D Koth
2836 Pinch Rd
Manheim PA 17545

Call Sign: W3WBQ
Robert K Famous
216 Maple Ave
Manheim PA 17545

Call Sign: KB3QYU
Jere D Lefever
1316 Newport Rd
Manheim PA 17545

Call Sign: N3LTP
Troy G Frey
204 Rapho St
Manheim PA 175451133

Call Sign: N3CKJ
William J Randolph
22 Miller Dr
Manheim PA 17545

Call Sign: N3NXX
Jere D Lefever
1316 Newport Rd
Manheim PA 17545

Call Sign: KB3SCD
Kyle J Hibshman
S Charlot St
Manheim PA 17545

Call Sign: KA3DBD
Peggy A Hoffer

Call Sign: WX3Y
Larry S Harman

Call Sign: W3MSS
Paul E Collier

3 S Charlotte St
Manheim PA 17545

Call Sign: KS3C
Ed A Rineer Jr
129 S Charlotte St
Manheim PA 17545

Call Sign: N3GNF
David M Miller
688 S Chiques Rd
Manheim PA 17545

Call Sign: N3HQR
Lorraine D Shellenberger
688 S Chiques Rd
Manheim PA 17545

Call Sign: K3LNG
J Harold Esbenshade
222 S Esbenshade Rd
Manheim PA 175459129

Call Sign: KB3RSM
Ronald D Baier
109 S Fulton St
Manheim PA 17545

Call Sign: KB3UAF
James G Mensch
44 S Linden St
Manheim PA 17545

Call Sign: WA3OTS
David E Ristenbatt
1224 Shumaker Rd
Manheim PA 17545

Call Sign: KB3LHS
Tammy L Roberts
2666 Shumaker Rd
Manheim PA 17545

Call Sign: N3VNO
Louis M Mangini

2274 Sunnyside Rd
Manheim PA 175459673

Call Sign: K3QCB
George H May
402 Thrush Dr
Manheim PA 17545

Call Sign: N3UEA
Christopher J Buchmoyer
73 Veterans Alley
Manheim PA 17545

Call Sign: WB2YIY
Joseph E Podlucky
25 W End Ave
Manheim PA 17545

Call Sign: KB3MEW
William D Mahan
253 W Hernley Rd
Manheim PA 17545

Call Sign: K3QF
Jonathan E Rudy
608 W High St
Manheim PA 17545

Call Sign: K3CIP
Carolyn P Rudy
608 W High St
Manheim PA 17545

Call Sign: KB3NRQ
David Rudy
608 W High St
Manheim PA 17545

Call Sign: K3SOL
Solomon J Rudy
608 W High St
Manheim PA 17545

Call Sign: K3OGX
D Ernest Weinhold

107 W Sun Hill Rd
Manheim PA 175452352

Call Sign: KB3YHZ
Cory M Gehr
1843 Wisgarver Rd
Manheim PA 17545

Call Sign: WA3MGO
William E Storck
3506 Echo Valley Rd
Manhiem PA 17545

Call Sign: KB3PBU
Walter D Roth
521 Graystone Rd
Manhiem PA 17545

FCC Amateur Radio Licenses in Manns Choice

Call Sign: KA3AKH
Dennis C Wertz
Box 159
Manns Choice PA 15550

Call Sign: KA3BNF
Janet L Wertz
Box 159
Manns Choice PA 15550

Call Sign: KB3UUT
Joseph L Prugh
205 Main St
Manns Choice PA 15550

Call Sign: AB3LP
Joseph L Prugh
205 Main St
Manns Choice PA 15550

Call Sign: KB4MQO
H Clay Thomas III
4432 Milligans Cove Rd

Manns Choice PA 15550

Call Sign: N3BNJ
Donald E James
6466 Milligans Cove Rd
Manns Choice PA 15550

Call Sign: KA3UDR
Steven G Elliott
368 Rest Home Rd
Manns Choice PA 15550

FCC Amateur Radio Licenses in Mansfield

Call Sign: WB2DLR
Clifton T Holmes
19 3rd St
Mansfield PA 16933

Call Sign: WB3DDO
Morris F Morgan
73 4th St
Mansfield PA 16933

Call Sign: N3JTK
Ryan M Giles
24 Bailey Creek Rd
Mansfield PA 169339105

Call Sign: K3PSO
Edward S Smith
Box 1074
Mansfield PA 16933

Call Sign: K3ZWA
Eugene S Kraybill
Box 1942
Mansfield PA 16933

Call Sign: KB3KBA
Ryan M Giles
Box 2045
Mansfield PA 16933

Call Sign: N3NQV
Gary L Gravatt
Box 262
Mansfield PA 16933

Call Sign: KA3AHA
Harry L Wimbrough
Box 462
Mansfield PA 16933

Call Sign: K3CKB
Howard J Wimbrough Jr
Box 463
Mansfield PA 16933

Call Sign: WB3DLK
Lenore M Wimbrough
Box 463
Mansfield PA 16933

Call Sign: N3YMQ
Ben J Briggs
Box 996
Mansfield PA 16933

Call Sign: WB2LPC
Anthony J Kiessling
57 Coles St
Mansfield PA 16933

Call Sign: KB3IEG
Susan L Greene
293 Daniels Rd
Mansfield PA 16933

Call Sign: K3ESK
Eugene S Kraybill
122 Drovers Ln
Mansfield PA 169330000

Call Sign: KA3OMI
George W Wheeler III
Kellytown Rd
Mansfield PA 16933

Call Sign: WB3DGI
Ernest D Johnston
373 Mulberry Hill Rd
Mansfield PA 16933

Call Sign: WA3TLP
Robert E Dalton Sr
263 Mulberry Ln
Mansfield PA 16933

Call Sign: WB3AJD
Carol J Dalton
263 Mulberry Ln
Mansfield PA 16933

Call Sign: KA3BCJ
Eleanor C Zagozewski
72 N Main St
Mansfield PA 16933

Call Sign: KA3AWN
Coralee L Owlett
15724 Rt 6
Mansfield PA 16933

Call Sign: W3VEG
John B Owlett
15724 Rt 6
Mansfield PA 16933

Call Sign: KD3NY
Margaret A Cleveland
962 S Main St Lot 1
Mansfield PA 169330433

Call Sign: KB3MYF
Joshua M Kunzmann
8 Sherwood St
Mansfield PA 16933

Call Sign: KA3UDV
James L Weiskopff
1635 Spencer Rd
Mansfield PA 16933

Call Sign: N3RSY
Michael J Weiskopff
1635 Spencer Rd
Mansfield PA 16933

Call Sign: N3FE
Corey H Dean
175 Warren Ln
Mansfield PA 16933

Call Sign: KG4P
James Casto
151 Welch Rd
Mansfield PA 169338424

Call Sign: WB3DLM
James L Ames
Mansfield PA 16933

Call Sign: N3WFD
Jeffrey L Evans
Mansfield PA 16933

Call Sign: KD3NU
Ralph J Cleveland
Mansfield PA 169330433

Call Sign: KF3Q
Ralph J Cleveland
Mansfield PA 169330433

FCC Amateur Radio Licenses in Mapleton Depot

Call Sign: N3QXD
Richard L Heaster
9534 Birdvale Rd
Mapleton Depot PA 17052

Call Sign: K3PPN
Richard L Heaster
9534 Birdvale Rd
Mapleton Depot PA 17052

Call Sign: KB3PG
Hartsel G McClain
17804 Hares Valley Rd
Mapleton Depot PA 17052

Call Sign: WA3LEM
Richard C Wise
Hill St
Mapleton Depot PA 17052

Call Sign: K3PPM
Merrill W Rohrer
Mapleton Depot PA 17052

FCC Amateur Radio Licenses in Marietta

Call Sign: KB3MGE
William M Eckman Jr
83 Ashley Dr
Marietta PA 17547

Call Sign: KB3ENR
Matthew J Drybred
14 E Market St Apt 2
Marietta PA 17547

Call Sign: KB3OGT
Charles J Paetz
78 Engle Rd
Marietta PA 17547

Call Sign: KB3PIJ
Robin C Bradley
385 Essex St
Marietta PA 17547

Call Sign: N3KND
Robert C Spangler
26 Fairview Ave
Marietta PA 17547

Call Sign: N3MJW
Alphonse E Fischer III
28 Kline Rd

Marietta PA 17547

Call Sign: KB3DUA
Shawn M Brown
23 Lorraine Ave
Marietta PA 17547

Call Sign: N3RXW
Dennis E Ebersole
2750 Maytown Rd
Marietta PA 17547

Call Sign: WD3K
William A Stock
164 Nicole St
Marietta PA 17547

Call Sign: KB3WIK
Edward J Shelton
257 Red Cedar Ln
Marietta PA 17547

Call Sign: AB3MX
Earl W Beeler
1720 River Rd
Marietta PA 17547

Call Sign: N3CGX
Earl W Beeler
1720 River Rd
Marietta PA 17547

Call Sign: KB3GAG
Edward Smith
85 Stackstown Rd
Marietta PA 17547

Call Sign: N3NMJ
Richard S Bair
36 Thornapple Dr
Marietta PA 17547

Call Sign: WA3OUF
Richard S Stoutzenberger
23 W Market St

Marietta PA 17547

Call Sign: W3NPF
Miriam S Lenhert
135 W Market St
Marietta PA 17547

Call Sign: KB3MYJ
Evstratios G Stephanis
219 W Walnut St
Marietta PA 17547

Call Sign: N3PD
John E Begg
228 W Walnut St
Marietta PA 17547

Call Sign: N3ZSL
Allan J Begg
228 W Walnut St
Marietta PA 17547

Call Sign: K3GKB
Jesse C Wagner II
Marietta PA 175470507

FCC Amateur Radio Licenses in Marion Heights

Call Sign: KB3NYA
Larry G Stump
103 E Melrose St
Marion Heights PA 17832

Call Sign: N3GUS
George Romania
406 Melrose St
Marion Heights PA 17832

FCC Amateur Radio Licenses in Markleton

Call Sign: KB3IAT
John D Younkin

1035 Casselman Rd
Markleton PA 19551

Call Sign: N3JFE
Blair E Younkin Jr
139 Humbert Rd
Markleton PA 15551

Call Sign: N3NVK
Catherine A Ansell
259 Old Bethel Rd
Markleton PA 15551

FCC Amateur Radio Licenses in Martinsburg

Call Sign: KA3PPP
Raymond G Wolfe
Box 114A
Martinsburg PA
166629652

Call Sign: KB3JIH
William R Davis
Box 68
Martinsburg PA 16662

Call Sign: N3LAS
Robert H Wareham
Box 91
Martinsburg PA 16662

Call Sign: WB2DPC
George J Fest
515 Hershberger St
Martinsburg PA
166621007

Call Sign: AB3BX
George Fest
515 Hershberger St
Martinsburg PA
166621007

Call Sign: KB3DUU

Warren R Tenley
136 Madison Rd
Martinsburg PA 16662

Call Sign: WB3FIA
James J Ritchey
603 Meadow Ln
Martinsburg PA 16662

Call Sign: KB3SSJ
Ryan P Blough
606 Meadow Ln
Martinsburg PA 16662

Call Sign: KB3MZM
Daniel J Lipko
1702 Pulpit Rd
Martinsburg PA 16662

Call Sign: KB3YEO
Thomas J Hickey Jr
406 S Market St
Martinsburg PA 16662

Call Sign: K3AFA
Steven L Diehl
228 Village Way
Martinsburg PA 16662

FCC Amateur Radio Licenses in Marysville

Call Sign: N3QZD
Karl T Zimmerman
432 Cameron St
Marysville PA 17053

Call Sign: KB3NBU
Ashley E Olvera
5 Kemper Dr
Marysville PA 17053

Call Sign: KB3MWO
Laura C Leidig
100 Kings Hwy

Marysville PA 17053

Call Sign: KA3EET
Frederick S Horanic
200 Kings Hwy
Marysville PA 170539411

Call Sign: K3WSE
Truman H Wolf Jr
304 Myrtle Ave
Marysville PA 17053

Call Sign: KB3OZP
Alexandra M Flurie
1575 New Valley Rd
Marysville PA 17053

Call Sign: KB3EJZ
Gary L Hammaker
311 Pine St
Marysville PA 17053

Call Sign: KB3PBA
Gregory E Vodzak
3 Reed Dr
Marysville PA 17053

Call Sign: KB3LWN
Matthew R Schmick
135 Reed Dr
Marysville PA 17053

Call Sign: KB3IWY
Christina M Bottorf
222 S State Rd
Marysville PA 17053

Call Sign: KB3IYX
Tiffany M Stoudt
318 Spruce St
Marysville PA 17053

Call Sign: WA3WBU
John M Gayman
1869 Valley Rd

Marysville PA 17053

Call Sign: KB3LAI
Samuel D Palm
2908 Valley Rd
Marysville PA 17053

Call Sign: WA3BLJ
Richard E Sheaffer
3350 Valley Rd
Marysville PA 17053

Call Sign: AA3T
Nicholas J Rylatt
15 Weaver Dr
Marysville PA 17053

Call Sign: KB3OAG
Joshua N Gaidos
102 Woods Dr
Marysville PA 17053

Call Sign: N3CAV
Tyrone E Ditzler
Marysville PA 17053

FCC Amateur Radio Licenses in Maytown

Call Sign: KB3SCW
Jody C Spackman
120 S Arnold St
Maytown PA 17550

Call Sign: KB3TPK
Anthony D Jantzi
Maytown PA 17550

FCC Amateur Radio Licenses in McAlisterville

Call Sign: KA3ZJD
Rick W Bates
Box 158
McAlisterville PA 17049

FCC Amateur Radio Licenses in McClure

Call Sign: K3KDK
Robert L Dudick
10 Blair Ln
McClure PA 178419250

Call Sign: W3MCC
Mifflin County ARC
10 Blair Ln
McClure PA 17841

Call Sign: N3LUO
James W Holzman
Box 2175
McClure PA 17841

Call Sign: KA3UOL
Michael E Snook
58 Ertley Crossover Ln
McClure PA 17841

Call Sign: N3PFM
Marjorie J Snook
1047 Ertley Rd
McClure PA 17841

Call Sign: N3PJB
Larry L Snook
1047 Ertley Rd
McClure PA 17841

Call Sign: WB3IXP
Quentin T Wagner
High St
McClure PA 17841

Call Sign: WA3TRE
Donald E Swank
10 Oak Hill Dr
McClure PA 17841

Call Sign: N3XET

Glen E Wray Jr
Old Stage Rd
McClure PA 17841

Call Sign: WB3IOT
James A Wert
226 Pine Crest Dr
McClure PA 17841

Call Sign: N3TRR
Clifton H Bell III
180 Shawver Rd
McClure PA 17841

Call Sign: KB3GDJ
Jeffrey S Martin
7826 US Hwy 522 N
McClure PA 17841

Call Sign: AA3JM
Jeffrey S Martin
7826 US Hwy 522 N
McClure PA 17841

Call Sign: KA3DFB
Harold L Sharadin
McClure PA 17841

FCC Amateur Radio Licenses in McConnellsburg

Call Sign: KB3IJH
Nicholas P Erickson
162 Aughwick Rd
McConnellsburg PA 17233

Call Sign: KB3DJW
Mark S Eigendrode
251 Eigenbrode Dr
McConnellsburg PA 17233

Call Sign: KB3FYG
Trent K Clugston
19842 Great Cove Rd

McConnellsburg PA 17233

Call Sign: N3ZAJ
Rene W Clugston
20044 Great Cove Rd
McConnellsburg PA 17233

Call Sign: N3ZSO
Jennifer L Clugston
20044 Great Cove Rd
McConnellsburg PA 17233

Call Sign: KB3FYN
Warren E Clugston
20162 Great Cove Rd
McConnellsburg PA 17233

Call Sign: N3ZPY
Alan E Clugston
20164 Great Cove Rd
McConnellsburg PA 17233

Call Sign: KB3FYM
Wade A Clugston
279 Penns Dr
McConnellsburg PA 17233

Call Sign: K3PQX
Alex G Rouzer
223 S 7th St
McConnellsburg PA
172338787

Call Sign: KB3FYF
Kenton C Yoder
227 Tritle Dr
McConnellsburg PA 17233

Call Sign: KB3OMP
Esther L Brooks
McConnellsburg PA 17233

Call Sign: W3PAW
Paul A Wachter

McConnellsburg PA
172330062

FCC Amateur Radio Licenses in McElhattan

Call Sign: KB6QE
Hugh L Franklin
300 Cochise Trl
McElhattan PA 177480443

Call Sign: N8VBW
Wayne S Mathis
442 McElhattan Dr Lot 891
McElhattan PA 17748

FCC Amateur Radio Licenses in McKnightstown

Call Sign: KA4FED
Thomas T Cole
251 Pine Valley Rd
McKnightstown PA
173430047

FCC Amateur Radio Licenses in McSherrystown

Call Sign: KA3MOW
Miles B Brooks
30 Conewago Dr
McSherrystown PA 17334

Call Sign: KA3VGV
Patrick A Taylor
135 Main St
McSherrystown PA 17344

Call Sign: KB3HAX
Jerome J Kornaski
624 Main St
McSherrystown PA 17344

Call Sign: KB3VWU
David P Jacoby
136 N 2nd St
McSherrystown PA 17344

Call Sign: KA3ZVF
Gerald D Yoder
39 Littlebrick Rd
McVeytown PA 17051

Call Sign: N3TRQ
Melvin B Adams
9 N Water St
McVeytown PA
170510303

Call Sign: KB3ZN
Thomas L Mank
303 Turkey Dr
McVeytown PA 17051

Call Sign: KB3LPT
Robert F Ahern
266 Acorn Ct
Mechanicsburg PA 17055

Call Sign: W3OWL
William Frantz
813 Acri Rd
Mechanicsburg PA 17050

Call Sign: KB3FCR
Robert W Frantz
813 Acri Rd
Mechanicsburg PA 17055

Call Sign: KB3RZB

Kathleen M Steele
821 Acri Rd
Mechanicsburg PA 17050

Call Sign: KB3TSX
David J Bennett
859 Acri Rd
Mechanicsburg PA 17050

Call Sign: KB3NBW
Michael M Sariano
866 Acri Rd
Mechanicsburg PA 17050

Call Sign: KB3QPN
Kaitlin A Bolster
921 Acri Rd
Mechanicsburg PA 17050

Call Sign: KB3OVH
Michael R Bolster
921 Acri Rd
Mechanicsburg PA 17050

Call Sign: KB3QXA
Matthew J Donahue
3508 Ada Dr
Mechanicsburg PA 17050

Call Sign: KB3MWC
Anthony J Gabriel
3511 Ada Dr
Mechanicsburg PA 17050

Call Sign: KB3LWR
Patrick J Larkin
704 Alberta Ave
Mechanicsburg PA 17050

Call Sign: N3KYQ
Keith L Blaisdell
3612 Alberta Ave
Mechanicsburg PA 17055

Call Sign: N3BKI

Paul W McDonnell
508 Albright Dr
Mechanicsburg PA 17055

Call Sign: W3DAE
Champe C Pool
514 Albright Dr
Mechanicsburg PA
170554301

Call Sign: KB3KLZ
Michael T Delaney
912 Alison Ave
Mechanicsburg PA 17055

Call Sign: N3EZQ
William E Wertz
913 Alison Ave
Mechanicsburg PA 17055

Call Sign: KB3LPW
Amanda K Beauduy
905 Allendale Rd
Mechanicsburg PA 17055

Call Sign: W3CAJ
Robert E Brenizer
Allendale Rd
Mechanicsburg PA
170554466

Call Sign: KB3KYA
David B Jacoby
24 Andersontown Rd
Mechanicsburg PA 17055

Call Sign: WA3VPJ
Carl G Lex
202 Andersontown Rd
Mechanicsburg PA 17055

Call Sign: KB3LAM
Peter M Sawyer
14 Andes Dr
Mechanicsburg PA 17055

Call Sign: W9UWL
Peter M Sawyer
14 Andes Dr
Mechanicsburg PA 17055

Call Sign: N2RWD
Michael L Mahar
822 Anthony Dr
Mechanicsburg PA 17055

Call Sign: N2GQ
Herbert J Lapp Jr
824 Anthony Dr
Mechanicsburg PA 17055

Call Sign: KB3SUH
Rina Song
325 Antilles Ct
Mechanicsburg PA 17050

Call Sign: KB3OPL
Jon Angle
988 Antrim Dr
Mechanicsburg PA 17050

Call Sign: KB3IXE
Daniel J Mullin
5003 Apache Dr
Mechanicsburg PA 17050

Call Sign: KB3MVX
Kathleen N Descours
523 Appalachian Ave
Mechanicsburg PA 17055

Call Sign: KB3LPZ
Boden A Carter
1207 Apple Dr
Mechanicsburg PA 17055

Call Sign: KB3NLL
Christopher J Shadle
34 Argali Ln
Mechanicsburg PA 17055

Call Sign: N7HHS
John F Flynn
2207 Aspen Dr
Mechanicsburg PA 17055

Call Sign: AA3AJ
Matthew D Kylen
6302 Auburn Dr
Mechanicsburg PA 17055

Call Sign: AA3DZ
David J Kylen
6302 Auburn Dr
Mechanicsburg PA 17055

Call Sign: KB3OZR
Jessica L Hammaker
1776 Autumnwood Dr
Mechanicsburg PA 17055

Call Sign: KB3QDH
Krista E Hammaker
1776 Autumnwood Dr
Mechanicsburg PA 17055

Call Sign: KB3LQO
Robert M Garofalo
1780 Autumnwood Dr
Mechanicsburg PA 17055

Call Sign: KB3SUJ
Jennifer L Zielonis
1786 Autumnwood Dr
Mechanicsburg PA 17055

Call Sign: KB3MXH
Jessica A Zielonis
1786 Autumnwood Dr
Mechanicsburg PA 17055

Call Sign: KB3OZY
Brianne K Keel
5006 Balmoral Ct
Mechanicsburg PA 17050

Call Sign: WB3JKP
Arthur D Murray Jr
34 Bare Rd
Mechanicsburg PA 17055

Call Sign: KB3KLS
Gaurav K Bashyakarla
2107 Beacon Cir
Mechanicsburg PA 17055

Call Sign: KB3LRZ
Blake F Stock
5492 Bearcreek Dr
Mechanicsburg PA 17050

Call Sign: KB3MWH
Hyuk Joo Ham
539 Bedford Ct
Mechanicsburg PA 17050

Call Sign: N3TUB
Elwood A Altmeyer Jr
3513 Beech Run Ln
Mechanicsburg PA 17055

Call Sign: N3QCC
Jaffar M Annab
3606 Beech Run Ln
Mechanicsburg PA 17055

Call Sign: KB3PAO
Michelle S Pryzie
4 Belvedere Dr
Mechanicsburg PA 17055

Call Sign: KB3MVQ
Leonard A Burg II
6358 Bennington Rd
Mechanicsburg PA 17050

Call Sign: N3AKQ
Charles R Thurner
435 Bethany Dr
Mechanicsburg PA 17055

Call Sign: KT3Q
Robert S Bogar
470 Bethany Dr
Mechanicsburg PA
170554359

Call Sign: AA3BP
James G Miller
3505 Beverly Ln
Mechanicsburg PA 17050

Call Sign: KB3LRH
Samuel P Messinger
16 Birch St
Mechanicsburg PA 17050

Call Sign: KB3RZW
Matthew J Rickards
6214 Blackfriars Way
Mechanicsburg PA 17050

Call Sign: KB3APA
Edgar A Dilks
44 Blue Mtn Vista Dr
Mechanicsburg PA 17050

Call Sign: N3RLA
Freda L Dilks
44 Blue Mtn Vista Dr
Mechanicsburg PA 17050

Call Sign: N3YQA
William S Lyter
104 Bluebell Dr
Mechanicsburg PA 17050

Call Sign: WB3BYJ
John P Tutka
955 Boiling Springs Rd
Mechanicsburg PA 17055

Call Sign: NZ3N
David C Armstrong
1128 Boiling Springs Rd

Mechanicsburg PA 17055

Call Sign: N3QDM
Robert C Schanke
911 Bonny Ln
Mechanicsburg PA 17055

Call Sign: AB3LA
Casey L Shearer
418 Boxwood Ct
Mechanicsburg PA 17050

Call Sign: KB3STZ
Lindsay M Moore
2214 Boxwood Ln
Mechanicsburg PA 17055

Call Sign: KB3IBW
Benjamin H Tiedgen
5 Bradford Ct
Mechanicsburg PA 17055

Call Sign: KA3VWP
John A Fieseler III
6460 Brandy Ln
Mechanicsburg PA 17055

Call Sign: KA3QBF
Mary M Price
920 Brandywine Way
Mechanicsburg PA 17050

Call Sign: WA5MQM
Arnold C Price
920 Brandywine Way
Mechanicsburg PA 17050

Call Sign: KB3RZI
Gregory F Alba
12 Bridgeport Dr
Mechanicsburg PA 17050

Call Sign: WB3GDT
Robert N Guarini
576 Brighton Pl

Mechanicsburg PA 17055

Call Sign: KB3MVV
Amanda M Connolly
115 Brindle Rd
Mechanicsburg PA 17055

Call Sign: KB3MWP
Taylor T Leonard
272 Brindle Rd
Mechanicsburg PA 17055

Call Sign: KB3GZN
Connie J Dixon
430 Brookview Ct
Mechanicsburg PA 17050

Call Sign: KB3LQB
Julia K Chasler
4137 Burns Rd
Mechanicsburg PA 17055

Call Sign: KC3IN
James L Richey
9 Canterbury Ct
Mechanicsburg PA 17050

Call Sign: WB3KQF
Meredith R Jones
12 Canterbury Ct
Mechanicsburg PA 17055

Call Sign: KB3MWQ
Bridget J Mahoney
2137 Canterbury Dr
Mechanicsburg PA 17055

Call Sign: KB3QXI
Brian T Johnson
2200 Canterbury Dr
Mechanicsburg PA 17055

Call Sign: KB3OVT
Martin P Shull
2225 Canterbury Dr

Mechanicsburg PA 17055

Call Sign: KB3RZC
John-Michael Talarico
2227 Canterbury Dr
Mechanicsburg PA 17055

Call Sign: WA1DQ
David D Quinn
18 Cardamon Dr
Mechanicsburg PA 17050

Call Sign: KG3BW
David D Quinn
18 Cardamon Dr
Mechanicsburg PA 17050

Call Sign: KG4NUC
Benjamin C Zink
419 Cascade Rd
Mechanicsburg PA 17055

Call Sign: KB3KMR
Kristi R Mennitto
4 Cedar Ave
Mechanicsburg PA 17055

Call Sign: N3URP
James J Mann
626 Cedar Rdg Ln
Mechanicsburg PA 17055

Call Sign: KB3OVG
Benjamin J Andres
6109 Charing Cross
Mechanicsburg PA 17050

Call Sign: N3PTM
John E Kurtinecz Jr
900 Charles St
Mechanicsburg PA 17055

Call Sign: N3XIX
Charles J Grew
905 Charles St

Mechanicsburg PA 17055

Call Sign: N3URC
Charles S Fries
1114 Charles St
Mechanicsburg PA 17055

Call Sign: KB3IXC
Keith E Comrey
402 Cherokee Dr
Mechanicsburg PA 17050

Call Sign: KA3QFI
Richard J ONeill
512 Cherry Cir
Mechanicsburg PA 17055

Call Sign: K3EAZ
Robert H Frank
3921 Cherylbrook Dr
Mechanicsburg PA 17055

Call Sign: KB3PAZ
Megan E Tocci
9 Cicada Dr
Mechanicsburg PA 17050

Call Sign: W3ZKL
Robert E Wech
20 Circle Dr
Mechanicsburg PA 17055

Call Sign: N3NIL
Samuel N Carmichael
23 Circle Dr
Mechanicsburg PA 17055

Call Sign: KB3RKM
Edmund Letersky
3811 Claverton Rd
Mechanicsburg PA 17050

Call Sign: K3AAU
Harper O Swartley Jr
2461 Cocklin Ct

Mechanicsburg PA
170555361

Call Sign: KB3IXA
Christine M Gillis
1114 Cocklin St
Mechanicsburg PA 17055

Call Sign: KB3LQR
Daivd A Gillis
1114 Cocklin St
Mechanicsburg PA 17055

Call Sign: KB3LQP
Andrew T Gess
1524 Collingdale Cir
Mechanicsburg PA 17050

Call Sign: W3DBH
David B Hultberg
1407 Concord Rd
Mechanicsburg PA
170501955

Call Sign: KB3QXF
Matthew R Gilson
1431 Concord Rd
Mechanicsburg PA 17050

Call Sign: WA3LIV
Richard J Harris
6354 Concord Rd
Mechanicsburg PA
170501993

Call Sign: KB3MVZ
Dustin J Eagle
917 Conely Dr
Mechanicsburg PA 17055

Call Sign: KB3LSD
Adam M Swetra
16 Cottage Ct
Mechanicsburg PA 17050

Call Sign: KA3UEZ
Stephen J Vergot
1418 Country Dr
Mechanicsburg PA 17055

Call Sign: KB3KMO
Allison K Luttermoser
1506 Country Dr
Mechanicsburg PA 17055

Call Sign: KB3IXF
Joshua E Selfe
1112 Cross Creek Dr
Mechanicsburg PA 17050

Call Sign: KB3LJA
Murali Narayanan
1195 Cross Creek Dr
Mechanicsburg PA 17050

Call Sign: KB3QXS
Emily A Miceli
418 Darla Rd
Mechanicsburg PA 17055

Call Sign: KB3OWB
Brittney R Evans
504 David Dr
Mechanicsburg PA 17050

Call Sign: KB3QWV
Matthew J Brosious
5209 Deerfield Ave
Mechanicsburg PA 17050

Call Sign: KB3QXH
Greg J Hychko
5269 Deerfield Ave
Mechanicsburg PA 17050

Call Sign: KB3SNV
Josiah A Frankford
14 Dewberry Ct
Mechanicsburg PA 17055

Call Sign: KB3SBY
Gregory J Frankford
14 Dewberry Ct
Mechanicsburg PA
170555600

Call Sign: K9XTC
Gregory J Frankford
14 Dewberry Ct
Mechanicsburg PA
170555600

Call Sign: KB3MWA
Amanda A Fontana
1 Drayton Ct
Mechanicsburg PA 17055

Call Sign: KB3LQD
Jonathan E Danko
1123 Dry Powder Cir
Mechanicsburg PA 17050

Call Sign: KB3MVR
Patrick W Burket
1138 Dry Powder Cir
Mechanicsburg PA 17050

Call Sign: N3MMG
Edward F Joyce
5 E Elmwood Ave
Mechanicsburg PA 17055

Call Sign: KB3NIL
Nicole M Zeigler
1112 E Lisburn Rd
Mechanicsburg PA 17055

Call Sign: KB3KNL
Lauren K Wagner
1106 E Powderhorn Rd
Mechanicsburg PA 17050

Call Sign: AA3HB
Joseph J Buckwalter
1106 E Simpson Rd

Mechanicsburg PA 17055

Call Sign: KB3QXT
Ashley J Murtha
120 E Simpson St
Mechanicsburg PA 17055

Call Sign: N3SFU
Robert A Young III
5130 E Trindle Rd Rear
Mechanicsburg PA 17050

Call Sign: KA3HOS
Glenn H Haagen
516 E Winding Hill Rd
Mechanicsburg PA 17055

Call Sign: N3OSC
Edward G Forguson
601 E Winding Hill Rd
Mechanicsburg PA 17055

Call Sign: KB3MQJ
Charles M Roesner
609 E Winding Hill Rd
Mechanicsburg PA 17055

Call Sign: KB3QXM
Nolan A Kauffman
2315 Elgin Cir
Mechanicsburg PA 17055

Call Sign: KB3RZS
Martin F Jackson Jr
116 Ellesmere Ln
Mechanicsburg PA 17055

Call Sign: WB0QZG
Gilbert G Humphrey
909 Emily Dr
Mechanicsburg PA
170555708

Call Sign: W3FH
Russell E Mummert

915 Emily Dr
Mechanicsburg PA 17055

Call Sign: KB3STK
Eric W Dethlefs Jr
6 Emlyn Ln
Mechanicsburg PA 17055

Call Sign: KB3KND
Margaret M Ryan
19 Emlyn Ln
Mechanicsburg PA 17055

Call Sign: KB3PAS
Timothy J Ryan
19 Emlyn Ln
Mechanicsburg PA 17055

Call Sign: KE4LKN
Nicholas E Alger
210 Ewe Rd
Mechanicsburg PA 17055

Call Sign: KB3UNI
Steven F Uhler
417 Fairway Dr
Mechanicsburg PA 17055

Call Sign: KB3NBO
Bernard W Girman III
3707 Falkstone Dr
Mechanicsburg PA 17050

Call Sign: KB3NBV
Brice A Robertson
3707 Falkstone Dr
Mechanicsburg PA 17050

Call Sign: N3YLE
Jeffery A Johnson
28 Fieldcrest Dr
Mechanicsburg PA 17055

Call Sign: KB3LQN
Joshua T Fry

1881 Fisher Rd
Mechanicsburg PA 17055

Call Sign: KB3QXC
Elliott P Fry
1981 Fisher Rd
Mechanicsburg PA 17055

Call Sign: KB3LQI
Christen M Dileonardo
723 Florence Cir
Mechanicsburg PA 17050

Call Sign: KB3LQE
Catherine K Davis
727 Florence Cir
Mechanicsburg PA 17050

Call Sign: KB3NLJ
Rosemarie E Perry
2105 Foxfire Dr
Mechanicsburg PA 17055

Call Sign: KB3QXV
Thomas Perry IV
2105 Foxfire Dr
Mechanicsburg PA 17055

Call Sign: KB3SJB
Christopher A Curwen
5519 General Jenkins Dr
Mechanicsburg PA 17050

Call Sign: W3DAB
Dale A Bair
Geneva Dr 22
Mechanicsburg PA 17055

Call Sign: KA3QYK
David S Fieseler
101 George St
Mechanicsburg PA 17055

Call Sign: KA3AJC
William L Leitzel

12 Gettysburg Pike
Mechanicsburg PA 17055

Call Sign: KB3IOS
Gayle C Green
Gloucester St
Mechanicsburg PA 17055

Call Sign: KB3PQT
Frank C Mellott
1010 Good Hope Rd
Mechanicsburg PA
170502120

Call Sign: N3DXR
John G Herbert
930 Grandon Way
Mechanicsburg PA 17050

Call Sign: N3TKO
Tore R Johnson
1090 Green Ln
Mechanicsburg PA 17055

Call Sign: W3KJS
Walter S Smuszkiewicz
1210 Gross Dr
Mechanicsburg PA 17055

Call Sign: N3URI
Alfred C Roesner
1105 Gunstock Ln
Mechanicsburg PA 17055

Call Sign: KB3LFB
Tyler Stephens
1106 Gunstock Ln
Mechanicsburg PA
170502008

Call Sign: W3HP
Richard J Harris
1109 Gunstock Ln
Mechanicsburg PA
170502009

Call Sign: KB3STI
Angelo M Barbush
1110 Gunstock Ln
Mechanicsburg PA 17055

Call Sign: KB3KMG
Ellen R Hanger
5 Harpers Ferry Way
Mechanicsburg PA 17050

Call Sign: KE4VIK
Paul M Betts
546 Harvest Ln
Mechanicsburg PA
170554487

Call Sign: KB3KMV
Kathryn S Palovick
864 Hawthorn Ave
Mechanicsburg PA 17055

Call Sign: KB3MVS
Charles L Casner
881 Hawthorne Ave
Mechanicsburg PA 17055

Call Sign: KB3LQU
Erna B Jablonski
901 Hawthorne Ave
Mechanicsburg PA 17055

Call Sign: KB3RSI
George W Craft II
6260 Haydon Ct
Mechanicsburg PA
170508104

Call Sign: N3YHD
Michael J Metz
6123 Haymarket Way
Mechanicsburg PA 17050

Call Sign: N3OFI
Brad Robertson

467 Heisey Rd
Mechanicsburg PA 17055

Call Sign: KB3VMH
Tomas A Volk
904 Hertzler Rd
Mechanicsburg PA 17055

Call Sign: WB3BWZ
Michael B Volk
904 Hertzler Rd
Mechanicsburg PA 17055

Call Sign: KM3Y
Michael B Volk
904 Hertzler Rd
Mechanicsburg PA 17055

Call Sign: KB3QPV
Nicholas J Mirando
6 Hidden Meadow Dr
Mechanicsburg PA 17050

Call Sign: KB3QDJ
Karsten E Hansen
10 High Ridge Trl
Mechanicsburg PA 17050

Call Sign: KA3TCR
William C Clapper
1032 Highland Dr
Mechanicsburg PA 17055

Call Sign: W3HCR
Bryan W Grant
116 Hill Ln
Mechanicsburg PA 17055

Call Sign: KB3SQW
Todd S Burnham
507 Hogestown Rd
Mechanicsburg PA 17050

Call Sign: KA3SCR
Philip B Neff

710 Hogestown Rd
Mechanicsburg PA 17055

Call Sign: N3KZY
Nicholas C Grable
116 Holly Dr
Mechanicsburg PA 17055

Call Sign: N3KZZ
William D Grable
116 Holly Dr
Mechanicsburg PA 17055

Call Sign: N3NTE
Sheri M Grable
116 Holly Dr
Mechanicsburg PA 17055

Call Sign: KB3QDG
Kaitlyn M Eberhart
55 Honeysuckle Dr
Mechanicsburg PA 17050

Call Sign: KB3MWT
John L Moloney
532 Ichabod Ct
Mechanicsburg PA 17050

Call Sign: KB3LSC
Melissa L Sutliff
1431 Inverness Dr
Mechanicsburg PA 17050

Call Sign: KB3OPP
John S Turner
708 Jenna Ct
Mechanicsburg PA 17055

Call Sign: AB3PS
John S Turner
708 Jenna Ct
Mechanicsburg PA 17055

Call Sign: NX3N
Brian W Rosenberg

5420 Joshua Rd
Mechanicsburg PA 17050

Call Sign: N3INS
Frederick M Thumma
2 Juniper Dr
Mechanicsburg PA 17055

Call Sign: KB3KNE
Joshua T Sechrist
4 Keefer Way
Mechanicsburg PA 17055

Call Sign: KB3GYH
Jesse A Sayre
66 Keefer Way
Mechanicsburg PA 17055

Call Sign: N3GQB
Charles S Moody Jr
43 Kensington Sq
Mechanicsburg PA 17050

Call Sign: KB3JAU
Robert N Grant Jr
808 Kent Dr
Mechanicsburg PA
170502281

Call Sign: KB3JAV
Robert N Grant III
808 Kent Dr
Mechanicsburg PA
170502281

Call Sign: KB3QXL
Kathleen Kardos
1003 Kent Dr
Mechanicsburg PA 17050

Call Sign: KB3SUF
Aimee M Seitz
1223 Kings Cir
Mechanicsburg PA 17050

Call Sign: KA3FUD
William K Whitlock Sr
5008 Kylock Rd
Mechanicsburg PA 17055

Call Sign: KB3KLX
Elizabeth A Curtis
127 Lancaster Blvd
Mechanicsburg PA 17055

Call Sign: WA3LPF
Ronald F Nordstrom
138 Lancaster Blvd
Mechanicsburg PA 17055

Call Sign: WB3KEQ
Melvin G Austin Jr
148 Lancaster Blvd
Mechanicsburg PA 17055

Call Sign: WB3KGY
Helen E Austin
148 Lancaster Blvd
Mechanicsburg PA 17055

Call Sign: K3WMX
Francis R Kumler
923 Larch Loop
Mechanicsburg PA
170558612

Call Sign: KA2SZK
Edward R Draucik
25 Lilac Dr
Mechanicsburg PA 17050

Call Sign: N3TUC
Matthew M Fisher
28 Lilac Dr
Mechanicsburg PA 17050

Call Sign: N3MSL
Rodger G Shanafelter
82 Linda Dr Lot 18
Mechanicsburg PA 17050

Call Sign: KB3IYY
Jennifer R Sacoman
412 Linden St
Mechanicsburg PA 17050

Call Sign: W3WZB
George T Wood
443 Linden St
Mechanicsburg PA 17055

Call Sign: KB3CRF
Mechanicsburg ARC
1101 Lindham Ct 102
Mechanicsburg PA 17055

Call Sign: KA3YLY
Dennis M Sheppard
7 Lismore Pl
Mechanicsburg PA 17050

Call Sign: KB3KLW
Patrick A Conrad
5 Lois Ln
Mechanicsburg PA 17050

Call Sign: KB3QWX
Adam J Conrad
5 Lois Ln
Mechanicsburg PA 17050

Call Sign: WA3UJS
Larry B Herlt
603 Louisa Ln
Mechanicsburg PA 17050

Call Sign: N3URK
Philip C Hitchcock
6155 Ludgate
Mechanicsburg PA 17055

Call Sign: N3ECF
Sandra L Goodman
199 Maple Ln
Mechanicsburg PA 17055

Call Sign: WA3USG
Richard E Goodman
199 Maple Ln
Mechanicsburg PA 17055

Call Sign: KB3NLE
Sarah R Goetz
1117 McCormick Rd
Mechanicsburg PA 17055

Call Sign: N3ZSK
Eric D Berry
2179 Merrimac Ave
Mechanicsburg PA 17055

Call Sign: N3VPJ
Donna Lee Hoover
566 Miller Blvd
Mechanicsburg PA 17055

Call Sign: KB3PAG
Katelyn A Mock
14 Monarch Ln
Mechanicsburg PA 17050

Call Sign: KB3IRF
A Edwin Dyer
3 Mt Allen Dr
Mechanicsburg PA 17055

Call Sign: K3DVM
Melvin K Ensminger
3965 Mtn View Rd
Mechanicsburg PA
170552133

Call Sign: N3URO
Larry C Eslinger
4060 Mtn View Rd
Mechanicsburg PA
170502134

Call Sign: K3ROY
Marvin J Edris

99 Mulberry Dr
Mechanicsburg PA 17055

Call Sign: KB3OVI
Mark B Bruening Jr
1102 Musket Ln
Mechanicsburg PA 17050

Call Sign: KB3RZL
Stephen R Bruening
1102 Musket Ln
Mechanicsburg PA 17050

Call Sign: KB3LSF
Kyle M Witman
1103 Musket Ln
Mechanicsburg PA 17050

Call Sign: KF4AZQ
Earl D Hance
108 N Arch St
Mechanicsburg PA 17055

Call Sign: W3PLI
George B Kabroth
218 N Arch St
Mechanicsburg PA 17055

Call Sign: KB3VFF
Adam L Dawson
117 N Madder Dr
Mechanicsburg PA 17050

Call Sign: WB3DIE
Robert L Swartz
407 N Market St
Mechanicsburg PA 17055

Call Sign: KB3QWS
Abigale A Adams
1769 N Meadow Dr
Mechanicsburg PA 17055

Call Sign: KB3PJX
Nicholas A Douty

1774 N Meadow Dr
Mechanicsburg PA 17055

Call Sign: KB3KMB
James P Dougherty Jr
6341 N Powderhorn Rd
Mechanicsburg PA 17050

Call Sign: KB3OOM
Harold R Underwood
2621 N Rosegarden Blvd
Mechanicsburg PA 17055

Call Sign: W3URG
Tolbert V Prowell
413 N York Rd
Mechanicsburg PA 17055

Call Sign: KA3DZW
Joseph P Joynes
10 Nittany Dr
Mechanicsburg PA 17055

Call Sign: N3URJ
David A Bartlett
902 Norway St
Mechanicsburg PA 17055

Call Sign: KA3VFD
Ira B Sollenberger
704 Oak Oval
Mechanicsburg PA 17055

Call Sign: KB3FHC
Theodore R Williams
4532 Old Gettysburg Rd
2nd Fl
Mechanicsburg PA 17055

Call Sign: KB3FNK
Theodore R Williams
4532 Old Gettysburg Rd
2nd Fl
Mechanicsburg PA 17055

Call Sign: WA2PJE
Neil A Wolvin
2244 Old Hollow Rd
Mechanicsburg PA 17055

Call Sign: K3NAW
Neil A Wolvin
2244 Old Hollow Rd
Mechanicsburg PA 17055

Call Sign: KZ3U
Tay K Tambolas
104 Orchard St
Mechanicsburg PA
170554167

Call Sign: KB3HLA
Brent M Gobat
5328 Oxford Cir Apt 32
Mechanicsburg PA 17055

Call Sign: KA3GRF
Kevin S Goff
5228 Oxford Dr
Mechanicsburg PA 17055

Call Sign: KB3LWM
Ruth E Constantine
5230 Oxford Dr
Mechanicsburg PA 17055

Call Sign: KB3IZB
Ryan M Gillespie
3806 Pamay Dr
Mechanicsburg PA 17050

Call Sign: KB3OZG
Eugenia Cervantes
3831 Pamay Dr
Mechanicsburg PA 17050

Call Sign: KB3LQA
Jorge Cervantes
3831 Pamay Dr
Mechanicsburg PA 17050

Call Sign: KB3OZK
Adam M Davis
3900 Pamay Dr
Mechanicsburg PA 17050

Call Sign: N3CCV
David E Wolfe
4004 Pamay Dr
Mechanicsburg PA
170509179

Call Sign: KB3QXD
Richard A Gatesman
4006 Pamay Dr
Mechanicsburg PA 17050

Call Sign: KB3QDN
Carlee A Otto
7 Patton Rd
Mechanicsburg PA 17055

Call Sign: W3MZ
Charles A Harris
436 Pawnee Dr
Mechanicsburg PA 17055

Call Sign: KA3FVH
George J Lawrence
454 Pawnee Dr
Mechanicsburg PA 17055

Call Sign: KB3OZS
Lauren R Herman
1 Penns Way Rd
Mechanicsburg PA 17050

Call Sign: KA3ERY
Jane OKeefe
12 Poplar Dr
Mechanicsburg PA 17055

Call Sign: KR3D
Michael F OKeefe
12 Poplar Dr

Mechanicsburg PA 17055

Call Sign: N3JYQ
Adam D Whitsel
529 Quail Ct
Mechanicsburg PA
170502083

Call Sign: KB3LQL
Ashleigh P Fisher
3504 Raintree Ln
Mechanicsburg PA 17050

Call Sign: KB3STQ
Austin B Gullo
3508 Raintree Ln
Mechanicsburg PA 17050

Call Sign: N3HR
Michael C Wacker
22 Raspberry Dr
Mechanicsburg PA
170502792

Call Sign: KB3NLM
Paul T Surry
5055 Ravenwood Rd
Mechanicsburg PA 17055

Call Sign: AD3L
Charles J Hooker Jr
16 Redbud Dr
Mechanicsburg PA
170501803

Call Sign: WB3DLO
William H Devore Jr
199 Ridge Hill Rd
Mechanicsburg PA 17050

Call Sign: ND3O
Jasper R McDonald Jr
221 Ridge Hill Rd
Mechanicsburg PA 17055

Call Sign: KB3QDW
Diana R Mitchell
839 Ridgewood Dr
Mechanicsburg PA 17050

Call Sign: KB3MWE
Michael R Giannelli
608 Riverstix Ln
Mechanicsburg PA 17050

Call Sign: KB3QPT
Marino A Magaro
614 Robert St
Mechanicsburg PA 17055

Call Sign: W3HMS
John A Jaminet
912 Robert St
Mechanicsburg PA
170553451

Call Sign: KB3MWL
Leah M Hirsch
1002 Robert St
Mechanicsburg PA 17055

Call Sign: KB3DCV
Barton R Shenck
12 Robin Ct
Mechanicsburg PA 17055

Call Sign: KB3SUL
Randall L Valk
4225 Roth Ln Apt 107
Mechanicsburg PA 17050

Call Sign: KB3RZE
Devin V Walker
102 Round Ridge Rd
Mechanicsburg PA 17055

Call Sign: W3BQ
Robert A Young Jr
5227 Royal Dr
Mechanicsburg PA 17055

Call Sign: KB3PAQ
Caitlyn M Ragni
1451 Ryland Dr
Mechanicsburg PA 17050

Call Sign: KB3RZV
Andrew T Perry
226 S High St
Mechanicsburg PA 17055

Call Sign: KB3DMH
Marc K Seeley Sr
410 S High St
Mechanicsburg PA
170556430

Call Sign: KB3OZU
Jennifer L Hnatuck
1779 S Meadow Dr
Mechanicsburg PA 17055

Call Sign: KB3RYT
Kenneth L Kostelac Jr
1783 S Meadow Dr
Mechanicsburg PA 17055

Call Sign: KB3RZZ
Edward J Spinelli
6350 S Powderhorn Rd
Mechanicsburg PA 17050

Call Sign: KB3FSZ
Paul T Bolock
311 S Sporting Hill Rd
Mechanicsburg PA
170503062

Call Sign: KB3RCZ
Heewon Park
435 S Washington St
Mechanicsburg PA 17055

Call Sign: N3RWT
Charles J Wilson

1012 S Waterford Way
Mechanicsburg PA 17055

Call Sign: KB3KNI
Lindsay N Teves
1012 Saffron Dr
Mechanicsburg PA 17050

Call Sign: KB3OZQ
Kelly L Greenway
1107 Saffron Dr
Mechanicsburg PA 17050

Call Sign: KC2RQS
Darryl H Arbeit
6901 Salem Park Cir
Mechanicsburg PA 17050

Call Sign: KB3QDS
Marlene E Smith
518 Salmon Rd
Mechanicsburg PA 17050

Call Sign: N3MKB
Richard J Prestia
21 San Juan Dr
Mechanicsburg PA 17055

Call Sign: KB3LQS
Jacqueline M Hilton
7 Sand Pine Ct
Mechanicsburg PA 17050

Call Sign: KB3QDY
Lindsay M Hilton
7 Sand Pine Ct
Mechanicsburg PA 17050

Call Sign: N3URN
Joseph J OHaren Jr
1232 Scenery Dr
Mechanicsburg PA 17055

Call Sign: KB3STL
Ersikha G Eugene

906 Scottish Ct
Mechanicsburg PA 17050

6 Sna Ln
Mechanicsburg PA 17055

405 Spring Run Dr
Mechanicsburg PA 17055

Call Sign: WB8ZZN
Michael W Rothwell
1803 Signal Hill Dr
Mechanicsburg PA 17050

Call Sign: KB3LRF
Danielle A Mccollum
6103 Sommerton Dr
Mechanicsburg PA 17050

Call Sign: W3ZIF
Royal W Kramer
2208 Spring Run Dr
Mechanicsburg PA 17055

Call Sign: KB3NYY
Michael W Rothwell
1803 Signal Hill Dr
Mechanicsburg PA 17050

Call Sign: KB3KGD
Harvey A Tannenbaum
6110 Sommerton Dr
Mechanicsburg PA 17050

Call Sign: KB3MXA
Viviana A Pino Gonzalez
1778 Springwillow Dr
Mechanicsburg PA 17055

Call Sign: K3MWR
Michael W Rothwell
1803 Signal Hill Dr
Mechanicsburg PA 17050

Call Sign: N3BVR
Brenda M Kylen
14 South Rd
Mechanicsburg PA 17050

Call Sign: KB3NPF
Joel X Zeiger
6314 Stephens Crossing
Mechanicsburg PA 17050

Call Sign: KB3QPQ
Shannon M Crane
1812 Signal Hill Rd
Mechanicsburg PA 17050

Call Sign: KB3QXZ
Andrew M Stokes
332 Southview Dr
Mechanicsburg PA 17055

Call Sign: KB3TTB
Joshua P Hamme
312 Stonehedge Ln
Mechanicsburg PA 17055

Call Sign: KA2PVE
Robert P Troy
1417 Silvercreek Dr
Mechanicsburg PA 17050

Call Sign: KB3QXW
Joseph M Perry
333 Southview Dr
Mechanicsburg PA 17055

Call Sign: KB3MWG
Kristen S Gunnison
10 Stratford Ln
Mechanicsburg PA 17050

Call Sign: KB3NLD
Megan E Gallagher
5514 Silvercreek Dr
Mechanicsburg PA 17050

Call Sign: KB3NLO
Hannah C Wenger
4 Southwatch Ln
Mechanicsburg PA 17050

Call Sign: WB3ICZ
Michael F Acri
3600 Sullivan St
Mechanicsburg PA 17055

Call Sign: N3TUD
James R Reynolds
60 Skyline Dr
Mechanicsburg PA 17055

Call Sign: KB3QQC
Jacob A Wenger
4 Southwatch Ln
Mechanicsburg PA 17050

Call Sign: WA3PIW
Robert E Kenny
5208 Terrace Rd
Mechanicsburg PA 17055

Call Sign: KB3OZW
James J Hoellman III
6 Sna Ln
Mechanicsburg PA 17050

Call Sign: KB3KNN
Rachel E Wenger
4 Southwatch Ln
Mechanicsburg PA 17050

Call Sign: KB3IZK
Mark J Saltus
5224 Terrace Rd
Mechanicsburg PA 17050

Call Sign: KB3RZQ
Jordan P Hoellman

Call Sign: W3BOH
Bernard F Bailey

Call Sign: KC3KW
Fred D Fike Jr

31 Texaco Rd
Mechanicsburg PA 17055

Call Sign: WB3DWQ
Shirley G Fike
31 Texaco Rd
Mechanicsburg PA 17055

Call Sign: K3RYV
Donald L Birx
208 Texaco Rd
Mechanicsburg PA 17055

Call Sign: WA3ASE
Adele S Birx
208 Texaco Rd
Mechanicsburg PA 17055

Call Sign: KB3QDZ
Seunghyun Pyun
9 Thyme Ct
Mechanicsburg PA 17050

Call Sign: KB3KMQ
Amanda B Martin
1014 Tiverton Rd
Mechanicsburg PA 17050

Call Sign: N2RFE
Andrew R Walker
1025 Tiverton Rd
Mechanicsburg PA 17050

Call Sign: KB3MWZ
Cara E Petruzzi
1101 Tiverton Rd
Mechanicsburg PA 17050

Call Sign: KB3LRG
Garrett R Mcgrath
7 Truffle Glen Rd
Mechanicsburg PA 17050

Call Sign: KB3OVO
Ivan Martak

1021 Turnbridge Ln
Mechanicsburg PA 17050

Call Sign: WB3BYI
Wayne H Lengel
112 Valley View Dr
Mechanicsburg PA 17050

Call Sign: WB3GCE
Richard L Barrick
130 Victoria Dr
Mechanicsburg PA
170553526

Call Sign: KB3KNK
Van D Tran
3 Virginia Cir
Mechanicsburg PA 17050

Call Sign: KA3ACI
Randy S George
438 Virginia Rd
Mechanicsburg PA
170553069

Call Sign: KB3PBC
James B Musselman Jr
512 W Keller St
Mechanicsburg PA 17055

Call Sign: K3XLT
James B Musselman Jr
512 W Keller St
Mechanicsburg PA 17055

Call Sign: K3KS
James B Musselman Jr
512 W Keller St
Mechanicsburg PA 17055

Call Sign: KA3UUU
Kevin C Ceaver
428 W Main St
Mechanicsburg PA 17055

Call Sign: KB3MVT
Hyun A Cho
111 W Powderhorn Rd
Mechanicsburg PA 17050

Call Sign: N3WEE
William S Graham Jr
215.5 W Simpson St
Mechanicsburg PA 17055

Call Sign: N3XUG
William P Reilly
955 W Trindle Rd
Mechanicsburg PA 17055

Call Sign: KB3OZF
Chelsea Brett
6105 Wallingford Way
Mechanicsburg PA 17050

Call Sign: KB3STJ
Kevin T Brett
6105 Wallingford Way
Mechanicsburg PA 17050

Call Sign: KB3LQW
Daniel S Joyce
1118 Wansford Rd
Mechanicsburg PA 17050

Call Sign: KB3MVW
Brett A Depalma
1024 Waterford Way
Mechanicsburg PA 17050

Call Sign: WA3KTI
David K Peters
509 Wayne Dr
Mechanicsburg PA 17055

Call Sign: W3ALS
Albert L Sites Sr
209 Westview Dr
Mechanicsburg PA
170555757

Call Sign: KB3LRC
Eric P Mangol
7 Wheatland Dr
Mechanicsburg PA 17050

Call Sign: KB3OIT
Mark A Foster
44 White Oak Blvd
Mechanicsburg PA 17050

Call Sign: KB3STM
Taylor J Ezzi
926 Willcliff Dr
Mechanicsburg PA 17050

Call Sign: WA3KTA
Albert S Hodge
6032 William Dr
Mechanicsburg PA 17055

Call Sign: N3OSN
Anthony A Bakogios
6036 William Dr
Mechanicsburg PA 17055

Call Sign: KB3MVE
Anthony A Bakagios
6036 William Dr
Mechanicsburg PA 17055

Call Sign: N3OSN
Anthony A Bakagios
6036 William Dr
Mechanicsburg PA 17055

Call Sign: K3SUN
Lan W Richter Sr
21 Willow Mill Park Rd
Mechanicsburg PA 17055

Call Sign: KB3LQM
Kieth P Fisher
501 Wilson Ln
Mechanicsburg PA 17055

Call Sign: W3KPF
Earl P Conley
5225 Wilson Ln
Mechanicsburg PA 17055

Call Sign: KB3OZX
Rachael L Holt
1 Winchester Ct
Mechanicsburg PA 17050

Call Sign: KB3PAK
Ye Oh
2 Winding Hill Dr
Mechanicsburg PA 17055

Call Sign: KE3BE
William R McCurdy
322 Wister Cir
Mechanicsburg PA 17055

Call Sign: W0KOG
Allen J Daniel Jr
451 Woodcrest Dr
Mechanicsburg PA
170506809

Call Sign: KB3SUD
Maureen S Reilly
470 Woodcrest Dr
Mechanicsburg PA 17050

Call Sign: K3MSH
James H Funkhouser
182 Woods Dr
Mechanicsburg PA
170552749

Call Sign: KB3JTM
David W Witsil
429 Wren Ct
Mechanicsburg PA 17050

Call Sign: W3UX
John L Pantaloni

1425 Yorktowne Rd
Mechanicsburg PA 17050

Call Sign: W3IWP
Paul H Hertzler
Mechanicsburg PA 17055

Call Sign: KB3KLF
Sean R Forsythe
Mechanicsburg PA
170551101

FCC Amateur Radio Licenses in Mercersburg

Call Sign: KB3BDZ
Michael B Musser
2855 Brooklyn Rd
Mercersburg PA 17236

Call Sign: KB3GOR
Dean W Shenberger
10065 Buchanan Trl W
Mercersburg PA 17236

Call Sign: KB3NOF
Troy D Fawley
13494 Buchanan Trl W
Mercersburg PA 17236

Call Sign: N3VGP
Donald W Rohrer Jr
14914 Buchanan Trl W
Mercersburg PA 17236

Call Sign: KA3UQS
Jason H Risser
10369 Corner Rd
Mercersburg PA 17236

Call Sign: K4WOP
James A Brinson
300 E Seminary St
Mercersburg PA 17236

Call Sign: N3TYR
Alan W Shoemaker
9208 Garnes Rd
Mercersburg PA 17236

Call Sign: KA3FSR
Kay Casteel
252 Johnston Ln
Mercersburg PA 17236

Call Sign: KC3GI
Neil M Coleman
252 Johnston Ln
Mercersburg PA 17236

Call Sign: KB3ICW
Brian L Hoover
13131 Karper Rd
Mercersburg PA 17236

Call Sign: KB3OES
Gerald E Berney
11129 Little Cove Rd
Mercersburg PA 17236

Call Sign: KA9JRR
Leonard W Smith
8605 Meyers Rd
Mercersburg PA 17236

Call Sign: WA3PTV
Joseph E Lockbaum
10376 Reeder Rd
Mercersburg PA 17236

Call Sign: KB3TFH
Jonathan D Springer
1924 W Orchard Rd
Mercersburg PA 17236

Call Sign: WD4FQS
John J Bethel
7990 Ward Dr
Mercersburg PA 17236

FCC Amateur Radio Licenses in Mexico

Call Sign: KA3EGB
Robert C Grening
Mexico PA 17056

FCC Amateur Radio Licenses in Meyersdale

Call Sign: KA3IUS
Richard L Irwin
330 Beachley St
Meyersdale PA 15552

Call Sign: N3IOJ
Jonathan W Beachy
330 Beachley St
Meyersdale PA 15552

Call Sign: N3SQM
Zachary S Holliday
Box 189
Meyersdale PA 15552

Call Sign: N3NDC
Dale E Smiley
Box 306
Meyersdale PA 15552

Call Sign: N3VYQ
Barry L Hutzell Sr
409 Cherry St
Meyersdale PA 15552

Call Sign: KB3DHA
Kathy A Stairs
3329 Cumberland Hwy
Meyersdale PA 15552

Call Sign: WA3WWG
Curtis R Kerns
160 Duncan St
Meyersdale PA 15552

Call Sign: KB3JEI
James P Gallagher Jr
343 Glade City Rd
Meyersdale PA 15552

Call Sign: KB3VDC
Philip L Burt
238 Large St
Meyersdale PA 15552

Call Sign: N3BSA
Grant E Atwell II
132 Meyers Ave
Meyersdale PA 15552

Call Sign: W3TZM
Shimer E Darr
1261 Murray Rd
Meyersdale PA 15552

Call Sign: KB3MBE
Doris L Valentine
1261 Murray Rd
Meyersdale PA 15552

Call Sign: N3HEY
Willard Broadwater
114 North St
Meyersdale PA 15552

Call Sign: KB3SDC
Dennis C Wertz
162 Roush Mt Rd
Meyersdale PA 15552

Call Sign: W3DCW
Dennis C Wertz
162 Roush Mt Rd
Meyersdale PA 15552

Call Sign: N3OUZ
Raymond F Helinski Jr
50 Salisbury St
Meyersdale PA 15552

Call Sign: N3RKM
Mark R Kirchner
500 Salisbury St
Meyersdale PA 15552

Call Sign: KA3ZBY
Robert A Kirchner
509 Salisbury St
Meyersdale PA 15552

Call Sign: K3DYR
William J Heffern
602 Salisbury St
Meyersdale PA 15552

Call Sign: W3ZCO
Kenneth E Beal
301 Schoolhouse Rd
Meyersdale PA 15552

Call Sign: KB3ULP
Kenneth A Klink
310 Thomas St
Meyersdale PA 15552

Call Sign: N3NQO
Howard J Nicklow
150 Vim Rd
Meyersdale PA 15552

FCC Amateur Radio Licenses in Middleburg

Call Sign: KB3ICK
Christian T Cochran
Box 11
Middleburg PA 17842

Call Sign: KB3JZE
Tonia D Clark
Box 203 Bickel Rd
Middleburg PA 17842

Call Sign: WA3DTV
Wilbur A Hain

1131 E Market Rd
Middleburg PA 17842

Call Sign: WB3CGH
Michael V Chisholm
664 E Ridge Rd
Middleburg PA 17842

Call Sign: N3SHP
Timothy A Yoder
45 Jackson Rd
Middleburg PA 17842

Call Sign: N3SHU
Vernon N Gingerich
45 Jackson Rd
Middleburg PA 17842

Call Sign: K3RRC
Ronald R Clark
165 Kissimmee Rd Apt 2
Middleburg PA 17842

Call Sign: N3CHV
Ricky L Eister
975 Middle Rd
Middleburg PA 17842

Call Sign: KB3EVZ
Donald D Pinci
4491 Middle Rd
Middleburg PA 17842

Call Sign: KD3MC
William T Moyer
1318 Mountain Rd
Middleburg PA 17842

Call Sign: WA2SWL
Peter H Lawrence
275 Peach Orchard Rd
Middleburg PA 17842

Call Sign: KB3JZD
Ronald R Clark

8301 Rt 522
Middleburg PA 17842

Call Sign: KB2IRO
Anthony J Portera
1219 S Hill Dr
Middleburg PA 17842

Call Sign: W3IRO
Anthony J Portera
1219 S Hill Dr
Middleburg PA 17842

Call Sign: K3KBB
Clayton H Best
311 Schoch
Middleburg PA 17842

Call Sign: N3LEP
Thomas F Shambach Jr
308 Schoch St
Middleburg PA 17842

Call Sign: KA3PYZ
John L Lebo
308 Schoch St
Middleburg PA 17842

Call Sign: N3XJY
Donna L Lebo
308 Schoch St
Middleburg PA 17842

Call Sign: KB3NYV
Caleb M Minium
250 W Oak Ave
Middleburg PA 17842

FCC Amateur Radio Licenses in Middlebury Center

Call Sign: AA3HI
Richard W Kinnan
Box 212A

Middlebury Center PA
16935

Call Sign: N3TKW
Barbara P Kinnan
Box 212A
Middlebury Center PA
16935

Call Sign: N3COL
Arthur Galan
Box 240 P
Middlebury Center PA
16935

Call Sign: KB3JTP
Richard J Carl Jr
Box 2526
Middlebury Center PA
16935

Call Sign: N3OTO
Vernon L Gardner
Box 252B
Middlebury Center PA
16935

Call Sign: N3NED
James R Bockus
Box 315A
Middlebury Center PA
16935

Call Sign: N2MIR
William A Constantine
Middlebury Center PA
16935

Call Sign: N2VKX
Theresa C Constantine
Middlebury Center PA
16935

**FCC Amateur Radio
Licenses in Middletown**

Call Sign: KA3AAA
Terry L Phillips
123 Adelia St
Middletown PA 17057

Call Sign: KC8YOP
Andrew M Pulaski
346 Aspen St
Middletown PA 17057

Call Sign: K3VLR
Walter J Maidl
5 Berkley Dr
Middletown PA 17057

Call Sign: N3MTM
Jackie A Stalter
1863 Bonnie Blue Ln
Middletown PA 17057

Call Sign: N3KRD
James J Policino
83 Bradford Ave
Middletown PA 17057

Call Sign: KB3OTY
Rodney E Gallagher
1941 Brentwood Dr
Middletown PA 17057

Call Sign: WA3RHO
Tildon F Sides
304 Burd
Middletown PA
170571601

Call Sign: N3UTO
William G De Wolfe
8 Caravan Ct
Middletown PA 17057

Call Sign: K3YIJ
Kenneth A Bachman
1345 Carriage House Rd

Middletown PA 17057

Call Sign: N3HLK
Michael J Kalbaugh
119 Catalpa St
Middletown PA 17057

Call Sign: N3IXJ
Donald E Witmer
945 Cola Rd
Middletown PA 17057

Call Sign: K3DAV
David W Witsil
132 Columbia St Apt 2
Middletown PA 17057

Call Sign: KB3HUB
Jared M Taylor
4006 E Harrisburg Pike
Middletown PA 17057

Call Sign: KC2FQK
Richard Araujo
1800 E Harrisburg Pike 10
Middletown PA 17057

Call Sign: KB3SPT
James J Hresko
234 E High St
Middletown PA 17057

Call Sign: W2SZA
Charles H Dauphin
416 Edinburgh Rd
Middletown PA
170573495

Call Sign: N3CGA
Charles K Leto
1501 Farmhouse Ln
Middletown PA
170572910

Call Sign: N3YHL

Carol A Kitlan
1001 Georgetown Rd
Middletown PA 17057

Call Sign: K3OPX
Donald R MacLeod
1629 Geyers Church Rd
Middletown PA 17057

Call Sign: W3CEI
Lawrence E Robbins
118 Grandview Ave
Middletown PA 17057

Call Sign: KA3CCO
Kurt R Farr
10 Greenwood Cir
Middletown PA 17057

Call Sign: N3CXW
William L Kennedy Jr
3753 Hedge Ln
Middletown PA 17057

Call Sign: KA3JKB
Eugene R Oldham
505 Laurel Ave
Middletown PA 17057

Call Sign: N3FCW
Horace B Tatem Jr
1593 Longview Dr
Middletown PA 17057

Call Sign: WA3FOR
Charles H Shearer
2005 Market St Ext
Middletown PA 17057

Call Sign: W3VOG
Charles Zito
520 N Lawrence St
Middletown PA 17057

Call Sign: KB3QJG

Christopher R Mcnamara
711 N Pine St
Middletown PA 17057

Call Sign: W9NYG
George W Sturgen
1020 N Union St
Middletown PA 17057

Call Sign: WA3WUC
Walter W Crawford
1020 N Union St Frey
Village
Middletown PA
170572158

Call Sign: KA3NJO
Peter J De Hart
523 N Wood St
Middletown PA 17057

Call Sign: KA3SWS
Scott G Cross
157 Nisley St
Middletown PA 17057

Call Sign: W3RWP
Joseph A Tatkovski Sr
32 Nissley Dr
Middletown PA 17057

Call Sign: WD3R
Howard C Crawford
1431 Old Reliance Rd
Middletown PA 17057

Call Sign: WA3JPL
Earl D Showalter
2912 Orchard Ln
Middletown PA 17057

Call Sign: N3XGR
Joshua R Adams
2966 Orchard Ln

Middletown PA
170575113

Call Sign: WD4ALU
John J Esak
41 Peters Ave Apt 27
Middletown PA 17057

Call Sign: KA3YCD
Robert W Gregg
26 Pine St
Middletown PA 17057

Call Sign: KC3LD
Thomas A Wagner
457 Plane St
Middletown PA 17057

Call Sign: KB3VFG
Robert N Whiteman Jr
1031 Plane St
Middletown PA 17057

Call Sign: K9JW
Steven D Dunwoody
6 Ray Rd
Middletown PA
170573332

Call Sign: N3ZXC
Joshua D Peterson
106 Richardson Rd
Middletown PA 17057

Call Sign: N3RMK
Timothy J Shirk
116 Richardson Rd
Middletown PA
170575511

Call Sign: N3SCZ
Charles E Fies
1711 S Geyers Church Rd
Middletown PA
170574304

Call Sign: N3RLB
Ruth P Walter
14 Vagabond Rd
Middletown PA 17057

Call Sign: N3PAC
Matthew C Miller Sr
30 W High St
Middletown PA 17057

Call Sign: N3PHO
Amber K Miller
30 W High St
Middletown PA 17057

FCC Amateur Radio Licenses in Mifflin

Call Sign: KA3EFV
Robert K Keiser
Box 82
Mifflin PA 17058

Call Sign: N3DXL
George R Keiser
Box 82
Mifflin PA 17058

Call Sign: K3ABR
Adam B Repsher
34 Hillcrest Dr
Mifflin PA 17058

FCC Amateur Radio Licenses in Mifflinburg

Call Sign: N3KCR
David P Swaney
5 Bogar Ln
Mifflinburg PA 17844

Call Sign: N3KCS
David P Swaney II
5 Bogar Ln

Mifflinburg PA 17844

Call Sign: N3MGY
Erin M Swaney
5 Bogar Ln
Mifflinburg PA 17844

Call Sign: N3XLK
Dwight J Swaney
5 Bogar Ln
Mifflinburg PA 178441427

Call Sign: KB3HCC
Erin R Henry
Box 49
Mifflinburg PA 17844

Call Sign: KB3YCF
Joshua Troup
114 Chestnut St
Mifflinburg PA 17844

Call Sign: KA3PYV
Chad L Bowersox
125 Chestnut St
Mifflinburg PA 178441313

Call Sign: KB3KDP
Chad L Bowersox
125 Chestnut St
Mifflinburg PA 178441313

Call Sign: WA3GPG
Charles J Spaid
357 Chestnut St
Mifflinburg PA 17844

Call Sign: KB3SLP
Marlin A Troup
601 Chestnut St
Mifflinburg PA 17844

Call Sign: W3TE
Domenick N Ronco
871 Church Rd

Mifflinburg PA 17844

Call Sign: N3MKC
John E Noss
2770 Dietrich Rd
Mifflinburg PA 17844

Call Sign: KB3YCB
Thomas L Duke
2565 Green Ridge Rd
Mifflinburg PA 17844

Call Sign: WB3IPS
Louis J Pietrandrea
1051 Green St
Mifflinburg PA 17844

Call Sign: KB3IGN
Robert D Poust
730 Johnstown Rd
Mifflinburg PA 17844

Call Sign: KB3DZK
Michael A Weber
81 Laney St
Mifflinburg PA 178441417

Call Sign: N3MOP
Robert E Klingman
93 Laney St
Mifflinburg PA 17844

Call Sign: N3MGV
Melinda J Van Fleet
222 Market St
Mifflinburg PA 17844

Call Sign: N3MFW
James A Van Fleet
222 Market St
Mifflinburg PA 178441333

Call Sign: KB3WST
Daniel E Leach
248 Market St

Mifflinburg PA 17844

Call Sign: WA3YKD
Howard R Hartzell Jr
8561 Old Tpke Rd
Mifflinburg PA 17844

Call Sign: WA2CPM
Emre E Dluhos
1058 Pine Needle Ln
Mifflinburg PA 17844

Call Sign: KB3MRL
Cody M Goddard
311 Powderhouse Ln
Mifflinburg PA 17844

Call Sign: N3PGB
John W Wagner
Rd 2
Mifflinburg PA 17844

Call Sign: KB3YBY
Jon C Arneson
31 Saratoga Ln
Mifflinburg PA 17844

Call Sign: KB3YBZ
Philip J Arneson
31 Saratoga Ln
Mifflinburg PA 17844

Call Sign: WD3L
Harry L Burkland
407 Swarey Rd
Mifflinburg PA 17844

Call Sign: WB3GDH
Donald R Girton
403 Ward Way
Mifflinburg PA 178441143

**FCC Amateur Radio
Licenses in Mifflintown**

Call Sign: KI3D
William N Bratton Jr
24 9th St
Mifflintown PA 17059

Call Sign: K3AUS
Hayes W Eckard
Box 1538
Mifflintown PA
170599210

Call Sign: KB3ND
R Robert Laubach
Box 1572
Mifflintown PA 17059

Call Sign: N3CFN
Donna L Laubach
Box 1572
Mifflintown PA 17059

Call Sign: KB3KUO
Ralph R Laubach
Box 1572
Mifflintown PA 17059

Call Sign: AB3CC
Ralph R Laubach
Box 1572
Mifflintown PA 17059

Call Sign: N3JFK
Paul R Fleisher
Box 3
Mifflintown PA 17059

Call Sign: K3TAR
Tuscarora ARA
Box 31E
Mifflintown PA 17059

Call Sign: KB3BWO
Tuscarora ARA
Box 31E
Mifflintown PA 17059

Call Sign: K3IAZ
Homer W Swartz
Box 472
Mifflintown PA 17059

Call Sign: N3XEU
Jesse L Myer
Box 669
Mifflintown PA 17059

Call Sign: WA3TTU
Larry C McCoy
Box 707
Mifflintown PA 17059

Call Sign: N3NVB
Donald H Wheeler
Box 83
Mifflintown PA 17059

Call Sign: AA3UH
Donald H Wheeler
Box 83
Mifflintown PA 17059

Call Sign: KB3THR
Gregory J Stottle
1 Breezy Ln
Mifflintown PA
170591226

Call Sign: WA3PLR
Fredrick M Gross
155 Mayapple Ln
Mifflintown PA
170595901

Call Sign: N3AGI
Jeffrey L Nale
713 Miller Hill Rd
Mifflintown PA 17059

Call Sign: N3GPL
Deborah K Nale

713 Miller Hill Rd
Mifflintown PA
170599650

Call Sign: N3HXW
Stephen J Ober
33 Muddy Run Rd
Mifflintown PA 17059

Call Sign: KB3THC
David L Hockenbroch
323 Ridge Rd
Mifflintown PA 17059

Call Sign: KA2HOU
Louis R Di Giulio
25 Scenic View Dr
Mifflintown PA 17059

Call Sign: AA3AK
Andrew A Zimmerman
492 Singer Hill Rd
Mifflintown PA 17059

FCC Amateur Radio Licenses in Mifflinville

Call Sign: KB3PNJ
Elvin J Leiby Jr
203 E 7th St
Mifflinville PA 18631

Call Sign: KA3RKO
Richard C Slusser
Fair St 801
Mifflinville PA 186310381

Call Sign: W3JLV
Jere L Vietz
127 W 5th St
Mifflinville PA 18631

Call Sign: KB3GTZ
Jere L Vietz
Mifflinville PA 18631

FCC Amateur Radio Licenses in Milesburg

Call Sign: AL7BC
Paul W Bittengle
207 Darrell St
Milesburg PA 16853

Call Sign: W3MOY
Charles G Weidow
Front St
Milesburg PA 16853

Call Sign: KA3PPK
Gerald H Goodhart Sr
307 Hazel St
Milesburg PA 168530582

FCC Amateur Radio Licenses in Mill Creek

Call Sign: N3JFC
Paul A Brown
Box 557
Mill Creek PA 17060

Call Sign: KA3NVH
William E Frain
Mill Creek PA 17060

FCC Amateur Radio Licenses in Mill Hall

Call Sign: KB3SIZ
Brenden R Hunter
260 Beagle Rd
Mill Hall PA 17751

Call Sign: KB3DMM
Betty J Sonnie
Box 257A
Mill Hall PA 17751

Call Sign: W8PSS

Joseph Matich
Box 30 E Haven Pines Dev
Mill Hall PA 17751

Call Sign: KB3EDB
Roger W Maull
92 Campbell Rd
Mill Hall PA 17751

Call Sign: KB3CBL
Larry D Sonnie
223 Campbell Rd
Mill Hall PA 17751

Call Sign: KB3JCS
Brent A Smith
239 Campbell Rd
Mill Hall PA 17751

Call Sign: KB3CTI
Scott P Jodun
239 Campbell Rd
Mill Hall PA 17751

Call Sign: KB3NUV
Bruce A Dorner
80 Cottage Ln
Mill Hall PA 17751

Call Sign: K3STP
Bruce A Dorner
80 Cottage Ln
Mill Hall PA 17751

Call Sign: KB3PWG
Kathy J Dorner
80 Cottage Ln
Mill Hall PA 17751

Call Sign: K3SCD
Kathy J Dorner
80 Cottage Ln
Mill Hall PA 17751

Call Sign: W3OHS

Francis A Rossman
229 Gwynned Wynd
Mill Hall PA 17751

Call Sign: KF4AKD
Duane K Shaffer
507 Keystone Central Dr
Mill Hall PA 17751

Call Sign: N3IM
Keith I Adams
416 Munro Rd
Mill Hall PA 17751

Call Sign: N3YMO
Amy Lusk
416 Munro Rd
Mill Hall PA 17751

Call Sign: KB3GGC
Randall E Mcintosh
5269 Nittany Valley Dr
Mill Hall PA 17751

Call Sign: KB3GGD
Pamela A Mcintosh
5269 Nittany Valley Dr
Mill Hall PA 17751

Call Sign: W4ZGG
Robert D McClaran
219 Pennsylvania Ave
Mill Hall PA 17751

Call Sign: N3LEO
Judith A Taylor
Mill Hall PA 17751

Call Sign: N3IIW
Mahlon G Taylor Jr
Mill Hall PA 17751

**FCC Amateur Radio
Licenses in Millersburg**

Call Sign: KC2HLG
Kevin C Miller
123 Brenda Dr
Millersburg PA 17061

Call Sign: KF3DN
Richard M Goldberg
398 Landis Rd
Millersburg PA 17061

Call Sign: N3VSN
Gary E Brosius
304 Market St Apt 2
Millersburg PA 17061

Call Sign: N3ZEV
Jason D Koppenhaver
446 River St
Millersburg PA 17061

Call Sign: KC3BB
Murry D Walthour
3320 Rt 147 N
Millersburg PA 17061

Call Sign: KB3UVH
John A Brabits
2674 Rt 209
Millersburg PA 17061

Call Sign: WA3EYQ
Joseph M Steppy
1527 Shippen Dam Rd
Millersburg PA 17061

Call Sign: WB3DWT
Cathy C Steppy
1527 Shippen Dam Rd
Millersburg PA 17061

Call Sign: W3KJA
Elliott E Martin Jr
150 Walnut St
Millersburg PA 17061

Call Sign: ND3I
Charles H Oldland III
539 Wert Rd
Millersburg PA 17061

Call Sign: AA3SJ
Edwin R Kessler
950 Woodside Station Rd
Millersburg PA 17061

Call Sign: KB3UVI
Shelby K Minier
Millersburg PA 17061

Call Sign: K3EMT
Shelby K Minier
Millersburg PA 17061

**FCC Amateur Radio
Licenses in Millerstown**

Call Sign: N3QCV
Dan S Hinkel
Box 173
Millerstown PA 17062

Call Sign: N3SDZ
John S Hinlal
Box 173
Millerstown PA 17062

Call Sign: N3YHE
Christian C White
Box 320
Millerstown PA 17062

Call Sign: WA3NLA
Douglas Wood
Box 478
Millerstown PA 17062

Call Sign: N3VYI
Loren B Wright
Box 740
Millerstown PA 17062

Call Sign: KB3CEA
Victor A Wolfe
112 Cherry Valley Rd
Millerstown PA 17062

Call Sign: KB3DNT
Christine E Carter
112 Cherry Valley Rd
Millerstown PA
170620281

Call Sign: N3LJQ
Michael D Hodge
101 Nace St
Millerstown PA 17062

Call Sign: N3LJR
Christine M Hodge
101 Nace St
Millerstown PA 17062

Call Sign: KB3FUL
Katherine G Hodge
101 Nace St
Millerstown PA 17062

Call Sign: KB3MTP
Christopher M Hodge
101 Nace St
Millerstown PA 17062

Call Sign: N3CMY
Larry A Willow
705 Poplar St
Millerstown PA 17062

Call Sign: KB3IKA
Shawn S Willow
705 Poplar St
Millerstown PA 17062

Call Sign: N3PFO
Randan L Nace
714 Poplar St

Millerstown PA 17062

Call Sign: N3VMU
Aric A Adlon
1544 Raccoon Valley Rd
Millerstown PA 17062

Call Sign: KB3TUW
Rick L Ward
6071 St Samuels Rd
Millerstown PA 17062

Call Sign: KC3JR
Dennis R Stauffer
Walnut St
Millerstown PA
170620169

Call Sign: WA3YTT
Robert L Greenfield
Millerstown PA 17062

Call Sign: KJ3F
Randall W Spriggle
Millerstown PA 17062

Call Sign: N3COH
Susan R Spriggle
Millerstown PA 17062

Call Sign: N3VSZ
Robert G Shipp
Millerstown PA 17062

Call Sign: KB3MWU
Jenna L Moore
Millerstown PA 17062

**FCC Amateur Radio
Licenses in Millersville**

Call Sign: KB3KPV
Kenneth P Delucca
206 Creek Dr
Millersville PA 17551

Call Sign: WA3KD
Kenneth P Delucca
206 Creek Dr
Millersville PA 17551

Call Sign: N3UEC
Steven L MacFeat
150 Elizabeth St
Millersville PA 17551

Call Sign: AA3LB
Albert F Williams Jr
23 Landis Ave
Millersville PA 175512009

Call Sign: N3UNV
Jeremy D Williams
23 Landis Ave
Millersville PA 175512009

Call Sign: KB3KKB
Allen C Rossi Jr
15 Laurelgate Pl
Millersville PA 17551

Call Sign: KB3UUC
Terry M Auspitz
3302 Lynne Ln
Millersville PA 17551

Call Sign: K3TMA
Terry M Auspitz
3302 Lynne Ln
Millersville PA 17551

Call Sign: AC3U
Graham F Todd
30 Manor Oaks Dr
Millersville PA 17551

Call Sign: N0JSC
Janet E Todd
30 Manor Oaks Dr
Millersville PA 17551

Call Sign: N3PIP
Carrie O Phillips
344 N George St
Millersville PA 17551

Call Sign: W3CWE
David A Phillips
344 N George St
Millersville PA 17551

Call Sign: K3MTF
Harry J Woodrow
17 N Prince St
Millersville PA 17551

Call Sign: KB3GAZ
Jason R Benedick
108 Oak Knoll Cir
Millersville PA 17551

Call Sign: KB0EC
Scott M Kohr
19 Sunrise Ter
Millersville PA 17551

Call Sign: N3RCF
Jacob A Weiler III
23 Sunrise Ter
Millersville PA 17551

Call Sign: N3UZU
Sheila L Weiler
23 Sunrise Ter
Millersville PA 17551

Call Sign: N3XPA
Joseph B Poole Jr
66 W Charlotte St
Millersville PA 175511414

Call Sign: KB3EYP
Paul E Sirbak
127 W Frederick St
Millersville PA 17551

Call Sign: KB3EYT
Karen L Sirbak
127 W Frederick St
Millersville PA 17551

Call Sign: KB3RPV
Tony R Heidbreder
151 W Frederick St
Millersville PA 17551

Call Sign: KB3CMF
Robert R Detwiler
48 Walnut Hill Rd
Millersville PA 17551

Call Sign: WA3SZU
Earl E Breneman
Millersville PA 17551

FCC Amateur Radio Licenses in Millerton

Call Sign: N3TAG
Richard A Huber
Box 100J
Millerton PA 16936

Call Sign: K3LZS
Loren M Dunham
Box 102
Millerton PA 16936

Call Sign: KB3KKW
Carissa N Ganong
Box 106F
Millerton PA 16936

Call Sign: KB3UNZ
James M Nixdorf II
Box 197J
Millerton PA 16936

Call Sign: KA3WUQ
Pamela L Achey

498 Dunkleberger Rd
Millerton PA 16936

Call Sign: W3HMK
George A Silvaney
Rd 1
Millerton PA 16936

Call Sign: WA3CSP
Lawrence E Brown Sr
6875 Rt 549
Millerton PA 16936

Call Sign: WB3GQC
Arlene L Brown
6875 Rt 549
Millerton PA 16936

Call Sign: K3DTE
Sam J Anastasio
41 White Rd
Millerton PA 16936

Call Sign: N3XJF
Patrick H Spencer
Millerton PA 16936

FCC Amateur Radio Licenses in Millheim

Call Sign: KB3HUZ
James S Turner III
101 Frazier St
Millheim PA 16854

Call Sign: N3IW
William A Morgan Jr
103 Walter St
Millheim PA 16854

FCC Amateur Radio Licenses in Millmont

Call Sign: KB3FWP
Scott A Susan

Box 692
Millmont PA 17845

Call Sign: N3MFU
David E Ebersole
Box 71
Millmont PA 17845

Call Sign: KA3CRI
Gerald J Badinger
915 Hassenplug Rd
Millmont PA 17845

Call Sign: KB3UYT
Eric A Bergmueller
1020 Orchard Rd
Millmont PA 17845

**FCC Amateur Radio
Licenses in Millville**

Call Sign: KB3UIK
Donald E Cicero
20 Black Birch Rd
Millville PA 17846

Call Sign: KB3TAX
Shirley A Cicero
20 Black Birch Rd
Millville PA 17846

Call Sign: KB3JKU
H Matthew Lunger
18 Eyersgrove Rd Apt 9
Millville PA 178469885

Call Sign: K3JOS
Oliver B Pettebone III
48 Haven Ln
Millville PA 178460320

Call Sign: KB3SLQ
Joseph S Warunek Jr
1516 Hill Rd
Millville PA 17846

Call Sign: W3JSW
Joseph S Warunek Jr
1516 Hill Rd
Millville PA 17846

Call Sign: KB3OVV
Robert E Schultz
196 Kashner Rd
Millville PA 17846

Call Sign: WB3KRH
Peter E Yastishock
232 Rote Hollow Rd
Millville PA 17846

Call Sign: N3BKX
John R Koenig Jr
252 White Horse Pike
Millville PA 17846

Call Sign: N3PEI
Bruce I Shoemaker
Millville PA 17846

Call Sign: W2APC
Anders P Christensen
Millville PA 17846

Call Sign: KB3NKK
Tyler M Breech
Millville PA 17846

**FCC Amateur Radio
Licenses in Milroy**

Call Sign: N1EWQ
Jeffrey L Decker
36 A St
Milroy PA 17063

Call Sign: KB3QGE
Joshua A Miller
16 Acacia Ct
Milroy PA 17063

Call Sign: W3MJO
Joshua A Miller
16 Acacia Ct
Milroy PA 17063

Call Sign: K3GVB
Carrie I Grove
Box 119
Milroy PA 17063

Call Sign: W3FKI
Thurman L Grove
Box 119
Milroy PA 17063

Call Sign: W3FKJ
Thurman S Grove
Box 119
Milroy PA 17063

Call Sign: N3TRS
David A Dutcher
Box B1
Milroy PA 17063

Call Sign: KB3HJI
Michael W Glantz
109 Hill St
Milroy PA 17063

Call Sign: N3ZWB
Kenneth E Klimek
3965 New Lancaster
Valley Rd
Milroy PA 17063

Call Sign: N3HID
Kenneth F Klimek
3965 New Lancaster
Valley Rd
Milroy PA 170639547

Call Sign: N3GSX
Gerald F Klimek

3965 New Lancaster Vly
Rd
Milroy PA 170639745

FCC Amateur Radio Licenses in Milton

Call Sign: K3VRH
Walter H Neuhard
Astro Village
Milton PA 17847

Call Sign: N3NCG
Tim H Longan
Box 1
Milton PA 17847

Call Sign: N3IHQ
Russell E Davis
Box 2030
Milton PA 17847

Call Sign: WB3JQA
Michael J Weisner
Box 224
Milton PA 17847

Call Sign: N3MGZ
Nicholas R Nelson
Box 297C
Milton PA 17847

Call Sign: N3MHA
Theodore P Nelson
Box 297C
Milton PA 17847

Call Sign: N3MHC
Robert D Nelson
Box 297C
Milton PA 17847

Call Sign: N3MHD
Martha K Nelson
Box 297C

Milton PA 17847

Call Sign: KB3LEA
Scott D Neuhard
430 Broadway
Milton PA 17847

Call Sign: W3DBB
Edward V Dobb
530 Center St
Milton PA 17847

Call Sign: N2MXM
Edward B Bearce Sr
113 Hepburn St
Milton PA 178471709

Call Sign: K3LTI
Raymond R Ravert
329 Hepburn St
Milton PA 17847

Call Sign: KB3YCA
Joshua S Bailey
506 Hepburn St
Milton PA 17847

Call Sign: K3VG
Scott A Bucher
13 Honeysuckle Ln
Milton PA 17847

Call Sign: KE3IL
Scott A Bucher
13 Honeysuckle Ln
Milton PA 17847

Call Sign: AA3UY
Scott A Bucher
13 Honeysuckle Ln
Milton PA 17847

Call Sign: N3RYD
Joseph L Smith
1095 Jefferson St

Milton PA 17847

Call Sign: NX3V
Fred A Simon Jr
444 King St
Milton PA 17847

Call Sign: KB3ICL
Charles R Everitt Jr
385 Locust St
Milton PA 17847

Call Sign: KB3IHM
Charles R Everitt Jr
385 Locust St
Milton PA 17847

Call Sign: K3ZZI
Charles R Everitt Jr
385 Locust St
Milton PA 17847

Call Sign: WA3AMI
John E Waldron
803 Mahoning St
Milton PA 17847

Call Sign: WN3FFP
Steven J Trapane
615 S Turbot Ave
Milton PA 178472225

Call Sign: KB3SLO
Barry G Huss
946 Sunset Dr
Milton PA 17847

Call Sign: WA3BZO
Harvey C Follmer Jr
800 Upper Market St
Milton PA 178472536

Call Sign: N3RFT
Donald A Cicero
449 Walnut St

Milton PA 17847

Call Sign: N3RFW
Keith Brown
Milton PA 17847

FCC Amateur Radio Licenses in Mineral Point

Call Sign: WB3ISA
Harry L Hughes Jr
374 Adams Ave
Mineral Point PA
159425801

Call Sign: WB3HRW
Peggy L Hughes
374 Adams Ave
Mineral Point PA
159425801

Call Sign: KF3BY
Robert L Burkett
873 Wess Rd
Mineral Point PA 15942

Call Sign: KB3OUM
Thomas L Brew
127 Zurenda Ln
Mineral Point PA 15942

Call Sign: KB3PJG
Holli E Brew
Mineral Point PA 15942

Call Sign: K3TLB
Thomas L Brew
Mineral Point PA 15942

Call Sign: K3WS
Thomas L Brew
Mineral Point PA 15942

Call Sign: KB3BLF
Cambria County ARES

Mineral Point PA
159420053

Call Sign: WA3WGN
Cambria Radio Club
Mineral Point PA
159420053

FCC Amateur Radio Licenses in Monroe Township

Call Sign: KB3OJU
Mark E Roote
5569 Sr 309
Monroe Township PA
18618

FCC Amateur Radio Licenses in Mont Alto

Call Sign: KC7MRY
John E Stein
328 Park St
Mont Alto PA 17237

Call Sign: KE3QT
James B Tabor
7 Penn St
Mont Alto PA 17237

Call Sign: K3KIT
Karen S Wyzewski
Mont Alto PA 17237

Call Sign: W3TED
Theodore Wyzewski
Mont Alto PA 17237

FCC Amateur Radio Licenses in Montandon

Call Sign: N3QKS
Richard D Buckles
Montandon Tc

Montandon PA 17850

FCC Amateur Radio Licenses in Montgomery

Call Sign: N3SFE
Arthur L Fritz
104 2nd St
Montgomery PA 17752

Call Sign: N3NUT
Arthur L Fritz
104 2nd St
Montgomery PA 17752

Call Sign: N3ZIO
Dale A Brendle
102 Broad St
Montgomery PA 17752

Call Sign: WA3IRS
Leon E Aunkst
185 Dogwood Ridge Rd
Montgomery PA 17752

Call Sign: WB3FWM
Michael K Brown
115 High St
Montgomery PA 17752

Call Sign: N3LEQ
Leslie M Gruver
102 Kinsey St
Montgomery PA 17752

Call Sign: N3ZCJ
Kenneth E Swinn
153 Montgomery St
Montgomery PA 17752

Call Sign: KB3IAY
Sandra L Johnson
153 Montgomery St
Montgomery PA 17752

Call Sign: KB3LIO
Brandon H Parkyn
315 Old Rd
Montgomery PA 17752

Call Sign: N3XUO
James J Bower
111 Pinchtown Rd
Montgomery PA 17752

Call Sign: KB3KUK
Walter S Steinbacher Jr
586 Ridge Rd
Montgomery PA 17752

Call Sign: N3NEP
Walter S Steinbacher Jr
586 Ridge Rd
Montgomery PA 17752

Call Sign: KB3FCO
Dennis M Gruver
553 School House Rd
Montgomery PA 17752

Call Sign: KB3ETE
James R Boose
215 Tiebohl Rd
Montgomery PA
177528772

Call Sign: KA4NIS
Robert M Fox
4968 US Hwy 15
Montgomery PA 17752

**FCC Amateur Radio
Licenses in Montoursville**

Call Sign: N3SFF
Christina L Carson
2515 4 Mile Dr
Montoursville PA 17754

Call Sign: KB3MRN

Brooke B Osborne
1325 Adele Rd
Montoursville PA 17754

Call Sign: KB3TIK
J Ralph Hoyt Jr
1328 Adele Rd
Montoursville PA 17754

Call Sign: N3GRR
Charles W Logan
117 Allendale Dr
Montoursville PA 17754

Call Sign: W2DHY
Howard C Aderhold
1108 Arthur Rd
Montoursville PA 17754

Call Sign: W3VZG
Howard C Aderhold
1108 Arthur Rd
Montoursville PA 17754

Call Sign: KC8PTB
James P Morris
191 Baxter Rd
Montoursville PA 17754

Call Sign: N3MXN
James F Keefer
2760 Blair St
Montoursville PA 17754

Call Sign: N3SFH
Carleton L Polk Jr
Box 414
Montoursville PA 17754

Call Sign: WB3ECT
Joyce K Dover
Box 439
Montoursville PA 17754

Call Sign: N3PFB

Timothy M Gingrich
316 Broad St
Montoursville PA 17754

Call Sign: KB3IPY
David E Brown
1201 Cherry St
Montoursville PA
177542125

Call Sign: KB3IPZ
Robert P Brown
1201 Cherry St
Montoursville PA
177542125

Call Sign: N3PVU
Christopher S Smurl
745 Clarence Fry Rd
Montoursville PA 17754

Call Sign: W3NOB
John A Mallory
119 Confair Pky
Montoursville PA 17754

Call Sign: WC3AAN
Lycoming Co Emerg
Management Agcy
2130 County Farm Rd
Montoursville PA 17754

Call Sign: KB3DXU
Lycoming County Ema
Dcs
542 County Farm Rd Ste
101
Montoursville PA 17754

Call Sign: KB3FTV
Joy A Walls
1950 Eldon Rd
Montoursville PA 17754

Call Sign: KB9KFZ

Walter D Stroop Jr
571 Fairfield Church Rd
Montoursville PA
177548116

Call Sign: KD3PF
Howard P Reisdorf
22 Fairview Ct
Montoursville PA 17754

Call Sign: WD4AII
Kenneth B Webster
1104 Fairview Dr
Montoursville PA 17754

Call Sign: KA3UBU
Kevin C Stabler
1320 Fairview Dr
Montoursville PA 17754

Call Sign: WA3KPI
Steven L Bonnell
1523 Good Shepherd Rd
Montoursville PA 17754

Call Sign: WA3SLN
Michael J Calvert
167 Hillcrest Dr
Montoursville PA 17754

Call Sign: W3IAD
Richard E Montis
1980 Inverness Rd
Montoursville PA 17754

Call Sign: KB3AUQ
Donald E Montis
1980 Inverness Rd
Montoursville PA 17754

Call Sign: K3RJP
Robert J Paulhamus
125 Irion Ln
Montoursville PA 17754

Call Sign: KB3IGO
Joshua A Larson
145 Irion Ln
Montoursville PA 17754

Call Sign: KB3IGP
Jeffrey Williamson
334 Jordan Ave
Montoursville PA 17754

Call Sign: KB3IIS
Mindi L Williamson
334 Jordan Ave
Montoursville PA 17754

Call Sign: N3NUU
Keith H Meckley
512 Jordan Ave
Montoursville PA
177542310

Call Sign: KB3YAD
Ron Behar
62 Katie Ln
Montoursville PA 17754

Call Sign: WB3DKC
John A Dover
234 Kuhns Rd
Montoursville PA 17754

Call Sign: KB3FTR
Qixian Pan
2529 Lincoln Dr
Montoursville PA 17754

Call Sign: KA3SDG
Josef M Wagner
2825 Lincoln Dr Rd 3
Montoursville PA 17754

Call Sign: N3YSN
Ronald R Kennedy
1108 Locust St

Montoursville PA
177541020

Call Sign: KD4CAG
Manuel Barrera Jr
95 Madden Rd
Montoursville PA
177549310

Call Sign: KB3RJD
James L Silver
1112 Monroe Rd
Montoursville PA 17754

Call Sign: K1JLS
James L Silver
1112 Monroe Rd
Montoursville PA 17754

Call Sign: KA3QEB
John T Nettling Jr
140 Mountain Rd
Montoursville PA 17754

Call Sign: N3PFD
John M Staron
928 Mulberry St
Montoursville PA 17754

Call Sign: N3MGI
David M Frei
109 N Loyalsock Ave
Montoursville PA 17754

Call Sign: KB3FIC
Robert W Paulhamus
652 Old Cement Rd
Montoursville PA 17754

Call Sign: K3RWP
Robert W Paulhamus
652 Old Cement Rd
Montoursville PA 17754

Call Sign: KB3GNT

Gregory L Madden
179 Old Cement Rd 32B
Montoursville PA 17754

Call Sign: N3UXH
Todd D Isernhagen
1011 Pearl Blvd
Montoursville PA 17754

Call Sign: KB3FTS
Joseph Sawucci
2875 Pine Ridge Rd
Montoursville PA 17754

Call Sign: W3HXV
Robert C Gray
70 Pine Tree Ln
Montoursville PA
177549053

Call Sign: K3EVS
Harry Gottschall Jr
2341 Quaker State Rd
Montoursville PA
177549703

Call Sign: WB3EKI
Fred L Le Fever
51 Rawle St
Montoursville PA 17754

Call Sign: KA3TTH
Kim W Dockey
305 South Alley
Montoursville PA 17754

Call Sign: KB3SYM
Ann M Lucas
305 South Alley
Montoursville PA 17754

Call Sign: K3KWD
Kim W Dockey
305 South Alley
Montoursville PA 17754

Call Sign: WA3HGT
Herbert W Raemsch
2016 Spruce Brook Ln
Montoursville PA 17754

Call Sign: KC3NW
Edward F Kelley
1937 Summit Courft
Montoursville PA 17754

Call Sign: N3GNP
John S Cillo
101 Sunset Dr
Montoursville PA 17754

Call Sign: KB3ORJ
Conrad H Pinches
87 Tallman Hollow Rd
Montoursville PA 17754

Call Sign: K3QFW
Donnell M Godfrey
1009 Tule St
Montoursville PA 17754

Call Sign: KA3LYP
Ange R Detato
1840 Warrensville Rd
Montoursville PA 17754

Call Sign: KB3WKF
Arlene F Havens
4802 Warrensville Rd
Montoursville PA 17754

Call Sign: N3TQS
Paul M Heaton
108 Willow St
Montoursville PA 17754

Call Sign: KA3SZJ
Brian Yarwood
1930 Woodland Rd Rd 2
Montoursville PA 17754

Call Sign: N3KVS
Anders P Christensen
Montoursville PA 17754

FCC Amateur Radio Licenses in Morris

Call Sign: WB3GAU
Bruno J Tibolla Jr
Box 90
Morris PA 169389619

Call Sign: N3ZLH
Eric A Broughton
327 Nauvoo Rd
Morris PA 16938

Call Sign: KB3UIQ
Ransford J Broughton
3312 Rt 414
Morris PA 16938

Call Sign: KB3VXG
Ryan J Broughton
5395 Rt 414
Morris PA 16938

Call Sign: KA3BAA
Ransford J Broughton
Morris PA 16938

Call Sign: N3ZLI
Ryan J Broughton
Morris PA 16938

Call Sign: KB3DQQ
Dennis J Williams
Morris PA 169380122

FCC Amateur Radio Licenses in Morrisdale

Call Sign: KA3DWR
Douglas A Rowles

3319 Allport Cutoff
Morrisdale PA 16858

Call Sign: W3DWR
Douglas A Rowles
3319 Allport Cutoff
Morrisdale PA 16858

Call Sign: KA3FHV
Jeffrey D Rowles
3319 Allport Cutoff
Morrisdale PA 168587509

Call Sign: N3ZQG
Edwena K Eger
Box 400 B
Morrisdale PA 168589511

Call Sign: KR2RK
Riku J Kalinen
Crowsfoot Ln
Morrisdale PA 16858

Call Sign: K3MGC
David S Posmoga
Morrisdale PA 16858

FCC Amateur Radio Licenses in Moshannon

Call Sign: KB3ITG
Mark A Herman
131 Oak Ln
Moshannon PA
168590086

Call Sign: KA2BBL
George A Salvanish Sr
218 Spruce Rd
Moshannon PA 16859

Call Sign: KB3PJA
Michele L Miles
Moshannon PA 16859

FCC Amateur Radio Licenses in Mount Bethel

Call Sign: WA2VBX
Michael A Nazzaro
415 Belvidere Corner Rd
Mount Bethel PA
183436223

Call Sign: KB3NGQ
Tracey Heffren
556 Belvidere Corner Rd
Mount Bethel PA 18343

Call Sign: NA2I
Howard C Lee
168 Frutchey Ct
Mount Bethel PA
183436235

Call Sign: N3UNJ
Frank E Adams
642 Hemlock Dr
Mount Bethel PA 18343

Call Sign: N3VJB
Raymond G Templeton
235 Independence Way
Mount Bethel PA 18343

Call Sign: WA2LIV
Lester W Baumgartner
216 Molly Pitcher Ln
Mount Bethel PA 18343

Call Sign: N2AAE
Michael Watley
37 Red Fox Ln
Mount Bethel PA 18343

Call Sign: KD3FT
Anthony R Ladzinski
4210 River Rd
Mount Bethel PA 18343

Call Sign: W7KRJ
Philip F Margulies
4246 River Rd
Mount Bethel PA 18343

Call Sign: KA3SFZ
Scott D Luzzi
491 Sunrise Blvd
Mount Bethel PA 18343

Call Sign: WG3F
Glenn J Luzzi
491 Sunrise Blvd
Mount Bethel PA 18343

Call Sign: AA3JU
George C Cook
Mount Bethel PA 18343

FCC Amateur Radio Licenses in Mount Carmel

Call Sign: KB3HRG
Sueellen Lamb
651 E 4th St
Mount Carmel PA 17851

Call Sign: W3RQU
Benjamin T Trefsgar
653 E 4th St
Mount Carmel PA 17851

Call Sign: W3LJD
Ray E Williard
210 E 7th St
Mount Carmel PA 17851

Call Sign: KB3HOC
Ronald J Siko
413 N Market St
Mount Carmel PA 17851

Call Sign: N3KFV
Ronald J Shopinski

320 N Oak St
Mount Carmel PA 17851

Call Sign: WA3IMH
Albert M Sebes
33 S Chestnut St
Mount Carmel PA 17851

Call Sign: KB3AVT
Jerome M Sassani
316 S Lemon St
Mount Carmel PA 17851

Call Sign: KA3SQF
Jean M Pulaski
225 S Vine St
Mount Carmel PA 17851

Call Sign: N3TQM
Thomas R Davis
418 W Cherry St
Mount Carmel PA 17851

Call Sign: KB3UGQ
Rcct Team 38380
478 W Girard St
Mount Carmel PA 17851

Call Sign: KB3PIN
Scott E Weaver
478 W Girard St Atlas
Mount Carmel PA 17851

FCC Amateur Radio Licenses in Mount Gretna

Call Sign: N3HGP
Sandra C Bowman
3rd & Weaver Sts Box 636
Mount Gretna PA 17064

Call Sign: WA3REY
Thomas B Bowman Jr
307 3rd St

Mount Gretna PA 17064

Call Sign: W3REY
Thomas B Bowman Jr
307 3rd St
Mount Gretna PA 17064

Call Sign: N3MJL
John C Balmer
109 5th St
Mount Gretna PA 17064

Call Sign: N3ELJ
Larry F Widmer
195 Birch Ave
Mount Gretna PA
170640398

Call Sign: WA2ITP
David J Mayercik
219 Village Ln
Mount Gretna PA 17064

FCC Amateur Radio Licenses in Mount Holly Springs

Call Sign: KB3BNO
Qrp Society Of Central PA
20 Brenely Ln
Mount Holly Springs PA
17065

Call Sign: W3HAH
Robert B Wicks
24 E Pine St
Mount Holly Springs PA
17065

Call Sign: N3DHK
William R Gabel II
642 Highland Ave
Mount Holly Springs PA
17065

Call Sign: WA3VFD
Charles H Kesner
103 Hillside Dr
Mount Holly Springs PA
170651802

Call Sign: KA3HWX
June E March
644 Holly Pike
Mount Holly Springs PA
17065

Call Sign: N3UTN
Douglas R Motter
28 Holly St
Mount Holly Springs PA
170651315

Call Sign: N3THG
Jeffrey M Kuklinski
8 Ian Dr
Mount Holly Springs PA
17065

Call Sign: WA3RFL
Albert F Hoffman Jr
100 McLand Rd
Mount Holly Springs PA
17065

Call Sign: KB3MVP
Caitlynne L Brophy
111 Moreland Ave
Mount Holly Springs PA
17065

Call Sign: KB3MVO
Emily C Baehr
192 Mtn View Rd
Mount Holly Springs PA
17065

Call Sign: N3EAG
Edward C Blake
4 Park St

Mount Holly Springs PA
17065

Call Sign: KA3TFK
Clarence A Bricker
231 Pine Rd
Mount Holly Springs PA
17065

Call Sign: KB3HCU
Clarence E Butterworth Jr
502 Sand Bank Rd
Mount Holly Springs PA
17065

Call Sign: KB3LRB
Anastasia V Mallios
715 Sand Bank Rd
Mount Holly Springs PA
17065

Call Sign: KB3MWR
Joanna T Mallios
715 Sandbank Rd
Mount Holly Springs PA
17065

Call Sign: KB3VUU
Michael H Berk
206 Sunset Dr
Mount Holly Springs PA
17065

Call Sign: K3NYY
Michael H Berk
206 Sunset Dr
Mount Holly Springs PA
17065

Call Sign: KB3WIE
Bryan A Gembusia
7 Woodview Dr
Mount Holly Springs PA
17065

Call Sign: KB3IUS
Michael G Endres
1 Yankee Dr
Mount Holly Springs PA
17065

Call Sign: N3TWT
South Mountain Radio
Amateurs
Mount Holly Springs PA
17065

Call Sign: KA3IDS
Judith A Tracey
Mount Holly Springs PA
170650088

Call Sign: KC3EK
Jo Glenn Tracey
Mount Holly Springs PA
170650088

**FCC Amateur Radio
Licenses in Mount Jewett**

Call Sign: N3PYN
Dorette M Brandes
43 Anderson St
Mount Jewett PA 16740

Call Sign: KB3LNQ
Linda J Greek
560 Warner Brook Rd
Mount Jewett PA 16740

Call Sign: W3WS
Karl P Baumler Sr
560 Warner Brook Rd
Mount Jewett PA 16740

Call Sign: KB3HDC
Allison T Bowman
Mount Jewett PA 16740

Call Sign: KB3LTP

Craig M Simons
Mount Jewett PA 16740

Call Sign: KB3LTQ
Steve A Warren
Mount Jewett PA 16740

Call Sign: KB3GLW
Stanley R Bowman
Mount Jewett PA 16740

Call Sign: KF4BKT
Frederick S Strickland
Mount Jewett PA
167400053

**FCC Amateur Radio
Licenses in Mount Joy**

Call Sign: WB3CUC
Michael W Zelinski
605 Alcott Dr
Mount Joy PA 17552

Call Sign: KE3FA
John G Bice
425 Anderson Ferry Rd
Mount Joy PA 17552

Call Sign: N3TJR
Thomas K Pesters
253 Brian Ave
Mount Joy PA 17552

Call Sign: KN3A
Scott A Lithgow
874 Center St
Mount Joy PA 17552

Call Sign: N3XPC
Jack A Clayton
906 Center St
Mount Joy PA 175529371

Call Sign: KB3KVQ

Brandon S West
483 Charter Ln
Mount Joy PA 17552

Call Sign: KB3VIE
David A Boucher
302 Crestwyck Cir
Mount Joy PA 17552

Call Sign: KB3SIQ
Gary L Devonshire Jr
2012 Crestwyck Cir
Mount Joy PA 17552

Call Sign: KB3RYK
Jared S Heinly
118 David St
Mount Joy PA 17552

Call Sign: KB3TLW
Roxanne M Emswiler
38 Dietz Ln
Mount Joy PA 17552

Call Sign: KA3JMA
John F Way Jr
836 Donegal Springs Rd
Mount Joy PA 17552

Call Sign: N3UDW
Jerry A Keener
1239 Donegal Springs Rd
Mount Joy PA 17552

Call Sign: N3TPL
Jeffrey S Ishler
1375 E Main St
Mount Joy PA 17552

Call Sign: N3DDF
John A Rylatt
1558 Emerson Dr
Mount Joy PA 17552

Call Sign: W3SXO

Harry E Zink Jr
462 Fairview Rd Apt 32
Mount Joy PA 17552

Call Sign: N3WTH
Gary S Barb Jr
235 Farmcrest Ln
Mount Joy PA 17552

Call Sign: KB3JPI
Peter B Bibawy
715 Farmdale Rd
Mount Joy PA 17552

Call Sign: KA3CMH
Dorothy I McElrea
918 Farmdale Rd
Mount Joy PA 175529352

Call Sign: WA3CUN
William J McElrea
918 Farmdale Rd
Mount Joy PA 175529352

Call Sign: WF3R
Scott D Felton
324 Farmview Ln
Mount Joy PA 17552

Call Sign: N3APD
Paul A Miller
344 Florin Ave
Mount Joy PA 17552

Call Sign: WA3VXG
John P Kling
727 Harold Ave
Mount Joy PA 17552

Call Sign: N3JPG
Louis L Toth
1819 Harrisburg Ave
Mount Joy PA 17552

Call Sign: N3XAI

Daniel G Trump
2057 Harrisburg Ave
Mount Joy PA 17552

Call Sign: WA3ZHR
Terry L Zink
654 Hawthorne Ln
Mount Joy PA 17552

Call Sign: N3KVG
Mark L Starner
835 Hilltop Dr
Mount Joy PA 17552

Call Sign: N3EPO
John K Bryson Jr
885 Hilltop Dr
Mount Joy PA 17552

Call Sign: KB3CQJ
Philip A Colvin
7 Jewel Dr
Mount Joy PA 17552

Call Sign: N3JPD
John A Gainer
19 Jewel Dr
Mount Joy PA 17552

Call Sign: KE3ZQ
James M Miller
838 Knoll Dr
Mount Joy PA 17552

Call Sign: WB8ZDF
Samuel J P Laube
434 Lefever Rd
Mount Joy PA 175529306

Call Sign: W3IHM
Samuel J P Laube
434 Lefever Rd
Mount Joy PA 175529306

Call Sign: N3XDN

Douglas O Kesser
355 Locust Ln
Mount Joy PA 17552

Call Sign: KB3HUD
Rex L Kesser
355 Locust Ln
Mount Joy PA 17552

Call Sign: KB3DWG
Phillip A Wright
4096 Marietta Ave
Mount Joy PA 17552

Call Sign: KB3KTS
John M Yost
4112 Millbrook Rd
Mount Joy PA 17552

Call Sign: KE3KH
David L Lockard
1956 Milton Grove Rd
Mount Joy PA 17552

Call Sign: N3QJW
Angela M Hoffer
1942 Misty Dr
Mount Joy PA 17552

Call Sign: K3AWY
Stanley M Godshall
1891 Mt Pleasant Rd
Mount Joy PA 17552

Call Sign: N2EWG
Paul E Collier
389 N Barbara St Apt 1
Mount Joy PA 17552

Call Sign: KB3JCV
Paul E Collier
389 N Barbara St Apt 1
Mount Joy PA 17552

Call Sign: N3VKQ

Kenneth M Nissley
127 N Market St
Mount Joy PA 17552

Call Sign: WQ3P
Carl R Denlinger
3675 Nolt Rd
Mount Joy PA 17552

Call Sign: K2HRS
George Roberts
4155 Nolt Rd
Mount Joy PA 17552

Call Sign: KA3TAM
Deborah S Fogal Zink
43 Old Market St
Mount Joy PA 17552

Call Sign: KB3CHA
Edward J Petts
820 Penny Ln
Mount Joy PA 175529229

Call Sign: KB3EYM
Ronald M Grose
210 Pinkerton Rd
Mount Joy PA 17552

Call Sign: KZ0H
Gary L Zeller
333 Pinkerton Rd
Mount Joy PA 17552

Call Sign: KA3GAU
Thomas L Miller
1843 Rhoda Ave
Mount Joy PA 17552

Call Sign: KB3KSS
Daniel C Whitsel
308 S Market Ave
Mount Joy PA 17552

Call Sign: N3OGM

Joy B Fry
463 S Plum St
Mount Joy PA 17552

Call Sign: KF3AT
Ronald W Vang
483 S Plum St
Mount Joy PA 17552

Call Sign: KA3TAN
Warren H Stehman Jr
619 Square St
Mount Joy PA 17552

Call Sign: N3GTR
Sandra J Stehman
619 Square St
Mount Joy PA 175520224

Call Sign: AI9I
Ronald J Rudolph
1170 Stellar Dr
Mount Joy PA 17552

Call Sign: KB3SCA
Margaret R Hamm
755 Terrace Ave
Mount Joy PA 17552

Call Sign: KB3SCB
Richard S Hamm
755 Terrace Ave
Mount Joy PA 17552

Call Sign: N3EPI
Donald J Robinson
569 W Main St
Mount Joy PA 17552

Call Sign: KB3FCL
Desiree L Douglas
36 W Main St Apt C
Mount Joy PA 17552

Call Sign: N3OFA

Robert E Bard
620 Water St
Mount Joy PA 17552

Call Sign: KB3SSZ
Gerald W Wagner
1309 Willow Creek Dr
Mount Joy PA 17552

Call Sign: KB3EYI
Hans D Gehman
1224 Wissler Ln
Mount Joy PA 17552

Call Sign: KB3LJK
Aimee L Stehman
Mount Joy PA 17552

Call Sign: K3SAB
Shannon Brown
Mount Joy PA 17552

FCC Amateur Radio Licenses in Mount Pleasant Mills

Call Sign: KE3BP
Thomas B Spangler
Box 223Ab
Mount Pleasant Mills PA
17853

Call Sign: N3CVQ
Roger L Dietz
Box 310
Mount Pleasant Mills PA
17853

Call Sign: N3VZT
Daniel J Weaver
Box 388
Mount Pleasant Mills PA
17853

Call Sign: KB3DPJ

Shirley B Spangler
851 Clark Hill Rd
Mount Pleasant Mills PA
17853

Call Sign: KB3CXP
Rebecca Spangler
851 Clark Hill Rd
Mount Pleasant Mills PA
17853

Call Sign: N3ZCX
Barbara J Weaver
1944 Pine Swamp Rd
Mount Pleasant Mills PA
17853

Call Sign: KD3OA
John C Tobias
3433 Red Bank Rd
Mount Pleasant Mills PA
17853

FCC Amateur Radio Licenses in Mount Union

Call Sign: N3YQN
Scott D Nearhood
Box 1295
Mount Union PA 17066

Call Sign: N3YQO
Crystal M Nearhood
Box 1295
Mount Union PA 17066

Call Sign: W3OKN
E Merle Glunt
Box 303
Mount Union PA 17066

Call Sign: N3YZF
David A Gaisior
14423 Carl St
Mount Union PA 17066

Call Sign: N3YZD
Ronald A Dell
580 Country Club Rd
Mount Union PA 17066

Call Sign: K3HKS
Frederick G Stewart
102 Dale Rd
Mount Union PA 17066

Call Sign: W2TL
Frederick G Stewart
102 Dale Rd
Mount Union PA 17066

Call Sign: W3DY
Frederick G Stewart
102 Dale Rd
Mount Union PA 17066

Call Sign: N3YQP
Bruce J Smith III
275 Dale Rd
Mount Union PA 17066

Call Sign: N3YQQ
Bruce J Smith IV
275 Dale Rd
Mount Union PA 17066

Call Sign: AA3X
Bruce J Smith III
275 Dale Rd
Mount Union PA 17066

Call Sign: KA3WBF
Andrew D Kurey Jr
118 E Market St
Mount Union PA 17066

Call Sign: N3OGT
Andrew J Ketner
38 E Milford St
Mount Union PA 17066

Call Sign: W3VI
Huntingdon County ARC
38 E Milford St
Mount Union PA 17066

Call Sign: WA3YVL
James A Cohenour
834 Kistler Rd
Mount Union PA 17066

Call Sign: W3JAC
James A Cohenour
834 Kistler Rd
Mount Union PA 17066

Call Sign: N3YZJ
George J Drobnock
213 S Jefferson St
Mount Union PA 17066

Call Sign: KR3C
Timothy W Clapper
W Shirley St
Mount Union PA 17066

Call Sign: K3KZE
David H Ross
Mount Union PA 17066

Call Sign: KA3KXR
Thomas J McGovern
Mount Union PA 17066

Call Sign: KA3RBX
Patricia A Ross
Mount Union PA 17066

Call Sign: KI3X
Richard L Jordan
Mount Union PA 17066

**FCC Amateur Radio
Licenses in Mount Wolf**

Call Sign: AH8P
Sandra S Peterson
920 2nd St
Mount Wolf PA 17347

Call Sign: KH8CN
Andrew P Peterson
920 2nd St
Mount Wolf PA 17347

Call Sign: N3SDH
Joel W Klinedinst
80 4th St Saginaw
Mount Wolf PA 17347

Call Sign: KB3EEM
Douglas J Hura
155 Abbey Dr
Mount Wolf PA 17347

Call Sign: KA3EMD
James C Myers
31 Acorn Dr
Mount Wolf PA 17347

Call Sign: N3TRA
Michael J Myers
5190 Board Rd
Mount Wolf PA 17347

Call Sign: N3VTX
Charles F Falkenhan
15 Coventry Cross Rd
Mount Wolf PA 17347

Call Sign: KB3SSS
John A Moramarco
165 Donrene Rd
Mount Wolf PA 17347

Call Sign: N3DX
Robert S Simpson
920 Jerusalem School Rd
Mount Wolf PA 17347

Call Sign: K3TXA
Charlotte I Brown
703 Lake Dr Starview Mhp
Mount Wolf PA 17347

Call Sign: K3TXB
Herald F Brown
703 Lake Dr Starview Mhp
Mount Wolf PA 17347

Call Sign: N3OHR
David G Mitchell
20 Laurel Dr
Mount Wolf PA 17347

Call Sign: KB3JSK
Glenn E Almoney
780 Market St
Mount Wolf PA 17347

Call Sign: KB3HBA
James R Rauch Jr
785 Market St
Mount Wolf PA 17347

Call Sign: WB3CGF
James R Rauch Jr
785 Market St
Mount Wolf PA 17347

Call Sign: AB3S
David W Prichard
335 Pebble Beach Dr
Mount Wolf PA
173479577

Call Sign: WA3YDF
Philip R Botterbusch
106 S 4th St
Mount Wolf PA 17347

Call Sign: N3SEB
Gary E Roberts
172 S 4th St
Mount Wolf PA 17347

Call Sign: KA3IUO
Donald S Miller II
260 S 4th St
Mount Wolf PA 17347

Call Sign: N3MUA
Kaye F Flenner
66 S 4th St Box 292
Mount Wolf PA 17347

Call Sign: N3WQV
Patrick H Rambeau
22 S 7th St
Mount Wolf PA 17347

Call Sign: WB5RDC
Jon A Winborn
130 Steffie Dr
Mount Wolf PA 17347

Call Sign: KT3A
Cameron C R Bailey
Mount Wolf PA 17347

Call Sign: N3NBW
Deborah A Bailey
Mount Wolf PA 17347

**FCC Amateur Radio
Licenses in Mountville**

Call Sign: KB3VCM
David J Bonafede
372 Blue Bell Dr
Mountville PA 17554

Call Sign: N3IDS
Michael J Wissler
306 Central Manor Rd
Mountville PA 17554

Call Sign: N3PIR
Arthur E Kalbach
3651 Clear Stream Dr

Mountville PA 17554

Call Sign: AD9E
Richard J Long
335 Curby Dr
Mountville PA 17554

Call Sign: W3EOJ
J Frank Enders
173 E Main St
Mountville PA 17554

Call Sign: N3TUR
Michael L Graybill
104 Froelich Ave
Mountville PA 17554

Call Sign: N3LTN
John P Murray Sr
112 Hampden Dr
Mountville PA 17554

Call Sign: KA3TLB
George J Russo Jr
Hershey Mill Rd
Mountville PA 17554

Call Sign: W3TLB
George J Russo Jr
Hershey Mill Rd
Mountville PA 17554

Call Sign: N3UNT
David A Weaver
420 Highland Dr
Mountville PA 17554

Call Sign: KA3ULQ
Christopher S
Blechschmidt
421 Highland Dr
Mountville PA 17554

Call Sign: KD4ADT
John C Spaulding

3624 Keen Ave
Mountville PA 17554

Call Sign: WB2JDU
Robert R Best
300 Millstone Dr
Mountville PA 17554

Call Sign: N3ROE
Vincent J Henry
3540 Mtn View Dr
Mountville PA 17554

Call Sign: KB3NYI
Jay M Johnson
327 Oakridge Dr
Mountville PA 17554

Call Sign: KB3RPU
Nancy Jo Johnson
327 Oakridge Dr
Mountville PA 17554

Call Sign: W3RLT
Ray H Enders
375 Primrose Ln
Mountville PA 17554

Call Sign: KB3JNL
Thomas L Mccurdy Jr
218 Ruby St
Mountville PA 17554

Call Sign: WA3ZHG
C Douglas Hengst
316 Spring Hill Ln
Mountville PA 17554

Call Sign: N3ZRY
John C Strickler
1855 Stony Battery Rd
Mountville PA 17554

Call Sign: KB3DWW
James C Strickler

1855 Stony Battery Rd Ste
1
Mountville PA 175541318

Call Sign: KG3X
Nathan M Murry
507 Talon Dr
Mountville PA 17554

Call Sign: KA0JQO
Kevin R Magloughlin
Mountville PA 17554

Call Sign: KB3GMY
Don Carman
Mountville PA 175540493

Call Sign: AB3HS
Don Carman
Mountville PA 175540493

FCC Amateur Radio Licenses in Muncy

Call Sign: N3JUI
James M OBrien
Box 224
Muncy PA 17756

Call Sign: N3RFV
Matthew L Burkhart
Box 538
Muncy PA 17756

Call Sign: N3ZHC
Francis E Burke II
123 Carpenter St
Muncy PA 17756

Call Sign: K3LYC
Francis E Burke II
123 Carpenter St
Muncy PA 17756

Call Sign: WA3GDK

Thomas L Rhoat
875 Chippewa Rd
Muncy PA 17756

Call Sign: WA3BHK
John E Young Jr
911 Chippewa Rd
Muncy PA 17756

Call Sign: N3CUB
Alan C Wheal
1604 Clarkstown Rd
Muncy PA 17756

Call Sign: WB3HOI
Kenneth R Frey
526 E Penn St
Muncy PA 177569113

Call Sign: KB3GIE
Michael A Puderbaugh
30 Green St
Muncy PA 17756

Call Sign: K3MAP
Michael A Puderbaugh
30 Green St
Muncy PA 17756

Call Sign: WD9BBV
Stanley G Boler
19 Larson Rd
Muncy PA 17756

Call Sign: AB3BL
Stanley G Boler
19 Larson Rd
Muncy PA 17756

Call Sign: KB5QJJ
Dean L Robbins
5 Moreland Baptist Rd
Muncy PA 17756

Call Sign: W3DLR

Dean L Robbins
5 Moreland Baptist Rd
Muncy PA 17756

Call Sign: KB3HPY
Wayne L Robbins
2476 Moreland Twp Rd
Muncy PA 17756

Call Sign: AB3AM
Wayne L Robbins
2476 Moreland Twp Rd
Muncy PA 17756

Call Sign: N3MFM
James E Powell
780 Muncy Exchange Rd
Muncy PA 17756

Call Sign: W3SDZ
Victor A Michael
4205 Muncy Exchange Rd
Muncy PA 17756

Call Sign: KA3FYX
William C Lewis
615 Oxbow Rd
Muncy PA 177567332

Call Sign: K3MSG
Milo H Frey
200 Quarry Rd
Muncy PA 17756

Call Sign: N2SCD
Stanley J Nierzwicki
105 Quarry Rd
Muncy PA 17756

Call Sign: N3KCQ
Gary L Burkhart
4010 Rabbittown Rd
Muncy PA 17756

Call Sign: N3PFF

John M Rymell
6175 Rt 405 Hwy
Muncy PA 17756

Call Sign: KB3GNY
Raymond E Girardi
1635 Rt 442 Hwy Lot B 19
Muncy PA 17756

Call Sign: N3WGQ
Glenn W Fronk
528 Ruben Kehrer Rd Lot
71
Muncy PA 17756

Call Sign: KB3FTA
Robert J Paulhamus
528 Ruben Kehrer Rd Lot
80
Muncy PA 17756

Call Sign: W8GRH
William C Whitney
124 S Main St
Muncy PA 17756

Call Sign: KB3KDO
Katie L Updegraff
104 S Main St Apt 6
Muncy PA 17756

Call Sign: K3KLG
Katie L Updegraff
104 S Main St Apt 6
Muncy PA 17756

Call Sign: WB3FGX
Robert H Myers
211 S Washington St
Muncy PA 17756

Call Sign: K3LTM
Bruce D Weaver
621 Shuttle Hill Rd
Muncy PA 17756

Call Sign: KB3BRU
Keystone ARA
6175 State Rt 405 Hwy
Muncy PA 17756

Call Sign: WB3JQJ
Geoffrey R Forester
166 Van Horn Blvd
Muncy PA 17756

Call Sign: N3ZEU
Lawrence G Wertman
173 W Water St
Muncy PA 177569115

Call Sign: W3LGW
Lawrence G Wertman
173 W Water St
Muncy PA 177569115

Call Sign: N3MFN
Birch B Phillips III
53 Waldron Ln
Muncy PA 17756

**FCC Amateur Radio
Licenses in Munson**

Call Sign: KB3MNU
Joseph M Maynard
Box 254
Munson PA 16860

**FCC Amateur Radio
Licenses in Myerstown**

Call Sign: W2KZT
Fred W Harnisch
61 Arbor Dr
Myerstown PA 170673133

Call Sign: N3UCV
Jeron L Reed
Box 66

Myerstown PA 17067

Call Sign: N3XNQ
John D Mellinger Jr
188 Deep Run Rd
Myerstown PA 17067

Call Sign: N3OUJ
Mark L Witmer
190 Deep Run Rd
Myerstown PA 17067

Call Sign: N3OUK
Miriam Witmer
190 Deep Run Rd
Myerstown PA 17067

Call Sign: N3OUI
Melody A Mellinger
188 Deep Run Rd
Myerstown PA 17067

Call Sign: N3UBC
Jeff L Martin
216 E Carpenter Ave
Myerstown PA 17067

Call Sign: N3TSU
Daryl G Martin
721 E Lincoln Ave
Myerstown PA 17067

Call Sign: N3VYL
Galen M Martin
721 E Lincoln Ave
Myerstown PA 17067

Call Sign: KB3ACK
Doi Van Vo
14 E Main St
Myerstown PA 17067

Call Sign: W3PU
Le Roy H Shreffler
58 E Rosebud Rd

Myerstown PA 17067

Myerstown PA 17067

Myerstown PA 17067

Call Sign: N3WFR
Kerry E Rapp
403 E Rosebud Rd
Myerstown PA 17067

Call Sign: N3IIT
Thomas R Centini
500 Hentztown Rd 43
Myerstown PA 17067

Call Sign: W3RUS
Russell S Wolfe Jr
280 Long Rd
Myerstown PA 17067

Call Sign: N3ZYR
Nevin M Nolt
384 Frystown Rd
Myerstown PA 17067

Call Sign: N3UWQ
Matthew R Burkholder
791 Houtztown Rd
Myerstown PA 17067

Call Sign: KA3RRQ
Keith W Lehman
612 N College St
Myerstown PA 17067

Call Sign: N3XAP
Thomas C Fox
369 Golf Rd
Myerstown PA 17067

Call Sign: N3UWR
J Andrew Burkholder
791 Houtztown Rd
Myerstown PA 17067

Call Sign: KA3RRR
Debra L Lehman
612 N College St
Myerstown PA 17067

Call Sign: N3OBF
Roger L Martin
17 Greble Rd
Myerstown PA 17067

Call Sign: W3EIA
Van S Miller II
500 Houtztown Rd Box 30
Myerstown PA 170672133

Call Sign: W3HLG
Howard J Rittle
207 N Railroad St
Myerstown PA 17067

Call Sign: N3OUN
Anthony L Martin
17 Greble Rd
Myerstown PA 17067

Call Sign: KB3DXC
Donald F McCole Jr
500 Houtztown Rd Lot 77
Myerstown PA 17047

Call Sign: KB3VIL
Erin K Walker
320 N Railroad St
Myerstown PA 17067

Call Sign: N3OXT
Phebe G Martin
17 Greble Rd
Myerstown PA 17067

Call Sign: WA3KXY
Robert R Confair Sr
771 Kutztown Rd
Myerstown PA 17067

Call Sign: KB3WOF
Erin K Walker
320 N Railroad St
Myerstown PA 17067

Call Sign: N3ZKE
Jason L Baugher
182 Greble Rd
Myerstown PA 17067

Call Sign: KB3DLG
Robert B Burkholder Jr
7980 Lancaster Ave
Myerstown PA 17067

Call Sign: N3GLP
Kevin H Light
183 N Ramona Rd
Myerstown PA 17067

Call Sign: KB3HYJ
Mark F Rajchel
580 Halfway Dr
Myerstown PA 17067

Call Sign: KB3EDL
Melvin L Unger
730 Little Mtn Rd
Myerstown PA 17067

Call Sign: KE5PLD
Michael E Floyd
5 Quarryland Dr
Myerstown PA 17067

Call Sign: KB3RSX
Tiffany L Yorgensen
790 Halfway Dr

Call Sign: KB3DBK
Clayton P Swartzentruber
1102 Little Mtn Rd

Call Sign: KB3QZM
Adolph L Montanye
317 S Broad St

Myerstown PA 17067

Myerstown PA 17067

Myerstown PA 17067

Call Sign: WL7BQV
Wesley E Hornberger
50 S Ramona Rd
Myerstown PA 170672347

Call Sign: N3MLF
Adam R Sitler
535 W Lincoln Ave
Myerstown PA 17067

Call Sign: N3HHI
Ellen R Messerschmidt
Myerstown PA 17067

Call Sign: N2KYZ
Robert A Levin
46 Scenic Dr
Myerstown PA 170673175

Call Sign: KB3ILN
Edward R Shutter
12 W Maple Ave
Myerstown PA 17067

Call Sign: KA3RCS
Karl F Messerschmidt
Myerstown PA 17067

Call Sign: WD8QPO
John E Reed
36 Springhouse Dr
Myerstown PA 17067

Call Sign: N3PKP
David A Roof
207 W Maple Ave
Myerstown PA 17067

Call Sign: KB3EPW
B Tiga B L Armantrout
Myerstown PA 17067

Call Sign: KB3WZD
Jedrek D Nolt
401 Stracks Dam Rd
Myerstown PA 17067

Call Sign: WT3H
David M Strasz
216 W McKinley Ave
Myerstown PA 17067

Call Sign: KA3YVE
Julia R Messerschmidt
Myerstown PA 170670353

Call Sign: KA3ION
Paul A Long
893 Tulpehocken Rd
Myerstown PA 17067

Call Sign: W3CKD
James C Mohn
7 W Park Ave
Myerstown PA 17067

Call Sign: KB3HZJ
Jamie L Horn
1237 Cardiff Rd
Nanty Glo PA 15943

Call Sign: KB3SDO
Christopher W Hoffman
333 Valley View Rd
Myerstown PA 17067

Call Sign: KA3IQZ
Donald R Knepp
28 W Stracks Dr
Myerstown PA 170672162

Call Sign: N3ZQW
Robert W Dzielski
322 Lincoln Ave
Nanty Glo PA 15943

Call Sign: AB3IR
William H Hoffman Jr
333 Valley View Rd
Myerstown PA 17067

Call Sign: N3FOU
Nancy L Gockley
3979 Wintersville Rd
Myerstown PA 17067

Call Sign: KB3OXQ
Robert W Dzielski
322 Lincoln Ave
Nanty Glo PA 15943

Call Sign: KA3RSY
Rhonda C Zook
343 Valleyview Rd
Myerstown PA 17067

Call Sign: NF3S
Glenn L Gockley
3979 Wintersville Rd
Myerstown PA 17067

Call Sign: KB3HZI
Tom R Swartz
181 Sterling Ave
Nanty Glo PA 15934

Call Sign: N3MLE
Larry I Sitler
535 W Lincoln Ave

Call Sign: N3OGJ
Franklin L Fulk
349 Woleber Rd

Call Sign: K3GYR

Gerald E Wizon
476 Gault Rd
Narvon PA 17555

Call Sign: KA3STV
Irene M Wizon
476 Gault Rd
Narvon PA 17555

Call Sign: W3DVW
Robert L Wizon
476 Gault Rd
Narvon PA 17555

Call Sign: KB3YDN
Susan A Stauffer
5753 Glen Oaks Dr
Narvon PA 17555

Call Sign: KB3YKW
Stephen M Dijoseph
6165 Guy Rd
Narvon PA 17555

Call Sign: N3KNG
George D Kinckiner
2402 Longview Dr
Narvon PA 17555

Call Sign: N3ISB
Raymond K Tinney
2020 Lucinda Ln
Narvon PA 17555

Call Sign: WT3Q
Samuel M Harner Jr
893 Narvon Rd
Narvon PA 17555

Call Sign: KD7IVO
Lucas G Toews
1319 Oaklyn Dr
Narvon PA 17555

Call Sign: WK3A

Harry L Haas
2323 Poplar St
Narvon PA 17555

Call Sign: KB3VNF
Robert B Sheaffer
1954 Shady Ln
Narvon PA 17555

Call Sign: KB3SCK
Kazu Matsushita
105 Shirk Town Rd
Narvon PA 17555

Call Sign: N3WME
Merle R Weaver
136 Spook Ln
Narvon PA 17555

Call Sign: KB3ENS
Beth A Weaver
136 Spook Ln
Narvon PA 17555

FCC Amateur Radio Licenses in Needmore

Call Sign: KB3KSU
Richard D Robinson
417 Buck N Rut Ln
Needmore PA 17238

Call Sign: KA3PHK
Homer C Mellott
715 Chester Rd
Needmore PA 17238

Call Sign: N3DBY
Edward D Guyer
5799 Pigeon Cove Rd
Needmore PA 17238

Call Sign: KD8IKF
Benjamin A Bright
4235 Timber Ridge Rd

Needmore PA 17238

FCC Amateur Radio Licenses in Nelson

Call Sign: N3GYY
Terril A Doan
Lakeview Dr
Nelson PA 16940

Call Sign: N3OTN
Loren H Doan
Nelson PA 16940

FCC Amateur Radio Licenses in New Berlin

Call Sign: N3RFS
George L Foust
518 Vine St
New Berlin PA 17855

Call Sign: KB3FHR
Sandra J Foust
518 Vine St
New Berlin PA 17855

Call Sign: AA3FD
Wendell M Smith
New Berlin PA 17855

Call Sign: KB3ENW
Kevin J Dozpat
New Berlin PA 17855

FCC Amateur Radio Licenses in New Bloomfield

Call Sign: K3MRG
Thomas D Berquist
118 Arbutus Ln
New Bloomfield PA 17068

Call Sign: WA3DOG

William A Yeager
100 Church St
New Bloomfield PA 17068

Call Sign: KB3NLC
Lauren C Cook
1315 Clouser Hollow Rd
New Bloomfield PA 17068

Call Sign: K3SRZ
W Michael Greaney Sr
3228 Cold Storage Rd
New Bloomfield PA
170688624

Call Sign: N3KES
Preston R Perkey Sr
152 Dix Hill Rd
New Bloomfield PA 17068

Call Sign: KA2CJN
M Pat Hutchins
2170 Laurel Grove
New Bloomfield PA 17068

Call Sign: WD2AKI
Robert C Hutchins
2170 Laurel Grove
New Bloomfield PA 17068

Call Sign: N3JUO
Dale A Ballard
15 Meadowview Dr
New Bloomfield PA 17068

Call Sign: N3TAO
Samuel L Wertz
124 Rock Ledge Ln
New Bloomfield PA 17068

Call Sign: KE3IJ
Richard A Andersen
301 Veterans Dr
New Bloomfield PA 17068

FCC Amateur Radio Licenses in New Columbia

Call Sign: KA3BDL
Brenda J Hering
16 Deerfoot Ln
New Columbia PA 17856

Call Sign: WA3IJU
Kenneth E Hering
16 Deerfoot Ln
New Columbia PA 17856

Call Sign: K3FLT
Milton ARC
143 Deerfoot Ln
New Columbia PA 17856

Call Sign: K3COD
Raymond J Grant
5 Dogwood St
New Columbia PA 17856

Call Sign: K4KMI
Hedwig Grant
5 Dogwood St
New Columbia PA 17856

Call Sign: K3VDT
Paul E Platt
2644 Millers Bottom Rd
New Columbia PA 17856

Call Sign: KB3KUM
William A Michaels
557 New Columbia Rd
New Columbia PA 17856

Call Sign: K3PYN
Larry W Platt
125 Platt Ln
New Columbia PA 17856

Call Sign: KB3CVI

Timothy J Baker
2071 White Deer Pike
New Columbia PA 17856

Call Sign: KB3DSV
Jamey L Baker
2071 White Deer Pike
New Columbia PA 17856

Call Sign: KB3YAE
Charles R Puckett II
284 Wooded Hts Dr
New Columbia PA 17856

FCC Amateur Radio Licenses in New Cumberland

Call Sign: KB3RCX
Ernest F Schneider
304 10th St
New Cumberland PA
17070

Call Sign: KB3MIJ
Trayer J Rende
531 16th St
New Cumberland PA
17070

Call Sign: WB3AWM
Paul E De Walt
914 16th St
New Cumberland PA
17070

Call Sign: KB3DBM
Tammy L Klaus
319 2nd St
New Cumberland PA
170702102

Call Sign: KB3DBL
Thomas M Klaus
319 2nd St

New Cumberland PA
170702102

Call Sign: KB3PXW
Nathanial E Riggs
412 3rd St
New Cumberland PA
17070

Call Sign: KB3OVF
Olivia C Alford
510 3rd St
New Cumberland PA
17070

Call Sign: KB3NKZ
Trevor C Alford
510 3rd St
New Cumberland PA
17070

Call Sign: KB3STX
Jamel L Mcmillian
711 3rd St
New Cumberland PA
17070

Call Sign: KB3CDX
Joshua L Shindel
423 4th St
New Cumberland PA
17070

Call Sign: KU3H
Lawrence C Posavec
425 4th St
New Cumberland PA
17070

Call Sign: KB3IYZ
Elizabeth A Moser
600 4th St
New Cumberland PA
17070

Call Sign: KB3IZA
Charles W Moser
600 4th St
New Cumberland PA
17070

Call Sign: KB3LWT
Derek W Delaney
801 5th St
New Cumberland PA
170701825

Call Sign: KB3CHS
Brian W Kurtz
429 9th St
New Cumberland PA
17070

Call Sign: KB3PAP
Nicole R Przybylowski
302 Bailey St
New Cumberland PA
17070

Call Sign: KB3LRT
Amanda C Przybylowski
302 Bailey St
New Cumberland PA
17070

Call Sign: KB3RZY
Laura W Schwartzer
1726 Beckley Dr
New Cumberland PA
17070

Call Sign: KB3QVX
Harold E Hahn
510 Benyou Ln
New Cumberland PA
17070

Call Sign: K3RNK
Harold E Hahn
510 Benyou Ln

New Cumberland PA
17070

Call Sign: KB3SOL
Zachary C Ferree
537 Brandt Ave Apt C
New Cumberland PA
17070

Call Sign: KB3GGN
Luke Hasemeier
1612 Bridge St
New Cumberland PA
170701122

Call Sign: AA3RC
Walter K Rumbel Jr
904 Bridge St Fl 1
New Cumberland PA
170701628

Call Sign: N2ETD
Vincent Muoio
16 Carriage Rd
New Cumberland PA
17070

Call Sign: KB3TPM
Aaron H Mininger
18 Carriage Rd
New Cumberland PA
17070

Call Sign: K3SWZ
Glenn R Kurzenknabe
23 Carriage Rd
New Cumberland PA
17070

Call Sign: KB3PGX
Central Pa Contest Club
23 Carriage Rd
New Cumberland PA
170702302

Call Sign: K3UKO
Central Pa Contest Club
23 Carriage Rd
New Cumberland PA
170702302

Call Sign: WB3DPE
Paul H Phelabaum
521 Coolidge St
New Cumberland PA
17070

Call Sign: WB3HLP
Kenneth N Smith Jr
704 Drexel Hills Blvd
New Cumberland PA
170701740

Call Sign: KB3LRY
Rachel M Stachowiak
705 Drexel Hills Blvd
New Cumberland PA
17070

Call Sign: KB3MJV
Daniel G Lerew
1003 Drexel Hills Blvd
New Cumberland PA
17070

Call Sign: N3ITD
Alvin J Groft Jr
709 Elkwood Dr
New Cumberland PA
170700154

Call Sign: KA3OMQ
Douglas M Cameron
413 Evergreen Rd
New Cumberland PA
17070

Call Sign: KB3LFU
Peter W Cameron
413 Evergreen Rd

New Cumberland PA
17070

Call Sign: N8ZWZ
Peter F Kay
501 Evergreen Rd
New Cumberland PA
17070

Call Sign: KB3KMU
Ashlee M Nazzaro
505 Evergreen Rd
New Cumberland PA
17070

Call Sign: KB3MWV
Gina A Nazzaro
505 Evergreen Rd
New Cumberland PA
17070

Call Sign: KB3QXX
Douglas W Pursel
332 Evergreen St
New Cumberland PA
17070

Call Sign: KB3IXD
Jaclyn M Ginanni
823 Fishing Creek Rd
New Cumberland PA
170702706

Call Sign: KB3SOJ
Jake J Tunstall
617 Haldeman Ave
New Cumberland PA
17070

Call Sign: WB3EJZ
Robert M Scharding
733 Harding St
New Cumberland PA
170701437

Call Sign: KB3NBS
John J Lanphier
106 Harrison Dr
New Cumberland PA
17070

Call Sign: KB3RYV
Jennifer N Minahan
311 Hillcrest Dr
New Cumberland PA
17070

Call Sign: KA3TCU
Douglas A Berguson
323 Hillcrest Dr
New Cumberland PA
170703035

Call Sign: KC3TL
Pietro M De Volpi Sr
408 Hillside Ave
New Cumberland PA
170703036

Call Sign: KY3ORK
York County ARC
408 Hillside Ave
New Cumberland PA
170703036

Call Sign: K3PD
Pietro M De Volpi Sr
408 Hillside Ave
New Cumberland PA
170703036

Call Sign: KB3IMU
Pietro M De Volpi Jr
408 Hillside Ave
New Cumberland PA
170703036

Call Sign: W3GOP
Pietro M De Volpi Jr
408 Hillside Ave

New Cumberland PA
170703036

Call Sign: N3NHZ
James H Stoup
1701 Kathryn St
New Cumberland PA
17070

Call Sign: KB3MVU
Haley A Cline
1706 Kathryn St
New Cumberland PA
17070

Call Sign: KB3IOR
Thomas V Chesek
306 Lafayette Dr
New Cumberland PA
17070

Call Sign: K3TVC
Thomas V Chesek
306 Lafayette Dr
New Cumberland PA
17070

Call Sign: WA3MVF
Patricia A Nissel
596 Lewisberry Rd
New Cumberland PA
17070

Call Sign: KB3RZU
Sung M Nam
938 Limekiln Rd
New Cumberland PA
17070

Call Sign: KA3MXF
Joseph J Reid
807 Linwood St
New Cumberland PA
17070

Call Sign: KB3OBZ
Timothy R Adams
1703 Maple St
New Cumberland PA
17070

Call Sign: W3SAU
J Douglass Berry
1497 Maplewood Dr
New Cumberland PA
17070

Call Sign: W3BXO
Gilbert R Houck
325 Market St
New Cumberland PA
17070

Call Sign: KG4DZK
Jonathan K Peek
6 Meadowbrook Ct
New Cumberland PA
17070

Call Sign: N3FAL
William H Trutt
121 Meadowbrook Rd
New Cumberland PA
17070

Call Sign: N3RZA
Brian L Simmons
107 Old York Rd Apt 31
New Cumberland PA
17070

Call Sign: KB3CKO
Timothy E Stoner
206 Orchard Rd
New Cumberland PA
17070

Call Sign: KB3DHJ
George R Stoner
206 Orchard Rd

New Cumberland PA
17070

Call Sign: W3AEA
Timothy E Stoner
206 Orchard Rd
New Cumberland PA
17070

Call Sign: KB3QDT
Christopher P Vittor
227 Orchard Rd
New Cumberland PA
17070

Call Sign: N3SW
Richard S Walker
610 Park Ave
New Cumberland PA
17070

Call Sign: KB3CWR
Carol A Walker
610 Park Ave
New Cumberland PA
170701724

Call Sign: N3XUC
Ron L Shuler
345 Pleasant View Rd
New Cumberland PA
17070

Call Sign: W3OBY
Herman A Hanemann Jr
101 Pleasantview Ter
New Cumberland PA
17070

Call Sign: KB3IHY
Leonard M Zazetski
412 Poplar Ave
New Cumberland PA
17070

Call Sign: W3IHY
Leonard M Zazetski
412 Poplar Ave
New Cumberland PA
17070

Call Sign: KB3QDK
Kailey B Maguire
414 Poplar Ave
New Cumberland PA
17070

Call Sign: KB3QDM
Alice V Miller
1108 Quincy Cir
New Cumberland PA
17070

Call Sign: KB3DWO
James W Carlisle Jr
1112 Quincy Cir
New Cumberland PA
17070

Call Sign: KA3FUG
Aubrey L Barber
27 Ross Ave
New Cumberland PA
17070

Call Sign: WA3AIB
Robert W Irvin
500 Ross Ave
New Cumberland PA
17070

Call Sign: WA3YWN
Jerry W Mcdonnell
1493 Simpson Ferry Rd
New Cumberland PA
17070

Call Sign: WB3ABV
Charles M Brandt
405 Summit Rd

New Cumberland PA
17070

Call Sign: KB3PAE
Allison E Mcmelvey
339 Timber Rd
New Cumberland PA
17070

Call Sign: K3IPW
Thomas H Rutland
1703 Warren
New Cumberland PA
17070

Call Sign: KB3HAZ
Michael S Walsh
403 Water St Apt C
New Cumberland PA
17070

Call Sign: N3XIJ
Paul C Nell
New Cumberland PA
17070

FCC Amateur Radio Licenses in New Enterprise

Call Sign: KB3DTJ
Doris K Butler
164 Flash Dr
New Enterprise PA 16664

Call Sign: KB3DTK
James L Butler
164 Flash Dr
New Enterprise PA 16664

Call Sign: KB3WSL
John P Neville
173 Pine Grove
New Enterprise PA 16664

FCC Amateur Radio Licenses in New Freedom

Call Sign: N3BSN
A Steven Meadows Sr
Box 2007 Keller Rd
New Freedom PA 17349

Call Sign: W3HGC
Raymond B Harris
Box 57
New Freedom PA 17349

Call Sign: KB3KGK
James D Morfe
12147 Diehl Ct
New Freedom PA 17349

Call Sign: K3JDM
James D Morfe
12147 Diehl Ct
New Freedom PA 17349

Call Sign: KB3SCY
Ron Kirchner Jr
90 E High St
New Freedom PA 17349

Call Sign: W3TSG
John C Anderson Sr
238 E Main St
New Freedom PA
173499211

Call Sign: KB3UTU
John G Lindley
110 Freedom Ave
New Freedom PA
173499753

Call Sign: NK0J
John G Lindley
110 Freedom Ave
New Freedom PA
173499753

Call Sign: KB3CTC
Tyler K Billingsley
1015 Harvest View Ct
New Freedom PA 17349

Call Sign: KB3CTD
Jarrett F Billingsley
1015 Harvest View Ct
New Freedom PA 17349

Call Sign: KB3CYF
Kris L Billingsley
1015 Harvest View Ct
New Freedom PA 17349

Call Sign: K3WIT
Ray W Tobias Jr
350 Hilltop Ct
New Freedom PA
173499066

Call Sign: W5JKH
Jeffrey K Halapin
54 Independence Dr
New Freedom PA 17349

Call Sign: WA3HMR
Ralph C Gilbert
14205 Ingham Rd
New Freedom PA 17349

Call Sign: WB8PDL
Arthur H Exner
4 Keesey Rd
New Freedom PA 17349

Call Sign: KX3M
Harry E Bates Sr
12 Keesey Rd
New Freedom PA 17349

Call Sign: N3FTN
Jonathan H Bates
12 Keesey Rd

New Freedom PA 17349

Call Sign: N3GZQ
Carolyn H Bates
12 Keesey Rd
New Freedom PA 17349

Call Sign: KA3NET
Harry E Bates Jr
12 Keesey Rd
New Freedom PA 17349

Call Sign: KB3HEZ
Vernon J Morgan Jr
212 Ken Rd
New Freedom PA 17349

Call Sign: N3VVK
Lori L Jankowiak
45 Logan Dr
New Freedom PA 17349

Call Sign: N3UJL
Larry G Linville
13 N 2nd St
New Freedom PA 17349

Call Sign: N3NSN
Richard A Snellinger
108 N 3rd St
New Freedom PA
173499438

Call Sign: N3UEK
Kathleen E Clagett
223 N 3rd St
New Freedom PA 17349

Call Sign: KE3SR
Leonard H Maynard III
9 Oakwood Rd
New Freedom PA 17349

Call Sign: W2AYP
Laurence J Cooper

359 Oakwood Rd
New Freedom PA 17349

Call Sign: KB3NDY
Michael T Rodeheaver
362 Oakwood Rd
New Freedom PA 17349

Call Sign: W3CDF
Michael T Rodeheaver
362 Oakwood Rd
New Freedom PA 17349

Call Sign: KB3GLT
Daniel C Mareck
478 Oakwood Rd
New Freedom PA 17349

Call Sign: KB3NXI
Cynthia M Mareck
478 Oakwood Rd
New Freedom PA 17349

Call Sign: KB3MOG
Rebecca A Mareck
478 Oakwood Rd
New Freedom PA 17349

Call Sign: WW3KW
Leonard H Maynard III
819 Oakwood Rd
New Freedom PA 17349

Call Sign: KB3BBZ
Susan R Mareck
478 Oakwood Rd
New Freedom PA 17349

Call Sign: WB2KIU
Daniel J Mareck
478 Oakwood Rd
New Freedom PA 17349

Call Sign: WN3F
Theodore R Vasilow

120 Penny Ln
New Freedom PA 17349

Call Sign: N3ZVV
Michael T Pedone
16103 Reese Rd
New Freedom PA 17349

Call Sign: N3TAM
April L Storm
13385 Richards Ct
New Freedom PA 17349

Call Sign: WB3EAF
Robert F Storm Jr
13385 Richards Ct
New Freedom PA 17349

Call Sign: KB3DVY
Wesley J Armstrong
36 S Charles St
New Freedom PA 17349

Call Sign: AA3TR
Wesley J Armstrong
36 S Charles St
New Freedom PA 17349

Call Sign: N3LZQ
Wayne A Hendrix
38 S Charles St
New Freedom PA 17349

Call Sign: KA3VSW
Dona E Smith
31 S Constitution Ave
New Freedom PA 17349

Call Sign: WA3JPN
William H Frost
37 S Constitution Ave
New Freedom PA 17349

Call Sign: KB3JA
Kenneth F Jones

S Constitution Ave
New Freedom PA 17349

Call Sign: KB3THB
Robert M Walker
26 S Main St
New Freedom PA 17349

Call Sign: N3QZQ
George Lovas Jr
109 S Shaffer Dr
New Freedom PA 17349

Call Sign: KB3WDK
Thomas E Throckmorton
1650 Sorrel Ridge Ln
New Freedom PA 17349

Call Sign: AB3OB
Thomas E Throckmorton
1650 Sorrel Ridge Ln
New Freedom PA 17349

Call Sign: K4IES
Ralph K Zimmerman
3653 Steltz Rd
New Freedom PA 17349

Call Sign: KD3ZM
Michael M Weidmayer
25 Still Pond Dr
New Freedom PA 17349

Call Sign: N3ZNW
Anna K Weidmayer
25 Still Pond Dr
New Freedom PA 17349

Call Sign: N8VKQ
Cleo W McLucas
1487 Sweitzer Rd
New Freedom PA 17349

Call Sign: N3LAY

Thomas E Throckmorton
Sr
42 Washington Rd
New Freedom PA 17349

Call Sign: KA3PGM
Lloyd H Furches
New Freedom PA 17349

Call Sign: KB3VAW
J Nolan Crowder
New Freedom PA 17349

Call Sign: AB3LX
J Nolan Crowder
New Freedom PA 17349

FCC Amateur Radio Licenses in New Germantown

Call Sign: W2BE
Bruce W Eichmann Sr
910 Lower Buckridge Rd
New Germantown PA
17071

FCC Amateur Radio Licenses in New Holland

Call Sign: K2IFX
Calvin C Peters
13 Ashlea Gardens
New Holland PA 17557

Call Sign: K3HLB
Roy K Smoker
108 Bergman Rd
New Holland PA 17557

Call Sign: N3XHC
Daniel M Foltz
328 Brimmer Ave
New Holland PA 17557

Call Sign: W3DMF
Daniel M Foltz
328 Brimmer Ave
New Holland PA 17557

Call Sign: W3KIM
Kimberly J Foltz
328 Brimmer Ave
New Holland PA 17557

Call Sign: KB3FQV
Kimberly J Foltz
328 Brimmer Ave
New Holland PA 17557

Call Sign: KA3AEC
William A Phreaner
122 Crestview Ave
New Holland PA 17557

Call Sign: KB3SCC
Michael K Haskett
88 Diller Ave 12
New Holland PA 17557

Call Sign: KB2BSQ
Harold J De Stefano
Don Dr
New Holland PA 17557

Call Sign: WA3VPS
Paul Nyul
346 E Cedar St
New Holland PA
175571305

Call Sign: KA3SDX
Leo E Peters Jr
108 E Conestoga St
New Holland PA 17557

Call Sign: KA3OFJ
Patrick J Naimoli
506 E Conestoga St
New Holland PA 17557

Call Sign: N3INB
Mervin N Zimmerman
492 E Farmersville Rd
New Holland PA 17557

Call Sign: N3PIQ
Mildred Z Zimmerman
492 E Farmersville Rd
New Holland PA 17557

Call Sign: W3ASC
Le Roy F Heckman Jr
319 E Jackson St
New Holland PA 17557

Call Sign: KB3DJT
Michael A Helms
594 E Jackson St
New Holland PA 17557

Call Sign: KB3ION
David A Hurst
401 E Main St
New Holland PA 17557

Call Sign: KD3YO
Peter J Molloy Jr
E Main St
New Holland PA 17557

Call Sign: KB3DXJ
Carl Z Brubaker
278 Gristmill Rd
New Holland PA 17557

Call Sign: KC3VG
Ivan R Troxel
58 Holly Dr
New Holland PA
175579473

Call Sign: N3NMS
Patricia H Ross
72 Holly Dr

New Holland PA 17557

Call Sign: K3OPE
Robert O Ross
72 Holly Dr
New Holland PA
175579475

Call Sign: N3SMU
Clyde Gantz
5235 Honeysuckle Ln
New Holland PA 17557

Call Sign: N3SMV
John J Gantz
5235 Honeysuckle Ln
New Holland PA 17557

Call Sign: N3SMW
Lucinda R Gantz
5235 Honeysuckle Ln
New Holland PA 17557

Call Sign: KA3YOG
Charles W Ulrich IV
224 Locust St
New Holland PA
175571615

Call Sign: WA3RKM
Steve R Houck
255 Locust St
New Holland PA 17557

Call Sign: KA3JGE
Allen H Martin
310 Martin Rd
New Holland PA 17557

Call Sign: N3RFY
Nevin J Bowman
541 Martindale Rd
New Holland PA 17557

Call Sign: KB3FBD

Bruce C Musser
731 Pleasant Dr
New Holland PA 17557

Call Sign: KB3BMP
Norma J Douglas
13 Rose Ct
New Holland PA 17557

Call Sign: KB3ARE
Trevor A Douglas
13 Rose Ct
New Holland PA 17557

Call Sign: KB3TIS
Darrell L Fisher
4 Runway Ave
New Holland PA 17557

Call Sign: WA2LQK
William H Alviti
894 S Custer Ave
New Holland PA
175579326

Call Sign: KB3VJ
Kier M Finlayson
433 S Kinzer Ave
New Holland PA 17557

Call Sign: KB3GHB
Stephen R Mcclure
115 Skyline Dr
New Holland PA 17557

Call Sign: KC0HRU
Benjamin J Peters
1624 Springville Rd
New Holland PA 17557

Call Sign: KA3WVE
Alec M Mercer
106 W Main St
New Holland PA 17557

Call Sign: N3PIT
Ricky D Horton
206 W Main St
New Holland PA 17557

Call Sign: W3DWS
John E Helenthal Jr
945 W Main St
New Holland PA 17557

Call Sign: KB3TJM
Dennis G Gaul Jr
101 W Main St Apt 4
New Holland PA 17557

Call Sign: WA3BKM
Glenn R Shonk
699 Wallace Rd
New Holland PA 17557

Call Sign: WB3HWK
Ernest M Orr Jr
37 Whisper Ln
New Holland PA 17557

Call Sign: N3QWR
Wendell N Nolt
579 White Oak Rd
New Holland PA 17557

Call Sign: N3TJI
Stephen C Van Art
New Holland PA 17557

Call Sign: W3LBS
Le Roy B Snader
New Holland PA 17557

FCC Amateur Radio Licenses in New Kingstown

Call Sign: KA3TCT
Kenneth J Ulmer
New Kingstown PA 17072

FCC Amateur Radio Licenses in New Oxford

Call Sign: KB3FQL
David W Eyler
91 Billerbeck St
New Oxford PA 17350

Call Sign: KJ3J
Robert W Gorseline
Box 128
New Oxford PA 17350

Call Sign: WB3LDJ
Dennis L Cullison
438 Brickcrafters Rd
New Oxford PA
173509670

Call Sign: KA3WED
Timothy L Toot
1060 Centennial Rd
New Oxford PA 17350

Call Sign: N3IZ
Timothy L Toot
1060 Centennial Rd
New Oxford PA 17350

Call Sign: K3NZZ
Gerald V Bate Jr
43 Creek Rd
New Oxford PA 17350

Call Sign: K3DJI
Alvin C Sipe
Cross Keys Vlg
New Oxford PA 17350

Call Sign: W3VTB
Harry W Rudolph
Cross Keys Vlg 206A
New Oxford PA 17350

Call Sign: KA1RTT
Daisy R Anderson
64 E Lowst Ln
New Oxford PA 17350

Call Sign: WA4RBQ
John F Hartman
36 Elizabeth Ln
New Oxford PA 17350

Call Sign: N3BVT
Richard E Harley
11 Fulton Dr
New Oxford PA 17350

Call Sign: N3NZF
Susan J Harley
11 Fulton Dr
New Oxford PA 17350

Call Sign: KB3DRM
Donald E Danner Sr
531 Grace Ter
New Oxford PA 17350

Call Sign: W3MZS
Harry C MacJilton
Grace Ter
New Oxford PA 17350

Call Sign: W1OU
Brian E Michael Md
740 Green Ridge Rd
New Oxford PA 17350

Call Sign: W3DFP
Charles R Sleighter
107 Hanover St
New Oxford PA 17350

Call Sign: KB3FYI
Robert E Bertrand Jr
106 Heritage Ct
New Oxford PA 17350

Call Sign: KB3BQT
Jefferey L Bowers Jr
77 Jaqueline Dr
New Oxford PA 17350

Call Sign: N3CVD
Richard W Taylor
50 Kimberly Ann Ln
New Oxford PA 17350

Call Sign: WB8WMU
Stanley E Yates
331 Kohler Mill Rd
New Oxford PA 17350

Call Sign: W3FRA
Stanley E Yates
331 Kohler Mill Rd
New Oxford PA 17350

Call Sign: N3VPW
Joseph G Heffron
240 Kohler School Rd
New Oxford PA 17350

Call Sign: KA3GUZ
Gregory R Shorb
115 Little Ave
New Oxford PA
173509461

Call Sign: KG3S
Gregory R Shorb
115 Little Ave
New Oxford PA
173509461

Call Sign: K3CXF
Francis R Huttinger
303 Matthew Dr
New Oxford PA 17350

Call Sign: W3JOH
William B Cullison
16 Oxen Ln

New Oxford PA 17350

Call Sign: KB3FIX
Douglas J Pierson
2228 Oxford Rd
New Oxford PA 17350

Call Sign: KA3MPX
Glenn W Millar Jr
2389 Oxford Rd
New Oxford PA 17350

Call Sign: KC3EN
Robert H Stover
40 Piper Dr
New Oxford PA 17350

Call Sign: KA3ZII
August C Schwab
370 Poplar Rd
New Oxford PA 17350

Call Sign: KA3MII
Ronald W Sullivan
304 S Hickory Ln
New Oxford PA
173509153

Call Sign: WA3FIX
Daniel L Sullivan
70 Walker Dr
New Oxford PA 17350

FCC Amateur Radio Licenses in New Paris

Call Sign: WA3BWJ
Joseph T Ream
Box 15
New Paris PA 15554

Call Sign: KB3GEF
Kent S Hammer
3191 Cortland Rd
New Paris PA 15554

Call Sign: KB3IAP
Mark A Baumgardner
1625 Crissman Rd
New Paris PA 15554

Call Sign: K7CI
Joseph V Gardner
315 Ridgewood Dr
New Paris PA 155548665

Call Sign: AB3GX
Arthur J Costigan Jr
448 Ridgewood Dr
New Paris PA 15554

Call Sign: W2BAP
Arthur J Costigan Jr
448 Ridgewood Dr
New Paris PA 15554

FCC Amateur Radio Licenses in New Park

Call Sign: KI3P
Greg N Sarris
170 Cedar Valley Rd
New Park PA 17352

Call Sign: WA3CDC
Arthur E Kirkpatrick
14 Stoney Ln
New Park PA 17352

FCC Amateur Radio Licenses in New Providence

Call Sign: W3FAL
Claude E Doner
2175 Beaver Valley Pike
New Providence PA 17560

Call Sign: WA3NRN
Paul W Harper

Box 514
New Providence PA 17560

Call Sign: N3LLZ
Timothy W Baldwin
310 Cinder Rd
New Providence PA
175609641

Call Sign: KC3LE
Paul Oliver
440 Daisy Dr
New Providence PA 17560

Call Sign: W3VCS
Philip R Reger
52 Kimberly Ave
New Providence PA 17560

Call Sign: KB3CQL
Robert R Farneth
65 Scott Rd
New Providence PA 17560

Call Sign: N3BF
Robert R Farneth
65 Scott Rd
New Providence PA 17560

Call Sign: KB3TNG
John C Kroener Sr
168 Sigman Rd
New Providence PA 17560

Call Sign: KB3MFB
Steve Weiss
737 Truce Rd
New Providence PA 17560

Call Sign: N3ATS
Steve Weiss
737 Truce Rd
New Providence PA 17560

Call Sign: N3NTO

Samuel E Mehaffey
New Providence PA 17560

Call Sign: KB3LKQ
Linda C Mehaffey
New Providence PA 17560

FCC Amateur Radio Licenses in New Salem

Call Sign: KA3ORK
Brenda S Stoner
Box 571
New Salem PA 15468

Call Sign: KB3GES
Robert E Vail
6890 National Pike
New Salem PA 15468

Call Sign: KB3KSD
Richard S Hoover
25 S Main St
New Salem PA 17371

FCC Amateur Radio Licenses in Newburg

Call Sign: K3IEZ
David R Henderson
10 Chestnut Rd Rr 1 Box 77
Newburg PA 17240

Call Sign: KB3IZG
Brady G Alleman
130 Jumper Rd
Newburg PA 17240

Call Sign: N3BGA
Brady G Alleman
130 Jumper Rd
Newburg PA 17240

Call Sign: WB2CPN

Cletus W Whitaker
112 Minick Dr
Newburg PA 17240

**FCC Amateur Radio
Licenses in
Newmanstown**

Call Sign: KB3LOM
Steven R Kline
218 Albright Rd
Newmanstown PA 17073

Call Sign: KB3CHE
James F Simmermon
Box 278
Newmanstown PA 17073

Call Sign: N3YKM
Nelson B Nolt
Box 318
Newmanstown PA 17073

Call Sign: KF4RQH
John D Moton
101 E Memorial Blvd
Newmanstown PA 17073

Call Sign: N3PTN
Joseph Lerman
53 Fox Rd
Newmanstown PA 17073

Call Sign: N3WKA
Diane Lerman
53 Fox Rd
Newmanstown PA 17073

Call Sign: N3JOZ
Daryl T Herr
1 Lost Acre Ln
Newmanstown PA 17073

Call Sign: KE3E
Edward M Fawver

128 Memorial Blvd
Newmanstown PA 17073

Call Sign: WA1SMG
Matthew J Popecki
Rd 1 Distillery Rd
Newmanstown PA 17073

Call Sign: N3ONP
Lynn V Ziegler
162 Schaeffer Rd
Newmanstown PA 17073

Call Sign: N3UZX
Kathleen M Ziegler
162 Schaeffer Rd
Newmanstown PA 17073

Call Sign: WA3OJA
David M Horvat
495 Sheep Hill Rd
Newmanstown PA 17073

Call Sign: N3JPJ
Larry D Keener
418 Sheephill Rd
Newmanstown PA
170738927

Call Sign: KA3RSC
Thomas E Hess
584 Stricklerstown Rd
Newmanstown PA 17073

Call Sign: KB3QYY
Todd B Muiznieks
127 Sweetwater Ln
Newmanstown PA 17073

Call Sign: N3YQG
Michael A Cholewa
21 Treeline Dr
Newmanstown PA 17073

Call Sign: KB3JWH

John F Gilbertson
24 Treeline Dr
Newmanstown PA 17073

Call Sign: N3ZFG
Dale R Dundore
217 Village Dr
Newmanstown PA 17073

Call Sign: N3BTS
Stephanie M Patschke
Newmanstown PA 17073

**FCC Amateur Radio
Licenses in Newport**

Call Sign: N3EBZ
Frank C Frey
48 Acker Rd
Newport PA 17074

Call Sign: WA3ENQ
Richard J Luxbacher
201 Buckwalter Rd
Newport PA 17074

Call Sign: WA3WCI
Donald J Halke II
500 Buttonwood Rd
Newport PA 17074

Call Sign: KI3YA
Lawrence S Hardy III
6 High Meadows Ln
Newport PA 17074

Call Sign: N3OSL
John E McNaughton
259 Honeysuckle Hollow
Rd
Newport PA 17074

Call Sign: KB3YDU
Jacob D Moench
86 Meadowgrove Rd

Newport PA 17074

Call Sign: KB3YDT
Timothy M Moench
86 Meadowgrove Rd
Newport PA 17074

Call Sign: WA3JMS
Robert W Craven
15 Milford Rd
Newport PA 170747476

Call Sign: KB3NGJ
Kevin R Campbell
1131 N Front St
Newport PA 17074

Call Sign: KB3LSG
Cameron J Zimmerman
668 Old Limekiln Ln
Newport PA 17074

Call Sign: KB3PBB
Spencer W Zimmerman
668 Old Limekiln Ln
Newport PA 17074

Call Sign: KD3PX
Eugene L Diveglia Jr
Rd 2
Newport PA 17074

Call Sign: N3XAK
Stephen M English
S 2nd St
Newport PA 17055

Call Sign: KI4YA
Lawrence S Hardy III
24 S Front St
Newport PA 17074

Call Sign: WA3ZRR
Michael E Byers
1432 Shull Hill Rd

Newport PA 17074

Call Sign: KB3FSW
James W Lowery
1479 Upper Bailey Rd
Newport PA 17074

FCC Amateur Radio Licenses in Newry

Call Sign: KB3TMV
Nickolas M Johnston
Newry PA 16665

FCC Amateur Radio Licenses in Newville

Call Sign: W2HZZ
Robert B Koehler
210 Big Spring Rd
Newville PA 17241

Call Sign: KB3SIR
John E Mccoy
201 Big Spring Ter
Newville PA 17241

Call Sign: N3ZQR
David L Myers
250 Blind Ln
Newville PA 17241

Call Sign: W3FQM
Lee H Pugh
Box 648
Newville PA 17241

Call Sign: N3GOX
Eric W Maul
7 Buchanan St
Newville PA 172411527

Call Sign: N3KDQ
Betty E Heckendorn
52 Carlisle Rd

Newville PA 17241

Call Sign: W3MXD
William M Heckendorn
52 Carlisle Rd
Newville PA 172419415

Call Sign: N3YPC
George B Dias
935 Center Rd
Newville PA 172419449

Call Sign: KB3WII
Steven A Orr
1310 Centerville Rd
Newville PA 17241

Call Sign: W4HSN
John J Bartko
143 Cherry Blossom Ln
Newville PA 17241

Call Sign: W3JJB
John J Bartko
143 Cherry Blossom Ln
Newville PA 17241

Call Sign: AE3I
James N Frey
10 Chestnut Rd
Newville PA 17241

Call Sign: KA3MNE
Barbara J Frey
10 Chestnut Rd
Newville PA 17241

Call Sign: KA3FAF
Patricia J McCann
14 Fox Ln
Newville PA 17241

Call Sign: WN3PIT
Kenneth D McCann
14 Fox Ln

Newville PA 17241

Call Sign: KB3YDB
Gary E Cribbs
21 Gettle Rd
Newville PA 172419556

Call Sign: KG4DIJ
Kemp J Beaty
584 Mt Rock Rd
Newville PA 17241

Call Sign: KB3IKK
Kemp J Beaty
584 Mt Rock Rd
Newville PA 17241

Call Sign: KB3OHZ
Jerome C Johnson
76 N Mountain Rd
Newville PA 172419738

Call Sign: N3KDR
John Barnes
317 N Mountain Rd
Newville PA 17241

Call Sign: N3SWD
William C Beck
13 Parsonage St
Newville PA 17241

Call Sign: KB3YDM
John W Roscinski
32 Parsonage St
Newville PA 17241

Call Sign: N3OTS
Joey L Orner
1805 Pine Rd
Newville PA 17241

Call Sign: W2FLI
Philip E Fox
84 Plum Tree Cir

Newville PA 17241

Call Sign: WA3ZXG
Wayne S Myers
119 Southside Dr
Newville PA 17241

Call Sign: KB3HFU
David J Barrick
27 Weist Rd
Newville PA 17241

Call Sign: K3QNS
Raymond H Hurley Jr
2 Westfield Ln
Newville PA 17241

Call Sign: KB3JHW
Michele E Brandt
Newville PA 17241

FCC Amateur Radio Licenses in Nicktown

Call Sign: N3QBU
James J Platko Jr
Box 274
Nicktown PA 15762

Call Sign: KB3AQO
Ross J Fleming
196 Freidhof Ln
Nicktown PA 15762

Call Sign: N3KLC
Donna J Ligas
3221 Killen School Rd
Nicktown PA 15762

Call Sign: N3ZTV
Chad A Ligas
3221 Killen School Rd
Nicktown PA 15762

Call Sign: WA3BDR

Walter J Ligas Jr
3221 Killen School Rd
Nicktown PA 15762

Call Sign: KB3AFZ
James J Platko
840 Kline Rd
Nicktown PA 15762

Call Sign: KB4JLE
G Monte Kirsch
125 St Joseph St
Nicktown PA 15762

FCC Amateur Radio Licenses in Northern Cambria

Call Sign: KA3TSD
Ron R Gelormino
3011 Bigler Ave
Northern Cambria PA 15714

Call Sign: W3PLM
Clyde T Kirsch
3301 Bigler Ave
Northern Cambria PA 157142117

Call Sign: KB3HZL
Edward G Mulligan
190 Bird Ln
Northern Cambria PA 157149046

Call Sign: N3SJP
Richard G Nalisnick
1408 Chestnut Ave
Northern Cambria PA 15714

Call Sign: KE4PJX
Mario J Vella
2314 Crawford Ave

Northern Cambria PA
15714

Call Sign: N3JSE
Barry L Pugh
3618 Crawford Ave
Northern Cambria PA
15714

Call Sign: N3SJY
Kathleen B Lute
736 Elm Rd
Northern Cambria PA
157148921

Call Sign: N3PHX
Roger V Lute
736 Elm Rd
Northern Cambria PA
157148921

Call Sign: KB3DMJ
Guy A Fleming
1064 Main St
Northern Cambria PA
15714

Call Sign: KB3ANT
Pearl J Fleming
1071 Main St
Northern Cambria PA
15714

Call Sign: KE3DR
Paul R Fleming
1071 Main St
Northern Cambria PA
15714

Call Sign: KB3MFQ
Jeffrey E Marshall
1504 Martin Ave
Northern Cambria PA
15714

Call Sign: N3WYZ
Allan W Varner
Mountain Dr
Northern Cambria PA
15714

Call Sign: N3LAD
Charles J Englody
148 Nancy St
Northern Cambria PA
15714

Call Sign: N3MWH
Sandra K Englody
148 Nancy St
Northern Cambria PA
15714

Call Sign: WA3QKO
Andrew J Klapak Jr
909 Oak St
Northern Cambria PA
157141442

Call Sign: N3PUM
Todd M Miller
522 Philadelphia Ave Apt
2
Northern Cambria PA
15714

Call Sign: N3XIQ
Gregory B Lagoda
1803 Tower Hill Rd
Northern Cambria PA
15714

FCC Amateur Radio Licenses in Nuthumberland

Call Sign: WA3WHX
Donald B Houtz
532 3rd St
Northumberland PA 17857

Call Sign: KB3UCW
David A Ferster
354 4th St
Northumberland PA 17857

Call Sign: KA3THE
Margaret D Stahl
452 4th St
Northumberland PA 17857

Call Sign: KA3THD
David A Stahl
452 4th St
Northumberland PA
178571108

Call Sign: N3CGE
Chester C Hunt
350 8th St
Northumberland PA 17857

Call Sign: W3BHC
William E Ulp
109 9th St
Northumberland PA 17857

Call Sign: N3MGH
Richard E Smith
Box 372Z Mtn Rd
Northumberland PA 17857

Call Sign: KA3GQM
Ronald A Beam
Box 489B
Northumberland PA 17857

Call Sign: N3YFB
Randy A Paul
583 Front St
Northumberland PA 17857

Call Sign: KB3NFY
Louis G Van Gilder
300 Ivy Ln

Northumberland PA 17857

Call Sign: KA3DNM
Fred P Siemsen
270 King St
Northumberland PA 17857

Call Sign: N3FOQ
Theodore C Koppen
290 Prince St
Northumberland PA 17857

Call Sign: KB3AAB
Timothy A Botts
537 Queen St
Northumberland PA 17857

Call Sign: WA3WHW
Birdie L Craven
Rd 1
Northumberland PA 17857

Call Sign: W3AVJ
David T Zweier
120 Ridgway
Northumberland PA
178579202

Call Sign: KC3QH
Harry M Bingaman
209 Stone School Rd
Northumberland PA 17857

Call Sign: K3NWH
Clarence E Walter
790 Strawbridge Rd
Northumberland PA 17857

Call Sign: W2ACM
Samuel E Craig
182 Viewpoint Ln
Northumberland PA
178578547

Call Sign: WY3M

Robert E Stahl
373 Wallace St
Northumberland PA 17857

FCC Amateur Radio Licenses in Numidia

Call Sign: K3BZG
George S Beaver
Numidia PA 178580011

FCC Amateur Radio Licenses in Oberlin

Call Sign: W3JVW
Earl W Eshenauer Jr
165 Hanshue St
Oberlin PA 17113

Call Sign: N3PHR
Wasyl Kadenko
1266 Ober St
Oberlin PA 17113

FCC Amateur Radio Licenses in Olanta

Call Sign: N3KLK
Daniel L Hubler
4566 Oak Ridge Rd
Olanta PA 16863

FCC Amateur Radio Licenses in Orangeville

Call Sign: N3GZG
Albert M Mahn
Box 132A
Orangeville PA 17859

Call Sign: N3MXO
Raymond L Miller
Box 80
Orangeville PA 17859

Call Sign: KB3ERH
Belinda M Daring
219 Meadow Ln
Orangeville PA 17859

Call Sign: KB3EUR
Richard N Daring
219 Meadow Ln
Orangeville PA 17859

Call Sign: K3BD
Belinda M Daring
219 Meadow Ln
Orangeville PA 17859

Call Sign: K3RND
Richard N Daring
219 Meadow Ln
Orangeville PA 17859

Call Sign: WA3SPL
James S Giger
210 Mill St
Orangeville PA 17859

Call Sign: KB3CVH
Dale K Morris
163 Old Greenwood Rd
Orangeville PA 17859

Call Sign: KB3PSP
Kenneth R Lewis Jr
Overlook St
Orangeville PA 17859

Call Sign: KA3BPK
G Rebecca Westover
141 Pealertown Rd
Orangeville PA 17859

Call Sign: N3MXL
Sandra I Yost
1096 Ridge Rd
Orangeville PA 17859

Call Sign: N3KWC
Byron L Yost
1101 Ridge Rd
Orangeville PA 178599630

Call Sign: WB3HFX
Donna M Adams
73 W Cedar St
Orangeville PA 17859

Call Sign: N3KPL
Gerard M Gallagher
Orangeville PA 17859

FCC Amateur Radio Licenses in Orbisonia

Call Sign: N3WIL
Terry L Jamison
Box 135
Orbisonia PA 17243

Call Sign: KA3DCN
Ellen S Cheslock
Box 315
Orbisonia PA 17243

Call Sign: KA3EAR
Charles J Cheslock
Box 315
Orbisonia PA 17243

Call Sign: N3YQS
Mary G Jamison
11165 Pogue Rd
Orbisonia PA 17243

FCC Amateur Radio Licenses in Orrstown

Call Sign: KB3QBR
James A Sikes
10064 Cardinal Dr
Orrstown PA 17244

Call Sign: KB3VVU
Barry E Mohler
12826 Sandy Mt Rd
Orrstown PA 17244

Call Sign: WA3DUS
Charles A Bender Jr
10379 Sandy Mtn Rd
Orrstown PA 17244

FCC Amateur Radio Licenses in Orrtanna

Call Sign: KB3TUF
Peter A Diaz
421 Buchanan Valley Rd
Orrtanna PA 17353

Call Sign: N3YGG
Todd A Waite
800 Orrtanna Rd
Orrtanna PA 17353

Call Sign: KB3TUG
William M Sipling
835 Ortanna Rd
Orrtanna PA 17353

Call Sign: N3ZLB
John F Chiuchiolo
195 Peach Tree Rd
Orrtanna PA 173539753

FCC Amateur Radio Licenses in Osceola

Call Sign: WE3L
William A Buckingham
1 Hammond St
Osceola PA 16942

Call Sign: N3JWH
Darold L Elliott
218 Holden St

Osceola PA 16942

Call Sign: KG4GEX
Rodney L Drabert
7491 Rt 49
Osceola PA 16942

Call Sign: KB3DOK
Audrey J Graham
204 Tuscarora Rd
Osceola PA 16942

Call Sign: KB3EAR
Northern Tier Repeater System
204 Tuscarora Rd
Osceola PA 16942

FCC Amateur Radio Licenses in Osceola Mills

Call Sign: N3SPE
Gregory A Granville
99 Blanchard St
Osceola Mills PA 16666

Call Sign: K3YAW
Clifford H Kanour
Box 522
Osceola Mills PA 16666

Call Sign: N3CLB
Bernard A Ropchock
Box 790C
Osceola Mills PA 16666

Call Sign: WA3GFL
Jerry I Bush
192 Centre Rd
Osceola Mills PA 16666

Call Sign: KA3YHT
Jerry R Dullen
310 Coal St
Osceola Mills PA 16666

Call Sign: N3CVE
Frank J Raftovich Jr
407 Spike Island Rd
Osceola Mills PA 16666

Call Sign: W3BAR
Bernard A Ropchock
201 Violet Ln
Osceola Mills PA 16666

FCC Amateur Radio Licenses in Osterburg

Call Sign: KB3OIF
Joshua T Brown
995 S Imler Valley Rd
Osterburg PA 16667

Call Sign: N3SSG
Tina K Blasko
9319 William Penn Rd
Osterburg PA 16667

FCC Amateur Radio Licenses in Palmyra

Call Sign: N3TAN
Michael W Moyer
10 Behren Dr
Palmyra PA 17078

Call Sign: N3TDB
Kenneth S Wolfe Jr
Box 197C Villa Ln
Palmyra PA 17078

Call Sign: AA3LY
Daniel A Farrell
320 Brookwood Dr
Palmyra PA 17078

Call Sign: KA3ZNI
Colleen E Farrell
320 Brookwood Dr

Palmyra PA 17078

Call Sign: KB3WIB
Kenneth L Bechtel II
845 Buttonwood St
Palmyra PA 17078

Call Sign: NJ3Z
Michael R Morrow
109 Campbelltown Rd
Palmyra PA 17078

Call Sign: W3QT
Michael R Morrow
109 Campbelltown Rd
Palmyra PA 17078

Call Sign: NC1E
John A Makuch
2 Clover Ln
Palmyra PA 17078

Call Sign: KA3UCW
Robert G Owens
102 Community Park Dr
Palmyra PA 17078

Call Sign: KA3DFI
Kathryn H Lanz
124 Community Park Dr
Palmyra PA 170783615

Call Sign: WB3DPG
John C Lanz
124 Community Park Dr
Palmyra PA 170783615

Call Sign: N3MKG
James S Bower
1030 Debra Dr
Palmyra PA 17078

Call Sign: K3WFW
Dennis M Shaak
4 Dogwood Ln

Palmyra PA 17078

Call Sign: WA3OBZ
Martha J Shaak
4 Dogwood Ln
Palmyra PA 17078

Call Sign: WA3MHL
Samuel W Brown
110 E Cherry St
Palmyra PA 17078

Call Sign: W3CWT
Charles W Tapley
E Main St
Palmyra PA 17078

Call Sign: KB3DLF
Robert S Strawderman
804 E Maple St
Palmyra PA 17078

Call Sign: W3ZJH
Paul P Troxell
624 E Oak St
Palmyra PA 17078

Call Sign: N3GFM
Warren W Bobb III
1439 Earlys Mill Rd
Palmyra PA 170789209

Call Sign: W3WWB
Warren W Bobb III
1439 Earlys Mill Rd
Palmyra PA 170789209

Call Sign: KE3EZ
Georg W Bakalorz
142 Eisenhower Rd
Palmyra PA 17078

Call Sign: KC3AK
Terry A Mills
148 Eisenhower Rd

Palmyra PA 17078

Call Sign: KB3QKP
Linda P Mills
148 Eisenhower Rd
Palmyra PA 17078

Call Sign: N3WCY
Christopher S Eichfeld
335 Fencepost Ln
Palmyra PA 17078

Call Sign: N4FSH
Leslie E Sheppard
402 Gold Finch Dr
Palmyra PA 17078

Call Sign: KA3RKW
Barry A Richmond
237 Gravel Hill Rd
Palmyra PA 17078

Call Sign: KA9VGW
Jill K Dietrich
2725 Horseshoe Pike
Palmyra PA 17078

Call Sign: W3MKV
Wilbur J Miller
118 Kettering Dr
Palmyra PA 17078

Call Sign: WA3GRQ
Walter W Hiester
73 Knight Ct
Palmyra PA 17078

Call Sign: KB3TLU
Brandy M Stone
193 Lindbergh Dr
Palmyra PA 17078

Call Sign: KB3NYB
Christopher S Peters
44 My Way Dr

Palmyra PA 17078

Call Sign: W3ESN
Robert L Cassel
21 N Grant St
Palmyra PA 17078

Call Sign: N3OSP
Donald E Barry Jr
711 N Grant St
Palmyra PA 17078

Call Sign: K3IUY
Irvin M Sanders
100 N Larkspur Dr Apt
119
Palmyra PA 17078

Call Sign: WB3JWS
Joseph W Smith Jr
226.5 N Railroad St
Palmyra PA 170780229

Call Sign: N3POT
Donald E Hartman Jr
619 N Railroad St
Palmyra PA 17078

Call Sign: KB3BYJ
Michael D Waters
30 N Railroad St 2nd Fl
Palmyra PA 17078

Call Sign: N3RQQ
John E Carbutt Jr
30 Oakwood Dr
Palmyra PA 17078

Call Sign: K3CPL
John W Peffley
802 Pajabon Dr
Palmyra PA 170783010

Call Sign: KB3OJC
Michael E Ferris

1321 S Duke St
Palmyra PA 17078

Call Sign: KB3DLI
Jack Kelly
2077 S Forge Rd
Palmyra PA 17078

Call Sign: N3WFP
Kristofer A Miller
S Grant St
Palmyra PA 170783208

Call Sign: W3TPM
Richard W Trautman
1071 S King St
Palmyra PA 17078

Call Sign: KA3KER
Dennis L Shank
1304 S Prince St
Palmyra PA 17078

Call Sign: KB3DXI
Billie A Burns
1343 S Queen St
Palmyra PA 17078

Call Sign: WI3X
Dane S Burns
1343 S Queen St
Palmyra PA 17078

Call Sign: KB3PYG
Robert J Bankey Jr
148 Schoolhouse Rd
Palmyra PA 17078

Call Sign: AK3P
Gary Hoffmann
25 Shirks Church Rd
Palmyra PA 17078

Call Sign: N3FDY
Marla N Hoffmann

25 Shirks Church Rd
Palmyra PA 17078

Call Sign: N3QZG
Daniel P Spengler
Shirks Church Rd Rd 1
Palmyra PA 17078

Call Sign: N3OGL
Dennis W Mills
130 Sunflower Ln
Palmyra PA 17078

Call Sign: N3GKY
Jim A Goshert
62 Sycamore Ln
Palmyra PA 17078

Call Sign: N3IER
Shirley A Grosh
62 Sycamore Ln
Palmyra PA 17078

Call Sign: N3JDB
James A Grosh
62 Sycamore Ln
Palmyra PA 17078

Call Sign: N3OFB
Cynthia L Goshert
62 Sycamore Ln
Palmyra PA 17078

Call Sign: N3YOS
Michael A Goshert
62 Sycamore Ln
Palmyra PA 17078

Call Sign: N3YOT
Aaron M Goshert
62 Sycamore Ln
Palmyra PA 17078

Call Sign: KB3TKM
Benjamin B Cooperson II

124 Trillium Dr
Palmyra PA 17078

Call Sign: N3ZSH
Robert J Millar
308 W Main St
Palmyra PA 17078

Call Sign: WA3VFN
Jere D Proctor Jr
433 W Main St Front
Palmyra PA 17078

Call Sign: NY3O
Richard M Schreffler
505 W Maple St
Palmyra PA 17078

Call Sign: KB3BCY
Richard A OLeary
2006 Wexford Rd
Palmyra PA 170789252

FCC Amateur Radio Licenses in Paradise

Call Sign: KH2SX
Joshua D White
1039 Georgetown Rd
Paradise PA 17562

Call Sign: KA3YWR
James V Houck Sr
15 Hershey Ave
Paradise PA 175620174

Call Sign: WL7DW
Marcus W Zito
7 N Vintage Rd
Paradise PA 17562

Call Sign: KB3HHT
Joshua M Rauch
12 Paradise Ln
Paradise PA 17562

FCC Amateur Radio Licenses in Patton

Call Sign: KB3UIZ
Vincent J Vescovi
305 6th Ave
Patton PA 16668

Call Sign: KB3IAN
Gregory J Ropp
264 Beech Rd
Patton PA 16668

Call Sign: KB3BMW
Dividing Ridge ARC Inc
199 Bender Rd Apt 1
Patton PA 16668

Call Sign: AB3FG
Anthony J Vescovi
141 Candle Ln
Patton PA 16668

Call Sign: KB3SXQ
William Strittmatter
151 Candle Ln
Patton PA 16668

Call Sign: WB3JQD
Armie T James
4713 Colonel Drake Hwy
Patton PA 16668

Call Sign: N4HKQ
Lewis E Robinson
764 Eckenrode Mill Rd
Patton PA 16668

Call Sign: K3AHE
Lewis E Robinson
764 Eckenrode Mill Rd
Patton PA 16668

Call Sign: K3MLE

Kenneth B Holtz
379 Glendale Lake Rd
Patton PA 16668

Call Sign: N3CQO
Carol K Holtz
379 Glendale Lake Rd
Patton PA 16668

Call Sign: KA3JIB
Chris A Venesky
513 Kerr Ave
Patton PA 16668

Call Sign: N3VRN
Emma M Venesky
513 Kerr Ave
Patton PA 16668

Call Sign: KB3T
Jerome H Humphrey
618 Magee Ave
Patton PA 16668

Call Sign: NX2Y
Jerome H Humphrey
618 Magee Ave
Patton PA 16668

Call Sign: W3QQ
Jerome H Humphrey
618 Magee Ave
Patton PA 16668

Call Sign: N3VRL
Thomas J Smith
1071 Magee Rd
Patton PA 16668

FCC Amateur Radio Licenses in Paxinos

Call Sign: N3MEK
Virginia C Sinclair
Box 154

Paxinos PA 17860

Call Sign: N3PEG
Veryl L Sinclair
Box 154
Paxinos PA 17860

Call Sign: N3SDA
James W Hoffman
Box 339
Paxinos PA 17860

Call Sign: N3EFB
Duane R Donmoyer
Box 352
Paxinos PA 17860

Call Sign: K3SJK
Robert C Aurand
Box 460
Paxinos PA 17860

Call Sign: WA4THR
Victor H Klein III
163 Frederick Rd
Paxinos PA 17860

FCC Amateur Radio Licenses in Peach Bottom

Call Sign: WA3EUD
Jeffrey E Nesbitt
110 Cornwall Ln
Peach Bottom PA 17563

Call Sign: KB3IRW
Jack L Thomas Jr
455 Peach Bottom Rd
Peach Bottom PA 17563

Call Sign: KC7PCX
Christopher T Sharp
Pilottown Rd
Peach Bottom PA 17563

Call Sign: KA3IGZ
Michael P Lane
117 Plum Hill Rd
Peach Bottom PA 17563

Call Sign: K3KZY
William J Kalin
2318 Robert Fulton Hwy
Peach Bottom PA
175639702

FCC Amateur Radio Licenses in Penfield

Call Sign: N3MYX
Mark A Maines Sr
Box 14
Penfield PA 15849

Call Sign: KB3UGD
Richard S Hasty
39 Ponderosa Dr
Penfield PA 15849

FCC Amateur Radio Licenses in Penns Creek

Call Sign: N3ZHG
John I Straub
180 Memory Ln
Penns Creek PA 17862

Call Sign: KB3QEE
Joseph L Corrall
Penns Creek PA 17862

Call Sign: W3JLC
Joseph L Corrall
Penns Creek PA 17862

FCC Amateur Radio Licenses in Pennsdale

Call Sign: KB3TQR
Richard C Laubach

706 Lycoming Mall Rd
Pennsdale PA 17756

FCC Amateur Radio Licenses in Pennsylvania Furnace

Call Sign: K1GFX
Kenneth C Gray
12 Beaver Branch
Pennsylvania Furnace PA
16865

Call Sign: N3SOW
Janice Perison
778 Beaver Branch Rd
Pennsylvania Furnace PA
16865

Call Sign: N2AVH
Richard J Stoller
782 Beaver Branch Rd
Pennsylvania Furnace PA
16865

Call Sign: K3RBH
Robert B Hazelton
406 Beaver Brook Dr
Pennsylvania Furnace PA
16865

Call Sign: KC1JL
William C Culp Jr
104 Fairbrook Dr
Pennsylvania Furnace PA
16865

Call Sign: KA3TTS
Todd F Walker
106 Gardner Ln
Pennsylvania Furnace PA
16865

Call Sign: N3NBM
Ellen M Bingham

145 Goddard Cir
Pennsylvania Furnace PA
16865

Call Sign: NV3N
Stuart C Bingham
145 Goddard Cir
Pennsylvania Furnace PA
168659729

Call Sign: K3IOQ
Michael R Mulauski
238 Meadow Ln
Pennsylvania Furnace PA
16865

Call Sign: KB3IFL
Thomas S Ertsgaard
197 Val Verda Dr
Pennsylvania Furnace PA
16865

Call Sign: KA3DCB
Charles O Crawford
215 Val Verda Dr
Pennsylvania Furnace PA
16865

Call Sign: KB3HWU
Christopher J Bourne
225 Val Verda Dr
Pennsylvania Furnace PA
16865

Call Sign: KA3MLF
Joseph L Loomis
4836 Whitehall Rd
Pennsylvania Furnace PA
16865

Call Sign: N3OWF
Joseph D Cochran
530 Wyandotte Ln
Pennsylvania Furnace PA
16865

Call Sign: K3DGT
Richard D Koontz
Pennsylvania Furnace PA
16865

FCC Amateur Radio Licenses in Pequea

Call Sign: KE3SB
Richard M Noll
56 4 Oaks Dr
Pequea PA 17565

Call Sign: KA3LQE
Ronald E Leisey Sr
233 Frogtown Rd
Pequea PA 17565

Call Sign: KB3LOL
Robert L Garner
322 House Rock Rd
Pequea PA 17565

Call Sign: WA3PTE
Barry M Bauman
764 Marticville Rd
Pequea PA 17565

Call Sign: KA8ZOO
Jerome E Broad
101 Oak Glen Dr
Pequea PA 17565

Call Sign: KA3YHC
Glenda C Broad
101 Oakglen Dr
Pequea PA 17565

Call Sign: WA3JGR
Patrick A Forestell
81 Westview Rd
Pequea PA 17565

FCC Amateur Radio Licenses in Petersburg

Call Sign: KA3TDX
Jeffery L Hensor
Box 46
Petersburg PA 16669

Call Sign: N3MCV
P Ganter
Box 766
Petersburg PA 16669

Call Sign: AB3PO
Edward E Allison
9316 Playhouse Rd
Petersburg PA 16669

Call Sign: KA3TCM
Jeremy J Kroll
Petersburg PA 16669

Call Sign: N3JCT
Terry L Hutchison
Petersburg PA 16669

Call Sign: K3AYV
Thomas E Howell
Petersburg PA 16669

Call Sign: N3YUZ
Keith T Stevens
Petersburg PA 16669

FCC Amateur Radio Licenses in Philipsburg

Call Sign: W3CDP
John T Shultz
Box 61
Philipsburg PA 16866

Call Sign: KB3MAI
Filip J Cerny
284 Copelin Rd

Philipsburg PA 16866

Call Sign: AB3HK
Filip J Cerny
284 Copelin Rd
Philipsburg PA 16866

Call Sign: W3PHB
Philipsburg Amateur Radio
Assoc
284 Copelin Rd
Philipsburg PA 16866

Call Sign: KB3CLZ
Philipsburg Amateur Radio
Assoc
284 Copelin Rd
Philipsburg PA 16866

Call Sign: AA3EJ
David G Runk
887 Decatur St
Philipsburg PA 16866

Call Sign: KB3RCJ
Steven M Lazar
238 Game Reserve Rd
Philipsburg PA 16866

Call Sign: N3HBJ
George N Patrick
206 Hemlock St
Philipsburg PA 16866

Call Sign: KB3OAV
John M Fetters Jr
414 Keystone Hill Rd
Philipsburg PA 16866

Call Sign: N3SPU
Thomas Foreman
904 Locust St
Philipsburg PA 16866

Call Sign: KB0CLZ

Scott T Vandewalle
150 Martin St
Philipsburg PA 16866

Call Sign: KB3CBN
Joseph M Howe Jr
14 N 2nd St
Philipsburg PA 16866

Call Sign: KB3FKK
Phyllis A Witherite
14 N 2nd St
Philipsburg PA 16866

Call Sign: N3SFJ
Russel M Franek
300 N Front St
Philipsburg PA 168662152

Call Sign: N3QLE
William J Foreman
703 Pauline St
Philipsburg PA 16866

Call Sign: N3ZCN
William N Marcoux Jr
1226 Philipsburg Bigler
Hwy
Philipsburg PA 16866

Call Sign: W3CDR
Boyd W Houck
131 S 2nd St
Philipsburg PA 16866

Call Sign: AB3PD
Andrew T Catherine
15 S 8th St
Philipsburg PA 16866

Call Sign: N3ONE
Jamison B Warg
215 S Front St
Philipsburg PA 16866

Call Sign: K3BIE
Richard L Thompson
814 Sleepy Hollow Rd
Philipsburg PA 16866

Call Sign: N3KFL
Alfred M Moyle Jr
1128 Tyrone Pike
Philipsburg PA 168669316

Call Sign: K3UMT
Leo W Kalinosky
125 Windsor St
Philipsburg PA 16866

FCC Amateur Radio Licenses in Picture Rocks

Call Sign: KB3IZN
Richard W Sprout
209 Center St
Picture Rocks PA
177620003

Call Sign: KB3JDK
Susan E Sprout
209 Center St
Picture Rocks PA
177620003

FCC Amateur Radio Licenses in Pine Grove

Call Sign: KB3POC
Joseph Ryan
Birds Hill Rd
Pine Grove PA 17963

Call Sign: K3JLX
Eugene A Derfler
Box 183
Pine Grove PA 17963

Call Sign: WB3HNX
Roland F Wiggins

Box 374
Pine Grove PA 17963

Call Sign: WB3GOW
Oscar K Heinbach
Box 600
Pine Grove PA 17963

Call Sign: KC3YD
Thomas J Mitchell
Box 95
Pine Grove PA 17963

Call Sign: KA3YCI
Marianne K Graham
821 Canal Dr
Pine Grove PA 17963

Call Sign: N3PTR
Dennis R Moore
44 E Pottsville St
Pine Grove PA 17963

Call Sign: N3EUK
David W Reed
35 E Pottsville St 2
Pine Grove PA 17963

Call Sign: AB9LG
Mark D Watson
108 High St
Pine Grove PA 17963

Call Sign: KB3TOK
Terry L Fetterman Jr
10 Jarrett Ln
Pine Grove PA 17963

Call Sign: N3FDX
Earl W Shollenberger
Lake Rd
Pine Grove PA 17963

Call Sign: N3QCE
Charles R Donmoyer

8 Mason Dr
Pine Grove PA 17963

Call Sign: WA3FKY
Joseph E Fisher
107 Molleystown Rd
Pine Grove PA 17963

Call Sign: KB3QDC
Anthony C Kauffman
170 N Tulpehocken St
Pine Grove PA 17963

Call Sign: KB3CSK
Ronald J Reidler
1517 Panther Valley Rd
Pine Grove PA 17963

Call Sign: N3FZO
Randolph R Rehrer
34 Ponderosa Ln
Pine Grove PA 17963

Call Sign: WB3FTU
Henry F Koenig
Rd 2
Pine Grove PA 17963

Call Sign: WB3FTV
Shirley A Koenig
Rd 2
Pine Grove PA 17963

Call Sign: KB3RJV
Joseph J Svrcek
84 S Tulpehocken St
Pine Grove PA 17963

Call Sign: WA3YID
Henry G Snyder
139 S Tulpehocken St
Pine Grove PA 17963

Call Sign: K3HZR
Ronald R Rehrer

108 Snyder Ave Apt 5
Pine Grove PA 17963

Call Sign: WB3BYC
Ledyard Thompson
730 Suedberg Rd
Pine Grove PA 17963

Call Sign: KA3ANG
Pierce J Banonis
3727 Sweet Arrow Lake
Rd
Pine Grove PA 17963

Call Sign: KB3QGR
React Of Schuylkill And
North Central Pa
314 Tremont Rd
Pine Grove PA 17963

Call Sign: KB3QZA
C J Ryan
314 Tremont Rd
Pine Grove PA 17963

Call Sign: N2ZVX
John V Povilaitis
716 Union Ct
Pine Grove PA 17963

Call Sign: KA3WDG
Jackie L Barr
33 W Pottsville St
Pine Grove PA 17963

Call Sign: WA3YMU
Homer F Luckenbill Jr
105 Walnut St
Pine Grove PA 17963

FCC Amateur Radio Licenses in Pine Grove Mills

Call Sign: N3IUF

Philip J Coolick
278 W Pine Grove Rd
Pine Grove Mills PA
16868

Call Sign: K3CHI
George W Swavely III
Pine Grove Mills PA
16868

Call Sign: KB3ESG
David A Harpster
Pine Grove Mills PA
16868

Call Sign: KB3VSF
Matthew R Heller
Pine Grove Mills PA
16868

FCC Amateur Radio Licenses in Plainfield

Call Sign: KB3FYO
Christopher J Ilgenfritz
Plainfield PA 17081

Call Sign: KB3GGK
Jonathan J Ilgenfritz
Plainfield PA 17081

Call Sign: N3PRG
Douglas F Stewart
Plainfield PA 170810178

FCC Amateur Radio Licenses in Pleasant Gap

Call Sign: K3EDD
Edward J Hinkle
108 Chapel Hill Cir
Pleasant Gap PA 16823

Call Sign: WA3YFN
Ernest L McIntosh

140 Colby Cir
Pleasant Gap PA 16823

Call Sign: KB3EFC
Jarryd W Beard
184 E College Ave
Pleasant Gap PA 16823

Call Sign: KA3HRS
Terry R Lindquist Sr
231 Harrison Rd
Pleasant Gap PA 16823

Call Sign: KB3NDI
Ryan M Misliuski
106 Heather Cir
Pleasant Gap PA 16823

Call Sign: N3EB
Eric L Brooks
170 Jodon Ave
Pleasant Gap PA 16823

Call Sign: N3EMD
Janice E Brooks
170 Jodon Ave
Pleasant Gap PA 16823

Call Sign: K3PMK
Paul A Frantz
123 Locust St
Pleasant Gap PA 16823

Call Sign: KB3NZP
David Conklin
119 Middle St
Pleasant Gap PA 16823

Call Sign: KB3SHW
Anthony A Peiffer
126 S Harrison Rd
Pleasant Gap PA 16823

Call Sign: WB3DND
William G Murphy III

127 West St
Pleasant Gap PA 16823

Call Sign: N3FVM
James E Rankin Jr
Box 220
Port Allegany PA 16743

Call Sign: K3BH
John G Hall
Box 341
Port Allegany PA 16743

Call Sign: KB3FFD
James L Lewis
Box 343
Port Allegany PA 16743

Call Sign: KA3ZDO
Susan W Haagen
Box 532
Port Allegany PA 16743

Call Sign: N3MWE
Neil B Haagen Jr
Box 532
Port Allegany PA 16743

Call Sign: KB3MFZ
Brady W Owens
100 Chestnut St
Port Allegany PA 16743

Call Sign: KB3SVH
Charles W Hallows
103 Chestnut St
Port Allegany PA 16743

Call Sign: N3RTY
Richard K Peterson
76 Church St
Port Allegany PA 16743

Call Sign: KB8LET
John S Coxen
207 E Arnold Ave
Port Allegany PA 16743

Call Sign: KB3FOI
Ryan T Smith
81 Katherine St
Port Allegany PA 16743

Call Sign: KB3FFC
Roydon D Hallock
85 Katherine St
Port Allegany PA 16743

Call Sign: KB3UOD
Stephen W Smith
796 Lower Grimes Rd
Port Allegany PA 16743

Call Sign: K3SWS
Stephen W Smith
796 Lower Grimes Rd
Port Allegany PA 16743

Call Sign: NJ3K
Bruce A Manning
784 Pine Grove Rd
Port Allegany PA 16743

Call Sign: KA3NQH
Wayne R Wright
962 Pine Grove Rd
Port Allegany PA 16743

Call Sign: N3NOV
Scott A Undercofler
36 S Elm St
Port Allegany PA 16743

Call Sign: N0HNJ
David A Corio
178 Two Mile Rd
Port Allegany PA 16743

Call Sign: KB3MOW
Dave A Corio
178 Two Mile Rd
Port Allegany PA 16743

Call Sign: N3GYX
Daniel R Williams
Port Allegany PA 16743

Call Sign: N3BXQ
David M Carre III
Box 118
Port Matilda PA 16870

Call Sign: WB3BKU
Jackson A Gabany
Box 92B
Port Matilda PA 16870

Call Sign: KB3JEF
Robert E Leonard
50 Charlotte St
Port Matilda PA 16870

Call Sign: WB9QZC
James R Zuhlke
111 Charlotte St
Port Matilda PA 16870

Call Sign: KF3EA
James R Zuhlke
111 Charlotte St
Port Matilda PA 16870

Call Sign: KB3NYH
Emma E Zuhlke
111 Charlotte St
Port Matilda PA 16870

Call Sign: N3UJM
Thomas A Majewski

15 Cornfield Ln
Port Matilda PA 16870

Call Sign: KD6GUF
Joel A Christensen
70 Darrich Ct
Port Matilda PA 16870

Call Sign: KB3JAX
Joel A Christensen
70 Darrich Ct
Port Matilda PA 16870

Call Sign: KA3EDZ
William E Ames
302 E Spruce St
Port Matilda PA 16870

Call Sign: KB3FAN
Cale F Brownstead
124 Forest Glen Cir
Port Matilda PA 16870

Call Sign: KB3JEG
Tyler K Stimely
2148 Halfmoon Valley Rd
Port Matilda PA 16870

Call Sign: AA3LT
Walter Mong
508 High St
Port Matilda PA 16870

Call Sign: KB3PZH
Julio Urbina
146 Hunter Wood Way
Port Matilda PA 16870

Call Sign: N3KSP
Keith L Smith
140 Lutz Ln
Port Matilda PA 16870

Call Sign: KB3GDQ
James F Breakall

264 Lutz Ln
Port Matilda PA 16870

Call Sign: W3FET
James F Breakall
264 Lutz Ln
Port Matilda PA 16870

Call Sign: KC3R
Nittany Contest Club
264 Lutz Ln
Port Matilda PA 16870

Call Sign: WA3FET
James K Breakall
264 Lutz Ln
Port Matilda PA 16870

Call Sign: KB3MQM
Sven Schulz
21 Morris Rd
Port Matilda PA 16870

Call Sign: KB3KJ
James C Mankin
30 Peggy Cir
Port Matilda PA
168709576

Call Sign: W3EVM
Raymond W Vogt
197 Potters Ln
Port Matilda PA 16870

Call Sign: KC7PYT
Thomas R Neff
1648 Reese Hollow Rd
Port Matilda PA 16870

Call Sign: KB3DSY
Susan L Person
281 Saddle Ridge Rd
Port Matilda PA 16870

Call Sign: KB3CFD

Floyd W Ringer
134 Susan Ln
Port Matilda PA 16870

Call Sign: KB3ESL
David J Ondrejik
382 Tow Hill Rd
Port Matilda PA 16870

Call Sign: K3NWS
David J Ondrejik
382 Tow Hill Rd
Port Matilda PA 16870

Call Sign: KB3KPP
Jason E Terosky
50 Winesap Dr
Port Matilda PA 16870

Call Sign: WB3GPJ
Richard A Sutton
Port Matilda PA 16870

FCC Amateur Radio Licenses in Port Royal

Call Sign: K3GOO
David B Esh
Box 750
Port Royal PA 170829746

Call Sign: N3ODW
Norma J Brackbill
Box 905
Port Royal PA 17082

Call Sign: K3VMS
Frederick C Shetler
235 Cross Rd
Port Royal PA 17082

Call Sign: N3KPW
Garth E Brackbill
Rd 1
Port Royal PA 17082

Call Sign: KA3TIW
Darwin C Heaps Jr
Port Royal PA 17082

FCC Amateur Radio Licenses in Port Trevorton

Call Sign: N3PWK
Amy C Buck
Box 437W
Port Trevorton PA 17864

Call Sign: N3CGU
Ronald E Etzweiler
1109 Kerstetter Ridge Rd
Port Trevorton PA 17864

FCC Amateur Radio Licenses in Portage

Call Sign: KA3ZFV
John M Havrilla
1121 Blair St
Portage PA 15946

Call Sign: N3LEU
Matthew J Stith
Box 399
Portage PA 15946

Call Sign: N3TGW
Catherine E Mrozek
1112 Center SE
Portage PA 15946

Call Sign: KB3WDN
Raymond J Hazlett
507 Farren St
Portage PA 15946

Call Sign: W3WGY
Howard W Smith
1312 Gillespie Ave

Portage PA 15946

Call Sign: N3KNB
Stephen M Voss
396 Jamestown Rd
Portage PA 15946

Call Sign: WA3YMZ
Raymond C McConnell
1404 Jefferson Ave
Portage PA 15946

Call Sign: N3KNA
Robert C Stith
1414 Munster Rd
Portage PA 15946

Call Sign: KB3LBG
David M Mrkich
1833 Munster Rd
Portage PA 15946

Call Sign: N3LSK
John W Havrilla
1121 N Blair St
Portage PA 15946

Call Sign: W3TGR
Stanley W Rapski
123 Rapski Ln
Portage PA 159466722

Call Sign: N3KMZ
Patrick J Sweeney
1203 Spring Hill Rd
Portage PA 15946

Call Sign: KB3MGB
Michael J Pisarski
1000 Stanley Dr
Portage PA 15946

Call Sign: N3QQK
Patrick J Sweeney Jr
910 Washington Ave

Portage PA 15946

Call Sign: KB3YHN
Dennis M Mainhart
1037 Willow Beach Rd
Portage PA 15946

FCC Amateur Radio Licenses in Quarryville

Call Sign: N3RJG
Stephen C Basciano III
104 Black Bear Rd
Quarryville PA 17566

Call Sign: K3IP
Henry Shaubach Jr
1004 Buck Rd
Quarryville PA 17566

Call Sign: N3BLM
Wesley D Curry
292 Cardinal Dr
Quarryville PA 17566

Call Sign: N3WWQ
Adam J Bilheimer
790 Church Rd
Quarryville PA 17566

Call Sign: KB3FRQ
Kevin W Baylor
186 Clendenin Rd
Quarryville PA 17566

Call Sign: K3KWB
Kevin W Baylor
186 Clendenin Rd
Quarryville PA 17566

Call Sign: KA3UPE
P Lyn Prange
536 Conowihgo Rd
Quarryville PA 17566

Call Sign: KA4HNE
Matthew W Jones Jr
1132 Fishing Creek Rd
Quarryville PA 17566

Call Sign: KB3JDQ
David L Hanks
1502 Lancaster Pike
Quarryville PA 175669771

Call Sign: K2JEI
William A Mierop
625 Robert Fulton Hwy
Quarryville PA 17566

Call Sign: KB4YUZ
Linda R Jones
1132 Fishing Creek Rd
Quarryville PA 17566

Call Sign: KB3DIY
Merton O Deaver Jr
110 Larkspur Dr
Quarryville PA 17566

Call Sign: WA1ZIT
George M Soresina
1252 Robert Fulton Hwy
Quarryville PA 175669628

Call Sign: N3VCO
Charles W Gross Jr
19 Greenview Cir
Quarryville PA 175669291

Call Sign: N3NEG
Sharon E MacIntire
34 Laurel Hill Dr
Quarryville PA 17566

Call Sign: N3TNI
Warren S Keeney
51 Sunset Dr
Quarryville PA 17566

Call Sign: N3WWR
Terry L Besancon
18 Hartwicke Dr
Quarryville PA 17566

Call Sign: N3CU
Kenneth E MacIntire
34 Laurel Hill Dr
Quarryville PA 175669285

Call Sign: N3KID
Ed De Garay
126 Tanglewood Dr
Quarryville PA 17566

Call Sign: KB3JOJ
Ellis C Nesbitt
16 Hartwood Ln
Quarryville PA 17566

Call Sign: KB3GEC
Casey W Bridwell
119 Marlton Ln
Quarryville PA 17566

Call Sign: N3KRJ
Chris E De Garay
126 Tanglewood Dr
Quarryville PA 17566

Call Sign: K3FYX
Charles E Curry
19 Hartwood Ln
Quarryville PA 17566

Call Sign: KB3DIX
Carl V Messano Dr
361 Nottingham Rd
Quarryville PA 17566

Call Sign: WA3DMH
Earl E Eshleman
679 Truce Rd
Quarryville PA 17566

Call Sign: KB3EYR
Greg S Sollenberger
874 Kirkwood Pike
Quarryville PA 17566

Call Sign: W3MQC
Edward S Wyatt
527 Park Ave
Quarryville PA 17566

Call Sign: N3EIO
Harry L Work Jr
628 Valley Rd
Quarryville PA 17566

Call Sign: K3CIB
Ralph W Haneman
737 Lancaster Pike
Quarryville PA 17566

Call Sign: AA2OH
Edward A Graetz
527 Park Ave
Quarryville PA 17566

Call Sign: N3NOB
Virginia S Work
628 Valley Rd
Quarryville PA 17566

Call Sign: KB3AES
William A Cook
1052 Lancaster Pike
Quarryville PA 17566

Call Sign: AG4RG
Joe Tolbert
527 Park Ave
Quarryville PA 17566

Call Sign: KG6AEP
Carmela Pryluck
Quarryville PA 17566

FCC Amateur Radio Licenses in Qunicy

Call Sign: KB1JT
Howard A Baxter
Chesapeake Dr
Quincy PA 17247

Call Sign: W3OIO
William L Freienmuth
Wesley Dr
Quincy PA 172470128

FCC Amateur Radio Licenses in Railroad

Call Sign: KB3OYQ
Jeffrey A Slagle
35 E Main St
Railroad PA 17355

FCC Amateur Radio Licenses in Ralston

Call Sign: WB3IFX
Robert K Leonard
Green St
Ralston PA 17763

FCC Amateur Radio Licenses in Ramey

Call Sign: N3PUJ
Lawrence Gallo
Miriam St
Ramey PA 16671

Call Sign: N3QBR
Daniel L Gallo
Miriam St
Ramey PA 16671

FCC Amateur Radio Licenses in Ranshaw

Call Sign: W3KDU
George M Olley
130 Main
Ranshaw PA 17866

FCC Amateur Radio Licenses in Reamstown

Call Sign: KD3RS
Raphael J Gomez
6 S Main St
Reamstown PA 17567

FCC Amateur Radio Licenses in Rebersburg

Call Sign: W3EJA
Francis P Chadick
Box 128
Rebersburg PA 16872

Call Sign: KA3TTQ
Douglas L Ripka
Rebersburg PA 16872

FCC Amateur Radio Licenses in Rebuck

Call Sign: KB3JYN
John R Borkoski
Hc Box 2
Rebuck PA 17867

FCC Amateur Radio Licenses in Red Lion

Call Sign: KB3LAL
Delores R Smeltzer
314 1st Ave
Red Lion PA 17356

Call Sign: KA3KAR
Kerry D Smeltzer

314 1st Ave
Red Lion PA 173561518

Call Sign: KB3DBU
Joni M Smeltzer
314 1st Ave
Red Lion PA 173561518

Call Sign: W3VXI
Henry B Downs
739 Atlantic Ave
Red Lion PA 17356

Call Sign: K3TSX
Richard D Jennings
816 Atlantic Ave
Red Lion PA 173561516

Call Sign: KB3LAN
Michael W Azzarello
615 Bahns Mill Rd
Red Lion PA 17356

Call Sign: K3RVX
Don R Goughnour
Box 112
Red Lion PA 17356

Call Sign: KA3UKI
Paul H Dailey
Box 230 Trinity Rd
Red Lion PA 17356

Call Sign: KA3YCP
Darryl C Snyder
Box 572A
Red Lion PA 17356

Call Sign: N3KNE
Danielle R Snyder
Box 572A
Red Lion PA 17356

Call Sign: N3NEN
Larry D Sechrist

Box 575
Red Lion PA 17356

Call Sign: KB3EPJ
Richard B Orem
8865 Camp Rd
Red Lion PA 17356

Call Sign: WP3SS
Josue Fontanez
2406 Cape Horn Rd Apt
A94
Red Lion PA 17356

Call Sign: KA3MIT
Barbara B Smith
9635 Chapel Church Rd
Red Lion PA 17356

Call Sign: WJ3N
Geoffrey S Smith
9635 Chapel Church Rd
Red Lion PA 17356

Call Sign: WA3FRF
Joseph P Curilla
4005 Charity Dr
Red Lion PA 17356

Call Sign: KA3TFI
Michael Yasovsky
105 Circle Dr
Red Lion PA 17356

Call Sign: WB3ADC
Robert L Manton
772 Delta Rd
Red Lion PA 17356

Call Sign: KA3RFI
Montel M Tyler
102 Devon Ln
Red Lion PA 173568792

Call Sign: N3VCM

David S Stine
111 Dixie Dr
Red Lion PA 17356

Call Sign: K3VDB
Charles E Heisler
115 Dixie Dr
Red Lion PA 17356

Call Sign: K3IIB
Carey S Green Jr
59 E High St
Red Lion PA 17356

Call Sign: N3RMI
Barbara A Green
59 E High St
Red Lion PA 17356

Call Sign: KB3RFH
Andrew J Hertz
321 E Lancaster St
Red Lion PA 17356

Call Sign: KB3NDZ
Nathaniel L Armstrong
21 East Ave
Red Lion PA 17356

Call Sign: KB3VUS
James C Thompson III
1011 Felton Rd
Red Lion PA 17356

Call Sign: KB3QOS
Craig P Devono
1139 Felton Rd
Red Lion PA 17356

Call Sign: KA3SPV
William E Mundis
15 Forest Hills Rd
Red Lion PA 17356

Call Sign: KE3BQ

Dennis L Davis
2910 Freysville Rd
Red Lion PA 17356

Call Sign: KB3CHQ
Nathan R Arnold
6619 Herbst Rd
Red Lion PA 17356

Call Sign: WB3EWA
Thomas C Wood
14 Hunters Run Ct
Red Lion PA 17356

Call Sign: KB3EHP
Randy J Starr
740 Jefferson Ln
Red Lion PA 17356

Call Sign: W3NER
Jeffrey T Walters
8 Jonathan Way
Red Lion PA 17356

Call Sign: KB3TGL
Patrick E Carter
316 Kendale Rd
Red Lion PA 17356

Call Sign: KB3VUY
James P Wilson
309 Larkin Dr
Red Lion PA 17356

Call Sign: N3QWP
Benjamin R Byers Jr
206 Lartry Dr
Red Lion PA 17356

Call Sign: WB3GRE
Gregory R Mundis
365 Manor Rd
Red Lion PA 173568748

Call Sign: KF3AI

Robert E Mundis
365 Manor Rd
Red Lion PA 173569245

Call Sign: AA3VP
Robert E Mundis
365 Manor Rd
Red Lion PA 173569245

Call Sign: KB3UIC
Thomas B Macintosh
400 Marlowe Garth
Red Lion PA 17356

Call Sign: K3TBM
Thomas B Macintosh
400 Marlowe Garth
Red Lion PA 17356

Call Sign: KY8P
James H Pressel
163 Martin St
Red Lion PA 17356

Call Sign: KA3LIK
Robert M Klinedinst
360 Myers Rd
Red Lion PA 173568597

Call Sign: K3VGX
Brian M Manns
120 N Charles St Apt 708
Red Lion PA 173561632

Call Sign: KB3JXY
Charles I Hepfer Jr
150 N Main St
Red Lion PA 17356

Call Sign: N3KZJ
Georgianne Boswell
422 Oak Hollow Rd
Red Lion PA 17356

Call Sign: N3ZNV

Michael E Slack
502 Orchard Ct
Red Lion PA 17356

Call Sign: KB3SNH
Curtis E Miller
2041 Parson Ct
Red Lion PA 173569417

Call Sign: KB3VSO
Curtis E Miller
2041 Parson Ct
Red Lion PA 173569417

Call Sign: N3XDL
Gregg O Ramble
930 Pleasant Grove Rd
Red Lion PA 17356

Call Sign: K3TWR
Gregg O Ramble
930 Pleasant Grove Rd
Red Lion PA 17356

Call Sign: K3JPT
James P Thompson
5804 Pleasant View Rd
Red Lion PA 17356

Call Sign: N3IKA
Melvin E Taylor Sr
130 Rain Dove Dr
Red Lion PA 17356

Call Sign: N3RBS
Terry E Shenberger
Rd 1 Chaple Church Rd
Red Lion PA 17356

Call Sign: K9MDY
Stanley D Short Jr
1140 Richmond Rd
Red Lion PA 17356

Call Sign: KB3WRH

Stanley D Short Jr
1140 Richmond Rd
Red Lion PA 173568898

Call Sign: KB3RJG
Boone W Morgan
1313 Richmond Rd
Red Lion PA 17356

Call Sign: KB3VVB
Stephen C Paules
504 S Main St
Red Lion PA 17356

Call Sign: KA3RVR
Robert S Dailey
537 S Main St
Red Lion PA 17356

Call Sign: KA3UDJ
Joseph A Dailey
537 S Main St
Red Lion PA 17356

Call Sign: WA3SOR
Stephen B Kennick
830 S Park St
Red Lion PA 17356

Call Sign: N3UNU
Troy D Hildebrand
211 S Pine St
Red Lion PA 17356

Call Sign: KB3PSX
Phyllis W Smeltzer
608 S Pine St
Red Lion PA 17356

Call Sign: KB3PSW
Joan Nuzum
614 S Pine St
Red Lion PA 17356

Call Sign: W3GZD

Gerald J Ryan Sr
360 Steinfelt Rd
Red Lion PA 17356

Call Sign: AI3Y
Donald L Attig
400 Steinfelt Rd
Red Lion PA 17356

Call Sign: K3SRP
Philip W Steinfelt Jr
425 Steinfelt Rd
Red Lion PA 17356

Call Sign: KB3VUW
Wilbur C Brown
520 Sterling Dr
Red Lion PA 17356

Call Sign: N3YFK
Joanna L Hildebrand
204 W Broadway
Red Lion PA 173562009

Call Sign: N3OAK
Kevin J La Brie
233 W Broadway
Red Lion PA 17356

Call Sign: K3OAP
Donald W Zarfos
752 W Broadway
Red Lion PA 17356

Call Sign: KB3CLS
Jedidiah D Adams
126 W High St
Red Lion PA 173561606

Call Sign: KB3SCS
Southern York County
Contest Club
18 W Prospect St
Red Lion PA 17356

Call Sign: W3EC
Southern York County
Contest Club
18 W Prospect St
Red Lion PA 17356

Call Sign: KB3OFF
Lesa S Tracey
18 W Prospect St
Red Lion PA 17356

Call Sign: N3NRN
Brad L Tracey
18 W Prospect St
Red Lion PA 17356

Call Sign: KB3BUJ
Jonathan M McGovern
215 Wimbleton Way
Red Lion PA 17356

Call Sign: K3HIL
Robert E Ream
110 Windsor Rd
Red Lion PA 17356

Call Sign: KA3FNH
Kenneth L Ness
1450 Windsor Rd
Red Lion PA 173569639

Call Sign: N3THT
Betty J Ness
1450 Windsor Rd
Red Lion PA 173569639

Call Sign: K3JIM
James J Walsh
231 Winterstown Rd
Red Lion PA 17356

Call Sign: N3KVE
Charles H Miller III
851 Zimmerman Rd
Red Lion PA 17356

Call Sign: N3MBC
Harlan E Abbott Jr
220 Betty Cir
Reedsville PA 17084

Call Sign: K3DNA
Juniata Valley ARC
220 Betty Cir
Reedsville PA 17084

Call Sign: KA3ANJ
Thomas R Brumbaugh
281 Betty Cir
Reedsville PA 17084

Call Sign: W3ANJ
Thomas R Brumbaugh
281 Betty Cir
Reedsville PA 17084

Call Sign: WA3BNB
Robert P Snider
78 Church Ln
Reedsville PA 17084

Call Sign: WA3TSH
Richard P Stimely
N Main St
Reedsville PA 17084

Call Sign: WB3COB
Richard C Yingling
85 Prince St
Reedsville PA 17084

Call Sign: W3OMB
Leroy W Orner Sr
Rd 1
Reedsville PA 17084

Call Sign: KB3BBL

Edward M Leeper Jr
65 Taylor Dr
Reedsville PA 17084

Call Sign: WB9UGP
Gilbert R Halbleib Jr
49 Tilbury Ln
Reedsville PA 17084

Call Sign: WA3VAR
Joseph M Molek
4293 US Hwy 322
Reedsville PA 170848710

Call Sign: K3RB
Robert L Burns
149 Walnut St
Reedsville PA 17084

Call Sign: WA3WAT
Richard C Burns
313 Walnut St
Reedsville PA 17084

**FCC Amateur Radio
Licenses in Reinholds**

Call Sign: KB3DXH
John D De Remer
126 Adamstown Rd
Reinholds PA 17569

Call Sign: KB3GKH
Tammy L Deremer
126 Adamstown Rd
Reinholds PA 17569

Call Sign: N3HXA
Timothy A Zimmerman
180 Blue Lake Rd
Reinholds PA 17569

Call Sign: KZ3X
Thomas J Balon
15 Buck Run Rd

Reinholds PA 17569

Call Sign: KB3EXC
Joseph R Kurpiel
5 Circle Dr
Reinholds PA 17569

Call Sign: KB3IWW
Robert J Kurpiel
5 Circle Dr
Reinholds PA 17569

Call Sign: W3GWX
Ralph L Bailey
10 Clearview Dr
Reinholds PA 17569

Call Sign: N3VQY
Clyde L Weaver
3 Dennis Dr
Reinholds PA 17569

Call Sign: KA3DSV
Herbert W Speck
Fritztown Rd Rd 1
Reinholds PA 17569

Call Sign: N3XNX
Richard R Wright
101 Furlow Rd
Reinholds PA 17569

Call Sign: N3XNR
Joel D Weinhold
121 Furlow Rd
Reinholds PA 17569

Call Sign: KB3DXG
Kristy L De Remer
317 Holtzman Rd
Reinholds PA 17569

Call Sign: KB3WIC
Greg A Chown
255 Laurel Ridge Rd

Reinholds PA 17569

Call Sign: N3XAQ
Gerald L Weinhold
15 Martins Dr
Reinholds PA 17569

Call Sign: N3IRJ
Mark E Clark
94 Mechanic St
Reinholds PA 17569

Call Sign: KB3RBL
James S Miller
98 Mechanic St
Reinholds PA 17569

Call Sign: N3XAO
Howard E Null
605 Mohns Hill Rd
Reinholds PA 17569

Call Sign: KB3MGL
Mitch L Merkel
240 N Blainsport Rd
Reinholds PA 17569

Call Sign: KB3JWC
Karen F Winter
Swamp Church Rd
Reinholds PA 17569

Call Sign: N3WCW
John F Winter
Swamp Church Rd
Reinholds PA 17569

Call Sign: KA3PVK
Maximo W Rey
230 Village Spring Ln
Reinholds PA 17569

Call Sign: KB3VOC
Lawrence H Gero Jr
370 W Rt 897

Reinholds PA 17569

Call Sign: KB3UJM
George E Dula
Reinholds PA 17569

FCC Amateur Radio Licenses in Renovo

Call Sign: W3KTH
Clyde V Haupt
218 6th St
Renovo PA 177641014

Call Sign: WA3ABF
Dam Operators Alvin R
Bush Dam
Box 94
Renovo PA 17764

Call Sign: KC4VJS
Frank E Morton Sr
152 Susquehanna Ave
Renovo PA 177641522

FCC Amateur Radio Licenses in Revloc

Call Sign: N3XVV
Charles J Devett
53 Penn Ave
Revloc PA 159480184

Call Sign: K3CJD
Charles J Devett
53 Penn Ave
Revloc PA 159480184

FCC Amateur Radio Licenses in Rew

Call Sign: KB3GGR
Kevin L Waid
1278 Sumit Rd
Rew PA 167440184

FCC Amateur Radio Licenses in Rexmont

Call Sign: KB3QZC
Christopher S Stutzman
264 Rexmont Rd Apt 3r
Rexmont PA 17085

FCC Amateur Radio Licenses in Rheems

Call Sign: N4GSR
Walter Cooke
155 Broad St
Rheems PA 17570

FCC Amateur Radio Licenses in Richfield

Call Sign: KA3TKM
Wilbur A Hain IV
Box 383
Richfield PA 170869617

Call Sign: KB3SKF
Stephen W Bordner
1878 Ridge Rd
Richfield PA 17086

Call Sign: KB3TTE
Joshua N Martin
36086 Rte 35 N
Richfield PA 17086

Call Sign: N3ZHF
Joel E Renninger
32 Valley View Ln
Richfield PA 17086

Call Sign: KB3EVY
Chad E Shaffer
Richfield PA 17086

FCC Amateur Radio Licenses in Richland

Call Sign: KA2SYS
Carl W Sensenig
604 Elm St
Richland PA 17087

Call Sign: N2PAN
Joseph G Sabia
105 Hickory Rd
Richland PA 17087

Call Sign: N3UDB
Victor P Brubacker
257 Millardsville Rd
Richland PA 17087

Call Sign: N3NWA
David N Brubacker
Millardsville Rd
Richland PA 17087

Call Sign: N3SWH
Strangers And Pilgrims
Amateur Radio Kindred
Millardsville Rd
Richland PA 17087

Call Sign: K3OWL
Outlaw Wireless League
204 Poplar St
Richland PA 17087

Call Sign: KM3D
Harry B Bump
204 Poplar St
Richland PA 17087

Call Sign: N3VTA
Catherine A Bump
204 Poplar St
Richland PA 17087

Call Sign: N3TRV

Robert H Beaver
208 Walnut St Box 276
Richland PA 17087

Call Sign: N3WFQ
Linda A Bump
Richland PA 17087

**FCC Amateur Radio
Licenses in Ridgway**

Call Sign: N3SGY
Robert A Devilling
Box 134 H
Ridgway PA 15853

Call Sign: KA3OGP
Raymond A Fannin
Box 330
Ridgway PA 15853

Call Sign: KB3VGD
Vincent A Borrello
331 Dewey Cir
Ridgway PA 15853

Call Sign: KB3UOC
Richard C Skellen
423 E Main St
Ridgway PA 15853

Call Sign: N3NIA
Elk County ARA
Elk County Courthouse
Ridgway PA 15853

Call Sign: KA3SQB
David J Wirth
538 Florence St
Ridgway PA 15853

Call Sign: KA3SOJ
Robert C Sprague
605 Front St
Ridgway PA 15853

Call Sign: N3UGD
Don E Hoffman
102 Grant St
Ridgway PA 15853

Call Sign: N3UDM
Berniece E Jarbeck
28392 Lake City Rd
Ridgway PA 15853

Call Sign: KB3HZY
Wayne T Steele
306 Little Ave
Ridgway PA 15853

Call Sign: WW3O
Peter S Carr
329 Little Ave
Ridgway PA 158531220

Call Sign: KB3AOG
Shawna M Lutton
225 Montmorenci Ave
Ridgway PA 15853

Call Sign: KB3BGB
Vivian J Lutton
225 Montmorenci Ave
Ridgway PA 15853

Call Sign: N3NWL
Lee C Lewis
1455 Montmorenci Rd
Ridgway PA 15853

Call Sign: N3UDN
Mary A Lewis
1455 Montmorenci Rd
Ridgway PA 15853

Call Sign: N3UGB
Joseph E Lewis
1455 Montmorenci Rd
Ridgway PA 15853

Call Sign: KB3EWT
Shari L Lewis
1455 Montmorenci Rd
Ridgway PA 15853

Call Sign: KB3RKV
Robert A Devilling
607 N Maple Ave
Ridgway PA 15853

Call Sign: N3SGY
Robert A Devilling
607 N Maple Ave
Ridgway PA 15853

Call Sign: N3WRN
Lois J Devilling
607 N Maple Ave
Ridgway PA 15853

Call Sign: WB3EMV
Rudolph T Melzer
44 Paddocks Dr
Ridgway PA 15853

Call Sign: KB3MGY
Connie W Fannin
2008 Ridgway
Johnsonburg Rd
Ridgway PA 15853

Call Sign: W2FAN
Raymond A Fannin
2008 Ridgway
Johnsonburg Rd
Ridgway PA 15853

Call Sign: N3NBK
Veronica A Joiner
41 W Cardott
Ridgway PA 15853

Call Sign: KB3FFA
Joni L Lewis

40 W Main St
Ridgway PA 15853

Call Sign: N3UGC
William P Estus
119 W Main St
Ridgway PA 15853

Call Sign: KB3EVF
Todd J Lewis
40 W Main St Apt 3
Ridgway PA 15853

Call Sign: KA3SHB
Wayne J Klawuhn
506 Walnut St
Ridgway PA 15853

Call Sign: N3HYW
Dale E Anderson
415 Washington St
Ridgway PA 15853

Call Sign: KF8XT
Steven M Fox
612 Willard St
Ridgway PA 158539744

Call Sign: KA3SRO
Michael L Allenbaugh
Ridgway PA 15853

Call Sign: N3IFO
Richard D Cronk
Ridgway PA 15853

Call Sign: KB3BOE
Elk County ARA
Ridgway PA 15853

Call Sign: N3DWN
Marie C Rennecke
Ridgway PA 15853

FCC Amateur Radio Licenses in Riverside

Call Sign: W2LQR
Richard B Bunnell
1031 Ave D
Riverside PA 17868

Call Sign: N3KLU
Eris Marie B Bunnell
1031 Ave D
Riverside PA 178680157

Call Sign: AA3M
John A Mattesini Jr
Riverside PA 17868

Call Sign: N3DIB
Rosemary J Mattesini
Riverside PA 17868

FCC Amateur Radio Licenses in Rixford

Call Sign: KB3FKA
Mark E Burns
1225 Looker Mt Trl
Rixford PA 16745

Call Sign: KB3CXY
Eric J Farr
Rixford PA 16745

FCC Amateur Radio Licenses in Roaring Branch

Call Sign: KA3EMP
Margaret L Jolly
Box 254A
Roaring Branch PA 17765

Call Sign: KA3FWM
John O Jolly
Box 254A

Roaring Branch PA 17765

Call Sign: KB3MSE
Matthew S Hoppes
5575 Roaring Branch Rd
Roaring Branch PA 17765

FCC Amateur Radio Licenses in Roaring Spring

Call Sign: KB3BNA
Jonathan R Erb
Box 351
Roaring Spring PA 16673

Call Sign: N3NKS
Kenneth P Reed Jr
329 Cherry St
Roaring Spring PA 16673

Call Sign: KB3EVP
Reid E Ritchey II
554 Cove Ln
Roaring Spring PA 16673

Call Sign: W3ZUG
Ferdinand J Hasenstab
621 Cove Ln
Roaring Spring PA
166732209

Call Sign: W3KFD
Silas R Koofer
210 June Dr Apt 361
Roaring Spring PA 16673

Call Sign: WS3D
George W Ebersole
536 New St
Roaring Spring PA 16673

Call Sign: WA3MTT
John G Thompson
801 New St

Roaring Spring PA 16673

Call Sign: WK3R
Robert A Miller
1301 Plum Creek Rd
Roaring Spring PA 16673

Call Sign: W3UBP
Kenneth E Thompson
709 Rockingham
Roaring Spring PA 16673

Call Sign: N3MHK
George M Wareham
719 Roosevelt Ave
Roaring Spring PA 16673

Call Sign: N3IAV
John K Stern Jr
1489 S Main St
Roaring Spring PA 16673

Call Sign: N3HCR
David E Randolph
6488 Woodbury Pike
Roaring Spring PA 16673

Call Sign: N3HBK
Richard M Gunsallus
6519 Woodbury Pike
Roaring Spring PA 16673

FCC Amateur Radio Licenses in Robertsdale

Call Sign: KA3YTV
David H Everetts
Box 10
Robertsdale PA 16674

Call Sign: KF4BLP
John S Disbrow
Box 31A Coles Valley Rd
Robertsdale PA 16674

FCC Amateur Radio Licenses in Rockhill Furnace

Call Sign: N3ZHH
Michael R Welsh
198 Valley St
Rockhill Furnace PA
17249

Call Sign: KB3SML
Terry L Lantz
Rockhill Furnace PA
17249

Call Sign: W3TLL
Terry L Lantz
Rockhill Furnace PA
17249

FCC Amateur Radio Licenses in Rockton

Call Sign: N3PVE
Charles E Robinson
Box 12B
Rockton PA 15856

Call Sign: N3GJZ
Ronald N Reed
Box 24
Rockton PA 15856

Call Sign: KA3YHW
Boyce A Hollopeter
Box 33
Rockton PA 15856

Call Sign: KA3YCB
Kevin D Snyder
118 Huey Ln
Rockton PA 158562322

Call Sign: N3WWT
Michael G Smith

2386 S Continental Dr
Rockton PA 15856

Call Sign: N3WWU
Angel D Smith
2386 S Continental Dr
Rockton PA 15856

FCC Amateur Radio Licenses in Rockwood

Call Sign: N3SYI
Krystal G Trice
Box 157A
Rockwood PA 15557

Call Sign: K3BGI
George B Kimmel
510 Broadway St
Rockwood PA 15557

Call Sign: KB3IHP
Michael D Pressley
221 Galico Rd
Rockwood PA 15557

Call Sign: NG3S
Jacob L Leonard
2271 Newcenterville Rd
Rockwood PA 15557

Call Sign: KC3HB
Kenneth V De Vore
807 Somerset Ave
Rockwood PA 15557

Call Sign: K3JQO
William L Casteel
1360 Trent Rd
Rockwood PA 15557

Call Sign: N3BLY
Luthera P Casteel
1360 Trent Rd
Rockwood PA 15557

Call Sign: WA3P
Lester D Trice
3921 Waterlevel Rd
Rockwood PA 15557

Call Sign: N3YVB
John G Thompson
612 White Oak St
Rockwood PA 15557

Call Sign: K3RCI
Theodore J Leonberger
Rockwood PA 15557

FCC Amateur Radio Licenses in Ronks

Call Sign: W2HQX
James H Hall
15 Peach Ln
Ronks PA 17572

Call Sign: N3PIM
Antoni M Wortel
39 Peach Ln
Ronks PA 17572

Call Sign: N3ELV
Keith R Miller
2554 Siegrist Rd
Ronks PA 17572

FCC Amateur Radio Licenses in Roulette Township

Call Sign: KB3RGC
Milton F Swift
20 White Chopin Rd
Roulette Township PA
16746

FCC Amateur Radio Licenses in Roxbury

Call Sign: N3PQN
Luke D Holtry
Roxbury PA 17251

FCC Amateur Radio Licenses in Sabinsville

Call Sign: N3NWG
Robert S Lloyd
Box 447
Sabinsville PA 16943

Call Sign: KB3AEM
E Linda Berkowitz
Box 793
Sabinsville PA 16943

Call Sign: N3AKA
John S Dettleff
395 Butler Rd
Sabinsville PA 16943

Call Sign: WB3IFZ
Ruth A Dettleff
395 Butler Rd
Sabinsville PA 16943

Call Sign: K3LIZ
Martin J Dwyer
1220 Meeker Rd
Sabinsville PA 16943

Call Sign: KB3TUU
Daryl W Mccullough
2502 Rt 349
Sabinsville PA 16943

Call Sign: KB3RGA
Therese Aigner
379 Summit Ridge
Sabinsville PA 16943

FCC Amateur Radio Licenses in Saint Marys

Call Sign: KB3CUZ
Donald J Hoehn
801 Birch Rd
Saint Marys PA 15857

Call Sign: N3LQA
Robert R Schauer Jr
1562 Bucktail Rd
Saint Marys PA 15857

Call Sign: N3OCD
Sandra A Metzler
1562 Bucktail Rd
Saint Marys PA 15857

Call Sign: NM3B
Wayne G Ginther
1765 Bucktail Rd
Saint Marys PA 15857

Call Sign: KD3LM
Franklin A Metzler
1562 Bucktail Tr
Saint Marys PA 15857

Call Sign: KB3CWJ
Kristin J Lynch
617 Center St
Saint Marys PA 15857

Call Sign: KB3VTY
Mark S Wagner
428 Chestnut St
Saint Marys PA 15857

Call Sign: WA8RZR
Jan A Blair
262 Church St
Saint Marys PA
158571010

Call Sign: KB3UGC
Shawn L Lecker
215 Columbus St

Saint Marys PA 15857

Call Sign: N3UYX
Glenn P Metzler
303 El Co Glen 759
Johnsonburg Rd
Saint Marys PA 15857

Call Sign: N3RJH
Richard J Wehler
920 Fern Rd
Saint Marys PA 15857

Call Sign: KB3MGX
Christopher J Earle
1288 Glen Hazel Rd
Saint Marys PA 15857

Call Sign: KB3CIM
William J Lynch
175 Grace Rd
Saint Marys PA 15857

Call Sign: KE3JE
Helen R Schneider
204 Grandview Rd
Saint Marys PA 15857

Call Sign: WS3T
Mark L Schneider
204 Grandview Rd
Saint Marys PA 15857

Call Sign: KB3UGB
Renee C Buerk
357 Grant St
Saint Marys PA 15857

Call Sign: KB3JCO
Bradley G Miller
126 Jackson Rd
Saint Marys PA 15857

Call Sign: KB3JED
Richard A Miller

126 Jackson Rd
Saint Marys PA
158573230

Call Sign: N3UDL
Mark P Cunningham
123 Jersey Rd
Saint Marys PA 15857

Call Sign: N3UGE
Gerianne M Cunningham
123 Jersey Rd
Saint Marys PA 15857

Call Sign: KB0UXI
Jacob G Farabaugh
562 John Rd
Saint Marys PA 15857

Call Sign: W4ESS
Virgil P Quirk
828 Johnsonburg Rd
Saint Marys PA 15857

Call Sign: N3UDJ
Virgil P Quirk
828 Johnsonburg Rd
Saint Marys PA 15957

Call Sign: N3YVA
Terence E Pontzer
134 Locust Rd
Saint Marys PA 15857

Call Sign: KB3IYT
Jeffrey N Reeser
128 Lynch Rd
Saint Marys PA 15857

Call Sign: KB3JEE
Steven R Fingado
41 Mark St
Saint Marys PA 15857

Call Sign: N3WRJ

Alexander J Quirk
247 N Michael St
Saint Marys PA 15857

Call Sign: KB3MYS
Mark A Rhines Jr
439 N Michael St
Saint Marys PA 15857

Call Sign: N3RHE
Allison J Esenwine
152 Rambler Rd
Saint Marys PA 15857

Call Sign: NO3D
Maurice G Herbstritt
345 S St Marys St
Saint Marys PA 15857

Call Sign: KB3LUR
Stephen A Delaquila
149 Teaberry Rd
Saint Marys PA 15857

Call Sign: KB3TCL
Mark T Greenthaner
640 Theresia St
Saint Marys PA 15857

Call Sign: ND3R
Paul W Ginther
713 Vine Rd
Saint Marys PA 15857

Call Sign: W3GJ
John H Guthrie
606 Virginia Rd Rd 1
Saint Marys PA 15857

Call Sign: N3PQF
William R Stock
501 Washington St
Saint Marys PA 15857

Call Sign: W3KXP

Paul P Lesser
461 Wolfel Ave
Saint Marys PA 15857

Call Sign: W8KTH
Keith R Schreiber
473 Wolfel Ave
Saint Marys PA 15857

Call Sign: N3LVG
Scott A Logue
Saint Marys PA 15857

FCC Amateur Radio Licenses in Saint Michael

Call Sign: KA3HJQ
Joseph F Delso Jr
125 Fox Dr
Saint Michael PA 15951

Call Sign: KA3RLL
James C Patterson
705 Franklin St
Saint Michael PA
159510047

Call Sign: KB3NME
Brian D Schmidt
937 Locust St Box 104
Saint Michael PA 15951

Call Sign: KA3LFT
Roscoe F Glacken
136 Water St
Saint Michael PA 15951

FCC Amateur Radio Licenses in Saint Thomas

Call Sign: KB3ECV
Devon R Geyer
1345 Apple Way
Saint Thomas PA 17252

Call Sign: N3QBI
Darrell E Lingenfield III
1688 Apple Way Rd
Saint Thomas PA
172529766

Call Sign: N3NRI
Gregory L Harbaugh Sr
5622 Frankin Ave
Saint Thomas PA 17252

Call Sign: N3POP
Rebecca J Harbaugh
5622 Franklin Ave
Saint Thomas PA 17252

Call Sign: KB3MUN
D. Daniel Mcglothin
6315 Gehr Rd
Saint Thomas PA 17252

Call Sign: N8PGS
Beth J Dixon
3201 Keller Rd
Saint Thomas PA 17252

Call Sign: N3CXC
Gary L Leab
2402 McDowell Rd
Saint Thomas PA 17252

Call Sign: N3XGG
Keith E Rosenberry
2226 Pioneer Dr
Saint Thomas PA 17252

Call Sign: KB3QAA
Griffith A Glover
1675 Shields Rd
Saint Thomas PA 17252

Call Sign: W3ESV
Griffith A Glover
1675 Shields Rd
Saint Thomas PA 17252

Call Sign: N3TLI
George R Naugle
32 St Thomas Edenville
Rd
Saint Thomas PA 17252

Call Sign: KG4DAZ
Charles Bihun
1242 Summerswood Dr
Saint Thomas PA 17252

FCC Amateur Radio Licenses in Salisbury

Call Sign: KB3BDJ
Shawn D Wingard
Box 33A
Salisbury PA 15558

Call Sign: KA8EIV
Craig D Robinette
108 Grant St
Salisbury PA 155580285

FCC Amateur Radio Licenses in Salix

Call Sign: KB3LBT
Stanley H Avramis Jr
762 Forest Hills Dr
Salix PA 15952

Call Sign: KB3JOY
John Sivec III
157 Maple Ct
Salix PA 159529419

Call Sign: W3POE
Walter M Allen
102 Taylor Ln
Salix PA 15952

FCC Amateur Radio Licenses in Salladasburg

Call Sign: AA3NA
John F Clark
Main St Box 436
Salladasburg PA
177400436

Call Sign: N3UHV
Clyde R Confair
84 Water St
Salladasburg PA 17740

FCC Amateur Radio Licenses in Salona

Call Sign: KB3TYU
Christopher Myers
22 McClintick Rd
Salona PA 17767

FCC Amateur Radio Licenses in Salunga

Call Sign: KB3PBV
Edward J Mccauley Sr
71 Autumn St
Salunga PA 17538

Call Sign: WB3LAN
John K Bender
85 Autumn St
Salunga PA 17538

Call Sign: N3ROC
James R Adams
158 Broad St
Salunga PA 17538

FCC Amateur Radio Licenses in Sandy Ridge

Call Sign: WB3AAI
Louis D Trubiani Jr
608 Oak St
Sandy Ridge PA 16677

FCC Amateur Radio Licenses in Saxton

Call Sign: KB3CQY
Marlin L Walters
Box 183X
Saxton PA 16678

Call Sign: N3SSC
Michele A Weimert
Box 47
Saxton PA 16678

Call Sign: N3SYJ
Fred E Weimert Jr
Box 47
Saxton PA 16678

Call Sign: W3HRC
Allen C Detwiler
704 Church St
Saxton PA 166781212

Call Sign: N3SPF
David B Crawshaw
106 Commerce Dr
Saxton PA 16678

Call Sign: KB3GHW
Michael B Simpson
613 Mifflin St
Saxton PA 16678

FCC Amateur Radio Licenses in Aaronsburg

Call Sign: N3HCP
Gary R Wells
336 S Market St
Schaefferstown PA 17088

Call Sign: K3QGT
George F Mentzer
8 Sportsman Ln

Schaefferstown PA
170880043

Call Sign: K3HFP
William C Zehring
Schaefferstown PA 17088

FCC Amateur Radio Licenses in Schellsburg

Call Sign: N3WQT
Steven M Beegle
Box 184E
Schellsburg PA 15559

Call Sign: KB3VMG
David A Boozer
749 Mill Rd
Schellsburg PA 15559

Call Sign: N3IHD
David A Boozer
749 Mill Rd
Schellsburg PA 15559

Call Sign: KB3KYC
Neil E Snyder
752 Mtn View Dr
Schellsburg PA 15559

Call Sign: KB3NZT
William F B Latz
133 Ringo Rd
Schellsburg PA 15559

Call Sign: KA3PXS
Albert Hayes
Schellsburg PA 15559

FCC Amateur Radio Licenses in Scotland

Call Sign: KB3WOX
Anthony L Ogburn
Scotland PA 17254

Call Sign: KB3ISL
Peter A Guldin
Scotland PA 17254

Call Sign: KB3LKC
Snyder County ARES
Box 130 K
Selinsgrove PA 17870

Call Sign: KB3LLN
Snyder County ARES
Box 130 K
Selinsgrove PA 17870

Call Sign: KB3LLO
Snyder County ARES
Box 130 K
Selinsgrove PA 17870

Call Sign: KA3TJA
Terry R Gugger
Box 157C
Selinsgrove PA 17870

Call Sign: N3IJL
William C Foust
Box 208 6
Selinsgrove PA 17870

Call Sign: KB3MST
Jeffrey W Brabant
Box 266 C
Selinsgrove PA 17870

Call Sign: WB3GDG
Charles H Bender
Box 83
Selinsgrove PA 17870

Call Sign: KA3QCG
Christian L Hehn

802 Broad St Apt 13C
Selinsgrove PA 17870

Call Sign: N3LUH
Mark A Johnson
110 Carousel Dr
Selinsgrove PA 117877084

Call Sign: WB3DXG
Paul E Swartz
10 Countryside Village
Old Trl
Selinsgrove PA 178708902

Call Sign: WB3IEM
Robert B Fetter
200 E Pine St
Selinsgrove PA 17870

Call Sign: KB3AJW
Rhysann J Conrad
Line Rd I
Selinsgrove PA 17870

Call Sign: KD3CT
Charles R Schofield
28 Macintosh Rd
Selinsgrove PA 17870

Call Sign: NR3U
Clement J Rohrer Jr
6 Melody Ln
Selinsgrove PA 17870

Call Sign: KB3WGF
Justin P Blocker
300 N High St
Selinsgrove PA 17870

Call Sign: N3SEX
Roy C Cox II
100 N Market S Apt 2R
Selinsgrove PA 17870

Call Sign: KB3MSQ

Kirsta M Reisinger
2 N Stonebridge Dr
Selinsgrove PA 17870

Call Sign: N3YHH
Bryan W Harker
2092 N Susquehanna Trl
Apt 1
Selinsgrove PA 17870

Call Sign: KB3FXG
Barbara E Yessel
601 Orange St
Selinsgrove PA 17870

Call Sign: AB3CE
C Allen Yessel
601 Orange St
Selinsgrove PA 17870

Call Sign: N3XKI
George W Inch Jr
2 Park Ave
Selinsgrove PA 17870

Call Sign: N3YYD
Shawn M Cooper
2700 Park Rd
Selinsgrove PA 17870

Call Sign: KB3AJX
Keith Conrad
Rd 2
Selinsgrove PA 17870

Call Sign: N3QWD
Raymond T Stanton
880 Rt 522
Selinsgrove PA 17870

Call Sign: KB3MSP
Susan M Reisinger
620 Stonebridge Dr
Selinsgrove PA 17870

Call Sign: KB3MSO
Gene W Reisinger
602 Stonebridge St
Selinsgrove PA 17870

Call Sign: N3PNI
Gary E Klase
214 Sunset Dr
Selinsgrove PA 17870

Call Sign: K3SNY
Snyder County Auxiliary
Communications Service
30 Universal Rd
Selinsgrove PA 17870

Call Sign: W3SNY
Snyder County Auxiliary
Communications Service
30 Universal Rd
Selinsgrove PA 17870

Call Sign: WS3SNY
Snyder County Auxiliary
Communications Service
30 Universal Rd
Selinsgrove PA 17870

Call Sign: KB3KUL
Bethann L Mull
105 W Elm St
Selinsgrove PA 17870

Call Sign: W3MGL
Lawrence E Boellhoff
12 W Mill St
Selinsgrove PA 17870

Call Sign: WA3MHE
G Daniel Heiser
204 Water St Apt B2
Selinsgrove PA 17870

Call Sign: AA2IP
William D Dilks

44 Wood Lynn Dr
Selinsgrove PA 17870

Call Sign: KF2HN
Jeril L Dilks
44 Woodlynn Dr
Selinsgrove PA 17870

FCC Amateur Radio Licenses in Seven Valleys

Call Sign: KB3PSV
Gail A Bollinger
1395 Bollinger Ln
Seven Valleys PA 17360

Call Sign: KB3MSC
Gregory L Bollinger
1395 Bollinger Ln
Seven Valleys PA 17360

Call Sign: KA3VEU
Carl R Johnson
Box 582A
Seven Valleys PA 17360

Call Sign: N3WQR
Scott M Wohler
Box 6605
Seven Valleys PA
173609690

Call Sign: KA3EZE
Thomas N Saxmann
1019 Brighton Cir
Seven Valleys PA
173609333

Call Sign: KA3RNU
Bruce R Norton
1328 Brighton Cir
Seven Valleys PA 17360

Call Sign: N3UON
Barry A Price

975 Brighton Dr
Seven Valleys PA
173609326

Call Sign: N3ZOV
Ann E Price
975 Brighton Dr
Seven Valleys PA
173609326

Call Sign: N3UUI
Kevin L May Sr
202 Claremont Dr
Seven Valleys PA 17360

Call Sign: K3JAW
Philip Hoeflich
300 Claremont Dr
Seven Valleys PA 17360

Call Sign: WB3KVR
Ronald W Berwager
9292 E Springfield Rd
Seven Valleys PA 17360

Call Sign: N3BHL
Alexander R Krause
7759 Grand Lake Dr
Seven Valleys PA 17360

Call Sign: KB3GMX
Beverly A Jones
2845 Larue Rd
Seven Valleys PA
173609274

Call Sign: WB5YLQ
Huey A Holden
162 Lindy Rd
Seven Valleys PA
173609223

Call Sign: KB3AKC
Louis A Vecchioni Jr
2851 Myers Rd

Seven Valleys PA 17360

Call Sign: N3EXZ
Richard G Piepoli
442 Oakwood Dr
Seven Valleys PA
173609397

Call Sign: KA3FYR
Paul E Pitzer
57 Park St
Seven Valleys PA 17360

Call Sign: NX3E
Theodore Kopey Jr
69 Park St
Seven Valleys PA 17360

Call Sign: WA2ORG
William P Molnar
1395 Springfield Ln
Seven Valleys PA 17360

Call Sign: KB3JAT
Seven Valleys Amateur
Group
510 White Ln
Seven Valleys PA 17360

Call Sign: N3VYV
Anthony R Piccione
510 White Ln
Seven Valleys PA 17360

**FCC Amateur Radio
Licenses in Shade Gap**

Call Sign: KA3JXW
Judith I Rockwood
22084 Deer Run Ln
Shade Gap PA 17255

Call Sign: KJ3H
Frederick D Rockwood
22084 Deer Run Ln

Shade Gap PA 17255

Call Sign: KA3RGM
Joseph D Eaton
Shade Gap PA 17255

**FCC Amateur Radio
Licenses in Shamokin**

Call Sign: N3ECY
Richard J Staugaitis
415 Balsam St
Shamokin PA 17872

Call Sign: K3QHL
Frank B Chaundy
Box 369
Shamokin PA 17872

Call Sign: K3MLD
Jon D Sten
Box 432
Shamokin PA 17872

Call Sign: KW3MD
Jon D Sten
Box 432
Shamokin PA 17872

Call Sign: W3GDK
Donald E Trego
Box 434
Shamokin PA 17872

Call Sign: K3LIB
Daniel Kolody
Box 477
Shamokin PA 17872

Call Sign: N3QFO
Stephen G Bielskie Jr
Box 49
Shamokin PA 17872

Call Sign: KA3PZA

Joseph M Miller Jr
Box 526
Shamokin PA 17872

Call Sign: K3RED
Robert E Donahue
Box 642
Shamokin PA 17872

Call Sign: K3KOQ
Joseph E Bohr
905 Center St
Shamokin PA 17872

Call Sign: W3WCB
William C Barrett
1132 Chemung St
Shamokin PA 17872

Call Sign: KA3VDB
Charles H Anoia
1008 E Dewart St
Shamokin PA 17872

Call Sign: N3QJQ
Nadine Markovich
309 E Sunbury St
Shamokin PA 17872

Call Sign: WB3JZK
Joseph W Latovich
1504 Mohawk St
Shamokin PA 17866

Call Sign: N3DUK
Carl E Fetterhoff
37 N 7th St
Shamokin PA 17872

Call Sign: KA3GVJ
Warren B Kline Jr
135 N 8th
Shamokin PA 17872

Call Sign: KG4GOV

Roy W Black
6 N Coal St
Shamokin PA 17872

Call Sign: N3KFW
Pamela A Dobak
1006 N Orange St
Shamokin PA 17872

Call Sign: WB3AMG
Stephen H Dobak
1006 N Orange St
Shamokin PA 17872

Call Sign: K3DFU
Gary L McCarney
1010 N Pearl St
Shamokin PA 17872

Call Sign: W3JSC
Walter A Holt
612 N Shamokin St
Shamokin PA 17872

Call Sign: N3RGA
Robert A Knowles Sr
126 N Vine St
Shamokin PA 17872

Call Sign: W3MJB
Michael J Barrett
1207 Pulaski Ave
Shamokin PA 17872

Call Sign: K3REB
Rich E Barrett Jr
1420 Pulaski Ave
Shamokin PA 17872

Call Sign: W3REB
Richard E Barrett Sr
1420 Pulaski Ave
Shamokin PA 17872

Call Sign: KC3JE

Ernest J Sabotchick
1922 Rt 61 St Hwy
Shamokin PA 17872

Call Sign: W3MOZ
Glen A Filer
110 S 2nd St
Shamokin PA 17872

Call Sign: N3BUF
Dolores R Kosmer
517 S Bay St
Shamokin PA 17872

Call Sign: KB3TDE
Glen Filer Memorial ARC
300 S Coal St
Shamokin PA 17872

Call Sign: W3MOZ
Glen Filer Memorial ARC
300 S Coal St
Shamokin PA 17872

Call Sign: WA3SYR
William F Grow
300 S Coal St
Shamokin PA 178726343

Call Sign: WB3LQS
Richard M Shipe
637 S Diamond St
Shamokin PA 17872

Call Sign: N3ZYD
Gerald Simpson
319 S Market St
Shamokin PA 17872

Call Sign: N3SFO
Gregory J Berholtz
205 S Market St
Shamokin PA 17872

Call Sign: KB3SZR

Richard S Fowler
308 W Mulberry St
Shamokin PA 17872

Call Sign: W3FSY
Ronald B Kerstetter
243 W Pine St
Shamokin PA 17872

Call Sign: N3PNE
Patricia Huntington
Shamokin PA 17872

FCC Amateur Radio Licenses in Shanksville

Call Sign: N3GTO
Dennis W Steckman
Shanksville PA 15560

FCC Amateur Radio Licenses in Shermans Dale

Call Sign: KA3LJT
Harry W Overholtzer II
515 Bentzel Rd
Shermans Dale PA 17090

Call Sign: N3GQR
Carol L Hepford
1055 Bower Rd
Shermans Dale PA 17090

Call Sign: N3RPM
Mark E Feltman
Box 152
Shermans Dale PA 17090

Call Sign: KA3UYX
Earle H Moore
Box 196 Airy View Rd
Shermans Dale PA 17090

Call Sign: KB3KMS

Timothy B Misicko
6 Bretz Cir
Shermans Dale PA 17090

Call Sign: N2RKW
Bruce L Walker
670 Losh Rd
Shermans Dale PA 17090

Call Sign: N3YBK
Donald S Taylor
437 Meadow Ln
Shermans Dale PA 17090

Call Sign: KB3YDI
Scott E Mcclintock
4802 Spring Rd
Shermans Dale PA 17090

Call Sign: N3YYB
Charles E Thiemann
5307 Spring Rd
Shermans Dale PA 17090

Call Sign: WA3OWC
William H Richey Jr
7244 Spring Rd
Shermans Dale PA 17090

Call Sign: KB3HAJ
Jerry L Lesher
501 Windy Hill Rd Lot 29
Shermans Dale PA 17090

Call Sign: N3RPK
Ralph J Webster Jr
Shermans Dale PA 17090

**FCC Amateur Radio
Licenses in Shinglehouse**

Call Sign: KB3YJP
Carl S Sottolano
1989 11 Mile Rd

Shinglehouse PA
167488423

Call Sign: N3DLS
Donald L Serkleski
2165 11 Mile Rd
Shinglehouse PA
167488425

Call Sign: KB3GQO
Paul A Rathbun
2270 11 Mile Rd
Shinglehouse PA 16748

Call Sign: KB3IPU
Donald L Serkleski
Box 160
Shinglehouse PA
167489611

Call Sign: N3MHV
Eric D Swartwout
Box 40
Shinglehouse PA 16748

Call Sign: KB3GQN
Gerald H Weber
144 Pinneo Hill Rd
Shinglehouse PA 16748

Call Sign: KA3DFA
Steven R Bell
216 S Lincoln St
Shinglehouse PA 16748

Call Sign: W3JRR
Joseph M Zias
118 S Oswayo St
Shinglehouse PA 16748

Call Sign: N3SFK
James E Schultz
SR Box 34
Shinglehouse PA 16748

Call Sign: KB3AUW
Marilyn F Shrift
Tr 348
Shinglehouse PA 16748

Call Sign: KB3AUX
James J Yust
Tr 348
Shinglehouse PA 16748

Call Sign: KB3PUJ
Mitchell H Ruback
308 W Academy St Box
614
Shinglehouse PA 16748

Call Sign: KB3MHR
Mitchell H Ruback
308 W Academy St Box
614
Shinglehouse PA 16748

Call Sign: N3HYX
Ann E Bell
122 W Honeoye St
Shinglehouse PA 16748

Call Sign: NG3W
Chris A Bell
122 W Honeoye St
Shinglehouse PA 16748

Call Sign: KB3HAI
Brian M Bell
Shinglehouse PA 16748

Call Sign: KB3RYB
Danielle R Bell
Shinglehouse PA 16748

Call Sign: KB3IPV
David J Bell
Shinglehouse PA 16748

Call Sign: KB3MMX
Charles S Pyatt
1236 Ashton Dr
Shippensburg PA 17257

Call Sign: KA3POL
Philip D Sollenberger
10674 Blind Ln
Shippensburg PA 17257

Call Sign: AB2HO
Donald G McCall Jr
721 Brenton St
Shippensburg PA 17257

Call Sign: KB3GCX
Eric S Clippinger
425 Clifton Rd
Shippensburg PA 17257

Call Sign: N3OKU
Robert E Fleming
137 Cottage Rd
Shippensburg PA 17257

Call Sign: WA3HYC
Wilbur C Chamberlin
75 Deadend Ln
Shippensburg PA 17257

Call Sign: W3QDJ
William R Stark
201 E Burd St Apt H109
Shippensburg PA
172571444

Call Sign: KA3FJI
Beatrice L Kelley
9554 Forest Ridge Rd
Shippensburg PA 17257

Call Sign: KC3EG

William R Kelley
9554 Forest Ridge Rd
Shippensburg PA 17257

Call Sign: KB3ISQ
Theodore R Ackerman
9567 Forest Ridge Rd
Shippensburg PA 17257

Call Sign: KB3TTI
Joshua C Shaul
45 Hale Rd
Shippensburg PA 17257

Call Sign: KB3IZJ
Douglas E Warner
93 Horse Killer Rd
Shippensburg PA 17257

Call Sign: W3DEW
Douglas E Warner
93 Horse Killer Rd
Shippensburg PA 17257

Call Sign: N3TMU
Charles P Scott IV
221 Lurgan Ave
Shippensburg PA 17257

Call Sign: W3IFR
Jack Mayo
891 Means Hollow Rd
Shippensburg PA 17257

Call Sign: W3JKZ
Charles L Coover
9690 Molly Pitcher Hwy
Shippensburg PA 17257

Call Sign: W3ESV
Ray F Coover
9718 Molly Pitcher Hwy
Shippensburg PA 17257

Call Sign: N3LNX

Rodney D Simon I
303 N Prince St
Shippensburg PA 17257

Call Sign: N3TWU
Raymond L Smith Jr
27 N Queen St
Shippensburg PA 17257

Call Sign: KB3SWW
Bradly A Jones
219 Neil Rd
Shippensburg PA 17257

Call Sign: N3PAH
Ginger S Burkholder
1517 Orrstown Rd
Shippensburg PA 17257

Call Sign: KB3SSN
Veronica M Latham
1602 Pinola Rd
Shippensburg PA 17257

Call Sign: KB3SSM
Victoria C Latham
1602 Pinola Rd
Shippensburg PA 17257

Call Sign: W3SML
Shannon M Latham
1602 Pinola Rd
Shippensburg PA 17257

Call Sign: KB3FWC
Rachel M Latham
1602 Pinola Rd
Shippensburg PA 17257

Call Sign: KB3RNP
Rachel M Latham
1602 Pinola Rd
Shippensburg PA 17257

Call Sign: KB3EBA

Michael P Harlow
9120 Possum Hollow Rd
Shippensburg PA 17257

Call Sign: K3XH
Michael P Harlow
9120 Possum Hollow Rd
Shippensburg PA 17257

Call Sign: W3BD
Keystone Radio Amateurs
Of Pa
146 Pugh Dr
Shippensburg PA 17257

Call Sign: KC2BCG
George D Harris
146 Pugh Dr
Shippensburg PA 17257

Call Sign: N3GH
George D Harris
146 Pugh Dr
Shippensburg PA 17257

Call Sign: KB3UEU
Albert J Potter Jr
165 Pugh Dr
Shippensburg PA 17257

Call Sign: AB3LJ
Albert J Potter Jr
165 Pugh Dr
Shippensburg PA 17257

Call Sign: K5FQ
Albert J Potter Jr
165 Pugh Dr
Shippensburg PA 17257

Call Sign: KC2CKJ
Kathleen L Harris
146 Pugh Dr
Shippensburg PA 17257

Call Sign: KB3MWX
Jamie L Pattison
2048 Rither Hwy
Shippensburg PA 17257

Call Sign: N3UPG
Sandra A Browne
88 S M E
Shippensburg PA 17257

Call Sign: KB3VJV
Clarence G Toigo
750 S Mt Estates Rd
Shippensburg PA 17257

Call Sign: KB3UHV
Nicholas W Caler
111 S Prince St
Shippensburg PA 17257

Call Sign: KA3USK
David J Lindenmuth
22 S Washington St
Shippensburg PA 17257

Call Sign: KC8MCX
Noel A Tenney III
46 Sme
Shippensburg PA 17257

Call Sign: N3ZXE
John W Phelan
275 Smith Rd
Shippensburg PA
172579626

Call Sign: KB3VVE
Emily J Saldana
11408 Spring Ridge Rd
Shippensburg PA 17257

Call Sign: N3POW
Robert L Adams
2102 Stillhouse Hollow Rd
Shippensburg PA 17257

Call Sign: KB3EQO
Rene Kedrowitsch
11336 Thornwood Rd
Shippensburg PA 17257

Call Sign: W3RKX
Rene Kedrowitsch
11336 Thornwood Rd
Shippensburg PA 17257

Call Sign: N3POU
David B Femlee
619 W King St
Shippensburg PA 17257

Call Sign: KA3LUT
William B Smyser
404 Walnut Bottom Rd
Shippensburg PA 17257

Call Sign: KB3BNY
South Mountain Repeater
Assn
404 Walnut Bottom Rd
Shippensburg PA 17257

Call Sign: N3ZJO
Curtis J Smyser
404 Walnut Bottom Rd
Shippensburg PA 17257

Call Sign: KB3GSJ
Dorothy J Smyser
404 Walnut Bottom Rd
Shippensburg PA 17257

Call Sign: KB3GSK
Cristina L Smyser
404 Walnut Bottom Rd
Shippensburg PA 17257

Call Sign: N3DOT
Dorothy J Smyser
404 Walnut Bottom Rd

Shippensburg PA 17257

Call Sign: K3RAE
Cristina L Smyser
404 Walnut Bottom Rd
Shippensburg PA 17257

Call Sign: KB3KGR
Nancy A Smyser
404 Walnut Bottom Rd
Shippensburg PA 17257

Call Sign: AA3LG
Steven R Burkholder
409 Westover Rd
Shippensburg PA 17257

Call Sign: W9GZV
Merton N Baird
410 Westover Rd
Shippensburg PA
172571012

Call Sign: KB3TFF
Lucas W Kalathas
1454 Woods Rd
Shippensburg PA 17257

Call Sign: K3SMP
The South Mountain
Project
Shippensburg PA 17257

Call Sign: WA1HHN
Walter J Nero
Shippensburg PA 17257

Call Sign: K3EAR
South Mountain Contest
Club
Shippensburg PA
172570368

FCC Amateur Radio Licenses in Shiremanstown

Call Sign: KB3MXE
Kristin M Steele
304 Pinewood Dr
Shiremanstown PA 17011

Call Sign: N3HCZ
Jeffrey W Kisner
202 W Green St
Shiremanstown PA 17011

Call Sign: W3JWK
Jeffrey W Kisner
202 W Green St
Shiremanstown PA 17011

Call Sign: KB3LPV
Tyler P Beaty
205 W Main St
Shiremanstown PA 17011

Call Sign: K3TZV
Steven M Cutshall
314 W Main St
Shiremanstown PA
170116332

FCC Amateur Radio Licenses in Shirleysburg

Call Sign: KA3OOJ
Crist C Flasher
Box 95A
Shirleysburg PA 17260

Call Sign: WA3HSM
Robert W Mock
Rd 1
Shirleysburg PA 17260

Call Sign: N3YSO
Wilbur D Hardy

Shirleysburg PA 17260

FCC Amateur Radio Licenses in Shrewsbury

Call Sign: WA3ODU
Lester W Shaffer
705 Bollinger Dr
Shrewsbury PA 17361

Call Sign: KB3BBN
Kimberly A Bobbitt
21 Brandywine Dr
Shrewsbury PA 17361

Call Sign: KB2HUL
Michael W Goddard
110 Brook Meadow Cir
Shrewsbury PA 17361

Call Sign: KA3MJY
Glenn L Stevens
38 Charles St
Shrewsbury PA
173611506

Call Sign: KA3PHG
Bonnie S Stevens
38 Charles St
Shrewsbury PA
173611506

Call Sign: K2YJP
Lloyd H Yost
25 Crosswind Dr
Shrewsbury PA 17361

Call Sign: K3BDF
Robert D Freeman
116 E Clearview Dr
Shrewsbury PA
173611206

Call Sign: N3SIC
Mahlon L Fritz

16 E Wood
Shrewsbury PA 17361

Call Sign: KB3JSJ
Jennifer L Geary
10 Eastwood Dr
Shrewsbury PA 17361

Call Sign: KB3OQL
Charlotte B Walters
26 Essex Cir Dr
Shrewsbury PA 17361

Call Sign: K2BOK
Charlotte B Walters
26 Essex Cir Dr
Shrewsbury PA 17361

Call Sign: KB3THA
Patrick S Walters
26 Essex Cir Dr
Shrewsbury PA 17361

Call Sign: KB3TOE
York County React 6123
26 Essex Cir Dr
Shrewsbury PA 17361

Call Sign: W3YCR
York County React 6123
26 Essex Cir Dr
Shrewsbury PA 17361

Call Sign: KB3NXM
Stanton L Walters
26 Essex Cir Dr
Shrewsbury PA 17361

Call Sign: AB3EM
Stanton L Walters
26 Essex Cir Dr
Shrewsbury PA 17361

Call Sign: KB3VBJ
Donald B Siperko

16581 Kennedy Cir
Shrewsbury PA 17361

Call Sign: K3AQK
Marion E Bollinger
Luther Rd
Shrewsbury PA
173611726

Call Sign: KD3SM
George P Larson
131 N Highland Dr
Shrewsbury PA
173611404

Call Sign: K3WLK
John J La Martina Sr
18 Plank Rd
Shrewsbury PA 17361

Call Sign: K3NXU
John J La Martina
18 Plank Rd
Shrewsbury PA 17361

Call Sign: WB3EBD
Eleanore L La Martina
18 Plank Rd
Shrewsbury PA 17361

Call Sign: WB3ATE
James M Carman
136 S Main
Shrewsbury PA 17361

Call Sign: N3SPD
Tyler J Harpster
505 S Main St
Shrewsbury PA 17361

Call Sign: KB3JKK
Loralie S Harpster
505 S Main St
Shrewsbury PA 17361

Call Sign: KM3G
Tyler J Harpster
505 S Main St
Shrewsbury PA 17361

Call Sign: K3TUX
Robert J Levine
657 S Main St
Shrewsbury PA 17361

Call Sign: KC6GMN
Carol G Kirschman
1 Shetland Dr
Shrewsbury PA 17361

Call Sign: N3ZNT
Aaron S Kirschman
1 Shetland Dr
Shrewsbury PA 17361

Call Sign: N6PHW
Nathan F Kirschman
1 Shetland Dr
Shrewsbury PA 17361

Call Sign: N3EFM
Michael W Ridgely
94 Skyview Dr
Shrewsbury PA 17361

Call Sign: KB3IRD
Donald G Fortner
103 Skyview Dr
Shrewsbury PA 17361

Call Sign: KB3UUB
Doug R Walters
111 Skyview Dr
Shrewsbury PA 17361

Call Sign: N3VCL
Carol A Owens
117 Strassburg Cir
Shrewsbury PA 17361

Call Sign: W6ORZ
Gene R Owens
117 Strassburg Cir
Shrewsbury PA 17361

Call Sign: KB3OBX
Matthew R Wagner
237 W Forrest Ave
Shrewsbury PA 17361

Call Sign: N3ZOX
John A Oswald Jr
103 Westview Dr
Shrewsbury PA
173611420

Call Sign: AB3U
William E Winfree
4 Whitcraft Ln
Shrewsbury PA 17361

Call Sign: KB3JMW
John A Fornadel
9 Whitcraft Ln
Shrewsbury PA 17361

Call Sign: N3PAI
Craig D Nemeth
15 Whitcraft Ln
Shrewsbury PA 17361

Call Sign: K3AE
Southern PA
Communications Group
Shrewsbury PA
173610024

Call Sign: WA3HDW
David C Landis
Shrewsbury PA
173610172

**FCC Amateur Radio
Licenses in Sidman**

Call Sign: KA3DAT
William R Botteicher
180 Beaver Run Ave
Sidman PA 15955

Call Sign: K3RRH
David F Brown
1125 Cameron Ave
Sidman PA 15955

Call Sign: KB3EBD
Collins Radio Assn
760 Forest Hills Dr
Sidman PA 15955

Call Sign: W3CRA
Collins Radio Assn
760 Forest Hills Dr
Sidman PA 159550034

Call Sign: N3WR
William E Rogers
945 Frankstown Rd
Sidman PA 15955

Call Sign: KB3NLZ
Sean R Nagy
106 Penn St
Sidman PA 15955

Call Sign: KA3OAC
Gary E Galbreath
321 Pine Bluff Rd
Sidman PA 15955

Call Sign: KK3U
Gary E Galbreath
321 Pine Bluff Rd
Sidman PA 15955

Call Sign: K3YQU
John T Mondick
364 Pine Bluff Rd
Sidman PA 15955

Call Sign: KB3UIU
Ryan C Nagy
390 Pine Bluff Rd
Sidman PA 15955

Call Sign: K3IBA
Arthur A Vidrich
1131 Railroad Ave
Sidman PA 15955

Call Sign: W3ST
David A Knepper
Sidman PA 15955

**FCC Amateur Radio
Licenses in
Sinnamahoning**

Call Sign: KB3MQW
Jesse M Coffman
47 1st Fork Rd
Sinnamahoning PA 15861

Call Sign: W3BGI
Mae L Metzger
Sinnamahoning PA 15861

Call Sign: W3ZYK
Harry L Metzger
Sinnamahoning PA 15861

**FCC Amateur Radio
Licenses in Sipesville**

Call Sign: KE3VE
Mark J Matthews
Sipesville PA 15561

**FCC Amateur Radio
Licenses in Slate Run**

Call Sign: WA3RSU
Charles R Segraves
Slate Run PA 17769

FCC Amateur Radio Licenses in Smethport

Call Sign: KA3TES
Melanie S Geiser
1278 Baker Rd
Smethport PA 16749

Call Sign: KB3LTN
Steven S Nelson
108 Bank St
Smethport PA 16749

Call Sign: N3XST
John M Miller Jr
Box 184 Wolfrun Rd
Smethport PA 16749

Call Sign: W2FVH
Clement R Alderfer
Box 21
Smethport PA 16749

Call Sign: KA3ZQI
Herman C Bisnett Jr
Box 27
Smethport PA 16749

Call Sign: N3VLG
Lori L Sander
Box 82 A
Smethport PA 16749

Call Sign: KA3WJB
Clarence W Strabel Jr
414 E King St
Smethport PA 16749

Call Sign: WB3DJM
Richard V Burt
210 E Main St
Smethport PA 16749

Call Sign: NJ7T
Roger B Keifer

897 E Main St
Smethport PA 16749

Call Sign: KB3TCS
Jeffrey A Wolfe
534 E Valley Rd
Smethport PA 16749

Call Sign: N3BXK
David C Mallison
3 Rosehill Ave
Smethport PA 16749

Call Sign: KB3NFC
Ward H Fitzsimmons
8223 Rt 46
Smethport PA 16749

Call Sign: KB3LAE
Curtis L Curcio
15911 Rt 6
Smethport PA 16749

Call Sign: KA3UXU
Larry M Cliver
43 Stickles Hollow Rd
Smethport PA 16749

Call Sign: N3QMS
David C Yoder
508 W King St
Smethport PA 16749

Call Sign: N3RIM
Josephine E Yoder
508 W King St
Smethport PA 16749

Call Sign: N3NIA
John M Miller
Wolf Run Rd
Smethport PA 16749

Call Sign: N3XSS
Barbara M Miller

948 Wolfrun Rd
Smethport PA 16749

Call Sign: N3PDB
Waldemar L Sander Jr
24 Woodsmen Dr
Smethport PA 16749

Call Sign: N3IUN
David L Yoder
Smethport PA 16749

Call Sign: KB3ILU
Curtis J Wallace
Smethport PA 16749

FCC Amateur Radio Licenses in Smithmill

Call Sign: N3ZSM
Elizabeth C Nestlerode
Smithmill PA 16680

FCC Amateur Radio Licenses in Snow Shoe

Call Sign: KB3UCL
Carrie A Sotak
111 E Sunset Ave
Snow Shoe PA 16874

Call Sign: KB3NDL
Paul D Saylor
202 Fountain Rd
Snow Shoe PA 16874

Call Sign: KC2BOI
Mark A Herman
102 N 4th St
Snow Shoe PA 168740085

Call Sign: W3NTL
Boyd E Paul
112 W Nectarine
Snow Shoe PA 16874

FCC Amateur Radio Licenses in Snydertown

Call Sign: K3FRY
John P Smink
N Main St
Snydertown PA 17877

Call Sign: KB3JKV
Patrick C Moyer
Snydertown PA 17877

FCC Amateur Radio Licenses in Somerset

Call Sign: WB3FBC
Arthur L Brown
173 Amber Ln
Somerset PA 155019374

Call Sign: KB3MTI
Hilltop Repeater Club
135 Baxter Dr
Somerset PA 15501

Call Sign: N3LZX
Hilltop Repeater Club
135 Baxter Dr
Somerset PA 15501

Call Sign: NJ3T
Jim R Crowley
135 Baxter Dr
Somerset PA 155013506

Call Sign: NJ3L
Dudley G Daniels
560 Blossom View Hts
Somerset PA 15501

Call Sign: W3WGX
Kenneth K Custer
120 Bopie Ln
Somerset PA 15501

Call Sign: KA1GZ
Joachim G Sacksen
Box 122
Somerset PA 15501

Call Sign: N3DUT
Eleanor G Morris
Box 231
Somerset PA 15501

Call Sign: KB3OUX
Robert K Hersch
97 Chaunceys Woods Rd
Somerset PA 15501

Call Sign: KB3MBK
Donald R Johnson
102 Chaunceys Woods Rd
Somerset PA 15501

Call Sign: KC3SF
David H Bowers
226 Cherry Ln
Somerset PA 15501

Call Sign: N3EDS
Jeffrey L Pritts
379 Chippewa Rd
Somerset PA 15501

Call Sign: N3YNW
Carol O Pritts
379 Chippewa Rd
Somerset PA 15501

Call Sign: KB3JYP
Ray H Miller
1485 Coxes Creek Rd
Somerset PA 15501

Call Sign: KB3DEF
Rebecca A Wilmotte
1602 Crestview Dr
Somerset PA 15501

Call Sign: WA3BKF
Dean D Mickey
525 Davis Ave
Somerset PA 155011717

Call Sign: W3BKF
Dean D Mickey
525 Davis Ave
Somerset PA 155011717

Call Sign: NG3N
Robert M Wiltrout
144 Drum Ave
Somerset PA 155012418

Call Sign: KB3SSH
Thomas P Kennedy Jr
1448 Gardner Rd
Somerset PA 15501

Call Sign: KB3CNI
Stefan M Difrancesco
6193 Glades Pike
Somerset PA 15501

Call Sign: KB3CWX
Brad Hoover
938 Hoover Rd
Somerset PA 155017635

Call Sign: N3ZVN
Le Ann Knepper
1298 Indiantown Rd
Somerset PA 155015524

Call Sign: KB3IEB
Matthew V Palguta
1122 James St
Somerset PA 15501

Call Sign: NB3E
Arthur K Cook
134 Jolico Rd
Somerset PA 15501

Call Sign: KD3OR
Rodney K Schrock
402 Lincoln St
Somerset PA 15501

Call Sign: NN3A
John D Robson
1308 Maplehurst Dr
Somerset PA 155012705

Call Sign: N3FPE
Evalyn A Gelpi
1401 N Center Ave
Somerset PA 15501

Call Sign: NI3D
Ernest B Gelpi
1401 N Center Ave
Somerset PA 15501

Call Sign: KB3JBE
Benjamin C Brinton
507 N Edgewood Ave
Somerset PA 15501

Call Sign: K3NOV
Benjamin C Brinton
507 N Edgewood Ave
Somerset PA 15501

Call Sign: WA3MYA
William J Weimer
1310 New Centerville Rd
Somerset PA 155018637

Call Sign: KB3MBD
Richard G Shinholt
2050 New Centerville Rd
Somerset PA 15501

Call Sign: K3SRT
Samuel S Foglesong
640 Piedmont Rd
Somerset PA 15501

Call Sign: WB3HGL
Richard A Warren
1190 Piedmont Rd
Somerset PA 15501

Call Sign: NI3W
Richard F Nicholson
428 S Columbia Ave
Somerset PA 15501

Call Sign: KB3DEG
Christine M Demorest
1206 S Columbia Ave
Somerset PA 155012705

Call Sign: KK3AN
Daniel R Simmonds
1551 Sheep Ridge Rd
Somerset PA 15501

Call Sign: KT3E
Richard H Gibbs
860 Sherwood Dr
Somerset PA 155019743

Call Sign: W3WK
Walter Kocinski
10314 Somerset Pike
Somerset PA 15601

Call Sign: KB3NHY
James W Ringdal
391 Stadium Dr
Somerset PA 15501

Call Sign: N3SQH
Jack N Humberson
355 Stoystown Rd
Somerset PA 15501

Call Sign: N3UVD
Bradley J Lorence
1231 Terrilin Dr
Somerset PA 15501

Call Sign: KB3RKD
Brad J Lorence
1231 Terrilin Dr
Somerset PA 15501

Call Sign: W3ADJ
Brad J Lorence
1231 Terrilin Dr
Somerset PA 15501

Call Sign: KB3MIO
Thomas Foley
162 Top Of Hickory Hill
Ln
Somerset PA 15501

Call Sign: K3FPX
George E Bowersox Jr
390 W Church St
Somerset PA 15501

Call Sign: KF3CG
Steven G Pender
390 W Patriot St
Somerset PA 15501

Call Sign: NI3Z
Melvin L Day
W Patriot St
Somerset PA 15501

Call Sign: KB3GUN
William F Smith
434 W Patriot St Rear
Somerset PA 15501

Call Sign: W3PVG
Harold P Showman
336 W Sanner St
Somerset PA 15501

Call Sign: N3JHB
Glenn W Peiffer
Somerset PA 15501

FCC Amateur Radio Licenses in South Fork

Call Sign: W3NXS
Albert Mrsnik
106 Maple St
South Fork PA 15956

Call Sign: KB3FBV
Joseph T Smiach
210 Maple St
South Fork PA 15956

FCC Amateur Radio Licenses in South Mountain

Call Sign: KB3ONJ
John H Staley
4745 Spruce Rd Box 5
South Mountain PA 17261

FCC Amateur Radio Licenses in South Williamsport

Call Sign: W3MTF
Richard J Pasco
475 Brown St
South Williamsport PA
17701

Call Sign: W3NZG
Jerry L Eischeid
530 Clinton St
South Williamsport PA
17702

Call Sign: KB3SAK
Deborah L Covey
330 E 1st Ave
South Williamsport PA
17702

Call Sign: W3HEL
Frank J Giordano
450 E 2nd Ave
South Williamsport PA
17701

Call Sign: W3WAL
Will J Waldstein
480 E 5th Ave Apt 5
South Williamsport PA
17702

Call Sign: KB3UBR
William J Waldstein
480 E 5th Ave Apt 5
South Williamsport PA
17702

Call Sign: K3RLK
Alfred C Schramm
311 E Mountain Ave
South Williamsport PA
17701

Call Sign: KM5YC
William C West
537 Fairmont Ave
South Williamsport PA
17702

Call Sign: N3SHX
Alvin M De Canio
513 Grandview Kpl
South Williamsport PA
17701

Call Sign: WB2TGW
James G Thomas
364 Hastings St
South Williamsport PA
17702

Call Sign: N3YPQ
Susan E Frei
519 Hastings St

South Williamsport PA
177027604

Call Sign: N8SRX
Adele J Stanley
502 Main St
South Williamsport PA
17702

Call Sign: KA3IFG
Joseph M Pfirman
709 Main St
South Williamsport PA
17702

Call Sign: N3WU
Joseph M Pfirman
709 Main St
South Williamsport PA
17702

Call Sign: N3YUT
Raymond R Patterson
615 S Howard St
South Williamsport PA
17701

Call Sign: N3YUU
Anna K Patterson
615 S Howard St
South Williamsport PA
17701

Call Sign: KG4VXN
Johnnie J Baker Jr
3149 State Rt 654
South Williamsport PA
17702

Call Sign: KM5PQ
William C West
552 Sylvan Dr
South Williamsport PA
17702

Call Sign: N3KVH
Jonathan W Parker
1027 W Central Ave
South Williamsport PA
17702

Call Sign: KB3PIT
Thomas N Williams
1015 W Mountain Ave
South Williamsport PA
177027516

Call Sign: K3NUT
Thomas N Williams
1015 W Mountain Ave
South Williamsport PA
177027516

Call Sign: KA8YQZ
Thomas D Inman
1533 W Southern Ave
South Williamsport PA
17702

Call Sign: N3NUR
Robin C Shearer
405 Winthrop St
South Williamsport PA
17702

Call Sign: N3MFK
Franklin S Ritter
South Williamsport PA
17702

Call Sign: N3PFC
Timothy P Bryan
South Williamsport PA
177020855

FCC Amateur Radio Licenses in Spangler

Call Sign: N3WZA
Cary J Solinski

71 Mtn Dr
Spangler PA 15775

Call Sign: N3BEG
Frank Sidwar
680 Nicktown Hill Rd
Spangler PA 15775

FCC Amateur Radio Licenses in Spring Grove

Call Sign: N3TVL
Monte R Schaszberger
4558 Beard School Rd
Spring Grove PA 17362

Call Sign: N3TVS
Melissa A Schaszberger
4558 Beard School Rd
Spring Grove PA 17362

Call Sign: N3ZCV
Judith D Miller
Box 2206
Spring Grove PA 17362

Call Sign: N3PXX
David A Fetters
Box 2298
Spring Grove PA 17362

Call Sign: N3KRZ
Mark S King
Box 2683A
Spring Grove PA 17362

Call Sign: N3YZX
Jimmy N Moffitt Jr
Box 2778
Spring Grove PA 17362

Call Sign: KA3UNO
Daniel G Smith
Box 4233 Leedy Rd
Spring Grove PA 17362

Call Sign: KA3UDD
Jacob L Miller III
Box 4332A
Spring Grove PA 17362

Call Sign: KB3NEA
Timothy A Bolinger
1249 Grandview Rd
Spring Grove PA 17362

Call Sign: KB3PVR
Tyler M Hoover
502 Hamlet Dr W
Spring Grove PA 17362

Call Sign: WB3BGK
Timothy R Hansen
6051 Hayrick Rd
Spring Grove PA 17362

Call Sign: KB3QLQ
Duane E Sterner
7197 Hershey Rd
Spring Grove PA 17362

Call Sign: N3JKY
George B Johns
6265 Hoff Rd
Spring Grove PA
173628941

Call Sign: KD3BH
John E Nicholson
6277 Hoff Rd
Spring Grove PA 17362

Call Sign: KB3KIW
Kevin M Henning
832 Jackson Sq Rd
Spring Grove PA 17362

Call Sign: KB3PFT
Timothy S Hilfiger
1668 Jefferson Rd

Spring Grove PA 17362

Call Sign: N3VWC
Kevin F White
1880 Jefferson Rd
Spring Grove PA 17362

Call Sign: N3RBO
Gale J Livelsberger
1479 Kbs Rd
Spring Grove PA 17362

Call Sign: N3OEZ
Fredrick W Christensen
4962 Lehman Rd
Spring Grove PA
173627706

Call Sign: KB3LOZ
George N Bollinger Jr
722 Mill Rd
Spring Grove PA 17362

Call Sign: KB3PXE
Matthew A Bollinger
730 Mill Rd
Spring Grove PA 17362

Call Sign: KB3SNM
Robert W Whyland
7 N Walnut St
Spring Grove PA
173621025

Call Sign: AA3QY
Robert A Peters
8442 Orchard Rd
Spring Grove PA
173628549

Call Sign: N3ZQP
Kristina S Peters
8442 Orchard Rd
Spring Grove PA
173628549

Call Sign: KJ3S
Matthew Easterling
2696 Pentland Rd
Spring Grove PA 17362

Call Sign: KB3SSW
Kenneth E Brown
7151 Pigeon Hill Rd
Spring Grove PA 17362

Call Sign: KB3UJY
Ryan P Keeney
2113 Pine Tree Rd
Spring Grove PA 17362

Call Sign: N3XZV
Ray A Wagner
5282 Sinsheim Rd
Spring Grove PA
173627957

Call Sign: WB3FVT
Malcolm H Laughead
6238 Thoman Dr
Spring Grove PA 17362

Call Sign: KB3NXL
Todd M Laughead
6238 Thoman Dr
Spring Grove PA 17362

Call Sign: KB3MZI
Tyler A Shearer
334 Three Hill Rd
Spring Grove PA 17362

Call Sign: KB3MSB
Jeremy E Dettinger
4645 View Dr
Spring Grove PA 17362

Call Sign: KB3NEC
Jacob C Kilgore
5056 Walters Hatchery Rd

Spring Grove PA 17362

Call Sign: KB5UOV
Linda J Stump
7575 Woodland Dr
Spring Grove PA 17362

Call Sign: N5QZD
Gerald E Stump
7575 Woodland Dr
Spring Grove PA 17362

Call Sign: KA2NLA
Richard D Kollmar
6423 York Rd
Spring Grove PA 17362

FCC Amateur Radio Licenses in Spring Mills

Call Sign: N3ZXU
Rebecca E Decker
131 Bear Springs Rd
Spring Mills PA 16875

Call Sign: N3ZXV
Devin Decker
131 Bear Springs Rd
Spring Mills PA 16875

Call Sign: N3CYL
William H Tucker
Box 71
Spring Mills PA 16875

Call Sign: N3OJD
Larry D Wolken
145 Greenbriar Gap Rd
Spring Mills PA 16875

Call Sign: KC0GUL
Joseph L Rowles
764 Lower Geos Valley Rd
Spring Mills PA 16875

Call Sign: WA3GYG
Gerald L Stover
264 Old Fort Rd
Spring Mills PA
168759112

Call Sign: N2WEO
Joseph M Pawell
401 Orndorf Rd
Spring Mills PA 16875

Call Sign: W2AWB
Joseph M Pawell
401 Orndorf Rd
Spring Mills PA 16875

Call Sign: W3EWX
William H Tucker
123 Pat Ln
Spring Mills PA 16875

Call Sign: AE3PA
Amateur Elmers Of PA
3568 Penns Valley Rd
Spring Mills PA 16875

Call Sign: AG3HH
Hungry Hams ARC
3568 Penns Valley Rd
Spring Mills PA 16875

Call Sign: K3YV
Ellwood E Brem
3568 Penns Valley Rd
Spring Mills PA 16875

Call Sign: N3SG
Sharon L Gaisler
3568 Penns Valley Rd
Spring Mills PA 16875

Call Sign: KB3VVQ
Tibben J Zerby
155 Sunrise Dr
Spring Mills PA 16875

Call Sign: KB3DLK
Timothy R Simkins
637 Upper Georges Valley
Rd
Spring Mills PA 16875

FCC Amateur Radio Licenses in Spring Run

Call Sign: KB3NPH
Timothy A Browning
16600 Dry Run Rd S Box
147
Spring Run PA 17262

FCC Amateur Radio Licenses in Spruce Creek

Call Sign: WB0YJS
Richard P Bouley
Box 59
Spruce Creek PA 16683

Call Sign: WA3HUD
Samuel E Hayes Sr
Spruce Creek
Spruce Creek PA 16683

Call Sign: KB3JII
Tracey E Brown
3860 Spruce Creek Rd
Spruce Creek PA 16683

Call Sign: KB3PKX
Abigail V Testament
4478 Tpke Rd
Spruce Creek PA 16683

FCC Amateur Radio Licenses in State College

Call Sign: KB3PSO
Nathaniel J Hobbs
430 Airport Rd

State College PA 16801

Call Sign: KA3YJQ
Robert S Hatten
138 Alkens Pl
State College PA 16801

Call Sign: KA3PNC
Darling F Kissel
1520 Ash Ave
State College PA 16801

Call Sign: WB3CBV
Andrew M Kissel
1520 Ash Ave
State College PA 16801

Call Sign: KC2PXA
Dominick J Marrone
143 Azalea Dr
State College PA 16803

Call Sign: N5GJM
Daryl L Biberdorf
613 Beaumont Dr
State College PA 16801

Call Sign: WA3YDC
Joseph P Portelli
609 Benjamin Ct
State College PA 16803

Call Sign: KA3DBY
Dorothy M Pelick
609 Berkshire Dr
State College PA 16803

Call Sign: KA3DBZ
Thomas J Pelick
609 Berkshire Dr
State College PA 16803

Call Sign: N3LLP
Robert D Jones
616 Berkshire Dr

State College PA 16803

Call Sign: KC8HYE
Bruce A Cromell Jr
638 Berkshire Dr
State College PA 16803

Call Sign: WB3GDX
Daniel E Crust
2528 Bernel Rd
State College PA 16803

Call Sign: KB3LUM
Robert P Stenerson
151 Black Bear Ln
State College PA 16803

Call Sign: KR3ORY
Robert P Stenerson
151 Black Bear Ln
State College PA 16803

Call Sign: KB3DTD
Richard L Neff
154 Black Bear Ln
State College PA 16803

Call Sign: KB3UCK
Daniel P Dewitt
348 Blue Course Dr Apt
340
State College PA 16803

Call Sign: N3TMI
Martha W Supina
415 Brandywine Dr
State College PA 16801

Call Sign: K3EZS
Robert M Peters
491 Breezewood Dr
State College PA
168012447

Call Sign: K3ZS

Robert M Peters
491 Breezewood Dr
State College PA
168012447

Call Sign: KB3IMH
Robert J La Verghetta
1730 Bristol Ave Apt 424
State College PA 16801

Call Sign: NK8Q
Mark J Schreiner
3002 Broadmoor Ln
State College PA 16801

Call Sign: KB3FAY
Prem Kumar
Calder Sq
State College PA 16805

Call Sign: KA1WLC
Frazier Newlin
Calder Sq 10293
State College PA 16805

Call Sign: KA1VZN
Adam Newlin
Calder Sq Box 10293
State College PA 16805

Call Sign: WD9GYC
K T Newlin
Calder Sq Box 10293
State College PA 16805

Call Sign: N8ZZ
John M Lipski
1742 Cambridge Dr
State College PA 16803

Call Sign: KA3LTZ
Timothy E Kohler
205 Camelot Ln
State College PA 16803

Call Sign: WB8ORB
Stephen D Clinger
312 Canterbury Dr
State College PA 16803

Call Sign: KB3GQW
David J Clinger
312 Canterbury Dr
State College PA 16803

Call Sign: N7FAT
Melvin D Andrews
2365 Charleston Dr
State College PA 16801

Call Sign: KB3HCN
Thomas B Gabrielson
2400 Chatham Ct
State College PA 16803

Call Sign: K3TBG
Thomas B Gabrielson
2400 Chatham Ct
State College PA
168032401

Call Sign: WX3TG
Thomas B Gabrielson
2400 Chatham Ct
State College PA
168032401

Call Sign: KB3DTB
Nathan W Wrye
105 Cherry Ridge Rd
State College PA 16803

Call Sign: N3YUO
Thomas E Sterling
215 Circle Dr
State College PA 16801

Call Sign: W3SLY
Lillie Z Hunter
225 Circle Dr

State College PA 16801

Call Sign: KB3ESD
Michael R Daley
1653 Circleville Rd
State College PA 16803

Call Sign: WB3BGG
Charles S Labor
2492 Circleville Rd
State College PA 16803

Call Sign: N3KSB
Dean E Arnold
Circleville Rd
State College PA
168033328

Call Sign: KB3RJW
Matthew R Steinbugl
116 Clemson Ct
State College PA 16803

Call Sign: K3MRS
Matthew R Steinbugl
116 Clemson Ct
State College PA 16803

Call Sign: KB3ROR
J Eric Boyer
140 Clover Rd
State College PA 16801

Call Sign: KB3EME
Scott W Irvin
152 Clover Rd
State College PA 16801

Call Sign: N3VKU
Vincent Scalamonga Jr
158 Clover Rd
State College PA
168017041

Call Sign: KB2HBO

Scott E Thomas
271 Conover Ln
State College PA 16801

Call Sign: N3YUM
Cynthia C Nucciarone
730 Cornwall Rd
State College PA 16803

Call Sign: N2BSS
Jeffrey J Nucciarone
730 Cornwall Rd
State College PA
168031427

Call Sign: N3BLF
Arnold M Rosenshine
731 Cornwall Rd
State College PA 16803

Call Sign: WB2YWQ
Jeffrey L Schiano
907 Crabapple Dr
State College PA 16801

Call Sign: N3SPT
Roy E Gilham
191 Creekside Dr
State College PA 16801

Call Sign: KC8KVD
Jerry R Logan
136 Creekside Dr
State College PA 16801

Call Sign: KB3WZC
Robert I Michniak II
659 Cricklewood Dr
State College PA 16803

Call Sign: KB3GGA
James H Rayburn
745 Cricklewood Dr
State College PA 16803

Call Sign: W3SAY
Wilber D Files
1422 Curtin St
State College PA 16803

Call Sign: KB3TBW
F Thomas Brown Jr
144 Dahlia Dr
State College PA 16803

Call Sign: K3FTB
F Thomas Brown Jr
144 Dahlia Dr
State College PA 16803

Call Sign: KB3TBY
Donald E Brown
144 Dahlia Dr
State College PA 16803

Call Sign: N3DBN
Donald E Brown
144 Dahlia Dr
State College PA 16803

Call Sign: KB3LPK
Robert J Talarico Jr
144 Dahlia Dr
State College PA 16803

Call Sign: KB3PWK
Joshua P Jackson
1348 Deerfield Dr
State College PA 16803

Call Sign: KB3RRD
Charles R Maggi
591 Devonshire Dr
State College PA 16803

Call Sign: N3CRM
Charles R Maggi
591 Devonshire Dr
State College PA 16803

Call Sign: KC3PD
Carl M Antonik
604 Devonshire Dr
State College PA
168031215

Call Sign: K3CBZ
John R Leeson
628 Devonshire Dr
State College PA
168033201

Call Sign: KB3SHX
Nathan E Wise
684 Devonshire Dr
State College PA 16803

Call Sign: N3RWR
Donald S Curtis
690 Devonshire Dr
State College PA 16803

Call Sign: N3YUY
James M Vogelsong
1645 Dogwood Cir
State College PA 16803

Call Sign: KB3QJD
Happy Valley ARC
1649 Dogwood Cir
State College PA 16803

Call Sign: K3PSU
Happy Valley ARC
1649 Dogwood Cir
State College PA 16803

Call Sign: KB3QQU
Happy Valley ARC
1649 Dogwood Cir
State College PA 16803

Call Sign: AA3PA
Happy Valley ARC
1649 Dogwood Cir

State College PA 16803

Call Sign: KB3RSL
Happy Valley ARC
1649 Dogwood Cir
State College PA 16803

Call Sign: W3CCN
Happy Valley ARC
1649 Dogwood Cir
State College PA 16803

Call Sign: KB3VJQ
Happy Valley ARC
1649 Dogwood Cir
State College PA 16803

Call Sign: K3SPY
Happy Valley ARC
1649 Dogwood Cir
State College PA 16803

Call Sign: WA3SMA
John Paul Devereaux
1649 Dogwood Cir
State College PA 16803

Call Sign: KB3UFN
Maria D Hibbert
1649 Dogwood Cir
State College PA 16803

Call Sign: KT3INA
Maria D Hibbert
1649 Dogwood Cir
State College PA 16803

Call Sign: KB3OGS
Robert L Hibbert
1649 Dogwood Cir
State College PA 16803

Call Sign: K3RLH
Robert L Hibbert
1649 Dogwood Cir

State College PA 16803

Call Sign: K3BOB
Robert L Hibbert
1649 Dogwood Cir
State College PA 16803

Call Sign: KA3BMU
William J Wrbican
1172 Dorum Ave
State College PA 16801

Call Sign: N3QKO
Jason R Nolan
347 Douglas Dr
State College PA 16803

Call Sign: K3AT
James D Petlock
400 Douglas Dr
State College PA 16803

Call Sign: KB3FAM
Christopher Cho
309 E Beaver Ave Apt 702
State College PA 16801

Call Sign: KK5GH
John A Telford
1916 E Branch Rd
State College PA 16801

Call Sign: KD4ZUC
Charles V Bartlett
188 E Cherry Ln
State College PA 16803

Call Sign: KC2JET
Blake Teitelbaum
444 E College Ave Ste 560
State College PA 16805

Call Sign: KB3FAP
Matthew T Ozalas
736 E Foster Ave Apt 110

State College PA 16801

Call Sign: N3YUQ
Thomas E Gesell
604 E Hamilton Ave
State College PA
168015708

Call Sign: KA3TUN
Sherrill K Graham
210 E Hamilton Ave Apt
32
State College PA 16801

Call Sign: KE3KD
Robert G Melton
532 E Irvin Ave
State College PA 16801

Call Sign: W3JNO
Paul B Weisz
500 E Marylyn Ave Apt
A1
State College PA 16801

Call Sign: W3GA
Robert P Hunter
500 E Marylyn Ave Apt
E70
State College PA 16801

Call Sign: KA1VWS
Shirley L Leopold
500 E Marylyn Ave Apt
F94
State College PA 16801

Call Sign: WB3AME
J Dean Jansma
500 E Marylyn Ave Unit
58
State College PA 16801

Call Sign: NB3W
Robert M Balonis

525 E McCormick Ave
State College PA
168016616

Call Sign: KA3JDW
James H Miller
321 E Mitchell Ave
State College PA 16803

Call Sign: KA3JDX
Bradford J Miller
321 E Mitchell Ave
State College PA 16803

Call Sign: W3DDM
Ronald E Gibson
353 E Outer Dr
State College PA 16801

Call Sign: W3ZZO
Douglas S Vonada
1243 E Park Hills Ave
State College PA
168033241

Call Sign: K3VGS
Howard F Keck
1425 E Park Hills Ave
State College PA 16803

Call Sign: KB3FGT
Lionel C Tauszig
600 E Pollock Rd 3202
State College PA 16801

Call Sign: KB3CZB
Connie A Curilla
112 E South Hills Ave
State College PA 16801

Call Sign: KB3SIY
Ming Shih Huang
559 Easterly Pkwy
State College PA 16801

Call Sign: KJ4JUQ
Philip J Gorman
Easterly Pkwy
State College PA 16801

Call Sign: WB3KZA
William L Caplan
1260 Edward St
State College PA 16801

Call Sign: WA3RHM
Eugene S Lindstrom
236 Ellen Ave
State College PA 16801

Call Sign: W3SUC
Harold R Hackman
237 Ellen Ave
State College PA 16801

Call Sign: AB7QV
Randy A Rogers
1021 Evergreen Rd
State College PA 16801

Call Sign: WA3UOE
J Patrick Campbell
651 Exeter Ct
State College PA 16803

Call Sign: KB3VRZ
John P Morgan Jr
2293 Fairfield Cir
State College PA 16801

Call Sign: N3VKT
Brian L Hassinger
1997 Fairwood Ln
State College PA 16803

Call Sign: KB3SOE
Abdulrahman Almutawa
130 Farmstead Ln 213
State College PA 16803

Call Sign: K3GQ
Fredric I Graham
300 Farmstead Ln F
State College PA 16803

Call Sign: KB3OVX
Shannon B Allison
303 Farmstead Ln Unit 5
State College PA 16803

Call Sign: K3VOT
Robert C Aurand
257 Florence Way
State College PA 16801

Call Sign: WA3JYN
Michael T Fitzgerald
375 Gerald St
State College PA 16801

Call Sign: KA3OAB
William M Culp
444 Gerald St
State College PA
168017486

Call Sign: KA3JDU
David P Robb
501 Glenn Rd
State College PA 16803

Call Sign: K3ARL
Karl F Hosterman
309 Goldfinch Dr
State College PA 16801

Call Sign: KB3HDE
Brandon G Hosterman
309 Goldfinch Dr
State College PA 16801

Call Sign: K3BGH
Brandon G Hosterman
309 Goldfinch Dr
State College PA 16801

Call Sign: KB3GOK
Sujarinee Kochawattana
Graduate Cir
State College PA 16801

Call Sign: N1GME
George H Webber
511 Gregor Cir
State College PA 16801

Call Sign: KB3HQO
Zikri Bayraktar
262 Hamilton Hall
State College PA 16802

Call Sign: KB3NDH
Sinan Aral
Hamilton Hall A047
State College PA 16802

Call Sign: W3KJM
John O Rigo
214 Harris Dr
State College PA
168018203

Call Sign: KA3GBC
Joseph T Pelick
1300 Harris St
State College PA 16803

Call Sign: KB3YID
Fan Wu
317 Hartranft Hall
State College PA 16802

Call Sign: KB3ESK
Duane A Moberg
2448 Harvest Ridge Dr
State College PA 16803

Call Sign: KB3WYY
Paul W Hay
1605 Hawthorn Dr

State College PA 16801

Call Sign: N5FKM
Dr Ryl
165 Haymaker Cir
State College PA 16801

Call Sign: WA0OCJ
Robert A Killoren Jr
846 Hedgerow Dr
State College PA 16801

Call Sign: W3WHC
William H Culp
136 Hickory Rd
State College PA
168017209

Call Sign: KB3FKJ
Joseph S Sherman
371 High Pt Cove
State College PA 16801

Call Sign: N3EVB
Brett D Saylor
375 High Pt Cove
State College PA 16801

Call Sign: W3DN
John A Nelson
1756 High Ridge Cir
State College PA 16803

Call Sign: KB3UUG
James P Dugan V
215 Hill Dr
State College PA 16801

Call Sign: K3CM
Charles W McMullen
7 Holly Cir
State College PA 16801

Call Sign: N3MJZ
George Hromnak

805 Holmes St
State College PA 16803

Call Sign: N6CX
Richard E Essen
241 Homan Ave
State College PA 16801

Call Sign: KD3PN
Diana Hershberger
257 Homan Ave
State College PA 16801

Call Sign: KB3TBX
James J Alles Jr
905 Houserville Rd
State College PA
168017163

Call Sign: KB6FOX
Gregory M Bower
1232 Houserville Rd
State College PA 16801

Call Sign: N3YUV
Michael G Trimmer
1300 Houserville Rd
State College PA 16801

Call Sign: KB3ROQ
Lorn M Ray
126 Hoy St
State College PA 16801

Call Sign: KA3RNA
Craig R Watkins
1883 Huntington Ln
State College PA 16803

Call Sign: KC0HHY
Delio D Vidal
1803 James Ave
State College PA 16801

Call Sign: KC0HVY

Anisia F Vidal
1803 James Ave
State College PA 16801

Call Sign: N3VSM
Fraser Bonnett
1814 James Ave
State College PA 16801

Call Sign: KB3FBB
Fraser Bonnett
1814 James Ave
State College PA 16801

Call Sign: N3PHN
Robert D Fenner
1823 James Ave
State College PA 16801

Call Sign: N3RJW
Patti L Fenner
1823 James Ave
State College PA 16801

Call Sign: K3RDF
Robert D Fenner
1823 James Ave
State College PA 16801

Call Sign: K3PLF
Patti L Fenner
1823 James Ave
State College PA 16801

Call Sign: KB3ESI
Ryan A Tancibok
1873 James Ave
State College PA 16801

Call Sign: KB3ESJ
Daniel A Tancibok
1873 James Ave
State College PA 16801

Call Sign: KC2DZQ

Owen M Christensen
108 Jules Dr
State College PA 16801

Call Sign: N2KBI
Thomas E Dunham
1530 Kennelworth Ct
State College PA 16801

Call Sign: KB3ESR
James A Wasson
544 Lanceshire Ln
State College PA
168031434

Call Sign: KD6TBB
Susan E Leska
1959 Lauck St
State College PA 16803

Call Sign: KB3RAL
Susan E Anderson
1959 Lauck St
State College PA 16803

Call Sign: KB3CTJ
Grace A Eberhardt
1312 Linn St
State College PA 16803

Call Sign: W2IBH
Francis H Yonker
160 Lions Hill Rd 101
State College PA
168031859

Call Sign: N3RUX
Eric T Nelson
200 Lions Hill Rd Apt
E015
State College PA 16803

Call Sign: W3ECM
Eugene C McGuire

200 Lions Hill Rd Apt
E017
State College PA 16803

Call Sign: W3NUO
Robert E Skipper
330 Lions Hill Rd W315
State College PA
168031898

Call Sign: W3ZX
David E Harris
300 Lions Hill Rd W409
State College PA 16803

Call Sign: KB3MPV
Edward D Peterson
320 Madison St
State College PA 16801

Call Sign: KA3ETX
Rosanna M Mutzabaugh
555 Marjorie Mae St
State College PA 16803

Call Sign: WB3CXR
John C Mutzabaugh
555 Marjorie Mae St
State College PA 16803

Call Sign: KA3TTR
Jeffrey S Medina
565 Marjorie Mae St
State College PA 16803

Call Sign: KB3IOU
Corrie I Nichol
1400 Martin St 3091
State College PA 16803

Call Sign: KB3BJG
Ryan T Ohlson
2050 Mary Ellen Ln
State College PA 16803

Call Sign: KB3OIG
Thomas Skerl Jr
213 McBath St
State College PA 16801

Call Sign: KB3CZC
Michael A Kreuter
319 McBath St
State College PA 16801

Call Sign: WA3ENK
Rodney A Kreuter
319 McBath St
State College PA 16801

Call Sign: AA3VS
Michael A Kreuter
319 McBath St
State College PA 16801

Call Sign: AA3SQ
Joyce Kreuter
319 McBath St
State College PA
168012744

Call Sign: K3POI
Robert J Moser
332 McBath St
State College PA 16801

Call Sign: N3ZYJ
Daniel P Komisarek
9 McKee Hall U Park
State College PA
168021793

Call Sign: W3MX
Carroll L Key Jr
923 McKee St
State College PA 16801

Call Sign: KB3YIF
Xiang Li
608 Mifflin Hall

State College PA 16802

Call Sign: KB3QGF
David W Decapria
155 Mitch Ave
State College PA
168017275

Call Sign: K3DWD
David W Decapria
155 Mitch Ave
State College PA
168017275

Call Sign: KB3ROS
Brian J Evans
2162 Mtn View Ave
State College PA 16801

Call Sign: KB3PVF
Dragos M Nistor
2023 Muncy Rd
State College PA 16801

Call Sign: KA3JEA
Carl R Chelius
625 N Allen St
State College PA
168033505

Call Sign: W3NEM
Robert E Gawryla
1463 N Allen St
State College PA
168033012

Call Sign: N3LET
Wade J Claar
N Atherton St 62
State College PA 16803

Call Sign: KD3SY
Kenneth J Richardson
1535 N Atherton St Apt 16
State College PA 16803

Call Sign: KA3HRN
Charles D Bolan
25 N Barkway Ln
State College PA 16803

Call Sign: KB3PVE
Kyle L Labowski
145 N Brook Ln Apt 107
State College PA 16803

Call Sign: N3BCA
Stephen Mershon
1346 N Foxpointe Dr
State College PA
168032407

Call Sign: WB3GEE
Phi D Trinh
121 N Hill Pl
State College PA 16803

Call Sign: KB3OYD
Robert L Hibbert Jr
1951 N Oak Ln
State College PA 16203

Call Sign: W3RLH
Robert L Hibbert Jr
1951 N Oak Ln
State College PA 16803

Call Sign: WB3HXK
John H Golbeck
415 Nimitz Ave
State College PA 16801

Call Sign: WB3LKQ
Carolyn L Wilhelm
415 Nimitz Ave
State College PA 16801

Call Sign: W3JHG
John H Golbeck
415 Nimitz Ave

State College PA 16801

Call Sign: W3CLW
Carolyn L Wilhelm
415 Nimitz Ave
State College PA 16801

Call Sign: KB3MTQ
Thomas R Harmon
120 Norle St
State College PA 16801

Call Sign: KB3VNH
Jeffrey Stalzer
1283 Northampton St
State College PA 16803

Call Sign: WB3BZH
Paul L Boyer
230 Oak Ln
State College PA 16801

Call Sign: N3GDP
Richard J La Palme
236 Oakley Dr
State College PA 16803

Call Sign: W3KNF
Jean V Cameron
121 Oakmont Rd
State College PA 16801

Call Sign: W3RNH
Donald L Cameron
121 Oakmont Rd
State College PA 16801

Call Sign: N3EMC
David N Richards
188 Oakwood Ave
State College PA 16803

Call Sign: KB3GZR
Jared R Kloda
911 Oakwood Ave

State College PA 16803

Call Sign: K3OOL
Craig S Miller
134 Oakwood Dr
State College PA 16801

Call Sign: KA3WCA
Peter S Wyckoff
230 Oakwood Dr
State College PA 16801

Call Sign: KB3VQA
Cathrine A Jenkins
1222 Old Boalsburg Rd
State College PA 16801

Call Sign: W3EDP
Eric D Prescott
1143 Oneida St
State College PA 16801

Call Sign: KA3MLG
John A Hargleroad II
482 Outer Dr
State College PA 16801

Call Sign: KB3UCN
Hashim N Akeel
9 Packer
State College PA 16802

Call Sign: AA3RS
Ronald A Strouse
3346 Pamela Cir
State College PA 16801

Call Sign: N3YZK
Andrew B Strouse
3346 Pamela Cir
State College PA 16801

Call Sign: AB3NC
Tracy L Kendall
1864 Park Forest Ave

State College PA 16803

Call Sign: N3AAP
David L Phillips
471 Park Ln
State College PA 16801

Call Sign: W3TJ
John W Telford
472 Park Ln
State College PA 16803

Call Sign: KA3VPQ
Luis M Jourdain
1437 Park Ln
State College PA 16803

Call Sign: KB3YIK
Zhichen Xu
104 Parker Hall
State College PA 16802

Call Sign: KB3VRU
Xiang Yu
411 Pennypacker Hall
State College PA 16802

Call Sign: KB3YIG
Yu Jin
513 Pennypacker Hall
State College PA 16802

Call Sign: KB3WPC
Cameron A Mchenry
532 Pike St
State College PA 16801

Call Sign: KB3WEU
Dean A Mchenry
532 Pike St
State College PA 16801

Call Sign: N3BXM
Joann W Snell
537 Pike St

State College PA 16801

Call Sign: N3HQD
John D Snell
537 Pike St
State College PA 16801

Call Sign: N3LLQ
David E Snell
537 Pike St
State College PA 16801

Call Sign: W2ELH
Lawrence E Yont
2425 Pine Hurst Dr
State College PA
168033383

Call Sign: KF2XR
Eugene C McGuire
1705 Plaza Dr
State College PA
168014651

Call Sign: KB3PVM
Ibrahim Al Ismaili
2507 Plaza Dr
State College PA 16801

Call Sign: KB3WRM
Ayan Beuzhanov
2000 Plaza Dr Apt 707B
State College PA 16801

Call Sign: KB3VDE
David M Ritz
2352 Raven Hollow Rd
State College PA 16801

Call Sign: KB3DWY
Jeremy S Morony
117 Ridge Ave
State College PA 16801

Call Sign: N3WS

Walter R Supina
525 Ridge Ave
State College PA 16803

Call Sign: WB3IVP
Supello ARC
525 Ridge Ave
State College PA 16803

Call Sign: KA3HRO
John M Herrmann
568 Ridge Ave
State College PA 16801

Call Sign: N3SPS
George B Gurney
1705 S Allen St
State College PA 16801

Call Sign: WA3GXA
Hoben Thomas
310 S Allen St 502
State College PA 16801

Call Sign: KB3FAW
Joseph M Scavona
825 S Allen St Apt 4
State College PA 16801

Call Sign: KB3PZE
William A Fabanich Jr
1231 S Allen St Apt 5
State College PA 16801

Call Sign: N3YUJ
Kathleen J Muhonen
1117 S Allen St Upper
State College PA 16801

Call Sign: N3YUK
Michael S Babst
1117 S Allen St Upper Apt
State College PA 16801

Call Sign: KB3MTS

Thomas P Keller
300 S Atherton St
State College PA 16801

Call Sign: KB3GDS
Matthew G Bray
710 S Atherton St
State College PA 16801

Call Sign: N3SWC
Isra A Chaiyasena
1700 S Atherton St
State College PA
168016211

Call Sign: K3ALE
Lorn M Ray
S Butz St
State College PA 16801

Call Sign: KB3SNQ
Karen P Brooks
250 S Carl St Apt 4C
State College PA 16801

Call Sign: W3XC
Charles R Krepps Jr
1650 S Cherry Hill Rd
State College PA
168033214

Call Sign: KB3SUW
Erin J Ames
209 S Coral St
State College PA 16801

Call Sign: KB3LFQ
Roger K Sporre
314 S Corl St
State College PA 16801

Call Sign: KA3VHR
Rita L Foderaro
301 S Gill St
State College PA 16801

Call Sign: N3IHL
Anthony H Foderaro
301 S Gill St
State College PA 16801

Call Sign: KA8EUF
David E Beyerle
331 S Gill St
State College PA
168013963

Call Sign: KC9AQC
Robert P Schroeder
903 S Pugh St
State College PA 16801

Call Sign: N3YUL
Robert L Passow
1114 S Pugh St
State College PA 16801

Call Sign: NT3O
David A Sibley
132 S Sparks St
State College PA 16801

Call Sign: W3BDD
J Edwin Davies Jr
961 S Sparks St
State College PA 16801

Call Sign: KB3GFZ
Anthony Ghaffari
1317 Sandpiper Dr
State College PA 16801

Call Sign: KA3WRQ
Vera M Sneff
119 Sandy Ridge Rd
State College PA 16803

Call Sign: KA3WRR
Eugene M Sneff
119 Sandy Ridge Rd

State College PA 16803

Call Sign: KC6TVX
Denise V Lanning
905 Saxton Dr
State College PA 16801

Call Sign: N3XVW
Ray J Lunnen Jr
1018 Saxton Dr
State College PA 16801

Call Sign: KB3JYD
Dominic M Geleskie
370 Selders Cir
State College PA
168012536

Call Sign: W3DDD
Dominic M Geleskie
370 Selders Cir
State College PA
168012536

Call Sign: KB3GGE
Mark Geleskie
370 Selders Cir
State College PA
168012536

Call Sign: W3MEG
Mark Geleskie
370 Selders Cir
State College PA
168012536

Call Sign: KM3G
Mark Geleskie
370 Selders Cir
State College PA
168012536

Call Sign: W6MG
Mark Geleskie
370 Selders Cir

State College PA
168012536

Call Sign: W3MG
Mark Geleskie
370 Selders Cir
State College PA
168012536

Call Sign: NE0S
Stephen D Turner
113 Seymore Ave
State College PA 16803

Call Sign: K3HPA
Stephen D Turner
113 Seymore Ave
State College PA 16803

Call Sign: KB3MLX
Charles J Turner
113 Seymore Ave
State College PA 16803

Call Sign: N3VJ
James A Vuccolo
1231 Shamrock Ave
State College PA 16801

Call Sign: N3FEB
Arthur F Hogrefe
3140 Sheffield Dr
State College PA 16801

Call Sign: K3EMI
Budd L Hoy
3301 Shellers Bend 904
State College PA
168013068

Call Sign: KB3OQF
Faraz Ahmad
33 Simmons Hall
State College PA 16802

Call Sign: KA3TTK
Alexander H Raye
2634 Sleepy Hollow Dr
State College PA 16803

Call Sign: N3SPR
Gilbert L Sanders
2652 Sleepy Hollow Dr
State College PA 16803

Call Sign: KB3YIV
Robert D Simon
1212 Smithfield Cir
State College PA 16801

Call Sign: W3OST
Matthew T Shamonsky
1125 Smithfield St
State College PA
168016428

Call Sign: N3YUN
Elaine R Prestia
1265 Smithfield St
State College PA
168016432

Call Sign: K3ERP
Elaine R Prestia
1265 Smithfield St
State College PA
168016432

Call Sign: KB3EBE
Nittany ARC
1265 Smithfield St
State College PA
168040332

Call Sign: K3CWP
Carmine W Prestia Jr
1265 Smithfield St
State College PA
168040332

Call Sign: W3GA
Nittany ARC
1265 Smithfield St
State College PA
168040332

Call Sign: KB3IVI
Dong J Lim
721 Snyder Hall
State College PA 16802

Call Sign: KE4OKZ
Jason M Becker
727 Southgate Dr
State College PA 16801

Call Sign: KB3UCT
Christian W Heinemann
745 Southgate Dr
State College PA 16801

Call Sign: KB3GDK
Ammar H Mohamed
849 Southgate Dr
State College PA 16801

Call Sign: KB3PSU
Ammar H Mohamed
849 Southgate Dr
State College PA 16801

Call Sign: N3LUB
Ralph F Poorman
322 Spring Lea Dr
State College PA 16801

Call Sign: N3BCH
Ralph F Poorman
322 Spring Lea Dr
State College PA 16801

Call Sign: N3YUW
Randall G Bitner
2320 Stafford Cir
State College PA 16801

Call Sign: N3HTP
Gi T Kim
803 Stratford Dr 4
State College PA 16801

Call Sign: KB3WPI
Michael E Crouse Jr
749 Struble Rd
State College PA 16801

Call Sign: WA7HUB
Richard R Plut
820 Struble Rd
State College PA
168017432

Call Sign: KB3KZQ
Adam G Ryan
144 Sunrise Ter
State College PA 16801

Call Sign: N1LOT
Matthew L Albert
Sunrise Ter
State College PA 16801

Call Sign: N3WMH
Lisa M Hilbert
256 Sycamore Dr
State College PA 16801

Call Sign: KA3NZX
John J Swords
716 Tanager Dr
State College PA 16803

Call Sign: KB3ESP
Jean W Bemis
1009 Taylor St
State College PA 16803

Call Sign: WB3EDI
Wilber G Bemis Jr
1009 Taylor St

State College PA
168033482

Call Sign: KB3OTS
Salvatore R Riggio Jr
810 Teaberry Ln
State College PA
168033176

Call Sign: WA3SAL
Salvatore R Riggio Jr
810 Teaberry Ln
State College PA
168033176

Call Sign: KB3UFM
Emma C Watts
214 Tener Hall
State College PA 16802

Call Sign: KF5HFR
Matthew J Woodruff
144 Thornton Rd
State College PA 16801

Call Sign: N5IVU
Eric O Scheie
510 Toftrees Ave 130
State College PA 16803

Call Sign: N3OCY
Rosemary A Miller
308 Toftrees Ave 331
State College PA 16803

Call Sign: KB3LPR
William J Glessner
518 University Dr Apt 9
State College PA 16801

Call Sign: KB3CBM
John A Vogelsang
Vairo Blvd
State College PA 16803

Call Sign: KB3TPW
Nathaniel Nazareno
201 Vairo Blvd 127G
State College PA 16803

Call Sign: KU1J
Kuninori Togai
10 Vairo Blvd Apt 11D
State College PA 16803

Call Sign: KB3LSO
Faisal H Abdal
501 Vairo Blvd Apt 2014D
State College PA 16803

Call Sign: KA3FSW
Kathryn L Hyatt
10 Vairo Blvd Apt 214A
State College PA 16803

Call Sign: KB3PVJ
Sattam S Al Otaibi
501 Vairo Blvd Apt 2211
State College PA 16803

Call Sign: KB3MCF
Feras A Alshehri
501 Vairo Blvd Apt 2314
State College PA 16803

Call Sign: KB3ODX
Gloria Mugisha
201 Vairo Blvd Apt 327 G
State College PA 16803

Call Sign: KB3FAQ
Asia M Johnson
601 Vairo Blvd Apt 337
State College PA 16803

Call Sign: KB3NDG
Murtadha A Hameed
201 Vairo Blvd Apt 353
State College PA 16803

Call Sign: N4FZP
Takuji Sudo
150 Village Dr
State College PA 16803

Call Sign: WB2LOU
Theodore C Trostle
150 Village Dr
State College PA 16803

Call Sign: N3YAV
Michael W Jacobs
218 W Aaron Dr
State College PA 16803

Call Sign: N3BST
Scott R Hazel
760 W Aaron Dr
State College PA 16803

Call Sign: KB3ESO
William H Parsonage
798 W Aaron Dr
State College PA 16803

Call Sign: KB3WHP
William H Parsonage
798 W Aaron Dr
State College PA 16803

Call Sign: KB3GIY
Kyle M Gabel
801 W Aaron Dr Apt D 8
State College PA 16803

Call Sign: KA3TTL
Krishna J Fisher
623 W Beaver Ave
State College PA 16801

Call Sign: N3FYF
Robert L Hirsch
1631 W Branch Rd
State College PA 16801

Call Sign: KB3IQZ
Sungyun Yoo
447 W Clinton Ave 404
State College PA 16803

Call Sign: KB3FAS
Shawn P Dugan
349 W Clinton Ave Apt
358
State College PA 16803

Call Sign: W3ENT
Lawrence C Pharo Jr
3670 W College Ave
State College PA 16801

Call Sign: KB8VIZ
Jakkrit Kunthong
312 W College Ave 3
State College PA 16801

Call Sign: N3ODN
Azmi Hashim
415 W College Ave 301
State College PA 16801

Call Sign: KB3TQI
Siming Zhao
600 W College Ave Apt
107
State College PA 16801

Call Sign: KB3UHJ
Tariq L Alturkestani
331 W College Ave Apt 23
State College PA 16801

Call Sign: KB3UCU
Sultan A Aboalela
331 W College Ave Apt 36
State College PA 16801

Call Sign: AB3GL
Sven G Bilen
435 W Fairmount Ave

State College PA 16801

Call Sign: N3VHN
Mark T Shirey
215 W Fairmount Ave Apt
201
State College PA
168015247

Call Sign: KB3YIM
Yongsuk Lee
127 W Hall
State College PA 16802

Call Sign: N3SPA
Joseph M Jimick
W Hamilton Ave
State College PA 16801

Call Sign: WL7BII
David R Maneval
126 W Lytle Ave
State College PA 16801

Call Sign: K3AME
Ronald D Brokloff
132 W Lytle Ave
State College PA
168015925

Call Sign: K3HOY
Ann K Brokloff
132 W Lytle Ave
State College PA
168015925

Call Sign: N3PKV
Justin J Olexy
101 W Nittany Ave
State College PA 16801

Call Sign: N3EPB
Aura Lee Supina
525 W Ridge Ave
State College PA 16803

Call Sign: KB3PZI
Charles R Philbrick
425 W Shadow Ln
State College PA 16803

Call Sign: W3JXP
John E Passaneau
2231 W Whitehall Rd
State College PA 16801

Call Sign: K3HKK
Nittany ARC Inc
2231 W Whitehall Rd
State College PA 16804

Call Sign: W2QNU
Roger K Sporre
2462 W Whitehall Rd
State College PA 16801

Call Sign: WB6KNU
Bruce Pincus
914 Walnut Spring Ln
State College PA 18801

Call Sign: KB3YIH
Abdulla Alhashmi
424 Waupelani Dr
State College PA 16807

Call Sign: KJ4JKO
Kyle C Etters
425 Waupelani Dr Apt 104
State College PA 16801

Call Sign: K4NTT
Kyle C Etters
425 Waupelani Dr Apt 104
State College PA 16801

Call Sign: KC0EYD
Kerry C Michael
424 Waupelani Dr Apt E
24

State College PA 16801

Call Sign: AA3XS
Alexander E Avramov
445 Waupelani Dr Apt E15
State College PA 16801

Call Sign: AA3AX
Alexander E Avramov
445 Waupelani Dr Apt E15
State College PA 16801

Call Sign: KB3JEK
Alexander A Avramov
445 Waupelani Dr Apt E15
State College PA 16801

Call Sign: WF9A
Alexander E Avramov
445 Waupelani Dr Apt E15
State College PA 16801

Call Sign: KC8KIP
Scott P Porter
424 Waupelani Dr Apt
H21
State College PA 16801

Call Sign: AA3TI
Hampton S Langdon
612 Wayland Pl
State College PA 16803

Call Sign: W3JMW
Edward S Kenney
625 Wayland Pl
State College PA 16803

Call Sign: N3ODP
Daniel V Roberts
851 Webster Dr
State College PA 16801

Call Sign: K3OXT
Helen B Volz

123 Wellington Dr
State College PA
168017680

Call Sign: KA3FXG
Frederick C Volz
123 Wellington Dr
State College PA
168017680

Call Sign: W3SMV
Carl Volz Jr
123 Wellington Dr
State College PA
168017680

Call Sign: KB3ORM
William M Mertens
1106 Westerly Pkwy
State College PA
168014157

Call Sign: K3WMM
William M Mertens
1106 Westerly Pkwy
State College PA
168014157

Call Sign: KB3HCZ
Michael J Beacham
1457 Westerly Pkwy
State College PA 16802

Call Sign: W3WAB
Wayne A Bicehouse
1126 Westerly Pky
State College PA 16801

Call Sign: KB3YBI
State College ARS
455 Westgate Dr
State College PA 16803

Call Sign: AJ0PA
State College ARS

455 Westgate Dr
State College PA 16803

Call Sign: KB3EIA
Michael J Coslo
455 Westgate Dr
State College PA 16803

Call Sign: N3LI
Michael J Coslo
455 Westgate Dr
State College PA 16803

Call Sign: KB3DTE
Joseph S Broniszewski
1201 William St
State College PA 16801

Call Sign: KB3DTF
Lisa A Broniszewski
1201 William St
State College PA 16801

Call Sign: W3NLU
Anthony J Ferraro
1204 William St
State College PA 16801

Call Sign: W3AJF
Anthony J Ferraro
1204 William St
State College PA 16801

Call Sign: WA3OXS
John E Evans Jr
612 Wiltshire Dr
State College PA
168031448

Call Sign: KS3S
Helen C Villano
625 Wiltshire Dr
State College PA 16803

Call Sign: N3GOI

Steven E Eslinger
721 Windsor Ct
State College PA 16801

Call Sign: KA3TTJ
Frank G Bamer Jr
143 Woodside Dr
State College PA 16801

Call Sign: N3MUY
J Michael George
State College PA 16804

Call Sign: KD3XZ
Eric L Schott
State College PA 16868

Call Sign: KB3NYG
Gregory E Miller
State College PA 16804

Call Sign: N3TLB
Arthur A Person
State College PA 16804

Call Sign: W3DPH
Raymond W Whetstine
State College PA 16804

Call Sign: W3PKE
P H Licastro
State College PA 16804

Call Sign: W3YA
The Nittany Amat Rad Clb
Inc
State College PA 16804

Call Sign: K3EKT
Eric L Schott
State College PA 16804

Call Sign: K3GEM
Gregory E Miller
State College PA 16804

Call Sign: KB3SUY
William E Ames
State College PA 16804

Call Sign: N3VMW
Michael E Buerger
State College PA 16805

Call Sign: KB3RMH
Justin M Locke
State College PA
168041193

FCC Amateur Radio Licenses in State Line

Call Sign: N3QAP
Donna H Young
State Line PA 17263

Call Sign: WB3FXI
Kenneth L Baer
State Line PA 17233

FCC Amateur Radio Licenses in Steelton

Call Sign: K3MRD
Joseph Jordan
157 Adams St
Steelton PA 171132214

Call Sign: N3JDT
Anthony N Zupanovic Jr
570 Chambers St
Steelton PA 17113

Call Sign: KB3UYN
Mark G Mattern
911 Gibson Blvd
Steelton PA 17113

Call Sign: K3BHL
Anthony W Malesic

517 Highland St Enhaut
Steelton PA 17113

Call Sign: WA3QJL
Gerry M Farmer Sr
491 Monroe St
Steelton PA 17113

Call Sign: K3PDY
Charles E Leidig
415 N 3rd St
Steelton PA 17113

Call Sign: KB3GGL
John H Jones
324 Riverview St
Steelton PA 17113

Call Sign: N3HVG
Gaza J Szekeres
451 S 2nd St
Steelton PA 17113

Call Sign: N3NJB
Richard H Bordner
2501 S 2nd St
Steelton PA 17113

Call Sign: KB3GRL
Harrisburg Area React
2611 S 2nd St
Steelton PA 17113

Call Sign: WA3MMD
Robert M Kurtinecz
2121 S 3rd St
Steelton PA 17113

Call Sign: N3NJB
Harrisburg Area React
2121 S 3rd St
Steelton PA 17113

Call Sign: KB3SDW
Daniel W Mcneil II

511 S Front St
Steelton PA 17113

Call Sign: KA3RTY
Sharon L Knepp
109 Summit Ave
Steelton PA 17113

Call Sign: WB5TTG
Mark D Knepp
109 Summit Ave
Steelton PA 17113

FCC Amateur Radio Licenses in Stevens

Call Sign: KB3NLQ
Kevin M Stanley
20 Blue Jay Dr
Stevens PA 17578

Call Sign: N3YAG
David L Meadath
8 Bunker Hill Rd
Stevens PA 17578

Call Sign: N3ZDZ
Shawn D Diamond
41 Cardinal Dr
Stevens PA 17578

Call Sign: KB3WPS
Jared L High
939 Daniel Dr
Stevens PA 17578

Call Sign: N3MSO
Brian K Miller
1020 Daniel Dr
Stevens PA 17578

Call Sign: N3VKO
Tyann R Miller
1020 Daniel Dr
Stevens PA 17578

Call Sign: N4NHH
Barbara A Mast
380 E Church St
Stevens PA 17578

Call Sign: N3JPM
Gerald R Burkman
9 E Summit Dr
Stevens PA 17578

Call Sign: WK3Q
Joseph P Ross
10 E Summit Dr
Stevens PA 17578

Call Sign: KB3EYS
Michael G Mccauley
31 E Summit Dr
Stevens PA 17578

Call Sign: N2BHC
William R Fitch
981 Forest Hill Rd
Stevens PA 175780981

Call Sign: K3IFL
William R Fitch
981 Forest Hill Rd
Stevens PA 175780981

Call Sign: N3YZZ
Jonathan E Sauder
595 Hopeland Rd
Stevens PA 17578

Call Sign: K3MNX
Leon R Robinson
1630 Kleinfel Tersville Rd
Stevens PA 17578

Call Sign: N3TUO
Paul W Landis
1555 Kleinfelterville Rd
Stevens PA 17578

Call Sign: N3ROH
Sheldon K Zeiset
142 N Reamstown Rd
Stevens PA 17578

Call Sign: AA1QP
Ronald J Focia
157 N Reamstown Rd
Stevens PA 17578

Call Sign: KB3QLA
Frank N Wright
83 Park St
Stevens PA 17578

Call Sign: K3ZRF
David L Wenger
11 Stevens Rd
Stevens PA 175780123

Call Sign: KB3HCE
Edwin F Motter
15 Stevens Rd
Stevens PA 17578

Call Sign: N3JQV
Dail R Granholm
4 Wild Deer Dr
Stevens PA 17578

**FCC Amateur Radio
Licenses in Stewartstown**

Call Sign: N3FOL
Michaelangelo D Raras
1 Aspen Ct
Stewartstown PA 17363

Call Sign: N3QYY
Russell E De Rose
126 Berkshire Ln
Stewartstown PA 17363

Call Sign: KB3WUR

Stephen C Wollett Jr
1411 Blue Ball Rd
Stewartstown PA 17363

Call Sign: KA3UDF
Howard H Merkel
Box 105 Draco Airport
Stewartstown PA 17363

Call Sign: KA3UDE
Jonathan P Merkel
Box 105 Draco Airport
Stewartstown PA 17367

Call Sign: N3OGB
Walter S Makush
Box 4162
Stewartstown PA 17363

Call Sign: KA3UDH
Brett A McElwain
Box 463A 1
Stewartstown PA 17363

Call Sign: K4JLD
Bertran D Walton II
12552 Brillstrick Rd
Stewartstown PA 17363

Call Sign: AA3VB
Galen R Lathrem
120 Charles Ave
Stewartstown PA 17363

Call Sign: KA3UIN
Jeff F Kearns Jr
Draco Rd Box 1409
Stewartstown PA 17363

Call Sign: N3YIX
John F Malachowski
19779 Dutton Rd
Stewartstown PA 17363

Call Sign: K3VGX

Brian M Manns
14228 Ebaugh Rd
Stewartstown PA
173638567

Call Sign: N3LPE
Daniel R Friese
108 Gateshead Dr
Stewartstown PA
173638997

Call Sign: KB3IRE
Craig W Snook
6141 Hickory Rd
Stewartstown PA 17363

Call Sign: N3VUL
Stephen L Hawkins
6209 Hickory Rd
Stewartstown PA 17363

Call Sign: K3HG
Harry B Graver Jr
7525 Hickory Rd
Stewartstown PA 17363

Call Sign: N3EZM
Douglas J Graham Sr
137 Hollow Rd
Stewartstown PA 17363

Call Sign: KB3CHN
Greg A McElhaney
295 Hollow Rd
Stewartstown PA 17363

Call Sign: N0YTU
Charles N Sullivan II
1826 Orwig Rd
Stewartstown PA 17363

Call Sign: KB3UTI
Paul E Roscosky
30 Poplar Springs Blvd

Stewartstown PA
173634105

Call Sign: KB3RVY
David A Leeper
18766 Rosewood Dr
Stewartstown PA 17363

Call Sign: KB3KGG
William C Thompson
S Main St Box 502
Stewartstown PA 17363

Call Sign: KA3QHA
Kurt P Mezger
3 Scarborough Fare
Stewartstown PA 17363

Call Sign: KB3GTR
William R Crawford
18 Scarborough Fare
Stewartstown PA 17363

Call Sign: N3XVK
Kenneth M Beard
2955 Shangrila Rd
Stewartstown PA 17363

Call Sign: KI3W
Steven M Scott
173 Switchpoint Dr
Stewartstown PA 17363

Call Sign: WB2FFY
James A Muller
5 Trout Ln
Stewartstown PA 17363

Call Sign: K3NK
James A Muller
5 Trout Ln
Stewartstown PA 17363

Call Sign: KE4VVN
Kenneth G Warren

Stewartstown PA
173630281

Call Sign: W3EME
Brian M Manns
Stewartstown PA
173630486

FCC Amateur Radio Licenses in Stillwater

Call Sign: N3CNB
Emerson R Bonham
Box 72
Stillwater PA 17878

Call Sign: N3CDJ
Alfred S Wilson
3960 Maple Grove Rd
Stillwater PA 17878

Call Sign: KD3MI
Thomas M Talanca
Rd 1
Stillwater PA 17878

Call Sign: WB3DUC
Donald V Boudman
3805 State Rt 487
Stillwater PA 17878

Call Sign: KB3OQO
Donald B Yarmul
60 Valley View Rd
Stillwater PA 17878

FCC Amateur Radio Licenses in Stoystown

Call Sign: KB1IXM
Candy L Couture
163 1st St
Stoystown PA 15563

Call Sign: KB1IXN

Daniel V Couture
163 1st St
Stoystown PA 15563

Call Sign: W3IXN
Daniel V Couture
163 1st St
Stoystown PA 15563

Call Sign: K3DKQ
Robert S Shaver
127 E Main St
Stoystown PA 15563

Call Sign: KB3JJK
John W Farkosh Jr
257 Folly Ln
Stoystown PA 15563

Call Sign: N3LZV
Brian E Leventry
604 Forbes Rd
Stoystown PA 15563

Call Sign: N3EVP
Gary W Valentine
473 Old Forbes Rd
Stoystown PA 15563

Call Sign: KB3MFN
Zachary L Rosenbaum
325 Rosenbaum Rd
Stoystown PA 15563

Call Sign: KB3TUP
Scott A Raszewski
116 Two Cylinder Ln
Stoystown PA 15563

Call Sign: K9RAS
Scott A Raszewski
116 Two Cylinder Ln
Stoystown PA 15563

Call Sign: WB3KNY

Nathan B Zimmerman
Stoystown PA 15563

**FCC Amateur Radio
Licenses in Strasburg**

Call Sign: AA2OE
Randall W Pearson
410 Canterbury Pl
Strasburg PA 175791027

Call Sign: N2VNX
Shirley J Pearson
410 Canterbury Pl
Strasburg PA 175791027

Call Sign: KB3DNU
Kristine E Shirk
210 Dallas Ave
Strasburg PA 17579

Call Sign: KB3FXU
Samuel R Bailey III
44 Denlinger Ave
Strasburg PA 17579

Call Sign: KB3IMO
Karen D Bailey
44 Denlinger Ave
Strasburg PA 17579

Call Sign: KB3IGM
Mark E Naudain
242 Julia Ave
Strasburg PA 17579

Call Sign: K3SXC
Robert A Kryder
952 May Post Office Rd
Strasburg PA 17579

Call Sign: KB3DWL
Robert M Gaynor
312 Miller St
Strasburg PA 17579

Call Sign: KB4YAL
John F Bush
321 Mindy Ave
Strasburg PA 17579

Call Sign: WB3BWF
John M Raub
234 N Fulton St
Strasburg PA 17579

Call Sign: K3JMR
John M Raub
234 N Fulton St
Strasburg PA 17579

Call Sign: KB3OWF
Edward C Albright
237 N Fulton St
Strasburg PA 17579

Call Sign: KA3DJJ
Floyd I Zook
245 N Fulton St
Strasburg PA 17579

Call Sign: K3KVM
Ralph D Lockard
322 W Sunset Ave
Strasburg PA 17579

Call Sign: KB3WOC
John R Schein
112 Washington St
Strasburg PA 17579

Call Sign: WA3UJM
George J Dierking
115 Washington St
Strasburg PA 17579

Call Sign: KA3SUL
Susan M Shaw
110 Wilton Dr
Strasburg PA 17579

Call Sign: KD3CN
Karl A Schoenknecht
110 Wilton Dr
Strasburg PA 17579

**FCC Amateur Radio
Licenses in Sugarloaf**

Call Sign: WB3BAW
Mary B Schatz
Box 62
Sugarloaf PA 18249

Call Sign: WA3GWY
Richard L Schatz
Box 69
Sugarloaf PA 18249

Call Sign: WB3CNZ
Sandra L Schatz
Box 69
Sugarloaf PA 18249

Call Sign: WB3AVF
Richard C Ague
Box 710
Sugarloaf PA 18249

Call Sign: KB3KIH
Christopher R Pollard
Box 718
Sugarloaf PA 18249

Call Sign: KA3WXX
David J De Martino
Box 85
Sugarloaf PA 18249

Call Sign: W2LHS
Anton G Frey
37 Center Hill Rd
Sugarloaf PA 18249

Call Sign: KB2SBX

Frank S Podlaski
130 Kraska Rd
Sugarloaf PA 18249

Call Sign: N3NAX
Thomas W Vernasco
15 Lakeview Trl
Sugarloaf PA 18249

Call Sign: K3MDC
Alfred L Senape
153 Mountain Rd
Sugarloaf PA 18249

Call Sign: N3PFV
James J Poncheri
60 Prospect Rd
Sugarloaf PA 18249

Call Sign: KA3GTB
Bernard C Dill
100 Prospect Rd
Sugarloaf PA 18249

Call Sign: WB3CNY
Jack F Schatz
Rd 1
Sugarloaf PA 18249

Call Sign: N3CDE
William D Shellhamer
108 Sidehille Ct
Sugarloaf PA 18249

Call Sign: WB3AOR
Raymond S Beishline
10 Spruce Ln
Sugarloaf PA 18249

Call Sign: KB3FGY
Andrew D Wesner
Sugarloaf PA 18249

FCC Amateur Radio Licenses in Summerdale

Call Sign: N3NUC
Richard L Keammerer
303 5th St
Summerdale PA 17093

Call Sign: N3JRS
Wilhelm H Mabius
7 Americana Ln
Summerdale PA 17093

Call Sign: N3JRP
Cathy H Mabius
7 Americana Ln
Summerdale PA
170930150

FCC Amateur Radio Licenses in Summerhill

Call Sign: KB3PCQ
Lucas M Mccoy
376 Benshoff Rd
Summerhill PA 15958

Call Sign: KB3AGU
Ronald D Rhoades II
Box 311C
Summerhill PA 15958

Call Sign: N3PUC
Mark A Snyder
2158 Fieldstone Ave
Summerhill PA 15958

Call Sign: N3UHH
David P Hersh
Summerhill PA 15958

FCC Amateur Radio Licenses in Sunbury

Call Sign: N3VDP
George P Machesic
130 Bainbridge St

Sunbury PA 178013309

Call Sign: WB3HCO
David J Patrick
Box 193A1
Sunbury PA 17801

Call Sign: N3HHP
Lynd A Gemberling Jr
Box 315A
Sunbury PA 17801

Call Sign: W3ZIG
Dennis F Ziegenfuss
Box 374
Sunbury PA 17801

Call Sign: W3NDB
John W Keller Jr
Box 453
Sunbury PA 17801

Call Sign: WB3KCW
Central Penna ARC
Box 509
Sunbury PA 17801

Call Sign: KA3THG
Adam R Klock
220 Broadway St
Sunbury PA 17801

Call Sign: KB3AJZ
Dave L Groat
67 Catawissa Ave
Sunbury PA 17801

Call Sign: WE4ME
Clarence E Badman
144 Catawissa Ave
Sunbury PA 17801

Call Sign: N3QDH
Marcie A Giesen
128 Chestnut St

Sunbury PA 17801

Sunbury PA 17801

Sunbury PA 17801

Call Sign: W3FZ
Fritz A Giesen
128 Chestnut St
Sunbury PA 17801

Call Sign: N3FLI
Daniel W Snyder
420 Grant St
Sunbury PA 17801

Call Sign: W3JJL
John J Lamb
666 N 5th St
Sunbury PA 17801

Call Sign: N3JS
John E Swank Sr
725 Chestnut St Apt 1204
Sunbury PA 17801

Call Sign: KA3SGH
James K Osman
955 Greenough St
Sunbury PA 17801

Call Sign: KB3KAW
Lynn V Bellve
666 N 5th St
Sunbury PA 17801

Call Sign: KB3MSS
Jason M Griffin Sr
244 Church St
Sunbury PA 17801

Call Sign: N3HHN
Bradley T Miller
262 Larch Rd
Sunbury PA 17801

Call Sign: N3LYN
Lynn V Bellve
666 N 5th St
Sunbury PA 17801

Call Sign: KB3NGA
Jason M Griffin Sr
244 Church St
Sunbury PA 17801

Call Sign: N3SLG
Maureen M Miller
262 Larch Rd
Sunbury PA 17801

Call Sign: N3PBK
Frank A Metzger
840 N 6th St
Sunbury PA 17801

Call Sign: NB3K
Jason M Griffin Sr
244 Church St
Sunbury PA 17801

Call Sign: KB3SZQ
Christopher D Feaster
1301 Market St Apt 2
Sunbury PA 17801

Call Sign: N3GER
Robert A Kerlin
37 N 8th St
Sunbury PA 17801

Call Sign: K3RIT
Donald F Sorber
240 Corcyra Rd
Sunbury PA 17801

Call Sign: K3ARR
William M Beck Jr
913 Masser St
Sunbury PA 178011519

Call Sign: N3IJE
David A Ney
122 N Front St
Sunbury PA 17801

Call Sign: AA3QZ
Patricia L Franklin
1000.5 E Chestnut St
Sunbury PA 17801

Call Sign: KB3DZL
Randy L Moyer
1064 Masser St
Sunbury PA 178011658

Call Sign: KB3UUF
Robert L Dunkle
137 N River Ave
Sunbury PA 17801

Call Sign: KA3JUV
Patricia H Haines
104 Fairmont Ave
Sunbury PA 17801

Call Sign: AB3AX
Gordon T Lamb
241 N 12th St
Sunbury PA 17801

Call Sign: K2SGF
John G Labosky
665 Park Dr
Sunbury PA 17801

Call Sign: KB3CRT
Robert K Parker
140 Fairmount Ave

Call Sign: WA3ONH
Robert A Reitz
218 N 4th St

Call Sign: N3VTE
John M Mailleue Jr
Rd 1

Sunbury PA 17801

Call Sign: KC3NO
Dennis F Ziegenfuss
Rd 2
Sunbury PA 17801

Call Sign: KA3ZXT
William A Moyer
608 Reagan St
Sunbury PA 17801

Call Sign: KB3WAU
Charles J Shrader
825 Reagan St
Sunbury PA 17801

Call Sign: K3SI
David A Welker
229 Ridge Ave
Sunbury PA 17801

Call Sign: KB3WON
Douglas E Fessler
300 Ridge Ave
Sunbury PA 17801

Call Sign: KB3IEE
James M Kauffman
227 S 10th St
Sunbury PA 17801

Call Sign: K3IEM
Robert B Fetter
130 S Front St Apt 1512
Sunbury PA 17801

Call Sign: W3RGA
Patrick C Moyer
3423 Snydertown Rd
Sunbury PA 17801

Call Sign: KB3LFP
Barry E Lewis
162 South St

Sunbury PA 17801

Call Sign: N3HLM
Michael C Migliaccio
1942 State Rt 61
Sunbury PA 178016521

Call Sign: WA3KFO
John P Glass
920 Susquehanna Ave
Sunbury PA 17801

Call Sign: K3TRK
Dale R Hane
110 Union St
Sunbury PA 17801

Call Sign: KC3BY
Gerald A Dowd
207 Union St
Sunbury PA 17801

Call Sign: AA3DS
Robert E Groat
Sunbury PA 17801

FCC Amateur Radio Licenses in Swatara

Call Sign: W3JWP
Lantz A Hoffman
1041 Pennsylvania Ave
Swatara PA 17111

Call Sign: W3KBR
Donald A Klingler
801 S 60th St
Swatara PA 17111

FCC Amateur Radio Licenses in Talmage

Call Sign: N3OLU
Steven W Plasko
Elizabeth Ave

Talmage PA 17580

FCC Amateur Radio Licenses in Terre Hill

Call Sign: NK3O
Jeffrey L Zell
302 Park Cir
Terre Hill PA 17581

Call Sign: N3FOO
Andrew D Dornes
Terre Hill PA 175810009

FCC Amateur Radio Licenses in Thomasville

Call Sign: KA3UDY
Catherine V Wagner
Box 212P
Thomasville PA 17364

Call Sign: N3QWM
Timothy R Serrano
Box 212P
Thomasville PA 17364

Call Sign: KA3UBZ
Teresa L Fahs
Box 250K
Thomasville PA 17364

Call Sign: K3YCT
Gerald L Zeigler
43 Cedar Ln
Thomasville PA 17364

Call Sign: WS3C
Michael H Sullivan Sr
4939 E Berlin Rd
Thomasville PA
173649326

Call Sign: N3TJB
David C Wood

Emig School Rd
Thomasville PA 17364

Call Sign: KB3VVH
Lance A Biesecker
6854 Lincoln Hwy
Thomasville PA 17364

Call Sign: N3TUN
Wendell G Martin
939 Meeting House Rd
Thomasville PA 17364

Call Sign: KB3GTS
Bryce C Warner
8140 Orchard Rd
Thomasville PA 17364

Call Sign: KB3VVA
Robert W Nivens
6883 Pleasant View Dr
Thomasville PA 17364

Call Sign: KB3VUX
Babette J Schuchart
7528 Ruth Farm Ln
Thomasville PA 17364

Call Sign: KB3SSV
Barry L Schuchart
7528 Ruth Farm Ln
Thomasville PA 17364

Call Sign: KB3OER
Thomasville Amateur
Radio
Thomasville PA 17364

FCC Amateur Radio Licenses in Thompsontown

Call Sign: WB3IPQ
Nancy L Walters
Box 154

Thompsontown PA 17094

Call Sign: WB3IQJ
Donald C Walters
Box 154
Thompsontown PA 17094

Call Sign: KA3TIO
Michael J Walters
Box 158
Thompsontown PA 17094

Call Sign: KA3ICA
Karen L Barnes
Box 2B
Thompsontown PA 17094

Call Sign: KB3THS
G Tyler Supplee
2503 Jonestown Rd
Thompsontown PA 17094

Call Sign: K3AKN
Wayne L Leiter
6 Pine St
Thompsontown PA
170940171

Call Sign: WA3DEM
Samuel R Helwig
12 S Mill St
Thompsontown PA 17094

FCC Amateur Radio Licenses in Three Springs

Call Sign: N3SZA
Denny R Cohenour
Ashman St
Three Springs PA 17264

Call Sign: N3BXS
Emile A De Camp
Box 1096

Three Springs PA 17264

Call Sign: K3QMY
John S Stains
Box 1456
Three Springs PA 17264

Call Sign: KD3ES
Charles J Stains
Box 1456
Three Springs PA
172649801

Call Sign: N3YSL
Michael D Boozel
Box 1641
Three Springs PA 17264

Call Sign: N3YZB
Tyrel A Greenland
Box 2946
Three Springs PA 17264

Call Sign: N3QFV
Larry W Stains
Box 336
Three Springs PA 17264

Call Sign: WB3JIY
Charles T Fields
Box 456
Three Springs PA 17264

Call Sign: WB3CZW
James E Benson
20826 Church St
Three Springs PA 17264

Call Sign: KA3AAC
Norma J Fields
20100 Sugar Grove Rd
Three Springs PA 17264

Call Sign: WC3F
Charles T Fields

20100 Sugar Grove Rd
Three Springs PA 17264

Call Sign: KB3VNI
Rocco Panosetti Jr
18454 Yankee Dr
Three Springs PA 17264

Call Sign: WA3YMH
Louis A Mamakos
Three Springs PA
172640264

FCC Amateur Radio Licenses in Tioga

Call Sign: K3UZY
Anthony J Maggitti
Box 120A
Tioga PA 16946

Call Sign: N3VAA
Jeffrey J Wilson
Box 124B
Tioga PA 16946

Call Sign: N3VQQ
Donna M Wilson
Box 124B
Tioga PA 169469754

Call Sign: WB3DEU
Dam Operators At
Cowanesque Dm
Box 65 Cowanesque Lk
Tioga PA 16946

Call Sign: WA3SFP
Dam Operators Tioga
Hammond Dm
Box 65 Tioga Hammond
Lks Engrs
Tioga PA 16946

Call Sign: N3TKY

Timothy A Pelton
143 Cole Rd
Tioga PA 16946

Call Sign: K3KGW
George W Wheeler
15 Crooked Creek Est Rd
Tioga PA 16946

Call Sign: K3WJV
William P Stravinsky Jr
60 Deer Ln Lot 39
Tioga PA 16946

Call Sign: KD3KP
Jeffrey G Lynn
21 Summit St
Tioga PA 16946

Call Sign: N3WNM
D Esta C Farr
Tioga PA 16946

FCC Amateur Radio Licenses in Tipton

Call Sign: N3LZM
Todd W Plummer
Tipton PA 16684

FCC Amateur Radio Licenses in Tire Hill

Call Sign: N3DAD
David J Horvath
Tire Hill PA 15959

Call Sign: KB3NLT
Nathaniel T Simonton
Tire Hill PA 15959

FCC Amateur Radio Licenses in Todd

Call Sign: N3YZE

David H Theys
Box 20D
Todd PA 16685

Call Sign: N3YZG
Marlene K Theys
Box 20D
Todd PA 16685

FCC Amateur Radio Licenses in Trevorton

Call Sign: N3TQL
Pamela K Schieber
220 10th St
Trevorton PA 17881

Call Sign: N3ZQK
Howard J Miller
277 E Market St
Trevorton PA 18818

Call Sign: N3SIA
James L Thorpe
220 S 10th St
Trevorton PA 17881

FCC Amateur Radio Licenses in Trout Run

Call Sign: KB3WRQ
Greg S Brown
2000 Murray Run Rd
Trout Run PA 17771

Call Sign: KB3OXJ
Paul F Calvert
914 Old Cemetary Rd
Trout Run PA 17771

Call Sign: W3PFC
Paul F Calvert
914 Old Cemetery Rd
Trout Run PA 17771

Call Sign: N3RJX
Clair W Matter
5752 Rose Valley Rd
Trout Run PA 177718985

Call Sign: KB3PIU
Robert J Howard
12626 Rose Valley Rd
Trout Run PA 177718552

Call Sign: KB3ETF
James E Temple
Trout Run PA 17771

FCC Amateur Radio Licenses in Troutville

Call Sign: KA3BAU
David B Swauger
Troutville PA 15866

Call Sign: KA3WSX
James F Byrne
Troutville PA 15866

FCC Amateur Radio Licenses in Turborville

Call Sign: KB3UHM
Derek T Applegate
248 Broadway St
Turbotville PA 17772

Call Sign: KD6SIO
Robert W Vitolo
355 Pleasant View Ests
Turbotville PA 177729711

Call Sign: WB3BNY
Kenneth L Balliet
515 Warrior Run Blvd
Turbotville PA 17772

FCC Amateur Radio Licenses in Twin Rocks

Call Sign: KB3DJQ
Thomas S Wixner
138 Park Ln
Twin Rocks PA 15960

FCC Amateur Radio Licenses in Tyrone

Call Sign: KB3DRI
Donna L Glunt
508 3rd St
Tyrone PA 16686

Call Sign: KC3XO
Paul W Glunt
508 3rd St
Tyrone PA 16686

Call Sign: KA3KBE
Carol R Cupper
Box 115
Tyrone PA 16686

Call Sign: W3TEO
Jack B Cupper
Box 115
Tyrone PA 16686

Call Sign: WB3DRL
Terry L Alley
Box 146
Tyrone PA 16686

Call Sign: K3FGL
James A Young
Box 161
Tyrone PA 16686

Call Sign: KE3XC
Vaughn R Imler
Box 170
Tyrone PA 16686

Call Sign: N3ZVT

Gerald S Wagner Jr
Box 313
Tyrone PA 16686

Call Sign: KB3OIJ
Matthew J Lehner
Box 32
Tyrone PA 16686

Call Sign: KB3OII
Don E Stewart
Box 347
Tyrone PA 16686

Call Sign: N3LAR
Grant W Gordon
Box 39A
Tyrone PA 16686

Call Sign: KA3VWD
Ray L Rumbarger
Box 434
Tyrone PA 16686

Call Sign: N3YPY
Terry L Hribik
Box 468B
Tyrone PA 16686

Call Sign: K6RDQ
Oliver G Langer
Box 518
Tyrone PA 16686

Call Sign: KA3KXT
Daniel O Yonkin
Box 521
Tyrone PA 16686

Call Sign: WO3U
Wade L Laird
Box 605A Stetter Rd
Tyrone PA 16686

Call Sign: K4MI

Jack E Kear
Box 612 Bell Tip Rd
Tyrone PA 166869805

Call Sign: KB3PSF
George L Wertman
Box 82
Tyrone PA 16686

Call Sign: K3LZR
Wilbur F Walk Jr
Box 91
Tyrone PA 16686

Call Sign: N3MON
Edward J Hribik Jr
1697 Decker Hollow Rd
Tyrone PA 16686

Call Sign: KB3GUR
Charles E Noble
4602 E Pleasant Vly Blvd
Tyrone PA 166867033

Call Sign: WF3B
Donald L Myers
822 General Jones Dr
Tyrone PA 16686

Call Sign: N3JXU
Carol A Troxell
112 N 12th St
Tyrone PA 16686

Call Sign: KA3FKK
Jerry L Troxell
112 N 12th St Rd 2
Tyrone PA 16686

Call Sign: N3LZO
Robert H Schmittle
752 N Douglass Ln
Tyrone PA 16686

Call Sign: N3IBQ

Robert E Stroup
1362 Pa Ave Apt 2
Tyrone PA 16686

Call Sign: KB3FAX
Sean M Bietz
13604 S Eagle Valley Rd
Tyrone PA 16686

Call Sign: N3JYA
Alois H Poppenwimer
1721 Stetter Rd
Tyrone PA 16686

Call Sign: W4IXL
Randall D Atchison
8 Stewart St Rear
Tyrone PA 16686

Call Sign: KB9OCQ
Dale E Catron
831 Teaberry St
Tyrone PA 16686

Call Sign: AB2FH
Mathew R Palmonka
5903 Tyrone Pike
Tyrone PA 166869433

Call Sign: AB3DB
Mathew R Palmonka
5903 Tyrone Pike
Tyrone PA 166869433

Call Sign: N3IOW
David J Snyder Sr
704 W 15th St
Tyrone PA 16686

Call Sign: W3AOL
Norman L Swayne
815 W 15th St
Tyrone PA 16686

Call Sign: KB3GGB

Michael L Fink
Tyrone PA 166860305

FCC Amateur Radio Licenses in Ulysses

Call Sign: K3MOE
David E Weiss
271 Center & Main
Ulysses PA 16948

Call Sign: N3MZS
Bradley D Carlin
390 Hardscabble Rd
Ulysses PA 16948

Call Sign: KB3GQM
Fay E Wood
420 Main St
Ulysses PA 16948

FCC Amateur Radio Licenses in Unionville

Call Sign: KA3QJJ
Helen E Martin
302 Lamborntown Rd
Unionville PA 19375

Call Sign: K3BRF
Charles W Stewart
Unionville PA 19375

Call Sign: K3JJG
Edward J Chance
Unionville PA 19375

Call Sign: K3YJA
Franklin R Knox Jr
Unionville PA 19375

Call Sign: KA3STH
Susan E Scimeca
Unionville PA 19375

Call Sign: KA3TRI
Russell E Gibson
Unionville PA 19375

FCC Amateur Radio Licenses in Unityville

Call Sign: N2EZR
Bernard C Kocher
Box 562
Unityville PA 17774

Call Sign: N3VTG
Scott A Lawuere
Unityville PA 17774

FCC Amateur Radio Licenses in University Park

Call Sign: KB3FAT
Ashok N Hariharan
144 Atherton Hall
University Park PA 16802

Call Sign: KB3RTM
Ye Gu Kang
329 Atherton Hall
University Park PA 16802

Call Sign: KB3UCM
Abdulaziz B Aldamanhori
Beam Hall
University Park PA 16802

Call Sign: KB3UCQ
Motheeb M Alkhashram
Beam Hall N Halls
University Park PA 16802

Call Sign: KB3SOF
Xiaoli Guo
734 Beaver Hall
University Park PA 16802

Call Sign: KB3VRX
James J Mayeski
815 Beaver Hall
University Park PA 16802

Call Sign: KB3JEA
Michael A Newman
Beaver Hall
University Park PA 16802

Call Sign: KB3VXL
James P Ambrose
912 Brumbaugh Hall
University Park PA 16802

Call Sign: KB3NDM
Muhammad K Arif
703 Geary Hall
University Park PA 16802

Call Sign: KB3KVM
Dikshant P Desai
506 Geary Halls E Halls
University Park PA 16802

Call Sign: KB3RAF
Satoshi Kawana
Hamilton Hall
University Park PA 16802

Call Sign: KB3YIJ
Tianyi Chen
212 Hartranft Hall Pollock
University Park PA 16802

Call Sign: K3CR
Penn State ARC
Hub Activities Desk
University Park PA 16802

Call Sign: KB3FOH
Jmaes C Perlingiero
304 Jordan Hall
University Park PA 16802

Call Sign: KA3TTP
Donald J Szczur
312 Jordon Hall
University Park PA 16802

Call Sign: KB3VRY
Tj Rumbaugh
107 Lyons Hall
University Park PA 16802

Call Sign: KB3SIW
Azri Azhar
56 McElwain Hall
University Park PA 16802

Call Sign: KB3SJA
Xiangyan Kong
135 McElwain Hall
University Park PA 16802

Call Sign: KB3FOM
Stephen J Driscoll II
114 McKean Hall
University Park PA 16802

Call Sign: KB3HQP
Joel T Shibata
310 McKean Hall E Halls
University Park PA 16802

Call Sign: KB3KVP
Abhijeet Agarwal
312 McKee Hall
University Park PA 16802

Call Sign: KB3GDR
Daniel M Logue
502 Packer Hall
University Park PA 16802

Call Sign: KB3JEC
Yoonseon Yang
Pennypacker Easthalls
Penn State U
University Park PA 16802

Call Sign: KB3RAP
Vishal H Patel
612 Pennypacker Hall
University Park PA 16802

Call Sign: KB3JEB
Seok Woo Choi
Pinchot Easthalls
University Park PA 16802

Call Sign: KB3GDO
Sean A Benson
409 Pinchot Hall
University Park PA 16802

Call Sign: KB3GDL
Abel E Astley
809 Pinchot Hall
University Park PA 16802

Call Sign: KB3GDP
Andre Vieira
1004 Pinchot Hall
University Park PA 16802

Call Sign: KB3SOC
Ibrahim M Al Mulhim
Runkle Hall
University Park PA 16802

Call Sign: KB3VXM
Boyuan Ding
504 Shunk Hall
University Park PA 16802

Call Sign: KB3JDZ
Ho Kei So
Shunk Hall
University Park PA
168022090

Call Sign: KB3OTO
Pratik Bang
418 Shunkh Pollock Halls

University Park PA 16802

Call Sign: KB3FOC
Michael A Carter
140 Simmons Halls S
Halls
University Park PA 16802

Call Sign: KB3VRV
Akash Duseja
321 Snyder Hall E Halls
University Park PA 16802

Call Sign: KB3HQQ
Srimath S Subasinghe
510 Stuart Hall E Halls
University Park PA 16802

Call Sign: KB3YIE
Anant Koul
103 Stuat Hall
University Park PA 16802

Call Sign: KB3FOQ
Yashar D Fakhari
706 Tener Hall
University Park PA 16802

FCC Amateur Radio Licenses in Upper Straburg

Call Sign: WA3JKC
Dennis W Urban
11855 Lower Horse Valley
Rd
Upper Strasburg PA 17265

FCC Amateur Radio Licenses in Ursina

Call Sign: KA3CXR
Paul A Woods
Ursina PA 15485

FCC Amateur Radio Licenses in Vintondale

Call Sign: W3VXK
Joseph A Anderson Sr
127 6th St
Vintondale PA 15961

Call Sign: KB3NMB
Ryan S Bailey
2854 Barkley Church Rd
Vintondale PA 15961

Call Sign: W3VIS
Wilbert L Misner
Box 195
Vintondale PA 15961

Call Sign: N3TLP
Adam L Stiffler
90 Main St
Vintondale PA 15961

Call Sign: N3XHE
Bonnie M Lucas
858 Main St
Vintondale PA 15961

Call Sign: KA3MZE
Edward S Lucas
858 Main St
Vintondale PA 15961

FCC Amateur Radio Licenses in Wallaceton

Call Sign: K3LYJ
Marshal L Shaw
Reed St
Wallaceton PA 16876

FCC Amateur Radio Licenses in Walnut Bottom

Call Sign: KB3DCU
Billy J Norman
18 Maple Ave
Walnut Bottom PA 17266

Call Sign: WA3KCP
John R Luthy
60 Water St
Walnut Bottom PA 17266

Call Sign: N3BVQ
Heung J Kil
Walnut Bottom PA 17266

FCC Amateur Radio Licenses in Warfordsburg

Call Sign: WT3G
Loran R Bittman
Box 785
Warfordsburg PA 17267

Call Sign: KD3QG
George J Farndell
Box 785
Warfordsburg PA
172679736

Call Sign: N3XJL
Richard G Sauter
15156 Buckvalley Rd Apt
2
Warfordsburg PA 17267

Call Sign: KD4SD
Robert E Hendershot
556 Fairview Rd
Warfordsburg PA
172678189

Call Sign: AA3CY
Michael L Spinoe
1558 Stoneybreak Rd
Warfordsburg PA 17267

Call Sign: N3LJN
Patricia M Spinoe
1558 Stoneybreak Rd
Warfordsburg PA 17267

Call Sign: N3ULB
Greg E Barry
Warfordsburg PA 17267

Call Sign: W3KGO
Greg E Barry
Warfordsburg PA 17267

FCC Amateur Radio Licenses in Warriors Mark

Call Sign: AA3YP
James H Rayburn
1812 Centre Line Rd
Warriors Mark PA 16877

Call Sign: W3JIM
James H Rayburn
1812 Centre Line Rd
Warriors Mark PA 16877

Call Sign: WN1G
Linda J Haft
166 Cow View Ln
Warriors Mark PA 16877

Call Sign: K0LO
Mark J Wharton
595 Dry Hollow Rd
Warriors Mark PA
168776030

Call Sign: KB3ESF
John A Rossman
1025 Dry Hollow Rd
Warriors Mark PA 16877

Call Sign: WA3IBO

James M Trostle
1027 Dry Hollow Rd
Warriors Mark PA 16877

Call Sign: K3PCE
William H Long Jr
1516 Marengo Rd
Warriors Mark PA 16877

Call Sign: KB3IVJ
Cathy C Kaltenbaugh
1655 Mtn Laurel Ct
Warriors Mark PA 16877

Call Sign: KD3VO
Bernard V Ward
Warriors Mark PA 16877

Call Sign: K3RDU
John C Swiderski
Warriors Mark PA
168770130

FCC Amateur Radio Licenses in Washington Boro

Call Sign: N3XOZ
Jerald S Fry
2 3rd St
Washington Boro PA
17582

Call Sign: WB3FKM
James J Eshleman
Box 420
Washington Boro PA
17582

Call Sign: KB3CQH
Norman D Welch
2010 Franklin Rd
Washington Boro PA
175829770

Call Sign: KB3CQK
Marilyn K Welch
2010 Franklin Rd
Washington Boro PA
175829770

Call Sign: KB3MTR
Daniel T Reist
2352 Gamber Rd
Washington Boro PA
17582

Call Sign: N3XOW
Clyde K Neal
1802 Hilltop Rd
Washington Boro PA
17582

Call Sign: N3AXI
Charles D Ament
3251 Kauffman Rd
Washington Boro PA
17582

Call Sign: KB3QVU
Thomas R Francis
3036 Miller Rd
Washington Boro PA
17582

Call Sign: K3TRF
Thomas R Francis
3036 Miller Rd
Washington Boro PA
17582

Call Sign: AA3H
Thomas R Francis
3036 Miller Rd
Washington Boro PA
17582

Call Sign: KB3SXN
Gail L Francis
3036 Miller Rd

Washington Boro PA
17582

Call Sign: KA3FSG
Patrick B Douglas
14 Rockfish St
Washington Boro PA
17582

FCC Amateur Radio Licenses in Waterfall

Call Sign: KB3OUK
Shelby L Brant
2540 N Hess Rd
Waterfall PA 16689

Call Sign: K3UNA
Roswell G Ritchey
451 Northwood Dr Box 31
Waterfall PA 16689

FCC Amateur Radio Licenses in Watsontown

Call Sign: KB3NXD
Robert P Hoops
110 Berkeley Dr
Watsontown PA 17777

Call Sign: W3EGL
Robert P Hoops
110 Berkeley Dr
Watsontown PA 17777

Call Sign: KB3NEZ
William J Hoops
110 Berkeley Dr
Watsontown PA 17777

Call Sign: K3WJH
William J Hoops
110 Berkeley Dr
Watsontown PA 17777

Call Sign: W3YFP
Glenn E Starr
Box 304
Watsontown PA 17777

Call Sign: KB3EQN
Robert C Torluccio
3 E 10th St
Watsontown PA 17777

Call Sign: N3CY
Clair E Yeagle
222 E 8th St
Watsontown PA
177771024

Call Sign: KB3PWD
Debra J Mccoy
105 Hickory Grove Rd
Watsontown PA 17777

Call Sign: KB3KGT
Gary E Mccoy
105 Hickory Grove Rd
Watsontown PA 17777

Call Sign: K3GMC
Gary E Mccoy
105 Hickory Grove Rd
Watsontown PA 17777

Call Sign: WL7LN
Carl S Jenkins
315 Main St
Watsontown PA 17777

Call Sign: N1NDE
Norman D Eisley III
142 Main St Apt 3
Watsontown PA 17777

Call Sign: KB3SEQ
Norman D Eisley III
113 Maple Ln
Watsontown PA 17777

Call Sign: N3NPL
Kathy L Stump
42 Pennsylvania Ave
Watsontown PA 17777

Call Sign: KA3HVA
Mary W Wehr
3380 River Rd
Watsontown PA 17777

Call Sign: KB3COF
Randy C Cromley
15280 State Rt 405
Watsontown PA 17777

FCC Amateur Radio Licenses in Waynesboro

Call Sign: KB3WFJ
Francis E Ford Jr
8526 Anthony Hwy
Waynesboro PA 17268

Call Sign: WB3KII
John L Manges
9108 Anthony Hwy
Waynesboro PA 17268

Call Sign: WB3DNE
Joseph A Cluck
329 Antietam Dr
Waynesboro PA 17268

Call Sign: N3UG
Dane R Morris
10655 Bailey Springs Ln
Lot 7
Waynesboro PA 17268

Call Sign: KB3BTI
Franklin J Larson
12142 Bayer Dr
Waynesboro PA 17268

Call Sign: KB3TAA
Anthon H Williamson
12126 Blue Ridge Ct
Waynesboro PA 17268

Call Sign: W3TES
Jesse R Baugher
180 Briar Ridge Dr
Waynesboro PA 17268

Call Sign: WS0U
Anthony L Shaver
11386 Buhrman Dr E
Waynesboro PA 17268

Call Sign: KX3C
Anthony L Shaver
11386 Buhrman Dr E
Waynesboro PA 17268

Call Sign: KB3MIQ
Michael W Glaze
11565 Buhrman Dr W
Waynesboro PA 17268

Call Sign: KB3TAC
Jeffery A Powell
14124 Charles Dr
Waynesboro PA 17268

Call Sign: KB3TAB
Sandra R Simkins
14124 Charles Dr
Waynesboro PA 17268

Call Sign: N1RHK
Martha A Macfarland
433 Clayton Ave
Waynesboro PA
172682017

Call Sign: N1QCE
Willard C Macfarland Jr
433 Clayton Ave

Waynesboro PA
172682017

Call Sign: KE3VM
Curtis B Spessard
315 Cleveland Ave
Waynesboro PA 17268

Call Sign: N3MGM
Helen M Foreman
141 Coquina Sands Dr
Waynesboro PA 17268

Call Sign: W0QPS
C Dale Dermott Jr
11341 Country Club Rd
Waynesboro PA
172689273

Call Sign: N3MPB
Shane N Rouzer
11387 Country Club Rd
Waynesboro PA 17268

Call Sign: KA3ZKV
Eleanore S Shaffer
14020 Crest Ave
Waynesboro PA 17268

Call Sign: N3LCI
Richard G Shaffer
14020 Crest Ave
Waynesboro PA 17268

Call Sign: N3NVU
Michael J Cermak Sr
135 E 2nd St
Waynesboro PA 17268

Call Sign: N3ONY
Sandra L Cermak
135 E 2nd St
Waynesboro PA 17268

Call Sign: N3LWK

Leonard C Boyer
13 E 7th St
Waynesboro PA 17268

Call Sign: WB3FVP
Hughie P Chavis Jr
121 E Main St
Waynesboro PA
172681636

Call Sign: N3SNB
James G Harbaugh
330 Fairmount Ave
Waynesboro PA 17268

Call Sign: AA3QL
Herbert D Greenlee
133 Fairview Ave
Waynesboro PA 17268

Call Sign: N3QHY
Sylvia A Warrenfeltz
200 Fairview Ave
Waynesboro PA 17260

Call Sign: K7GMR
Michael J Rentfrow
200 Fairview Ave
Waynesboro PA
172681931

Call Sign: KB3GMM
John D Morton
316 Fairview Ave
Waynesboro PA 17268

Call Sign: KB3RBO
John A Mcferren
328 Fairview Ave
Waynesboro PA
172681933

Call Sign: KB3PXR
John R Mcferren
328 Fairview Ave

Waynesboro PA
172681933

Call Sign: WB3BXH
Dennis E Bonner
9266 Gap Rd
Waynesboro PA 17268

Call Sign: N3TVE
Hilton K Ernde
9357 Gap Rd
Waynesboro PA
172689265

Call Sign: N0TXU
Ralph D Opitz
225 Geiser Ave
Waynesboro PA 17268

Call Sign: KA3QIN
Edward G Schuit
13183 Grandview Dr
Waynesboro PA 17268

Call Sign: KB3BBT
Joshua L Carter
13297 Grandview Dr
Waynesboro PA 17268

Call Sign: N3NEQ
David A Schuit
13297 Grandview Dr
Waynesboro PA 17268

Call Sign: WA3KUM
William A Hyslop
14096 Harbaugh Church
Rd
Waynesboro PA 17268

Call Sign: W3QI
William A Hyslop
14096 Harbaugh Church
Rd
Waynesboro PA 17268

Call Sign: KB3TBQ
Derek L Noll
9257 Harlee Rd
Waynesboro PA 17268

Call Sign: N3TMJ
Derek L Noll
9257 Harlee Rd
Waynesboro PA 17268

Call Sign: KA3FJN
Harvey E Scott
6177 Iron Bridge Rd
Waynesboro PA 17268

Call Sign: N3KZA
Michael F Foreman
128 Kristyn Ct
Waynesboro PA 17268

Call Sign: K1ZJF
Ralph D Pryor
14057 Lower Edgemont
Rd
Waynesboro PA 17268

Call Sign: N1RAT
Leonard E Manson
Main St Apt 19
Waynesboro PA 17268

Call Sign: N3LTQ
Milton C Engle
5765 Manheim Rd
Waynesboro PA 17268

Call Sign: K3LN
Ellen J Engle
5765 Manheim Rd
Waynesboro PA 17268

Call Sign: KA3NJJ
Charles A Davis Jr
519 Maple St

Waynesboro PA 17268

Call Sign: N3TGV
Mary A Davis
519 Maple St
Waynesboro PA 17268

Call Sign: KF3BX
Anton M Giroux
14061 Mar Penn Ave
Waynesboro PA 17268

Call Sign: KA3LJW
Darrell L Zeger
6365 Marsh Rd
Waynesboro PA
172689565

Call Sign: N2HBR
Fred A Bennett
6629 Marsh St
Waynesboro PA 17268

Call Sign: K3JLG
Bruce Francis
9365 Meadowbrook Dr
Waynesboro PA
172689206

Call Sign: WA3MXG
George B Newcomer
13384 Meadowview Ave
Waynesboro PA 17268

Call Sign: N3FAS
Norman L Walker
7603 Mentzer Gap Rd
Waynesboro PA 17268

Call Sign: NN3AS
Norman L Walker
7603 Mentzer Gap Rd
Waynesboro PA 17268

Call Sign: KB3FGH

Gary A Baker
12863 Mentzer Gap Rd
Waynesboro PA
172689326

Call Sign: WD3W
Gary A Baker
12863 Mentzer Gap Rd
Waynesboro PA
172689326

Call Sign: W3OG
Gary A Baker
12863 Mentzer Gap Rd
Waynesboro PA
172689326

Call Sign: KD4SAV
Maureen J Rosenberry
10436 Monta Vista Dr
Waynesboro PA 17268

Call Sign: N3VZY
Linda C Nalley
10469 Monta Vista Dr
Waynesboro PA 17268

Call Sign: KB3GPG
Beverly A Spicer
252 Mt Airy Ave
Waynesboro PA 17268

Call Sign: N3KYV
Jack W Spicer
252 Mt Airy Ave
Waynesboro PA
172681321

Call Sign: KB3TUE
Brendon A Craig
100 N Church St
Waynesboro PA 17268

Call Sign: KB3GMJ
Miguel A Zurita

304 N Franklin St 2nd Fl
Waynesboro PA 17268

Call Sign: N3HEX
William H Moore
11411 N Garfield St Ext
Waynesboro PA 17268

Call Sign: WA3QHR
Christopher N Snively
238 N Grant St
Waynesboro PA
172681130

Call Sign: KA3KOU
Jon O Newcomer
305 Northfield Ave Rear
Waynesboro PA 17268

Call Sign: W3JFQ
David H Bender
3052 Oak Hill Rd
Waynesboro PA 17268

Call Sign: KB3MYB
James R Salko
11948 Oakton Dr
Waynesboro PA 17268

Call Sign: K3VPJ
James R Salko
11948 Oakton Dr
Waynesboro PA 17268

Call Sign: N3ISU
Michael R Pippenger
11985 Old Forge Rd
Waynesboro PA 17268

Call Sign: KB3KRN
Thomas E Wynkoop
12097 Old Forge Rd
Waynesboro PA 17268

Call Sign: N3VGR

David S Brown
12615 Old Germantown
Rd
Waynesboro PA
172689463

Call Sign: KA3WCE
Donald E Shockey Sr
12210 Old Pen Mar Rd
Waynesboro PA 17268

Call Sign: K3QIF
Harold R Gardenhour Sr
9305 Oyer Ct
Waynesboro PA 17268

Call Sign: KA8WIV
Charles Kennedy
605 Park St
Waynesboro PA 17268

Call Sign: N3TOQ
Matthew S Datcher
610 Park St
Waynesboro PA
172682145

Call Sign: KB3ISH
Eric A Stouffer
13188 Redbud Ct
Waynesboro PA 17268

Call Sign: KB3FHD
Shane G Phillips
141 S Church St
Waynesboro PA 17268

Call Sign: KB3PCB
James M Graham
458 Scott Ave
Waynesboro PA 17268

Call Sign: KB7THL
Michael A Stern
13201 Shawnee Cir

Waynesboro PA 17269

Call Sign: N3YSP
Randall L Sanders
6634 Slabtown Rd
Waynesboro PA
172688912

Call Sign: AA3EX
Reginald A Gossert
6850 Slabtown Rd
Waynesboro PA 17268

Call Sign: KB3COA
Winona Huber
5695 Tick Ridge Rd
Waynesboro PA 17268

Call Sign: N3ZHJ
Kevin J McAllister
338 W 2nd St Apt 2
Waynesboro PA 17268

Call Sign: N3KOF
Amos S Gossard
33 W 6th St
Waynesboro PA 17268

Call Sign: WB3HBC
Edward C Jones
313 W 6th St
Waynesboro PA
172682103

Call Sign: W3VTF
Reginald H Diller
531 W 6th St
Waynesboro PA 17268

Call Sign: WA3CMF
Otis S Brown
11286 Weatherstone Dr
Waynesboro PA 17268

Call Sign: KB3FIE

Christian P Nygard
11645 Woodlea Dr
Waynesboro PA 17268

Call Sign: N3POS
Pedro A Rodriguez
Waynesboro PA 17268

Call Sign: WB3JPZ
Daniel H Hill
Waynesboro PA 17268

FCC Amateur Radio Licenses in Weedville

Call Sign: WB3DCZ
Theodore P Irwin
Gardner Hill Rd Rd 2
Weedville PA 15868

Call Sign: N3FXU
Ricky R Rimer
163 Rita Ln
Weedville PA 15868

Call Sign: N3VFC
Catherine L Rimer
163 Rita Ln
Weedville PA 15868

Call Sign: N3VWS
David R Rimer
163 Rita Ln
Weedville PA 15868

Call Sign: N3ZQZ
Daniel E Rimer
163 Rita Ln
Weedville PA 15868

Call Sign: KB3HZZ
Martin M Mcdonnell
121 Russles Hideaway Rd
Weedville PA 15861

Call Sign: AD2L
Lawrence S Mommicco
14 2nd St
Wellsboro PA 169018155

Call Sign: AA3VK
Walter E Minschwaner Jr
372 Airport Rd
Wellsboro PA 16901

Call Sign: NR3K
Pa Grand Canyon Repeater
Group
66 American St
Wellsboro PA 16901

Call Sign: KA2VSR
Joyce M Howey
66 American St
Wellsboro PA 169011305

Call Sign: WB3DLN
Dale L Howey
66 American St
Wellsboro PA 169011305

Call Sign: N3PDD
Paula A Clemens
2 Antrim St
Wellsboro PA 16901

Call Sign: W4PLO
Ivan E Smith
3 Bacon St
Wellsboro PA 16901

Call Sign: N3ZLJ
James S Monks Jr
10 Bacon St
Wellsboro PA 16901

Call Sign: KB3UIR

Curtis A Werline
43 Bell Rd
Wellsboro PA 16901

Call Sign: K3CVW
Curtis A Werline
43 Bell Rd
Wellsboro PA 16901

Call Sign: N3RSX
John L Pier
31 Bodine St
Wellsboro PA 16901

Call Sign: KA3KUT
Frank L Ellis
Box 104
Wellsboro PA 16901

Call Sign: WB3DKY
Emil J Solotko
Box 116
Wellsboro PA 16901

Call Sign: KA3SWH
Steven G Gastrock
Box 16
Wellsboro PA 16901

Call Sign: WE3M
Stephen E Finestone
Box 167
Wellsboro PA 16901

Call Sign: KE4MNS
Mark T Hitsman
Box 186
Wellsboro PA 16901

Call Sign: KA1QU
Jack E Kissinger
Box 196
Wellsboro PA 169010697

Call Sign: KB3CAM

Tioga County ARC
Box 200
Wellsboro PA 169018972

Call Sign: N3NWF
Robert D Borzok
Box 212
Wellsboro PA 16901

Call Sign: KF3DY
Corey H Dean
Box 220
Wellsboro PA 16901

Call Sign: N3GZW
Corey H Dean
Box 220
Wellsboro PA 16901

Call Sign: KA3SCE
Jennifer G Worthington
Box 236B
Wellsboro PA 16901

Call Sign: W2IXH
William N Plimpton
Box 264
Wellsboro PA 16901

Call Sign: KA3TMY
Jeffrey L Winkler
Box 267
Wellsboro PA 16901

Call Sign: N3RTB
Aaron M Fuhrer
Box 269
Wellsboro PA 16901

Call Sign: KA3BOW
James C Bump
Box 28
Wellsboro PA 16901

Call Sign: N3PDC

Preston L Patterson
Box 301
Wellsboro PA 16901

Call Sign: NQ3O
Boyd W Ferry
Box 310
Wellsboro PA 169019198

Call Sign: N3XJH
John D Bockus
Box 311
Wellsboro PA 16901

Call Sign: KB3EVU
James W Johnson
Box 315
Wellsboro PA 16901

Call Sign: N3ZLK
Edward A Pinchock II
Box 323
Wellsboro PA 16901

Call Sign: KA3SCD
Walter L Reese
Box 338A
Wellsboro PA 16901

Call Sign: N3TKX
William McCoy
Box 456
Wellsboro PA 16901

Call Sign: KB3HQL
Ross E Bellinger
Box 54
Wellsboro PA 16901

Call Sign: N3NAO
John M Carson
Box 61
Wellsboro PA 16901

Call Sign: N3HKH

Harold S Dean
Box 65 Fischler St
Wellsboro PA 16901

Call Sign: N3FVP
Gerald B Crawford
59 Broughton Hollow Rd
Wellsboro PA 16901

Call Sign: N3FVQ
Deborah A Crawford
59 Broughton Hollow Rd
Wellsboro PA 16901

Call Sign: KB3WUU
Pete J Boergermann
98 Buena Vista St
Wellsboro PA 16901

Call Sign: N3ZAE
Raymond J Thomas
68 Central Ave
Wellsboro PA 16901

Call Sign: KA3SCF
Jo Howey Thomas
68 Central Ave
Wellsboro PA 169011817

Call Sign: N3RSZ
David F Boyce
1125 Charleston Rd
Wellsboro PA 16901

Call Sign: N3RYV
Cynthia L Boyce
1125 Charleston Rd
Wellsboro PA 16901

Call Sign: NM3O
Michael D Wilson
1697 Charleston Rd
Wellsboro PA 16901

Call Sign: N3KVT

Richard A Kerestes
27 Conway St
Wellsboro PA 16901

Call Sign: WA3HGD
Carl L Borden
9 D St
Wellsboro PA 16901

Call Sign: N3WFB
Joseph Thomas A Bergen
1952 Deanhill Rd
Wellsboro PA 16901

Call Sign: KB3IED
Thomas M Conte Sr
1314 Dutch Hill Rd
Wellsboro PA 16901

Call Sign: KB3MEL
Elaine M Hemenway
96 Gas Company Rd
Wellsboro PA 16901

Call Sign: KB3VRW
Elaine M Hemenway
96 Gas Company Rd
Wellsboro PA 16901

Call Sign: KB3VJA
Tioga County ARC
96 Gas Company Rd
Wellsboro PA 16901

Call Sign: WB3GPY
Tioga County ARC
96 Gas Company Rd
Wellsboro PA 16901

Call Sign: KA3VRW
Philip E Hemenway
96 Gas Company Rd
Wellsboro PA 16901

Call Sign: WB3GPZ

Douglas B Bowen
138 Gas Company Rd
Wellsboro PA 16901

Call Sign: N3JOS
John R Bair
110 Hickory Nut Ln
Wellsboro PA 16901

Call Sign: N3NGF
Carolyn J Bair
110 Hickory Nut Ln
Wellsboro PA 16901

Call Sign: WB3LBR
Carolyn J Bair
110 Hickory Nut Ln
Wellsboro PA 16901

Call Sign: KK5SS
Robin P Ertl
141 Hills Creek Dr
Wellsboro PA 16901

Call Sign: N3VHA
Charlotte M Ertl
141 Hills Creek Dr
Wellsboro PA 169019607

Call Sign: N3SMS
Raymond H Corse
585 Hills Creek Lake Rd
Wellsboro PA 16901

Call Sign: KA3SAZ
Peter A Ott
29 Ingerick Rd
Wellsboro PA 16901

Call Sign: KE3KI
Robert E Dalton Jr
8 Ives St
Wellsboro PA 16901

Call Sign: KA3SCC

William L Shaw
33 Jackson St
Wellsboro PA 16901

Call Sign: KB3VXF
William A Kilmer Jr
43 Jackson St
Wellsboro PA 16901

Call Sign: N3TQO
Richard McCoy
5 Kelsey St
Wellsboro PA 16901

Call Sign: N3VGU
Kim Weber
5 Kelsey St
Wellsboro PA 16901

Call Sign: N3VGW
Lacey G McCoy
5 Kelsey St
Wellsboro PA 16901

Call Sign: NO3R
John E Wilcox
35 Kelsey St
Wellsboro PA 16901

Call Sign: KB3RDM
Aaron M Fuhrer
18 Maries Ln
Wellsboro PA 16901

Call Sign: N3ZLG
Robert P Fisher
1430 Marsh Creek Rd
Wellsboro PA 16901

Call Sign: K3EMT
Robert B Reilly
8 Morgan Ter
Wellsboro PA 169011803

Call Sign: WB3DKZ

Durwood R Learn
4 Morris Ln
Wellsboro PA 16901

Call Sign: KB3EVT
Jan A Seely
260 Old Tioga St
Wellsboro PA 16901

Call Sign: KB3OUR
Linda A Stager
266 Old Tioga St
Wellsboro PA 16901

Call Sign: KB3OUQ
Lawrence D Stager
266 Old Tioga St
Wellsboro PA 16901

Call Sign: W3QD
Kevin J Hritz
263 Park Rd
Wellsboro PA 169017185

Call Sign: KA3YLC
Robert Mattison
404 Pinnacle Towers
Wellsboro PA 16901

Call Sign: KA3TMX
Kenneth R Watson Sr
3087 Princeton St
Wellsboro PA 169019423

Call Sign: KB3IEC
David C Moore
11 Queen St
Wellsboro PA 16901

Call Sign: N3NXD
Gregory L Root
1226 Rt 362
Wellsboro PA 169017215

Call Sign: KA3MMM

Elwood H Austin
231 Rt 660
Wellsboro PA 16901

Call Sign: KB3BFD
Alex W Borzok
1 Shumway Hill Rd
Wellsboro PA 16901

Call Sign: N3UPJ
Cynthia B Borzok
1 Shumway Hill Rd
Wellsboro PA 16901

Call Sign: N3ZMM
Paul Georg Blickle
1 Shumway Hill Rd
Wellsboro PA 16901

Call Sign: AA3JR
James L Kilduff
1634 Shumway Hill Rd
Wellsboro PA 16901

Call Sign: KB3GST
Brandon J Kilduff
1634 Shumway Hill Rd
Wellsboro PA 16901

Call Sign: N3RTA
Allan L Hammond
473 Shumway Hill Rd
Wellsboro PA 16901

Call Sign: W3UAQ
John J Antonio
36 Skyline Dr
Wellsboro PA 169010101

Call Sign: N3FVK
Lester A English
412 Spring Brook Rd
Wellsboro PA 16901

Call Sign: N3NXT

Michael R Mattison
25 Tioaa St
Wellsboro PA 16901

Call Sign: N3VGV
Patrick S Dexter
54 W Ave
Wellsboro PA 16901

Call Sign: N3JYR
Pamela F Peterson
881 W Hill Rd
Wellsboro PA 16901

Call Sign: WO3C
Darlene L Rahn
34 W Water St
Wellsboro PA 169011015

Call Sign: AA3RD
David L Burge
47 Waln St
Wellsboro PA 16901

Call Sign: N3NXC
David K Shultz
354 Ward Rd
Wellsboro PA 169017424

Call Sign: N3SFG
Jean M Shultz
354 Ward Rd
Wellsboro PA 169017424

Call Sign: KB3NFV
Chad D Shultz
354 Ward St
Wellsboro PA 16901

Call Sign: K3VRP
Donald W Bottomstone
226 Welsh Rd
Wellsboro PA 169016875

Call Sign: K3WKG

Agatha B Bottomstone
226 Welsh Rd
Wellsboro PA 169016875

Call Sign: WB3GPY
John T Winkler
210 Whitneyville Rd
Wellsboro PA 16901

Call Sign: KA3FEW
Melany J Winkler
210 Whitneyville Rd
Wellsboro PA 169017038

Call Sign: KA3WUR
Simon P Shaw
27 Woodland Ave
Wellsboro PA 16901

Call Sign: KB3UBQ
Audrey J Patterson
30 Woodland Ave
Wellsboro PA 16901

Call Sign: N3AJP
Audrey J Patterson
30 Woodland Ave
Wellsboro PA 16901

Call Sign: N3KCM
Jason R Patterson
30 Woodland Ave
Wellsboro PA 169011930

Call Sign: KB3IAG
Sueanne Carson
2017 Yale St
Wellsboro PA 16901

Call Sign: W3BGK
Nessmuck Amateur Radio
Assoc
Wellsboro PA 16901

Call Sign: KA1PRA

Robert P Williams
Wellsboro PA 16901

Call Sign: KA3SAX
William P Miller
Wellsboro PA 16901

Call Sign: N3QNG
Gary A Goodreau
Wellsboro PA 16901

Call Sign: N3SNM
Bertha A Miller
Wellsboro PA 16901

Call Sign: N3UPH
Alexander K Bertram
Wellsboro PA 16901

Call Sign: N3VGZ
Isaac B Shaffer
Wellsboro PA 16901

Call Sign: N1QCM
Heather A Kissinger
Wellsboro PA 169010697

FCC Amateur Radio Licenses in Wellsville

Call Sign: KB3FTE
Reagan C Stoddard
1250 Fickes Rd
Wellsville PA 17365

Call Sign: KF3CU
Michael J Scherden
1745 Pinetown Rd
Wellsville PA 17365

Call Sign: KB3TCM
Joseph J Imgrund
295 Quaker Meeting Rd
Wellsville PA 17365

Call Sign: KB3STT
Mary H Imgrund
295 Quaker Meeting Rd
Wellsville PA 17365

Call Sign: KB3FYL
Frederick M Leader
45 Thundergust Mill Rd
Wellsville PA 17365

Call Sign: W3FML
Frederick M Leader
45 Thundergust Mill Rd
Wellsville PA 17365

Call Sign: KA6ZPD
John B Hundley
810 Zeigler Rd
Wellsville PA 17365

FCC Amateur Radio Licenses in West Becatur

Call Sign: N3ZCP
Matthew Undercofler
1236 Salem Rd
West Decatur PA 16878

Call Sign: N3XTT
James B Undercofler Jr
1236 Salem Rd
West Decatur PA 16878

FCC Amateur Radio Licenses in Westfield

Call Sign: KB3BSM
Daniel C Skinner
Box 322
Westfield PA 16950

Call Sign: N3JCA
Thomas S Davis
Box 470
Westfield PA 16950

Call Sign: N3WOX
Evelyn V Goebel
Box 716
Westfield PA 16950

Call Sign: N3YMP
Douglas C Skinner
333 California Rd
Westfield PA 16950

Call Sign: N3GYR
James D Smith
258 Church St
Westfield PA 16950

Call Sign: KB3CRO
Benjamin M Heyler
626 E Main St
Westfield PA 16950

Call Sign: KB3BRH
Gwen M Heyler
704 E Main St
Westfield PA 16950

Call Sign: K3QEY
Kathryn K Campbell
224 Elm St
Westfield PA 16950

Call Sign: N3XJC
Howard A Nixon Sr
99 Gilbert Rd
Westfield PA 16950

Call Sign: N3XRC
Susan J Nixon
99 Gilbert Rd
Westfield PA 16950

Call Sign: N3XJG
Louise A Jordon
121 Mason St
Westfield PA 16950

Call Sign: N3VYX
Margaret S Willis
121 Mason St
Westfield PA 169501109

Call Sign: KB3WAR
Lee Brooke
337 N Fork Rd
Westfield PA 16950

Call Sign: KB3WAS
Dale L Tubbs
997 N Fork Rd
Westfield PA 16950

Call Sign: KB3JSO
Robert J Mccaslin
185 Potterbrook Rd
Westfield PA 16950

Call Sign: N3UGF
Charles C Goebel
Rd4
Westfield PA 16950

Call Sign: KB3BRT
Cowanesque Valley
School ARC
Rte 49
Westfield PA 16950

Call Sign: N3QNH
Louis C Moon
39 Sr 49
Westfield PA 16950

Call Sign: KB3EVV
Dale E Niles Jr
121 Stevenson St
Westfield PA 16950

Call Sign: KE3JI
Kurt R Heisey
121 Walnut St

Westfield PA 16950

Call Sign: KB3DUK
Michael H Plank
253 Whitaker Rd
Westfield PA 16950

FCC Amateur Radio Licenses in Wiconisco

Call Sign: KR3H
Charles L Dietrich
721 Mountain St
Wiconisco PA 170970147

FCC Amateur Radio Licenses in Wilburton

Call Sign: WA3PCS
Andrew J Yakubik
452 Main St
Wilburton PA 17888

Call Sign: KB3JPJ
Matthew R Price
6 Marion Acres
Wilburton PA 178889702

FCC Amateur Radio Licenses in Wilcox

Call Sign: KB3CQS
Robert J Biel
Box 15A
Wilcox PA 15870

Call Sign: N3NWP
Harold S Dowdle
6434 Glenhazel Rd
Wilcox PA 15870

Call Sign: WB3AIT
Edward C Wickett
121 Hill Rd
Wilcox PA 158709750

Call Sign: KB3UGA
Thomas W Mehalko
514 Horner Rd
Wilcox PA 15870

Call Sign: KB3AQB
David E Krise
378 Old Kane Rd
Wilcox PA 15870

FCC Amateur Radio Licenses in Williamsburg

Call Sign: KB3WDM
Michael A Kauruter
305 Biddle Rd
Williamsburg PA 16693

Call Sign: N3YUR
Rowdy C Kagarise
Box 154 A
Williamsburg PA 16693

Call Sign: N3VJW
Marvin R Anderson
Box 18
Williamsburg PA
166939618

Call Sign: N3YUS
Glenn F Kagarise
Box 201
Williamsburg PA 16693

Call Sign: N3RXM
John R Bollinger
Box 22B
Williamsburg PA 16693

Call Sign: N3JFB
Joanne C Peca
186 High Pt Dr
Williamsburg PA
166937905

Call Sign: WO3T
Carmen J Peca Jr
186 High Pt Dr
Williamsburg PA
166937905

Call Sign: WY3R
Kathleen J Peca
186 High Pt Dr
Williamsburg PA
166937905

Call Sign: KB3ABR
David W Shanholtz
1015 N Plum St
Williamsburg PA 16693

Call Sign: KB3AHC
Julia H Shanholtz
1015 N Plum St
Williamsburg PA 16693

Call Sign: N3DWV
Galen R Reigh
19 Sage Hill Dr
Williamsburg PA 16693

Call Sign: KA3DRN
Chris E Detweiller
838 W 3rd St
Williamsburg PA 16693

Call Sign: NU3T
David S Love
1375 Windy Ridge Dr
Williamsburg PA 16693

**FCC Amateur Radio
Licenses in Williamsport**

Call Sign: KB3FQF
N Clifford Smith Jr
835 1st Ave
Williamsport PA 17701

Call Sign: K3NCS
N Clifford Smith Jr
835 1st Ave
Williamsport PA 17701

Call Sign: W3JBJ
Marshall D Welch Jr
941 1st Ave
Williamsport PA 17701

Call Sign: N3CYW
Donald E King
641 5th Ave
Williamsport PA
177014760

Call Sign: KB3LIN
Robert H Deisenroth
1405 Almond St
Williamsport PA 17701

Call Sign: N3MFO
John C Porcello
1309 Almond St Apt 2
Williamsport PA 17701

Call Sign: KA3JFA
Joseph B Shank
784 Antler Ln
Williamsport PA
177018504

Call Sign: KA3JFB
Angela J Shank
784 Antler Ln
Williamsport PA
177018504

Call Sign: KA3RNL
Elmer S Steppy
306 Arch St
Williamsport PA 17701

Call Sign: AA3FS

James W Diehl
1111 Avalon Pkwy
Williamsport PA 17701

Call Sign: W3LWS
Max V Ritter
1032 Baldwin St
Williamsport PA 17701

Call Sign: N3GGW
Steven M Harder
1024 Beechnut Pky
Williamsport PA 17701

Call Sign: K3EYQ
William G Hamm
2440 Blair St
Williamsport PA 17701

Call Sign: AB4UD
Paul H Thomas
2450 Blair St
Williamsport PA 17701

Call Sign: W3PJO
Paul H Thomas
2450 Blair St
Williamsport PA 17701

Call Sign: KB3FTY
Keenan P Knaur
1750 Bloomingrove Rd
Williamsport PA 17701

Call Sign: N3JDI
Phillip M Cook
Box 227
Williamsport PA 17701

Call Sign: KA3VXI
Jocelyn E Getgen
Box 54
Williamsport PA 17701

Call Sign: KB3CWL

Scott E Bower
Box 625
Williamsport PA 17702

Call Sign: KB3CVF
Greg M Bower
Box 625
Williamsport PA 17702

Call Sign: WB3GPB
James C Fink
2025 Boyd St
Williamsport PA 17701

Call Sign: KD3CR
Daven Kreifeldt
30 Brandon Pl
Williamsport PA 17701

Call Sign: KB3WBC
Janet M Feigles
242 Brandon Pl
Williamsport PA 17701

Call Sign: K3JMF
Janet M Feigles
242 Brandon Pl
Williamsport PA 17701

Call Sign: KB3PIV
Paul F Feigles
242 Brandon Pl
Williamsport PA 17701

Call Sign: K3PFF
Paul F Feigles
242 Brandon Pl
Williamsport PA 17701

Call Sign: KB3FTU
Corey W Gailit
119 Brittany Pkwy
Williamsport PA 17701

Call Sign: N3ZET

Donald H Stahl
1890 Caldwell Ave
Williamsport PA 17701

Call Sign: W3DVX
Alan D Wilcox
1669 Campbell St
Williamsport PA 17701

Call Sign: N3CX
Eric K Albert
1807 Campbell St
Williamsport PA 17701

Call Sign: KB3NNF
Garrett E Schneider
1035 Canterbury Rd
Williamsport PA 17701

Call Sign: KB3AWQ
John W Springman III
672 Cemetery St
Williamsport PA 17701

Call Sign: K3UWJ
Paul J Eck
2108 Central Ave
Williamsport PA 17701

Call Sign: N3RUD
Robert S Markle Jr
409 Chatham Pk
Williamsport PA 17701

Call Sign: W3CDT
Anthony J Stanzione
1639 Chestnut Ave
Williamsport PA 17701

Call Sign: KB3LEY
John J Comerford
1709 Clarion Dr
Williamsport PA 17701

Call Sign: KB3FZL

Foster J Bonnell Jr
401 Clayton Ave
Williamsport PA 17701

Call Sign: W3FJB
Foster J Bonnell Jr
401 Clayton Ave
Williamsport PA 17701

Call Sign: KB3GQX
Zena L Carson
231 Cold Water Town Rd
Williamsport PA 17702

Call Sign: KB3BCK
Stuart T Hague
214 Cottage Ave
Williamsport PA
177011114

Call Sign: N3WYB
Robert W Thomas
1001 Country Club Dr
Williamsport PA 17701

Call Sign: KB3VNP
Robert J Haefner Sr
447 Curtin St
Williamsport PA 17702

Call Sign: KA3UFK
David J Bloom
1905 Devon Rd
Williamsport PA 17701

Call Sign: W3VZB
Floyd L Kendall
1040 Dewey Ave
Williamsport PA 17701

Call Sign: KB3VU
Thomas S Forker
280 Dunkleberger Rd
Williamsport PA 17701

Call Sign: N3MHE
Howard E McGee
1738 E 3rd St
Williamsport PA 17701

Call Sign: WA3MIX
Louis J Kolb
334 E 4th St
Williamsport PA 17701

Call Sign: WB3KRN
Kathy M Kolb
334 E 4th St
Williamsport PA 17701

Call Sign: KB3GOB
Edward T Ploy Jr
2620 E Hills Dr
Williamsport PA 17701

Call Sign: W3WKM
Herman H Hess Jr
135 E Wilcox Rd
Williamsport PA
177018486

Call Sign: KB3PIR
Joshua A Boring
161 East St
Williamsport PA 17701

Call Sign: KB3MVG
Michael J Eck
1035 Elizabeth St
Williamsport PA 17701

Call Sign: WA3QQY
David T Jennings
1510 Elliott St
Williamsport PA
177012626

Call Sign: N3FON
Richard J Lockridge
1400 Elmira St

Williamsport PA 17701

Call Sign: KC3Q
Augustus O Thomas
1608 Elmira St
Williamsport PA 17701

Call Sign: W3NEY
George M Mraz
2320 Fairview Ter
Williamsport PA 17701

Call Sign: N3PDY
A Neale Winner
2360 Fairview Ter
Williamsport PA 17701

Call Sign: KB3PSH
James W Boring
2216 Federal Ave
Williamsport PA 17701

Call Sign: N3JWB
James W Boring
2216 Federal Ave
Williamsport PA 17701

Call Sign: KB3SAM
Thomas J Swigart Sr
819 Franklin St
Williamsport PA 17701

Call Sign: KB3SAO
Samuel W Hessert
306 Glenwood Ave
Williamsport PA 17701

Call Sign: KB3TIJ
Harry D Mintzer
125 Grampian Blvd
Williamsport PA 17701

Call Sign: K3LPX
Martin G Maurer Jr
1410 Grampian Blvd

Williamsport PA 17701

Call Sign: N3QWF
Timothy E Fronk
2525 Grand St
Williamsport PA 17701

Call Sign: N3EYZ
Howard J Lamade Jr
52 Grandview Rd
Williamsport PA 17701

Call Sign: N3KLV
David A Steele
606 Grier St
Williamsport PA 17701

Call Sign: KC3M
John V Preston
1420 Harding Ave
Williamsport PA 17701

Call Sign: N3NUS
Brian S Bidelspach
605 Hawthorne Ave
Williamsport PA 17701

Call Sign: KB3FCN
Brian A Lowmiller
927 Henrietta St
Williamsport PA 17701

Call Sign: KB3SAL
Linda S Utter
1052 Hepburn St
Williamsport PA 17701

Call Sign: KB0AUI
Timothy C Shepherd Jr
1132 Hepburn St
Williamsport PA 17701

Call Sign: KB3NOX
Ashleigh L Caldera
2500 Heshbon Rd

Williamsport PA 17701

Call Sign: W0ZD
Jerry T Booth
25 Hillcrest Ln
Williamsport PA 17701

Call Sign: KB3BEW
Kerri D Shepherd
2128 Hillside Ave
Williamsport PA 17701

Call Sign: W2DUC
Frederick B Cupp
1834 Homewood Ave
Williamsport PA
177013935

Call Sign: WA3THB
David B Strickler
27 Hoover Rd
Williamsport PA 17701

Call Sign: N7QCX
William D Haggerty
1050 Isabella St
Williamsport PA 17701

Call Sign: N3ZST
Bruce L Bower
4121 Jacks Hollow Rd
Williamsport PA
177028441

Call Sign: WB3EKV
James L Pfirman
389 Johnson Dr
Williamsport PA 17701

Call Sign: W3TO
James L Pfirman
389 Johnson Dr
Williamsport PA 17701

Call Sign: AA3MI

Michael J Pars
2350 Kenwood Ave
Williamsport PA 17701

Call Sign: KB3FCK
Keith T Bair
1932 Lacomic St
Williamsport PA
177011546

Call Sign: KB3FTW
Craig A Waltman
2863 Leona Ln
Williamsport PA 17701

Call Sign: K3PMY
Michael R McDowell
810 Leuisa St
Williamsport PA 17701

Call Sign: WA0UMB
Philinda H Snethen
1810 Liberty Dr
Williamsport PA 17701

Call Sign: KB3YAF
Thomas C Mahoney
247 Lincoln Ave
Williamsport PA 17701

Call Sign: K3KAA
Thomas C Mahoney
247 Lincoln Ave
Williamsport PA 17701

Call Sign: W3NMK
William T Colville III
2148 Lincoln Dr
Williamsport PA 17701

Call Sign: KB3SAN
David R Wright
2339 Linn St
Williamsport PA 17701

Call Sign: W3TOG
Angelo L Martinozzi
2700 Linn St
Williamsport PA 17701

Call Sign: KB3ITD
Daniel L Young
626 Livermore Rd
Williamsport PA 17701

Call Sign: N3GKQ
Jason R McBride
10 Longview Dr
Williamsport PA 17701

Call Sign: W3ILG
Paul D McBride
10 Longview Dr
Williamsport PA 17701

Call Sign: WB3FUR
Althea M McBride
10 Longview Dr
Williamsport PA 17701

Call Sign: W3ILG
Jason R McBride
10 Longview Dr
Williamsport PA 17701

Call Sign: W3FJ
Paul D McBride
10 Longview Dr
Williamsport PA 17701

Call Sign: W3AMM
Althea M McBride
10 Longview Dr
Williamsport PA 17701

Call Sign: K3AMM
Althea M McBride
10 Longview Dr
Williamsport PA 17701

Call Sign: KC3EC
William G Hitchens Jr
850 Lousia St Apt 1
Williamsport PA
177013067

Call Sign: N3TFF
Allen E Kaplan
300 Lower Barbours Rd
Williamsport PA 17701

Call Sign: K3APY
Allen E Kaplan
300 Lower Barbours Rd
Williamsport PA 17701

Call Sign: W3GPR
Edward C Crowe
1734 Loyal Sock Dr Apt 1
Williamsport PA
177012889

Call Sign: KB2NA
Robert D Seagrave
42 Maple Ave
Williamsport PA 17701

Call Sign: KB3OTT
Caleb R Hill
810 Market St
Williamsport PA 17701

Call Sign: W3JVP
Donald F Cook
940 Market St
Williamsport PA 17701

Call Sign: W3YYF
Calvin W Tilley
1207 Market St
Williamsport PA 17701

Call Sign: K3VFZ
Harry E Kieser
923 Mary

Williamsport PA 17701

Call Sign: KE3TP
James F Cendoma
2895 McKinney St
Williamsport PA 17701

Call Sign: N3XHS
Scott E Swinn
710 McMinn Ave
Williamsport PA 17701

Call Sign: KB3RLY
Richard E Stahl
1453 Memorial Ave
Williamsport PA 17701

Call Sign: K3RCL
John H Ellis
1783 Memorial Ave
Williamsport PA 17701

Call Sign: K3MHW
Michael H Weymer
1370 Morgan Ave
Williamsport PA 17701

Call Sign: WA3SAM
Michael H Weymer
1370 Morgan Ave
Williamsport PA 17701

Call Sign: W3OOO
Michael H Weymer
1370 Morgan Ave
Williamsport PA 17701

Call Sign: K3UQ
Michael H Weymer
1370 Morgan Ave
Williamsport PA
177012850

Call Sign: W3DEW
William E McErn

2123 Mosser Ave
Williamsport PA 17701

Call Sign: KB3TXE
Donald S Foye
1916 Newberry St
Williamsport PA 17701

Call Sign: N3SSL
Malvin R Gross
2629 Newberry St
Williamsport PA 17701

Call Sign: N3ZUP
Ronald A Cline
1524 Oakmount Dr
Williamsport PA
177019548

Call Sign: N3PFK
Clyde T Hammer
1523 Park Ave
Williamsport PA 17701

Call Sign: KG4LZP
Justin J Fetter
324 Pearson Ave
Williamsport PA 17701

Call Sign: KB3JTS
Shawn D Mccloskey
735 Pennsylvania Ave
Williamsport PA 17701

Call Sign: KB3JTR
Zachary R Wessner
1349 Pennsylvania Ave
Williamsport PA 17701

Call Sign: KB3JDI
Wildcat ARC
Pennsylvania Coll Of Tech
I College Ave
Williamsport PA 17701

Call Sign: N3GZO
Robert B Dayton Jr
Poco Farm
Williamsport PA 17701

Call Sign: W3OYB
Arthur L Altemose Jr
1500 Princeton Ave
Williamsport PA
177011307

Call Sign: K3MCT
Eugene D Morehart
916 Race St
Williamsport PA 17701

Call Sign: W3HC
Carl F McDaniel
2116 Reed St
Williamsport PA 17701

Call Sign: K3JJN
Gladys T McDaniel
2116 Reed St
Williamsport PA
177013904

Call Sign: K3RMF
Floyd A Cohick
941 Ridge Ave
Williamsport PA 17701

Call Sign: KB3AHS
John S Cendoma
9 Ridgedale Ave
Williamsport PA 17701

Call Sign: N3SFD
Jason S Kirk
151 Round Hill Rd
Williamsport PA 17701

Call Sign: K3UL
Robert B Garrett
8131 S Rt 44 Hwy

Williamsport PA 17702

Call Sign: WS3M
Daniel A Witz
320 Sherman St
Williamsport PA 17701

Call Sign: KG3G
Jeffrey F Ulman
379 St Davids Rd
Williamsport PA 17701

Call Sign: W3KRU
James B Wilson Jr
1185 St Davids Rd
Williamsport PA 17701

Call Sign: KB3IKS
Aislinn M Hayes
325 Susquehanna St
Williamsport PA 17701

Call Sign: KB3IKT
Eoin J Hayes
325 Susquehanna St
Williamsport PA 17701

Call Sign: KB3IIY
Edward Hayes
325 Susquehanna St
Williamsport PA
177015760

Call Sign: KA3VXJ
Jeff M Thayer
1828 Sweeley Ave
Williamsport PA 17701

Call Sign: AE3F
Richard L Burger
103 Tiffany Dr
Williamsport PA
177019622

Call Sign: KA3WMW

Delmar L Sauder
330 Tinsman Ave
Williamsport PA 17701

Call Sign: KA3CAA
Jeffrey J Allison
1180 Vallamont Dr NW
Williamsport PA 17701

Call Sign: W3NEN
Robert A Stout
11 Valley Hts Dr
Williamsport PA 17701

Call Sign: KB3PST
Harry A Jarrell III
938 Vine Ave Apt 1
Williamsport PA 17701

Call Sign: KB3UDH
Calvin W Tilley
18 W 3rd St
Williamsport PA 17701

Call Sign: N3GHQ
Paul B Kulik
2134 W 3rd St
Williamsport PA 17701

Call Sign: W3VH
Wendell P Pyle
412 W 3rd St 1
Williamsport PA 17701

Call Sign: W3SHP
James A Herb
424 W 4th St
Williamsport PA
177016002

Call Sign: KB3NQK
Susquehanna Valley Dx
Assn
800 W 4th St
Williamsport PA 17701

Call Sign: K3IPT
Susquehanna Valley Dx
Assn
800 W 4th St
Williamsport PA 17701

Call Sign: KA3SFX
John E Smertneck
2515 W 4th St
Williamsport PA 17701

Call Sign: W3KDK
Joseph A Smertneck
2515 W 4th St
Williamsport PA 17701

Call Sign: KB3CIV
Bryan C Baird
2829 W 4th St
Williamsport PA 17701

Call Sign: KA3EFF
Vance M Miller
3344 W 4th St
Williamsport PA
177014103

Call Sign: WQ3I
Robert L Hamaker
612 W Edwin St
Williamsport PA 17701

Call Sign: KA3PSM
Eric T Donnell
100 W Hills Dr
Williamsport PA 17701

Call Sign: KA3VZB
Anna L Shellenberger
117 W Hills Dr
Williamsport PA 17701

Call Sign: KB3YAG
Alan D Kaufman

2101 W Southern Ave
Williamsport PA 17702

Call Sign: KB3IAZ
Forest E Hafer Jr
714 Walnut St
Williamsport PA 17701

Call Sign: WY3I
Daniel C Wurster
1214 Walnut St
Williamsport PA 17701

Call Sign: KB3IBA
Forest G Hafer
21 Washington Blvd
Williamsport PA 17701

Call Sign: KB3SEB
Hilton W Smith Jr
808 Wayne Ave
Williamsport PA
177014227

Call Sign: W3HWS
Hilton W Smith Jr
808 Wayne Ave
Williamsport PA
177014227

Call Sign: K3EJK
Charles E Hanford
913 Wayne Ave
Williamsport PA 17701

Call Sign: KA3VZX
Diane H Bardsley
6 Wedgwood Knoll
Williamsport PA 17701

Call Sign: KB3OM
H Vincent Bardsley
6 Wedgwood Knoll
Williamsport PA
177019678

Call Sign: KB3IAX
Robert E Fisher
1942 Wells Rd
Williamsport PA 17702

Call Sign: N3FPN
Paul M McBride
2221 Wheatland Ave
Williamsport PA 17701

Call Sign: KB3NNG
Dennis P Beck
1271 Windfield Dr
Williamsport PA 17701

Call Sign: N3MFL
Kevin E Bennardi
59 Wither Hollow Ln
Williamsport PA 17701

Call Sign: KB3GNU
Andrea L Mcentire
59 Wither Hollow Ln
Williamsport PA 17701

Call Sign: AB3EZ
Kevin E Bennardi
59 Wither Hollow Ln
Williamsport PA 17701

Call Sign: KA3FPI
Barry J Opdahl
33 Woodbryn Dr
Williamsport PA 17701

Call Sign: WA3VUE
Gary R Hafer
1206 Woodmont Ave
Williamsport PA 17701

Call Sign: WA3ZTE
Anthony H Visco Jr
1401 Woodmont Ave
Williamsport PA 17701

Call Sign: K3IPT
Anthony H Visco Jr
1401 Woodmont Ave
Williamsport PA 17701

Call Sign: W3TYN
Robert W Dannelley
Williamsport PA 17701

Call Sign: KB3HLL
Bald Eagle Repeater Assoc
Williamsport PA 17701

Call Sign: N3MFJ
Bill Fullmer
Williamsport PA 17703

FCC Amateur Radio Licenses in Williamstown

Call Sign: KB3VCX
Steven J Perzia
145 East St
Williamstown PA 17098

Call Sign: WA3HFR
Gerald K Shaffner Sr
195 Lenker Dr
Williamstown PA 17098

Call Sign: KB3VDL
Berry Mountain ARC
9115 State Rt 209
Williamstown PA 17098

Call Sign: KB3NFZ
Paul D Coleman
9115 State Rt 209
Williamstown PA 17098

Call Sign: KB3GPW
Scott A Ferris
211 Tunnel St
Williamstown PA 17098

Call Sign: KA3AWV
Robert J Boyer
220 W Boyer St
Williamstown PA 17098

Call Sign: KA3MVI
Clarence A Heberling Jr
435 W Broad St
Williamstown PA 17098

Call Sign: WB3ECS
Robert I Bensinger Jr
1254 W Broad St
Williamstown PA 17098

Call Sign: W2FZD
William P Koll
201 Walnut St
Williamstown PA 17098

FCC Amateur Radio Licenses in Willow Street

Call Sign: KB3CQG
Dorothy B Houser
436 Beaver Valley Pike
Willow Street PA 17584

Call Sign: WA3PPH
H Robert Houser
436 Beaver Valley Pike
Willow Street PA 17584

Call Sign: KB3BYV
William J White IV
110 Broadmoor Dr
Willow Street PA 17584

Call Sign: KB3CDW
C Edward Baylor III
57 Carriage House Dr
Willow Street PA 17584

Call Sign: N3ZYY

F Ernest Thompson
57 Cobblestone Dr
Willow Street PA 17584

Call Sign: KB3PYR
Terri L Trimble
314 Edgemont Dr
Willow Street PA 17584

Call Sign: KB3GWI
Nathan M Murry
1606 Eshelman Mill Rd
Apt G
Willow Street PA 17584

Call Sign: K3GHL
John A Janisak
355 Flintlock Dr
Willow Street PA 17584

Call Sign: N3VZS
Kurtis A Shank
21 Hawthorne Cir
Willow Street PA 17584

Call Sign: N3CFO
Victor W Sinopoli
186 Linestown Rd
Willow Street PA 17584

Call Sign: K3FCT
Jesse L Silvius
1 Maplewood Cir
Willow Street PA 17584

Call Sign: WB0NNO
Garry M Foster
1012 Millwood Rd
Willow Street PA 17584

Call Sign: K3QGX
H Edward Yeagley Jr
11 Mylin Ave
Willow Street PA 17584

Call Sign: KA3ROC
Gerald R Handel
25 Pleasant View Ave
Willow Street PA 17584

Call Sign: N3QGK
Christopher J Smucker
57 Ridgeview Dr
Willow Street PA 17584

Call Sign: N3EJG
James B Williams
79 W Boehms Rd
Willow Street PA 17584

Call Sign: W0RBT
Michael L Burcin
25 W Kendig Rd
Willow Street PA 17584

Call Sign: WB2RMB
Mark E Scherer
616 Willow Valley Lakes
Dr
Willow Street PA 17584

Call Sign: W3RER
John L Gardner
718 Willow Valley Lakes
Dr
Willow Street PA 17584

Call Sign: K3VPA
G Yale Eastman
830 Willow Valley Lakes
Dr
Willow Street PA 17584

Call Sign: K6RER
John L Gardner
918 Willow Valley Lakes
Dr
Willow Street PA 17584

Call Sign: N3BQ

William G Quinn
Willow Valley Lakes Dr
Willow Street PA 17584

Call Sign: N3SWK
Earl K Metzler
300 Willow Valley Lakes
Dr Apt E 105
Willow Street PA 17584

Call Sign: K2DPK
William L Engstrom
950 Willow Valley Lakes
Dr Apt I 105
Willow Street PA
175849663

Call Sign: W2OTM
Walter E Vreeland
950 Willow Valley Lakes
Dr Apt K 405
Willow Street PA 17584

Call Sign: N8RD
Ronald D Dillon
950 Willow Valley Lakes
Dr H 404
Willow Street PA 17584

Call Sign: KB3QC
Marvin R Hohenstein
950 Willow Valley Lakes
Dr J303
Willow Street PA 17584

Call Sign: W3GPQ
Preston J Schoon
710 Willow Vly Lks Dr
Willow Street PA 17584

Call Sign: W9HPT
Willis J Kramer
Wycliffe Dr
Willow Street PA 17584

Call Sign: W3HXY
Roy W Shetter
Willow Street PA 17584

Call Sign: KB3DPC
John T Frimenko
Willow Street PA 17584

FCC Amateur Radio Licenses in Windber

Call Sign: KB3JIG
Pamela M Foglesong
201 11th St
Windber PA 15963

Call Sign: KB3JBF
Samuel S Foglesong
201 11th St
Windber PA 15963

Call Sign: N3KLD
Joseph J Boburchuk
209 6th St
Windber PA 15963

Call Sign: KA3BWO
John J Balogh
202 8th St
Windber PA 15963

Call Sign: N3XHZ
Brenda H Davis
303 8th St
Windber PA 15963

Call Sign: KB3AGV
Coy R Shaffer
Box 4A
Windber PA 15963

Call Sign: KB3UIX
Shawn M Sabo
112 Catherine Dr
Windber PA 15963

Call Sign: KB3MFR
Jesse J Mishka
3743 Dark Shade Dr
Windber PA 159635905

Call Sign: KB3NMH
Joseph J Oresko II
2707 Graham Ave
Windber PA 15963

Call Sign: KB3LBL
Christopher A Herron
2306 Graham Ave Apt 4
Windber PA 15963

Call Sign: KB3JOZ
Zachary J Zankey
262 Hayes St
Windber PA 15963

Call Sign: WA3BLM
Donald R Cowher
1238 Horn Rd
Windber PA 15963

Call Sign: KA3PYA
Mike Horwitz
68 Mine 30
Windber PA 15963

Call Sign: KA3TXR
Richard Faust
145 Mt Carmel Dr
Windber PA 15963

Call Sign: N3MAR
Jane A Faust
145 Mt Carmel Dr
Windber PA 15963

Call Sign: KB3FBN
Mike V Allisopn
3736 Mt Carmel Dr
Windber PA 15963

Call Sign: WA3YXV
Grant G Moore
179 Old Luther St
Windber PA 159638204

Call Sign: KA3SEP
Vernon W Click
1738 Seanor Rd
Windber PA 15963

Call Sign: WB3LUO
Lewis D Lenart
1914 Seanor Rd
Windber PA 15963

Call Sign: KA3EAI
Dennis L Doebler
1005 Somerset Ave
Windber PA 15963

Call Sign: KB3FBU
Chad P Bunk
623 Sunny Dr
Windber PA 15963

Call Sign: WA3FMX
Carl J Bunk
147 Velma Ln
Windber PA 15963

Call Sign: KB3MFK
Brett N Yonish
1813 Washington St
Windber PA 15963

FCC Amateur Radio Licenses in Windsor

Call Sign: WA3QEZ
Robert L Rauch
Box 192A
Windsor PA 17366

Call Sign: KA3RVJ

Arthur H Barry
Box 232 5
Windsor PA 17366

Call Sign: K3MMI
Frederick W Wise
1366 Craley Rd
Windsor PA 17366

Call Sign: KB3EYN
Paul G Kline
2 Edith Dr
Windsor PA 17366

Call Sign: N3SDK
Martin F Hoak
229 Graham Ln
Windsor PA 17366

Call Sign: KD4DVP
Janet M Blomquist
337 Graham Ln
Windsor PA 173667473

Call Sign: KD4DVQ
Richard H Blomquist
337 Graham Ln
Windsor PA 173668473

Call Sign: WA4EED
James F Overdorff
93 Kennick Dr
Windsor PA 17366

Call Sign: WA3HNR
Paul W Klinedinst Sr
375 Newcomer Rd
Windsor PA 173668486

Call Sign: KB3JMX
Gregory L Gillespie
1025 Richmond Rd
Windsor PA 17366

Call Sign: KB3JMY

Jodi V Nispel
1025 Richmond Rd
Windsor PA 17366

Call Sign: WB3DSD
Greg L Towson
405 S Blacksmith Ave
Windsor PA 17366

Call Sign: W3RLR
Robert L Rauch
1764 Snyder Corner Rd
Windsor PA 17366

Call Sign: KA3FEI
Richard A Becker
622 Taylor Rd
Windsor PA 173669763

Call Sign: WB3GOC
Dawn E Berrevoets
160 Valley Rd
Windsor PA 17366

Call Sign: KK3S
Jacobus J Berrevoets
160 Valley Rd
Windsor PA 173668904

Call Sign: N3UOP
Lloyd V Klinedinst
Windsor Acres
Windsor PA 17366

Call Sign: KB3IDG
Edward L Behrensen
Windsor PA 17366

**FCC Amateur Radio
Licenses in Winfield**

Call Sign: KB3DRP
Matthew J Bolduc
Box 140
Winfield PA 17889

Call Sign: N3CVT
Anthony J De Santis
Box 17
Winfield PA 17889

Call Sign: N3SHY
Levi M Beachy
Box 184
Winfield PA 17889

Call Sign: N3SHZ
Ervin A Beachy
Box 184
Winfield PA 17889

Call Sign: N3SHS
Kore L Beachy
Box 190
Winfield PA 17889

Call Sign: N3SHT
Perry M Beachy
Box 202
Winfield PA 17889

Call Sign: WA3JHF
Terrence J Splitt
Box 368
Winfield PA 17889

Call Sign: KB3TTF
James L Mowery
6130 New Berlin Hwy
Winfield PA 17889

Call Sign: KA3GCB
Neil B Hess
1111 Park Rd
Winfield PA 17889

Call Sign: AJ3D
Anthony J De Santis
1859 Park Rd
Winfield PA 17889

Call Sign: K3MD
John W Thompson
598 Reichley Rd
Winfield PA 17889

Call Sign: WB4MQR
Felix C Miles
3 Ridge Rd
Winfield PA 17889

Call Sign: KB3RUY
Harry E Holliday
109 Ridge Rd
Winfield PA 17889

**FCC Amateur Radio
Licenses in Woodbury**

Call Sign: W3JYM
Edwin D Sell
4686 Woodbury Pike
Woodbury PA 16695

Call Sign: N3VWQ
Justin M Kovalick
Box 290
Woodland PA 16881

Call Sign: N3RJV
Anthony W Brindel
Rd
Woodward PA 16882

**FCC Amateur Radio
Licenses in Woolrich**

Call Sign: KB3UZW
Michael J Wolfe
219 Park Ave
Woolrich PA 17779

**FCC Amateur Radio
Licenses in
Wormleysburg**

Call Sign: W3TOL
Arthur R Geisler
35 Beach Farm Rd
Wormleysburg PA 17043

Call Sign: KB3OJA
Ashlyn N Stumpf
73 Greenwood Cir
Wormleysburg PA 17043

Call Sign: KB3RVM
John T Galinac III
529 N 2nd St
Wormleysburg PA
170431011

Call Sign: N3KVB
Robert L Newmyer
8 N Front St
Wormleysburg PA 17043

Call Sign: WB7UGB
Tracy N Stuart
202 N Front St
Wormleysburg PA 17043

Call Sign: N3ESF
Susan L Stuart
202 N Front St
Wormleysburg PA 17043

Call Sign: WB3LKS
David E Winston
504 N Front St
Wormleysburg PA 17043

Call Sign: KB3JIC
Michael T Hoang
26 S Front St
Wormleysburg PA 17043

Call Sign: KB3NLG
Catherine T Hoang
26 S Front St

FCC Amateur Radio Licenses in Wrightsville

Call Sign: N3HUE
Richard S Bair Sr
700 Almoney Rd
Wrightsville PA
173689629

Call Sign: W3OWW
Geary O Russell
Box 48R
Wrightsville PA 17368

Call Sign: N3LHL
Fred Hagens Jr
317 Brook Ln
Wrightsville PA 17368

Call Sign: N3UBW
Dee A Townsley
317 Brook Ln
Wrightsville PA 17368

Call Sign: KB3ETG
Thomas A Graybill Jr
209 Chestnut St
Wrightsville PA 17368

Call Sign: KB3EVC
Susan L Graybill
209 Chestnut St
Wrightsville PA 17368

Call Sign: N3OFH
Pauline A Norton
29 Cool Creek Manor Dr
Wrightsville PA 17368

Call Sign: N3ONA
Vincent E Norton
29 Cool Creek Manor Dr
Wrightsville PA 17368

Call Sign: KC2EOC
Robert M Tiller
74 Cool Creek Manor Dr
Wrightsville PA 17368

Call Sign: KB3DWI
Jeffrey B Sicher
2586 Craley Rd
Wrightsville PA 17356

Call Sign: N3RBP
David S Marino
28 Derby Ct
Wrightsville PA 17368

Call Sign: N3UED
Joseph W Smith Jr
146 Jonathan Ct
Wrightsville PA 17368

Call Sign: W3GES
Ben C Zarfos
6368 Lincoln Hwy
Wrightsville PA 17368

Call Sign: KB3SQM
Larry D Bunner
113 Livia Ln
Wrightsville PA 17368

Call Sign: WA3EJH
Richard S Bair Jr
418 Locust St
Wrightsville PA 17368

Call Sign: KB3RGK
Nathan C Jones
207 Mulberry St
Wrightsville PA 17368

Call Sign: KB3BXD
Elizabeth Mckonly
413 S 6th St
Wrightsville PA 17368

Call Sign: N3SUB
Donald E McKonly
413 S 6th St
Wrightsville PA 17368

Call Sign: KB3STB
Donald E Mckonly
413 S 6th St
Wrightsville PA 17368

Call Sign: KA2JNH
Domenic J Pizzirusso
38 Stonewyck Hill Rd
Wrightsville PA 17368

Call Sign: NG3X
Harry F Sieber Jr
6732 Sunrise Ln
Wrightsville PA 17368

Call Sign: N3UAB
Frederick L Salzman Jr
30 Surrey Dr
Wrightsville PA
173689080

Call Sign: WA3WOT
Dennis G Bartch
415 Vine St
Wrightsville PA 17368

Call Sign: KA3GLG
Stephen D Paduhovich
67 W Maple St
Wrightsville PA
173689164

FCC Amateur Radio Licenses in Yeagertown

Call Sign: WB3JAD
John H Gibboney
20 S Locke Ave Box B
Yeagertown PA 17099

Call Sign: NC3R
Dennis S Dillon
41 S Mann Ave
Yeagertown PA 17099

Call Sign: KU3C
Susan M Laurino
Yeagertown PA 17099

FCC Amateur Radio Licenses in Yoe

Call Sign: N3SUF
Cynthia D Manns
30 E High St
Yoe PA 17313

Call Sign: N3OSV
Bruce G Manns
30 E High St
Yoe PA 17313

Call Sign: W3YOE
Charles G Landis Jr
134 S Maple St
Yoe PA 17313

FCC Amateur Radio Licenses in York

Call Sign: WB3LTF
Donald P Cheever
1415 3rd Ave
York PA 174031906

Call Sign: K3FOB
Stanley K Hoffman
1687 4th Ave
York PA 17403

Call Sign: WA3LNA
Anthony P Spinelli
437 4th St
York PA 17512

Call Sign: N3GIB
Ronald L Cohen Sr
729 Academy Rd
York PA 174062316

Call Sign: KB3TPX
Thierry G Matthieu
1029 Accomac Rd
York PA 17406

Call Sign: KC3PS
James R Kinsey
2160 Aslan Dr
York PA 17404

Call Sign: KB3DNV
Roy E Wolfhope
438 Atlantic Ave
York PA 17404

Call Sign: KA3RAJ
Donald E Slenker
2410 Baker Rd
York PA 17404

Call Sign: KB3FVP
Donald A Selack
Barachel Dr
York PA 17402

Call Sign: KA3USN
Mark W Goodson
3333 Barwood Rd
York PA 17406

Call Sign: KA3ZHH
Stacey J Blouse
928 Beaverton Dr
York PA 17402

Call Sign: KA3PQI
Lloyd L Kiger
1330 Beeler Ave
York PA 174044503

Call Sign: WY6Z
Christopher R Palm
1360 Beeler Ave
York PA 17408

Call Sign: KG6ADM
Nicholas C Palm
1360 Beeler Ave
York PA 17408

Call Sign: K3PKD
Leon E Paxton
2455 Beeler Ave
York PA 17404

Call Sign: KB3IHZ
Melissa J Emig
14 Biesecker Rd
York PA 17404

Call Sign: WA3ISD
Howard J Baker
360 Blue Ridge Dr
York PA 17402

Call Sign: N3RJK
Michael A Stanhope
1359 Bon Bar Rd
York PA 17403

Call Sign: KA3ZBI
Kurt W Miller Sr
Box 177
York PA 17402

Call Sign: N3UOR
Christopher A Wright
Box 329
York PA 17404

Call Sign: N3OZX
Mark A Gladfelter
Box 377
York PA 17404

Call Sign: K3WDB
Dam Operatrs At Indian
Rock Dm
Box 6 Indian Rock Dam
York PA 17403

Call Sign: N3CNC
Wilbur J Routson
2429 Bradford Dr
York PA 17402

Call Sign: K3OCW
Robert A Carbaugh
317 Brentwood Dr Apt C
York PA 174034322

Call Sign: N3MTS
Paul Mudrock
4335 Briarwood Ct
York PA 17404

Call Sign: KB3KGI
Samuel P Fleischer
105 Bridlewood Way C33
York PA 17402

Call Sign: N3TVR
Jeffrey R Shaffer Jr
1320 Brittany Dr
York PA 17404

Call Sign: KB3LAK
Sybil R Tate
2465 Brookmar Dr
York PA 17404

Call Sign: KB3IQO
Ken Brody
121 Camelot Arms Bldg O
York PA 17402

Call Sign: N3JRT
Richard A Williams
608 Campbell Rd

York PA 17402

Call Sign: WF3D
James L Rowe
1067 Canadochly Rd
York PA 17406

Call Sign: KG4DUZ
James W Beamer
741 Carl St
York PA 17404

Call Sign: KB3TGY
Micah E Neff
457 Carlisle Ave
York PA 17404

Call Sign: KB3RGQ
Jamin Neff
457 Carlisle Ave
York PA 17404

Call Sign: WB3LJW
Francis L Dohm
1960 Carlisle Rd
York PA 17404

Call Sign: N3YSM
Jeffrey S Chapman
1960 Carlisle Rd
York PA 174041510

Call Sign: N3BSM
Marie C Hagens
2030 Carlisle Rd
York PA 17404

Call Sign: KB3OCA
Paul E Schreck
2426 Carllyn Dr
York PA 17403

Call Sign: N3VI
Paul E Schreck
2426 Carllyn Dr

York PA 17403   York PA 17402   York PA 174048270

Call Sign: KB3WZU Call Sign: W3EDO Call Sign: KB3VHY
Joseph J Pisciello George H Gable Paul D Zenkowich
2673 Carnegie Rd 80 Claystone Rd 608 Courtland St
York PA 17402   York PA 17404   York PA 17403

Call Sign: KD7MG Call Sign: N3NEM Call Sign: KB3TPZ
Michael E Tucker Jeffrey D Heller Daryl L Hancock
821 Cedar Village Dr 2605 Coldspring Rd 617 Courtland St
York PA 17402   York PA 17404   York PA 17403

Call Sign: K3YSL Call Sign: KD0AEY Call Sign: WB3CAB
William F Corse Timothy S Melton Glenn R Miller
604 Chambers Ridge 553 Colonial Ave 1749 Crescent Rd
York PA 17402   York PA 17403   York PA 17403

Call Sign: KB3WRL Call Sign: N3LAW Call Sign: KB3IDD
Justin M Snyder Diane Y Delozier Suzanne J Garrety
3442 Chardonnay Dr 770 Colonial Ave 2460 Crollschool Rd
York PA 17404   York PA 17403   York PA 17403

Call Sign: K3TKQ Call Sign: KA3TRV Call Sign: N3FDW
George W Collier Melissa J Fauth Edwin F Classen
290 Chestnut Hill Rd 75 Copenhaffer Rd 2230 Dandridge Dr
York PA 174029562 York PA 17404   York PA 17403

Call Sign: WA3YVR Call Sign: WB7VIZ Call Sign: KB3DEI
David N Eckman Charles M Fults Belinda A Jackson
680 Chronister St 300 Cortleigh Dr Apt A1 4665 Darlington Rd
York PA 17406   York PA 174024022 York PA 17404

Call Sign: KA3THU Call Sign: N4FAI Call Sign: N5FCR
Michael L McCullough Jr John T Elicker Joel W Winer
232 Church Rd 772 Country Club Rd 2897 Deer Chase Ln
York PA 17402   York PA 17403   York PA 17403

Call Sign: N3ZMO Call Sign: W3ADE Call Sign: KB3EBB
Terri L Zech John T Elicker Brie A Luttenberger
1996 Church Rd 772 Country Club Rd 4141 Deerhil Dr
York PA 17404   York PA 17403   York PA 17402

Call Sign: KB3WDL Call Sign: N3PRH Call Sign: K3BRE
Nicholas A Coby Marlyn E Warren Brie A Luttenberger
22 Circle Dr 221 Country Rige Dr 4141 Deerhil Dr

York PA 17402

Call Sign: NO3C
Sterling L Tate
2154 Derry Rd
York PA 17404

Call Sign: WA3WOH
Ivan L Fillmore
1020 Detwiler Dr
York PA 17404

Call Sign: KB3IIW
Martin A Rexroth
1060 Detwiler Dr
York PA 174041104

Call Sign: N3ZVK
Frans Delhez
1774 Devers Rd
York PA 17404

Call Sign: KB3EBY
Samuel J Zolin
29 Dew Drop Rd
York PA 174039511

Call Sign: AI3W
Richard L Graham
60 Dietz Ests Dr
York PA 17404

Call Sign: KB2IQX
William T Donegan
2833 Dove Dr
York PA 17408

Call Sign: N3IZS
Michael W Kacala
1604 Druck Valley Rd
York PA 17402

Call Sign: KA3ZIJ
Jason E MacDonald
2361 Druck Valley Rd

York PA 17402

Call Sign: N3ESD
Eleanor G Driscoll
4696 Druck Valley Rd
York PA 174068740

Call Sign: WB3GRN
Joseph A Lewis
780 Ducktown Rd
York PA 174069114

Call Sign: WB3GRO
Ann C Lewis
780 Ducktown Rd
York PA 174069114

Call Sign: KB3GIX
Sarah G Riese
324 Duke St
York PA 17403

Call Sign: N0VBU
Patricia A Brandick
2800 Durham Rd
York PA 174023809

Call Sign: W3GKJ
Joseph A Brandick
2800 Durham Rd
York PA 174023809

Call Sign: KB3PRD
Calvin B Miller
55 E 5th Ave
York PA 17404

Call Sign: KB3YEY
Patrick S Colvin
700 E Boundary Ave
York PA 17403

Call Sign: W3HLD
William E Hurst
825 E Boundary Ave

York PA 17403

Call Sign: K3MOA
Fred D Smith Jr
420 E Butter Rd
York PA 17404

Call Sign: KB3MPP
Thomas B Mitcheltree
575 E Canal Rd
York PA 17404

Call Sign: KA3OBR
John H Toomey
334 E College Ave
York PA 17403

Call Sign: KB3ICZ
Charles R Faucette
541 E Hillcrest Rd
York PA 17403

Call Sign: WB3EOE
Ralph A Serrano
440 E King St Apt 143
York PA 17403

Call Sign: K3HBN
John W Wagaman
107 E Locust Ln
York PA 17402

Call Sign: KB3VVN
John H Chronister
331 E Locust St
York PA 17403

Call Sign: KA3WSN
Ronald L Hamme
241 E Maple St
York PA 17403

Call Sign: KA3LJL
Edward L Swank Sr
312 E Maple St

York PA 17403

Call Sign: N3SWW
Michael J Dohm
838 E Market St
York PA 17403

Call Sign: KD3XB
Jack E Stabley
125 E Phila St
York PA 174031437

Call Sign: KF3AV
Larry L Shaw
4996 E Prospect Rd Apt 2
York PA 17406

Call Sign: KB3HZR
Victoria A Perry
929 E Prospect St
York PA 17403

Call Sign: KA3CCA
William G Hopkins
1745 East St
York PA 17402

Call Sign: KA3YHA
Jeffrey R Lander
2340 Eastern Blvd
York PA 17402

Call Sign: K3PQZ
Alan W Goughnour
3025 Eastern Blvd
York PA 17402

Call Sign: WA3KYD
Timothy B Burk
3102 Eastern Blvd
York PA 17402

Call Sign: KA3KAQ
Craig L Wisherd
111 Eastland Ave

York PA 174021102

Call Sign: KB3ETJ
Rodney P Mcclellan
1205 Eberts Ln
York PA 17402

Call Sign: N3GTU
Roger J Perry
2531 Edgewood Ln
York PA 17403

Call Sign: KA3IUB
Charles J Shultz
618 Edison St
York PA 17403

Call Sign: KA3VID
William H Hax
173 Edward Rd
York PA 17403

Call Sign: N3MFR
John W Ness
38 Eisenhower Dr
York PA 17402

Call Sign: KB3TLV
David W Bird
96 Eisenhower Dr
York PA 17402

Call Sign: N3ZYQ
Harry B Graver Jr
1996 Elim St
York PA 17404

Call Sign: K3BZK
August A Gabriele
200 Elmwood Blvd
York PA 17403

Call Sign: K3KDJ
Rose R Gabriele
200 Elmwood Blvd

York PA 17403

Call Sign: W2DGZ
George W Moran
950 Erlen Dr
York PA 17402

Call Sign: N3ZMQ
Daniel A Rutherford
2165 Esbenshade Rd
York PA 17404

Call Sign: K3WOW
Daniel A Rutherford
2165 Esbenshade Rd
York PA 17404

Call Sign: AA3G
Daniel A Rutherford
2165 Esbenshade Rd
York PA 17404

Call Sign: K3UKR
Antonio Pantano
639 Evergreen Dr
York PA 17402

Call Sign: N3PJE
Wayne E Jonosky
2945 Exeter Dr S
York PA 17403

Call Sign: N3QZP
Alisa A Jonosky
2945 Exeter Dr S
York PA 17403

Call Sign: K8UYC
John R Magar
4175 Exton Ln
York PA 17402

Call Sign: KB3SSA
Bryan M Hull
2439 Fairway Dr

York PA 17408

Call Sign: KB3TXJ
Aline M Harrison
2607 Fairway Dr
York PA 17402

Call Sign: KA3OCC
Gail M Crow
1633 Filbert St
York PA 17404

Call Sign: K1TUX
Jeffrey V Salzman
1651 Filbert St
York PA 17404

Call Sign: N3DVO
Pete J Chantiles
700 Fireside Rd
York PA 17404

Call Sign: KB3OWR
Natasha C Shortencarrier
830 Florida Ave
York PA 17404

Call Sign: N3TIZ
Joyce E Moss
275 Folkstone Way
York PA 17402

Call Sign: N3UOT
Thomas F Balanda Jr
772 Foxtail Dr
York PA 17404

Call Sign: KB3OCB
Jay R Reich Jr
5740 Furnace Rd
York PA 17406

Call Sign: W3PNZ
Jay R Reich Jr
5740 Furnace Rd

York PA 17406

Call Sign: K3ZEH
Girard E Moore
5819 Furnace Rd
York PA 17406

Call Sign: N3KDS
Robert E Moore
5819 Furnace Rd
York PA 17406

Call Sign: N3LZS
Virginia L Moore
5819 Furnace Rd
York PA 17406

Call Sign: KB3DXN
Robert W Hoke
500 Gatehouse Ln E
York PA 17402

Call Sign: KB3CHR
Marc W Mckinley
3022 Gemstone Ln
York PA 17404

Call Sign: KB3IDF
Henry P Groat
2817 Glen Hollow Dr
York PA 17402

Call Sign: N3NBT
Robert H Gundlach
2829 Glen Hollow Dr
York PA 174069706

Call Sign: N3RBT
Mary E Gundlach
2829 Glen Hollow Dr
York PA 174069706

Call Sign: N3LKJ
Joseph C Horvath

10 Governors Pl At
Waterford
York PA 17402

Call Sign: W3FLD
John A Zett
2740 Grandview Ave
York PA 17404

Call Sign: N3JPK
Richard W Gleitz
2390 Grandview Dr
York PA 17403

Call Sign: KB3MNF
Paul G Sipe
800 Grantley Ct
York PA 17403

Call Sign: KB3TZU
Christina L Gilchrist
2342 Grantley Rd
York PA 17403

Call Sign: N3DVS
Michael S Euculano
843 Green Briar Rd
York PA 17404

Call Sign: K3TZJ
Ronald L Boltz
619 Green Springs Rd
York PA 17404

Call Sign: N3DYT
Louis J Wawro
374 Greendale Rd
York PA 17403

Call Sign: KB3HXX
H Robert Derrick
592 Greendale Rd
York PA 174034065

Call Sign: W3WBL

H Robert Derrick
592 Greendale Rd
York PA 174034065

Call Sign: WB3EPJ
Frank J Iati
1505 Greenmeadow Dr
York PA 17404

Call Sign: WA3BXU
Kenneth E Shank
600 Greenwood Rd
York PA 17404

Call Sign: KB3WOD
Scott A Kuhn
451 Gun Club Rd
York PA 17406

Call Sign: AB3BG
Ken Brody
2978 Harford Cir
York PA 17404

Call Sign: N3FPJ
Jeffrey R Shaffer Sr
3600 Harrowgate Rd
York PA 174024230

Call Sign: N3SWV
Brandon P Gotwalt
130 Haybrook Dr
York PA 17402

Call Sign: KB3SSX
Fern I Sardegna
2268 Heather Rd
York PA 17408

Call Sign: N3YEE
Christopher J Davis
2458 Hepplewhite Dr
York PA 17404

Call Sign: N3IHU

Charles W Kuster Jr
2080 Herman Dr
York PA 17404

Call Sign: W3JHC
Harold S Hollander
421 Hill N Dale
York PA 17403

Call Sign: WX3S
Dana Kay Conner
370 Hill N Dale Dr S
York PA 174034740

Call Sign: WB3CAL
Kerry L Smith
3 Hill St
York PA 17403

Call Sign: KB3NVO
Yolanda U Ogena-Stevens
429 Hillcrest Rd
York PA 17403

Call Sign: K3YOS
Yolanda U Ogena-Stevens
429 Hillcrest Rd
York PA 17403

Call Sign: N3ASA
Scott H Stevens
429 Hillcrest Rd
York PA 174034711

Call Sign: KB3AW
Leo P Eck
213 Hillside Ter
York PA 17404

Call Sign: K3LNI
Richard F Blom
1771 Hilltop Dr
York PA 17402

Call Sign: W3HRP

Ronald F Mease
104 Homewood Dr
York PA 17403

Call Sign: WB3DRV
David E Duffan
111 Homewood Dr
York PA 17403

Call Sign: KB3HCT
Benjamin L Heyser
3017 Honey Run Dr
York PA 17408

Call Sign: KB3RSN
Joel B Hummel
3139 Honey Run Dr
York PA 17408

Call Sign: K3UVJ
Robert G Hildebrand Jr
4725 Horn Rd
York PA 17406

Call Sign: N3UAE
Daniel P Andrews
2820 Ironstone Hill Rd
York PA 17403

Call Sign: AB3IV
Daniel P Andrews
2820 Ironstone Hill Rd
York PA 17403

Call Sign: WB3AE
Daniel P Andrews
2820 Ironstone Hill Rd
York PA 17403

Call Sign: N3HIK
Robert E Moore Sr
108 Irving Rd
York PA 17403

Call Sign: W3HFF

Charles C Hyde
11 Jean Lo Way
York PA 17042

Call Sign: W3YPS
Richard F Bernd
57 Jean Lo Way
York PA 174066710

Call Sign: K3JGF
Charles E Hummer
225 Jody Dr
York PA 17402

Call Sign: N3CAR
Orland C Augburn
2425 Joppa Rd
York PA 17403

Call Sign: N3EYG
Sandra L Augburn
2425 Joppa Rd
York PA 17403

Call Sign: N3QZL
Robert A Carn
1930 Kenneth Rd Apt 210
York PA 174049122

Call Sign: KB3WOT
Nicole E Davis
160 Kern Rd
York PA 17406

Call Sign: KB3MVD
Dean J Marmian
44 Kevin Dr
York PA 17404

Call Sign: KB3HWL
Jeffrey T Walters
115 Keymar Dr
York PA 17402

Call Sign: KB3PRM

Walter D Kloker
130 Keymar Dr
York PA 174029552

Call Sign: N2AMK
Walter D Kloker
130 Keymar Dr
York PA 174029552

Call Sign: KB3RDP
Walter D Kloker
130 Keymar Dr
York PA 174029552

Call Sign: KG3ICP
Walter D Kloker
130 Keymar Dr
York PA 174029552

Call Sign: KA3YOS
John C Meerbach
1953 Kimes Rd
York PA 17402

Call Sign: KB3ROM
Francis T Plaza
122 Kings Arms At
Waterford
York PA 17402

Call Sign: KB3FKE
Lonna J Mellinger
3856 Kings Arms Ln
York PA 17402

Call Sign: N3ZCW
Ernest L Mellinger
3856 Kings Arms Ln
York PA 17402

Call Sign: K3ELM
Ernest L Mellinger
3856 Kings Arms Ln
York PA 17402

Call Sign: N3IZD
Harold F Heywood
3415 Kingston Rd
York PA 17402

Call Sign: N3UAD
Terence C Holtzinger
3455 Kingston Rd
York PA 17402

Call Sign: W3LSG
David J Wilke Sr
167 Kirch Rd
York PA 17402

Call Sign: WB3BEF
Dale M Unger
807 Kylemore Way
York PA 17402

Call Sign: KB3GPX
Michael A Schiding
150 Lafayette St
York PA 17403

Call Sign: NR3V
Marvin W Simkins
3030 Lakefield Rd
York PA 17402

Call Sign: KA3NVG
A Wayne Conger
Lark Cir
York PA 17404

Call Sign: K3MHJ
John G Bauman
3130 Lark Dr
York PA 17404

Call Sign: KB3TTM
Bryan C Wiley
225 Leader Hts Rd
York PA 17402

Call Sign: K3DJC
Robert C Riese
100 Leeds Rd
York PA 17403

Call Sign: KB3TTA
John W Gibson
1315 Livingston Rd
York PA 174041925

Call Sign: W3AGU
Dean L Paules
102 Lyn Cir
York PA 17403

Call Sign: KA3WUG
Stewart A Stevens
100 Lexington Rd
York PA 17402

Call Sign: KB3PIK
Samuel E Brands
471 Locust Grove Rd
York PA 17402

Call Sign: WB3HBN
Thomas E Minnich
331 Lynbrook Dr N
York PA 17402

Call Sign: KA3THC
Kathleen M Dellinger
115 Lexington Rd
York PA 17402

Call Sign: K3MJN
George W Adams
2295 Locust Ln
York PA 17404

Call Sign: KB3SWK
Alexander D Ahmadi
3012 Mackenzi Ln Apt 4
York PA 174089240

Call Sign: KA3UDI
Andrew W Spuker
115 Lexington Rd
York PA 17402

Call Sign: KA3PHX
Pamella P Elkins
2351 Log Cabin Rd
York PA 17404

Call Sign: KB3RQ
Dann S Johns
16 Maple Rd
York PA 17403

Call Sign: N3BQB
Carl E Dellinger
115 Lexington Rd
York PA 17402

Call Sign: N3WCQ
David A Elkins III
2351 Log Cabin Rd
York PA 17404

Call Sign: WB2VIE
Gerald J Zulewski
3576 Mark Dr
York PA 17402

Call Sign: KC3JD
Carl E Dellinger
115 Lexington Rd
York PA 17402

Call Sign: KD8CS
Jeffrey A Judd
2791 Loman Ave
York PA 17408

Call Sign: KA3UTB
Stephen W Busch
697 Maryland Ave
York PA 17404

Call Sign: KB3FWI
Gregory G Potter
4907 Lincolnwood Dr
York PA 17404

Call Sign: N3CLH
Ray L Ensminger
2116 Louise Ave
York PA 174034819

Call Sign: KB3DZI
Dave M Busch
697 Maryland Ave
York PA 17404

Call Sign: KB3SSQ
Daniel L Mitchell
4991 Lincolnwood Dr
York PA 17408

Call Sign: WB3DGR
Camp Shohola ARC
425 Ludlow Ave
York PA 174033535

Call Sign: K3GDI
Frank Bair
2602 Meadowbrook Blvd
York PA 17402

Call Sign: KA3THB
Cynthia M Rowe
152 Lisa Cir
York PA 17406

Call Sign: WA3HWY
Thomas K Gibson
425 Ludlow Ave
York PA 174033542

Call Sign: KB3CJQ
Jason M Howe
2703 Meadowbrook Blvd
York PA 17406

Call Sign: KB3EWN
Clifford R Frankenfield
238 Melinda Dr
York PA 17408

Call Sign: WA3ONG
Jay W Lyter
455 Melrie Dr
York PA 17403

Call Sign: W3NUA
Robert T Geist
1391 Memory Ln
York PA 17402

Call Sign: N3KDU
Cleveland C Wolfgang
1555 Memory Ln Extd Rd
22
York PA 17402

Call Sign: WB3IGF
Warren D Hale
824 Midland Ave
York PA 17403

Call Sign: WB2MMD
Richard M Grotkier Sr
1244 Midland Ave
York PA 17403

Call Sign: K2IC
Richard M Grotkier Sr
1244 Midland Ave
York PA 17403

Call Sign: KA3OBS
Patricia L Strausbaugh
2535 Midpine Dr
York PA 17404

Call Sign: KC3PR
Joseph E Strausbaugh
2535 Midpine Dr
York PA 174041223

Call Sign: KA3PAT
Patricia L Strausbaugh
2535 Midpine Dr
York PA 174041223

Call Sign: W3MMV
Frederick B Lowe
2635 Milford Ln
York PA 17402

Call Sign: KB3SBE
Ralph E Brandt
1705 Misty Dr
York PA 174084237

Call Sign: K3HQI
Ralph E Brandt
1705 Misty Dr
York PA 174084237

Call Sign: KA3JGW
Rodger G Henry
850 Moffett Ln
York PA 17403

Call Sign: WB3ERZ
James A Erisman
880 Moonlight Dr
York PA 17402

Call Sign: W3IXG
Elmer E Hauer
288 Moul
York PA 17402

Call Sign: KB3VGH
David K Tawaclras
640 Mundis Mill Rd
York PA 17406

Call Sign: KB3IDB
Moises Nieves
121 N Belvidere Ave
York PA 17404

Call Sign: W3PRG
Charles G W Arnold
34 N Findlay St
York PA 17402

Call Sign: WA1HEW
Craig R Dowling
301 N Forrest St
York PA 17404

Call Sign: WB3KVN
Richard K Renn
45 N George St
York PA 17404

Call Sign: N3RDL
Jacquelyn G Kraft
156 N George St
York PA 17401

Call Sign: N3UAA
Lee R Garrett
2628 N George St
York PA 17402

Call Sign: WB3GRD
Barry L Miller
3033 N George St
York PA 17402

Call Sign: KB3ULX
Jack Alan Dean
238 N George St Apt 304
York PA 17401

Call Sign: AC7PA
Allen W Berg
205 N Gotwalt St
York PA 17404

Call Sign: W3JIF
Richard N Toomey
326 N Gotwalt St
York PA 17404

Call Sign: N3TSJ
Timothy R Myers
21 N Hartley St
York PA 17404

Call Sign: WA3WSM
Steven K Botterbusch
2158 Narnia Dr
York PA 17404

Call Sign: N3USX
Richard D Fares
118 Old Orchard Rd
York PA 17403

Call Sign: N3TWR
Cathy R Myers
21 N Hartley St
York PA 17404

Call Sign: KB3JOG
Shawn T Beard
115 Nina Dr
York PA 17402

Call Sign: KA3CKZ
Barry L Poe
1473 Old Salen Rd
York PA 17404

Call Sign: N3UYN
Willard C Pope Jr
1800 N Hills Rd 513
York PA 174021848

Call Sign: N3QZF
Andrew K Blair
1561 North Dr
York PA 17404

Call Sign: KB3VWS
Marshall H Behrmann
335 Old Stone Way
York PA 17406

Call Sign: WB3IVW
John G Enders
139 N Marshall St
York PA 174022319

Call Sign: KB3TTG
Jonathan Polanco-Mueses
349 Oak Ln
York PA 17401

Call Sign: KB3MZK
David R Briddell
Olo Way
York PA 17403

Call Sign: W3END
John G Enders
139 N Marshall St
York PA 174022319

Call Sign: WD5BCL
Thomas C Steidel
8 Oak Ridge Dr
York PA 17402

Call Sign: KB3AVH
Mary E Frame
2430 Opal Rd
York PA 174044466

Call Sign: KB3IDC
David E Wagman
207 N Newberry St
York PA 17404

Call Sign: WB3EZT
Robert L Gotwalt
126 Oakleigh Dr
York PA 17402

Call Sign: WB3FTD
Alan J Frame
2430 Opal Rd
York PA 174084466

Call Sign: KB3EEZ
Jeremy V Sippel
2260 N Point Dr
York PA 17406

Call Sign: K3CET
Robert C Langeheine
745 Oatman St
York PA 17404

Call Sign: N3ODS
Geraldine M Stauch
2010 Orange St
York PA 17404

Call Sign: KB3AKL
Matthew R Schmuck
34 N State St
York PA 17403

Call Sign: WB3FHA
Thomas M Codori
771 Oatman St
York PA 174042419

Call Sign: KB3DZH
David J Zolin
164 Oriole Dr
York PA 174039511

Call Sign: N3PAJ
Belinda C Frederick
42 N Vernon St
York PA 174022341

Call Sign: KB3ITX
Thomas W Mcclain Jr
3841 Old Joseph Rd
York PA 17404

Call Sign: WA8WAL
David E Kennedy
623 Owen Rd
York PA 17403

Call Sign: N3LHK
Stephen O Laucks Md
631 Owen Rd
York PA 17403

Call Sign: KB3DCG
Gregory C Halpin
794 Pacific Ave
York PA 174042451

Call Sign: KB3HLD
Gabriel J Radzik
418 Park St
York PA 174012926

Call Sign: N3UGO
Mark W Breon
755 Parkway Blvd
York PA 174042635

Call Sign: N3KVC
Gerald W Regensburg
211 Pauline Dr
York PA 17402

Call Sign: KB3YGM
Tyler Roman
3127 Paulownia Ln
York PA 17404

Call Sign: KB3WDP
David F Saylor
2149 Pemberton Pl
York PA 17408

Call Sign: KB3RGI
Alexander J Miller
717 Pennsylvania Ave
York PA 17404

Call Sign: W3SAS
Stephanie A Stanhope
121 Penwood Rd
York PA 17406

Call Sign: W3RMS
Robert M Stanhope Sr
121 Penwood Rd
York PA 17406

Call Sign: KB3VVJ
Judith A Bassett
25 Percheron Dr
York PA 17406

Call Sign: K3WHC
Stephen H Cruse
2770 Pilgrim Rd
York PA 17402

Call Sign: N3LD
Lee G Driscoll
2527 Pin Oak Dr
York PA 174067563

Call Sign: WB3EGX
Douglas M Warner
203 Pine Ct
York PA 17408

Call Sign: W3ABN
Albert E Gibson Jr
2790 Pine Grove Rd 3314
York PA 174035153

Call Sign: K3QVW
Vincent L Shyblowski
2790 Pine Grove Rd Apt
3209
York PA 174035183

Call Sign: KB3RGR
Sara J Knudson
354 Pine Hill Ln
York PA 17403

Call Sign: WB3GRA
Roland E Mackley Jr
334 Pinehurst Rd

York PA 17402

Call Sign: N3MPG
Lester W Hagelgans
335 Pinehurst Rd
York PA 17402

Call Sign: KY3ARS
Y A R S
118 Pleasant Acres Rd
York PA 17402

Call Sign: KB3BIK
Y A R S
118 Pleasant Acres Rd
York PA 17402

Call Sign: W3HSR
John W Munnell
3620 Pleasant Valley Rd
York PA 17402

Call Sign: KB3TSZ
Larry D Frey
2435 Pleasant View Dr
York PA 174062304

Call Sign: N3LED
Larry D Frey
2435 Pleasant View Dr
York PA 174062304

Call Sign: KB3OYL
Kimball L Shaud
280 Point Cir
York PA 17406

Call Sign: K3KLS
Kimball L Shaud
280 Point Cir
York PA 17406

Call Sign: KB3PP
Donald E Wildasin

1765 Powder Mill Rd Apt
204
York PA 17403

Call Sign: K3DVL
George W Hubley
2650 Primrose Ln
York PA 174041228

Call Sign: N3GZJ
John F Smith Jr
2729 Primrose Ln E
York PA 17402

Call Sign: KA3VUZ
Jan A Smith
2729 Primrose Ln E
York PA 17402

Call Sign: KB3IDE
David A Perry Sr
929 Prospect St
York PA 17403

Call Sign: N3KVJ
Elizabeth R Troutman
60 Quail Run
York PA 17402

Call Sign: N3LAB
James G Troutman
60 Quail Run
York PA 17402

Call Sign: WD8DFD
Carol L Gottschalk
560 Quaker Dr
York PA 17402

Call Sign: K3UQJ
Lynn W Bortner Jr
1927 Queenswood Dr Apt
B 106
York PA 17403

Call Sign: K3RUL
Glenn P Groff
1927 Queenswood Dr Apt
E104
York PA 17403

Call Sign: NM3J
Garvin M Herigstad
1835 Radnor Rd
York PA 17402

Call Sign: AA3EF
Glenn W Winter
1847 Radnor Rd
York PA 17402

Call Sign: K3RSB
Norman M Metzler
1848 Radnor Rd
York PA 174024810

Call Sign: WA3BPR
Russell W Wilson Jr
1854 Radnor Rd
York PA 17402

Call Sign: N3TQY
Thomas A Eubank
1617 Rainbow Cir
York PA 17404

Call Sign: WA3CLV
Robert G Hildebrand Sr
3560 Raintree Rd
York PA 17404

Call Sign: WB3BLM
Richard M Kline
14 Ramsgate Ct
York PA 17404

Call Sign: K3DLK
William T Smeltzer
Rd 8
York PA 17403

Call Sign: WB3AZG
Randy L Stegemerten
111 Reynolds Mill Rd
York PA 17403

Call Sign: KB3JSG
Louis H Tateosian
209 Reynolds Mill Rd
York PA 174039549

Call Sign: KB3JEJ
Tom J Burkholder
278 Reynoldsmill Rd
York PA 17403

Call Sign: KB3QOR
Dawson C Stump Jr
138 Ridgefield Dr
York PA 17403

Call Sign: K3NBW
Corbin W Durham
158 Ridgefield Dr
York PA 17403

Call Sign: N3UOO
Chad M Mitzel
512 Ridgeview Dr
York PA 17402

Call Sign: K3NVI
Dennis L Cooper
1013 Ridgewood Rd
York PA 174021757

Call Sign: N3QZO
Charles M Feeney
3675 Rimrock Rd
York PA 17402

Call Sign: N3RCD
William P Hitchner Sr
102 Rockwood Ave
York PA 17402

Call Sign: N3CSV
Oscar R Bupp
3270 Roosevelt Ave
York PA 17404

Call Sign: WB3EIE
Craig M Diehl
21 Roselyn Dr
York PA 17402

Call Sign: K3CMD
Craig M Diehl
21 Roselyn Dr
York PA 17402

Call Sign: N3QZS
James A Woof
50 Roselyn Dr
York PA 174023232

Call Sign: K3PKG
Rebecca B Baker
2088 Rosewood Ln
York PA 17403

Call Sign: K3NUZ
Don C Baker Sr
2088 Rosewood Ln
York PA 174035902

Call Sign: KB3TBR
Christopher J Vandermark
129 Royal Ct At Waterford
York PA 17402

Call Sign: KA3MSZ
Roy F Ritchey
2500 Rutland Ave
York PA 17406

Call Sign: N3WEF
Constance L Cook
1625 S Dr
York PA 17404

Call Sign: N3WP
Willard C Pope Jr
311 S Findlay St
York PA 174023433

Call Sign: N3HKW
Lawrence J R Goldhahn
1001 S George St
York PA 17403

Call Sign: WB3HVV
Bruce A Collier
2680 S George St
York PA 174039794

Call Sign: W3EDU
York ARC Inc
S George St
York PA 17401

Call Sign: KB3EEL
Robin L Bobula
644 S Hampton At
Waterford
York PA 17402

Call Sign: N3DRQ
Shirley G Parker
16 S Harlan St
York PA 17402

Call Sign: N3DRR
John C Parker Jr
16 S Harlan St
York PA 17402

Call Sign: N3ESE
Peter O Sandberg
350 S Harlan St
York PA 174023442

Call Sign: KB3DXP
George E Reisinger Jr
330 S Kershaw St

York PA 174023448

Call Sign: KA3CCD
Robert D Miller
710 S Kershaw St
York PA 17402

Call Sign: KA3CEK
Shirley R J Miller
710 S Kershaw St
York PA 17402

Call Sign: W2RPV
Phillip H Ellis
63 S Pine St
York PA 17403

Call Sign: N3KEI
David L Gent
163 S Pine St
York PA 17043

Call Sign: KB3PTV
York County School Of
Technology ARC
2179 S Queen St
York PA 17402

Call Sign: WB2ITJ
Stephen F Nosoff
191 S Royal St
York PA 17402

Call Sign: K3JFE
Willard A Strayer
531 S Russell St
York PA 17402

Call Sign: KB3OYK
Christopher W Coulson
540 S Russell St
York PA 17402

Call Sign: KB3RGO
Christopher R Hartman

26 S Vernon St
York PA 17402

Call Sign: KB3BAR
Francis A Kimpel Sr
541 S Vernon St
York PA 17402

Call Sign: WB3EPL
Bryan C Poe
1473 Salem Rd
York PA 17404

Call Sign: N0TTJ
Peggy L Groeneveld
3890 Sandra Dr
York PA 17402

Call Sign: N3MTY
Scott A Caltagirone
740 Satellite Dr
York PA 17402

Call Sign: WA3SRE
John F Salony
131 Scott Rd
York PA 17403

Call Sign: KB3IDA
Alysia G Magness
140 Scott Rd
York PA 17403

Call Sign: KA3SPW
Charles A Fink Sr
165 Scott Rd
York PA 17403

Call Sign: N4NHQ
Robert J Furlong
410 Shady Dell Rd
York PA 17403

Call Sign: N3OFG
Terry R Drawbaugh

2558 Shagbark Ct
York PA 174067587

Call Sign: W8ZZZ
Lawrence M Pontious
4055 Sharoden Dr
York PA 17408

Call Sign: KB3FKG
Bruce D Budinger
182 Sharon Dr
York PA 17403

Call Sign: KB3JSH
Allen E Walker Jr
1865 Shiloh Dr
York PA 17404

Call Sign: KB3HPT
William E Davis
3793 Silverwood Dr
York PA 174024319

Call Sign: KB3WPJ
Aakash K Sham
3700 Skipton Cir
York PA 17402

Call Sign: N3AIV
Robert A Hotaling
3118 Skylight Dr E
York PA 17402

Call Sign: K3TID
Robert A Axe
260 Skyview Dr
York PA 17402

Call Sign: KB3VVL
Leo G Grenier
2391 Slater Hill Ln E
York PA 17406

Call Sign: KB3MVC
Andrew D Luther

861 Smith Dr
York PA 17408

Call Sign: KA3MMS
Robert M Carrick
925 Smith Dr
York PA 17408

Call Sign: KB3MAF
York Area Contest Club
125 Southciew Dr
York PA 17402

Call Sign: AD3PA
York Area Contest Club
125 Southview Dr
York PA 17402

Call Sign: AD3E
Gene C Warner Jr
125 Southview Dr
York PA 17402

Call Sign: KB3EBV
Linda L Warner
125 Southview Dr
York PA 17402

Call Sign: KI4IAK
Barry B Whittney
2039 Spring St
York PA 17408

Call Sign: WA3MCQ
Richard H Townsend
2090 Spring St
York PA 17404

Call Sign: KA3QXE
Peter P Carli II
100 Springdale Rd
York PA 17403

Call Sign: WA3EEN
Robert L Williams

2535 Springwood Rd
York PA 174029530

Call Sign: KB3QYV
Cathy Lehman
399 Stonewood Rd
York PA 17402

Call Sign: KB3DOG
Cathy Lehman
399 Stonewood Rd
York PA 17402

Call Sign: N3OFX
Mark Bender
3892 Stoney Brook Dr
York PA 17402

Call Sign: KB3HKY
Susquehanna Radio Club
5989 Susquehanna Plaza
Dr
York PA 174068910

Call Sign: W3YQJ
Edward H Kirby Jr
2325 Sycamore Rd
York PA 174044131

Call Sign: N3ZLC
William J Nugent
3895 Sylvan Dr
York PA 17402

Call Sign: KB3GGO
Jo-Ann Wrights
3895 Sylvan Dr
York PA 17402

Call Sign: KB3UJC
Bradley A Jacobs
100 Talisman Ct
York PA 17404

Call Sign: KB3DBT

Heather A Te Beau
3841 Tarpley Dr
York PA 17402

Call Sign: KB3DPF
Richard S Tebeau
3841 Tarpley Dr
York PA 17402

Call Sign: W3RAZ
William D Fulton
1701 Taxville Rd 22H
York PA 17404

Call Sign: KB3WZV
Gregory C Scarborough
1701 Taxville Rd Apt 1E
York PA 17408

Call Sign: W3NGN
Russell J Woodrow
2150 Teslin Rd
York PA 17404

Call Sign: KA3CLA
Nettie V Poe
808 Texas Ave
York PA 17404

Call Sign: KB3JSF
George E Sheffer
1900 Thelon Dr
York PA 17408

Call Sign: KA1ULG
Leroy W Thomas Jr
1941 Thelon Dr
York PA 17404

Call Sign: NN3Z
Millard J Martin
2070 Thelon Dr
York PA 174044224

Call Sign: KA3CLC

Gregory M Stough
2745 Thornbridge Rd W
York PA 17408

Call Sign: KB3JSE
Jere F Stahl
3731 Trout Run Rd
York PA 17402

Call Sign: N3VQI
David L Gutshall
2181 Twigden Ct
York PA 174034525

Call Sign: KB3RCT
Jeffrey D Patterson
1780 Valley Vista Dr
York PA 17406

Call Sign: KB3VVD
Kelly E Patterson
1780 Valley Vista Dr
York PA 17406

Call Sign: K3ZTT
John K Gray
2062 Village Cir E
York PA 17404

Call Sign: N3NBX
Charles E Anstine Jr
38 W 9th Ave
York PA 17404

Call Sign: KB3PIL
Whitley R Crenshaw
428 W College Ave
York PA 17404

Call Sign: WB3CFN
Joseph E Krepps
1027 W College Ave
York PA 174043536

Call Sign: KA3GRO

James W Haverstick
296 W Jackson
York PA 17403

Call Sign: KA3UVS
Jonathan E Bahn
810 W King St
York PA 17404

Call Sign: KE3NR
Robin W Stout
1561 W King St
York PA 17404

Call Sign: W3BRX
Carlton D Trotman
247 W Maple St
York PA 17401

Call Sign: K3JFL
James D Strauss
644 W Market St
York PA 17404

Call Sign: N3KWZ
James R Hamilton
646 W Market St
York PA 17404

Call Sign: W3JAD
Jack A Dean
1400 W Market St
York PA 17404

Call Sign: KB3CNF
Thomas A Brungard
1612 W Market St 2
York PA 17404

Call Sign: KA3HKI
Jeffrey E Ferree
1104 W Market St Apt 2
York PA 174043483

Call Sign: KB3OPT

Melissa A Corter
760 W Mason Ave
York PA 17401

Call Sign: KB3OFG
Rick L Corter
760 W Mason Ave
York PA 17401

Call Sign: N3XUA
Melony J Graham
764 W Mason Ave
York PA 17404

Call Sign: KB3WLT
Irvin Sanchez Montesano
478 W Philadelphia St
York PA 17401

Call Sign: N3JDP
Bryan T Flohr
2054 W Philadelphia St
York PA 17404

Call Sign: WB3EFA
Stephen E Steffan
310 W Philadelphia St 439
York PA 174012942

Call Sign: WB2EZL
Samuel P Fleischer
818 W Poplar St
York PA 17401

Call Sign: WB3KKF
Wayne D Coulson
722 W Princess St
York PA 174043641

Call Sign: K1KHF
Richard R Lanoue
2340 Warwick Rd
York PA 174084387

Call Sign: KB3KGF

Karl T Koch
2401 Warwick Rd
York PA 17404

Call Sign: KA3PQG
Marjorie V Thomas
2465 Warwick Rd
York PA 17404

Call Sign: KB3VSY
Brandon R Pepper
443 Weldon Dr
York PA 17404

Call Sign: WA3GWB
Jeffrey E Shank
700 Weldon Dr
York PA 174044828

Call Sign: NX1S
Andreas Fieber
Westgate Apt 201
York PA 17408

Call Sign: KB3IQN
Ezraella B Brody
1657 Westgate Dr 201
York PA 17404

Call Sign: KB3EZZ
Ezraella B Brody
1657 Westgate Dr 201
York PA 17404

Call Sign: N5QYQ
Michael R Fandell
1689 Westgate Dr 201
York PA 17408

Call Sign: KB8BDY
Nicholas F Szabo
1685 Westgate Dr 202
York PA 17408

Call Sign: N3GFY

James W Hauer
98 Westview Manor
York PA 17404

Call Sign: WB3HNA
Le Moyne V Lindsay
2772 Westwind Ln
York PA 17404

Call Sign: WA3TPX
Melvin L Rosenberg
220 Wheatfield Way
York PA 17403

Call Sign: WB3EPK
Clyde B Poe
2000 White
York PA 17404

Call Sign: N3LTZ
Dorothy F Barefoot
1434 Whiteford Rd
York PA 17402

Call Sign: W3UQJ
William E Barefoot Sr
1434 Whiteford Rd
York PA 174022122

Call Sign: WN8TIH
Charles E Spencer
25 Williamstown Cir
York PA 17404

Call Sign: N3OFD
Norman E Abramson
2320 Willow Rd
York PA 17404

Call Sign: N3LLT
Paul S Ness
889 Willow Ridge Dr
York PA 17404

Call Sign: W3FLM

Sol Dubin
4074 Wilshire Dr
York PA 17402

Call Sign: N3SUD
Dave F Jensenius
4160 Wilshire Dr
York PA 17402

Call Sign: N3SUE
Robert H Jensenius
4160 Wilshire Dr
York PA 17402

Call Sign: W3MYK
James R Shultz
1267 Wiltshire Rd
York PA 17403

Call Sign: KB3SSO
John A Shanabrook
2033 Winding Rd
York PA 17408

Call Sign: KB3SSP
Michael R Shanabrook
2033 Winding Rd
York PA 17408

Call Sign: N3TKJ
John H Green
325 Windsor Rd
York PA 174028674

Call Sign: KB3MZJ
Isaac Burke
2636 Winemiller Ln
York PA 17404

Call Sign: N3YRQ
Dilip G Patel
835 Woodbridge Raod
York PA 17402

Call Sign: KB3GXG

Jack A Dean
341 Woodland View Dr
York PA 17402

Call Sign: KB3DXO
Joshua D Hoke
2732 Woodmont Dr
York PA 17404

Call Sign: KB3VIH
John M Drasher
2916 Woodshead Ter
York PA 17403

Call Sign: N3YEG
Michael R Mitzel
2931 Woodshead Ter
York PA 17403

Call Sign: N3OFE
Joseph A Krenitsky
1937 Worth St
York PA 17404

Call Sign: N3OFF
Vicki Krenitsky
1937 Worth St
York PA 17404

Call Sign: W3VNJ
Dale R Smith Jr
1260 Wyndham Dr
York PA 17403

Call Sign: W3LUD
Royal M Gibson
219 Wynwood Rd
York PA 17402

Call Sign: KA3QFA
Richard L Partain
302 Wynwood Rd
York PA 17402

Call Sign: KA3PQH

James M Yost
York PA 17405

Call Sign: N0HTQ
John T Randall
York PA 17402

Call Sign: W3HZU
Keystone Vhf Club Inc
York PA 17402

Call Sign: KB3SNL
Frank W Segel
York PA 17404

Call Sign: KC3XE
William D Reis
York PA 17405

Call Sign: KB3WZW
Beverly D Nispel
York PA 17405

Call Sign: KA3VDM
Richard A March
York PA 174020255

Call Sign: N3LSN
Robert H Secrist
York PA 174040401

Call Sign: N3UAC
Jacob W Frederick Sr
York PA 174050445

**FCC Amateur Radio
Licenses in York Haven**

Call Sign: KA3SHW
Kevin W Quickel
1325 Cly Rd
York Haven PA 17370

Call Sign: KB3OFE
Tim M Beck

685 Cragmoor Rd
York Haven PA 17370

Call Sign: N3URR
Charlotte N Markley
190 Garriston Rd
York Haven PA 17370

Call Sign: N3XGF
Ernest S Markley
190 Garriston Rd
York Haven PA 17370

Call Sign: KB3KNA
Aaron J Reiprich
2465 Grand View Dr
York Haven PA 17370

Call Sign: KA3GGC
Clarence J Intrieri III
3410 Grandview Ave
York Haven PA 17370

Call Sign: N3BAS
Cathy R Clark
95 Iroquois Trl
York Haven PA 17370

Call Sign: WA3HUP
Mary A Crider
2485 Lewisberry Rd
York Haven PA 17370

Call Sign: KB3SRI
Robert N Mulfinger
40 Markley Dr
York Haven PA 17370

Call Sign: KA3TBP
Stephen J Bond Sr
85 River Rd
York Haven PA 17370

Call Sign: KB3CNH
Eric J Smyder

125 River Rd
York Haven PA 17370

Call Sign: N3IFH
Charles S Kirby
215 Roxberry Rd
York Haven PA 17370

Call Sign: K3HWH
Gordon P Moul
34 S Front St
York Haven PA 17370

Call Sign: KB3VMS
Joseph C Edgar
50 Shawnee Trl
York Haven PA 17370

**FCC Amateur Radio
Licenses in York Springs**

Call Sign: KB3QXR
Cameron F Martinez
439 County Line Rd
York Springs PA 17372

Call Sign: KB3MWS
Chelsea F Martinez
439 County Line Rd
York Springs PA 17372

Call Sign: KB3THD
Steven K Beard
445 County Line Rd
York Springs PA 17372

Call Sign: N3GFL
Arthur D Murray III
1768 County Line Rd
York Springs PA 17372

Call Sign: WB3EZW
Frederick V Dundore
2350 County Line Rd
York Springs PA 17372

Call Sign: KB3ONI
David L Baker
853 E Berlin Rd
York Springs PA 17372

Call Sign: W3LEL
Lloyd E Lichtenfels
1070 Fickes School Rd
York Springs PA 17372

Call Sign: WA3VXV
John L Gallagher
24 Greenbriar Rd
York Springs PA 17372

Call Sign: N8QVT
Valli M Hoski
134 Harrisburg St
York Springs PA 17372

Call Sign: K3EYL
Harry M Fasick Jr
134 Harrisburg St
York Springs PA 17372

Call Sign: N3XRH
Patricia A Mitchel
320 Main St
York Springs PA 17372

Call Sign: KA3IUF
C Edward Rothenhoefer
7173 Old Harrisburg Rd
York Springs PA 17372

Call Sign: KA3WWV
Holly A Williams
180 Roelker Rd
York Springs PA 17372

Call Sign: WB5RIB
Barry Pannebaker
York Springs PA 17372

Call Sign: N3WQQ
David J Mitchel
York Springs PA 17372

FCC Amateur Radio Licenses in Zullinger

Call Sign: WB3BXG
Paul R Johnson
11831 Shady Ln
Zullinger PA 17272

Call Sign: WN2R
Frederick A Bennett II
Zullinger PA 17272

www.ingramcontent.com/pod-product-compliance
Lightning Source LLC
Chambersburg PA
CBHW081346280326
41927CB00042B/3074